W9-BRV-877

Upper Austria
p151

Lower Austria
p108

★ Vienna
p54

The
Salzkammergut
p200

Burgenland
p138

Salzburg &
Salzburgerland
p218

Styria
p172

Vorarlberg
p334

Tyrol
p292

Hohe Tauern
National Park
p271

Carinthia
p248

Language

BASICS

THIS EDITION WRITTEN AND RESEARCHED BY

Anthony Haywood,
Caroline Sieg, Kerry Christiani

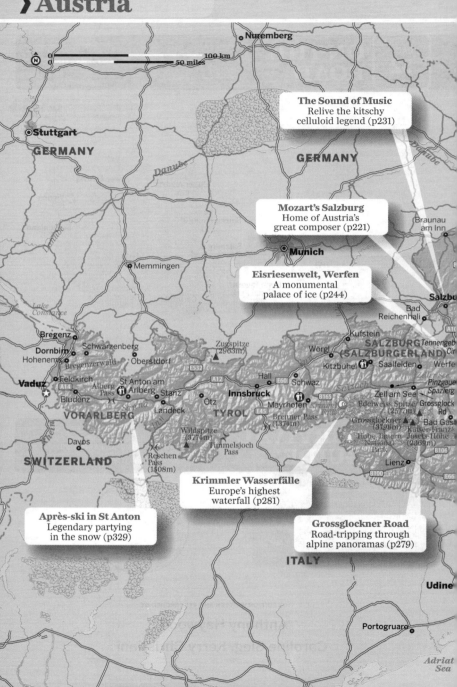

❭ Austria

Stuttgart
GERMANY

Nuremberg

0 ___ 100 km
0 ___ 50 miles

GERMANY

Danube

The Sound of Music
Relive the kitschy
celluloid legend (p231)

Mozart's Salzburg
Home of Austria's
great composer (p221)

Munich

Braunau
am Inn

Eisriesenwelt, Werfen
A monumental
palace of ice (p244)

Salzbu

Bad
Reichenhall

Memmingen

*Lake
Constance*

Bregenz
Dornbirn
Hohenems
Bregenzerwald
Schwarzenberg
Oberstdorf

Zugspitze
(2963m)▲

Kufstein

Wörgl

SALZBURG
(SALZBURGERLAND) Tennengeb

Kitzbühel
Saalfelden
Werfe

Vaduz
Feldkirch
Bludenz

Arlberg
Pass
St Anton am
Arlberg
Stanz

Landeck

A12

Ötz

Hall

Schwaz

B165

Zell am See

Pinzgau
Spazier

Zell See

Innsbruck

Mayrhofen

Brenner Pass
(1374m)

Edelweiss Spitze
(2577m)▲
Grossglock
Rd

VORARLBERG

TYROL

E45

Grossglockner
(3798m)▲▲
Hohe Tauern
National
Park

Bad Gas

Kaiser-Franz-
Josefs-Höhe
(2369m)

Davos

Wildspitze
(3774m)▲

Timmelsjoch
Pass

B106

SWITZERLAND

Reschen
Pass
(1508m)

Lienz

B100

E66

Krimmler Wasserfälle
Europe's highest
waterfall (p281)

Après-ski in St Anton
Legendary partying
in the snow (p329)

Grossglockner Road
Road-tripping through
alpine panoramas (p279)

ITALY

Udine

Portogruaro

*Adriat
Sea*

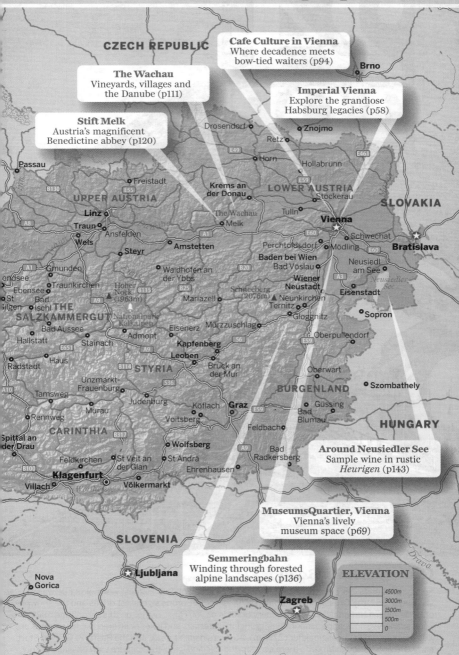

CZECH REPUBLIC

Cafe Culture in Vienna
Where decadence meets
bow-tied waiters (p94)

Brno

The Wachau
Vineyards, villages and
the Danube (p111)

Imperial Vienna
Explore the grandiose
Habsburg legacies (p58)

Stift Melk
Austria's magnificent
Benedictine abbey (p120)

Drosendorf   Znojmo

Retz

Passau   Horn   Hollabrunn

Freistadt   Krems an   LOWER AUSTRIA
der Donau   Stockerau

UPPER AUSTRIA

Linz   The Wachau   Tulln   Vienna   SLOVAKIA
Traun   Melk   Schwechat

Ansfelden   Bratislava

Wels   Perchtoldsdorf   Mödling

Amstetten   Baden bei Wien   Neusiedl
am See

Steyr   Bad Vöslau

Waidhofen an   Wiener   Eisenstadt
der Ybbs   Neustadt

Gmunden   Schneeberg   Neunkirchen   Sopron
(2076m)

Traunkirchen   Hoher   Mariazell   Ternitz
Nock
(1963m)   Gloggnitz

Ebensee   Oberpullendorf

St   Bad   THE   Nationalpark   Eisenerz   Mürzzuschlag
Gilgen   Ischl   SALZKAMMERGUT   Kalkalpen

Bad Aussee   Admont   Kapfenberg

Hallstatt   Stainach   Leoben   Oberwart

Radstadt   Haus   STYRIA   Bruck an
der Mur

Unzmarkt-   BURGENLAND   Szombathely
Frauenburg

Tamsweg   Oberwart

Judenburg   Köflach   Graz   Güssing

Rennweg   Murau   Voitsberg   Bad
Blumau

CARINTHIA   Feldbach   HUNGARY

Spittal an   Wolfsberg   Bad
der Drau   Radkersberg   **Around Neusiedler See**
Sample wine in rustic
Heurigen (p143)

Feldkirchen   St Veit an   St Andrä
der Glan   Ehrenhausen

Klagenfurt

Villach   Völkermarkt

MuseumsQuartier, Vienna
Vienna's lively
museum space (p69)

SLOVENIA

Nova   Ljubljana   **Semmeringbahn**
Gorica   Winding through forested
alpine landscapes (p136)

ELEVATION

Zagreb

4500m
3000m
1500m
500m
0

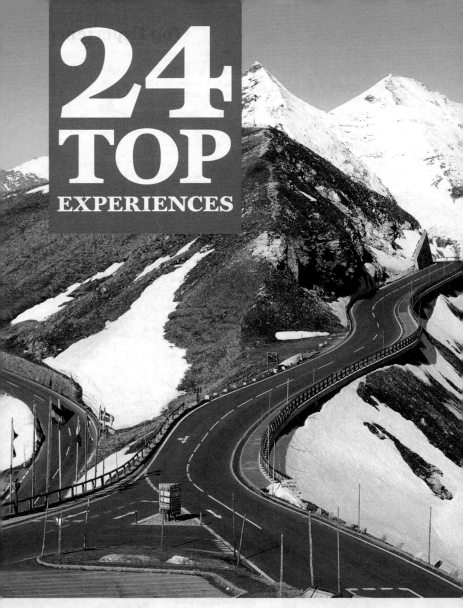

Grossglockner Road

1 Hairpin bends: 36. Length: 48km. Average slope gradient: 9%. Highest viewpoint: Edelweiss Spitze (2571m). Grossglockner Rcad (p279) is one of Europe's greatest drives and the showpiece of Hohe Tauern National Park. The scenery unfolds as you climb higher on this serpentine road. And what scenery! Snowcapped mountains, plunging waterfalls and lakes scattered like gemstones are just the build-up to Grossglockner (3798m), Austria's highest peak, and the Pasterze Glacier. Start early and allow enough time, as there's a stop-the-car-and-grab-the-camera view on every corner.

Imperial Vienna

2 Imagine what you could do with unlimited riches and Austria's top architects at your hands for 640 years and you'll have the Vienna of the Habsburgs. The monumentally graceful Hofburg (p59) whisks you back to the age of empires; marvel at the treasury's imperial crowns, the equine ballet of the Spanische Hofreitschule and the chandelier-lit apartments fit for Empress Elisabeth. The palace is rivalled in grandeur only by the 1441-room Schloss Schönbrunn (p78), a Unesco World Heritage site, and baroque Schloss Belvedere (p75), both set in exquisite gardens. Schloss Schönbrunn, below

Skiing

3 In a country where three year olds can snowplough, 70 year olds still slalom and the tiniest speck of a village has its own lift system, skiing is more than just a sport – it's a way of life. Why? Just look around you. There's St Anton am Arlberg (p329) for off-piste and après-ski, Mayrhofen (p313) for freestyle boarding and its epic Harakiri, Kitzbühel (p317) for its perfect mix – the scope is limitless and the terrain fantastic. Cross-country or back-country, downhill or glacier, whatever your ski style, Austria has a piste with your name on it.

KRZYSZTOF DYDYNSKI

Cafe Culture in Vienna

4 A pianist plays and bow-tied waiters bustle to and fro with cakes and encyclopaedic coffee menus. Ahhh, this is what the Viennese mean by *Gemütlichkeit* (cosiness), you realise, as you sip your *Melange* (milky coffee), rustle your newspaper and watch life go decadently by. Café Sacher (p96) for the richest of chocolate cakes, Café Jelinek (p98) for its quirky vibe, Café Hawelka (p96) for bohemian flavour – Vienna has a coffee house for every mood and occasion. Indulge, talk, read and dream; just as Trotsky and Freud, Hundertwasser and Warhol once did. *Café Sperl, left*

Castles & Palaces

5 On the most obscure of country roads, the sun suddenly spotlights a turreted castle clinging to a wooded hillside. It happens all the time in Austria, where kings, emperors and prince-archbishops collected fairy-tale castles and palaces the way others collect postcards. The lordly Hofburg (p59) in Vienna and Salzburg's baroque Residenz (p223) dazzle with their finery, history and art treasures. But if gloomy dungeons are more your scene, formidable fortresses such as 900-year-old Festung Hohensalzburg (p222) and cliff-top Burg Hohenwerfen (p244) will appeal.
Festung Hohensalzburg overlooking Salzburg, above

DIANA MAYFIELD

The Wachau

6 When Strauss composed 'The Blue Danube', he surely had the Wachau (p111) in mind. Granted Unesco World Heritage status for its harmonious natural and cultural beauty, this romantic stretch of the Danube Valley waltzes you through poetic landscapes of terraced vineyards, forested slopes and apricot orchards. Resplendent Benedictine abbey Stift Melk (p120) begs exploration, as does Dürnstein's Kuenringerburg (p116). This ruined hilltop castle is where the troubadour Blondel attempted to rescue Richard the Lionheart from the clutches of Duke Leopold V.

Après-Ski in St Anton

7 It's late afternoon and après-ski time in party-mad St Anton am Arlberg (p329); off come the jackets, out come the *Dirndl*-clad waitresses and the Jägermeister, on goes the Europop. You don't know how it happened, but within a matter of no time you're singing along to German bands, dancing on the tables and buying schnapps for the guy that cut you off on the slope. Buoyed by the fun at Sennhütte, Mooserwirt, Heustadl or Taps (p333), you'll believe your skiing technique has never been so, hic, fantastic.

Classical-Music Festivals

8 No country can outshine Austria when it comes to classical music. The country was a veritable production line of great composers in the 18th and 19th centuries. And there's always a reason to celebrate that great heritage, starting with the much-lauded Salzburg Festival (p232) and Vienna's Opernball (p83). Other highs in the classical calendar include lakeside opera at the Bregenzer Festspiele (p337), a feast of Schubert at Vorarlberg's Schubertiade (p343) and Bruckner at the Brucknerfest (p158) in Linz. Floating stage at the Bregenzer Festspiele, below

GARETH McCORMACK

Alpine Hiking

9 You're on the Pinzgauer Spaziergang (p277), a crisp blue sky overhead, snowy peaks crowding the horizon. You're waking up to a rose-tinted sunrise in the Dolomites (p286). You're thanking your lucky stars you packed your walking boots... Locals delight in telling you that the best – no, no, the only – way to see the Austrian Alps is on foot. And they're right. Here a peerless network of trails and alpine huts brings you that bit closer to nature.

Eisriesenwelt

10 The twinkling chambers and passageways of Eisriesenwelt (p244) are like something out of Narnia under the White Witch. Sculpted drip by drip over millennia, the icy underworld of the limestone Tennengebirge range is billed as the world's largest accessible ice cave. Otherworldly sculptures, shimmering lakes and a cavernous *Eispalast* (ice palace) appear as you venture deep into the frozen heart of the mountain, carbide lamp in hand. Even in summer, temperatures down here are subzero, so wrap up warm.

ANDY CHRISTIANI

The Sound of Music

11 Salzburg is a celebrity for those who have never even set foot in the city, thanks to its star appearance in *The Sound of Music*. Should you wish, you can fine-tune your own tour (p231) of the film locations. The sculpture-dotted Mirabellgarten of 'Do-Re-Mi' fame, the Benedictine nunnery Stift Nonnberg, the 'Sixteen Going on Seventeen' pavilion in Hellbrunn Park – it's enough to make you yodel out loud. For the truth behind the celluloid legend, stay the night at the original Villa Trapp (p233), a 19th-century mansion in the Aigen district. Schloss Leopoldskron, where the lake scene was filmed, left

JENNY JONES

Stift Melk

12 Austria's greatest works of art are those wrought for God, some say. Gazing up at the golden glory of Stift Melk (p120), Austria's must-see Benedictine abbey-fortress, you can't help but agree. The twin-spired monastery church is a baroque tour de force, swirling with prancing angels, gilt flourishes and Johann Michael Rottmayr's ceiling paintings. Such opulence continues in the library and marble hall, both embellished with illusionary *trompe l'oeil* tiers by Paul Troger. If you can, stay to see the monarch of monasteries strikingly lit by night.

RICHARD NEBESKY

Spa Time

13 With its crisp mountain air and thermal springs, Austria positively radiates good health. For an otherworldly spa experience, drift off in flying-saucer-shaped pools at crystalline Aqua Dome (p322) at the foot of the Ötztaler Alps, or in the fantastical hot springs of Hundertwasser's technicolor Rogner-Bad Blumau (p188). History bubbles to the surface in the Wienerwald's Römertherme (p131), where beauty-conscious Romans once took the sulphuric waters. The Victorians favoured belle-époque Bad Gastein (p282), whose radon-laced springs reputedly cure a multitude of ills. Aqua Dome in the Ötztal, below

MuseumsQuartier

14 Once the imperial stables, now one of the world's biggest exhibition spaces, Vienna's 60,000-sq-metre MuseumsQuartier (p69) contains more art than some small countries. Emotive works by Klimt and Schiele hang out in the Leopold Museum (p69), while the basalt MUMOK (p71) highlights provocative Viennese actionists, and the Kunsthalle (p71) new media. Progressive boutiques, workshops and cafes take creativity beyond the canvas. On warm days, Viennese gather in the huge courtyard to chat, drink and watch the artistic world go by.

ANDY CHRISTIANI

Outdoor Adventure

15 Anywhere where there's foaming water, a tall mountain or a sheer ravine, there are heart-pumping outdoor escapades in Austria. For a summertime buzz, you can't beat throwing yourself down raging rivers such as the Inn and Sanna (p326) in Tyrol, Austria's rafting mecca. Or strap into your harness and be blown away by the alpine scenery paragliding in the Zillertal (p310). Peak-baggers enjoy high-altitude rock climbing in the mighty three-thousanders of Hohe Tauern National Park (p271).

Wine Tasting in Heurigen

16 If you see an evergreen branch hanging on a door on your ramblings through Vienna's out-skirts and Burgenland, especially around the Neusiedler See (p143), you've probably stumbled across a traditional *Heuriger*. Pull up a chair in one of these cosy taverns to taste the local vintage of crisp white Grüner Veltliner and spicy Blaufränkisch wines. The experience is partly to do with the wine and partly what surrounds it – the atmosphere, the scenery, the chatty locals, the hearty food. September is the month for new wine and golden vineyard strolls. *Traditional Heuriger, above*

Krimmler Wasserfälle

17 No doubt you'll hear the thunderous roar of the 380m-high Krimmler Wasserfälle (p281), Europe's highest waterfall, before you see it. You can't help but feel insignificant when confronted with the sheer force and scale of this cataract, which thrashes immense boulders and produces the most photogenic of rainbows. As with all natural wonders, this one looks best from certain angles, namely from the Wasserfallweg (Waterfall Trail). The path zigzags up through moist, misty forest to viewpoints that afford close-ups of the three-tiered falls and a shower in its fine spray.

KOH/IMAGEBROKER

Semmeringbahn

18 The monumental Semmeringbahn (Semmering Railway; p136) is a panoramic journey through the Eastern Alps and a nostalgic trip back to early rail travel. Some 20,000 workers toiled to create the railway, an alpine first, in a feat of 19th-century engineering that is now a Unesco World Heritage site. Though steam has been replaced by electricity, you can still imagine the wonder of the first passengers as the train curves around 16 viaducts, burrows through 15 tunnels and glides across 100 stone bridges. The grandeur of the railway and landscapes is timeless.

Mozart's Salzburg

19 Mozart's spiritual home may have been Vienna, but the musical prodigy was born and bred in Salzburg's baroque *Altstadt* (p221). Here you can see where the 18th-century superstar lived, loved and composed. Orchestras wish the late Amadeus a happy (if rather belated) birthday at Mozartwoche (p230) in late January. Year-round there are chamber concerts of Mozart's music in the exquisite surrounds of Schloss Mirabell's Marmorsaal (Marble Hall; p227). Marionettes bring his operas magically to life at the nearby Salzburger Marionettentheater (p238). Mirabellgarten surrounding Schloss Mirabell, right

ROBERTO GEROMETTA

KRZYSZTOF DYDYNSKI

High-Rise Journeys

20 Whether rising above clouds in the Alps or above rooftops in cities, this is a land of head-spinning journeys. Vienna seems toy-town tiny as you turn gently in the 19th-century Riesenrad (p74) of *Third Man* fame, the Würstelprater's carousel music and candyfloss stands far below. Kufstein's rickety 1970s chairlift (p321) exhilarates with a treetop-skimming ride to the wild Kaisergebirge mountains. Linz may be flat, but that didn't stop its narrow-gauge Pöstlingbergbahn (p156) from slipping into Guinness World Records as Europe's steepest mountain railway. Vienna's Riesenrad, left

Food Markets

21 So is it to be the Vorarlberg cheese, the smoky mountain speck or the peppercorn-studded Tyrolean ham? Oh, what the heck, let's take all three... It's always the same conundrum in Austria's food markets, where locals gather to shop, gossip and trade seasonal recipes for chanterelles and asparagus. Get into the swing of things at Vienna's Naschmarkt (p94), stopping for lunch and people-watching between purchases of Turkish spices and fruit. Salzburg's open-air Grüner Markt (p237) and Innsbruck's Markthalle (p304) are other top spots to fill your picnic basket. Vienna's Naschmarkt, right

GREG ELMS

New Dimensions

22 Space age is the new baroque in many of Austria's cities. Zaha Hadid has captured the Zeitgeist in Innsbruck with her curvy glass-and-steel Nordketten Bahnen (funicular stations; p300), which appear to float above the city. Like some kind of futuristic ship, the Ars Electronica Center (p153) rises above the Danube in Linz and kaleidoscopically changes colour after dark. Sci-fi fans rave about Kunsthaus Graz (p176). Nicknamed the 'friendly alien', it resembles a magnificent space-age sea slug with its fluid form and acrylic skin. Kunsthaus Graz, above

Lake Escapades

23 From the jewel-coloured alpine lakes of Salzkammergut (p200) to the deliciously warm lakes of Carinthia (p248), Austria has literally hundreds of lakes to choose from. Let your sail catch the breeze on glassy Mondsee (p216), windsurf on Neusiedler See (p143) or dive into the turquoise Wörthersee (p256). If you'd prefer to keep your feet dry, pedal between borders on the expansive Bodensee (p340) or appreciate sublime mountain views from the beaches fringing Zeller See (p275). Diving platform at Zell am See, above

Foodie Trails

24 Austrians pride themselves on home-grown flavours, with almost every region leading to mouth-watering surprises. Taste farm-fresh cheeses on the Käsestrasse (p346), a scenic road that threads through the Bregenzerwald. Or sample poppy-filled specialities in the rural Waldviertel (p122), aromatic Schlegeisspeck ham from the Alps in Mayrhofen (p313) and tangy cider in the apple orchards of the Mostviertel (p127). Something stronger, you say? Head to the 650-person, 54-distillery village of Stanz (p327) for potent plum and apple schnapps. The Mostviertel region, above

welcome to Austria

Mountains, lakes and deep alpine valleys. Food and wine, and Vienna's gritty eloquence. Austria has lots of culture to get into, and iconic landscapes for getting away from it all.

Culture in Many Disguises

Austria is fabled for its cultural life, especially in Vienna, where white Lipizzaner horses move to the tunes of classical music, angelic choir boys pledge their innocence to the heavens, and innovative and provocative theatre, opera and classical music can be enjoyed in exciting seasonal programs. No less grandiose is the architecture, which is often combined with performance or visual arts in the one ensemble. But the cultural experience of Austria is also about the undiscovered, the regional and the grassroots – the artists and performers working in the provincial capitals. It's about geographically far-flung and unusual exhibition spaces huddled in long valleys – valleys dotted with small towns and which together form a heartland of the country. Anyone with an eye for the nuances of everyday life will also find much of informal cultural interest. This is definitely one country where the grandiose and the everyday, the provincial and the idiosyncratic, and the iconic and the concealed stand in poetic contrast.

Landscapes & the Great Outdoors

The mountains, valleys and lakes of Austria are legendary and provide one of the world's most spectacular backdrops for outdoor activities. Dominating the country is the towering eastern Alps, where in winter skiers and snowboarders test their mettle. Come summer, some of the winter ski trails complement vast networks of hiking or mountain-biking trails, often serviced by a cable car. The mountain meadows make for a perfect picnic spot in warm weather. Austria's thousands of lakes are also fine places in summer for swimming and relaxing – some are chilly and glacial, others warm, splashy playgrounds. Thanks to the modest size of most towns, the great outdoors is never far away.

Food & Wine Experiences

Austria is experiencing a renaissance in food and wine. Vienna is packed with exciting new places to eat and drink, and the long traditions of the coffee house and *Beisl* (tavern) are being imbued with new life. Outside the capital, regions such as the Waldviertel, Danube Valley and southern Styria beckon with food and wine experiences in picturesque landscapes. Traditional *Heurigen* (wine taverns) abound, and innovative producers are delivering the ingredients from regions such as these to the nation's tables. This is good news for the traveller, who can easily combine food and wine with city visits, outdoor activities, health and wellness, or with trips by bicycle or car through Austria's character-packed gourmet and wine regions.

need to know

Currency
» Euro (€)

Language
» German

When to Go

■ Mild to hot summers, cold winters
■ Warm to hot summers, mild winters
■ Mild year round
■ Cold Climate

Vienna
GO Late Mar–Oct

Kitzbühel
GO Jun–Sep for alpine hikes;
Dec–Mar for skiing

Salzburg
GO Jul & Aug for the Salzburg Festival;
rest of the year for fewer crowds

Innsbruck
GO Jun–Sep & Dec–Mar for outdoor pursuits;
rest of year for uncrowded sights

Graz
GO Apr–Oct

High Season
(Apr–Oct)

» High season peaks from July to August.

» In lake areas the peak runs from June to September.

» Ski resorts peak from mid-December to March.

» Prices rise over Christmas and Easter.

Shoulder Season (late Mar–May & late Sep–Oct)

» The weather's changeable, the lakes are chilly and the hiking's excellent.

» Sights are open and less crowded.

Low Season
(Nov–Mar)

» Many sights are closed at this time of year.

» There's a cultural focus in Vienna and the regional capitals.

» Ski resorts open from mid-December.

Your Daily Budget

Budget less than
€80

» Dorm beds or cheap doubles: about €25 per person

» Self-catering or lunch-time specials

» Stay in low-profile regions, enjoy free sights

Midrange
€80–140

» Hotel singles: €50–80 (€60–70 in cities)

» Explore the culinary scene (a good meal costs €20–30)

» High-profile sights and day trips

Top end over
€140

» Luxury suites and doubles in large cities

» Pamper yourself with wellness facilities

» Eat superbly, enjoy wines and antipasti in a *Vinothek* (wine bar)

Money

» ATMs widely available. Maestro direct debit and Visa credit cards accepted in most hotels and restaurants, MasterCard often accepted in midrange places.

Visas

» Austria is part of the Schengen Agreement. Generally, for stays of up to three months a visa is not necessary, but some nationalities need a Schengen visa.

Mobile Phones

» Travellers from outside Europe will need a quad band (world) mobile phone for roaming. Local SIM cards (about €10) are easily purchased for 'unlocked' phones.

Driving

» Drive on the right; the steering wheel is on the left side of the car.

Websites

» **Lonely Planet** (www.lonelyplanet. com/Austria) Destination information, hotel bookings, traveller forum and more.

» **Österreich Werbung** (www.austria.info) National tourism authority.

» **Tiscover** (www. tiscover.com) Information and accommodation booking.

» **Embassy of Austria** (www.austria.org) US-based website with current affairs and information.

» **Austrian National Tourist Office** (www. austriatourism.com) Aimed at media and business but with interesting information for everyone.

Exchange Rates

Australia	A$1	€0.71
Canada	C$1	€0.70
Japan	¥100	€0.87
New Zealand	NZ$	€0.56
Russia	RUB1	€0.02
UK	UK£1	€1.14
USA	US$1	€0.70

For current exchange rates see www.xe.com.

Important Numbers

To dial listings in this book from outside Austria, dial your international access code, the country code, the city code and then the number.

Country code	☑43
International access code	☑00
International operator & information	☑11 88 77 (EU & neighbouring countries), ☑0900 11 88 77 (other countries)
Mountain rescue	☑140
Emergency (police, fire, ambulance)	☑112

Arriving in Austria

» **Vienna International Airport** City Airport Train (CAT) – Every 30 minutes from 6.05am to 11.35pm; 16 minutes. Bus – Every 30 minutes from 6.20am to 12.20am; 22 minutes to Schwedenplatz (central Vienna).
See p106.

» **Graz Airport** Train – Departs at least hourly from 4.48am to 10.48pm Monday to Friday, 5.18am to 10.48pm Saturday and 5.40am to 9.48pm Sunday; 18 minutes. Bus – Less frequent but convenient between trains.. See p135.

Getting Around Austria

Small towns and even small cities often have limited or no car-hire services, so reserve ahead from major cities. Public transport is excellent for reaching even remote regions, but it takes longer. Austria's national railway system is integrated with the Postbus bus services. Plan your route using the Österreiche Bundesbahn (Austrian Federal Railway; ÖBB; www.oebb.at) or Postbus (www.postbus.at) websites.

what's new

For this new edition of Austria, our authors have hunted down the fresh, the revamped, the transformed, the hot and the happening. Here are a few of our favourites. For up-to-the-minute reviews and recommendations, see lonelyplanet.com/austria.

Pankratium

1 Nestled deep in the heart of Carinthia, medieval Gmünd surprises with its Pankratium exhibition space, immersing the visitor in an extraordinary world of water, light and haunting sound. (p266)

Dachstein Eispalast & Skywalk

2 The Dachstein Skywalk affords fantastic valley views, while a short but slippery walk away is the Dachstein Eispalast, a world of ice inside a glacier. (p196)

Pratersauna

3 Boogie down and sip a cocktail at the swimming pool and sauna turned nightclub and performance-art venue in Vienna's Leopoldstadt district. (p102)

Boutiquehotel Stadthalle

4 Vienna's most ecofriendly hotel boasts a lavender roof, solar-heated hot water and discounts for those arriving by bike or train. (p88)

Der Steirer

5 This Styrian *neo-Beisl* (tavern) and wine bar not only has excellent wines, its goulash is one of the best in the country – a delicious beef classic accompanied by fried polenta. (p181)

Villa Trapp

6 Say so long, farewell to Salzburg's crowds and spend the night at this beautifully restored 19th-century mansion, the original von Trapp family home. (p233)

Ars Electronica Center

7 Linz' new temple to digital wizardry and robotics. Like a space-age ship, it rears up above the Danube and is strikingly illuminated by night. (p153)

Area 47

8 With its Venice beach–style lido, water park and action-packed sports from rafting to canyoning, Area 47 in the Ötztal is Tyrol's ultimate outdoor playground. (p323)

Arlrock

9 This great new family attraction in St Anton am Arlberg brings together climbing walls, a kids' play area, tennis courts and outdoor activity centre called H20-Adventures. (p329)

RAJ

10 Raj means 'paradise' in Slovenian – this piece of it combines performance and the arts with good food and wine in Klagenfurt's oldest street. (p255)

Heritage.Hotel Hallstatt

11 Situated in Hallstatt on the Salzkammergut's spectacular Hallstätter See, this new upmarket hotel in three buildings offers views across the lake from most rooms, all of which have tasteful, modern interiors. (p205)

Joanneumsviertel

12 Graz' museum complex in the centre of the old town is going through changes – it will bring together a picturesque courtyard and museums to create a new mini-neighbourhood in the heart of Styria's capital. (p175)

K-Hof

13 Not only boasting great lakeside hotels, Gmunden in the Salzkammergut houses a fascinating, eclectic display of historic toilets, fossils, and a former Gothic church under the K-Hof's splendid roof. (p210)

if you like...

Museums & Palaces

Few countries in the world match Austria for palaces, castles and museums. Vienna has the most impressive grand residences, but others are scattered throughout the valleys and on mountain tops. The best palaces are now exciting museum spaces.

MuseumsQuartier Where baroque stables have morphed into Europe's finest modern museum quarter (p69)

Vienna's Hofburg Fortress, palace, home to the Habsburgs for over 600 years, and it now hosts magnificent museums (p59)

Schloss Belvedere Prince Eugene's Viennese masterpiece, with sensational art collections (p75)

Schloss Schönbrunn Vienna's premier palace and gardens where the Habsburgs are the focal point (p78)

Schloss Eggenberg Graz' magnificent Renaissance palace, with museums and gardens (p176)

Festung Hohensalzburg Salzburg's mighty 900-year-old fortress, complete with torture chamber (p222)

Residenz in Salzburg Opulence coupled with European grand masters (p223)

Hiking

Trails of all levels of difficulty can be accessed easily from most towns. Choose between strenuous mountain hikes, medium-difficulty walks through forest and meadows or easy hikes through vineyards to a tavern or a restaurant.

Lainzer Tiergarten A picturesque and easy walk outside Vienna to a wildlife park (p81)

Pinzgauer Spaziergang A great alpine walk affording mesmerising views of the snowcapped Hohe Tauern National Park and Kitzbühel Alps (p277)

Llama trekking A guided walk with gentle-natured camelids (p288)

Zillertal Circuit A classic alpine day hike starting at a jewel-coloured reservoir and offering fantastic views of the Zillertal Alps (p315)

Radsattel Circuit One of Vorarlberg's most spectacular hikes, exploring two valleys linked by a pass and taking you high into the realms of glaciers and 3000m mountains (p350)

Wining & Dining

The Danube Valley brings together food, wine and culture. Vienna has an extraordinary choice, and every major town and many smaller ones in Austria have much to offer. It's all about fresh and local – and sometimes organic – ingredients.

Aubergine Where a Viennese offal dish has been reinvented with snail caviar, plus a sensational wine list (p88)

Café Drechsler Legendary goulash in a designer coffee house to the tune of DJs in Vienna (p96)

Weinstube Josefstadt One of Vienna's best wine taverns (p97)

Wachau Dine in a restaurant or pack a picnic and head for the picturesque woods and vineyards (p112)

Der Steirer Wine and especially the art of goulash (p181)

Burgenland wines Reds galore (p148)

South Styrian wine roads Mostly white wine and some excellent food (p136)

Aiola Upstairs Modern and breezy, views over Graz (p181)

Viennese Beisln Eat at least once in a traditional tavern (p88)

RUSSELL MOUNTFORD

>> Staatsoper, Vienna (p100)

Winter Sports

Plowing, striding or riding through the snow is something you won't want to miss on a winter visit. Mostly little or no planning's required. Options (several with legendary après-ski) abound in Tyrol, western Styria and the Salzkammergut.

Major resorts Downhill skiing and snowboarding are a treat in Kitzbühel (p317), St Anton am Arlberg (p329) and Mayrhofen (p313)

Schladming Alpine skiing on pistes and on a glacier, plus gripping spectator events (p196)

Epic descents Streif in Kitzbühel (p317) and Harakiri in Mayrhofen (p313) will test your mettle

Igloo dreams Spend the night in an igloo at the Kitzsteinhorn Glacier (p278)

Après-ski Best in St Anton (p329) and Ischgl (p327)

Low key Snowshoeing, sledding and cross-country skiing in Seefeld, even for nonskiers (p310)

Cross-country Short loops and long treks in places such as Schladming (p196), Bad Gastein (p282) and Seefeld (p310)

Wellness & Good Living

Spa towns abound, and excellent wellness hotels combine creature comforts with sauna, activities, and health and beauty treatments. In some of them you can step right out of the pool and into a landscape of towering mountains.

Hotel Sacher Reminiscent of an expensive fin-de-siècle bordello; traditional luxury and high-tech wellness (p84)

Bad Gastein Belle-époque spa town in Hohe Tauern National Park (p282)

Semmering Spectacular railway, mountain activities and wellness offerings (p136)

Loisium Hotel Convenient to Vienna; wine, massages, and Danube Valley gourmet restaurants a short drive away (p123)

St Martins Therme & Lodge Burgenland mineral springs, with lake swimming (p147)

Therme Geinberg Upper Austrian spa with a Caribbean-style lagoon (p171)

Rogner-Bad Blumau Spa designed by Friedensreich Hundertwasser (p188)

Erzherzog Johann Large sauna area, 30m saltwater pool, kids' activities and hikes to Salzkammergut lakes from Bad Aussee (p209)

Musical Experiences

Vienna is renowned for classical music. Salzburg's most famous son is Mozart and elsewhere in Austria top-shelf events are a feature of the cultural landscape.

Vienna Boys' Choir The heavenly voices of the world's most enduring 'boy group' – founded five centuries ago (p101)

Staatsoper Vienna's premier venue for opera and classical music (p100)

Musikverein Home to the Vienna Philharmonic Orchestra, with dazzling acoustics (p100)

Mozart in Salzburg The boy wonder of classical is the focus of a festival and events at numerous venues in Salzburg (p232)

Alpine folk music and kitsch Check out the Zillertal (p310) or *Sound of Music* country (p228)

Hip and heavy The band Fuckhead will more than do the trick for the hard stuff, but listen in to other worthy acts, too (p380)

Styriarte Graz' series of classical concerts in June and July (p177)

Donauinselfest Three days of rock, pop, hardcore, folk and country music on the Donauinsel in Vienna (p83)

If you like... Christmas markets

Hit Vienna or Innsbruck in December and sip mulled wine (p105 and p301)

If you like... Sisi

Empress Elisabeth is more famous than Marilyn Monroe – visit the Kaiserappartements (p59)

The Wide Open Road

Despite its small size, Austria offers some great road trips – by car, motorbike or bicycle. The best wind through spectacular valleys and over mountain passes, and some of them are through wine-growing regions such as the Wachau and southern Styria.

Grossglockner Road One of Austria's greatest mountain drives. The super fit can bike it: it's worth the back-breaking uphill for the exhilarating downhill, some say (p279)

South Styrian wine roads Hidden away on the Slovenian border but easily reached from Graz, this wine route passes through a landscape reminiscent of Tuscany (p187)

Danube Valley The Wachau region combines culture, wine and of course good food. The route can be done by car from Vienna or by bicycle from Krems (p118)

Bregenzerwald Käsestrasse The Bregenz Forest Cheese Road takes you through a cheese-producing region of Vorarlberg with quaint villages (p346)

Lookouts & High Rides

With the Alps running like a jagged backbone across the country, splendid lookouts and gondola rides offer spine-chilling views and vertical rides.

Dachstein Eispalast and Skywalk Dangle precariously at the vertical rock face before reaching the viewing platform at the top (p196)

Millennium-Express cable car Six kilometres, with skiing or mountain biking down (p262)

Hintertux Glacier A cable-car ride to the glacier with views to die for (p313)

Riesenrad Vienna's iconic Ferris wheel combines a great ride with fantastic city views (p74)

Festung Hohensalzburg Views over the spires, domes and rooftops of Salzburg (p222)

Edelweiss Spitze (2571m) On the Grossglockner Road; 360-degree views of more than 30 peaks over 3000m (p279)

Balthazar im Rudolfsturm Fantastic views over the Hallstätter See complemented by a delicious light meal and a drink (p206)

Kaisergebirge Kufstein's retro-ride cable car – angst at its most satisfying (p321)

Mountain Biking & Cycling

Pedalling lazily through a valley or rolling landscape for a few hours, exploring Vienna by bicycle, winding along mountain trails or roaring down a hair-raising run. This is one of the best ways to experience the Austrian outdoors.

Vienna Cycle paths abound, making this a convenient way to take in the capital (p107)

Danube Valley cycle path The quintessential path, from the German border via the Wachau and Vienna to Slovakia (p111)

Schladming With 900km of bike trails and some challenging mountain-bike runs (p196)

Bodensee Radweg Highly scenic trail circumnavigating Lake Constance (p340)

Tauernradweg A 310km trail of mountain landscapes in Hohe Tauern National Park (p282)

Dachstein circuit Fab three-day mountain-bike trail (p245)

Nordkette Singletrail Innsbruck's tough trail, one of the most exhilarating downhill rides in the country (p301)

Millennium Express–Gmanberg Stash the bicycle in the cable car and zip 11.7km back down in Carinthia (p262)

month by month

January

The ski season is revving. One of the coldest months of the year in Austria, this is the right time to hit the peaks for downhill or cross-country skiing, or for snowshoe hikes.

 New Year Concerts

On 1 January the new year is welcomed with classical concerts. The Vienna Philharmonic's performance in Vienna's Staatsoper is the most celebrated.

Perchtenlaufen

Locals dress as *Perchten* (spirits crowned with elaborate headdresses) and parade through the streets across much of western Austria in a celebration to bring good fortune and bountiful harvests for the year. Salzkammergut's equivalent is Glöckerlauf (p213) in Ebensee.

Mozartwoche

Held in Salzburg in late January, the Mozart Weeks (www.mozarteum. at) celebrate the city's most famous son (p230).

February

The winter months are freezing, but in Vienna the museums and cultural scene are in full swing. Crowds are down except in the traditional cafes. On the slopes the skiing is usually still excellent.

Opernball

Of the 300 or so Vienna balls held in January and February, Opernball (Opera Ball; www.wiener -staatsoper.at) is number one. It's a supremely lavish affair, with the men in tails and women in shining white gowns (p83).

Schemenlaufen

Every four years, Imst in Tyrol plays host to a Shrovetide festival, the Schemenlaufen (ghost dance); one takes place on 12 February 2012. The highlight is the vibrant parade of ghostlike characters, from hunchback *Hexen* (witches) to impish *Spritzer* that squirt water at spectators (p324).

March

The sun is thawing the public squares in cities like Vienna, Salzburg and Graz. Hiking and cycling become possible in some places from late March, but many sights outside Vienna are still dormant.

 **Easter**

Easter is when families come together to celebrate. In Salzburg it is yet another excuse for a mammoth music festival, the Osterfestspiele (www. osterfestspiele-salzburg.at). In Vienna the OsterKlang Festival (www.osterklang. at) orchestral and chamber-music recitals are held. The opening concert features the Vienna Philharmonic.

May

Cities such as Vienna, Salzburg and Graz are a delight on bright days — uncrowded and often warm. A hike to a mountain *Alm* (meadow) becomes a romp through flowers, and since April all sights and activities have opened on a summer schedule.

Wiener Festwochen

In Vienna arts from around the world hit the stages until mid-June (p83).

Medieval Festival

In late May, Feldkirch revisits the Middle Ages with troubadours, knights and nonstop feasting at the Mittelaltermarkt (p345).

Linz Fest

In late May or early June contemporary and rock music of all descriptions is staged for free in Linz (p158).

Gauderfest

The festival takes place on the first weekend in May in Zell am Ziller, where farmers and urban cowboys do what they do best: make music, dance and drink (p312).

Musikwochen Millstatt

In Millstatt in Carinthia a string of concerts are held between May and September, mostly in the medieval abbey (p269).

June

Mountain lakes are still very chilly, but the Wörthersee and others have soaked up the summer weather. Other activities such as hiking or kayaking are also excellent. Big-hitting sights in Vienna and Salzburg start to get crowded.

Donauinselfest

Vienna gets down for a three-day festival of rock, pop, hardcore, folk and country music on the Donauinsel (www.donau inselfest.at; p83).

Innsbruck Summer Dance Festival

A selection of top international contemporary dance groups takes to the stage for a month during the Tanzsommer in June and July (p301).

Sommerszene

Salzburg's cutting-edge dance, theatre and music bash ignites from mid-June to mid-July (p231).

Rainbow Parade

In Vienna the Regenbogen Parade (Rainbow Parade) takes over the Ring and MuseumsQuartier at the end of June or in early July (p99).

Styriarte

Graz' most important cultural festival offers almost continuous classical concerts in June and July (p177).

July

School holidays begin in July, the time when families enjoy the warm weather on lakes and in the mountains. Cities can be sweltering and crowded, but restaurant dining is at its alfresco best.

Lehár Festival

Works by the composer Franz Lehár are the focus of a festival of music in Bad Ischl in July and August (p203).

Wörthersee Festspiele

Operas, ballets and pop concerts are staged over the water of the Wörthersee in Klagenfurt from late June to mid-August (p252).

ImPuls Tanz

Vienna's premier avant-garde dance festival takes place from mid-July to mid-August (p83).

Lienz Street Festival

Top circus and theatre acts from around the world descend on Lienz (Tyrol; p289). Summer also welcomes a series of events celebrating Tyrolean culture.

Salzburger Festspiele

World-class opera, classical music and drama take the stage across Salzburg from late July to August (p232).

Spectaculum

One of Austria's more unusual events takes place in the small town of Friesach in Carinthia, where on the last Saturday in July electric lights are extinguished and the town is closed off and lit by torches and flares as medieval characters stroll around performing (p263).

Seefestspiele

The sleepy town of Mörbisch am See in Burgenland shifts to centre stage from mid-July to August with the Seefestspiele, a summer operetta festival whose counterpart is the Opern Festspiele held 7km away near even sleepier St Margareten (p145).

Musikfilm Festival

Screenings of operas, operettas and concerts outside Vienna's Rathaus in July and August (p83).

August

School holidays continue to propel families into the resorts, which along with international visitors makes things a bit crowded. Hit some isolated spots in the fine weather – seek out a *Heuriger* (wine tavern) on a vineyard.

Bregenzer Festspiele

Beginning in late July and continuing until late August, this is Vorarlberg's top-class cultural event, where classical concerts, opera and theatre are performed on a floating, open-air stage (p337).

Kirchtag

On the first Saturday in August, Villach's pedestrian centre is transformed into a folk-music festival featuring international, national and local musicians (p258).

September

The temperatures are beginning a gradual descent and the crowds are tailing off now. Museums and most of the activities are still in season, however, and a couple of top-class festivals are revving into action.

Brucknerfest

Linz stages its most celebrated festival, a series of classical concerts based around composer Anton Bruckner (p156).

Internationale Haydntage

International and Austrian performers take the audience through the range of works by Josef Haydn throughout much of September in his home town of Eisenstadt (p142).

October

Goldener Oktober – the light reflects the golden browns of autumn, the mountains are growing chilly at night, the wine harvest is in and in some places the museums are preparing to close for winter.

Steirischer Herbst

Held in Graz (p177) each year, this avant-garde festival is the autumn highlight of the cultural calendar, with a program of music, theatre and film, plus exhibitions and art installations.

Viennale

For two weeks from mid-October, city cinemas host screenings of films from fringe ranging through documentaries to short and feature films (p83).

November

Many museums outside the capital have gone into winter hibernation, the days are getting short and the weather can be poor. The cafes, pubs and restaurants become the focal point.

St Martin's Day

Around 11 November the new wine is released and St Martin's Day is marked with feasts of goose washed down by the nectar of the gods.

December

Cold has set in, the ski resorts are filling and in Vienna and other capitals winter programs are being staged in the theatres and classical-music venues – often the best performances are during the coldest months.

Christmas Markets

Christkindlmärkte (Christmas markets) spring up around the country from early December until the 24th and Austrians rug themselves up and sip mulled wine from stands on public squares.

Silvester

Book early for the night of 31 December, celebrated with fireworks and a blaze of crackers and rockets on the crowded streets.

itineraries

Whether you've got six days or 60, these itineraries provide a starting point for the trip of a lifetime. Want more inspiration? Head online to lonelyplanet. com/thorntree to chat with other travellers.

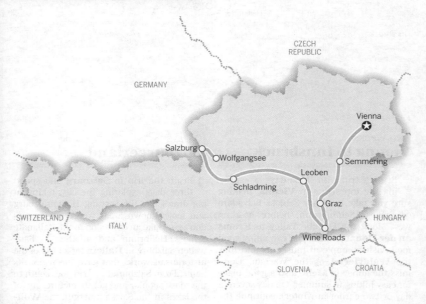

Two Weeks
Classic Austria

> Spend three days visiting top sights in **Vienna** before taking a train over the Semmering Pass to the spa town of **Semmering** (day four). During the ski season (from about mid-December to early March in this region), you might want to hit the snow here or relax in a hotel wellness area. In summer, take in the picturesque surroundings and fresh air on a walk before setting off for **Graz** late on day five or early on day six. In winter in Styria take advantage of the cultural scene, catching a performance or visiting a museum or two, and enjoying the local cuisine and nightlife. In summer, don't miss Schloss Eggenberg. After exploring Graz, the **wine roads** in the south or one of the surrounding sights, board the train by day nine for Schladming, breaking the journey for a few hours in **Leoben** to visit the MuseumsCenter Leoben. In **Schladming**, visit the skywalk and glacier, staying overnight (longer in winter for snow sports) before finishing the classic trip in **Salzburg** and (in summer) the nearby **Wolfgangsee**.

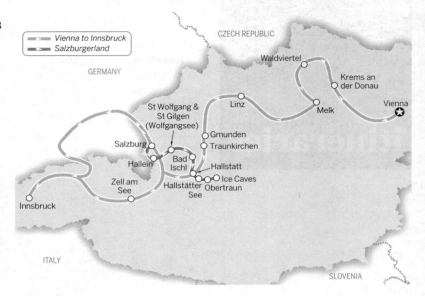

Two Weeks
Vienna to Innsbruck

❯ Begin a trip with three days of exploring the top sights in **Vienna**, making sure you take in either Schloss Belvedere or Schloss Schönbrunn, before heading west along the Danube Valley to **Krems an der Donau**, where you can enjoy good food, visit a couple of museums and tour the **Waldviertel** or the Wachau. Don't miss the abbey in **Melk**, also a good place for easy hiking in summer. On day seven (a day or two earlier in winter), continue the trip to **Linz** for an overnight stay in this industrial city with exciting museums such as the Lentos Kunstmuseum. The trail to **Hallstatt** and the lakes of the Salzkammergut will restore the feel for the picturesque landscape after Linz, and you can briefly break the journey in **Gmunden** or **Traunkirchen** on the Traunsee as a foretaste of the more spectacular landscapes to come. From Hallstatt you have a choice of travelling to **Salzburg** for the many cultural sights and crossing through Germany to Innsbruck, or bypassing Salzburg and stopping over in **Zell am See** before continuing to **Innsbruck**, where you can choose between culture or hiking trails.

10 Days
Salzburgerland

❯ Begin the trip in **Salzburg** and spend three days exploring the city, taking in big draws like the Festung Hohensalzburg and lesser-known areas where the crowds don't go. Make an excursion to the Italianate Schloss Hellbrunn and another to Salzwelten Salzburg in **Hallein** for a taste of the historic salt works that gave the region its name. From Salzburg the road goes south to the most popular and gently picturesque of the lakes in the Salzkammergut, the **Wolfgangsee**, where the summertime swimming, walking and cycling are splendid. Explore the lesser-known towns on hikes or rides over the next three to four days. From **St Wolfgang** or **St Gilgen** it's a short bus hop to **Bad Ischl**, an excellent base for exploring other lakes in the Salzkammergut. The most spectacular of these is the **Hallstätter See**, with **Hallstatt** or the quieter (but less historic) **Obertraun** perfect for overnighting if you are not based in Bad Ischl for the next three days. Near Obertraun, take in the **ice caves** on a cable-car ride and make sure you do one of the hikes in the area. Around Hallstatt you can visit another of the excellent salt works before returning to Salzburg.

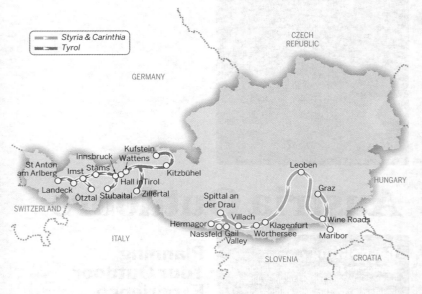

Styria & Carinthia
Tyrol

CZECH
REPUBLIC

GERMANY

St Anton
am Arlberg
Landeck
Ötztal
Imst
Stams
Innsbruck
Hall in Tirol
Stubaital
Kufstein
Wattens
Kitzbühel
Zillertal

SWITZERLAND

ITALY

Spittal an
der Drau
Villach
Hermagor
Nassfeld Gail
Valley
Klagenfurt
Wörthersee

Leoben
Graz
Wine Roads
Maribor

HUNGARY

SLOVENIA
CROATIA

10 Days
Styria & Carinthia

> Begin the trip in **Graz**, or in Klagenfurt if you're doing this itinerary in the other direction. Plan three or four days in Graz to get to know the city, its sights, culinary delights and the friendly Grazer. Explore the lively eating and drinking scenes or the formal cultural scene. On the third day take an excursion along the south Styrian **wine roads**, a Tuscan-like landscape hugging the Slovenian border with vineyards at every bend. A day trip to **Maribor** in Slovenia is possible, or you might like to spend a fifth day at one of the other places easily accessible from Graz. A train takes you to **Klagenfurt** via **Leoben** where you can break the journey for a few hours and check out its MuseumsCentre Leoben. The remaining five days can be divided between Klagenfurt and **Wörthersee**, **Villach** or **Spittal an der Drau**, all towns with a sprinkling of sights and good opportunities for activities nearby. Towns such as **Hermagor** in the **Gail Valley** have great cycling, hiking and (in winter) skiing possibilities at **Nassfeld**. For a food, wine and culture focus, plan more time around Graz in Styria. For swimming and other activities, plan more time for Carinthia.

Two Weeks
Tyrol

> Kick off with a few days laid-back **Innsbruck**. Stroll the lanes of the historic *Altstadt* (old town), taking in its galleries, Habsburg treasures and upbeat nightlife. On the third day, you might opt to take the futuristic funicular to the Nordkette for some hiking or skiing, or head out to Olympic ski jump, Bergisel. From Innsbruck, go south for scenic glacier skiing in the **Stubaital** or west to **Stams'** exquisite baroque abbey. Day five leads you further west to the spectacularly rugged **Ötztal**, where you can dip into prehistory at Ötzi Dorf and thermal waters at Aqua Dome spa. Spend the next couple of days rafting near **Landeck**, exploring the Rosengartenschlucht gorge at **Imst**, or hiking and skiing in **St Anton am Arlberg**. In week two, retrace your steps to Innsbruck and swing east. Factor in a day to tour the pristine medieval town of **Hall in Tirol** and Swarovski Kristallwelten, the heart of the Swarovski crystal empire in **Wattens**. The alpine scenery of the **Zillertal** will keep you occupied with outdoor activities, nature reserve and thigh-slapping folk music over the next few days. Finish your adventure in fortress-topped **Kufstein** and the legendary mountains of **Kitzbühel**.

Austria Outdoors

Best Skiing

St Anton am Arlberg A holy grail for adventurous skiers, with varied terrain, exhilarating off-piste opportunities, an impeccable snow record and the hottest après-ski in the Austrian Alps.

Best Cycling

Danube Cycle Path This smooth-as-silk trail shadows the Danube. Take in storybook castles, vineyards and majestic abbeys as you pedal gently along.

Best Climbing

Zillertal Alps Sheer granite cliffs, bizarre rock formations and boulders make the Zillertal Alps a wonderland for the ardent climber.

Best Rafting

Landeck A handy base for tackling the swirling waters of the Inn and Sanna Rivers.

Planning Your Outdoor Experience

One look at a map of Austria says it all: jagged peaks and glacier-gouged valleys, mighty rivers and lakes cover almost every last lovely inch of the country. Be it hiking in wildflower-strewn pastures, schussing down Tyrol's mythical slopes, whirling above the mountain tops from a parachute or freewheeling along the Danube, Austria will elevate, invigorate, thrill and amaze you. In this eminently accessible and delightfully compact country, you'll be itching to get outdoors and create your own adventure.

When to Go

» **May–June** Few crowds and often fine weather, especially for cycling. Snow patches linger above 2000m in the Alps. June is great for hiking: the weather is warm, days are long and wildflowers like hot-pink alpine roses brush the slopes. On the downside, huts are still closed and mountain transport is reduced or nonexistent.

» **July–August** This is the alpine rush hour and deservedly so. Snow melts from all but the highest peaks and all lifts and huts are open (book ahead), making this the best time for high-altitude and hut-to-hut hikes. The sun can be penetrating, but a crystal-clear lake or river is usually nearby for water sport fans. Muggy temperatures in August can bring sudden thunderstorms.

» **September–early October** On a good day, the hiking is glorious – skies are blue as blue,

TOP SLOPES

Cruise, carve, party and quake in your boots at some of these top spots:

» **Top descents** The Streif (p317), part of the epic Hahnenkamm, is Kitzbühel's king of scary skiing. Mayrhofen's Harakiri (p313) is Austria's steepest run, with a gradient of 78%. It's pitch-black and there's no turning baaaaaack...

» **Top family skiing** Filzmoos (p245) for its uncrowded nursery slopes, chocolate-box charm and jagged Dachstein mountains. Heiligenblut (p279) is refreshingly low-key and has the Bobo's Kids' Club.

» **Top snowboarding** Mayrhofen (p313) is a mecca to free riders, and some say it has Austria's most *awesome* terrain park.

» **Top après-ski** Join the singing, swinging, Jägermeister-fuelled fun in St Anton am Arlberg (p332), Austria's après-ski king. Wild inebriation and all-night clubbing are the winter norm in raucous rival Ischgl (p328).

» **Top glacier skiing** The Stubai Glacier (p309) has snow-sure pistes within easy reach of Innsbruck. Head to the Kitzsteinhorn Glacier (p273) for pre- and post-season skiing at 3203m, with arresting views of the snowy Hohe Tauern range.

temperatures mild, the forests a vibrant palette of reds and golds. On a bad day, you can hit rain, fog, even snow. Alpine huts are closed and mountain transport reduces to a trickle. That said, other accommodation is cheaper than in summer and trails are considerably less crowded.

» **Mid-October–December** The days are short and the weather is highly unpredictable, with rain, fog and snow above 1500m in the Alps. The lack of mountain transport limits your hiking to the lower regions. If you do hike, get an early start and plan your route carefully.

» **December–April** Skiers whiz down the slopes until Easter. There is *Winterwandern* (winter walking) in popular alpine resorts. For less crowded slopes and cheaper accommodation, avoid skiing in school holiday times: Christmas, New Year, February half-term and Easter. As a rule, the higher you go, the longer the season.

Skiing & Snowboarding

No matter whether you're a slalom expert, a fearless free rider or a beginner, there's a slope with your name on it in Austria. And, oh, what slopes! Granted, the Swiss and French Alps may have the height edge, but Austria remains Europe's best skiing all-rounder. This land is the origin of modern skiing (thanks to Hannes Schneider's dashing Arlberg technique), the birthplace of Olympic legends and the spiritual home of après-ski. Here you'll find intermediate cruising, knee-trembling black runs and summertime glacier skiing – in short, powdery perfection for every taste and ability.

Planning Your Skiing Trip

Ski Run Classifications

Piste maps are available on most tourist office websites and at the valley stations of ski lifts; runs are colour-coded according to difficulty as follows:

» **Blue** Indicates easy, well-groomed runs that are suitable for beginners.

» **Red** Indicates intermediate runs, which are groomed but often steeper and narrower than blue runs. Skiers should have a medium level of ability.

» **Black** For expert skiers with polished technique and skills. The runs are mostly steep, not always groomed and may have moguls and steep vertical drops.

Safety

» Avalanches are a serious danger in snowbound areas and can be fatal.

» If you're skiing off-piste, never go alone and take an avalanche pole, a transceiver or a shovel and – most importantly – a professional guide.

» See www.lawine.at (in German) for the avalanche risk and snow coverage by region.

» UV rays are stronger at high altitudes and intensified by snow glare; wear ski goggles and sunscreen.

Austria Outdoors

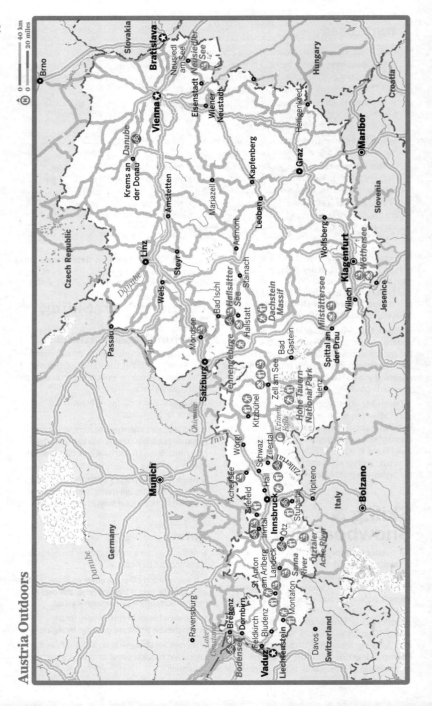

<table>
<tr><td>

SUMMER SNOW

If the thought of pounding the powder in summer appeals, hightail it to glaciers such as the Stubai Glacier (p309), Hintertux Glacier (p313) and Kitzsteinhorn Glacier (p273), where, weather permitting, there's fine downhill skiing year-round.

</td></tr>
</table>

» Get in good shape before hitting the slopes and build up gradually.

» Wear layers to adapt to the constant change in body temperature; make sure your head, wrists and knees are protected (preferably padded).

» Before you hurtle down that black run, make sure you're properly insured and read the small print: mountain-rescue costs, medical treatment and repatriation can soon amount to triple figures.

Resources

Books

Alpine Ski Mountaineering: Central and Eastern Alps (Bill O'Connor) Great guide detailing ski tours through the Silvretta, Ötztal, Stubai and Ortler ranges.

Where to Ski and Snowboard (Chris Gill and Dave Watts) Updated annually, this is an indispensable guide to the slopes, covering everything from terrain to lift passes.

Which Ski Resort – Europe: Our Top 50 Recommendations (Pat Sharples and Vanessa Webb) Written by a freestyle champ and a ski coach, this handy guide has tips on everything from off-piste to après-ski.

Websites

Bergfex (www.bergfex.com) A great website with piste maps, snow forecasts of the Alps and details of every ski resort in Austria.

If You Ski (www.ifyouski.com) Resort guides, ski deals and info on ski hire and schools. You can beat the slope-side queues by prebooking your lift pass online.

MadDog Ski (www.maddogski.com) Fun skiing website full of insider tips on everything from slopes to where to stay and après-ski.

On the Snow (www.onthesnow.co.uk) Reviews of Austria's ski resorts, plus snow reports, webcams and lift pass details.

Where to Ski & Snowboard (www.where toskiandsnowboard.com) Key facts on resorts, which are ranked according to their upsides and downsides, plus user reviews.

World Snowboard Guide (www.worldsnow boardguide.com) Snowboarder central, with comprehensive information on most Austrian resorts.

Lift Passes

Costing around €220 or thereabouts for a week, lift passes are a big chunk out of your budget. The passes give access to one or more ski sectors and nearly always include ski buses between the different areas. Lift passes for lesser-known places may be as little as half that charged in the jet-set resorts. Count on around €30 to €45 for a one-day ski pass, with substantial reductions for longer-term passes. Children usually pay half-price, while under-fives ski for free (bring a passport as proof of age).

Most lift passes are now 'hands-free', with a built-in chip that barriers detect automatically, and some can be prebooked online. You may need a passport-sized photo for multi-day (usually eight days or more) passes.

Equipment Hire

Skis (downhill, cross-country, telemark), snowboards, boots, poles and helmets can be rented at sport shops like **Intersport** (www.intersport.at) in every resort. Ski/snowboard/cross-country ski rental costs around €27/125 per day/week, or €33/156 for top-of-the-range gear. Boot hire is around €15/60 per day/week. With Intersport, children 15 and under pay half-price, under-10s get free ski hire when both parents rent equipment, and you can ski seven days for the price of six.

Ski Tuition

Most ski resorts have one or more ski schools; for a list of regional ski schools, visit www.skilehrer.at (in German) and click on 'Landesverbände'. Group lessons for both adults and children typically cost €60 per day (two hours in the morning, two hours in the afternoon), €160 for four days and €180 for six days. The more days you take, the cheaper it gets. Private instruction is available on request. Kids can start learning from the age of four.

Ski Regions & Resorts

The following are our pick of Austria's ski regions and resorts, but they're just a taste of what's up there. While this book features plenty of skiing information, it's not a dedicated skiing guide; Austria has hundreds of excellent ski resorts and no attempt has been made to cover them exhaustively.

SLOPE SAVERS

It's worth checking websites like www.igluski.com, www.skiingaustria.co.uk and www.j2ski.com for last-minute ski deals and packages. Local tourist offices and www.austria.info might also have offers.

If you're heading to Kitzbühel or Zell am See-Kaprun, you can save with a SnowBall Pass (www.snowballpass.com). Valid for the winter season, the pass costs €18 and gets you significant discounts on equipment hire, lift passes, tuition, insurance and more.

You can save time and euros by prebooking ski and snowboard hire online at Snow-brainer (www.snowbrainer.com), which gives a discount of up to 49% on shop rental prices.

Ski Amadé (Salzburgerland)

Salzburgerland's Ski Amadé (www.skiamade .com) is Austria's biggest ski area, covering a whopping 860km of pistes in 25 resorts divided into five snow-sure regions. Among them are low-key Radstadt (p246) and family-friendly Filzmoos (p245). Such a vast area means that truly every level is catered for: from gentle cruising on tree-lined runs to off-piste touring. One ski pass covers the entire region and costs €196 for six days.

Ski Arlberg (Tyrol/Vorarlberg)

With 280km of slopes, Ski Arlberg (www.ski arlberg.at) is one of Austria's most famous skiing regions and deservedly so. After all, this is the home of St Anton am Arlberg (p329), a mecca to expert skiers and boarders, with its great snow record, challenging terrain and terrific off-piste; not to mention *the* most happening après-ski in Austria, if not Europe. Its over-the-valley neighbours are the resorts of Lech and Zürs (p349) in Vorarlberg. A six-day pass costs €212.

Kitzbühel (Tyrol)

The legendary Hahnenkamm, 170km of groomed slopes, a car-free medieval town centre and upbeat nightlife all make Kitzbühel (p317) one of Austria's most popular resorts. Critics may grumble about unreliable snow – with a base elevation of 762m, Kitzbühel is fairly low by alpine standards – but that doesn't stop skiers who come for the varied downhill, snowboarding and off-piste. A six-day AllStarCard for Kitzbühel and nine other resorts in the region (a total 1067km of slopes) costs €217.

Zillertal Arena (Tyrol)

Mayrhofen (p313) is the showpiece of the Zillertal Arena (www.zillertalarena.at), which covers 166km of slopes and 49 lifts (some pretty high-tech) in the highly scenic Zillertal. As well as being intermediate heaven, Mayrhofen has Austria's steepest black run, the kamikaze-like Harakiri with a 78% gradient, and appeals to freestylers for its fantastic terrain park. Even if snow lies thin in the valley, it's guaranteed at the nearby Hintertux Glacier (p313). A six-day Zillertal Superskipass costs €199.

Zell am See–Kaprun (Hohe Tauern National Park)

The lakeside resort of Zell am See (p273) and its twin Kaprun (www.zellamsee-kaprun.com) share 138km of sunny slopes. Pistes tend to be more of the tree-lined and scenic kind, making this a sound choice for novices and families. Even if the snow coverage is thin on the lower slopes, there's fresh powder and a terrain park at the Kitzsteinhorn Glacier to play in. The après-ski in Zell am See's car-free old town is lively but not rowdy. The entire region affords gorgeous views of the glacier-capped Hohe Tauern range. A six-day pass costs €202.

Silvretta-Montafon (Vorarlberg)

The iconic arrow-shaped peak of Piz Buin (3312m) dominates the Silvretta-Montafon (http://winter.silvretta-montafon.at, in German) ski area (p349). Tucked away in the southeast corner of Vorarlberg, this serene and beautiful valley's low-key resorts appeal to families, cruisers and ski tourers. Besides 152km of downhill, there is plenty to do off-piste, from sledding to winter hiking. A six-day pass will set you back €189.50.

Ischgl–Silvretta Arena (Tyrol)

Ischgl (p327) is the centrepiece of the Silvretta Arena (www.silvretta.at), comprising 238km of prepared slopes and 41 ultramodern lifts. High slopes above 2000m mean guaranteed snow, mostly geared towards confident intermediates, off-piste fans and boarders. The resort has carved a name for itself as a party hot spot, with big-name season opening and closing concerts, and pumping (borderline sleazy) après-ski. For those seeking a quieter vibe, Galtür, Kappl and Samnaun (Switzerland) are nearby. A six-day pass for the whole area costs €236.

Ötztal–Sölden (Tyrol)

The Ötztal (p322) is defined by some of the wildest and highest mountains in Austria. Its main ski resort is snow-sure Sölden (www.soelden.com), with 150km of slopes between 1350m and 3340m, a state-of-the-art lift network and a crazy après-ski scene. The terrain is intermediate heaven, but presents more of a challenge on long runs such as the 50km Big 3 Rally and off-piste. A bonus to skiing here is the snow reliability on two glaciers – Rettenbach and Tiefenbach – making this a great pre- or late-season choice. A six-day lift pass costs €225.

Cross-Country Skiing

Cross-country skiing (*Langlauf*) in Austria is considerably greener and cheaper than skiing. Skis give you the traction to walk uphill at your own pace and experience the beauty of the forest and mountains in slow motion. The two main techniques are the classic lift-and-glide method on prepared cross-country tracks (*Loipen*) and the more energetic 'skating' technique. The basics are easy to master at a cross-country school and tracks are graded from blue to black according to difficulty.

Seefeld (p309) features among Austria's top cross-country skiing destinations, with 266km of *Loipen* criss-crossing the region including a floodlit track. Zell am See (p273) is another hot spot, with 200km of groomed trails providing panoramic views of the Hohe Tauern mountains. Other great resorts to test your stamina and stride include the Bad Gastein region (p282), with 90km of well-marked cross-country trails. To search for cross-country regions and packages, see www.langlauf-urlaub.at (in German).

Walking & Hiking

'*Der Berg ruft*' (the mountain calls) is what Austrians say as they gallivant off to the hills at the weekend, and what shopkeepers post on closed doors in summer. And what more excuse do you need? For Austrians, *Wandern* (walking) is not a sport, it's second nature. Kids frolicking in alpine pastures, nuns Nordic-walking in the hills, super-fit 70-somethings trekking over windswept 2000m passes – such universal wanderlust is bound to rub off on you sooner or later.

With its towering peaks, forest-cloaked slopes and luxuriantly green valleys, the country's landscapes are perfectly etched and the walking opportunities are endless. Strike into Austria's spectacularly rugged backyard, listen closely and you too will hear those mountains calling...

Planning Your Walk
Weather

If there's one rule of thumb in the Austrian Alps, it's to never take the weather for granted. It may *look* sunny but conditions can change at the drop of a hat – hail, lightning, fog, torrential rain, you name it. Check the forecast before embarking on long hikes at high altitudes. Tourist offices also display and/or provide mountain-weather forecasts.

Österreichischer Alpenverein (ÖAV; Austrian Alpine Club; www.alpenverein.at, in German) A reliable web source for forecasts for the alpine regions.

Snow Forecast (www.snow-forecast.com) Up-to-date snow forecasts for major Austrian ski resorts.

Wetter Österreich (www.wetter.at, in German) Day and three-day weather forecasts, plus up-to-date weather warnings.

BIG FOOT

Tired of the crowded slopes? Snowshoeing is a great alternative for nonskiers. On a sunny day, there's little that beats making enormous tracks through deep powder and twinkling forests in quiet exhilaration. If you imagine snowshoes as old-fashioned, tennis racquet–like contraptions, think again: the new ones are lightweight and pretty easy to get the hang of. Many resorts in the Austrian Alps have marked trails and some offer guided tours for a small charge. It costs roughly €15 to €20 to hire a set of snowshoes and poles for the day.

EQUIPMENT CHECK LIST

Clothing

- [ ] windproof and waterproof jacket
- [ ] breathable fleece
- [ ] loose-fitting walking trousers, preferably with zip-off legs
- [ ] hiking shorts
- [ ] T-shirts or long-sleeved shirts
- [ ] socks (polypropylene)
- [ ] sun hat
- [ ] sunglasses
- [ ] swimwear (optional)

Footwear

- [ ] walking boots with a good grip
- [ ] trekking sandals or thongs
- [ ] socks

Other Equipment

- [ ] backpack or daypack
- [ ] sleeping bag
- [ ] water bottle
- [ ] map
- [ ] compass
- [ ] Swiss Army knife

For Emergencies

- [ ] emergency food rations
- [ ] first-aid kit
- [ ] torch/flashlight (batteries and bulbs)
- [ ] whistle
- [ ] mobile phone

Miscellaneous Items

- [ ] camera and lenses
- [ ] umbrella

- [ ] insect repellent
- [ ] high-energy food (eg nuts, dried fruit, bread, cured meat)
- [ ] at least 1L of water per person, per day
- [ ] sunscreen (SPF15+)
- [ ] toiletries, toilet paper and towel
- [ ] stuff sacks

For Hikes above 2000m

- [ ] thermal underwear
- [ ] extra clothing
- [ ] gaiters
- [ ] gloves
- [ ] warm hat
- [ ] walking sticks

Walk Designations

Austria is criss-crossed with well-maintained *Wanderwege* (walking trails), which are waymarked with red-white-red stripes (often on a handy rock or tree) and yellow signposts. Bear in mind, though, that these are no substitute for a decent map and/or compass in the Alps. Like ski runs, trails are colour-coded according to difficulty:

» **Blue** The blue routes (alternatively with no colour) are suitable for everyone; paths are well marked, mostly flat and easy to follow.

» **Red** The red routes require a good level of fitness, surefootedness and basic mountain experience. They are sometimes steep and narrow, and may involve scrambling and/or short fixed-rope sections.

» **Black** For experienced mountain hikers with a head for heights, black routes are mostly steep, require proper equipment and can be dangerous in bad weather.

Walk Descriptions

» The times and distances for walks that appear in this book are provided only as a guide.

» Times are based on the actual walking time and do not include stops for snacks, taking photos,

rests or side trips. Be sure to factor these in when planning your walk.

» Distances should be read in conjunction with altitudes – significant elevation can make a greater difference to your walking time than lateral distance.

Safety

Most walker injuries are directly attributable to fatigue, heat exhaustion and inadequate clothing or footwear. A fall resulting from sliding on grass, scree or iced-over paths is a common hazard; watch out for black ice. On high-alpine routes, avalanches and rock falls can be a problem. A few common-sense rules will help you stay safe when walking:

» Always stick to the marked and/or signposted route, particularly in foggy conditions. With some care, most walking routes can be followed in fog, but otherwise wait by the path until visibility is clear enough to proceed.

» Study the weather forecast before you go and remember that weather patterns change suddenly in the mountains.

» Increase the length and elevation of your walks gradually, until you are acclimatised to the vast alpine scale; this will help prevent altitude sickness and fatigue.

» Where possible, don't walk in the mountains alone. Two is considered the minimum number for safe walking, and having at least one additional person in the party will mean someone can stay with an injured walker while the other seeks help.

» Inform a responsible person, such as a family member, hut warden or hotel receptionist, of your plans, and let them know when you return.

Resources

Books

While we cover some walks in the On the Road chapters of this book, you should consider investing in a dedicated walking guide if you're planning on doing a lot of hiking. Here are a few to get you started:

100 Mountain Walks in Austria (Kev Renolds) A useful guide, listing more than 100 walks in 10 regions (mostly in the Alps).

Alpine Flowers-Alpenblumen (NF 1300; Kompass) Become well-versed in the local flora with this handy pocket guide complete with colour illustrations.

Mountain Walking in Austria (Cecil Davies) This has long been the standard English-language walking guidebook to Austria, but some route descriptions can be out of date. The book covers 98 walks, from half-day to week-long hikes, focusing largely on alpine regions.

Walking Austria's Alps Hut to Hut (Jonathan Hurdle) An informative and inspirational guide covering multiday routes and Austria's alpine huts.

Walking Easy in the Swiss & Austrian Alps (Chet Lipton) Covers gentle two- to six-hour hikes in the most popular areas.

Websites

Get planning with the routes, maps and GPS downloads on the following websites:

> ### SOS SIX
>
> The standard Alpine distress signal is six whistles, six calls, six smoke puffs, six yodels – that is, six of whatever sign or sound you can make – repeated every 10 seconds for one minute. If you have a mobile phone, make sure you take it with you. Mountain rescue (📞140) in the Alps is very efficient but extremely expensive, so make sure you have adequate insurance (read the fine print).

Bergfex (www.bergfex.com) Plan your dream hike with detailed route descriptions (many are in German) and maps, searchable by region, fitness level and length. Free GPS downloads.

Naturfreunde Österreich (NFÖ, Friends of Nature Austria; www.naturfreunde.at, in German) Hundreds of walking routes, walk descriptions, maps and GPS downloads, including Nordic walking and snowshoeing routes. Also information on NFÖ huts, tips on mountain safety and up-to-date weather reports.

ÖAV (www.alpenverein.at, in German) Search for alpine huts and find information on events, tours, hiking villages and conservation. There's a section on the country's 10 *Weitwanderwege* (long-distance trails), which stretch from 160km to 1200km and showcase different areas of Austria's stunning landscape.

On Tour (www.on-tour.at, in German) Short and sweet walks searchable by region and graded according to difficulty. The site is in German but easy to navigate.

TOP HIKES

Grab your rucksack and get out and stride on the following trails:

» **Top day hikes** The Zillertal Circuit (p315) is especially beautiful in early summer, when the alpine roses are in bloom. A moderately challenging hike in the Silvretta Alps is the Radsattel Circuit (p350), taking in glaciers, jewel-coloured lakes and the iconic peak of Piz Buin.

» **Top high-alpine hike** A classic high-level trail is the Pinzgauer Spaziergang (p277), affording mesmerising views of the snowcapped Hohe Tauern and Kitzbühel Alps with little real effort.

» **Top short hike** Take a photogenic forest stroll for close-ups of the 380m-high Krimmler Wasserfälle (p281), Europe's highest waterfall. The Rosengartenschlucht Circuit (p325) is an easygoing hike through Imst's dramatic gorge.

» **Top kid-friendly hike** Kids in tow? Rent a gentle-natured llama for the day to explore the rugged splendour of the Dolomites near Lienz (p288).

Österreich Werbung (ANTO; Austrian National Tourist Office; www.austria.info) Excellent information on walking in Austria, from themed day hikes to long-distance treks. Also has details on national parks and nature reserves, hiking villages and special walking packages. Region-specific brochures are available for downloading.

Wander Magazin (www.wandern.at, in German) Handy website for walking trails and maps and walker-friendly accommodation, all searchable by region.

Maps

The best place to stock up on maps is a *Tabak* (tobacconist), newsagent or bookshop. Usually they only have local maps, although bookshops in the major cities offer a wider selection. Outdoor-activities shops usually sell a limited variety of walking maps. Many local tourist offices hand out basic maps that may be sufficient for short, easy walks.

A great overview map of Austria is Michelin's 1:400,000 national map No 0730 *Austria*. Alternatively, the ANTO (www.austria.info) can send you a free copy of its 1:800,000 country map. Visit www.austrianmap.at for a zoomable topographic country map. High-quality walking maps can be purchased online:

Freytag & Berndt (www.freytagberndt.at) Publishes a wide selection of reliable 1:50,000-scale walking maps.

Kompass (www.kompass.at, in German) Has a good series of 1:50,000 walking maps and includes a small booklet with contact details for mountain huts and background information on trails.

ÖAV (www.alpenverein.at, in German) Produces large-scale (1:25,000) walking maps that are clear, detailed and accurate.

Regions

In a land where even the tiniest of villages can have scores of fabulous walks, the question is not *where* you can walk in Austria, but *how*. For purists, that means the high-alpine trails which dominate in the mountainous west of the country, but lowland areas such as the vine-strewn Wachau can be just as atmospheric. Tourist offices are usually well armed with brochures, maps and information on local guides.

In summer, lots of places run themed guided hikes, which are sometimes free with a guest card; for instance in Innsbruck and Kitzbühel. Other regions such as Hohe Tauern National Park and Naturpark Zillertaler Alpen charge a small fee (usually around €5). The walks can range from herb spotting to wildlife spotting, half-day hikes to photo excursions.

Accommodation

Hiking Hotels

Gone are the days when hiking meant a clammy tent and week-old socks. Austria has seriously upped the ante in comfort with its so-called *Wanderhotels* (hiking hotels). These hotels are run by walking specialists who offer guided walks from leisurely strolls to high-alpine hikes, help you map out your route and have equipment (eg poles, flasks, rucksacks) available for hire. Most establishments are family-run, serve up regional cuisine and have a sauna or whirlpool where you can rest your weary feet. See www.wanderhotels.com and www.wandermagazin.com (in German) for some-

---

PILGRIM'S WAY

An historic path, the Pilgrim's Way (Pilgerweg), connects St Gilgen and St Wolfgang (p214) via the western shore of the Hallstätter Sea (Lake Hallstatt). In the past, pilgrims followed this path to honour St Wolfgang, the bishop who was said to have founded the church in St Wolfgang village by throwing his axe from the Falkenstein hill into the valley below and building the church on the spot where it fell.

The walk takes half a day and maps are available from the tourist offices in St Wolfgang and St Gilgen. The path starts from Furberg, near St Gilgen, and climbs the Falkenstein (795m) before continuing through the village of Reid to St Wolfgang. Apart from the fairly steep climb to the top of the Falkenstein, the walk isn't too strenuous (remind yourself that many pilgrims did it with lentils in their shoes or naked with iron rings around their necks as a sign of penance!). There are various things to see along the way, including a stone that still apparently bears the marks of St Wolfgang's buttocks. It became as soft as wax in a miracle sent by God to allow the saint to rest his weary bones.

To help preserve the ecology and beauty of Austria, consider the following tips when hiking.

Trail Etiquette

» Leave farm gates as you find them. In summer, low-voltage electric fences control livestock on the open alpine pastures; where an electric fence crosses a path, it usually has a hook that can be easily unfastened to allow walkers to pass through without getting zapped.

» Approach wildlife with discretion; moving too close will unnerve wild animals, distracting them from their vital summer activity of fattening up for the long winter.

» Greet your fellow walkers with a *Servus* (hello).

» On narrow paths, ascending walkers have right of way over those descending.

Rubbish

» Carry out all your rubbish, including easily forgotten items such as tinfoil, orange peel, cigarette butts and plastic wrappers. Empty packaging should be stored in a dedicated rubbish bag. Make an effort to carry out rubbish left by others.

» Never bury your rubbish: digging disturbs soil and ground cover, and encourages erosion. Buried rubbish will likely be dug up by animals, which may be injured or poisoned by it. It also takes years to decompose, especially at high altitudes.

» Minimise waste by taking minimal packaging and no more food than you will need. Take reusable containers or stuff sacks.

» Sanitary napkins, tampons, condoms and toilet paper should be carried out despite the inconvenience. They burn and decompose poorly.

Human Waste Disposal

» Make an effort to use toilets in huts and refuges where provided. Where there is none, bury your waste. Dig a small hole 15cm deep and at least 100m from any watercourse. Cover the waste with soil and a rock. In snow, dig down to the soil.

» Contamination of the local water sources by human faeces can lead to the transmission of giardiasis, a human bacterial parasite. It can cause severe health risks to other walkers, local residents and wildlife.

Erosion

» Hillsides and mountain slopes, especially at high altitudes, are prone to erosion. Stick to existing trails and avoid short cuts.

» If a well-used trail passes through a mud patch, walk through the mud so as not to increase the size of the patch.

» Avoid removing the plant life that keeps topsoils in place. Alpine wildflowers look lovelier on the mountainsides and many of them are protected species.

thing to suit every taste and pocket, from farmstays to plush spa hotels.

Going a step further are Austria's *Wanderdörfe* (www.wanderdoerfer.at), a countrywide network of 50 hiker-friendly villages and regions. Here, you can expect well-marked short and long-distance walks, beautiful scenery and alpine huts, good infrastructure (eg trains and/or hiking buses) and hosts geared up for walkers. You can order a free brochure online.

Hut-to-Hut Hiking

One of the joys of hiking in Austria is spending the night in a mountain hut. These trailside refuges give you the freedom to tackle multiday treks in the Alps with no more than a daypack. The highly evolved system means you're hardly ever further than a five- to six-hour walk from the next hut, so there's no need to lug a tent, camping stove and other gear that weighs hikers down. Huts generally open from mid-June to mid-September,

NAME	START	FINISH	DISTANCE	DURATION
Adlerweg	St Johann in Tirol near Kitzbühel	St Anton am Arlberg	280km	3-4 weeks
Berliner Höhenweg	Finkenberg near Mayrhofen	Mayrhofen	70km	8 days
Arnoweg	Salzburg	Salzburg	1200km	2 months
Stubai Höhenweg	Neustift in Stubaital	Neustift in Stubaital	120km	8 days
Salzburger Almenweg	Pfarrwerfen near Werfen	Pfarrwerfen	350km	1 month

when the trails are free of snow; the busiest months are July and August, when advance bookings are highly recommended. Consult the ÖAV (www.alpenverein.at, in German) for hut contact details and opening times.

Accommodation is in multibed dorms called *Matratzenlager,* or in the *Notlager* (emergency shelter – wherever there's space) if all beds have been taken. Blankets and pillows are provided but you might need to bring your own sleeping sheet. In popular areas, huts are more like mountain inns, with drying rooms and even hot showers (normally at an extra charge).

Most huts have a convivial *Gaststube* (common room), where you can socialise and compare trekking tales over drinks and a bite to eat. ÖAV members can order the *Bergsteigeressen* – literally 'mountaineer's meal' – which is low in price but high in calories, though not necessarily a gastronomic treat! It's worth bringing your own tea or coffee, as *Teewasser* (boiled water) can be purchased from the hut warden.

Cycling & Mountain Biking

Austria is one of Europe's most bike-friendly lands. It is interlaced with well-marked cycling trails that showcase the mountains, valleys and cities from their best angles.

MODERN-DAY SHERPAS

If you love long-distance hiking but find carrying a rucksack a drag, you might want to consider *Wandern ohne Gepäck* (literally 'walking without luggage'). Many regions in Austria now offer this clever scheme, where hotels transport your luggage to the next hotel for a small extra charge. Visit www.austria.info or www.wanderhotels.com for more details.

If you would prefer your Sherpa to be of the cute and woolly kind, llama trekking could be just the thing. Many towns, including Lienz (p288) in the Dolomites, now offer this family favourite. Nothing motivates kids to walk quite like these hikes, which reach from two-hour forest strolls to two-week treks on pilgrimage routes. The llamas carry your luggage and leave you free to enjoy the scenery. Contact local tourist offices for more options.

LEVEL	HIGHLIGHTS	RESOURCES
moderate	Classic alpine landscapes from the Kaisergebirge's limestone peaks to the Arlberg region's rugged mountainscapes	See www.adlerweg.tirol.at for maps, brochures and route descriptions.
demanding	High-alpine, hut-to-hut route taking in the beautiful lakes, glaciers and mountains of the Zillertal Alps	See www.naturpark-zillertal.at for a detailed route description in German; Alpenvereinskarte 1:25,000 map No 35 Zillertaler Alpen covers the route.
demanding	Epic circular tour of the Austrian Alps, taking in gorges, valleys and Hohe Tauern National Park's glacial landscapes	Rother's walking guide Arnoweg covers the trail in detail, or see www.arnoweg.com.
moderate-demanding	A classic circular hut-to-hut route passing glaciers, rocky peaks and wild alpine lakes	Download maps and route descriptions at www.stubaier-hoehenweg.at; Cicerone's Trekking in the Stubai Alps is a reliable guide.
moderate	A hut-to-hut route taking in Salzburgerland's fertile Almen (alpine pastures), karst scenery and the eternally ice-capped peaks of Hohe Tauern	See www.salzburger-almenweg.at for detailed route descriptions, maps and a virtual tour.

Whether you want to test your stamina on hairpin bends and leg-aching mountain passes, blaze downhill on a mountain bike in the Alps, or freewheel leisurely around the country's glorious lakes – Austria has routes that will take your breath away.

Planning Your Route

When to Go

Warmer temperatures from May to October beckon cyclists, while downhill mountain bikers head to the Alps from late June to mid-September. Snow rules out cycling at higher elevations in winter, but this can be a quiet time to explore Austria's low-lying valleys. Pedalling up alpine passes in July and August can be a hot, tiring, thirsty business; take ample sunscreen and water, and factor in time for breaks.

Resources

Websites

Here are some websites to (virtually) get your wheels spinning:

Radtouren (www.radtouren.at) An excellent site listing Austria's major cycling routes and hotels.

Radfahren (www.radfahren.at, in German) Easy-to-navigate website with descriptions on cycling trails (including long-distance routes), bike-friendly hotels, bike rental and transport throughout Austria. Has interactive maps.

Bike Holidays (http://bike-holidays.at) Search by region for mountain-bike (MTB) trails, cycling routes, free-ride parks and bike hotels in Austria.

Biken (http://bike-holidays.at) Handy source for information on cycling and mountain biking in Salzkammergut and Upper Austria. You can order free brochures including Cycling Country Austria.

Maps & Guides

Local tourist offices usually stock brochures and maps on cycling and mountain biking. Cycle clubs are another good source of information. For more detailed maps and guides try:

Esterbauer (www.esterbauer.com, in German) Produces the Bikeline series of cycling and mountain biking maps and guides which give comprehensive coverage on Austria's major trails.

Freytag & Berndt (www.freytagberndt.at) Stocks a good selection of cycling maps and produces the Austria Cycling Atlas detailing 160 day tours.

Kompass (www.kompass.at, in German) For cycle tour maps at scales between 1:125.000 and 1:50.000. Covers long-distance routes well, including those along the Bodensee, Danube and Inntal.

Rentals

City and mountain bikes are available for hire in most Austrian towns and resorts. **Intersport** (www.intersport.at) has a near monopoly on rental equipment, offering a selection of

ÖAV MEMBERSHIP

Before you hit the trail in the Austrian Alps, you might want to consider becoming a member of the Österreichischer Alpenverein (www.alpenverein.at, in German). Adult membership costs €52 per year and there are significant discounts for students and people aged under 25 or over 61. Membership gets you an up to 50% reduction at Austrian (ÖAV) and German (DAV) alpine huts, plus other benefits including insurance, workshops, access to climbing walls countrywide and discounts on maps. The club also organises walks. There is an arm of the club in England, the Austrian Alpine Club (www.aacuk.org.uk). You should allow at least two months for your application to be processed.

Of the 1000-odd huts in the Austrian Alps, 241 are maintained by the ÖAV.

quality bikes in 140 stores throughout Austria. Day rates range from €15 to €25. All prices include bicycle helmets and there's a 50% reduction on children's bikes. Those who want to plan their route ahead can search by region and reserve a bike online.

Transport

Look for the bike symbol at the top of timetables or on the ÖBB (Austrian Federal Railway; www.oebb.at) website to find trains where you can take your bike, or see p416. A day ticket for your bike on regional and S-Bahn trains costs €5, for IC and EC trains €10.

Many of Austria's leading resorts have cottoned onto the popularity of downhill mountain biking and now allow cyclists to take their bikes on the cable cars for free or for a nominal charge in summer, allowing you to enjoy the downhill rush without the uphill slog!

Accommodation

Throughout Austria you'll find hotels and pensions geared up for cyclists, particularly in the Alps. So-called *Radhotels* go a step further with everything from storage facilities to bike repairs and staff well informed on local routes. You can browse for bike-friendly hotels by region on www.bike-holidays.com and www.radtouren.at. Local tourist offices can also point you in the right direction and sometimes offer special packages.

Cycling Routes

There's more to cycling in Austria than the exhilarating extremes of the Alps, as you'll discover pedalling through little-explored countryside with the breeze in your hair and the chain singing. There are plenty of silky smooth cycling trails that avoid the slog without sacrificing the grandeur; many of them circumnavigate lakes or shadow rivers. Below are some of our long-distance favourites.

Danube Cycle Path

Shadowing the mighty Danube for 380km from Passau to Bratislava, this cycle route takes in some lyrical landscapes. Wending its way through woodlands, deep valleys and orchards, the trail is marked by green-and-white signs on both sides of the river. Esterbauer's Bikeline *Danube Bike Trail* is useful for maps and route descriptions. See www.donauradweg.at (in German) for details on the route and an interactive map, and www.donau-radweg.info for tours.

Inn Trail

Starting in Innsbruck and travelling 302km through Austria to Schärding, the trail (www.inn-radweg.com) sticks close to the turquoise Inn River. It's basically downhill all the way, passing through fertile farmland, alpine valleys and castle-topped towns in Tyrol, Bavaria and Upper Austria. The final stretch zips through bucolic villages and countryside to Schärding. The route is well marked, but signage varies between regions.

Bodensee Cycle Path

Touching base with Bregenz in Vorarlberg, this 270km cycleway encircles the Bodensee (Lake Constance), Europe's third largest lake. Marked with red-and-white signs, the mostly easygoing trail zips through Austria, Germany and Switzerland, passing through woodlands, marshes, orchards, vineyards and historic towns. Come in early autumn for fewer crowds, new wine and views of the Alps on clear days. Visit www.bodensee-radweg.com for details.

Salzkammergut Trail

This 345km circular trail explores the pristine alpine lakes of the Salzkammergut, including Hallstätter See (p204), Attersee (p213) and Wolfgangsee (p213). Though not exactly flat, the trail is well signposted (R2) and only moderate fitness is required. To explore in greater depth, pick up Esterbauer's Bikeline *Radatlas Salzkammergut*.

Tauern Trail
Rolling through some of Austria's most spectacular alpine scenery on the fringes of the Hohe Tauern National Park, the 310km Tauern Trail (www.tauernradweg.com) is not technically difficult, but cycling at high altitude requires stamina. It begins at Krimml, then snakes along the Salzach River to Salzburg, then further onto the Saalach Valley and Passau. The trail is marked with green-and-white signs in both directions. For maps and GPS tracks, see www.tauernradweg.com.

Mountain Biking
The Austrian Alps are an MTB (mountain biking) mecca, with hairpin bends, back-breaking inclines and heart-pumping descents. The country is crisscrossed with 17,000km of mountain bike routes, with the most challenging terrain in Tyrol, Salzburgerland, Vorarlberg and Carinthia. Below is a sample of the tours and regions that attract two-wheeled speed demons.

Dachstein Tour
Hailed as one of the country's top mountain bike routes; this three-day tour circles the rugged limestone pinnacles of the Dachstein massif and blazes through three provinces: Salzburgerland, Upper Austria and Styria. You'll need a good level of fitness to tackle the 182km trail that starts and finishes in Bad Goisern, pausing en route near Filzmoos. For details, see the website www.dachsteinrunde.at.

Salzburger Almentour
On this 146km trail, bikers pedal through 30 *Almen* (mountain pastures) in three days. While the name conjures up visions of gentle meadows, the route involves some strenuous climbs up to tremendous viewpoints like Zwölferhorn peak. Green-and-white signs indicate the trail from Annaberg to Edtalm via Wolfgangsee. Route details and highlights are given online (www.almentour. com, in German).

Silvretta Mountain Bike Arena
Sidling up to Switzerland, the Silvretta Mountain Bike Arena (p327) in the Patznauntal is among the biggest in the Alps, with 1000km of trails; some climbing to almost 3000m. Ischgl makes an excellent base, with a technique park and plenty of trail information available at the tourist office. The 15 free-ride trails for speed freaks include the Velill Trail, involving 1300m of descent. Tour details are available at www.ischgl-bikeacademy.at, in German.

Kitzbühel
Covering 750km of mountain bike trails, the Kitzbühel region ranks as one of Austria's top freewheeling spots. Routes range from 700m to 2300m in elevation and encompass trial circuits, downhill runs and bike parks. The must-experience rides include the Hahnenkamm Bike Safari from Kitzbühel to Pass Thurn, affording far-reaching views of Grossglockner and Wilder Kaiser.

Stubaital & Zillertal
These two broad valleys running south from the Inn River in Tyrol are flanked by high peaks crisscrossed with 800km of mountain bike trails. The terrain is varied and the landscape splendid, with gorges, waterfalls and glaciers constantly drifting into view. Highlights feature the alpine route from Mayrhofen to Hintertux Glacier and the dizzying roads that twist up from Ginzling to the Schlegeisspeicher.

Adventure & Water Sports
Rock Climbing & Via Ferrate

Synonymous with mountaineering legends like Peter Habeler and South Tyrolean Reinhold Messner, Austria is a summertime paradise for ardent *Kletterer* (rock climbers). In the Alps there's a multitude of climbs ranking all grades of difficulty. Equipment rental (around €10) and guided tours are widely available.

If you are not quite ready to tackle the three-thousanders yet, nearly every major resort in the Austrian Alps now has a *Klettersteig* (via ferrata). These fixed-rope routes, often involving vertical ladders,

---

GPS FREEWHEELING
It's easier to navigate Austria's backcountry and find little-known bike trails with a GPS tour. Surf www.bike-gps.com for downloadable cycling and mountain biking tours. Alternatively, click onto www.gps-tour.info for more than 200 tours in Austria.

zip-lines and bridges, are great for getting a feel for climbing; all you'll need is a harness, helmet and a head for heights.

Resources

ÖAV (www.alpenverein.at, in German) Check for information on Austria-wide climbing halls, tours and courses.

Bergsteigen (www.bergsteigen.at) Search by region or difficulty for climbing routes, via ferrate and ice-climbing walls.

Rock Climbing (www.rockclimbing.com) Gives details on around 1000 climbing tours in Austria, many with climbing grades and photos.

Regions

For serious mountaineers, the ascent of Grossglockner (3798m), Austria's highest peak, is the climb of a lifetime. Professional guides can take you up into the wild heights of the Hohe Tauern National Park (see p273), a veritable climbing nirvana.

Sheer granite cliffs, bizarre rock formations and boulders make the Zillertal Alps another hot spot, particularly Ginzling (p316) and Mayrhofen (p313).

Other climbing magnets include Pelstein in Lower Austria, the limestone peaks of the Dachstein and the Tennengebirge in Salzburgerland.

Water Sports

Austria may be landlocked but it offers plenty of watery action on its lakes and rivers in summer. You can windsurf on Neusiedler See, white-water raft in Tyrol or scuba dive in Wörthersee. Zipping across lakes by wind power is the most popular water sport in the country, and if Olympic medals are anything to go by, the locals aren't bad at it either.

Rafting & Canoeing

Rafting, canoeing or kayaking the swirling white waters of Austria's alpine rivers are much-loved summertime escapades. Big rivers which support these fast-paced sports include the Enns and Salza in Styria; the Inn, Sanna and Ötztaler Ache in Tyrol; and the Isel in East Tyrol. Tours start from around €30 and usually include transport and equipment.

Well-known rafting centres include Landeck, Innsbruck for adventures on the Inn, Zell am Ziller and St Anton am Arlberg.

PETER HABELER: MOUNTAINEER & SKI INSTRUCTOR

Peter Habeler (www.habeler.com) was born in Mayrhofen in 1942 and has been scrambling up the peaks of the Zillertal Alps since the age of six. After qualifying as a mountain guide aged 21, he struck up a partnership with Reinhold Messner in the 1960s, who once described him as being 'like a sky rocket – really impressive once the fuse is lit'.

Peak Performance

Extreme alpinism has always been my goal and I was lucky enough to have the best teachers there are. When Messner and I made the first-ever ascent of Everest without supplementary oxygen in 1978, we climbed quickly and took only the bare essentials. Other climbers said it was suicide, but we knew that if Sherpas could reach 8500m, Everest was only a couple of hundred metres higher.

Climbing Tips

Take time to acclimatise – adapt to the mountains, befriend them; they aren't enemies that need to be conquered. For me, alpinism is about technique, condition and the ability to predict. Listen to your instincts and know when to call it a day. There's freedom in the mountains but also restriction.

Zillertal Alps

I still love climbing in the Zillertal Alps where I grew up, especially the Olperer (3476m) and my 'little Everest', the Ahornspitze (2976m). When I'm not in Mayrhofen, I occasionally pop over to Nepal to guide an expedition or to Hohe Tauern to climb Grossglockner.

» **Go ahead, jump** The 152m-high platform of the capital's needle-thin Donauturm (www.donauturm.at) is one of the world's highest bungee jumps from a tower. Yo-yoing at speeds of 90km/h from this landmark sure is an original way to see Vienna. Daredevils also leap into oblivion from the 192m Europabrücke (p301) bridge above the Sill River, a thrilling upside-down bounce.

» **Get a grip** If you thought regular climbing was slippery, try ice climbing! Scaling frozen walls and waterfalls is pure adventure, but you'll need a decent pair of crampons and a good instructor. The Stubai Glacier (p309) and Lech (p351) are among the places where you can give it a go. Experts can search for ice-climbing locations countrywide on www.bergsteigen.at (in German).

» **Going down...** For a real heart-stopping moment, you can't beat rolling out of a plane at 4000m and freefalling for 60 seconds before your parachute opens. Tandem skydiving jumps are available all over Austria – from Vienna to Salzburg; see www.skydiveworld.com for details.

» **Alpine rush** Speed is of the essence in Tyrol, particularly on Igls' hair-raising Olympic bob run (p301). Add altitude to the equation by zip-lining over incredible scenery on the flying fox at Area 47 (p323).

» **Snow crazy** Swap your skis for a more novel way of whizzing down the mountains. Most resorts in the Austrian Alps, including Sölden (p323) and Mayrhofen (p313), offer snow tubing. Other snow-sports crazes to look out for include airboarding and snowbiking.

Windsurfing & Sailing

Sailing, windsurfing and kite-surfing are all extremely popular pursuits on Austria's lakes.

Close to Vienna lies Neusiedler See (p143), one of the few steppe lakes in Central Europe and the number-one place for windsurfing and kite-surfing thanks to its stiff winds. It hosts a heat of the Surf World Cup from late April to early May.

St Gilgen (p215) and Mondsee (p216) in Salzkammergut are highly scenic lakes for water sports; the latter harbours Austria's largest sailing school. Millstätter See in Carinthia (p268), Achensee (p316) in Tyrol and the vast Bodensee (p337) in Vorarlberg are other popular spots to set sail. The following websites will get you launched:

Österreichischer Segelverband (Austrian Sailing Federation; www.segelverband.at, in German) Can provide a list of clubs and locations in the country.

Kitesurfing (www.kitesurfing.at, in German) For the low-down on kite-surfing on Neusiedler See.

Segelkurs (www.segelkurs.at, in German) Has contact details for sailing schools in Austria.

Swimming & Diving

Bath-warm or invigoratingly cold? Alpine or palm-fringed? Much of Austria is pristine lake country and there are scores to choose from. Carinthia is famed for its pure waters, which can heat up to a pleasantly warm 28°C in summer; Millstätter See and Wörthersee offer open-water swimming and scuba diving with great visibility. You can also make a splash in lakes such as Hallstätter See and Attersee in Salzkammergut, and Bodensee in Vorarlberg.

Paragliding

Wherever there's a mountain and a steady breeze, you'll find paragliding and hang-gliding in Austria. On a bright day in the Alps, look up to see the sky dotted with people catching thermals to soar above peaks and forests. In many alpine resorts, you can hire the gear, get a lesson or go as a passenger on a tandem flight; prices for the latter start at around €100. Most people fly in summer, but a crystal-clear winter's day can be equally beautiful.

Tyrol is traditionally a centre for paragliding, with narrow valleys and plenty of cable cars. A good place to head is Zell am Ziller (p311). Another scenic paragliding base is

ON THE BEACH

There's no sea for miles, but nearly all of Austria's major lakes are fringed with *Strandbäder* (lidos) for an invigorating dip, many of which have beaches, outdoor pools and barbecue areas. Some are free, while others charge a nominal fee of around €3 per day. If you dare to bare all, *FKK* (nudist) beaches, including those at Hard (p337) on Bodensee, Hallstätter See (p204), Milstätter See (p268) and even the Donauinsel (p75) in Vienna, welcome skinny-dippers.

Zell am See (p275) in the rugged Hohe Tauern National Park.

Find the best place to spread your wings at www.flugschulen.at, giving a regional rundown of flight schools offering paragliding and hang-gliding.

Canyoning

For a buzz, little beats scrambling down a ravine and abseiling down a waterfall while canyoning. This wet, wild sport has become one of the most popular activities in the Austrian Alps. Guided tours costing between €50 and €75 for half a day abound. Most companies provide all the gear you need, but you'll need to bring swimwear, sturdy shoes, a towel and a head for heights. A good level of fitness is also recommended.

Top locations for canyoning include Mayrhofen (p313) in the Zillertal, the Ötztal (p322) and Lienz (p286).

regions at a glance

Vienna

Art & Architecture ✓✓✓
Music ✓✓✓
Drinking in Style ✓✓✓

Art & Architecture

Vienna's art has waltzed arm in arm with its architecture through the grand ballroom of history. The city's fin de siècle years spawned *Jugendstil* (art nouveau), synonymous in Vienna with the Secession (p69), art pushes boundaries at the Museums-Quartier (p69) and Albertina (p64), and it's literally impossible to turn a corner in the centre of the capital without bumping into a medieval or baroque building – the Hofburg (p59) is a particularly triumphant showpiece that

has been expanded upon over the centuries.

Music

You can listen to the music of Mozart at palatial venues across town, visit Mozart's former home (p67), embrace decadence and operatic masterpieces at the Staatsoper (p100) – one of the most spectacular opera houses in Europe – or head to the Klangforum (p100) where the up-and-coming composers perform. And then there's the equine ballet where you can watch white Lipizzaner stallions prance, as they've done for over five centuries (p65).

Drinking in Style

Viennese coffee houses are legendary: you sip, you read, you press pause in palatial surrounds such as Café Gloriette (p98) or at hip modern versions such as Café Drechsler (p96). Grab a cocktail in Secessionist architect Adolf Loos' brass and mirror masterpiece of a bar (p95) or indulge in freshly pressed wine at a *Stadtheuriger* (urban wine tavern; p94).

p54

Lower Austria

Food & Wine ✓✓✓
Culture ✓✓✓
Cycling ✓✓

Food & Wine

The Wachau region (p111) of the Danube Valley is famous for top-class restaurants, and the Kamptal (Kamp Valley) in the Waldviertel is brimming with specialities, including organic cheeses in Diendorf (p123) and Waldviertel poppy seed (p122).

Culture

Stift Melk (p120) in the Wachau region is the indisputable monarch among the abbeys of Austria, Schloss Grafenegg (p115) has reinvented itself as a top-class venue for outdoor music and opera, and Krems (p112) and Schloss Schallaburg (p120) host great exhibitions.

Cycling

The Mostviertel (p127) is a lesser-known region with picturesque cycling routes. The most popular path is along the Danube River, sprinkled with highlights of the Wachau region (p111), and Carnuntum with its Roman ruins (p128).

p108

Burgenland

Food & Wine ✓✓✓
Cycling ✓✓
Windsurfing ✓✓

Food & Wine
The regions of Burgenland around the Neusiedler See (p143) are famous for their wines, especially reds, and *Heurigen* (wine taverns) where the nectar of the gods washes down cold platters or classic Austrian dishes.

Cycling
In summer the reedy Neusiedler See offers a great escape into a steppe landscape replete with wetlands, water birds and a bicycle trail leading through national park, a small corner of Hungary and back around the reedy shores on the western flanks. It's a ride for the whole family.

Windsurfing
With stiff summer breezes blowing across the Pannonian Plain and stirring up the waters of the Neusiedler See, Europe's second-largest lake is a popular windsurfing getaway for the experienced and the beginner alike.

p138

Upper Austria

Art & Technology ✓✓✓
Churches & Abbeys ✓✓✓
Rural Retreats ✓✓

Art & Technology
Linz' strikingly lit Ars Electronica Center (p153) propels visitors into the future with robotic wizardry and virtual voyages, while the rectangular Lentos (p153) gallery hosts cutting-edge art exhibitions. Modern art and sculpture also hang out in the Landesgalerie (p154).

Churches & Abbeys
Kremsmünster's Benedictine abbey (p166) and St Florian's baroque Augustinian abbey (p163) hide ecclesiastical treasures. Linz has neo-Gothic Neuer Dom (p155) and opulent Alter Dom (p156), while Kefermarkt is known for the Gothic altar in its church (p170).

Rural Retreats
Rolling countryside is scattered with storybook towns like Steyr (p164) and spa retreats like Bad Hall (p166). Farmstays in the Mühlviertel (p168) and Traunviertel (p164) offer total peace. Hike in the limestone wilderness of the Nationalpark Kalkalpen (p166).

p151

Styria

Culture ✓✓
Outdoor Pursuits ✓✓✓
Food & Wine ✓✓✓

Culture
Famous for its festivals throughout the year, the capital, Graz, makes up for its small size with some big cultural hits and an ensemble of top-rate museums, including Schloss Eggenberg (p176).

Outdoor Pursuits
Hiking trails abound in Styria – some easy, others challenging – and some good hikes and mountain-bike rides can be had in the cleaved valleys of the remote Gesäuse National Park (p195), or in the more popular Schladming (p196). Here, the mountains soar to dizzying heights and the pistes rev to life in winter.

Food & Wine
Graz has some of the best food in the country. The wine at the tables often comes from the vineyards hugging the nearby Slovenian border. Fantastic whites are complemented by excellent restaurants on the The south Styrian wine roads (p187).

p172

The Salzkammergut

Lake Swimming ✓✓✓
Hiking & Cycling ✓✓✓
Culture ✓

Lake Swimming
With its contrast of soaring mountains and deep lakes nestled in steeply walled valleys, the Salzkammergut is the best place to slip into lake waters. Some of these are cold – very cold – but others such as the Hallstätter See (p204), the Wolfgangsee (p213) or Mondsee (p216) are perfect for challenging open-water swimming or quick dips.

Hiking & Cycling
Hallstatt (p204) and Obertraun (p206) are centres for lakeside hiking, forays into the heights of the Dachstein mountains by cable car or on foot, and winter ski hikes. The cycling is excellent in the Salzkammergut region, too – the mountain variety or easier touring.

Culture
Salt – the 'white gold' – is what has given the region its name, and above Hallstatt is Austria's best exhibition salt mine (p204), tracing mining back to ancient times.

p200

Salzburg & Salzburgerland

Culture ✓✓✓
Outdoor Pursuits ✓✓✓
Food ✓✓

Culture
Salzburg's regal Residenz (p223), the magnificent baroque *Altstadt* (old town; p221), and the 900-year-old Festung Hohensalzburg (p222) are high on every cultural agenda. The city hosts the world-renowned Salzburg Festival (p232).

Outdoor Pursuits
Hikers are mesmerised by the evocative landscapes of the Tennengebirge (p244). Underground lies Eisriesenwelt (p244), the world's largest accessible ice caves, and nearby is the precipitous Liechtensteinklamm (p245) gorge. Filzmoos (p245) appeals to families for its gentle skiing.

Food
Drink in history at grand coffee houses such as Bazar (p236) and Sacher (p236), or at monk-run brewpubs such as Augustiner Bräustübl (p237). Michelin-starred Obauer (p245) in Werfen serves regional cuisine in refined surrounds.

p218

Carinthia

Lake Swimming ✓✓✓
Winter Sports ✓✓✓
Cycling ✓✓✓

Lake Swimming
The Wörthersee (p253) is a summer playground for the rich, the famous and the rest of us. Warm in summer, with one of the country's best lake-swimming areas on the edge of Klagenfurt, this is where even the distance fanatics can get into a long swim.

Winter Sports
At the Nassfeld ski field near Hermagor (p262) skiers take the 6km-long Millennium-Express cable car up to the slopes for some top skiing. Nordic skiing and ski hikes are also possible in this rugged province with remote regions.

Cycling
Eleven kilometres downhill on a mighty run – mountain biking is a favourite pastime in Carinthia, but so too is touring on the trails and routes around Hermagor or outside Villach.

p248

Hohe Tauern National Park

Natural Wonders ✓✓✓
Outdoor Pursuits ✓✓✓
Spas ✓✓

Natural Wonders
Hohe Tauern National Park is a 'greatest hits' of alpine scenery, with wondrous glaciers, 3000m peaks and the 380m-high Krimmler Wasserfälle (p281), Europe's highest waterfall. The panoramic Grossglockner Road (p279) winds towards Grossglockner, Austria's highest peak, and the Pasterze Glacier.

Outdoor Pursuits
One of Hohe Tauern's most memorable hikes is the alpine Pinzgauer Spaziergang (p277). Swimmers cool off in mountain-rimmed Zeller See (p273) and rafters in the fast-flowing rivers of Lienz (p288). Winter brings skiing to the Kitzsteinhorn Glacier (p278) and Bad Gastein (p282).

Spas
Belle-époque Bad Gastein (p282) is renowned for its therapeutic springs. Take the radon-laced waters in Felsentherme Gastein (p283) or nearby Bad Hofgastein's Alpen Therme spa (p286).

p271

Tyrol

Skiing ✓✓✓
Hiking & Cycling ✓✓✓
Culture ✓✓

Skiing
Tyrol has Austria's finest slopes – quite some feat in this starkly mountainous country. Alpine resorts like St Anton am Arlberg (p329), Kitzbühel (p317), Mayrhofen (p313) and Ischgl (p327) excel in downhill, off-piste and upbeat après-ski. Seefeld (p309) has cross-country runs of Olympic fame.

Hiking & Cycling
Tyrol has some of the most scenic alpine hiking and cycling in Austria. Summer calls high-altitude walkers, cyclists and mountain bikers to the valleys and peaks of the ruggedly beautiful Zillertal (p310), Ötztal (p322) and Patznauntal (p327).

Culture
Palatial Hofburg (p297), Renaissance Schloss Ambras (p298) and galleries of Old Masters (p298) beckon in Innsbruck. Well-preserved medieval towns like Schwaz (p308) and Hall (p307) and the baroque interiors of the Cistercian abbey in Stams (p322) are other standouts.

p292

Vorarlberg

Rural Retreats ✓✓✓
Outdoor Pursuits ✓✓✓
Art & Architecture ✓✓

Rural Retreats
There's a back-to-nature feel in the rolling dairy country and wooded heights of the Bregenzerwald (p342), sprinkled with farmstays and chocolate-box villages like Schwarzenberg. The Käsestrasse (p346) is a deliciously cheesy drive taking in working dairies.

Outdoor Pursuits
Cyclists and beach-goers descend on the glittering Bodensee (p336) in summer. Clean air and scenery attract hikers to the rugged mountains of Montafon (p349). Those same peaks lure skiers in winter, as do glamorous resorts like Lech and Zürs in Arlberg (p349).

Art & Architecture
Vorarlberg is scattered with avant-garde buildings on the cutting edge of design. The glass-walled Kunsthaus Bregenz (p336) hosts contemporary art exhibitions, while Schwarzenberg hosts the work of Swiss-Austrian neoclassical painter Angelika Kauffmann (p342).

p334

Look out for these icons:

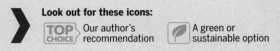

TOP CHOICE Our author's recommendation

A green or sustainable option

FREE No payment required

See the Index for a full list of destinations covered in this book.

On the Road

Vienna

AREA CODE 🎵1 / POP 1.7 MILLION

Best Places to Eat & Drink

» Neni (p94)

» Bitzinger Würstelstand am Albertinaplatz (p88)

» Figlmüller (p88)

» Café Drechsler (p96)

» 10er Marie (p98)

» Wein & Wasser (p97)

Best Places to Stay

» Boutiquehotel Stadthalle (p88)

» Pension Hargita (p86)

» Hotel Sacher (p84)

» Hotel Kaertnerhof (p86)

Why Go?

Few cities in the world glide so effortlessly between the present and the past like Vienna. Its splendid historical face is easily recognised: grand imperial palaces and bombastic baroque interiors, museums flanking magnificent squares.

But Vienna is also one of Europe's most dynamic urban spaces. A stone's throw from Hofburg, the MuseumsQuartier houses some of the world's most provocative contemporary art behind a striking basalt facade. Outside, a courtyard buzzes on summer evenings with throngs of Viennese drinking and chatting.

The city of Mozart is also the Vienna of Falco (Hans Hölzel), who immortalised its urban textures in song. Sushi and Austro-Asian fusion restaurants stand alongside the traditional *Beisl* (small tavern). In this Vienna, it's OK to mention poetry slam and Stephansdom in one breath.

Throw in the mass of green space within the city limits (almost half the urban expanse is given over to parkland) and the 'blue' Danube cutting a path east of the historical centre and this is a capital that is distinctly Austrian.

When to Go

In summer, you can catch some rays on the banks of the Danube and loll about drinking made-on-the-premises wine in the outdoor gardens of the *Heurigen* (wine taverns). Hiking among the Vienna woods in October yields a spectacular autumn view of the capital. In December, the city is lit up in all its festive glory – go ice skating in front of the *Rathaus* (town hall) or sip *Glühwein* (mulled wine) at one of the capital's atmospheric Christmas markets.

Planning Your Trip

If you're short on time and you only have two days, start with the **Stephansdom** (p58) in the morning. Then head to the **Hofburg** (p59), which is packed with sights. Your best approach to avoid museum and church fatigue is to mix it up – first the **Kaiserappartements** (p59) and Sisi Museum, then the Burgkapelle and the **Schatzkammer** (p62). Take a stroll outside around the **Burggarten** and grab a drink at the **Palmenhaus** (p95). Finish with a casual bite at **Café Drechsler** (p96). It's famous for its goulash.

On day two, hit the **Naschmarkt** (p94) before the crowds roll in. Then visit any of the museums in the **Museums-Quartier** (p69), followed by a stroll around Neubau. For dinner, head back to the Naschmarkt for dinner – Neni is an excellent bet. Finish the night with some bar-hopping through Wieden or some dancing at **Pratersauna** (p102).

DON'T MISS

The **Riesenrad** (p74), the world's most iconic Ferris wheel, is in the centre of the Würstelprater, Vienna's favourite old-school amusement park. Step into the gargantuan containers and spin slowly around, taking in sweeping views of the city, the neighbouring hills and the Danube.

One of Vienna's most convivial markets, the **Naschmarkt** (p94) boasts stalls and stalls of international food, a cacophony of vendors urging you to try their goodies and a slew of top-notch restaurants, many housed in modern glass cubes along the river.

Be sure to hit one of the area's **Heurigen** (wine taverns), but take note of their (notoriously unpredictable) opening hours and call in advance. Don't fret if one is closed, as another will surely be open.

Before You Arrive

Reserve your tickets for the **Spanische Hofreitschule** (Spanish Riding School; p62) at least six months in advance. Two to three months before you leave, check the calendar for concert performances at the **Staatsoper** (p100)and the **Musikverein** (p101), and secure your seats to whatever looks appealing. Last, a week before you depart, decide which day you'll visit **Schloss Schönbrunn** (p78) and book your tickets in advance online.

TRANSPORT PLANNING

For information about fares and routes around Vienna, consult www.wienerlineien.at. During clement weather, consider using Vienna's excellent city-bike scheme: www.citybikewien.at.

Where to Splurge

Pop over to off-the-beaten-path, Michelin-star-rated **Restaurant Vincent** (p90) for a classy but laid-back evening.

Plonk down those euros for a night in Vienna's most famous hotel, the **Sacher** (p96), home of its namesake *Sacher Torte*.

Coffee Decoder

» **Brauner** Black, with a splash of milk.

» **Melange** With milk or cream, like a cappuccino.

» **Maria Theresia** With orange liqueur and whipped cream.

Resources

» Austria Today (www.austriatoday.at) News and opinion.

» Austrian Times (www.austriantimes.at) News and opinion.

» Falter (www.falter.at, in German) Entertainment and social commentary.

» Vienna Tourist Board (www.wien.info) Chock-full of information.

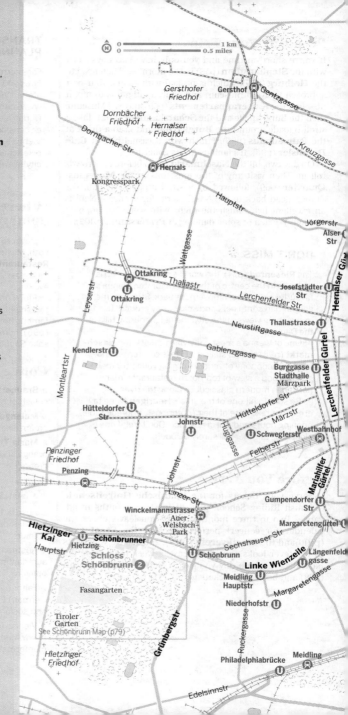

Vienna Highlights

1 Scaling **Stephansdom** (p58), Vienna's glorious Gothic cathedral and beloved icon

2 Savouring the bombastic pomp of **Schloss Schönbrunn** (p78) and the views from its gardens

3 Hanging out in the **MuseumsQuartier** (p69), an art space spiked with bars and alive with urban energy

4 Being provoked by naked bodies smeared with salad (among other modern-art flourishes) at Vienna's **MUMOK** (p71)

5 Slowing down and indulging in cake and coffee at Vienna's legendary **coffee houses** (p94)

6 Immersing yourself in Vienna's **Heurigen** (wine taverns; p94) on a night or day ramble

7 Spinning around in the giant rectangles dangling off the **Riesenrad** (p74), Vienna's oversized Ferris wheel, in the Prater outdoor area

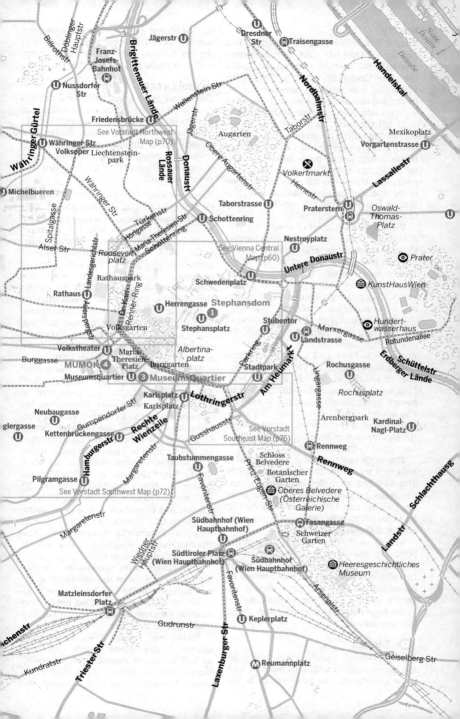

History

Vienna was probably an important trading post for the Celts when the Romans arrived around 15 BC. They set up camp and named the place Vindobona, after the Celtic tribe Vinid. The settlement blossomed into a town by the 3rd and 4th centuries, and vineyards were introduced to the surrounding area.

In 881 the town, then known as Wenia, surfaced in official documents. Over the ensuing centuries control of Vienna changed hands a number of times before the city fell under the rule of the Babenburgs (see p357). The Habsburgs inherited it, but none of them resided here permanently until Ferdinand I in 1533; the city was besieged by Ottoman Turks in 1529 (p368).

Vienna was a hotbed of revolt and religious bickering during the Reformation and Counter-Reformation and suffered terribly through plague and siege at the end of the 17th century. However, the beginning of the 18th century heralded a golden age for the city, with baroque architecture, civil reform and a classical-music revolution.

Things turned sour at the beginning of the 19th century – Napoleon occupied the city twice, in 1805 and 1809. His reign over Europe was brief, and in 1814–15 Vienna hosted the Congress of Vienna in celebration of his defeat. Vienna grew in post-Napoleonic Europe and in 1873 hosted its second international event, the World Fair. The advent of WWI stalled the city's architectural and cultural development and, by the end of the war, the monarchy had been consigned to the past (p361).

The 1920s saw the rise of fascism, and in 1934 civil war broke out in the city streets. The socialists were defeated and Vienna's city council dissolved. Austria was ripe for the picking, and Hitler came a-harvesting; on 15 March 1938 he entered the city to the cries of 200,000 ecstatic Viennese.

Vienna suffered heavily under Allied bombing, and on 11 April 1945 advancing Russian troops liberated the city. The Allies joined them until Vienna became independent in 1955, and since then it has gone from the razor's edge of the Cold War to the focal point between new and old EU member nations.

⊙ Sights

Most of Vienna's top attractions are inside the Innere Stadt or within 10 minutes' walk of its boundaries. The Innere Stadt is best tackled on foot as it's a maze of narrow one-way and pedestrian-only zones. The rest of the city is easily managed by public transport or, if you're feeling fit, by bicycle.

INNERE STADT

The Innere Stadt is a timeless and magical place where Vienna's past swirls and eddies in narrow ways and atmospheric cobblestone streets. The city-centre district is a Unesco World Heritage site. Though well trodden, it rewards close exploration, and if crowds distract then try exploring the streets at night.

Stephansdom   CATHEDRAL
(St Stephen's Cathedral; Map p60; ☑515 52-3520; www.stephanskirche.at; 01, Stephansplatz; ⊘6am-10pm Mon-Sat, 7am-10pm Sun) The most beloved and recognisable structure in Vienna is the Gothic masterpiece Stephansdom or Steffl (little Stephen), as the locals call it.

The cathedral was built on the site of a 12th-century church, of which the surviving Riesentor (Giant's Gate), main entrance and Heidentürme (Towers of the Heathens) are incorporated into the present building. These are Romanesque, but the cathedral's most distinctive features date from its being rebuilt in the Gothic style from 1359.

Dominating the cathedral is the skeletal Südturm (adult/under 14yr €3.50/1; ⊘9am-5.30pm), rising 136.7m and completed in 1433 after 75 years of work. Negotiating 343 steps brings you to a cramped viewing platform for a stunning panorama of Vienna. Originally this should have been matched on the north side by a companion tower, but the imperial purse withered and when the Gothic style went out of fashion the incomplete tower (adult/under 14yr €4/1.50; ⊘8.15am-6pm Jul & Aug, to 4.30pm Sep-Jun, closed 1-15 Jan) was topped off with a Renaissance cupola in 1579. (The tower is accessible by lift.) The **Pummerin** (boomer bell), Austria's largest bell, weighing in at a hefty 21 tonnes, was installed in 1952.

Look closely at the decorations and statues on the exterior of the cathedral: at the rear the agony of the Crucifixion is well captured, while the glorious **tiled roof** shows dazzling chevrons on one end and the Austrian eagle on the other.

Taking centre stage inside is the magnificent Gothic **stone pulpit**, fashioned in 1515 by Anton Pilgram. The expressive faces of the four fathers of the church (the saints Augustine, Ambrose, Gregory and

Vienna occupies 415 sq km in the Danube Valley, with the Wienerwald (Vienna Woods) forming a natural border to the north and west. The Danube (Donau) River flows northeast to southwest through the city. Vienna's heart, the Innere Stadt (inner city; first district), is south of the river on a diversion of the Danube, the Danube Canal (Donaukanal). It's encircled on three sides by the Ringstrasse, or Ring, a series of broad roads sporting an extravaganza of architectural delights. The Ring is at a distance of between 1.75km and 3km from the Gürtel (literally, 'belt'), a larger traffic artery that is fed by the flow of vehicles from outlying autobahn.

Stephansdom (St Stephen's Cathedral), with its slender spire, is in the heart of the Innere Stadt and is Vienna's principal landmark. Leading south from Stephansplatz station is Kärntner Strasse, an important pedestrian street that terminates at Karlsplatz, a major public-transport hub.

The Danube runs down a long, straight channel, built between 1870 and 1875 to eliminate flooding. This was supplemented 100 years later by the building of a parallel channel, the Neue Donau (New Danube), creating the Donauinsel (Danube Island) recreational area. The original Alte Donau (Old Danube) loops north of the Neue Donau to enclose the Donaupark, Vienna International Center (UNO City, home to the UN), beaches and water-sports centres. Squeezed between the Danube Canal and the Danube is the Prater, a large park and playground of the Viennese.

In terms of addresses, Vienna is divided into 23 *Bezirke* (districts), fanning out in approximate numerical order clockwise around the Innere Stadt. Note when reading addresses that the number of a building within a street *follows* the street name. Any number *before* the street name denotes the district. The middle two digits of postcodes correspond to the district. Thus a postcode of 1010 means the place is in district one, and 1230 refers to district 23.

Jerome) are at the centre of the design, but the highlight is Pilgram himself, peering out from a window below. He also appears at the base of the organ loft on the northern wall, seemingly holding up the entire organ on his narrow shoulders. The baroque **high altar** in the main chancel depicts the stoning of St Stephen; the left chancel contains a winged altarpiece from Wiener Neustadt dating from 1447; the right chancel houses the Renaissance-style red marble tomb of Friedrich III.

The cathedral's Katakomben (catacombs; tours adult/under 14yr €4/1.50; ⊙10-11.30am & 1.30-4.30pm Mon-Sat, 1.30-4.30pm Sun) house the remains of plague victims, kept in a mass grave and a bone house. Also on display are rows of urns containing the organs of the Habsburgs. One of the many privileges of being a Habsburg was to be dismembered and dispersed after death: their hearts are in the Augustinerkirche in the Hofburg, some organs are here and the rest was buried.

Hofburg
PALACE

Nothing symbolises the culture and heritage of Austria more than its Hofburg (Map p60). The Habsburgs were based here for over six centuries, from the first emperor (Rudolf I in 1273) to the last (Karl I in 1918). The Hofburg owes its size and architectural diversity to plain old one-upmanship: new sections were added by the new rulers, including the early-baroque **Leopold Wing**, the 18th-century **Imperial Chancery Wing**, the 16th-century **Amalia Wing** and the Gothic **Burgkapelle** (Royal Chapel).

The oldest section is the 13th-century **Schweizerhof** (Swiss Courtyard), named after the Swiss guards who used to protect its precincts. The Renaissance Swiss gate dates from 1553. The courtyard adjoins a larger courtyard, **In der Burg**, with a **monument to Emperor Franz II** in its centre. The palace now houses the offices of the Austrian president and a raft of museums.

Kaiserappartements
MUSEUM

(Imperial Apartments; Map p60; ✆533 75 70; 01, Innerer Burghof, Kaisertor; adult/student/under 19yr €9.90/8.90/5.90; ⊙9.30am-5.30pm Sep-Jun, 9am-6pm Jul & Aug) Once occupied by Franz Josef I and Empress Elisabeth, the Kaiserappartements are extraordinary for their opulence, fine furniture, tapestries and bulbous crystal chandeliers; only

VIENNA

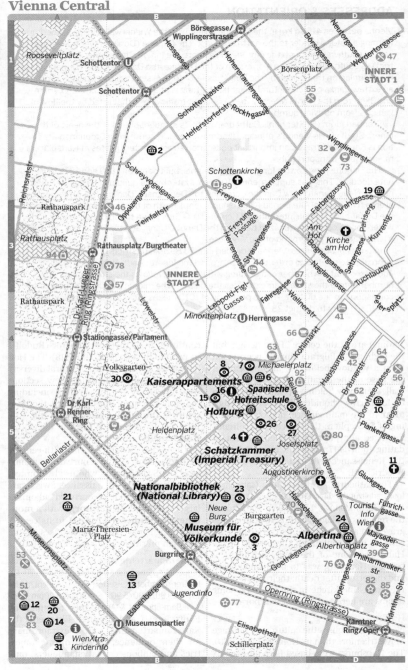

Rooseveltplatz
Schottentor Ⓤ
Schottentor 🚊
Börsegasse/ Wipplingerstrasse
Hohenstaufengasse
Hessgasse
Börsegasse
Neutorgasse
Werdertorgasse ✕47
Börsenplatz
INNERE STADT 1
55
43
Schottenbastei
Helferstorferstr Rockhgasse
Schottenstorferstr
🏛2
Wipplingerstr 32 ●
73
Schreyvogelgasse
Schottenkirche ✝
🔒89
Renngasse
Tiefer Graben
Färbergasse
Drahtgasse 19 🏛
Rathauspark ✕46
Freyung
Onpolzergasse
Teinfaltstr
Freyung Passage
Am Hof ⊕ Kirche am Hof
Pariserg
Kurrentg
Rathausplatz
🏛94
Rathausplatz/Burgtheater
Herrengasse
Strauchgasse
Bognergasse
Naglergasse
Seitzergasse
Tuchlauben
Peter splatz
Rathauspark
Dr-Karl-Lueger-Ring (Ringstrasse)
☆78
✕57
INNERE STADT 1
44
67
41
Leopold-Figl-Gasse
Fahregasse
Wallnerstr
Lowelstr
Minoritenplatz Ⓤ Herrengasse
66
Kohlmarkt
64
Stadiongasse/Parlament
63
42
Volksgarten
30 ◉
8 7◉ Michaelerplatz
Kaiserappartements 🏛🏛6
92
Reitschulstr
Habsburgergasse
Bräunerstr
56
Dr Karl-Renner-Ring
16 ❶ **Spanische**
15 ◉ **Hofreitschule**
Hofburg 🏛
62
Dorotheerg
10
Bellariastr
84
72 ☆
Heldenplatz
4 ⊕ ◉26
27 ◉
Josefsplatz
☆80
🏛88
Plankengasse
Spiegelgasse
Augustinerstr
11 ⊕
Schatzkammer (Imperial Treasury)
Augustinerkirche ⊕
Gluckgasse
21 🏛
Nationalbibliothek (National Library) 🏛 23 ◉
Neue Burg
Burggarten
Hanuschgasse
70
24 🏛 **Albertina** 🏛
Tourist Info Wien ⓘ
Führich-gasse
Maria-Theresien-Platz
Museum für Völkerkunde ◉
3
Albertinaplatz
Mayseder-gasse
Burgring 🚊
76 ☆
Philharmoniker-str
53 ✕
🏛13
Museumsplatz
Babenbergerstr
ⓘ Jugendinfo
Opernring (Ringstrasse)
82 ☆
85 ☆
51
🏛12 🏛20
☆77
Opergasse
Kärntner Str
83
🏛14 ⓘ
Ⓤ Museumsquartier
Elisabethstr
Kärntner Ring/Oper 🚊
🏛31 **WienXtra-Kinderinfo**
Schillerplatz

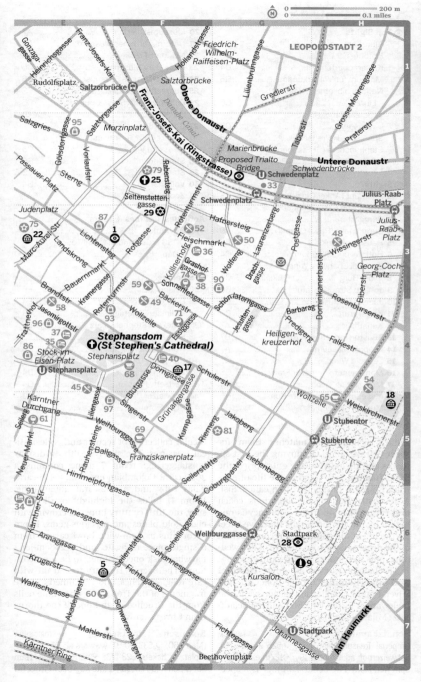

VIENNA

LEOPOLDSTADT 2

Gonzagagasse
Heinrichsgasse
Franz-Josefs-Kai
Hollandstrasse
Friedrich-Wilhelm-Raiffeisen-Platz
Lilienbrunngasse
Grosse Mohrengasse

Rudolfsplatz
Saltzorbrücke
Salzgries
Gölsdorfgasse
95
Saltzorgasse
Morzinplatz
Obere Donaustr
Salztorbrücke
Gredlerstr
Taborstr
Praterstr

Salzgries
Passauer Platz
Vorlaufstr
Sterng
Franz-Josefs-Kai (Ringstrasse)
Donau Canal
Marienbrücke
Proposed Trialto Bridge
Schwedenbrücke
Untere Donaustr
Schwedenplatz

Judenplatz
75
22
Marc-Aurel-Str
Landskrong
Lichtensteg
87
1
Rotgasse
Rabensteig
79
25
Seitenstettengasse
29
Rotenturmstr
Schwedenplatz
33
Julius-Raab-Platz
Julius-Raab-Platz

Hafnersteig
52
Fleischmarkt
50
Köllnerhof
36
Grashofgasse
74
38
90
Sonnenfelsgasse
Wollzeig
Laurenzerberg
Drachgasse
Schön Laternengasse
Postgasse
48
Wiesingerstr
Georg-Coch-Platz
Rosenbursenstr

Brandtstr
58
Bauernmarkt
Kramergasse
Rotenturmstr
59
49
93
Backerstr
71
Esslinggasse
Jesuitengasse
Heiligenkreuzerhof
Predigerg
Barbarag
Dominikanerbastei
Biberstr
Falkestr

Trattnerhof
Jasomirgottstr
96
35
37
86
Stock-im-Eisen-Platz
Stephansplatz
Stephansdom
(St Stephen's Cathedral)
Stephansplatz
68
40
17
Domgasse
Schulerstr

Kärntner Durchgang
45
61
Seilerg
Neuer Markt
Lilliengasse
97
Singerstr
Weihburggasse
69
Blutgasse
Grünangergasse
Kumpfgasse
Rienerg
81
Jakoberg
Wollzeile
65
54
18
Weiskirchnerstr
Stubentor
Stubentor

Rauhensteing
Ballgasse
Franziskanerplatz
Seilerstätte
Coburgbastei
Liebenberg

Himmelpfortgasse
91
34
Kärntner Str
Johannesgasse
Annagasse
Krugerstr
Seilerstätte
Schellinggasse
Johannesgasse
Weihburggasse
Weihburggasse
28
Stadtpark
9

Walfischgasse
Akademiestr
5
60
Fichtegasse
Schwarzenbergstr
Kursalon

Mahlerstr
Fichtegasse
Johannesgasse
Stadtpark
Am Heumarkt

Kärntner Ring
Beethovenplatz

Schloss Schönbrunn matches them for sheer extravagance. Occupying the first six rooms and included in the entry price, the **Sisi Museum** is devoted to the life of Austria's Empress Elisabeth, often called 'Sisi'. A reconstruction of the luxurious coach that carried her on many a journey is one highlight, but it's the details that give a feel for the life of the empress: a reconstruction of the dress she wore on the eve of her wedding, plus her sunshade, fans and gloves.

The highlight of the adjoining **Hoftafel und Silberkammer** (Court Tableware and Silver Depot), a collection of porcelain and tableware, is a 30m-long Mailänder Tafelaufsatz (Milan Table Piece).

Schatzkammer MUSEUM
(Imperial Treasury; Map p60; ☎525 24-486; 01, Schweizerhof; adult/under 19yr €12/free; ⊙10am-6pm Wed-Mon) The Schatzkammer is a spectacular collection of secular and ecclesiastical treasures. The sheer wealth on display is staggering: room 7 alone contains a 2680-carat Colombian emerald, a 416-carat balas ruby and a 492-carat aquamarine. Room 11 holds the highlight of the treasury, the 10th-century imperial crown, with eight gold plates and precious gems. Room 8 contains a 75cm-wide bowl carved from a single piece of agate, and a 243cm-long narwhal tusk once claimed to be a unicorn horn. The Sacred Treasury tops it off with rare religious relics, and is claimed to have fragments of the True Cross, one of the nails from the Crucifixion and one of the thorns from Christ's crown.

Spanische Hofreitschule HISTORIC SHOW
(Map p60; ☎533 90 31; www.srs.at; 01, Michaelerplatz 1; tickets €23-143; ⊙performances 11am Sat & Sun mid-Feb–Jun & late Aug-Dec) Graceful

stallions perform an equine ballet to a program of classical music while chandeliers shimmer above and the audience cranes to see from pillared balconies. Tickets can be ordered through the website, but be warned that performances are usually booked out months in advance. Unclaimed tickets are sold about two hours before performances, so you might try asking at the office about cancellations. Training or movement programs are open to the public at various times. The most regular is the **Morgenarbeit** (morning training; adult/child/family €12/6/24; ⊗10am-noon Tue-Sat Feb-Jun & mid-Aug–Dec) session. For these, tickets can be bought at the **visitor centre** (⊗9am-4pm Tue-Fri, to 7pm Fri on performance days) on Michaelerplatz, or the same day at gate 2 in Josefsplatz in the Hofburg. Queues are very long early in the day, but most people have disappeared by around 11am, when you can often get in quickly.

Nationalbibliothek LIBRARY
(Map p60; ☎534 10 397; www.onb.ac.at; 01, Josefsplatz 1; adult/under 19yr/family €7/free/12.50; ⊗10am-6pm Tue-Sun, to 9pm Thu) Austria's flagship library, the Nationalbibliothek contains an astounding collection of literature, maps, globes of the world and other cultural relics; its highlight, though, is the **Prunksaal** (Grand Hall), a majestic baroque hall built between 1723 and 1726. Commissioned by Karl VI (whose statue is under the central dome), it holds some 200,000 leather-bound scholarly tomes. Rare volumes (mostly 15th century) are stored within glass cabinets, with books opened to beautifully illustrated pages of text. The central fresco, by Daniel Gran, depicts the emperor's apotheosis.

Two Days

Jump on tram 1 or 2 and circle the **Ringstrasse** for a brief but rewarding informal tour of the boulevard's buildings. Get out at Kärntner Strasse and wander towards the heart of the city, where the glorious Gothic **Stephansdom** awaits. Make your way to the **Hofburg** before crossing the Ringstrasse to the **Kunsthistorisches Museum**, home to a breathtaking art collection. Recharge your batteries at one of the many Innere Stadt restaurants before attending a performance at the **Staatsoper**.

On day two visit imperial palace **Schönbrunn** before heading to the **Leopold Museum**, a treasure chest of Austrian artists. Take an early dinner at Vienna's celebrated **Naschmarkt**, then cross the city for a ride on the **Riesenrad** Ferris wheel. Finish the day with local wine and food at a *Heuriger*.

Four Days

Start the third day with an exploration of the **Schloss Belvedere**, an unequalled baroque palace, before lunching at Zu den Zwei Liesln. See Klimt's sumptuous *Beethoven Frieze* in the **Secession**, then end the night in one of the Gürtel's progressive bars.

If you're still up for unfathomable art collections in regal surroundings, a visit to **Palais Liechtenstein** is a must on the fourth day. Spend your last evening in the **Musikverein** experiencing the music of Beethoven or Mozart where it was originally played.

Neue Burg Museums MUSEUM
(Map p60; ☑525 24-484; 01, Heldenplatz; adult/under 19yr €12/free, audio guide €3; ☉10am-6pm Wed-Mon) An ensemble of three museums occupies part of the Neue Burg. The **Sammlung Alter Musik Instrumente** (Collection of Ancient Musical Instruments) is the best of the bunch and contains instruments in all shapes, sizes and tones. The **Ephesos Museum** features artefacts from Ephesus and Samothrace donated (some say 'lifted') by the sultan in 1900 after a team of Austrian archaeologists excavated Ephesus in Turkey. Last but not least is the **Hofjägd und Rüstkammer** (Arms and Armour) museum, with a fine collection of ancient armour dating mainly from the 15th and 16th centuries.

Museum für Völkerkunde MUSEUM
(Museum of Ethnology; Map p60; ☑534 30-0; www.ethno-museum.ac.at; 01, Heldenplatz; adult/under 19yr €8/free; ☉10am-6pm Wed-Mon) You can impress your children by taking them to this museum. Revamped a few years ago, it exudes a lightness of mood and has a thoughtful use of space that adults will appreciate too. Exhibits are on non-European cultures and divided into regions and nationalities, covering such countries as China, Japan and Korea, and also the Polynesian, Native American and Inuit cultures.

Albertina MUSEUM
(Map p60; ☑534 83-544; www.albertina.at; 01, Albertinaplatz 3; adult/under 19yr/student €9.50/free/7; ☉10am-6pm, to 9pm Wed) Once used to house imperial guests, the Albertina is now home to an astoundingly rich collection of graphic art. It contains 1½ million prints and 50,000 drawings, including 145 by Dürer (the largest collection in the world), 43 by Raphael, 70 by Rembrandt and 150 by Schiele. There are more by Leonardo da Vinci, Michelangelo, Rubens, Bruegel, Cézanne, Picasso, Klimt, Matisse and Kokoschka – of course, only a fraction of the collection is on display at any one time.

The enormous collection of graphics, architectural sketches, photographs, prints and drawings from the archive are used as the basis for temporary exhibitions on a particular theme, and these have been augmented since 2009 by a sensational permanent collection of paintings in the **Masterworks of Modern Art** section that is a who's who of 20th-century and contemporary art – Chagall, Nolde, Jawlensky and very many more.

Haus der Musik MUSEUM
(House of Music; Map p60; ☑516 48; www.hdm.at; 01, Seilerstätte 30; adult/under 12yr €10/5.50; ☉10am-10pm) The Haus der Musik is devoted in one form or another to music. The 1st floor pays homage, rather briefly, to the Vienna Philharmonic.

The 2nd floor is where the fun begins; the **Sonosphere** section delves into the physics of it all and uses touch screens and loads of hands-on displays to explain the mechanics of sound. Here you can test the limits of your hearing, play around with sampled audio and record your own CD (€0.99 per song, plus €2 for CD and cover). The 3rd floor features the stars of Vienna's classical music – Haydn, Mozart, Beethoven, Schubert, Strauss and Mahler all receive a room apiece. Best of all is the 'virtual conductor', where a video of the Vienna Philharmonic responds to a conducting baton and keeps time with your movements.

Kaisergruft   CHURCH
(Imperial Burial Vault; Map p60; ✆512 68 53; www. kapuziner.at/wien, in German; 01 Neuer Markt; adult/student/child €4/3/1.50; ☉10am-6pm)
The high-peaked Kaisergruft, beneath the Kapuzinerkirche (Church of the Capuchin Friars), was instigated by Empress Anna (1585–1618), and her body and that of her husband, Emperor Matthias (1557–1619), were the first to be placed here. Since then, all but three of the Habsburg dynasty members found their way here (in bits and pieces), the last being Empress Ziti in 1989. The only non-Habsburg to be buried here is the Countess Fuchs.

THE WHITE HORSE IN HISTORY

The Lipizzaner stallions date back to the 1520s, when Ferdinand I imported the first horses from Spain for the imperial palace. His son Maximillian II imported new stock in the 1560s and in 1580 Archduke Charles II established the imperial stud in Lipizza (Lipica, today in Slovenia), giving the horse its name. Austria's nobility had good reason for looking to Spain for its horses: the Spanish were considered the last word in equine breeding at the time, thanks to Moors from the 7th century who had brought their elegant horses to the Iberian Peninsula. Italian horses were added to the stock around the mid-1700s (these too had Spanish blood) and by the mid-18th century the Lipizzaner had a reputation for being Europe's finest horse.

The original baroque horses were not white or light grey but of various colours. In fact, it only became fashionable to breed white stallions during the 19th century, when Arab and various other horses were reintroduced into the line and the horses carefully selected.

Over the centuries, natural catastrophe, but more often war, caused the Lipizzaner to be evacuated from their original stud in Slovenia on numerous occasions. One of their periods of exile from the stud in Lipica was in 1915 due to the outbreak of WWI. Some of the horses went to Laxemburg (just outside Vienna), and others to Bohemia in today's Czech Republic (at the time part of the Austro-Hungarian Empire). When the Austrian monarchy collapsed in 1918, Lipica passed into Italian hands and the horses were divided up between Austria and Italy. The Italians ran the stud in Slovenia, while the Austrians transferred their horses to Piber, near Graz, which had been breeding military horses for the empire since 1798 – mostly at that time stallions crossed with English breeds. Today, Piber still supplies the Spanische Hofreitschule with its white stallions.

Things got no easier for the Lipizzaner after WWI, with Europe being carved up into ever-smaller pieces. Austrians, Hungarians, Czechs, Italians and the Yugoslavs developed their own studs, and even Romanians had their own Lipizzaner lineages. When WWII broke out, Hitler's cohorts goose-stepped in, requisitioned the Piber stud and started breeding military horses and – spare the thought! – pack mules there. They also decided to bring the different studs in their occupied regions together under one roof, and Piber's Lipizzaner wound up in Hostau, Bohemia.

Fearing the Lipizzaner would fall into the hands of the Russian army as it advanced towards the region in 1945, American forces seized the Lipizzaner and other horses in Hostau and transferred them to the safety of rural Upper Austria. The 'rescue' of the Lipizzaner was the basis for a rather kitsch Walt Disney film from 1963, *The Miracle of the White Stallions*. In 1952 our equine friends were finally returned to Piber, and as a result of this turbulent history there are Lipizzaner lineages in a handful of European countries, including Slovenia, of course, which in 2007 issued 20-cent coins with a Lipizzaner imprint.

VIENNESE ACTIONISM

Viennese actionism spanned the period from 1957 to 1968 and was one of the most extreme of all modern-art movements. It was linked to the Vienna Group, formed in the 1950s by HC Artmann, whose members experimented with surrealism and Dadaism in their sound compositions and textual montages. Actionism sought access to the unconscious through the frenzy of an extreme and very direct art; the actionists quickly moved from pouring paint over the canvas and slashing it with knives to using bodies (live people, dead animals) as 'brushes' and using blood, excrement, eggs, mud and whatever came to hand as 'paint'. The traditional canvas was soon dispensed with altogether and the artist's body instead became the canvas. This turned the site of art into a deliberated event (a scripted 'action', staged both privately and publicly) and even merged art with reality.

It was a short step from self-painting to inflicting wounds upon the body, and engaging in physical and psychological endurance tests. For 10 years the actionists scandalised the press and public, inciting violence and panic – but they got plenty of publicity. Often poetic, humorous and aggressive, the actions became increasingly politicised, addressing the sexual and social repression that pervaded the Austrian state. The press release for *Art in Revolution* (1968) gives the lowdown on what could be expected at a typical action: '[Günter] Brus undressed, cut himself with a razor, urinated in a glass and drank his urine, smeared his body with faeces and sang the Austrian national anthem while masturbating (for which he was arrested for degrading state symbols and sentenced to six months' detention).' This was, not entirely surprisingly, the last action staged in Vienna. For more, see p378.

The royals' fashion extends even to tombs: those in the vault range from the unadorned to the ostentatious. By far the most elaborate caskets are those in 18th-century baroque pomp, such as the huge double sarcophagus containing Maria Theresia and Franz I. The tomb of Charles VI has been expertly restored. Both were the work of Balthasar Moll.

Jüdisches Museum   MUSEUM
(Jewish Museum; Map p60; ☑535 04 31; www.jmw. at; 01, Dorotheergasse 11; adult/student & child €6.50/4, combined ticket €10/6; ☺10am-6pm Sun-Fri) Taking up three floors of Palais Eskeles, this museum uses holograms and an assortment of objects to document the history of the Jews in Vienna, from the first settlements at Judenplatz in the 13th century up to the present. The ground floor is filled with the Max Berger collection – a rich compilation of Judaica mainly dating from the Habsburg era. Temporary exhibitions are presented on the 1st and 2nd floors.

The combined ticket (students should bring ID) allows entry to the **Stadttempel** (Synagogue; Map p60; ☑535 04 31; www.jmw.at; 01, Seitenstettengasse 4; adult/student & child €3/2; ☺guided tours 11.30am & 2pm Mon-Thu) and the Museum Judenplatz.

Museum Judenplatz   MUSEUM
(Jewish Museum; Map p60; ☑535 04 31; www.jmw. at; 01, Judenplatz 8; adult/child €4/2.50; ☺10am-6pm Sun-Thu, to 2pm Fri) The Museum Judenplatz focuses on the excavated remains of a medieval synagogue (1421) once situated on Judenplatz. The basic outline of the synagogue can still be seen and a small model of the building helps to complete the picture. Documents and artefacts dating from 1200 to 1400 are on display, and spacey interactive screens explain Jewish culture. On Judenplatz is Austria's first Holocaust memorial, the 'Nameless Library'. This squat, box-like structure pays homage to the 65,000 Austrian Jews who were killed.

Ankeruhr   CLOCK
(Anker Clock; Map p60; Hoher Markt 10-11) Commissioned by the Anker Insurance Co, this picturesque art-nouveau clock was created by Franz von Matsch in 1911. Over a 12-hour period, figures such as Josef Haydn and Maria Theresia slowly pass across the clock face – details of who's who are outlined on a plaque on the wall below. Join the mass of tourists at noon when all the figures trundle past in turn, and organ music from the appropriate period is piped out.

FREE **Ruprechtskirche** CHURCH
(St Rupert's Church; Map p60; ☎535 60
03; www.ruprechtskirche.at, in German; 01, Seitenstettengasse 5; ⏱10am-noon & 3-5pm Mon, Wed &
Fri, 10am-noon Tue & Thu) A few steps north of
Ruprechtsplatz, Ruprechtskirche dates from
about 1137 or earlier, making it the oldest
church in Vienna. The lower levels of the
tower date from the 11th century, the roof
from the 15th century and the iron Renaissance door on the west side from the 1530s.
What makes this church attractive is its
unusually simple exterior of ivy-clad stone
walls in cobblestoned surrounds. The interior is just as sleek and worth viewing, with
a Romanesque nave from the 12th century.

Beethoven Pasqualatihaus NOTABLE BUILDING
(Map p60; ☎535 89 05; 01, Mölker Bastei 8;
adult/under 19yr €2/free; ⏱10am-1pm & 2-6pm
Tue-Sun) Beethoven's residence from 1804
to 1814 (he apparently occupied some
60 places in his 35 years in Vienna); he
composed Symphonies 4, 5 and 7 and the
opera *Fidelio* here. You can listen to works
and view some memorabilia.

Mozarthaus Vienna NOTABLE BUILDING
(Map p60; ☎512 1791; 01, Domgasse 5; adult/
under 14yr €9/7; ⏱10am-7pm) Three floors
covering Vienna during Mozart's era, the
musician himself and this former residence, where he penned *The Marriage of
Figaro*.

Neidhart-Fresken MURAL
(Map p60; ☎535 90 65; 01, Tuchlauben 19; adult/
child €2/free; ⏱10am-1pm & 2-6pm Tue, 2-6pm
Fri-Sun) The oldest extant secular murals
in Vienna, dating from 1398. They tell the
story of the minstrel Neidhart von Reuen-
tal (1180–1240) in lively and jolly scenes.

RINGSTRASSE
Emperor Franz Josef was largely responsible
for the monumental architecture around the
Ringstrasse, a wide, tree-lined boulevard encircling much of the Innere Stadt. In 1857 he
decided to tear down the redundant military
fortifications and exercise grounds and re-

MORE FOR YOUR MONEY 67

If you're planning on doing a lot of
sightseeing in a short period, consider
purchasing the **Wien-Karte** (Vienna
Card; €18.50), which provides 72 hours
of unlimited travel plus discounts at selected museums, attractions, cafes and
shops. It comes with an information
brochure and is available from hotels
and ticket offices.

The City of Vienna runs some 20
municipal museums (www.museum.
vienna.at) scattered around the city, all
of which are included in a free booklet
available at the Rathaus. Permanent
exhibitions in all are free on Sunday.

place them with grandiose public buildings
in a variety of historical styles. Work began
the following year and reached a peak in the
1870s. The stock-market crash in 1873 put a
major dampener on plans, and other grand
schemes were shelved due to lack of money
and the outbreak of WWI. The Ring is easily
explored on foot or bicycle; if you've not the
time, jump on tram 1 or 2, both of which run
the length of the boulevard and offer a snapshot of the impressive architecture.

Parlament MONUMENT
(Map p70; ☎40 110-2570; www.parlinkom.gv.at; 01,
Dr-Karl-Renner-Ring 3; tours adult/under 19yr €4/1)
The neoclassical facade and Greek pillars of
Parlament are the work of Theophil Hansen
in 1883 and make a striking impression,
complemented by the beautiful **Athena
Fountain** situated in front of the building.
Athena is flanked by statues of horse break-
ing (though some would say horse punch-
ing).

FREE **Rathaus** MONUMENT
(City Hall; Map p70; ☎525 50; www.wien.
gv.at; 01, Rathausplatz; ⏱tours 1pm Mon, Wed & Fri)
The neo-Gothic Rathaus, modelled on Flemish city halls, steals the Ringstrasse show. Its

TOURS OF THE PARLIAMENT

Tours of the parliament lasting almost one hour are conducted at 11am and on the hour
between 2pm and 4pm Monday to Thursday, at 11am and on the hour between 1pm and
4pm Friday and on the hour between 11am and 4pm Saturday September to mid-July.
The rest of the year tours are on the hour between 11am and 4pm Monday to Saturday.
A combined ticket for a tour of Parlament and entrance to Palais Epstein costs €7/3 per
adult/child.

VIENNA'S CITY WALLS

The Ringstrasse runs along the line of the former 16th-century city walls. These walls originally had the extra protection of a ditch or moat, beyond which a wide, sloped clearing allowed defenders to hurl the heavy stuff at their exposed invaders. Anyone living in the Vorstädte (inner suburbs) outside the fortress was expected to flee inside it as invading forces approached – or take their chances.

main spire soars to 102m, if you include the pennant held by the knight at the top. You're free to wander through the seven inner courtyards but you must join a guided tour to catch a glimpse of the interior, with its red carpets, gigantic mirrors and frescoes.

Kunsthistorisches Museum   MUSEUM
(Museum of Fine Arts; Map p60; ☑525 240; www. khm.at; 01, Burgring 5; adult/student €12/free; ☺10am-6pm Tue-Sun, to 9pm Thu) This ranks among the finest museums in Europe, if not the world, and should not be missed. The Habsburgs were great collectors, and the huge extent of lands under their control led to many important works of art being funnelled back to Vienna.

Peter Paul Rubens was appointed to the service of a Habsburg governor in Brussels, so it comes as no surprise that the museum has one of the best collections of his works. The collection of paintings by Pieter Bruegel the Elder (1525–69) is also unrivalled. In the building itself, the murals between the arches above the stairs were created by three artists, including a young Gustav Klimt (1862–1918; northern wall), painted before he broke with neoclassical tradition.

Ground Floor

In the west wing is the Egyptian collection, including the burial chamber of Prince Kaninisut and mummified animal remains. The Greek and Roman collection here includes the Gemma Augusta cameo made from onyx in AD 10.

The east wing contains sculpture and decorative arts covering a range of styles and epochs. This is closed indefinitely for renovation; when it reopens the collection will include 17th-century glassware, ornaments and lavish clocks from the 16th and 17th centuries.

First Floor

The Gemäldegalerie (Picture Gallery) on this floor is the most important part of the museum and features Bruegel, Dürer, Rubens, Rembrandt and many others. All works are labelled in English and German.

The East Wing is devoted mainly to German, Dutch and Flemish paintings. The exact locations of paintings change somewhat, but one room is set aside for the Bruegel collection, amassed by Rudolf II. A recurrent theme in Bruegel the Elder's work is nature, as in *The Hunters in the Snow* (1565). A gallery also displays the warm, larger-than-life scenes of Flemish baroque. The motto in *The Celebration of the Bean King* by Jacob Jordaens (1593–1678), a rollicking painting depicting revellers raising their glasses, translates as 'None resembles a fool more than the drunkard'. Works by Albrecht Dürer (1471–1528) feature prominently among the German painters. His brilliant mastery of colour is perhaps best illustrated in *The Adoration of the Trinity* (1511), originally an altarpiece.

The paintings by the mannerist Giuseppe Arcimboldo (1527–93), in rooms dedicated to Italian painting in the 15th and 16th century, use a device well explored later by Salvador Dalí (1904–89) – familiar objects arranged to be perceived in a new light. Dramatic baroque scenes by Rubens (1577–1640), who brought together northern European and Italian traditions, are showcased among the 17th-century Flemish painters. Several self-portraits by Rembrandt can be found among the 17th-century Dutch painters.

The West Wing contains evocative works by Titian (1485–1576), a member of the Venetian school. Never too far away is *The Three Philosophers* (1508), which is one of the few properly authenticated works by Giorgione (1478–1510). Also part of the 15th- and 16th-century Italian collection is Raphael's (1483–1520) harmonious and idealised *Madonna in the Meadow* (1505) – its triangular composition and the complementary colours are typical features of the Florentine high Renaissance. It's interesting to compare this with Caravaggio's (1571–1610) *Madonna of the Rosary* (1606), housed in the collection of Italian paintings from the 17th and 18th centuries, in which the supplicants' dirty feet illustrate a new realism in early baroque. The 18th-century Italian painter Bernardo Bellotto (1721–80) was commissioned by Maria Theresia to paint scenes of Vienna. Several are on show here, and some of these landscapes, such as a view from Schloss Belvedere, break away from faithful representation of the landscape.

Naturhistorisches Museum MUSEUM
(Museum of Natural History; Map p60; ☑521 77-0 www.nhm-wien.ac.at; 01, Burgring 7; adult/under 19yr €10/free; ☉9am-6.30pm Thu-Mon, to 9pm Wed) This is the scientific counterpart to the Kunsthistorisches Museum. Minerals, meteorites and animal remains are displayed in jars, while zoology and anthropology are covered in detail. There's also a children's corner. The 25,000-year-old *Venus of Willendorf* statuette is on display here (her 100th anniversary of discovery was celebrated in 2008), and also in room 11 is her older sister, the 32,000 BC statuette *Venus of Galgenberg* (the oldest figurative sculpture in the world).

Akademie der bildenden Künste MUSEUM
(Academy of Fine Arts; Map p72; ☑588 16-0; www.akademiegalerie.at, in German; 01, Schillerplatz 3; adult/under 10 yr €6/free, audio guide €2; ☉10am-6pm Tue-Sun) This small picture gallery's highlight is *The Last Judgement* altarpiece by Hieronymus Bosch (1450–1516). Flemish painters are well represented in this building, which itself sports an elegant facade. As fate would have it, this was the academy that turned down would-be artist Adolf Hitler. A statue of Schiller takes centre stage in front of the academy.

Secession MUSEUM
(Map p72; ☑587 53 07; www.secession.at; 01, Friedrichstrasse 12; adult/concession exhibition & frieze €8.50/5, exhibition only €5/4; ☉10am-6pm Tue-Sun) The year 1897 was a fateful one for Austrian art. This was the year 19 progressive artists broke away from the conservative art establishment that met in the Künstlerhaus gallery in Vienna and formed their own secession movement. Their aim was to present new trends in contemporary art and depart from backward-looking historicism. Among their number were Gustav Klimt, Josef Hoffman (1871–1956), Kolo Moser (1868–1918) and Josef M Olbrich (1867–1908), a former student of Otto Wagner (1841–1918).

In 1898, Olbrich designed the movement's **Secession Building**. Its most striking feature is the enormous golden sphere (prosaically described as a 'golden cabbage' by some Viennese) rising from a turret on the roof. Above the door are highly distinctive mask-like faces with dangling serpents instead of earlobes. The motto above the entrance postulates: *'Der Zeit ihre Kunst, der Kunst ihre Freiheit'* (To each time its art, to art its freedom).

The 14th exhibition held in the building, in 1902, featured the famous *Beethoven Frieze* by Klimt. This 34m-long work was intended only as a temporary exhibit but has been painstakingly restored and is permanently on show in the basement. The frieze shows willowy women with bounteous hair jostling for attention with a large gorilla, while slender figures float and a choir sings. The ground floor is still used for temporary exhibitions of contemporary art.

MuseumsQuartier CULTURAL PRECINCT
(Museum Quarter; Map p60; ☑523 58 81-173, 0820-600 600; www.mqw.at; 07, Museumsplatz 1; ☉information & ticket centre 10am-7pm) This remarkable ensemble of museums, cafes, restaurants and bars is located inside former imperial stables designed by Fischer von Erlach. A breeding ground of Viennese cultural life, it's the perfect place to hang out and watch or meet people on warm evenings. With over 60,000 sq metres of exhibition space, the complex is one of the world's most ambitious cultural spaces.

Of the combined tickets on offer, the MQ Kombi Ticket (€25) includes entry into every museum (Zoom only has a reduction) and a 30% discount on performances in the TanzQuartier Wien; MQ Art Ticket (€21.50) gives admission into the Leopold Museum, MUMOK, Kunsthalle and reduced entry into Zoom, plus 30% discount on the TanzQuartier Wien; and MQ Duo Ticket (€17) covers everything the Art ticket does, minus the Kunsthalle (a flexible version allows you to choose two from any of the museums).

Leopold Museum MUSEUM
(Map p60; ☑525 70-0; www.leopoldmuseum.org; 07, Museumsplatz 1; adult/under 7yr €10/free, audio guide €3; ☉10am-6pm, to 9pm Thu) In 1994 the Austrian government acquired the enormous private collection of 19th-century and modern Austrian paintings amassed by Rudolf Leopold, paying €160 million for 5266 paintings (sold individually, the paintings would have made him €574 million). It then went about building a museum to display this important collection, and the Leopold Museum was born.

Leopold began his art collection in 1950 with the purchase of his first Egon Schiele (1890–1918), so it comes as no surprise that

VIENNA

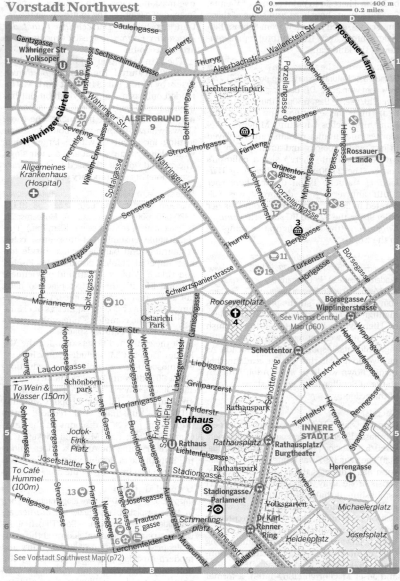

the Leopold owns the largest collection of the painter's work in the world. Most are usually on the ground floor; his *Kardinale und Nonne – Liebkosung* (Cardinal and Nun – Caress) is a delightful oil on canvas depicting the two figures kneeled in furtive embrace, their eyes fixed on the onlooker. Also on the ground floor is a large collection of works by Gustav Klimt; his large *Tod und Leben* (Death and Life) is just one highlight. Simple yet highly emotional sketches by both artists are displayed in the basement.

Vorstadt Northwest

realism, pop art and photo-realism. The best of expressionism, cubism, minimal art and Viennese actionism is represented in a collection of 9000 works that are rotated and exhibited on themes. On a visit you might glimpse, in the following order: a wearily slumped attendant (not part of any exhibit), photos of horribly deformed babies, a video piece of a man being led by a beautiful woman across a pedestrian crossing on a dog leash, naked bodies smeared with salad and other delights, a man parting his own buttocks, flagellation in a lecture hall, and an ultra-close-up of a urinating penis. The heavy stuff comes later. Be prepared.

Kunsthalle   MUSEUM

(Arts Hall; Map p60; ☎521 890; www.kunsthallewien.at; 07, Museumsplatz 1; adult/under 13yr Hall 1 €7.50/free, Hall 2 €6/free, combined ticket €10.50/free; ◑10am-7pm Fri-Wed, to 9pm Thu) The Kunsthalle showcases Austrian and international contemporary art. Programs, which run for three to six months, tend to focus mainly on photography, video, film, installation and new media.

Museum für Angewandte Kunst   MUSEUM

(MAK, Museum of Applied Arts; Map p60; ☎711 36-0; www.mak.at; 01, Stubenring 5; adult/under 19yr €7.90/free, Sat free, tours €2; ◑10am-6pm Wed-Sun, to midnight Tue, tours in English noon Sun) MAK is devoted to craftsmanship and art forms in everyday life. Each exhibition room showcases a different style, which includes Renaissance, baroque, orientalism, historicism, empire, art deco and the distinctive metalwork of the Wiener Werkstätte. Contemporary artists were invited to present the rooms in ways they felt were appropriate, resulting in eye-catching and unique displays. The 20th-century design and architecture room is one of the most fascinating, and Frank Gehry's cardboard chair is a gem. The collection encompasses tapestries, lace, furniture, glassware and ornaments; Klimt's *Stoclet Frieze* is upstairs.

The basement Study Collection has exhibits based on types of materials: glass and ceramics, metal, wood and textiles. Here you'll find anything from ancient oriental statues to unusual sofas (note the red-lips sofa).

Votivkirche   CHURCH

(Map p60; 09, Rooseveltplatz; ◑9am-1pm & 4-6pm Tue-Sat, to 1pm Sun) Commissioned by Franz Josef after he survived an assassination attempt, this neo-Gothic church has

Other artists well represented include Albin Egger-Lienz (1868–1926), Richard Gerstl (1883–1908) and, arguably Austria's third-greatest painter (after Klimt and Schiele), Oskar Kokoschka (1886–1980). Egger-Lienz had a knack for capturing the essence of rural life; this is seen in his stark *Pietà* (1926), considered by Leopold to be the artist's best work. Some of the most exciting pieces by Kokoschka were done early in his long career; his *Selbstportrait mit ein Hand* (Self-Portrait with One Hand) from 1918 is just one fine example. Works by Hoffmann, Loos, Otto Wagner, Waldmüller and Romako are also housed here.

MUMOK   MUSEUM

(Museum Moderner Kunst; Map p72; ☎525 00; www.mumok.at; 07, Museumsplatz 1; adult/student €9/free; ◑10am-6pm, to 9pm Thu) The dark basalt building that houses MUMOK is alive inside with Vienna's premier collection of 20th-century art, centred on fluxus, nouveau

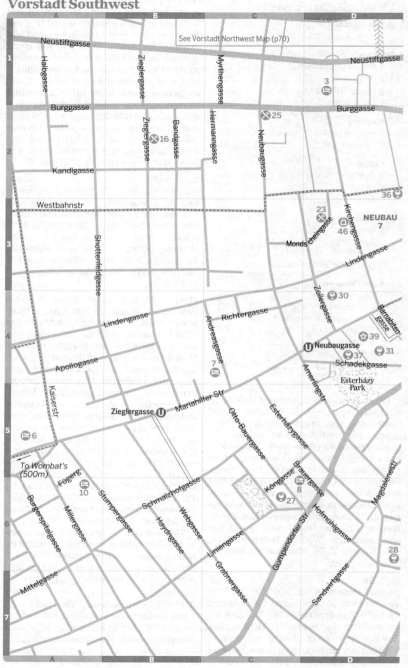

See Vorstadt Northwest Map (p70)

VIENNA

VIENNA

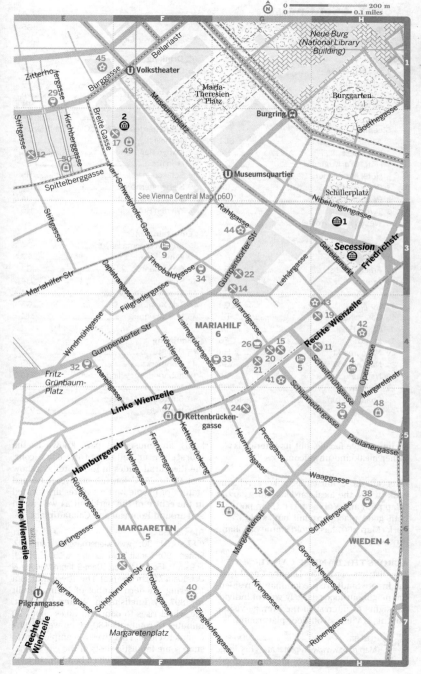

See Vienna Central Map (p60)

an impressive facade, but its interior is rather bleak and unwelcoming.

After all those museums, take a relaxing walk in one the local gardens. **Burggarten** (Map p60) and **Volksgarten** (Map p60) are both good places to chill out, and **Stadtpark** (Map p60) has a gold statue of Johann Strauss.

ACROSS THE DANUBE CANAL

The districts across the Danube Canal from the Innere Stadt are predominantly residential neighbourhoods, largely void of individual sights of interest to the average visitor. But this is Vienna's outdoor playground.

FREE **Prater**   AMUSEMENT PARK
(Map p56; www.wien-prater.at) This large park encompasses grassy meadows, wood-lands, an amusement park known as the **Würstelprater** and one of the city's icons, the Riesenrad. Rides in the Prater sideshow cost €1 to €5. Colourful, bizarre, deformed statues of people and creatures are located in the centre of the parkland as well as on and around Rondeau and Calafattiplatz.

Riesenrad   FERRIS WHEEL
(☎729 54 30; www.wienerriesenrad.com; 02, Prater 90; adult/child/family €8.50/3.50/21; ⊘9am-11.45pm May-Sep, 10am-9.45pm Mar, Apr & Oct, 10am-7.45pm Nov-Feb) The Riesenrad is a towering, modern symbol of Vienna. Built in 1897 by Englishman Walter B Basset, the wheel rises to 65m and takes about 20 minutes to rotate its 430-tonne weight one complete circle. This gives you ample time to snap some fantastic shots of the city spread out at your feet. It survived bombing in 1945

and has had dramatic lighting and a cafe added at its base. This icon achieved celluloid fame in *The Third Man,* in the scene where Holly Martins finally confronts Harry Lime, and also featured in the James Bond flick *The Living Daylights* and director Richard Linklater's *Before Sunrise.* The latter is an intriguing film with a lot of Vienna and a lot of love, but oddly for such a film, no sex scene worth writing home about.

A ride on the Riesenrad includes entry into the Panorama, a collection of disused wheel-cabins filled with models depicting scenes from the city's history, including Roman Vienna and the Turkish invasions. Close to the Riesenrad begins the 4km Liliputbahn (minirailway) connecting the Würstelprater with Ernst-Happel-Stadion.

Donauinsel & Alte Donau   RECREATION AREA
Dividing the Danube from the Neue Donau is the svelte Donauinsel, which stretches some 21.5km from opposite Klosterneuburg in the north to the Nationalpark Donau-Auen (p130) in the south. The island features long sections of swimming areas, concrete paths for walking and cycling, and restaurants and snack bars. The Alte Donau is a landlocked arm of the Danube, a favourite of sailing and boating enthusiasts, swimmers, walkers, fishermen and, in winter (when it's cold enough), ice skaters.

INSIDE THE GÜRTEL
The districts that lie inside the Gürtel are a dense concentration of apartment blocks pocketed by leafy parks, with a couple of grand baroque palaces thrown in for good measure.

Schloss Belvedere   MUSEUM
(Map p76; www.belvedere.at; combined ticket for both sections adult/student €13.50/9.50) Belvedere is a masterpiece of total art and one of the world's finest baroque palaces. Designed by Johann Lukas von Hildebrandt (1668–1745), it was built for the brilliant military strategist Prince Eugene of Savoy, conqueror of the Turks in 1718. The Unteres (Lower) Belvedere was built first (1714–16) with an orangery attached, and it was the prince's summer residence. Connected to it by a long, landscaped garden is the Oberes (Upper) Belvedere (1721–23), the venue for the prince's banquets and other big bashes.

The palace is now home to the Österreichische Galerie (Austrian Gallery), split between the Unteres Belvedere and Orangerie, which combine to house special exhibitions, and the Oberes Belvedere, housing primarily Austrian art from the Middle Ages to the present.

Oberes Belvedere   MUSEUM
(Map p56; ☎795 57-0; www.belvedere.at; 03, Prinz-Eugen-Strasse 27; adult/student €9.50/6.50, audio guide €4; ☺10am-6pm) Pride and joy of Oberes Belvedere are its paintings by Gustav Klimt, including his famous *The Kiss* (1908) and *Judith* (1901), which with their rich gold tones and highly ornamental style perfectly embody Viennese art nouveau. Masterpieces by Egon Schiele and Oskar Kokoschka also feature in this collection, while the Viennese Biedermeier school figures strongly through the works of Ferdinand Georg Waldmüller (1793–1865), Friedrich von Amerling (1803–87) and Peter Fendi (1796–1842). The gallery is a staggeringly beautiful who's who of Austrian art, with works by other artists of

HITLER IN VIENNA

Born in Braunau am Inn, Upper Austria, in 1889, with the name Adolf Schicklgruber (his father changed the family name when they moved to Germany in 1893), Adolf Hitler moved to Vienna when he was just 17. Six unsettled, unsuccessful, poverty-stricken years later he abandoned the city and moved to Munich to make a name for himself. He later wrote in *Mein Kampf* that his Vienna years were 'a time of the greatest transformation that I have ever been through. From a weak citizen of the world I became a fanatical anti-Semite'. Whether this had anything to do with being twice rejected by the Akademie der bildenden Künste (Academy of Fine Arts), who dismissed his work as 'inadequate', he did not say. Even though he was convinced that proper training would have made him into a very successful artist, these rejections caused Hitler to write to a friend that perhaps fate may have reserved for him 'some other purpose'. This 'purpose' became all too clear to everyone over time.

Hitler briefly returned to Vienna in 1938 at the head of the German army and was greeted by enthusiastic crowds on Heldenplatz. He left a day later.

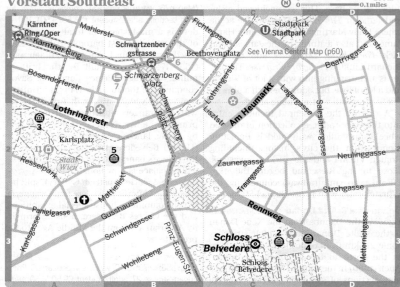

the calibre of Hans Makart (1840–84), Friedensreich Hundertwasser (1928–2000), Fritz Wotruba (1907–75) and many more.

The west wing of the Upper Belvedere goes beyond Austria's borders to showcase some stunning late-Gothic sculpture and panels, beginning from 1400 and culminating in the 16th century. Just one highlight here is the 15th-century Znaim Altar, probably originating from Znojmo in Czech Moravia.

The baroque era finds expression in the evocative and sometimes disturbing paintings of Johann Michael Rottmayr (1654–1730) and Paul Troger (1698–1762), and the bizarrely grimacing sculptured heads of Franz Xaver Messerschmidt (1736–83).

While visiting the Upper Belvedere, try to see the elaborately stuccoed and frescoed **Marmorsaal** (Marble Hall), offering superb views over the palace gardens and Vienna.

Unteres Belvedere MUSEUM
(Map p76; ☎795 57-0; www.belvedere.at; 03, Rennweg 6; adult/student €9.50/6.50; ◷10am-6pm Thu-Tue, to 9pm Wed) Built from 1714 to 1716, Unteres Belvedere is remarkable as Prince Eugene's former residential apartment and ceremonial rooms, with grandiose interiors such as in the **Groteskensaal** (Hall of the Grotesque), the **Marmorgalerie** (Mar-

ble Gallery) and the **Goldenes Zimmer** (Golden Room). Temporary exhibitions are held here and in the Orangery (Map p76); the latter has a walkway offering views over Prince Eugene's private garden and to Oberes Belvedere.

Belvedere Gardens GARDEN
(Rennweg/Prinz-Eugen-Strasse) The long garden between the two Belvederes was laid out in classical French style and has sphinxes and other mythical beasts along its borders. South of the Oberes Belvedere is the small alpine garden (adult/concession €3.20/2.50; ◷10am-6pm Apr-Jul), which has 3500 plant species and a bonsai section. North of here is the much larger Botanischer Gärten (Botanical Gardens; Map p56; admission free; ◷9am-1hr before dusk) belonging to Vienna University.

Palais Liechtenstein MUSEUM
(Liechtenstein Museum; Map p70; ☎319 57 67-0; www.liechtensteinmuseum.at; 09, Fürstengasse 1; adult/under 16yr €10/free; ◷10am-5pm Fri-Tue) After many years collecting dust in depot vaults, these days the private collection of Prince Hans-Adam II of Liechtenstein is displayed in this splendid museum. The magnificent collection consists of some 200

Vorstadt Southeast

paintings and 50 sculptures dating from 1500 to 1700.

Built between 1690 and 1712, the palace illustrates the audacious folly and extravagance of baroque architecture. Frescoes and ceiling paintings by the likes of Johann Michael Rottmayer (1654–1730) and Marcantonio Franceschini (1648–1729) decorate the halls, staircases and corridors.

The palace is in four sections. On the ground floor near the western staircase (on the left as you enter) is the **Gentlemen's Apartment Library**, a magnificent neoclassical hall containing about 100,000 books, frescoes by Johann Michael Rottmayr and a temple-like empire clock dating from 1795. From the library you can enter galleries I to III, which have changing exhibitions. You can also enter these directly from alongside the eastern staircase (near the cloak room). After that, climb the eastern staircase, which, like its western counterpart, is decorated with Rottmayr frescoes. Upstairs is the **Herkulessaal** (Hercules Hall), named for the Hercules motifs within its ceiling frescoes by renowned Roman painter Andrea Pozzo (1642–1709).

Surrounding the hall on three sides beginning from the eastern staircase and culminating at the western staircase are galleries IV to X, with the permanent collection

of the palace. And what a collection this is! Seven galleries intertwine to provide a trip through 200 years of art history, starting in 1500 with early Italian panel paintings in gallery IV. Gallery V is dedicated to late-Gothic and Renaissance portraits; Raphael's *Portrait of a Man* (1503) is a highlight here. The centrepiece of the upper floor is gallery VII, which is home to Rubens' *Decius Mus* cycle (1618). Consisting of eight almost life-size paintings, the cycle depicts the life and death of Decius Mus, a Roman leader who sacrificed himself so that his army could be victorious on the battlefield. Gallery VIII is devoted to Rubens and Flemish baroque painting; even more Rubens works – this time his portraits – are on display in gallery IX alongside those of Van Dyck and Fran Hals. The sheer exuberance and life captured by Rubens in his *Portrait of Clara Serena Rubens* (1616) is testament to the great artist's talent. Gallery X gives you a soft landing of ivory craftwork and Dutch still life.

Heeresgeschichtliches Museum MUSEUM
(Museum of Military History; Map p56; ☑795 61-60420; www.hgm.or.at; 03, Arsenal; adult/under 10yr €5.30/free; ☺9am-5pm) The superb Heeresgeschichtliches Museum is housed in the Arsenal, a large neo-Byzantine barracks and munitions depot.

Spread over two floors, the museum works its way from the Thirty Years' War (1618–48) to WWII, taking in the Hungarian Uprising and the Austro-Prussian War (ending in 1866), the Napoleonic and Turkish Wars, and WWI. Highlights on the 1st floor include the Great Seal of Mustafa Pasha, which fell to Prince Eugene of Savoy in the Battle of Zenta in 1697.

On the ground floor, the room on the assassination of Archduke Franz Ferdinand in Sarajevo in 1914 – which set off a chain of events culminating in the start of WWI – steals the show. The car he was shot in (complete with bullet holes), the sofa he bled to death on and his rather grisly blood-stained coat are on show. The eastern wing covers the republic years after WWI up until the Anschluss in 1938; the excellent displays include propaganda posters and Nazi paraphernalia, plus video footage of Hitler hypnotising the masses.

Wien Museum MUSEUM
(Map p76; ☑505 87 47-0; www.museum.vienna.at, in German; 04, Karlsplatz 5; adult/under 19yr €6/free; ☺10am-6pm Tue-Sun) The Wien Museum

Karlsplatz is the main building of the city museum and illustrates the development of the capital through a blend of art, illustrations and historic objects. Exhibits include maps and plans, artefacts and stunning paintings by Klimt and Schiele. Biedermeier painters like Waldmüller alone are worth the entrance fee.

Karlskirche
CHURCH

(St Charles' Church; Map p76; ☎712 44 56; www.karlskirche.at; 04, Karlsplatz; adult/under 10yr €6/free; ⊙9am-noon & 1-6pm Mon-Sat, 1-5.30pm Sun) Karlskirche was built between 1716 and 1739 to fulfil a vow made by Charles VI following the 1713 plague. The twin columns are modelled on Trajan's Column in Rome and show scenes from the life of St Charles Borromeo (who succoured plague victims in Italy), to whom the church is dedicated. The huge oval dome is 72m high and its interior is graced by cloud-bound celestial beings painted by Johann Michael Rottmayr; admission includes a ride in the lift up to the dome for a close-up look.

KunstHausWien
GALLERY

(Map p56; ☎712 04 91; www.kunsthauswien.com; 03, Untere Weissgerberstrasse 13; adult/11-18yr €9/4.50, incl temporary exhibitions €12/9, Mon half-price; ⊙10am-7pm) This gallery looks like something out of a toy shop. It was designed by Friedensreich Hundertwasser, whose highly innovative buildings feature uneven floors, coloured ceramics, patchwork decoration, irregular corners, and grass and trees on the roof. The permanent collection is something of a tribute to Hundertwasser, showcasing his paintings, graphics and tapestry, his philosophy on ecology, and his architecture.

Hundertwasserhaus
HISTORIC HOUSE

(Map p56; cnr Löwengasse & Kegelgasse) This residential block of flats was designed by Hundertwasser and is now one of Vienna's most prestigious addresses, even though it only provides rented accommodation and is owned by the city of Vienna. It's not possible to see inside, but you can visit the Kalke Village (www.kalke-village.at; ⊙9am-7pm), also the handiwork of Hundertwasser, created from an old Michelin factory. It contains overpriced cafes, souvenir shops and art shops, all in typical Hundertwasser fashion with colourful ceramics and a distinct absence of straight lines.

Sigmund Freud Museum
MUSEUM

(Map p70; ☎319 15 96; www.freud-museum.at; 09, Berggasse 19; adult/student €7/4.50; ⊙9am-5pm) Former house of the famous psychologist, now housing a small museum featuring some of his personal belongings.

Stadtbahn Pavillons
NOTABLE BUILDINGS

(Map p76; ☎505 87 47-84059; 04, Karlsplatz; adult/student & child €2/1; ⊙10am-6pm Tue-Sun Apr-Oct) *Jugendstil* (art nouveau) pavilions designed by Otto Wagner for Vienna's first public-transport system.

OUTSIDE THE GÜRTEL

The districts that fall outside the Gürtel are quite an unusual blend. Parts are rather dull and uninviting (by Viennese standards) – in particular towards the south – while others are beautiful beyond belief and home to some of Vienna's greatest treasures.

Schloss Schönbrunn
MUSEUM

(Map p56; ☎811 13-0; www.schoenbrunn.at; 13, Schloss Schönbrunn; tours adult/concession from €9.50/8.50; ⊙8.30am-6pm Jul & Aug, 8.30am-5pm Apr-Jun, Sep & Oct, 8.30am-4.30pm Nov-Mar) While Schloss Belvedere is mostly about its stupendous art collection and a handful of grand rooms, Schloss Schönbrunn focuses on the palace itself. This means grand rooms and background on the habits and quirks of Austria's famous Habsburg family.

Of the 1441 rooms within the palace, 40 are open to the public. The Imperial Tour takes you into 26 of these, and in the last room those on a Grand Tour show their tickets again and continue through the remaining rooms. Note that the Grosse Galerie, part of both tours, is being restored until late 2012. Despite the rather steep prices, both tours are well worth doing for an insight into the people and the opulence of the baroque age. Because of the popularity of the palace, tickets are stamped with a departure time, and there may be a delay before you're allowed to set off in summer, so buy your ticket straight away and then explore the gardens.

FREE Schloss Schönbrunn Gardens
GARDEN

(Map p79; 13, Schloss Schönbrunn; ⊙6am-dusk Apr-Oct, 6.30am-dusk Nov-Mar) The beautifully tended formal gardens of the palace, arranged in the French style, are a symphony of colour in summer and a combination of greys and browns in winter; all seasons are appealing in their own right. The grounds, which were opened to the public by Joseph II in 1779, hide a number of attractions in the tree-lined avenues (arranged according to a grid and star-shaped system between 1750

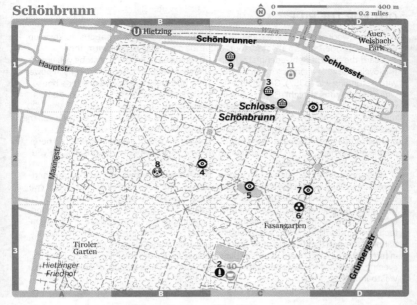

and 1755). From 1772 to 1780 Ferdinand Hetzendorf added some of the final touches to the park under the instructions of Joseph II: fake **Roman ruins** in 1778; the **Neptunbrunnen** (Neptune Fountain), a riotous ensemble from Greek mythology, in 1781; and the crowning glory, the **Gloriette** (rooftop access adult/student/child €2/1.70/1.40; ⊙9am-7pm Jul & Aug, to 6pm Apr-Jun & Sep, to 5pm Oct) in 1775. The view from the Gloriette, looking back towards the palace with Vienna shimmering in the distance, ranks among the best in the city. It's possible to venture onto its roof, but the view is only marginally superior.

The original **Schöner Brunnen fountain**, from which the palace gained its name, now pours through the stone pitcher of a nymph near the Roman ruins.

The garden's 630m-long **maze** (adult/student/child €2.90/2.40/1.70; ⊙9am-7pm Jul & Aug, to 6pm Apr-Jun & Sep, to 5pm Oct) is a classic hedge design based on the original maze that occupied its place from 1720 to 1892; adjoining this is the **labyrinth** (Map p79), a playground with games, climbing equipment and a giant mirror kaleidoscope.

To the east of the palace is the **Kronprinzengarten** (Crown Prince Garden; Map p79; adult/student/child €2/1.70/1.40; ⊙9am-6pm Jul & Aug, to 5pm Apr-Jun, Sep & Oct), a replica of

Schönbrunn

⊙ Top Sights

the baroque garden that occupied the space around 1750.

Wagenburg   MUSEUM
(Imperial Coach Collection; Map p79; ☎877 32 44; 13; Schloss Schönbrunn; adult/under 19yr

OUT FOR THE RIDE

With its network of over 30 lines, Vienna is ideal for exploration by tram. Just to spice up one possible ride, here's a 'mystery tour'. Set aside a half-day to do it with stops.

Board the tram at Schwedenplatz (Map p60) going east. After a few stops you cross the lovely bridge of a famous general who helped keep the Habsburg monarchy in power with a stunning win (p357). Get off here if you like and look or ask someone for a house where no line runs straight. Board again in the same direction, get out once you've reached the terminus and walk towards *the* major attraction here. It'll take you about 20 minutes. Along the way, there's a trampoline centre (in good weather). If it's open, tell the person at the booth you've got a brother who weighs 100kg and ask whether that's OK on the trampolines ('*Mein Bruder wiegt Einhundert Kilo, geht das überhaupt?*'). There are places to snack, eat or drink all along the way if your brother needs upsizing, or you can rent a bike to downsize him.

Press on until you reach the train station. Jump on tram 5 towards Westbahnhof and immediately look out for the lovely little bar named after a famous 1970s kitsch film (we don't really recommend this one). After a while, you cross the bridge Friedensbrücke. On the right is another masterpiece from our 'straight is not great' fellow. It was completed in 1971, and our architect wrote a famous manifesto called…? (Time you read that Architecture chapter, isn't it?) You've crossed the canal now and are weaving towards Westbahnhof through the districts of Alsergrund and Josefstadt (Vienna's smallest district in terms of area). You might get off at Blindengasse to explore the neighbourhood; if it's evening, try one of the bars beneath the Josefstädter U-Bahn station, or continue on to Westbahnhof.

€6/free; ⊙9am-6pm Apr-Oct, 10am-4pm Nov-Mar) The Wagenburg displays carriages ranging from tiny children's wagons up to sumptuous vehicles of state, but nothing can compete with Emperor Franz I Stephen's (1708–65) coronation carriage. Weighing in at 4000kg and dripping in ornate gold plating, it has Venetian glass panes and painted cherubs.

Zentralfriedhof   CEMETERY
(Central Cemetery; ☑760 41-0; 11, Simmeringer Hauptstrasse 230-244; ⊙information office 8am-3pm Mon-Sat, cemetery 7am-8pm May-Aug, to 7pm Apr & Sep, to 6pm Mar & Oct, 8am-5pm Nov-Feb) Opened in 1874, this has grown to become one of Europe's largest cemeteries – larger than the Innere Stadt and, with 2.5 million graves, far exceeding the population of Vienna itself.

It contains the lion's share of tombs of Vienna's greats, including numerous famous composers: Gluck, Beethoven, Schubert, Brahms, Schönberg and the whole Strauss clan are buried here in the cold ground. A monument to Mozart has also been erected, but he was actually buried in an unmarked mass grave in the St Marxer Friedhof (03, Leberstrasse 6-8; ⊙7am-7pm Jun-Aug, to 6pm May & Sep, to 5pm Apr & Oct, to dusk Nov-Mar). The Ehrengräber (Tombs of Honour) in the Zentral-

friedhof are just beyond Gate Two and, in addition to the clump of famous composers, those pushing up daisies include Hans Makart, sculptor Fritz Wotruba, architects Theophil Hansen and Adolf Loos, and *the* man of Austrian pop, Falco.

Kirche am Steinhof   CHURCH
(☑910 60-11 204; 14, Baumgartner Höhe 1; tours €6; ⊙public admission 4-5pm Sat, tours 3-4pm Sat) Situated in the grounds of the Psychiatric Hospital of the City of Vienna, Kirche am Steinhof, built from 1904 to 1907, is the remarkable achievement of Otto Wagner. Kolo Moser chipped in with the mosaic windows, and the roof is topped by a copper-covered dome that earned the nickname Limoniberg (Lemon Mountain) from its original golden colour. It's a bold statement in an asylum that has other art-nouveau buildings, and it could only be pushed through by Wagner because the grounds were far from the public gaze.

🏃 Activities

The Alte Donau is the main boating and sailing centre, but the Neue Donau also provides opportunities for boating, windsurfing and water skiing.

Vienna's layout and well-marked cycle lanes make cycling a pleasant and popular pastime, especially along the banks of the Danube, in the Prater and around the Ringstrasse. The Wienerwald (Vienna Woods) is popular for mountain biking; check the websites www.mbike.at and www.mtbwienerwald.at (both in German) for ideas and trails.

The Donauinsel, Alte Donau and Lobau (all free bathing) are hugely popular places for taking a dip on steamy hot summer days. Topless sunbathing is quite the norm, as is nude sunbathing, but only in designated areas; much of Lobau and both tips of the Donauinsel are *Frei Körper Kultur* (FKK, nude-bathing areas).

Hofbauer   BOAT HIRE
(☎203 86 80; www.hofbauer.at, in German; 22, Wagramerstrasse 49; ☺Apr–mid-Oct) This outfit rents sailing boats from €13.80 per hour, row boats for €7.80, and pedal boats for €11. It also provides sailing lessons (in English) for those wishing to learn or to brush up on their skills. Many options are available; call or visit the website for details.

Wienerwald   WALKING
To the west of the city, the rolling hills and marked trails of the Wienerwald are perfect for walkers. A good trail heading in the woods to the north of Vienna starts in Nussdorf (take tram D from the Ring) and climbs Kahlenberg (484m), a hill offering views of the city. On your return to Nussdorf you can undo all that exercise by imbibing at a *Heuriger*. The round trip is around 11km, or you can spare yourself the leg-work by taking the Nussdorf-Kahlenberg 38A bus in one or both directions.

Amalienbad   SWIMMING
(☎607 47 47; 10, Reumannplatz 23; adult/child incl locker rental €4.70/2.60; ☺9am-9:30pm Mon & Fri, to 6pm Tue, 7am-9:30pm Thu, to 8pm Sat, to 6pm Sun, seniors and disabled only 12.30-3pm Mon) This stunning *Jugendstil* bath is one of the numerous swimming pools owned and run by the city. For a full list of pools call ☎601 12 8044 between 7.30am and 3.30pm Monday to Friday or log on to www.wien.at/baeder (in German).

Strandbad Gänsehäufel   SWIMMING
(☎269 90 16; 22, Moissigasse 21) Occupies a section of island in the Alte Donau. Hours and admission prices as for Amalienbad.

Prater   WALKING
Has a wood with walking trails.

Lainzer Tiergarten   WALKING
This densely forested animal reserve, a wild park in the west of Vienna, is perfect for roaming.

☞ Tours

Vienna has everything from bus tours to horse-drawn carriage rides, so if you're looking for a guided tour of the city you'll find something to suit your taste. Bus tours are good if you're very short on time and want to pack in as much as possible, while the walking tours are perfect if you're interested in learning more on a specific topic.

Cityrama   BUS
(Map p60; ☎534 130; www.cityrama.at; 01, Börsegasse 1; Vienna adult €39-47, child €15-30, excursions beyond Vienna adult/child from €69/30) Half- and full-day bus tours of Vienna and attractions within a day's striking distance of the city, including Salzburg, Budapest and Prague. Some tours require an extra fee for admission to sights, such as training at the Spanische Hofreitschule.

Fiaker   CARRIAGE
(20min/40min/1hr tour €40/65/95) More of a tourist novelty than anything else, a *Fiaker* is a traditional-style open carriage drawn by a pair of horses. Drivers generally speak English and point out places of interest en route. Lines of horses, carriages and bowler-hatted drivers can be found at Stephansplatz, Albertinaplatz and Heldenplatz at the Hofburg.

Ring Tram   TRAM
(☎790 91 00; www.wienerlinien.at; adult/child €6/4; ☺10am-6pm, to 7pm Jul & Aug) This ring tram runs the length of the Ringstrasse and is a hop-on, hop-off service with video screens and guided commentary along the way. Tickets can also be combined to include 24 hours of public transport and other variations. Schwedenplatz (Map p60) is the start/end of the tour; the first tour of the day starts at the Staatsoper station, however. The tram arrives at Schwedenplatz at 15 and 45 minutes past each hour and the entire Ring tour is 24 minutes without disembarking.

City Segway Tours/Pedal Power   CYCLING
(☎729 72 34; www.pedalpower.at; 02, Ausstellungsstrasse 3; hired bike half-/full day €24/32) City Segway hires bikes from 10am April to October and provides maps for unguided tours in and around Vienna. Pick bikes up at the office just northeast of the centre or, for an extra €4, arrange for them to be

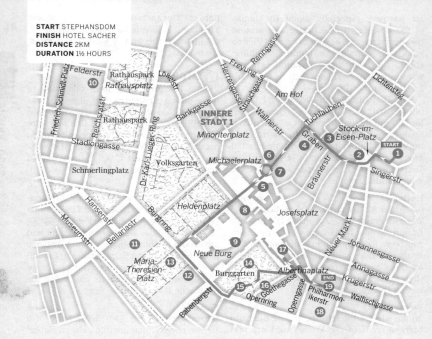

Walking Tour
The Historic Centre

❭ This walk takes you past recognisable sights that dominate this quarter of the Innere Stadt.

Start at Vienna's cathedral, the Gothic **1 Stephansdom**, offset by the unashamedly modern **2 Haas Haus**. Many Viennese were unhappy about the silver structure crowding their cathedral, but tourists seem happy to snap the reflections of Stephansdom's spire in its windows.

Leading northwest from Stock-im-Eisen-Platz is the broad pedestrian thoroughfare of plush shopping street **3 Graben**. It's dominated by the knobbly outline of the **4 Pestsäule**, completed in 1693 to commemorate the 75,000 victims of the Black Death. When you turn left into Kohlmarkt, the arresting sight of **5 Michaelertor**, the Hofburg's northeastern gate on Michaelerplatz, comes into view.

At Michaelerplatz, look out for the **6 Loos Haus**, a perfect example of the clean lines of Loos' work. Franz Josef hated it and described the windows, which lack lintels, as 'windows without eyebrows'. **7 Michaelerkirche** on the square portrays 500 years of architectural

styles, ranging from 1327 (Romanesque chancel) to 1792 (baroque doorway angels).

Pass through the imposing Michaelertor and past the **8 Schweizertor** to Heldenplatz and the impressive **9 Neue Burg**. Continue on past the line of *Fiakers* (horse-drawn carriages), noting the Gothic spire of the **10 Rathaus** to the right. Ahead, on the far side of the Ring, stand rival identical twins the **11 Naturhistorisches Museum** and the **12 Kunsthistorisches Museum**; between them is a proud **13 statue of Maria Theresia** surrounded by key figures of her reign.

Turn left onto the Ring and, once past the Neue Burg, turn left again into the peaceful **14 Burggarten**, formerly reserved for the imperial family and high-ranking officials. It contains **15 statues of Mozart** and **16 Franz Josef** and cafe-bar **17 Palmenhaus**.

It's not far down Philharmonikerstrasse, where you'll pass the rear of the grand **18 Staatsoper** and the frontage of **19 Hotel Sacher**, a perfect spot to rest those weary legs.

conveniently dropped off and picked up at your hotel. The outfit also offers Segway tours (€70) covering the main city highlights including the Ringstrasse, the Rathaus, Hofburg and more. The Segways look funny but function without a hitch, and staff make certain you're comfortable on the apparatus before you head off.

Vienna Tour Guides WALKING
(☎774 89 01; www.wienguide.at; adult/child €14/7) Group of highly knowledgeable guides who conduct 60 guided walking tours, some of which are in English. Everything from art-nouveau architecture to Jewish traditions in Vienna is covered; one of the most popular is the *Third Man* tour. The monthly *Wiener Spaziergänge* leaflet from the tourist office provides details of all the walks.

DDSG Blue Danube BOAT
(Map p60; ☎588 80; www.ddsg-blue-danube.at; 01, Schwedenbrücke; adult/child from €15/7.50, under 10yr free; ☺11am & 3pm Apr-Oct) Boat trips circumnavigating the districts of Leopoldstadt and Brigittenau via the Danube and Danube Canal.

Hop On-Hop Off Vienna Line BUS
(☎712 46 83; www.viennasightseeingtours.com; 01, Opernring; 1hr/2hr/all-day tickets adult €13/16/20, all tickets child €7; ☺10am-5pm) Bus tour passing 13 major sights. You can hop on and off the buses as many times as you wish. The main stop is outside the Staatsoper.

✦ Festivals & Events

Regardless of the time of year, there will be something special happening in Vienna; pick up a copy of the monthly booklet of events from the tourist office. Tickets for many events are available to personal callers at Wien-Ticket Pavillon (Map p60) in the hut by the Staatsoper.

Opernball OPERA BALL
(Opera Ball; ☎514 44-7880; 01, Staatsoper) Of the 300 or so balls held in January and February, the Opernball is the ultimate. It's a supremely lavish affair, with the men in tails and women in shining white gowns.

OsterKlang Festival MUSIC
(☎427 17; www.osterklang.at) Orchestral and chamber music recitals in some of Vienna's best music halls, the highlight of which is the opening concert featuring the Vienna Philharmonic. Held at the beginning of April.

Wiener Festwochen ARTS
(☎589 22-22; www.festwochen.or.at) Wide-ranging program of arts from around the world, from May to mid-June.

Donauinselfest MUSIC
Free three-day festival of rock, pop, hardcore, folk and country music on the Donauinsel in June.

Jazzfest Wien JAZZ
(☎408 60 30; www.viennajazz.org) The major jazz festival, held in June and July.

Musikfilm Festival OPERA
Screenings of operas, operettas and concerts outside the Rathaus in July and August.

ImPuls Tanz DANCE
(☎523 55 58; www.impulstanz.com) Vienna's premier avant-garde dance festival attracts an array of internationally renowned troupes and newcomers between mid-July and mid-August.

Volksstimmefest COMMUNISM
(www.kpoe.at, in German) Communist festival over a weekend at the end of August or the beginning of September in the Prater; features some 30 live acts and attracts a bizarre mix of hippies and staunch party supporters.

Lange Nacht der Museen MUSEUMS
(langenacht.orf.at; tickets adult/child €12/10) On one late-September or October evening some 500 museums nationwide open their doors to visitors between 6pm and 1am.

THE VIENNALE

Vienna's annual international film festival, the Viennale, is the highlight of the city's celluloid calendar. By no means as prestigious as Cannes or Berlin, it still attracts top-quality films from all over the world and is geared to the viewer rather than the filmmakers. For two weeks from mid-October city cinemas continuously play screenings that could broadly be described as fringe, ranging from documentaries to short and feature films. Tickets for the more popular screenings and most evening screenings can be hard to come by. Tickets can be bought two weeks before the festival starts from a number of stands around town. To get a jump on fellow festival goers, call ☎526 59 47 or check www.viennale.at.

VIENNA FOR CHILDREN

It was once said the Viennese love dogs more than they love children, and while this might be true for some folk, Vienna is actually quite child friendly. Its museums, attractions and theatres, such as the Kunsthistorisches Museum and the Albertina, arrange children's programs over the summer months.

The Prater, with its wide playing fields, giant Ferris wheel, playgrounds and funfair, is ideal for children. Just as fascinating for adults as for kids – and adults can also relax here over a drink and sausage while the kids see the animals – is the Tirolerhof, inside the Tiergarten (Map p79) at Schloss Schönbrunn. Actually a historic farmhouse from Tyrol deconstructed and rebuilt inside the zoo, it holds ancient Nordichorses, as well as goats, bulls, chickens and other farm animals. The Donauinsel is another place where kids can run off their energy. Swimming pools, located here and throughout Vienna, are free to children under 15 over the summer school holidays.

Two museums are aimed directly at kids. **Zoom** (Map p60; 524 79 08; www.kindermuseum.at; 07, Museumsplatz 1; child €5, accompanying adult free; 8.30am-4pm Tue-Sun), next door to the WienXtra-Kinderinfo in the MuseumsQuartier, is a bonanza for kids, with craft studio and ocean, lab, and science and exhibition sections (some of these multimedia) for exciting sessions of about 1½ or two hours aimed at kids up to the age of 14; book ahead. Schönbrunn's **Kindermuseum** (Map p79; 811 13-239; www.schoenbrunn.at; 13, Schloss Schönbrunn; adult/child/family €6.50/4.90/17; 10am-5pm Sat, Sun & school holidays) focuses quite understandably on the 16 children of Maria Theresia, and the kids dress up in costume. But it's not all hobnobbing – they'll also find out what aspects of life made the right royal Habsburgs different from mere low-life mortals. The obvious – fortune, fame, pets you can ride – are a start.

One ticket (available at the museums) allows entry to all of them.

Viennale
FILM

(526 59 47; www.viennale.at) The country's biggest and best film festival, featuring fringe and independent films from around the world in October. See boxed text, p83.

Christkindlmärkte
CHRISTMAS

Vienna's much-loved Christmas market season runs from mid-November to Christmas Day.

Silvester
NEW YEAR'S EVE

The Innere Stadt becomes one big party zone for Silvester, which features loads of alcohol and far too many fireworks in crowded streets.

🛏 Sleeping

From palatial abodes to swanky minimalism, from youth hostels to luxury establishments like the Hotel Imperial and Hotel Sacher, where chandeliers, antique furniture and original 19th-century oil paintings are the norm rather than the exception, Vienna's lodging covers it all. In between are homely Pensions and less ostentatious hotels, plus a small but smart range of apartments, many of which can be rented for only a few nights.

Standards remain high, and generally so do prices; bargains are few and far between. A private bathroom and breakfast (normally a Continental buffet) are invariably included in the price, but parking isn't, costing anything between €6 and €30 per 24 hours.

For more information on accommodation options, and hostel contact details, see p402.

INNERE STADT

Schweizer Pension
PENSION €

(Map p60; 533 81 56; www.schweizerpension.com; 01, Heinrichsgasse 2; s/d from €48/65;) Cheaper rooms here are without their own bathroom. This small, family-run pension is a superb deal, with homely touches and accreditation for being environmentally friendly. Book in advance, though, as it has only 11 rooms and is popular among those on squeezed budgets. Wi-fi is only available in the common areas.

TOP CHOICE Hotel Sacher
HOTEL €€€

(Map p60; 514 56-0; www.sacher.com; 01, Philharmonikerstrasse 4; d from €375; U1, U2, U4 Karlsplatz) Walking into the Sacher is like turning back the clocks 100 years. The reception, with its dark-wood panelling, deep red shades and heavy gold chandelier, is reminiscent of an expensive fin-de-siècle bordello. The smallest rooms are surprisingly large, with beds the size of small ships; suites are truly palatial and everything has received a recent upgrade. All boast baroque furnishings and genuine 19th-century oil paintings (the hotel has the largest private oil-painting collection in Austria). Your arrival is sweetened further with a tiny cube of *Sacher Torte* in each room. The top floor is a high-tech spa complex, with herbal sauna, ice fountain and fitness room.

Pension Nossek
PENSION €€

(Map p60; ☎533 70 41-0; www.pension-nossek.at, in German; 01, Graben 17; s/d from €65/120; ☎) When it comes to real estate, it's all about location, location, location. And with a front door facing the Graben, and Stephansdom within sight, Nossek has oodles of all three. Service is professional, polite, a little stiff but typically Viennese. Rooms are spotless, highly adequate, generally spacious and enhanced with baroque-style furnishings; views are either of the pedestrian street below or the quiet inner courtyard. Note that the hotel doesn't accept credit cards.

Aviano
PENSION €€

(Map p60; ☎512 83 30; www.secrethomes.at; 01, Marco-d'Aviano-Gasse 1; s/d €104/148; ☎) Aviano earns its points for a supremely central position, high standards, and all-round value for money. Rooms are small without being claustrophobic and feature high ceilings, decorative moulding and whitewashed antique furnishings; corner rooms have a charming alcove overlooking Vienna's main pedestrian street. The breakfast room is sunny and bright, and in summer utilises a small balcony on the inner courtyard. Its

---

DESIGN HOTELS

In a city noted for its architecture, it's no surprise that Vienna boasts a number of design hotels – our favourites are listed here:

DO & CO (Map p60; ☎241 88; www.doco.com; 01, Stephansplatz 12; r from €310) Swanky and sexy with views of Stephansdom.

Style Hotel (Map p60; ☎22 780-0; www.stylehotel.at; 01, Herrengasse 12; r from €250) Top contender for the title 'most fashionable hotel address' in Vienna, with overtones of art nouveau and art deco.

---

sister hotel, the **Baronesse** (☎405 10 61; 08,Lange Gasse 61; ☎; ☐1, 2) in Josefstadt offers the same ambience at slightly lower prices.

Pertschy Pension
PENSION €€

(Map p60; ☎534 49-0; www.pertschy.com; 01, Habsburgergasse 5; s/d from €79/119; ☎) It's hard to find fault with Pertschy. Its quiet yet central location, just off the Graben, is hard to beat, staff are exceedingly able, willing and friendly, and children are welcomed with gusto (toys for toddlers and high chairs for tots are available). Rooms are not only spacious but also filled with a potpourri of period pieces and a rainbow of colours; you'll find one bedecked in subtle hues of pink, while its neighbour is awash in yellow. A little gem in the Innere Stadt.

Holmann Beletage
PENSION €€

(Map p60; ☎961 19 60; www.hollmann-beletage.at 01, Köllnerhofgasse 6; r from €140; ☎; ⑤U1, U4 Schwedenplatz, ☐1, 2) A minimalist establishment of sorts, Holmann Beletage is a *Pension* for guests with an eye for style and a penchant for clean lines. Rooms are slick units, with natural wood floors, bare walls, simple, classic furniture and designer lamps and door handles. Space is utilised to the max; bathrooms and cupboards are cleverly hidden behind tall double doors, creating a Tardis-like effect. Beyond is a garden terrace and a home cinema screening Vienna-focused films three times per day.

Hotel am Stephansplatz
HOTEL €€€

(Map p60; ☎534 05-0; www.hotelamstephansplatz.at; 01, Stephansplatz 9; s/d from €170/220; ⑤U1, U3 Stephansplatz; ☎) You'd think you can't beat the view – it overlooks the Gothic spires of Stephansdom – yet the hotel's interior almost tops its location. The entire structure is also a model of ecofriendly design – all building materials used, right down to the glue, were subject to environmental restrictions – and the breakfast is a compilation of organic produce. Rooms are filled with modern furniture and warmed with earthy colours, while the bedding is a treat – thick, snug and *über* skin-friendly. Room 702 steals the show: a rooftop suite with balcony views across to the hallowed doors of Stephansdom.

König von Ungarn
HOTEL €€

(Map p60; ☎515 84-0; www.kvu.at; 01, Schulerstrasse 10; s/d €150/219; ☎; ⑤U1, U3 Stephansplatz) The oldest hotel in Vienna (1746) balances class and informality with a wonderful inner courtyard (its pyramid sky-light, wood panelling and leather furniture will easily impress) and excellent service. Little acts of decadence – like gold-plated, free-standing ashtrays everywhere (even in the lift) – are all around. Rooms are individually furnished with antiques and range in style from rather plain to downright extravagant; the best face Domgasse.

RINGSTRASSE

TOP CHOICE Hotel Kaertnerhof HOTEL €€
(Map p60; ☑512 19 23; www.karntnerhof.com; 01, Grashofgasse 4; s/d from €95/140; @ ☎) Tucked away from the bustle down a side street, this tall treasure fuses old Vienna charm with cosy ambience, from the period paintings lining the walls to the wood- and frosted glass–panelled lift to the surprising roof terrace. Rooms mix a few plain pieces with antiques, chandeliers and elegant curtains, but all exude warmth and charm. With Stephansplatz less than five minutes away, this place is a steal.

Pension Wild PENSION €
(Map p70; ☑406 51 74; www.pension-wild.com; 08, Lange Gasse 10; s/d from €41/43) Wild is one of the very few openly gay-friendly pensions in Vienna, but the warm welcome extends to all walks of life. The top-floor Luxury rooms are simple yet appealing, with plenty of light-wood furniture and private bathrooms, the latter a big advantage over Wild's other two categories, Standard and Comfort. All, however, are spotlessly clean and kitchens are available for guests to use and abuse. Note that 'Wild' is the family name, not a description.

Hotel am Schubertring HOTEL €€
(Map p76; ☑717 02-0; www.schubertring.at; 01, Schubertring 11; s/d from €99/128; ☎) Of the highly sought after hotels on the Ringstrasse, Am Schubertring is the only option available to the average Joe. Rooms are either Biedermeier or art nouveau; the former are characterised by floral designs and graceful lines and may look disturbingly similar to your Granny's flat, while the latter are more dynamic, with flowing lines and little flourishes. All are in very good condition and the hotel spreads itself across the upper floors of two buildings. Staff are friendly while keeping a healthy professional distance.

Hotel Imperial HOTEL €€€
(Map p76; ☑50110-333; www.luxurycollection.com/imperial; 01, Kärntner Ring 16; r from €350; @ ☎)

A mere mention of the Imperial makes most Viennese nod in awe and respect. This former palace, with all the glory and majesty of the Habsburg era, gives any respectable classical museum a run for its money. The Fürsten Stiege, cloaked in rich red carpet, is a flamboyant opening, leading from the reception to the Royal suite. Suites are filled with 19th-century paintings and genuine antique furniture (and come with butler service), while 4th- and 5th-floor rooms in Biedermeier style are far cosier and some come with balcony.

ACROSS THE DANUBE CANAL

Gal Apartments APARTMENTS €
(☑561 19 42; www.apartmentsvienna.net; 02, Grosse Mohrengasse 29; apt from €80; ☎) For a superb home away from home, check into these modern apartments smack in the action of up-and-coming Leopoldstadt. Spaces range from 30 to 60 sq metres – all apartments in the renovated Biedermeier structure feature modern furniture flanked by tasteful, *Jugendstil*-inspired paintings. It's a short walk to the Karamelitermarkt, the Riesenrad and the Augarten, and the subway whips you to the centre of town in less than 10 minutes.

All You Need Vienna 2 HOTEL €€
(Map p60; ☑212 16 68; www.allyouneedhotels.at; 02, Grosse Schiffgasse 12; s/d from €69/89; ☎) This modern, multi-floor high-rise only a short walk from the Innere Stadt is sleek, modern and vibrant. The youngish clientele lounges in the art-filled reception, and rooms (on the small side) are fitted with light wood and large windows – some include balconies. In warm weather, the expansive garden is ideal for breakfast and plotting your day of sightseeing.

INSIDE THE GÜRTEL

TOP CHOICE Pension Hargita PENSION €
(Map p72; ☑526 19 28; www.hargita.at; 07, Andreasgasse 1; s/d from €57/68; ☎) Ignore the bland exterior – one step into the wood-panelled lobby and you'll think you've entered a mountain chalet. Named after the Hargita region in the Carpathians, this Hungarian-Austrian family-operated space is tasteful simplicity: fresh, crisp blues and whites. with touches like delicate paper flowers in tiny vases, make each room homey, and Hungarian plates hanging on walls in the breakfast room lend a country feel.

Hotel Fürstenhof
HOTEL €€

(Map p72; ☎523 32 67; www.hotel-fuerstenhof.com; 07, Neubaugürtel 4; s/d from €70/120; ☎) This family-run affair overflowing with personality has been the choice of touring alternative bands (see the reception for proof) and knowledgeable visitors for years – don't be surprised if you encounter a burgeoning rock star in the reception-lounge, which doubles as a library (oodles of used books to peruse). Rooms are basic but blood-red carpets, full-length curtains and deep colours create a warm feel; furniture is simple yet highly functional. The house dates from 1906, so ceilings are higher than average and the lift is a museum piece (the motor, thankfully, isn't).

Altstadt
PENSION €€

(Map p72; ☎522 66 66; www.altstadt.at; 07, Kirchengasse 41; s/d from €149/249; @☎) Altstadt is arguably the finest pension in Vienna. Each room is individually decorated, with one thing in common; charming, tasteful, quirky, arty, welcoming decor that's not overcooked, and the right combination of practicality, comfort and warmth. Add to this high ceilings, plenty of space and natural light, and a cosy lounge with free afternoon tea and cakes. Staff are genuinely affable, art is from the owner's personal collection and at press time a hopping bar was being built on the ground floor below the hotel.

Hotel Drei Kronen
PENSION €€

(Map p72; ☎587 32 89; www.hotel3kronen.at; 04, Schleifmühlgasse 25; s/d €79/100; @☎) Within stumbling distance of the Naschmarkt (some rooms overlook it), this family-owned abode is one of Vienna's best-kept secrets on the lodging scene. Tiny palatial touches (shiny marble, polished brass, white-and-gold wallpaper) are distinctly Viennese, but nonetheless a casual feel prevails. Rooms are fitted with *Jugendstil* furniture and art (including many prints by Klimt). The breakfast buffet is gargantuan and includes free *Sekt* (sparkling wine), an unheard-of luxury in a three-star hotel.

Pension Kraml
PENSION €

(Map p72; ☎587 85 88; www.pensionkraml.at; 06, Brauergasse 5; s/d from €35/76, apt from €99; ☎) A cosy pension in a quiet neighbourhood, Kraml is family run and from the old school of hospitality, where politeness is paramount and the comfort of guests a top priority. Rooms are surprisingly large, accommodating twin beds, bedside tables and a solid wardrobe while leaving plenty of room for a close waltz. Furniture and fittings, including those in the bathroom, are a little dated but by no means past their use-by dates. Internet is only available in the common areas.

Westend City Hostel
HOSTEL €

(Map p72; ☎597 67 29; www.westendhostel.at; 06, Fügergasse 3; s/d €52/62, dm from €20.50; @☎) This independent hostel received a head-to-toe revamp in 2009 and the change is evident everywhere – bright walls, splashes of colour and comfy, Ikea-style furnishings. All dorm rooms are en suite, with wooden bunks bright red lockers, and ample space for moving around and the ivy-lined inner courtyard is superb.

Tyrol
HOTEL €€

(Map p72; ☎587 54 15; www.das-tyrol.at; 06, Mariahilferstrasse 15; s/d from €109/149; ☎) Das Tyrol ranks among the top design hotels in the city. Each floor is devoted to a theme (one floor is humorously dedicated to Donald Duck and his love, Daisy; another is an ode to modern art with splashes of colour everywhere). The cosy rooms are a subdued mix of greens and yellows and spacious enough to fit a small couch and desk, while bathrooms are a spotless combination of white-and-black tiling. Try for a corner room, which enjoy a small balcony overlooking busy Mariahilferstrasse. Breakfast – served with Champagne – will keep you going for most of the day.

Theaterhotel
HOTEL €€

(Map p70; ☎405 36 48; http://cordial-theaterhotel-wien.h-rsv.com; 08, Josefstädter Strasse 22; s/d €184/196; ☎) A hotel for theatre and music lovers. Theatre memorabilia lines the hallways, stairwells and rooms, art-nouveau touches hark back to the days when the stage was all the rage and rooms (all with kitchenette) are filled with dark-wood furniture. Each room is inspired by a different composer (Mozart, Schubert, etc), with elements like sketches of the master or a print of a famous composition's notes. The hotel also has sauna and solarium; internet is only available in the bar and cafe-restaurant.

Das Triest
HOTEL €€€

(Map p72; ☎589 18-0; www.dastriest.at; 04, Wiedner Hauptstrasse 12; s/d €224/289; @☎) This Sir Terence Conran creation is a symbiosis of history and modern design. The 300-year-old building (former stables) is cutting edge with an overall nautical theme; portholes replace spy holes and windows, and stairwell railings would be just at home on the *Queen Mary* 2. Rooms are stylish in their simplicity and bathed in pastel warmth, while touches such as fresh flowers polish the scene off. Staff are professional but informal.

OUTSIDE THE GÜRTEL

Altwienerhof HOTEL €€
(☑892 60 00; www.altwienerhof.at; 15, Herklotzgasse 6; s/d €79/99) Altwienerhof, a pseudo-plush family-run hotel just outside the Gürtel ring, offers ridiculously romantic abodes that hark back to a bygone era when the Orient Express was all the rage; miniature chandeliers, antique pieces, floral bed covers and couches, and lace table-cloths all do a fine job of adding a touch of old-fashioned romance. Breakfast is taken either in the conservatory or in the large inner courtyard on sultry summer days.

Boutiquehotel Stadthalle HOTEL €€
(☑982 42 72; www.hotelstadthalle.at; 15, Hackengasse 20; s/d from €68/98) The most sustainable hotel in Vienna: solar panels heat all the hot water, cisterns collect rain (for flushing toilets and watering the hotel garden and lavender roof, Vienna's largest lavender plantation), the new wing has no traditional heat or air con – special water pipes in the walls cool and heat the structure – and LED lights are used throughout. The hotel encourages green transport: anyone who arrives by bike or train receives a 10% discount. Rooms are modern with polished antiques. The owners also run a cheap pension down the street at Hackengasse 33 (singles/doubles from €39/49; reception is at the main hotel).

Wombat's HOSTEL €
(☑897 36 23; www.wombats.at; 05, Mariahilferstrasse 137; dm €20, r €56; @🎧) Offering up a bit of Australian hostel vibe in the Capital of Culture, Wombat's is the choice for the savvy backpacker. The interior is a rainbow of bright colours; common areas include a bar, pool tables, music and comfy leather sofas; and all dorms are en suite and superbly out-fitted with modern furnishings. Bike rental is available and staff are experienced and relaxed. A second **Wombat's** (☑897 23 36; 15, Grangasse 6; @🎧; 🚇52, 58, 🚋12A) is a prime choice if this one fills up (prices are the same as at the main location), and a third branch near the Naschmarkt is slated to open in late 2011 – check the website for updates.

Eating

Vienna has thousands of restaurants covering all budgets and styles of cuisine, but dining doesn't stop there. *Kaffeehäuser* (coffee houses; see p385) and *Heurigen* (see p391) are almost defining elements of the city, and just as fine for a good meal. The humble *Beisl*, Vienna's equivalent of a beer house or tavern, is normally a simple restaurant serving the best of Viennese cuisine in unhealthy portions.

If you've no time to sit around and wait, a *Würstel Stand* (sausage stand) will suffice; conveniently located on street corners and squares, these are at the ready with sausages, bread and beer. Otherwise you could try the ubiquitous Schnitzelhaus chain, which serves up fast food Viennese style.

Self-caterers will have no problem stocking up on provisions; Hofer, Zielpunkt, Billa, Spar and Merkur supermarkets are commonplace throughout the city. Some have well-stocked delis that make sandwiches to order – the perfect cheap lunch on the run. Vienna is also dotted with markets (see p91 and p94).

INNERE STADT

TOP CHOICE **Figlmüller** BEISL €€
(Map p60; ☑512 61 77; 01, Wollzeile 5; mains €7-15; ☉11am-10.30pm, closed Aug) Vienna, and the Viennese, would simply be at a loss without Figlmüller. This famous *Beisl* has some of the biggest – and best – schnitzels in the business. Sure, the rural decor is contrived for its inner-city location, and beer isn't served (only wine from the owner's own vineyard), but it's a fun Viennese eating experience and one you won't find anywhere else in the world.

TOP CHOICE **Bitzinger Würstelstand am Albertinaplatz** SAUSAGE STAND €
(Map p60; 01, Albertinaplatz; sausages €2.80-3.50; ☉10am-4am Nov-Mar, 24hr Apr-Oct) Vienna has very many sausage stands, but this one – located behind the Staatsoper – offers the contrasting spectacle of ladies and gents dressed to the nines and sipping wine while enjoying sausage at outdoor tables after performances. It's no coincidence that here you find Moet & Chandon (€19.90 for 0.2mL); for the less well heeled, there's house wine (€2.80) and Stiegl Goldbräu beer (€2.90). Prime winter position is at the heated counter.

Aubergine FRENCH, AUSTRIAN €€€
(Map p60; ☑968 31 83; 01, Gonzagagasse 14; 3-course business lunch €21.50, mains €21-24, 3-5 course evening menus €42-62; ☉11.30am-2.30pm

& 6pm-midnight Mon-Fri, 6pm-midnight Sat Dec) Aubergine greets you with its namesake, a delicate slither of salted, marinated eggplant to whet the appetite. After that it leads you into a culinary wonderland that might include *Kalbsbeuschel,* thin slices of offal accompanied by snails and garnished with snail caviar for €16.80 (it's less salty than sturgeon caviar and doesn't explode as easily when you bite on it). Plenty of delicate meats and accompaniments also feature on the menu. The wine list is mammoth – about 800 bottled Austrian wines.

Expedit
ITALIAN €€

(Map p60; 512 33 13 23; 01, Wiesingerstrasse 6; mains €8-25; 10am-1am Mon-Sat, to 10pm Sun;) Expedit has successfully moulded itself on a Ligurian *Osteria* and become one of the most popular Italian restaurants in town. Its warehouse decor, with shelves stocked full of oil, pesto, olives and wine from Liguria, helps to create a busy yet informal atmosphere and a clean, smart look. Every day brings new, seasonal dishes to the menu, but count on a few divine vegetarian, meat and fish specialities. Reservations are recommended. The affiliated Expedit Lager in the same building does takeaway.

Wrenkh
VEGETARIAN €€

(Map p60; 533 15 26; 01, Bauernmarkt 10; midday menus €9.50-10.50, mains €8.50-19.50; noon-4pm & 6-10pm Mon-Fri, 6-10pm Sat;) Wrenkh was long the cutting edge of vegetarian cuisine, and today it's still the serrated edge – owner Christian Wrenkh has more recently introduced a handful of meat and fish dishes. The quality and presentation can be exquisite and everything is prepared with organic produce. Choose from the vibrant front section with its glass walls and chatty customers, or the quieter back room with its intimate booths.

Griechenbeisl
BEISL €€

(Map p60; 533 19 77; 01, Fleischmarkt 11; mains €11-24; 11am-1am) The oldest guest house in Vienna (dating from 1447), Griechenbeisl was once frequented by the likes of Ludwig van Beethoven, Franz Schubert and Johannes Brahms and quite rightly aims at the tourist trade. It's a lovely haunt, with vaulted rooms, age-old wooden panelling and a figure of Augustin trapped at the bottom of a well just inside the front door. Every classic Viennese dish is on the menu, and in summer the plant-fringed front garden is pole position.

A SLICE OF ITALY IN THE INNERE STADT

One of the most useful places to know about in the Innere Stadt is **Zanoni & Zanoni** (Map p60; 512 79 79; 01, Lugeck 7; ice cream from €2; 7am-midnight). This Italian *gelataria* and *pasticceria* has some of the most civilised opening times around (365 days a year) and is just right when you realise you'd like a late-night dessert – there are about 35 varieties of gelati, with more cream than usual. It does breakfast and some great cakes with cream, but best of all it's a buzzing place on a Sunday where you can linger over a coffee and plan your moves for the day.

En
JAPANESE €€

(Map p60; 532 44 90; 01, Werdertorgasse 8; midday menus €8.20-9.70, mains €9-23; 11.30am-2.30pm & 5.30-10.30pm Mon-Sat;) A Tokyo chef and Hokkaido staff banded together to create this exceptionally relaxed Japanese restaurant in a quiet corner of the Innere Stadt. The many different varieties of sushi (including octopus and sweet shrimp) are among the best in Vienna. The *gyoza* are delightful and warm sake or *genmaicha* (green tea with roasted rice) makes a perfect accompaniment. It's completely nonsmoking during the day.

Soupkultur
SOUP & SALAD €

(Map p60; 532 46 28; 01, Wipplingerstrasse 32; soups €3.90-4.50, salads €5.80-7.20; 11.30am-3.30pm Mon-Thu, to 3pm Fri;) Soupkultur is popular among office workers seeking a healthy bite on the hop. Organic produce and aromatic spices are used to create eight soups and eight varieties of salad each week. Options range from red-lentil soup or a traditional Hungarian goulash to Caesar salad or chicken and orange salad. There's token seating, but count on taking away (a leafy park is just around the corner).

Trzesniewski
SANDWICHES €

(Map p60; 512 32 91; 01, Dorotheergasse 1; bread with 100g spread from €2.80; 8.30am-7.30pm Mon-Fri, 9am-5pm Sat) Possibly the finest sandwich shop in Austria, Trzesniewski has been serving spreads and breads to the entire spectrum of munchers (Kafka was a regular here) for over 100 years. Choose from 21 delectably thick spreads – paprika, tuna with egg, salmon, and Swedish herring are but a few examples – for your choice of bread, or simply pick a selection from those waiting ready made. Plan on sampling a few; two bites and they're gone. This branch is one of seven in Vienna.

Freyung (Map p60; 01, Freyung; ⊙9am-6pm Fri & Sat 1st & 3rd weekend of month) is a great market selling exclusively fresh organic produce. If you want a general supermarket, try **Interspar** (Map p60; 1st fl, cnr Rotenturmstrasse & Fleischmarkt) or **Billa** (Map p60; Singerstrasse).

RINGSTRASSE

Kantine CAFE €
(Map p60; ✆523 82 39; 07, Museumsplatz 1; soups €2.90-5.90, wraps €5.10-6.40, light mains €7.20-8.90; ⊙9am-2am Mon-Thu, to 4am Fri & Sat, to midnight Sun; 🖱🍴) This upbeat cafe-bar housed in the former stables of the emperor's personal steeds is the most laid-back spot to eat in the MuseumsQuartier. It has a couple of old sofas down the back where you can lounge about and surf in comfort, and you can grab a cocktail from the extensive list and make good use of the outdoor patio on MQ's main square. It's a versatile place, like most in the MQ, and a good place to meet up before moving on.

Halle INTERNATIONAL €€
(Map p60; ✆523 70 01; 07, Museumsplatz 1; midday menus €6.80-8.50, mains €6.90-16.50; ⊙10am-2am; 🖱🍴) Managed by the owners of Motto, Halle is the versatile resident eatery of the Kunsthalle with little kitchen downtime – the pots and pans are hung up at midnight. The interior has plenty of optical tricks, like cylindrical lamps and low tables, and the chefs churn out antipastos, pastas, salads, several Austrian all-rounders (breaded chicken, but not a *Wiener Schnitzel*) and pan-Asian dishes. On steamy summer days it's usually a fight for an outside table between the Kunsthalle and MUMOK. It sells Noan olive oil (€9.90), with proceeds flowing into children's projects.

Österreicher im MAK AUSTRIAN €€
(Map p60; ✆7140 121; 01, Stubenring 5; lunch specials €6.40, mains €14.50-20.80; ⊙8.30-1am) Österreicher im MAK is the brainchild of Helmut Österreicher, one of the country's leading chefs and a force behind the movement towards back-to-the-roots Austrian flavours. He goes beyond strictly classical Viennese dishes such as *Tafelspitz* (boiled

beef) by complementing them with exotic or non-regional ingredients. These are served in two sections of the restaurant – a lounge and bar area where you can also get breakfast from 8.30am until 11am, and the more formal restaurant out back. Sleek interior architectural lines create a modern flourish.

Vestibül INTERNATIONAL €€€
(Map p60; ✆532 49 99; 01, Dr-Karl-Lueger-Ring 2; evening menus from €39, mains €16-24; ⊙11am-midnight Mon-Fri, 6pm-midnight Sat; 🍴) The interior of Vestibül, which takes pride of place in the southern wing of the Burgtheater, is a heady mix of marble columns and chandeliers, topped off with a glorious sparkling mirrored bar. The menu has a strong focus on regional, seasonal produce, such as organic Waldviertel beef or a snack of *Presswurst* (head cheese) from Mangalitza ham. Reservations are recommended.

ACROSS THE DANUBE CANAL

Schöne Perle NEO-BEISL €
(Beautiful Pearl; ✆243 35 93; 02, Grosse Pfarrgasse 2; midday menus €7, mains €4-16; ⊙noon-11pm Mon-Fri, 10am-11pm Sat & Sun; 🍴) Schöne Perle has a simple look and serves everything from lentil soups through *Tafelspitz* to vegetarian and fish mains, and all are created with organic produce. Wines are from Austria, as is the large array of juices. Unusually for a Viennese restaurant, dogs are forbidden and kids welcome.

Pizza Mari' PIZZA €
(✆0676/687 49 94; Leopoldgasse 23a; pizzas €5.90-8.50; ⊙noon-11pm Tue-Sat; 🍴) The kitchen in this pizza restaurant closes between 2.30pm and 6pm, the choice of pizza isn't enormous and (oddly for a pizza restaurant) it *never* uses anchovies – that's the downside. The rest is good: Pizza Mari' serves some of the best pizzas this side of the canal, the inexpensive salads as side dishes are fresh and Mari' has a friendly, comfortable feel that makes you feel at home.

Restaurant Vincent INTERNATIONAL €€€
(✆214 15 16; 02, Grosse Pfarrgasse 7; 10-course menu €98, mains €20-30; ⊙6pm-midnight Mon-Sat; 🍴) Vincent began life as a student place and over the years evolved into its higher calling: providing the Viennese with fine food. Today it sports a Michelin star and serves an interesting range of dishes à la carte or from menus that can be put together by the diner in flexible courses based on seasonal produce. The focus tends to be on classic ingredients

such as lamb, beef or pheasant prepared expertly, but locally produced snails do feature. The ambience up front is historic and traditional, the back room is slightly bland, and beyond that is an atrium section.

Spezerei
TAPAS, MEDITERRANEAN €€

(☑218 47 18; Karmeliterplatz 2; tapas €6.90-10.90; ⏱11.30am-11pm Mon-Sat; ☑) This small *Vinothek* and Mediterranean tapas place specialises in Spanish fish tapas (€6.90 to €9.90), foccacia and panini (from €4.70) and quality wines to wash them down with – and what a selection of wines it is, too! About a dozen can be drunk by the glass and several hundred by the bottle, including four house varieties. The wall is full of them, mostly from Austria, and in summer you can enjoy your choice sitting outdoors soaking up the sun. (Karmeliterplatz is on Taborstrasse – not to be confused with nearby Karmelitermarkt.)

INSIDE THE GÜRTEL

Zu den Zwei Liesln
BEISL €

(Map p72; ☑523 32 82; 07, Burggasse 63; lunch menu €4.90-5.30, mains €6-11.90; ⏱11am-11pm; ☑) A classic, budget *Beisl* of legendary status, Zu den Zwei Liesln has been serving celebrities, politicians, office workers and students for decades. Six varieties of schnitzel crowd the menu (the *Haus Schnitzel,* filled with Gorgonzola, ham and pepperoni, is killer bee), but there are other Viennese options, and even two vegetarian choices. The wood panelling, simple wooden chairs and chequered tablecloths create a quaint and cosy interior, complemented by a tree-shaded inner courtyard.

Aromat
INTERNATIONAL €€

(Map p72; ☑913 24 53; 04, Margaretenstrasse 52; menus €7.90, mains €10-15; ⏱5-11pm Tue-Sun, closed mid-Jul–Aug) The mainstay of this funky little eatery is fusion cooking with a strong emphasis on Upper Austrian and Vietnamese cuisine, but you'll mostly find a menu that changes daily with the whims of the chef. It has an open kitchen and often caters for those with an intolerance to wheat and gluten. The charming surroundings feature simple Formica tables, 1950s fixtures, a blackboard menu, and one huge glass frontage. Personable staff help to create a convivial, barlike atmosphere.

St Josef
VEGETARIAN €

(Map p72; ☑526 68 18; 07, Mondscheingasse 10; small/large plates €6.80/8.20; ⏱8am-5pm Mon-Fri, to 4pm Sat; ☑☑) You'll find lots of places

All the markets below are open 6am to 7.30pm Monday to Friday and 6am to 5pm Saturday. See also p94.

Brunnenmarkt (16, Brunnengasse) West of the centre; one of Vienna's best produce and food markets, with lots of Turkish stands and some organic produce stalls.

Hannovermarkt (20, Hannovergasse) In Brigittenau, north of the centre.

Karmelitermarkt (02, Karmelitermarkt) North of the centre.

Meidlinger Markt (12, Niederhofstrasse) In Meidling, southwest of the centre.

Volkertmarkt (02, Volkertplatz) Northeast of the centre.

Vorgartenmarkt (02, Ennsgasse) Between the Danube Canal and the Danube River.

with vegetarian offerings in this neighbourhood, but St Josef is a canteen-like vegetarian place that cooks to a theme each day (Indian, for instance) and gives you the choice of a small or large plate filled with the various delights. It has a sparse, industrial character, which is part of its charm, and super-friendly staff who will point you in the right direction if you don't quite know where to start.

Zum Alten Fassl
BEISL €€

(☑544 42 98; 05, Ziegelofengasse 37; midday menus €5.70-6.80, mains €7.50-13.90; ⏱11.30am-3pm, 5pm-1am Mon-Fri, 5pm-1am Sat, noon-3pm & 5pm-midnight Sun) With its private garden amid residential houses and polished wooden interior (typical of a well-kept *Beisl*), Zum Alten Fassl is worth the trip south of the centre just for a drink. But while here sample the Viennese favourites and regional specialities, like *Eierschwammerl* and *Blunzengröstl.* When it's in season, *Zanderfilet* (fillet of zander) is the chef's favourite. Between 1974 and 1982 the singer Falco lived upstairs in this building – a plaque marks the spot.

Ra'mien
ASIAN €€

(Map p72; ☑585 47 98; 06, Gumpendorfer Strasse 9; mains €7-16; ⏱11am-midnight Tue-Sun, closed Aug; ☑) Picture a grey-white room in minimalist look and lots of bright, young,

TICHY ICE CREAM

It only takes one lick of **Tichy** (☑604 44 46; 10, Reumannplatz 13; ☺10am-11pm mid-Mar–Sep; ⑤U1 Reumannplatz) ice cream and you're hooked. In addition to the usual creamy suspects, this legendary *Eissalon* (ice-cream parlour) is known for pioneering *Eismaril-lenknödel* (ball of vanilla ice cream with apricot centre). It's a mere cone's throw away from the U-Bahn station – just look for Tichy's loyal patrons scattered around on park benches, grinning and enjoying their sweet treats. And be prepared to shove your way through crowds to reach the counter – it's all part of the fun.

hip things bent over piping-hot noodles and you have Ra'mien. The menu covers a good swath of Asia, with a choice of Thai, Japanese, Chinese and Vietnamese noodle soups and rice dishes. Ra'mien fills up quickly at night so it's best to book to avoiding having to wait for a table; the lounge bar downstairs has regular DJs and stays open until at least 2am. Next door, the affiliated **Shanghai Tan** (Map p72; ☑585 49 88; 06, Gumpendorfer Strasse 9; dim sum €3.50-4.50, lunch specials €6.90-9.50, mains €9.50-13.80; ☺11.30am-3pm & 6pm-2am Mon-Sat) does sushi, sashimi, noodle soups, fried noodles, satay and other excellent pan-Asian dishes. Downstairs is an opium den minus the opium – a chilled-out area with hidden corners and pillows for reclining.

Gasthaus Wild   NEO-BEISL €€

(☑920 94 77; 03, Radetzkyplatz 1; midday menus €7.50, mains €8.80-17.50; ☺9am-1am; ☑) Gasthaus Wild, formerly a dive of a *Beisl*, has in recent years morphed into a great *neo-Beisl*. Its dark, wood-panelled interior retains a traditional look, and the menu includes favourites like goulash and *Schnitzel mit Erdäpfelsalat* (schnitzel with potato salad), but also veal fillet with dumplings spiced with blood sausage. The menu changes regularly, the ambience is relaxed, the staff is welcoming and the wine selection is good. Wild is south of the river east of the centre.

Gaumenspiel   INTERNATIONAL €€

(Map p72; ☑526 11 08; 07, Zieglergasse 54; menus €32-40, mains €17.50-21.50; ☺6pm-midnight Mon-Sat; ☺☑) Gaumenspiel is an immaculate, modern *Beisl* with a menu that changes every three weeks. The food is international with a heavy Mediterranean influence, but here you might also find braised veal cheeks with polenta, potato dumplings and artichokes. The decor is light in detail, and the handful of street-side tables are popular in summer. Reservations are recommended.

Motto   INTERNATIONAL €€

(Map p72; ☑587 06 72; 05, Schönbrunner Strasse 30; mains €10-23; ☺6pm-2am Mon-Thu & Sun, to 4am Fri & Sat) A fusion of Asian, Austrian and Italian influences is the secret behind Motto's long-running success, with the likes of chicken satay with peanut sauce and coriander rice or expertly prepared Styrian baked chicken among the mouth-watering choices. One of the most fascinating is fillet steak with chocolate-chilli sauce. Motto is very popular, particularly with the gay crowd, so reservations are recommended. Entrance is through the forbidding chrome door on Rüdigergasse.

Stomach   AUSTRIAN €€

(Map p70; ☑310 20 99; 09, Seegasse 26; mains €10-18; ☺4pm-midnight Wed-Sat, 10am-10pm Sun) Stomach has been serving seriously good food for years. The menu brims with meat and vegetarian delights, such as Styrian roast beef, cream of pumpkin soup, and, when in season, wild boar and venison. The interior is authentically rural-Austrian, and the overgrown garden creates a picturesque backdrop. The name Stomach comes from the rearrangement of the word Tomaschek, the butcher's shop originally located here. Reservations are highly recommended.

Glacis Beisl   NEO-BEISL €€

(Map p72; ☑526 56 60; 07, Museumsplatz; mains €8.90-17.60; ☺11am-2am; ☑) Hidden downstairs behind the buildings along Breite Gasse (follow the signs from MUMOK) in the MuseumsQuartier, Glacis Beisl does an authentic goulash, an accomplished *Wiener Schnitzel* and some very decent other Austrian classics, which you can wash down with excellent reds and whites from Austria. If you're staying in the area, the chances are high this one will evolve into your regular *Beisl*.

Amacord
AUSTRIAN, INTERNATIONAL €

(Map p72; 587 47 09; 05, Rechte Wienzeile 15; breakfast €5.10-12.80, mains €8.90-14.90; 10am-2am;) The popularity of this small eatery stems from its convivial vibe, friendly staff, lovely vaulted ceilings, comfy surroundings and good, affordable food. Viennese classics are mixed in with a healthy range of Italian pastas, the odd curry and ragout, and an extensive salad selection. However, some will find the smoke overpowering as the evening rolls on, and trying to find a seat on a Saturday morning is a fruitless enterprise. Eat off-peak here.

Gasthaus Wickerl
BEISL €€

(Map p70; 317 74 89; 09, Porzellangasse 24a; midday menu €6.20, mains €7.90-16; 9am-midnight Mon-Fri, 10am-midnight Sat, 10am-4pm Sun) Wickerl is a beautiful *Beisl* with an all-wood finish and a warm, welcoming mood. Seasonal fare, such as *Kürbiscremesuppe* (cream of pumpkin soup) and *Kürbisgulasch* (pumpkin goulash) in autumn, *Marillenknödel* in summer and *Spargel* (asparagus) in spring are mixed in with the usual Viennese offerings of *Tafelspitz, Zwiebelrostbraten* (beef fried in onions) and veal and pork schnitzel.

Scala
ITALIAN €€

(Map p70; 310 20 79; 09, Servitengasse 4; pasta & meat mains €8.20-16.90; 11am-midnight) Scala is an unpretentious Italian restaurant where on a rainy day you can find refuge behind a plate of pasta, a pizza or a more substantial dish while warming up over a glass of wine. In summer there's outdoor seating. Alongside or further along Servitengasse you'll find a sprinkling of cafes and bars, as well as Xocolat (Servitengasse 5; 10am-6pm Mon-Fri, 9am-1pm Sat), where some of Vienna's finest local chocolate is manufactured and sold.

Café Sperl
COFFEE HOUSE

(Map p72; 586 41 58; 06, Gumpendorfer Strasse 11; 7am-11pm Mon-Sat, 11am-8pm Sun, closed Sun summer;) With its gorgeous *Jugendstil* fittings, grand dimensions, cosy booths and unhurried air, Sperl is one of the finest coffee houses in Vienna. And that's to say nothing of a menu that features *Sperl Torte* – a mouth-watering mix of almonds and chocolate cream. Grab a slice and a newspaper, order a strong coffee, and join the rest of the patrons people watching and day-dreaming.

Amerlingbeisl
BEISL €

(Map p72; 526 16 60; 07, Stiftgasse 8; midday menus €5, mains €7-10; 9am-2am) Serving solid Austrian fare (and a sprinkling of Italian pasta dishes), Amerlingbeisl is a lovely place situated in the pedestrian quarter of Spittelberg, an old-world spot of tight cobblestone streets and quirky shops. The inner courtyard of this *Beisl* is a lush oasis, and on balmy summer nights the roof slides back to create a lovely outdoor feel.

Ubl
BEISL €

(Map p72; 587 64 37; 04, Pressgasse 26; mains €9-15; noon-2pm, 6pm-midnight Wed-Sun;) This much-loved *Beisl* is a favourite of the Wieden crowd. Its menu is heavily loaded with Viennese classics, such as *Schinkenfleckerl, Schweinsbraten* and four types of schnitzel, and it's enhanced with seasonal cuisine throughout the year. You could do worse than finish the hefty meal off with a stomach-settling plum schnapps. The quiet, tree-shaded garden is wonderful in summer.

Schloss Concordia (Kleine Oper Wien)
AUSTRIAN €

(769 88 88; 11, Simmeringer Hauptstrasse 283; midday menu €8.75, mains €6.50-14; 10am-1am;) The gigantic stone Jesus that greets diners to Schloss Concordia is a fitting welcome mat, given the Zentralfriedhof directly opposite. It also sets the scene for inside; the bare wooden floors, gargantuan mirrors and stained-glass roof are suitably dated, and when candlelit in the evening it all creates a rather eerie picture. The overgrown garden at the rear adds to the effect. The menu, which is crowded with schnitzels, will suit meat lovers; for a memorable experience, try *Degustationsmenü*, a hefty plate of different kinds of schnitzel. Thankfully, there's a smattering of vegetarian options, too.

Kent
TURKISH €

(405 91 73; 16, Brunnengasse 67; mains €5-10; 6am-2am;) Kent means 'small town' in Turkish, an appropriate name considering the hordes that frequent this ever-expanding Turkish restaurant. In summer the tree-shaded garden is one of the prettiest in the city, and the food is consistently top-notch. The menu is extensive, but highlights include shish kebab, *Ispanakli Pide* (long Turkish pizza with sheep's cheese, egg and spinach) and *Büyük Meze Tabagi* (starter plate as big as a main with baked eggplant, carrots, zucchini, rice-filled vine leaves, green beans, hummus and other delights). The vegetarian and breakfast selections will please most, and everything is available for takeaway. For late-night desserts, try the Turkish bakery next door, which

NASCHING AT THE NASCHMARKT

The **Naschmarkt** (Map p72; O6, btwn Linke Wienzeile & Rechte Wienzeile; ⊙6am-6.30pm Mon-Fri, to 5pm Sat) – to *nasch* means to snack in German – is Vienna's biggest and boldest market and a food lover's dream come true. Not only are there food stalls selling meats, fruits, vegetables, cheeses and spices, but there's also a wide variety of restaurants. Here're a few:

Neni
BAR, CAFE €

(Map p72; ☑585 20 20; O6, Naschmarkt 510; breakfast €4-8.50, salads & snacks €4-11, mains €9-15; ⊙8am-midnight Mon-Sat) Some of Naschmarkt's 'stands' take on the proportions of Belvedere. Neni is no exception. The area downstairs is mostly used as a cafe and bar, and upstairs is a main eating area where tasty delights mostly have a Middle Eastern focus. Dishes such as caramelised aubergine with ginger and chilli (€9) are served alongside expertly prepared lamb chops with truffle-laced polenta (€14) or a pulse ragout with cranberries and rice (€9.50). Tables can be at a premium most nights, so reserve ahead or drop by outside prime time. Breakfast is served until 2pm.

Naschmarkt Deli
CAFE €

(Map p72; ☑585 08 23; O4, Naschmarkt 421; bagels €5, sandwiches €4-7, mains €6-12; ⊙7am-midnight Mon-Sat) Among the market's many enticing stands, Naschmarkt Deli has an edge on the others for its delicious snacks. Sandwiches, falafel wraps, big baguettes and quick soups (lentil soup is a good bet) fill the menu, but much space is dedicated to a heady array of breakfasts. Come Saturday morning this glass box overflows with punters waiting for the Continental or English breakfast.

Do-An
INTERNATIONAL €

(Map p72; ☑585 82 53; O6, Naschmarkt 412; breakfast €5-7, salads €4.80-6.60; ⊙7am-midnight Mon-Sat; ✎) Located in the heart of Naschmarkt, Do-An does an eclectic mix of sandwiches, rice and noodle dishes, delicious salads and meats with salads as well as some Turkish staples at affordable prices. Many of its diners head straight for the breakfasts from around the globe; the American reads more like a traditional English fry-up and the Continental is a nice, light starter of bread and spreads. Like Naschmarkt Deli, Do-An is a rectangular aquarium with huge glass walls and a steadfast following that enjoys the relaxed vibe and sunny corners.

keeps practical opening times: 24 hours a day, seven days a week.

OUTSIDE THE GURTEL
There are Billa supermarkets at Nisselgasse 4 near Schönbrunn Anschützgasse 26 and Thaliastrasse 85.

 Drinking

Vienna is riddled with late-night drinking dens, but you will find concentrations of pulsating bars north and south of the Naschmarkt, around Spittelberg (many of these double as restaurants) and along the Gürtel (mainly around the U6 stops of Josefstädter Strasse and Nussdorfer Strasse). The Bermuda Dreieck (Bermuda Triangle), near the Danube Canal in the Innere Stadt, also has many bars, but they are more touristy.

Also during the summer months, partygoers congregate at Copa Kagrana and Sunken City, an area around the U1 Donauinsel U-Bahn station. It's quite a tacky affair, but it can be a lot of fun. **Summer Stage** (☑315 52 02; O9, Rossauer Lände; ⊙5pm-1am Mon-Sat, 3pm-1am Sun May-Sep) and the **Alte AKH** (Map p70; ☑87 05 04; cnr Alser Strasse & Spitalgasse) also wage war against the threat of melting indoors.

Vienna's coffee houses are wonderful places for sipping tea or coffee, imbibing beer or wine, and catching up on gossip or news of the world. Most serve light meals, while most cafes have a good cake range.

Identified by a *Busch'n* (a green wreath or branch) hanging over the door, *Heurigen* nearly always have outside tables in large gardens or courtyards, while inside the atmosphere is rustic. Some serve light meals, which in Vienna can be a hot or cold buffet.

Concentrations of *Heurigen* can be found in the wine-growing suburbs to the north, southwest, west and northwest of the city. Grinzing, in the northwest, is the best-known *Heurigen* area, but it is also the most touristy. It's generally avoided by the Viennese, but if you like loud music and busloads of rowdy tourists, then it's the place for you.

INNERE STADT

Palmenhaus
BAR, CAFE

(Map p60; ☏533 10 33; 01, Burggarten; ⊙10am-2am Mar-Oct, closed Mon & Tue Jan & Feb) Housed in a beautifully restored Victorian palm house, complete with high arched ceilings, glass walls and steel beams, Palmenhaus occupies one of the most attractive locations in Vienna. The crowd is generally well-to-do, but the ambience is relaxed and welcoming. The outdoor seating in summer is a must, and there are occasional club nights.

Kleines Café
COFFEE HOUSE

(Map p60; 01, Franziskanerplatz 3; ⊙10am-2am) Designed by architect Hermann Czech in the 1970s, the Kleines Café exudes a bohemian atmosphere reminiscent of Vienna's heady *Jugendstil* days. It's tiny inside, but the wonderful summer outdoor seating on Franziskanerplatz is arguably the best in the Innere Stadt.

Vis-a-vis
WINE BAR

(Map p60; ☏512 93 50; 01, Wollzeile 5; ⊙4:30pm-10:30am Tue-Sat) Hidden down a narrow, atmospheric passage (and directly across from famed *Beisl* Figlmüller is this wee wine bar – it may only seat close to 10, but it makes up for it with over 350 wines on offer (with a strong emphasis on Austrian faves). A perfect spot to escape after a packed day of sightseeing – tapas, antipasto and gourmet olives round out the selection

Loos American Bar
COCKTAIL BAR

(Map p60; ☏512 32 83; 01, Kärntner Durchgang 10; ⊙noon-4am Sun-Wed, to 5am Thu-Sat) *The* spot for a classic cocktail in the Innere Stadt, expertly whipped up by talented mixologists. Designed by Adolf Loos in 1908, this tiny box (space for about 20) is head to toe in onyx and polished brass; mirrored walls trick you into thinking it's a far bigger space. Beware: gawkers popping in merely for a glimpse of the interior will be swiftly ejected.

Café Griensteidl
COFFEE HOUSE

(Map p60; ☏535 26 92; 01, Michaelerplatz 2; ⊙8am-11.30pm) Griensteidl holds a prestigious position between the Hofburg and the Loos Haus, and was once the *Stammlokal* (local haunt) for Vienna's late-19th-century literary set. It now caters mainly to tourists, but it still attracts with its *Jugendstil* lamps, wooden chairs and tables, and huge windows overlooking Michaelerplatz.

Haas & Haas
COFFEE HOUSE, TEAROOM

(Map p60; ☏512 26 66; 01, Stephansplatz 4; ⊙8am-8pm Mon-Fri, to 6.30pm Sat) The fragrance of tea from around the world greets customers on entry to Haas & Hass, Vienna's prime tea house. Green, herbal, aromatic, Assam, Ceylon, Darjeeling: the selection seems endless. The rear garden is a shaded retreat from the wind, rain, sun and tourist bustle, while the front parlour sports comfy cushioned booths and views of Stephansdom.

Café Bräunerhof
COFFEE HOUSE

(Map p60; ☏512 38 93; 01, Stallburggasse 2; ⊙8am-9pm Mon-Fri, 8am-7pm Sat, 10am-7pm Sun) Bräunerhof is an authentic coffee house of some standing amongst *Kaffeehäuser* aficionados. It remains little changed from the days when Austria's seminal writer Thomas-Bernhard frequented the premises: smoke-stained walls, tight tables, surly staff and a

EUROPE'S LAST BASTION OF SMOKING

Vienna is smoky. Despite the strict smoking bans that have swept across Europe over the last decade, Austria agreed on a multi-option compromise in 2009: in any locale under 50 sq metres, the proprietor is free to choose to be smoking or nonsmoking. If it's larger than 80 sq metres, a nonsmoking space must be provided with a partition and appropriate ventilation. Between 50 sq metres and 80 sq metres, establishments exist in a funny loophole (most escape the law on a variety of grounds; architecture is often cited). In practice, this partial ban means little – effective partitions rarely exist between smoking and nonsmoking areas. Many Viennese smoke and don't bat an eye about health risks or the effect of secondhand smoke on nonsmokers. Rumours of change in the smoky air rise up periodically, but for the moment expect to encounter thick smoke in most bars, clubs and coffee houses.

huge newspaper selection. Classical music from the Bräunerhof features 3pm to 6pm on weekends and holidays.

Café Hawelka
COFFEE HOUSE

(Map p60; ☎512 82 30; 01, Dorotheergasse 6; ☺8am-2am Mon & Wed-Sat, from 10am Sun) At first glance it's hard to see what all the fuss is about: dirty pictures, ripped posters, brown-stained walls, smoky air and cramped tables don't look too appealing. But a second glance explains it – the convivial vibe between friends and complete strangers. A traditional haunt for artists and writers, it attracts the gamut of Viennese society. You'll be constantly shunted up to accommodate new arrivals at the table. Be warned: the organising elderly *Frau* seizes any momentarily vacant chair (curtail your toilet visits!) to reassign elsewhere.

Café Sacher
COFFEE HOUSE

(Map p60; ☎541 56-0; 01, Philharmonikerstrasse 4; ☺8am-11:30pm) Sacher is the cafe every second tourist wants to visit. Why? Because of the celebrated *Sacher Torte* (€4), a rich chocolate cake with apricot jam once favoured by Emperor Franz Josef. Truth be told, as cafes go Sacher doesn't rate highly for authenticity, but it pleases the masses with its opulent furnishings, battalion of waiters, and air of nobility.

Demel
COFFEE HOUSE

(Map p60; ☎535 17 17; 01, Kohlmarkt 14; ☺10am-7pm) An elegant and regal cafe within sight of the Hofburg, Demel was once the talk of the town but now mainly caters to tourists. The quality of the cakes hasn't dropped, however, and it wins marks for the sheer creativity of its sweets. Demel's speciality is the *Ana Demel Torte,* a calorie bomb of chocolate and nougat that rivals Café Sacher's *Torte.*

Esterházykeller
STADTHEURIGER

(Map p60; ☎533 34 82; 01, Haarhof 1; ☺11am-11pm Mon-Fri, 4-11pm Sat & Sun) Esterházykeller is tucked away on a quiet courtyard just off Kohlmarkt. Its enormous cellar is a tad claustrophobic, but after a few glasses of excellent wine, direct from the Esterházy Palace cellar in Eisenstadt, no one seems to mind. The rustic decor, complete with medieval weaponry and farming tools, reeks of kitsch, but the individual wooden booths are its saving grace. Unlike most *Heurigen*, it offers beer.

Zwölf Apostelkeller
STADTHEURIGER

(Twelve Apostle Cellar; Map p60; ☎512 67 77; 01, Sonnenfelsgasse 3; ☺11am-midnight) Even though Zwölf Apostelkeller plays it up for the tourists, it still retains plenty of charm, dignity and authenticity. This is mostly due to the premises themselves: a vast, dimly lit multilevel cellar. The atmosphere is often lively and rowdy, helped along by traditional *Heuriger* music from 7pm daily.

RINGSTRASSE

Café Prückel
COFFEE HOUSE

(Map p60; ☎512 61 15; 01, Stubenring 24; ☺8.30am-10pm) Prückel's unique mould is a little different from that of other Viennese cafes: instead of a sumptuous interior, it features an intact 1950s design. Intimate booths, aloof waiters, strong coffee and diet-destroying cakes are all attractions, but the smoke can at times be bothersome; thankfully, there's a non-smoking room at the rear. Live piano music is offered 7pm to 10pm Monday, Wednesday and Friday.

Café Landtmann
COFFEE HOUSE

(Map p60; ☎241 00; 01, Dr-Karl-Lueger-Ring 4; ☺7.30am-midnight; ☎) Landtmann attracts both politicians and theatre goers with its elegant interior and proximity to the Burgtheater, Rathaus and Parlament. The list of coffee specialities is formidable and the dessert menu features classics like the *Sacher Torte* and *Apfelstrudel*. There's a huge selection of Austrian and international papers, and live piano music from 8pm to 11pm Sunday to Tuesday.

Volksgarten Pavillon
BAR, OUTDOOR BAR

(Map p60; ☎532 09 07; 01, Burgring 1; ☺11am-2am Apr–mid-Sep) Volksgarten's second venue (after the club Volksgarten p102) is a lovely 1950s-style pavilion with views of Heldenplatz. On Tuesday nights its ever-popular garden is packed to the gunnels.

INSIDE THE GÜRTEL

TOP CHOICE Café Drechsler
COFFEE HOUSE

(Map p72; ☎587 85 80; 06, Linke Wienzeile 22; ☺8am-2am Mon, 3am-2am Tue-Sat, 3am-midnight Sun) One of the liveliest coffee houses in town, Drechsler reopened with a smash after extensive renovations (Sir Terence Conran worked hips magic with polished marble bar and table tops, Bauhaus light fixtures and whitewashed timber panels – the result is stylish yet still distinctly Viennese). Besides the usual coffee-house suspects, the *Gulasch* (goulash) is legendary, as are the tunes the DJ spins, which seemingly change every few hours and always keep the vibe upbeat and hip.

TOP CHOICE **Wein & Wasser** WINE BAR
(Wine & Water; ☑403 53 45; 08, Laudongasse 57; ⊙6pm-1am Mon-Sat) The best place in Vienna to sample Austrian wine outside a *Heuriger*. Its philosophy is to teach customers what they know about wine, and the staff warmly guides you through the lengthy list. Over 20 Austrian wines are served by the glass. If you prefer to stick to what you know, check out the list's 'Foreigners' section for the usual suspects. Kick back in the subterranean space, its arched bricks flanked by lights oozing pale yellow and flickering candles. Nibbles and tapas round out the menu.

Weinstube Josefstadt STADTHEURIGER
(Map p70; ☑406 46 28; 08, Piaristengasse 27; ⊙4pm-midnight, closed Jan-Mar) Weinstube Josefstadt is one of the loveliest *Stadtheurigen* in the city. Its garden is a barely controlled green oasis among concrete residential blocks, and tables are squeezed in between the trees and shrubs. Food is typical, with a buffet-style selection and plenty of cheap

meats (chicken wings go for only €1). The friendly, well-liquored locals come free of charge. The location is not well signposted; the only clue to its existence is a metal *Buschel* hanging from a doorway.

Das Möbel BAR, CAFE
(Map p72; ☑524 94 97; 07, Burggasse 10; ⊙10am-1am; 🛜) Das Möbel wins points for its furniture, consisting entirely of one-off pieces produced by local designers. Half the fun is choosing a spot that takes your fancy – whether it be a swinging chair or a surfboard bench. Light fittings, bags and various odds and ends complete the look, and everything is for sale.

Europa BAR, CAFE
(Map p72; ☑526 33 83; 07, Zollergasse 8; ⊙9am-5am; 🛜) A long-standing fixture of the seventh district, Europa is a chilled spot any time, day or night. During the sunny hours, join the relaxed set at a window table for coffee and food, and in the evening take a pew at the bar and enjoy the DJ's tunes. Its breakfast, served between 9am and 3pm daily, caters to a hungover clientele; Sunday features a sumptuous breakfast buffet (€9.50).

VIENNA'S MICROBREWERIES

Venues where the beer is always fresh and the atmosphere boisterous, Vienna's microbreweries make for a hedonistic evening out. Most offer a healthy selection of beers brewed on the premises (and proudly display the shining brass brewing equipment), complimented by filling Austrian staples.

1516 Brewing Company (Map p60; ☑961 15 16; www.1516brewingcompany.com; 01, Schwarzenbergstrasse 2; ⊙11am-2am) Unfiltered beers and a few unusual varieties, such as Heidi's Blueberry Ale. Large choice of cigars. Frequented by city workers and UN staff.

Fischer Bräu (☑369 59 49; www.fischerbraeu.at, in German; 19, Billrothstrasse 17; ⊙4pm-1am Mon-Sat, 11am-1am Sun) A new beer every four to six weeks, and a *Helles* lager all year round. The large garden is a local fave and the live jazz on Sunday is perennially packed.

Salm Bräu (Map p76; ☑799 59 92; www.salmbraeu.com; 03, Rennweg 8; ⊙11am-midnight) Brews its own *Helles, Pils, Märzen, G'mischt,* and *Weizen*. Smack next to Schloss Belvedere and hugely popular, with a happy hour from 3pm to 5pm Monday to Friday and noon to 4pm Saturday.

Siebensternbräu (Map p72; ☑523 86 97; www.7stern.at; 07, Siebensterngasse 19; ⊙10am-midnight) Large brewery with all the main varieties, plus a hemp beer, chilli beer, and smoky beer (the malt is dried over an open fire); the hidden back garden is sublime in the warmer months.

Wieden Bräu (Map p60; ☑586 03 00; www.wieden-braeu.at, in German; 04, Waaggasse 5; ⊙11.30am-midnight year round, from 4pm Sat & Sun Jul & Aug; 🛜) *Helles, Märzen* and hemp beers all year round, plus a few seasonal choices, including a ginger beer. Happy hour 5.30pm to 7.30pm.

Futuregarden Bar & Art Club   BAR, CLUB

(Map p72; ☑585 26 13; 06, Schadekgasse 6; ☺6pm-2am Mon-Sat, from 8pm Sun) With white walls, an open bar and basic furniture, it's hard to find a simpler place. Its one decoration – apart from the occasional art exhibition by local artists – is its rectangular disco 'ball', which swings from the ceiling. Futuregarden attracts a late-20s and 30s crowd with a cool atmosphere and electric sounds.

Joanelli   BAR, WINE BAR

Map p72; ☑311 84 04; 06, Gumpendorferstrasse 47; ☺6pm-2am) Vienna's oldest *Eissalon* (the ancient sign still hangs above the entrance) has morphed into an arty hangout, with colourful lighting (sometimes pink, sometimes yellow) casting shadows on the plain white Formica tables and empty walls. In addition to relaxed tunes the drinks list contains over 20 quality wines by the glass (most of them Austrian) – staff expertly guide you between the Blauburgunders and the Veltliners. A full cocktail and beer menu is on offer, too.

Halbestadt Bar   COCKTAIL BAR

(☑319 47 35; 09, Stadtbogen 155; ☺6pm-2am Mon-Thu, 7pm-2am, to 4am Sat & Sun) It starts when you can't open the glass door. The host swings it forth, escorts you in, takes your coat and offers to advise you on what to order – impeccable hospitality with no trace of snobbery. Over 500 bottles grace the walls of the tiny space under the boden (subway arches) and mixologists hold court creating tongue-enticing works of art, shaken and poured into exquisite receptacles. South Pacific–inspired drinks arrive in a ceramic Polynesian goblet, and *Sekt* comes in a shallow, retro champagne glass.

Mon Ami   BAR

(Map p72; ☑585 01 34; 06, Theobaldgasse 9; ☺4pm-1am Mon-Sat) Don't let the dog and cat grooming sign fool ya: this former pet-grooming salon morphed into a lovely '60s-style bar mixes excellent cocktails, serves a short but decent beer, wine and snacks list, and attracts a laid-back and unpretentious crowd. The rear of the bar is a shop stocking young designer creations (open to 10pm), so you can pick up a groovy new top and knock a few back in fewer than 10 steps.

Schikaneder   BAR

(Map p72; ☑585 58 88; 04, Margaretenstrasse 22-24; ☺6pm-4am) Most of the colour in Schikaneder comes from the regularly projected movies splayed across one of its white walls – the students and arty crowd who frequent this grungy bar dress predominantly in black. But that's not to detract from the bar's atmosphere, which exudes energy well into the wee small hours of the morning. Schikaneder also hosts movies most nights.

Tanzcafé Jenseits   BAR, CLUB

(Map p72; ☑587 12 33; 06, Nelkengasse 3; ☺9pm-4am Mon-Sat) The red-velvet interior that might be out of a '70s bordello is a soothing backdrop for a night out at Jenseits. The tiny dance floor fills to overflowing on Friday and Saturday with relaxed revellers slowly moving around each other to soul and funk.

Café Hummel   COFFEE HOUSE

(☑405 53 14; 08, Josefstädter Strasse 66; ☺7am-midnight Mon-Sat, from 8am Sun; ☎) Unpretentious and classic, Hummel is a large *Kaffeehaus* catering to a regular crowd. The coffee is rich, the cakes baked on the premises, and the waiters typically snobbish. In summer, it's easy to spend a few hours at Hummel's outdoor seating area, mulling over the international papers and watching the human traffic on Josefstädter Strasse.

Café Jelinek   COFFEE HOUSE

(Map p72; ☑597 41 13; 06, Otto-Bauergasse 5; ☺9am-9pm) Walk in from the street here and everyone looks up as if keeping a secret about something shocking that happened 20 years ago. Newspapers fill a ledge near the doorway, the wood oven is fired up in winter and the cigarette smoke clings to you long after you've gone. There's food too, but drift across the street for Viennese nosh at **Steman**, run by the same people.

OUTSIDE THE GÜRTEL

TOP CHOICE 10er Marie   STADTHEURIGER

(☑489 46 47; 16, Ottakringerstrasse 222-224; ☺3pm-midnight Mon-Sat) The oldest *Heuriger* in Vienna has been going strong since 1740 – back in the day Schubert, Strauss and Crown Prince Rudolf all enjoyed a glass or three here; today it welcomes a grand mix of visitors and locals. Family run and operated, it offers the rustic ambience a *Heuriger* ought to without requiring you to trek to the far reaches of the city. The usual buffet is on offer plus a handful of schnitzels.

Café Gloriette   COFFEE HOUSE

(Map p79; ☑879 13 11; 13, Gloriette; ☺9am-1am) Café Gloriette occupies the Gloriette, a neoclassical construction high on a hill behind Schloss Schönbrunn, built for the pleasure of Maria Theresia in 1775. With sweeping views of the Schloss, its magnificent gardens

Vienna is reasonably tolerant towards gays and lesbians, and things get better each year. Even the Vienna Tourist Board does its bit; its *Queer Guide* booklet has listings of bars, restaurants, hotels and festivals, while its *Vienna Gay Guide* is a city map with gay locations marked up. *Xtra* and *Night Life* (www.nightlifeonline.at, in German), two free monthly publications, are additional supplements packed with news, views and listings (in German only).

The best organisation in town is the **Rosa Lila Villa** (☎586 8150; www.villa.at; 06, Linke Wienzeile 102), an unmissable pink house by the Wien River. Its **Lesbian Centre** (☎586 81 50; ⊙5-8pm Mon, Wed & Fri) is on the ground floor, while its **Gay Men's Centre** (☎585 43 43; ⊙5-8pm Mon & Fri, 1-8pm Wed) is on the 1st floor. **Homosexualle Initiative Wien** (HOSI; ☎216 66 04; www.hosiwien.at, in German; 02, Novaragasse 40), another helpful organisation, is politically minded and holds regular events.

Events to look out for on the gay and lesbian calendar include the **Regenbogen Parade** (Rainbow Parade), a colourful parade that takes over the Ring and MuseumsQuartier at the end of June, the **Life Ball** (www.lifeball.org), an AIDS-charity event around the middle of May, **Wien ist andersrum** (www.andersrum.at), a month-long extravaganza of gay and lesbian art in June, and **Identities – Queer Film Festival** (www.identities.at), a film festival showcasing queer movies, also in June.

Unfortunately there isn't much in the way of accommodation aimed at gay and lesbians; **Hotel-Pension Wild** is one option.

The Scene

Vienna has enough bars and clubs to entertain its gay and lesbian community, while some straight clubs, like U4, feature gay nights on a weekly basis. **Rainbow** (www.rainbow.at/guide) has a scene guide for large cities.

Café Berg   CAFE
(Map p70; ☎319 57 20; 09, Berggasse 8; ⊙10am-1am, to midnight Jul-Sep) With some of the nicest staff in Vienna, a lovely, open layout and all-round friendly vibe, it's no wonder Café Berg is often full with a gay and straight crowd. Its bookshop, Löwenherz, stocks a grand collection of gay magazines and books.

Café Willendorf   CAFE
(Map p72; ☎587 17 89; 06, Linke Wienzeile 102; ⊙6pm-2am Mon-Sat, 10am-3pm & 6pm-2am Sun) This is one of Vienna's seminal gay and lesbian bars, housed in the pink Rosa Lila Villa.

Frauencafé   CAFE
(Map p70; ☎406 37 54; 05, Lange Gasse 8; ⊙6pm-midnight Thu & Fri) A long-established strictly women-, lesbian- and transgender-only cafe-bar.

Mango Bar   BAR
(Map p72; ☎587 44 48; Laimgrubengasse 3; ⊙9pm-4am) Ever-popular bar open every day of the week.

Why Not?   BAR
(Map p60; ☎535 11 58; www.why-not.at; 01, Tiefer Graben 22; ⊙10pm-4am Fri & Sat) Small and very central, Why Not? pops at the seams on weekends, when it fills quickly, mainly with young gay guys.

and the districts to the north, Gloriette has arguably one of the best vistas in all of Vienna. And it's a welcome pit stop after the short but sharp climb up the hill.

Hirt   HEURIGER
(☎318 96 41; 19, Eisernenhandgasse 165, Kahlenberg; ⊙2pm-late Wed-Sat, from 10am Sun every odd month & first half of Dec) Hidden among the vineyards on the eastern slopes of Kahlenberg, Hirt is a simple *Heuriger* with few frills. Basic wooden tables, a small buffet and marginal service all help to create a traditional atmosphere, while views of Kahlenbergerdorf and the 21st district across the Danube are a pleasure to enjoy over a few glasses of wine in the early evening.

MOZART IN THE MAKING

Klangforum Wien (☎521 670; www.
klangforum.at) an ensemble of 24 artists from nine countries, celebrates a
unique collaboration between conductors, composers and interpreters who
produce a wide range of musical styles,
from improv to edgy jazz to classical
notes. Many up-and-coming composers are represented here (over 500
new pieces have premiered since its
opening in 1985), so don't be surprised
if you are wowed with a sneak peek at
the next best thing. The Klangforum
performs at various venues in the city –
check the website for dates and details.

Mayer am Pfarrplatz   HEURIGER

(☎370 12 87; 19, Pfarrplatz 2, Nussdorf; ⏱4pm-
midnight Mon-Sat, from 11am Sun) Fifteen minutes' walk from U4 Heiligenstadt U-Bahn
station, Mayer caters to tour groups but still
manages to retain an air of authenticity,
helped along by its ambience, vine-covered
surrounds and history (Beethoven lived here
in 1817). The huge shaded garden at the rear
includes a children's play area, and there's
live music from 7pm to 11pm daily.

Zawodsky   HEURIGER

(☎320 79 78; 19, Reinischgasse 3, Döbling; ⏱5pm-
midnight Mon & Wed-Fri, from 2pm Sat & Sun Mar-
Nov) Zawodsky is only a 15-minute walk from
the touristy haunts of Grinzing, yet light
years away in atmosphere. This stripped-
back setup features picnic tables surrounded
by apple trees and vineyards, and a small selection of hot and cold meats complemented
by various salads. From Grinzing, walk up
Strassergasse, take tiny Rosenweg on your
left past the Maria Schmerzen Kirche and
Reinischgasse appears on your right.

Edelmoser   HEURIGER

(☎889 86 80; www.edlmoser.at; 23, Maurer Lange
Gasse, Mauer; ⏱2.30pm-midnight last half of
month Apr-Nov) Dynamic young winemaker
Michael Edlmoser, who apprenticed under
California's highly respected Ridge Winery,
blends an outward-looking attitude with
a deep love of Austrian tradition to create
what he calls cult wines. Enjoy them in a
400-year-old house with clean lines, modern
wood furnishings and a superb swath of yellow fabric covering a vine-lined garden – a
fusion of old and new, just like his wines.

☆ Entertainment

Vienna is, and probably will be till the end of
time, the European capital of opera and classical music. The program of music events is
never-ending, and as a visitor in the centre
you'll continually be accosted by people in
Mozart-era costume trying to sell you tickets
for concerts or ballets. Even the city's busk-
ers are often classically trained musicians.

The city also sports a number of great
clubs, jazz bars and live-music venues. The
tourist office produces a handy monthly listing of concerts and other events.

Opera & Classical Music

The list of venues below is certainly not complete, and many churches and cafes are fine
places to catch a classical concert.

Tickets for the Akademietheater, Burgtheater, Schauspielhaus, Staatsoper and Volksoper can be purchased from the state ticket
office, **Bundestheaterkassen** (Map p60; ☎514
44-7881; www.bundestheater.at; 01, Operngasse 2;
⏱8am-6pm Mon-Fri, 9am-noon Sat & Sun). The
office charges no commission, and tickets for
the Staatsoper and Volksoper are available
here one month prior to the performance.

The **Wien-Ticket Pavillon** (Map p60; www.
wien-ticket.at, in German; 01, Herbert-von-Karajan-
Platz; ⏱10am-7pm) outside the Staatsoper
sells tickets for all venues. **Jirsa Theater
Karten Büro** (Map p70; ☎400 600; www.vienna
ticket.at; 08, Lerchenfelder Strasse 12; ⏱9.30am-
5.30pm Mon, Thu & Fri, to 1pm Tue & Wed, 10am-1pm
Jul & Aug) also covers most venues in town.

Staatsoper   OPERA & CLASSICAL MUSIC

(Map p60; ☎514 44 7880; www.wiener-staatsoper.
at; 01, Opernring 2; tours adult/child €5/2; ⏱box
office 9am-1hr before performance Mon-Fri, to 5pm
Sat) This is the premier opera and classical-
music venue in Vienna. Productions are
lavish affairs and the Viennese take them
very seriously and dress up accordingly.
Standing-room tickets (€3 to €4) can only
be purchased 80 minutes before the beginning of performances and any unsold tickets are available for €30 one day before a
performance (call ☎514 44 2950 for more
information).

Musikverein   CLASSICAL MUSIC

(Map p76; ☎505 81 90; www.musikverein.at; 01,
Bösendorferstrasse 12; ⏱box office 9am-8pm Mon-
Fri, to 1pm Sat) The Musikverein, home to the
Vienna Philharmonic Orchestra, is said to
have the best acoustics of any concert hall
in Austria. The interior is suitably lavish and
can be visited on the occasional guided tour.

Standing-room tickets in the main hall cost €4 to €6; there are no student tickets.

Konzerthaus
CLASSICAL MUSIC
(Map p76; ☑242 002; www.konzerthaus.at; 03, Lothringerstrasse 20; ☺box office 9am-7.45pm Mon-Fri, to 1pm Sat) This is a major venue in classical-music circles, but throughout the year ethnic music, rock, pop or jazz can also be heard in its hallowed halls. Students can purchase tickets for €14 from 30 minutes before the show.

Theater an der Wien
OPERA & CLASSICAL MUSIC
(Map p72; ☑588 85; www.musicalvienna.at; 06, Linke Wienzeile 6; ☺box office 10am-7pm) Once the host of monumental premieres such as Beethoven's *Fidelio*, Mozart's *Die Zauberflöte* and Strauss Jnr's *Die Feldermaus,* Theater an der Wien now showcases opera, dance and concerts. Tickets start from €7 for standing room, sold one hour before performances.

Volksoper
OPERA
(Map p70; ☑514 44 3670; www.volksoper.at; 09, Währinger Strasse 78; ☺box office 8am-6pm Mon-Fri, 9am-noon Sat) This is Vienna's second opera house and features operettas, dance and musicals. Standing tickets go for as little as €2 to €6, and there are discounts 30 minutes before performances.

Theatre & Dance

English Theatre
THEATRE
(Map p70; ☑402 12 60-0; www.englishtheatre.at; 08, Josefsgasse 12; tickets €22-42; ☺box office 10am-7.30pm Mon-Fri, 5-7.30pm Sat on performance days) Performances in English.

International Theatre
THEATRE
(Map p70; ☑319 62 72; www.internationaltheatre. at; 09, Porzellangasse 8; tickets €20-25; ☺box office 11am-3pm Mon-Fri, 6-7.30pm on performance days) Performances in English. Smaller than the English Theatre.

Burgtheater
THEATRE
(Map p60; ☑514 44-4140; www.burgtheater.at; 01 Dr Karl-Lueger-Ring; tickets €4-48; ☺box office 8am-6pm Mon-Fri, 9am-noon Sat & Sun) Best of the German theatres.

Schauspielhaus
THEATRE
(Map p70; ☑317 01 01-18; www.schauspielhaus. at; 09, Porzellangasse 19; tickets €18; ☺box office from 4pm Mon-Fri, from 6pm on performance days) Performances in German.

Volkstheater
THEATRE
(Map p72; ☑521 11-400; www.volkstheater.at, in German; 07, Neustiftgasse 1; tickets €8-45; ☺box office 10am-performance Mon-Sat Sep-Jun) Performances in German; limited opening hours in summer.

TanzQuartier Wien
DANCE
(Map p60; ☑581 35 91; www.tqw.at; 07, Museumsplatz 1; tickets €11-18; ☺box office 1hr before performances) Vienna's first ever dance institution hosts an array of local and international performances with a strong experimental nature.

Nightclubs

Goodmann
NIGHTCLUB
(Map p72; ☑967 44 15; www.goodmann.at, in German; 04, Rechte Wienzeile 23; ☺3am-10am Mon-Sat) Who cares that Goodmann keeps the

---

VIENNA BOYS' CHOIR

As with Manner Schnitten, Stephansdom, Lipizzaner stallions, and sausage stands, Vienna wouldn't be Vienna without the **Vienna Boys' Choir** (Wiener Sängerknaben; www.wsk. at). Founded over five centuries ago by Maximilian I as the imperial choir, its members over the ages included famed composers Schubert and Gallus and conductors Richter and Krauss; Mozart composed for them in his day; Haydn was a member of another local choir, but he occasionally stepped in to sing with them. Today, it's the most famous boys' choir in the world. It now consists of four separate choirs – hand selected each year and mainly Austrian – who share the demanding global tour schedule.

Catching the choir in concert takes some organisation. Tickets for the **Sunday performances** (☑533 99 27; www.bmbwk.gv.at, in German; tickets €5-32; ☺9.15am Oct-Jun) in the Burgkapelle (Royal Chapel) in the Hofburg should be booked around six weeks in advance. The choir also sings a mixed program of music in the **Musikverein** (tickets €36-56; ☺4pm Fri May, Jun, Sep & Oct). If you don't manage to obtain tickets, settle for a *Stehplatz* (standing-room space); simply show up by about 8:15pm for a spot – they give them out free, so if your legs get tired you can always leave early. In general, the only seats affording you an actual view of the choir are the most expensive ones – the boys are firmly ensconced in the organ loft.

strangest opening hours of any establishment in Vienna? This is where clubbers go when the clubs close; most come for a snack (food is served till 8am) before heading downstairs to dance till closing.

Palais Palffy
NIGHTCLUB

(Map p60; ☑512 56 81; www.palais-palffy.at; 01, Josefsplatz 6; ☺from 9pm Thu-Sat) This 550-sq-metre club occupies two floors of an illustrious old building used for live-music performances. The 1st-floor lounge bar – set with thousands of miniature glittering gemstones below a 12m chandelier with 80,000 Swarovski crystals – stocks over 700 spirits. Less glittery is the luxurious upstairs dance floor. Thursday is mixed electronic and pop, Friday features house, and the Jetlag Club (oldies, current dance) comes to town on Saturday.

Flex
NIGHTCLUB

(☑533 75 25; www.flex.at; 01, Donaukanal, Augartenbrücke; ☺6pm-4am) Flex still looks like a complete dive, but it has one of the best sound systems in Europe, puts on great shows and features the top DJs from Vienna and abroad. 'Messed Up' on Monday (techno) and London Calling (alternative and indie) on Wednesday and Friday are among the most popular.

Volksgarten
NIGHTCLUB

(Map p60; ☑532 42 41; 01, Burgring 1; ☺Tue-Sat) This club attracts a well-dressed crowd, keen to strut their stuff and scan for talent from the long bar. The quality sound system pumps out an array of music styles, which changes from night to night (as do the hours).

Pratersauna
NIGHTCLUB

(☑729 19 27;www.pratersauna.tv; 02, Waldsteingartenstrasse 135; ☺10-6pm Fri & Sat Jan-Apr, 9pm-6am Wed-Sun May-Sep) Pool, cafe, bistro and club converge in a former sauna – these days, you'll sweat it up on the dance floor. Any given night hosts light installations and performance art to check out before or after you groove to electronica spun by international DJs. On warm nights it all spills out onto the terrace, gardens and pool – if you need to cool down, nobody bats an eye if you take a quick dip

Roxy
NIGHTCLUB

(Map p72; ☑961 88 00; www.sunshine.at; 04, Operngasse 24; ☺11pm-4am Thu-Sat) Roxy's tiny dance floor reaches bursting point when DJs from the electronic scene guest here, though everything from Brazilian to jazzy grooves can be heard.

U4
NIGHTCLUB

(☑817 11 92; www.u-4.at; 12, Schönbrunner Strasse 222; cover €6-25; ☺8pm-late Mon, from 10pm Tue-Sun) Once the cutting edge of techno in Vienna, these days U4 pulls a young, studenty crowd – the edge has been blunted somewhat, but it's still very popular.

Live Music

Porgy & Bess
LIVE MUSIC

(Map p60; ☑512 88 11; www.porgy.at; 01, Riemergasse 11; ☺from 7pm) Quality is the cornerstone of Porgy & Bess' continuing popularity. Its program is loaded with modern jazz acts from around the globe, including many from nearby Balkan countries, and DJs fill spots on weekends. The interior is dim and the vibe velvety and very grown-up.

WUK
LIVE MUSIC

(Map p70; ☑40 121-0; www.wuk.at; 09, Währinger Strasse 59; cover free-€10) WUK is a space as much as a venue. You can catch Mieze Medusa & Tenderboy hip-hopping one night and classical concerts, film evenings, theatre or even children's shows another.

Arena
LIVE MUSIC

(☑798 85 95; www.arena.co.at, in German; 03, Baumgasse 80; cover varies; ☺2pm-late summer, 4pm-late winter) Arena normally hosts hard rock, metal and rock, which is well suited to its industrial location. The former slaughterhouse also shows films outdoors in summer and it holds once-a-month all-night parties; 'Iceberg', a German-British 1970s new wave bash, is popular.

Jazzland
LIVE MUSIC

(Map p60; ☑533 25 75; www.jazzland.at; 01, Franz-Josefs-Kai 29; ☺7pm-2am Mon-Sat, from 7.30pm Jul & Aug) Jazzland has been an institution of Vienna's jazz scene for the past 30 years. The music covers the whole jazz spectrum and the brick venue features a grand mixture of local and international acts.

Szene Wien
LIVE MUSIC

(☑749 33 41; www.szenewien.at; 11, Hauffgasse 26; ☺from 7.30pm) Good things happen in small places – this small venue hauls out a mixed bag that includes rock, reggae, funk, jazz and world music.

Cinemas

Vienna has a fine mix of cinemas featuring Hollywood blockbusters and art-house films in both German and English. *Falter, City* and *Der Standard* (daily newspaper) all contain film listings. Monday is *Kinomontag*, when many seats are discounted. Expect to pay about €8 to €12 for tickets.

Artis International
CINEMA

(Map p60; ☎535 65 70; www.cineplexx.at; 01, Schultergasse 5) Mainstream films in English.

Breitenseer Lichtspiele
CINEMA

(☎982 21 73; 14, Breitenseer Strasse 21) Opened in 1905; still contains the original fittings and plays old B&W classics and independents.

Burg Kino
CINEMA

(Map p60; ☎587 84 06; www.burgkino.at; 01, Opernring 19) English films; has regular screenings of *The Third Man*.

English Cinema Haydn
CINEMA

(Map p72; ☎587 22 62; www.haydnkino.at; 06, Mariahilfer Strasse 57) Features mainstream Hollywood-style films in their original language.

Filmcasino
CINEMA

(Map p72; ☎581 39 00-10; www.filmcasino.at; 05, Margareten Strasse 78) Art-house cinema with a mix of Asian and European independent films.

Österreichische Filmmuseum
CINEMA

(Map p60; ☎533 70 54; www.filmmuseum.at; 01, Augustinerstrasse 1; ☉Sep-Jun) Monthly retrospectives on directors or genres.

Top Kino
CINEMA

(Map p72; ☎208 30 00; www.topkino.at; 06, Rahlgasse 1) Shows European independent films and hosts the Vienna Short Film Festival each May. Also has a great bar.

Votivkino
CINEMA

(Map p70; ☎317 35 71; www.votivkino.at; 09, Währinger Strasse 12) Hollywood and art-house films in their original language.

Shopping

Vienna is one place where the glitz and glamour of shops selling high-end brands stand in stark contrast to some weird and idiosyncratic local stores. Specialities include porcelain, ceramics, handmade dolls, wrought-iron work and leather goods, and there are many shops selling *Briefmarken* (stamps), *Münze* (coins) and *Altwaren* (secondhand odds and ends).

The bustling Mariahilfer Strasse and Kärntner Strasse are lined with global high-street names and chain stores. Off Mariahilfer Strasse in Mariahilf itself and in Neubau are where some of the more interesting shops are located. Otto-Bauer-Gasse is a freak's paradise, while Neubaugasse is good for secondhand hunters and collectors, and Josefstädter Strasse is an old-fashioned shopping street filled with quaint shops selling anything from flowers to tea. Not to be forgotten, too, is the Flohmarkt (see the boxed text, p105).

gabarage upcycling design
FURNITURE, ACCESORIES

(Map p72; ☎585 76 32 20; 04, Schleifmühlgasse 6; www.gabarage.at; ☉10am-6pm Mon-Fri, to 3pm Sat) Recycled design, ecology and social responsibility are the mottoes at gabarage upcycling design. Old sealing rings become earrings, former outdoor rubbish bins get a new life as tables and chairs, advertising tarpaulins morph into carrying bags and

---

ALTWAREN AUCTIONS

Although you may never dream of dropping into Sotheby's for a quick browse, when in Vienna it seems perfectly natural to inspect what's on offer at the **Dorotheum** (Map p60; ☎515 60-0; www.dorotheum.com; 01, Dorotheergasse 17). Among the largest auction houses in Europe, this is the apex of Vienna's *Altwaren*-consumer culture, the Flohmarkt's wealthy uncle. Something between a museum and the fanciest car-boot sale you ever saw, the rooms are filled with everything from antique toys and tableware to autographs, antique guns and Old Masters paintings.

The stock changes weekly, and not everything is priced sky-high – there are also affordable household ornaments up for grabs. On the 2nd floor is the Freier Verkauf section, a massive antique gallery where you can buy on the spot at marked prices.

Auction proceedings are fun to watch even if you don't intend to buy, and scheduled dates for auctions and viewings are available online (or at the ground-floor reception). If you lack the confidence to bid, you can commission an agent to do it for you. The hammer price usually excludes VAT; you'll have to pay this, but you may be able to claim it back later.

fused ring binders reappear as recliners. Humans also receive a second shot at a new life: after completing substance-abuse therapy, former addicts receive jobs plus one year's training in various skills through gabarage's own occupational-therapy program.

Wie Wien
ACCESSORIES, GIFTS

(Map p72; ☎699 113 49 33 8; www.wiewien.at; 05, Kettenbrückegasse 5; ◷2-7pm Mon-Fri, 11am-6pm Sat) A Vienna concept store like no other – each piece in the shop represents the city in some way, from delicate ceramics with a Riesenrad stencilled upon them, to colouring books filled with Vienna scenes to whimsical buttons and T-shirts depicting the Naschmarkt, the Stephansdom, and other landmarks.

Das Studio
FASHION

(Map p72; ☎941 11 41; www.das-studio.at; 07, Kirchengasse 17; ◷noon-7pm Tue-Fri, 11am-5pm Sat; ◻49, ◻13A) This hub for the young Viennese fashion community in dynamic Kirchengasse includes collections by Igor Zeus, Monikova, Milch, Shinyblink and the Fairtrade label Göttin des Glücks, including the label's creative sock dress and shirt (created with repurposed socks sewn together to form remarkably stylish attire).

Unger und Klein
WINE

(Map p60; ☎532 13 23; www.ungerundklein.at; 01, Gölsdorfgasse 2; ◷3pm-midnight Mon-Fri, 5pm-midnight Sat) Unger und Klein's small but knowledgeable wine collection spans the globe, but the majority of its labels come from Europe. The best of Austrian wines – expensive boutique varieties to bargain-bin bottles – is available. It's also a small, laid-back wine bar, with a reasonable selection by the glass – it gets crowded on Friday and Saturday evenings.

Austrian Delights
FOOD

(Map p60; ☎532 16 61; www.austriandelights.at; 01, Judengasse 1a; ◷11am-7pm Mon-Fri, to 6pm Sat) Stocking Austrian-made items by mainly small producers, Delights has regional specialties – fine confectionary, local wine, schnapps and cognac, jams, jellies, chutneys, honey, vinegars and oils – that you can't find anywhere else in the capital. Be sure to check out the sparkling and still Schilcher wines made from Blauer Wildbacher grapes, an acidic but fruity off-pink tipple rarely found outside Austria. Most of it is manufactured by hand or, as the owner says, they're 'items Austrian grandmothers made

through the ages'. Samples of many foods are available to taste.

Manner
CONFECTIONERY

(Map p60; ☎513 70 18; 01, www.manner.com; 01, Stephansplatz 7; ◷10am-6.30pm Sun-Fri, 9.30am-8.30pm Sat) This concept store has been the favourite of Vienna's sweet teeth since 1898. The peachy pink is hard to ignore, but so too are the confectionery delights available in a variety of packaging and combinations.

Loden-Plankl
LEATHER

(Map p60; ☎533 80 32; 01, Michaelerplatz 6) Loden-Plankl is a specialist in *Trachten,* traditional folk wear like *Lederhosen* (leather trousers) and *Dirndln* (traditional women's dresses). It's been in operation for over 170 years, but the prices for quality stuff are less folkloric.

Lomoshop
PHOTOGRAPHY

(Map p72; ☎523 70 16; 07, Museumsplatz 1; ◷11am-7pm Mon-Sun) The first ever shop of the Lomographic Society (www.lomography.com) is in MuseumsQuartier. Lomo is a world-wide cult and the Lomoshop is considered its heart. There's all manner of Lomo cameras, gadgets and accessories for sale; an original Russian-made Lomo will set you back around €160, and you can get single-use disposable Lomo cameras for €14. There's also a wall full of Lomo photos on display, for inspiration.

Wein & Co
WINE

(Map p60; ☎535 09 16; www.weinco.at, in German; 01, Jasomirgottstrasse 3-5; ◷10am-2am Mon-Sat, 11am-midnight Sun) With a wide selection of quality European and New World wines, and a huge variety of local bottles, Wein & Co is probably your best bet for wine shopping – you should be able to pick up a bargain, as the specials here are always great. You can also buy cigars, and the wine bar has a terrace with a view of Stephansdom (try 'Happy Sunday', when all glasses are half-price 11am to 4pm). Seven other Wein & Co shops are scattered around town.

Woka
PORCELAIN

(Map p60; ☎513 29 12; www.woka.at; 01, Singerstrasse 16) Accurate recreations of Wiener Werkstätte lamps are the hallmark of Woka, using designs from the likes of Adolf Loos, Koloman Moser and Josef Hoffmann.

J&L LobmeyrVienna
PORCELAIN

(Map p60; ☎512 05 08; www.lobmeyr.com; 01, Kärntner Strasse 26) Around since the late

The atmospheric **Flohmarkt** (flea market; Map p72; O5, Kettenbrückengasse; ☉dawn-4pm Sat), in the mould of an Eastern European market, shouldn't be missed, with goods piled up in apparent chaos on the walkway. You can find anything you want (and everything you don't want): books, clothes, records, ancient electrical goods, old postcards, ornaments, carpets...you name it. Bargain for prices here.

From around the middle of November, *Christkindlmärkte* (Christmas markets) start to pop up all over Vienna. Ranging from kitsch to quaint in style and atmosphere, the markets all have a few things in common: plenty of people, loads of Christmas gifts to purchase, mugs of *Glühwein* and hotplates loaded with *Kartoffelpuffer* (hot potato patties) and *Maroni* (roasted chestnuts). Most close a day or two before Christmas Day. Some of the best:

Freyung market (Map p60) Austrian arts and crafts and an old-world feel.

Heiligenkreuzerhof market (Map p60) Oft-forgotten market which is arguably the most authentic and quaint of all the *Christkindlmärkte*.

Karlsplatz market (Map p76) Mainly sells arty gifts and is situated close to the Karlskirche.

Rathausplatz market (Map p60) Easily the biggest and most touristy Christmas market in Vienna, held on the square in front of the Rathaus. Most of the Christmas gifts on sale are kitschy beyond belief, unfortunately.

Schönbrunn market (Map p79) Circle of upmarket stalls, loads of events for the kids and daily classical concerts at 6pm (more on weekends).

Spittelberg market (Map p72) Traditional market occupying the charming cobblestone streets of the Spittelberg quarter. Stalls sell quality arts and crafts, but not at the cheapest prices.

19th century and supplying the imperial court with glassware, Lobmeyr now focuses on Werkstätten pieces.

Altmann & Kühne CONFECTIONERY (Map p60; ☎533 09 27; 01, Graben 30) Altmann & Kühne have been producing its handmade bonbons for over 100 years using a well-kept secret recipe. The packaging is designed by Wiener Werkstätten.

Information

Emergency

Police station (☎313 10; 01, Deutschmeisterplatz 3; ☉24hr)

ViennaMed hotline (☎513 9595; ☉24hr) Information in English and German on local doctors.

Women's Emergency Line (Frauennotruf; ☎71 719; ☉24hr)

Media

For gay-specific publications, see the boxed text, p99.

Falter (www.falter.at, in German) Weekly magazine; best resource for political commentary and entertainment listings in every genre imaginable.

Medical Services

If you require a *Zahnarzt* (dentist) after hours, call ☎512 20 78 (recorded message in German only); likewise if you need an *Apotheken* (pharmacy) outside shop hours, dial ☎1550 (in German only). The following *Krankenhäuser* (hospitals) have emergency rooms open 24 hours a day, seven days a week.

Allgemeines Krankenhaus (Map p70; ☎404 00; 09, Währinger Gürtel 18-20)

Hanusch-Krankenhaus (☎910 21-0; 14, Heinrich-Collin-Strasse 30)

Lorenz Böhler Unfallkrankenhaus (☎331 10; 20, Donaueschingenstrasse 13)

Unfallkrankenhaus Meidling (☎601 50-0; 12, Kundratstrasse 37)

Money

Banks and currency-exchange offices are located around town, but compare commission rates before changing money. *Bankomats* (ATMs) are found everywhere, including at the train stations and airport; most shut down at midnight.

Post

Franz-Josefs-Bahnhof Post Office (☎0577 677 1090; 09, Althanstrasse 10; ☉7am-8pm Mon-Fri, 9am-2pm Sat & Sun)

WANT MORE?

For in-depth information, reviews and recommendations at your fingertips, head to the Apple App Store to purchase Lonely Planet's *Vienna City Guide* iPhone app.

Alternatively, head to Lonely Planet (www.lonelyplanet.com/austria/vienna) for planning advice, author recommendations, traveller reviews and insider tips.

Main post office (Map p60; ☎0577 677 1010; www.post.at; 01, Fleischmarkt 19; ☉6am-10pm)

Tourist Information

Airport Information Office (☉6am-11pm) Located in the arrivals hall.

Jugendinfo (Map p60; ☎1799; www.jugend infowien.at; 01, Babenbergerstrasse 1; ☉noon-7pm Mon-Sat) Tailored to ages 14 to 26; tickets for a variety of events at reduced rates and tips on the young alternative scene in Vienna.

Tourist Info Wien (Map p60; ☎24 555; www .wien.info; 01, Albertinaplatz; ☉9am-7pm) Vienna's main tourist office, with a ticket agency, hotel-booking service, free maps and every brochure you could ever want.

WienXtra-Kinderinfo (Map p60; ☎4000 84 400; www.kinderinfowien.at; 07, Museumsplatz 1; ☉2-7pm Tue-Thu, 10am-5pm Fri & Sat) This child-friendly tourist office has loads of information on kids' activities and a small indoor playground.

Websites

About Vienna (www.aboutvienna.org) General website with cultural and sightseeing information.

City of Vienna (www.wien.gv.at) Comprehensive government-run website.

Falter (www.falter.at, in German) Online version of the ever-popular *Falter* magazine.

Vienna Online (www.vienna.at, in German) Site with info on parties, festivals and news.

Vienna Tourist Board (www.wien.info) One of the first ports of call for any visitor.

❶ Getting There & Away
Air

Vienna is the main centre in Austria for international flights. Flying domestic routes offers few benefits over trains. Although there are frequent flights to Graz, Klagenfurt, Salzburg and Linz with Austrian Airlines from Vienna, Innsbruck in Tyrol is the one place where flying (one hour, five times daily) is considerably faster than the train. Book early for the cheapest fares.

Boat

Steamers head west (mostly from Krems – see p112) and fast hydrofoils head east – see p415 and p115.

Bus

Vienna currently has no central bus station and national Bundesbuses arrive and depart from several different locations, depending on the destination. Bus lines serving Vienna include **Eurolines** (www.eurolines.com).

Train

Vienna is one of central Europe's man rail hubs. **Österreichische Bundesbahnen** (ÖBB; Austrian Federal Railway; ☎05 17 17; www.oebb.at) is the main operator. There are direct services and connections to many European cities. For train times and fares, see p414.

Vienna has multiple train stations. At press time, a massive construction project was in progress at **Südbahnhof** (see the boxed text, p415). Essentially, the station is shut but an eastern section has been set up as a temporary station called the **Südbahnhof Ostbahn**; this serves some regional trains to/from the east, including Bratislava. All long-distance trains are being rerouted among the rest of Vienna's train stations.

Westbahnhof is also undergoing major renovation; at press time a provisional station had been created so that the station could remain in operation. The revamped station is slated to open in late 2011. After the new **Hauptbahnhof** opens, the Westbahnhof will only handle regional trains.

Further stations include **Franz-Josefs-Bahnhof** (north of the centre; handles trains to/from the Danube Valley), **Wien Mitte**, **Wien Nord** and **Wien Meidling** (Meidling-Philadelphiabrücke, not Meidling Hauptstrasse; Meidling-Philadelphiabrücke is currently getting lots of trains, but this will change with the opening of the Hauptbahnhof).

❶ Getting Around
To/From the Airport

A standard taxi to/from central Vienna costs roughly €35 to €37.

Bus Link (☎05 17 17; www.postbus.at) Fares are €6/11 one-way/return (€3/5.50 for children aged six to 15; children under six ride free). The bus runs from Westbahnhof between 5am and 11pm, from Meidling between 5.15am and 11.15pm, from Schwedenplatz between 5am and 11.30pm, and from UNO City between 6.38am and 6.38pm, every 30 minutes. The

Westbahnhof service calls in at Wien Meidling station.

C&K Airport Service (☎444 44; www.ck-airportservice.at) This car service is a better, cheaper option than a taxi as its rates are fixed (€33 one way for up to four people). On arrival at the airport, head to its stand to the left of the exit hall; when leaving Vienna, call ahead to make a reservation.

City Airport Train (CAT; ☎252 50; www.cityairporttrain.com) Return fare is €18 (€16 if booked online; children under 15 ride free). Departs from Wien-Mitte every 30 minutes from 5.38am to 11.08pm. Luggage check-in facilities and a boarding card–issuing service.

Schnellbahn 7 (☎05 17 17; www.oebb.at) Cheapest way to get to the airport (one-way fare is €3.60; tickets are valid for one hour and include transfer to connecting city transport). Departs from Wien Nord and Floridsdorf every 30 minutes between 4.32am and 9.56pm Monday to Saturday; passes through Wien-Mitte.

Bicycle

Cycling is an excellent way to get around and explore the city – over 800km of cycle tracks crisscross the capital. Popular cycling areas include the 7km path around the Ringstrasse, the Donauinsel, the Prater and along the Donaukanal. There are a number of options for keen cyclists.

Over 60 **Vienna City Bike** (☎0810-50 05 00; www.citybikewien.at, in German) stands are scattered throughout the city. A credit card is required to rent bikes – just swipe your card in the machine and follow the instructions (in a number of languages). Rental is free for the first hour, €1 for the second, €2 for the third and €4 for four or more hours. Keep in mind that these bikes are mainly for use as an alternative to transport (unless you bring your own bike chain, they can only be locked up at a bike station). A lost bike will set you back €600.

Car & Motorcycle

Due to a system of one-way streets and expensive parking, you're better off using Vienna's excellent public transport. If you do plan to drive in the city, take special care of the trams; they always have priority and vehicles must wait behind trams when they stop to pick up or set down passengers.

Public Transport

Vienna has an efficient, unified public-transport network. Flat-fare tickets are valid for trains, trams, buses, the underground (U-Bahn) and the S-Bahn regional trains. Services are frequent

and you rarely have to wait more than 10 minutes. Sunday through Thursday, public transport starts around 5am or 6am; buses (with the exception of night buses) and trams finish between 11pm and midnight and S-Bahn and U-Bahn services between 12.30am and 1am. On Friday and Saturday nights the U-Bahn runs through the following morning at a reduced schedule. Free maps and information pamphlets are available from **Wiener Linien** (☎7909-100; www.wienerlinien.at, in German).

Tickets and passes can be purchased at U-Bahn stations and in *Tabakladen*. Once bought, tickets need to be validated before starting your journey (except for weekly and monthly tickets); look for small blue boxes at the entrance to U-Bahn stations and on buses and trams. It's an honour system and ticket inspection is infrequent, but if you're caught without a ticket you'll be fined €62, no exceptions.

Single Ticket (*Einzelfahrschein;* €1.80) Good for one journey, with line changes; costs €2.20 if purchased on trams and buses (correct change required).

Strip Ticket (*Streifenkarte;* €7.20) Gives you four single tickets on one strip.

24-Hour Ticket (*24 Stunden Wien-Karte;* €5.70) Offers 24-hour unlimited travel from time of validation.

48-Hour Ticket (*48 Stunden Wien-Karte;* €10) Offers 48-hour unlimited travel from time of validation.

72-Hour Ticket (*72 Stunden Wien-Karte;* €13.60) Offers 72-hour unlimited travel from time of validation.

Eight-Day Ticket (*8-Tage-Karte;* €28.80) Valid for eight days, but not necessarily eight consecutive days; punch the card as and when you need it.

Weekly Ticket (*Wochenkarte;* €14) Valid Monday through Sunday only.

Monthly Ticket (*Monatskarte;* €49.50) Valid from the first of the month to the last day of the month.

Taxi & Pedal Taxi

Taxis are reliable and relatively cheap by Western European standards. City journeys are metered; flag fall costs roughly €2.60 from 6am to 11pm Monday to Saturday and €2.70 any other time, plus a small per-kilometre fee. A small tip is expected; add about 10% to the fare. Taxis are easily found at train stations and taxi stands all over the city, or just flag them down in the street. To order one call ☎31 300, 60 160 or 40 100. Few accept credit cards.

Lower Austria

Best Places to Eat

» Filmbar im Kesselhaus (p113)

» Mörwald Kloster Und (p113)

» Restaurant zur Traube (p115)

» Restaurant Loibnerhof (p117)

» Brod (p135)

Best Places to Stay

» Restaurant & Hotel Schloss Grafenegg (p115)

» Arte Hotel Krems (p112)

» Hotel Schloss Dürnstein (p116)

» Hotel Nibelungenhof (p121)

» Panorama Hotel Wagner (p136)

Why Go?

Surrounding Vienna on all sides, Lower Austria is a cradle of Austrian culture. The region offers visitors one of the country's most lively cultural landscapes, a strong range of outdoor activities and at Carnuntum a glimpse into the age of the Romans.

The world-renowned Danube River (Donau) and its valley is a place of magnificent natural beauty and cultural achievement. The Wachau, which stretches between Melk and Krems an der Donau, is the prettiest section and truly a European highlight for its wines, castles, abbeys and medieval villages.

The north is an often neglected region of rich pastures, forested glens and pretty vineyards set upon gentle, rolling hills, lending itself to day trips from Vienna and touring. The region directly surrounding Vienna in the west and south forms the Wienerwald (Vienna Woods), and further southwest the mountains are ideal for hikes or riding the world-famous Semmeringbahn (Semmering Railway).

When to Go

The best time to visit Lower Austria is during the April to October warm season, when the Wachau is often bathed in a soft light and you can make the most of the Danube River and its sights and activities. The shoulder season periods (April to May and September to October) are quieter. Autumn is the best time to enjoy wine in the Wachau, and from 11 November (St Martin's Day) each year semifermented young wine is sold in open-topped bottles. Between November and April many sights are closed, but winter sport in the mountains around Semmering comes into its own.

Wine Experiences

The predominantly white wines of the Wachau complement perfectly the region's magnificent landscapes and excellent local foods. One way to enjoy the fruits of the vineyards is to visit a *Heuriger* (vineyard wine tavern). The *Heurigen* open on a rotating basis, and tourist offices (and many hotels) stock a local calendar listing the opening dates for each one. A highlight of the wine calendar is 11 November (St Martin's Day), when the new wine, known as *Sturm,* is traditionally released and drunk semifermented.

The **Weinstrasse Kamptal** (Kamptal Wine Rd), running north from Krems through the Kamp Valley, is more low key than the Wachau and has lots of vineyards. In Krems the **Weingut der Stadt Krems** (p112) also has tastings; in Langenlois at the **Loisium Weinwelt** (p123) you can walk through ancient cellars or take wine treatments; and **Schloss Grafenegg** (p115) has wine tastings at its Vinothegg wine bar. For restaurants, try inexpensive **Jell** (p113) in Krems or the more upmarket **Mörwald Kloster Und** (p113) and **Restaurant zur Traube** (p115).

DON'T MISS

The **Wachau**, the section of the Danube Valley between Krems an der Donau and Melk, is one of the world's great cultural landscapes. A ride or drive along the valley will take you past castle ruins, baroque churches and some stunning scenery.

Stift Melk, at the western end of the Wachau, is easily the most spectacular and celebrated of the abbeys in this Unesco Cultural Heritage region. It dates back to the 11th century and was later reshaped into a baroque masterpiece, with frescoes by Paul Troger and Johann Michael Rottmayr. A nice way to get there is by bicycle or on one of the regular ferries from Krems.

Hikes & Rides

» **Wachau** Cycling a stretch of the Wachau between Krems and Melk or taking a Danube boat trip is a great way to soak up the scenery.

» **Schneeberg** Lower Austria's highest mountain can be hiked or enjoyed on a ride on the cogwheel railway.

» **Petronell-Carnuntum to Hainburg** Cycling from Petronell-Carnuntum to Hainburg is the best way to take in the Romans.

» **Schlossbergweg** After visiting the ruins of Kuenringerburg, hike the Schlossbergweg to Fesselhütte.

» **Semmeringbahn** The railway can be enjoyed not only from the inside – walking trails abound in the region.

MEDIEVAL & LOW KEY

Drosendorf (p122), a far-flung village with Austria's only intact medieval town wall, and the Nationalpark Thayatal (p123), are two low-key places where you can escape the summer crowds, right on the Czech border.

Best Concert Location

The best place to enjoy a concert in Lower Austria is in the parks and gardens of **Schloss Grafenegg** (www.grafenegg.at; p115). A 15-metre Cloud Tower open-air stage is situated in the grounds, with seating for over 1700 spectators.

Transport Planning

Use the **ÖBB** (www.oebb.at) and **Postbus** (www.postbus.at) websites to plan your travel. Bus services often reduce to a trickle or dry up altogether on a Sunday, so plan travelling to more remote places during the week.

Resources

» Das Land Niederösterreich (www.noe.gv.at) Facts and figures.

» Lower Austria (www.lower-austria.info) Food, culture and outdoor themes.

» Schneebergbahn (www.schneebergbahn.at) Cogwheel railway.

Lower Austria Highlights

1 Exploring the historic Wachau in the **Danube Valley** (p118)

2 Meandering through **Stift Melk** (p120), a magnificent baroque monastery on the banks of the Danube at Melk

3 Indulging in the rustic pleasures of wine and *Wurst* in one of the *Heurigen* in **Krems an der Donau** (p113)

4 Riding the **Semmeringbahn** (p136), a remarkable engineering feat and Unesco World Heritage site

5 Hiking or catching the train up **Schneeberg** (p137), Lower Austria's highest peak

6 Exploring the Roman ruins on a bicycle in and around **Carnuntum** (p128)

7 Sampling wine and gourmet delights on a **Waldviertel** road trip (p123)

❶ Getting There & Around

Much of Lower Austria has excellent autobahn, rail and bus connections to the rest of the country. Travelling through the province can be done mostly by rail, but the Waldviertel north of the Danube and the Mostviertel south of the Danube have limited train connections. Here it's better to have your own car or bicycle, or use buses.

THE DANUBE VALLEY

The Danube, which enters Lower Austria from the west near Ybbs and exits in the east near Bratislava, Slovakia's capital, carves a picturesque path through the province's hills and fields. Austria's most spectacular section of the Danube is the dramatic stretch of river between Krems an der Donau and Melk, known as the Wachau. Here the landscape is characterised by vineyards, forested slopes, wine-producing villages and imposing fortresses at nearly every bend. The Wachau is today a Unesco World Heritage site, due to its harmonious blend of natural and cultural beauty.

Tourismusverband Wachau Nibelungengau (☑02713-300 60 60; www.wachau.at; Schlossgasse 3, Spitz an der Donau; ☺9am-4.30pm Mon-Thu, to 2.30pm Fri) can help with information on the Wachau and its surrounds.

❶ Getting Around

BICYCLE

A wonderfully flat cycle path runs along both sides of the Danube between Vienna and Melk, passing through Krems, Dürnstein, Weissenkirchen and Spitz on the northern bank. Many hotels and pensions (B&Bs) are geared towards cyclists and most towns have at least one bike-rental shop. For more information, pick up a free copy of *The Donauradweg – Von Passau bis Bratislava* (from tourist offices and some hotels), which provides details of distances, hotels and information offices along the route.

BOAT

A popular way of exploring the region is by boat, particularly between Krems and Melk; it's also possible to travel from Passau (in Germany) to Vienna (see p162 for details). The most convenient time to take a boat trip on the Danube is between May and September, when boat companies operate on a summer schedule. Children receive a 50% discount.

Brandner (☑07433-25 90-21; www.brandner. at; Ufer 50, Wallsee) Services the Krems–Melk route (one way/return €20/25) one to two times daily from mid-April to late October; stops include Spitz.

Many towns in Lower Austria are part of a bike hire network called **Leihradl**. After registering using Visa, Master-Card or AMEX credit cards (either by calling the hotline on ☑02742-229 901 or on the website www.leihradl.at, in German), a refunded €1 is deducted from your card and you can begin renting bicycles for €1/5 per hour/24 hours. It's easy:

» Choose a bike at a bicycle station

» Call the hotline and tell them the identification number on the bike

» Open the lock using the code you are given (note it down)

» Return the bike to any bicycle station, lock it and call the hotline to sign off

DDSG Blue Danube (☑01-588 80; www. ddsg-blue-danube.at; 01, Handelskai 265, Vienna) Operates boats between Krems and Melk, stopping in at Dürnstein and Spitz, from April to October. DDSG boats leave Krems at 10.15am all season, and from late April to September two extra sailings depart at 1pm and 3.45pm. Return sailings from Melk are at 1.50pm the whole season, and 11am and 4.15pm from late April to September (one way/return €20/25, three hours upstream, 1¾ hours downstream). Bikes can be taken on board all boats for free.

CAR

The roads on both sides of the Danube between Krems and Melk, where the B3 and the B33 hug the contours of the river, lend themselves well to touring. Vehicle bridges cross the river at Krems, Melk, Pöchlarn and Ybbs.

TRAIN

Direct trains from Franz-Josefs-Bahnhof in Vienna to Krems are the easiest way into the valley. For Dürnstein (Dürnstein-Oberloiben; €16, 1¼ hours, 15 daily) from Franz-Josefs-Bahnhof you need to change at Krems. Trains from Vienna's Westbahnhof (€16, 1¼ hours, 11 daily) direct to Melk go via St Pölton and don't follow the Danube Valley. From Krems to Melk (€3.60, one hour, three to six daily) a useful integrated rail connection with a change to bus in Spitz works best if you leave early morning. A rail track runs along the Danube's northern bank but while it's a scenic trip, it's slow.

Krems an der Donau

☎02732 / POP 23,800

Krems an der Donau is the prettiest of the larger towns on the Danube and marks the beginning of the Wachau. It has a small university and some good eating and drinking, and also offers a very attractive historical aspect. Resting on the northern bank of the Danube, surrounded by terraced vineyards, it has been a centre of the wine trade for most of its history.

Krems has three parts: Krems to the east, the smaller settlement of Stein (formerly a separate town) to the west, and the connecting suburb of Und. Hence the local witticism: *Krems und Stein sind drei Städte* (Krems and Stein are three towns).

◉ Sights & Activities

TOP CHOICE Kunsthalle   ART GALLERY
(www.kunsthalle.at; Franz-Zeller-Platz 3; adult/child/family €9/3.50/18, combined ticket for 3 Kunstmeile museums €11; ☉10am-6pm Apr-Oct, to 5pm Nov-Mar) Situated on the **Kunstmeile** (Art Mile), the section of Steiner Landstrasse with a collection of museums and space for art and media, the Kunsthalle is the flagship gallery and has small but excellent changing exhibitions on artists and themes.

Karikaturmuseum   MUSEUM
(www.karikaturmuseum.at, in German; Steiner Landstrasse 3a; adult/child/family €9/3.50/18; ☉10am-6pm Apr-Oct, to 5pm Nov-Mar) The Caricature Museum opposite the Kunsthalle features changing exhibitions and a large permanent collection of caricatures of prominent Austrian and international figures.

Weinstadt Museum   MUSEUM
(www.weinstadtmuseum.at; Körnermarkt 14; adult/child €4/2; ☉10am-6pm Wed-Sat, Sun 1-6pm Mar-Nov) Housed in a former Dominican monastery, the 'Wine Town' Museum has collections of religious and modern art (including works by Kremser Schmidt,

who painted the frescoes in Pfarrkirche St Veit), as well as winemaking artefacts.

Pfarrkirche St Veit   CHURCH
(Pfarrplatz 5; ☉dawn-dusk) This baroque parish church was resurrected from earlier Gothic and Romanesque forms. Its colourful frescoes are by Martin Johann Schmidt, an 18th-century local artist who was also known as Kremser Schmidt and occupied a house from 1756 near the Linzer Tor in Stein.

Piaristenkirche   CHURCH
(Frauenbergplatz; ☉dawn-dusk) Gothic church with vaulting, huge windows and baroque altars.

Weingut der Stadt Krems   WINE TASTING
(Stadtgraben 11; ☉9am-noon & 1-5pm Mon-Sat) City-owned vineyard yielding 200,000 bottles per year (90% is Grüner Veltliner and Riesling), some of which you can sample and buy.

⌑ Sleeping

Krems has plenty of places but book ahead in summer. Stein has a good selection of private rooms.

TOP CHOICE Arte Hotel Krems   HOTEL €€
(☎711 23; www.arte-hotel.at, in German; Dr-Karl-Dorrek-Strasse 23; s €89-105; d €128-162; P⊛@ⓦ) The large, well-styled rooms at this comfortable new art hotel close to the university have bright designs and a clever use of colour and natural lighting. The bathrooms are open plan. Rooms have LAN (bring your network cable), the lobby has wi-fi and the entire hotel is nonsmoking. There's a separately owned wellness studio in the building, and a grill restaurant (mains €7.50 to €29) in the same complex.

Hotel Unter den Linden   HOTEL €€
(☎821 15; www.udl.at; Schillerstrasse 5; s €50, d €74-98; P⊛@ⓦ) This big, yellow, family-run hotel has knowledgeable and helpful owners, bright comfortable rooms and a convenient location in Krems itself. Book ahead as

---

DON'T MISS

WALKING KREMS

A walk through the cobblestone streets of Krems and Stein, especially at night, is one of the delights of a visit. Some of the most atmospheric parts to explore are on and behind **Schürerplatz** and **Rathausplatz** in Stein (don't miss these two wonderful squares), dominated by the baroque Mazzettihaus and the 18th-century Steiner Rathaus respectively; here you could be forgiven for thinking you had stumbled upon an isolated Adriatic village. The tourist office has a useful multilingual **walk-by-numbers guide** to sights.

it gets bus groups and is arguably the best deal in town.

Gourmet-Hotel Am Förthof
HOTEL €€

(☑833 45; www.hotel-foerthof.at; Förthofer Donaulände 8; s €60-100, d €100-150; P⊜@⑦⑨) A country-style mansion about 500m west of Stein, combining cosy rooms, romantic ambience, a pretty garden and a superb restaurant (mains €16 to €22, menus €22 to €45) serving gourmet and seasonal menus as well as delicious Austrian classics such as *Tafelspitz* (boiled beef with radish sauce).

Gästehaus Einzinger
GUESTHOUSE €

(☑823 16; www.gaestehaus-einzinger.at, in German; Steiner Landstrasse 82; s €38, d €58-70; ⑦) The courtyard in this 16th-century guesthouse will blow away even the most history-hardened: blackbirds buzz and chirp, budgies taunt them from a cage, and one portico after another opens up around a courtyard spilling with foliage. Rooms are a little basic but some have views to night-lit Stift Göttweig.

ÖAMTC Donaupark Camping
CAMPGROUND €

(☑844 55; donaucampingkrems@aon.at; Wiedengasse 7; camp sites per adult/child/car/tent €4/2.70/3.90/4.60; ⊙Easter–mid-Oct; P) This camp site alongside the Danube rents bicycles for €6.50 per day.

Jugendherberge
HOSTEL €

(☑834 52; oejhv.noe.krems@aon.at; Ringstrasse 77; dm €18; ⊙Apr-Oct; P⊜⊛) This popular HI hostel close to the tourist office is well geared for cyclists; it features a climbing wall, a garage for bicycles and packed lunches.

Hotel Alte Poste
HOTEL €

(☑822 76; www.altepost-krems.at, in German; Obere Landstrasse 32; s €30-59, d €58-79; P) In a historic 500-year-old building, this friendly guesthouse has comfortable rooms, an enchanting courtyard and a good traditional restaurant.

Hotel-Garni Schauhuber
HOTEL €€

(☑851 69; www.gaestehaus-freisleben.at, in German; Steiner Landstrasse 16; s/d €40/80; ⊜⑦) The Schauhuber is bright and tastefully furnished, with sparkling tiled surfaces, large rooms and a small table in each where you can catch up on writing your travel journal.

✖ Eating & Drinking

You'll find a **Spar** (Obere Landstrasse 15) supermarket in Krems, and a second **Spar** (Schürerplatz) in Stein. Don't omit a *Heuriger* visit; most are out of the centre and provide an authentic eating and drinking experience. They're only open for two- or three-week bursts during the year; get the schedule from the tourist office.

⌐TOP⌐ CHOICE⌐ Filmbar im Kesselhaus
INTERNATIONAL €

(www.filmbar.at, in German; Dr-Karl-Dorreck-Strasse 30; mains €5-10; ⊙10am-2.30pm Mon & Tue, to midnight Wed-Sun; ⑦) This sleek student restaurant and bar is the hub of eating and drinking activity on the university campus; it also shows art-house films. Some dishes feature organic ingredients, and two-/three-course lunches cost €6.90/7.90.

⌐TOP⌐ CHOICE⌐ Mörwald Kloster Und
AUSTRIAN €€

(☑704 930; www.moerwald.at; Undstrasse 6; mains €20-33, 5-course menu €85, 3-course lunch €25; ⊙Tue-Sat; ⊜) Mörwald is the most central of a crop of restaurants run by Toni Mörwald; it offers exquisite delights ranging from roast pigeon breast to beef, poultry and fish dishes with French touches. A lovely yard and an impressive wine selection round off one of the best restaurants in the Wachau.

Jell
AUSTRIAN €€

(www.amon-jell.at, in German; Hoher Markt 8-9; mains €12-22; ⊙lunch & dinner Tue-Fri, lunch Sat & Sun) Occupying a gorgeous stone house, Jell is hard to beat for a rustic atmosphere and fine wine from its own vineyard. Its friendly staff also adds to a great regional experience; located just east of Pfarrkirche St Veit.

Sm.kunst.genuss
AUSTRIAN €

(www.moerwald.at; Steiner Landstrasse 3; pasta & salads €3.50-11, mains €12.50-15.50; ⊙9am-6pm) Another eatery in the Toni Mörwald stable, this one's excellent for lunch (some dishes are organic), salads or a quick coffee alongside the Kunsthalle.

Gasthaus zum Elefanten
AUSTRIAN €

(www.zum-elefanten.at, in German; Schürerplatz 10; mains €10.50-16.50; ⊙lunch & dinner Wed-Sat, lunch Sun) Situated on a romantic baroque town square, the 'Elephant' serves classics with an upmarket edge in a cosy atmosphere indoors or at outdoor tables.

Piano
BAR

(www.piano-krems.at; Steiner Landstrasse 21; ⊙5pm-2am Mon-Thu, to 3am Fri & Sat, to midnight Sun) A crossover crowd of students, young workers and mellow jazz types gather at this lively and off-beat pub. It does a couple of local sausage snacks to go with its great

Krems an der Donau

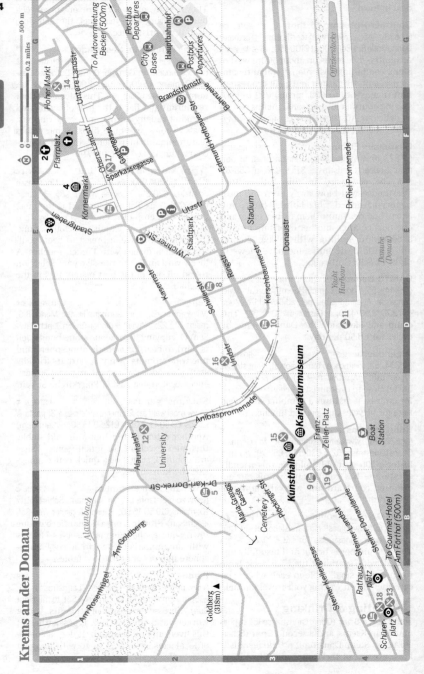

0   500 m
0   0.2 miles

Krems an der Donau

selection of beer. A few other decent bars and restaurants are on this street.

ℹ️ Information

Krems Tourismus (📞826 76; www.krems.info; Utzstrasse 1; ⊙9am-6pm Mon-Fri, 11am-5pm Sat, 11am-4pm Sun, closed Sat & Sun Nov-Apr) Has an excellent walk-by-numbers *Krems Stadtrundgang* (Krems city walk; in German) map with route descriptions. It also stocks a *Heurigen* calendar and culinary guide, and for those with a car or bike a *Weinstrasse Kremstal* map (in German) showing vineyards.

Main post office (Brandströmstrasse 4-6) Near the *Hauptbahnhof* (main train station).

ℹ️ Getting There & Around

BICYCLE Bicycles can be hired at ÖAMTC Donau Camping and some hotels.

BOAT The river station is near Donaustrasse, about 2km west of the train station.

CAR Autovermietung Becker (📞82433; www.rent.becker.at, in German; Wachauer Strasse 30) rents cars from €59 per day.

TRAIN & BUS Frequent daily trains connect Krems with Vienna's Franz-Josefs-Bahnhof (€13.90, one hour). The quickest way to Melk is by train to Spitz, continuing by bus (€7.30, one hour, five times daily).

Around Krems

STIFT GÖTTWEIG

Brooding from its hilltop opposite Krems, **Stift Göttweig** (Göttweig Abbey; 📞02732-85581-231; Furth bei Göttweig; adult/child/family €7/3.50/15; ⊙9am-6pm) was founded in 1083 and restored after a devastating fire in the early 18th century. Aside from the grand view back across the Danube Valley from its garden terrace and restaurant, the abbey's highlights include the **Imperial Staircase**, with a heavenly ceiling fresco painted by Paul Troger in 1739, and the over-the-top baroque interior of the **Stiftskirche** (Abbey Church), with a Kremser Schmidt work in the crypt. Guided tours at 11am and 3pm take in the abbey's Imperial Wing (per person €2); the church can be viewed without a tour.

Only two direct buses on weekdays travel between Krems' train station and Göttweig (€1.80, 25 minutes). The train is another possibility, but it's a steep walk uphill from the Klein Wien station (€2, 10 minutes, every two hours).

SCHLOSS GRAFENEGG

About 10km east of Krems near the road to Tulln is **Schloss Grafenegg** (www.grafenegg.com; Haitzendorf; entry adult/child/family €5/3/7.50; ⊙10am-5pm Tue-Sat, mid-Apr–Sep; 🅿), a castle with the look and feel of an ornate Tudor mansion set in English woods. Built in a revivalist (neo-Gothic) style by Leopold Ernst in the mid-19th century, it is now a venue for exhibitions and concerts but you can explore the interior, which includes a chapel and decadent state rooms. The castle is complemented by the addition of the innovative, modern **Wolkenturm** (Cloud Tower), which is used for concerts in the parkland in fine weather.

The wine bar **Vinothegg** (⊙11am-6pm Tue-Sat, 10am-6pm Sun Mar–mid-Dec) here has over 130 wines from the Kamptal. The castle's manicured gardens are perfect for a picnic, but for fine dining don't pass up **Restaurant & Hotel Schloss Grafenegg** (📞02735-2616-0; www.moerwald.at; Grafenegg 12; s €89-104, d €118-158, 3-/4-course menu €29/37; ⊙10am-10pm Wed-Sun Easter-Dec; 🅿😴🍴), owned by celebrity chef and winemaker Toni Mörwald. Two kilometres away in Feuersbrunn is Mörwald's **Hotel Villa Katharina** (☑02738-229 80; www.moerwald.at; Kleine Zeile 10; s €89-104, d €118-138; **P**🅿︎🛜😊), with its **Restaurant zur Traube** (☑02738-229 80; www.moerwald.at; Kleine Zeile 13-17; mains €16.50-24.50; ☺lunch & dinner, closed Mon-Wed Jul & Aug; **P**😊🅿︎).

To get to Schloss Grafenegg, catch the train to nearby Wagram-Grafenegg (€3.60, 18 minutes, seven to 10 daily) and walk 2km northeast to the castle.

Dürnstein

☑02711 / POP 900

The pretty town of Dürnstein, on a supple curve in the Danube, is not only known for its beautiful buildings but also for the castle above the town where Richard I (the Lionheart) of England was once imprisoned.

◉ Sights

Kuenringerburg   CASTLE

Kuenringerburg, the castle high on the hill above the town, is where Richard the Lionheart was incarcerated from 1192 to 1193. His crime was to have insulted Leopold V; his misfortune was to be recognised despite his disguise when journeying through Austria on his way home from the Holy Lands. His liberty was achieved only upon the payment of an enormous ransom of 35,000kg of silver (which partly funded the building of Wiener Neustadt). It was also here that the singing minstrel Blondel attempted to rescue his sovereign. There's not a lot to see but a heap of rubble, but the view is worth the 15- to 20-minute climb.

ⓘ HIKING FROM DÜRNSTEIN

After visiting the **Kuenringerburg**, where Richard the Lionheart was incarcerated, hike the Schlossbergweg (marked green) from there to **Fesselhütte** (www.fesslhuette.at, in German; Dürsteiner Waldhütten 23; goulash soup €2.30; ☺9.30am-6pm Wed-Sun Easter-Oct), about one hour by foot from the castle, to enjoy sausage, soup or wine at this forest tavern. A road also leads up here from Weissenkirchen.

Chorherrenstift   ABBEY

(Stiftshof; adult/child €2.50/1.50; ☺9am-6pm Apr-Oct) Of the picturesque 16th-century houses and other prominent buildings lining Dürnstein's streets, the meticulously restored Chorherrenstift is the most impressive. It's all that remains of the former Augustinian monastery originally founded in 1410; it received its baroque facelift in the 18th century (overseen by Josef Munggenast, among others). Kremser Schmidt did many of the ceiling and altar paintings. Entry includes access to the porch overlooking the Danube and an exhibition on the Augustinian monks who once ruled the roost here (up until the monastery was dissolved by Joseph II in 1788).

🛏 Sleeping & Eating

The tourist office has a list of private rooms, pensions and *Gasthöfe* (guesthouses) in Dürnstein and neighbouring Oberloiben and Unterloiben.

TOP **Hotel Schloss Dürnstein**
CHOICE

HISTORIC HOTEL €€€

(☑212; www.schloss.at; Dürnstein 2; s €166, d €198-276, apt €355-380; **P**😊🅿︎🛜🚪) This castle (with lift) is the last word in luxury in town and has a high-end restaurant. Most rooms are tastefully furnished with antiques, a massage can be arranged for your arrival, and it has a sauna and steam bath. Stay five nights and you will be treated to a free 'surprise menu' in the terrace restaurant (mains €16 to €30) with staggering views over the river. Stay 10 and you get a night on the house (which might be useful if you happen to be broke by that stage). Wi-fi is in the public areas and costs €7 per day.

Hotel Sänger Blondel   HOTEL €€

(☑253; www.saengerblondel.at; Klosterplatz/Dürnstein 64; s €68, d €86-112; **P**😊@) One of the nicest options in town, this hotel has good-sized rooms furnished in light woods, some with sofas. A couple have views to the Danube and others look out onto the castle or garden. Internet is with a laptop from reception.

Pension Böhmer   PENSION €

(☑239; pension.boehmer@i-one.at; Hauptstrasse 22; s/d €42/62; **P**) This small B&B in the heart of town has comfortable rooms at very reasonable prices.

Richard Löwenherz   HOTEL €€

(☑222; www.richardloewenherz.at; Dürnstein 8; s €96-116, d €166-201, apt €260-320; **P**😊@🚪)

One of the best hotels in town, the 'Lion-heart' has midsized rooms right on the Danube in a former monastery, these days with a lift. The walled garden is superb, and the Austrian restaurant (mains €14 to €23) serves classics.

Restaurant Loibnerhof AUSTRIAN €€
(✆828 90; Unterloiben 7; mains €15-26, 3- & 4-course menu €26-52; ☺Wed-Sun) Situated 1.5km east of Dürnstein in Unterloiben, this family-run restaurant inside a 400-year-old building has a lovely garden where you can enjoy delicious local specialities such as *Kalbsbeuschel* (veal lights).

ℹ Information

The **tourist office** (✆200; www.duernstein. at; Dürnstein Bahnhof; ☺9am-5pm) is near the train station, about five minutes' walk east of Hauptstrasse, the town's main street. The **rathaus** (town hall; ✆219; Hauptstrasse 25; ☺8am-noon & 1-4pm Mon-Fri) also has information.

ℹ Getting There & Away

BOAT Brandner (www.brandner.at; landing station near Chorherrenstift) boats connect Dürnstein with Krems (€10, 20 to 30 minutes) once or twice daily from mid-April to late October. Boats also sail to – but not from – Weissenkirchen (same price and times).

TRAIN Dürnstein's train station is called Dürnstein-Oberloiben, with connections to Krems (€2, 11 minutes, hourly) and Weissenkirchen (€2, seven minutes, hourly).

Weissenkirchen

✆02715 / POP 1450
In Weissenkirchen, 12km from Krems, the main attraction is the pretty hilltop **fortified parish church**, whose front doors are approached along a labyrinth of covered pathways. This Gothic church was built in the 15th century and has a baroque altar and a garden terrace with good views of the Danube. Below the church is the charming Teisenhoferhof arcaded courtyard, with a covered gallery and lashings of flowers and dried corn.

The **Wachau Museum** (Weissenkirchen 32; adult/child/concession €5/2.50/3.50; ☺10am-5pm Tue-Sun Apr-Oct) houses works by artists of the Danube school.

The **Raffelsberger Hof** (✆22 01; www.raffelsbergerhof.at; s €88-95, d €122-138, ste €145-170; ☺Apr-Nov; P☺@☺) is a four-star hotel

in a small but beautifully renovated Renaissance castle.

Weissenkirchen has boat and train connections to Dürnstein.

Spitz & Around

✆02713 / POP 1800
Situated 17km west of Krems on the north bank of the Danube, Spitz is a pleasant town that doesn't get as clogged with visitors as Dürnstein. It has a picturesque old town centre, and offers some good hiking in the surrounding forests and vineyards. To reach the old town, turn left after leaving the station then head right up Marktstrasse to Kirchenplatz.

If the Gothic **parish church** (Kirchenplatz 12; ☺8am-6pm) in Spitz is one too many Danube churches, pick up some maps from the tourist office and hike up to **Burgruine Hinterhaus** (Hinterhaus castle ruin) on the bluff for fantastic views of the valley; other trails run through the forests of **Jauerling Naturpark** (Jauerling Nature Reserve) behind the castle ruin. Hikes offering picturesque views also begin from **Rotes Tor** (Red Gate), a remnant of the town's gates and the last one to be taken by the Swedes in the Thirty Years' War in 1618–48 – it was reputedly red from the blood of battle.

Six kilometres west of Spitz in Mühldorf is the castle and hotel **Burg Oberranna** (✆8221; www.burg-oberranna.at; s/d/apt €85/133/148; P☺☝). Surrounded by woods and overlooking the valley, it is furnished with period pieces and has a refreshing old-worldly feel. Children receive discounts in an apartment.

If you decide to stay in Spitz, the tourist office can help with accommodation, or you can look for signs advertising private rooms. **Hotel Wachauer Hof** (✆2303; www.wachauerhof-spitz.at, in German; Hauptstrasse 15; s/d €47/78; P☺) is very centrally located, with comfortable rooms and a restaurant with outside seating in summer.

The helpful **tourist office** (✆2363; www.spitz-wachau.at, in German; Mittergasse 3a; ☺9am-noon & 1.30-7pm Mon-Sat, 2-6pm Sun) is situated 400m west of the station and has excellent free maps of the town with hiking trails marked.

Trains connect Spitz and Krems (€3.60, 30 minutes, hourly). Bicycles can be rented from the train station through **Wachau Touristik Bernhardt** (✆02713-2222;

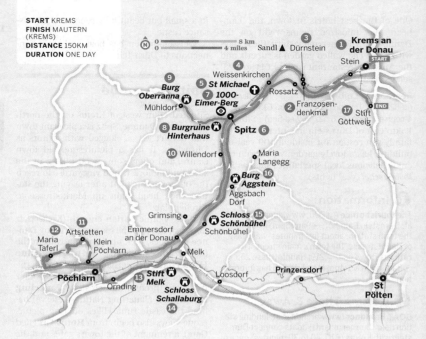

0 ——— 8 km
0 ——— 4 miles

Krems an der Donau ①
Stein
START

Sandl ▲ Dürnstein ③

Weissenkirchen
St Michael ⑤
1000-Eimer-Berg ⑦
Rossatz

Burg Oberranna ⑨
Mühldorf

Burgruine Hinterhaus ⑧
Spitz ⑥

② Franzosen-denkmal
Stift Göttweig ⑰
END

⑩ Willendorf

Maria Langegg

Burg Aggstein ⑯
Aggsbach Dorf

Artstetten ⑪
⑫ Maria Taferl
Klein Pöchlarn

Emmersdorf an der Donau
Grimsing

Schloss Schönbühel ⑮
Schönbühel

Melk

Pöchlarn
Ornding
⑬ **Stift Melk**
Schloss Schallaburg ⑭

Loosdorf

Prinzersdorf

St Pölten

Driving & Cycling Tour
The Danube Valley

❯ This road trip is almost all-weather and needs little preparation. It mostly follows the Danube, taking in towns and sights on a circuit between Krems an der Donau and Maria Taferl on the north bank, and Melk and several castles and ruins on the south bank. The junctions only get tricky around Melk; even if you only have limited experience driving on the right-hand side of the road, these shouldn't present a huge problem. The best time to do the trip is on a Monday or Tuesday, when traffic is light.

From the ① **Krems-Stein roundabout**, take the B3 southwest towards Spitz. About 3km from Krems-Stein you approach the small settlement of Unterloiben, where on the right you can see the ② **Franzosendenk-mal** (French Monument), erected in 1805 to celebrate the victory of Austrian and Russian troops here over Napoleon. Shortly afterwards the lovely town of ③ **Dürnstein**, 6km from Krems, comes into view and you can see the blue-towered Chorherrenstift backed

by Kuenringerburg, the castle where Richard the Lionheart was imprisoned in 1192.

The valley is punctuated by picturesque terraced vineyards as you enter the heart of the Wachau. In ④ **Weissenkirchen**, 12km from Krems, you'll find the pretty fortified parish church on the hilltop. The Wachau Museum here houses work by artists of the Danube school.

A couple of kilometres on, just after Wösendorf, you find the church of ⑤ **St Michael**, in a hamlet with 13 houses. If the kids are along for this ride, now's the time to ask them to count the terracotta hares on the roof of the church (seven, in case they're not reading this!).

Some 17km from Krems, the pretty town of ⑥ **Spitz** swings into view, surrounded by vineyards and lined with quiet, cobblestone streets. There are some good trails leading across hills and into *Heurigen* (wine taverns) here.

Turn right at Spitz onto the B217 (Ottenschläger Strasse). The terraced hill on your right is **7** **1000-Eimer-Berg**, so-named for its reputed ability to yield 1000 buckets of wine each season. On your left, high above the valley opening, is the castle ruin **8** **Burgruine Hinterhaus**. Continue along the B217 to the mill wheel and turn right towards **9** **Burg Oberranna**, 6km west of Spitz in Mühldorf. Surrounded by woods, this castle and hotel overlooking the valley is furnished with period pieces and has a refreshing old-worldly feel.

From here, backtrack down to the B3 and continue the circuit. The valley opens up and on the left, across the Danube, you glimpse the ruins of Burg Aggstein.

10 **Willendorf**, located 21km from Krems, is where a 25,000-year-old figurine of Venus was discovered. The original is today housed in the Naturhistorisches Museum in Vienna. Continuing along the B3, the majestic Stift Melk rises up across the river. There's some decent swimming in the backwaters here if you're game to dip into the Danube.

At Klein Pöchlarn a sign indicates a first turn-off on Artstettner Strasse (L7255), which you can follow for 5km to **11** **Artstetten**, unusual for its many onion domes. From here, the minor road L7257 winds 6.5km through a sweeping green landscape to **12** **Maria Taferl** high above the Danube Valley.

Backtrack 6km down towards the B3. Turn left at the B3 towards Krems and follow the ramp veering off to the left and across the river at the Klein Pöchlarn bridge. Follow the road straight ahead to the B1 (Austria's longest road) and turn left onto this towards Melk.

This first section along the south bank is uninteresting, but it will soon improve. Unless the weather isn't playing along, across the river you should be able to make out Artstetten in the distance, and shortly **13** **Stift Melk**, will rise up ahead in a golden shimmering heap.

From Stift Melk, a 7km detour leads south to the splendid Renaissance castle of **14** **Schloss Schallaburg**. To reach the castle from the abbey in Melk, follow the signs to the *Bahnhof* (train station) and Lindestrasse east, turn right into Hummelstrasse/Kirschengraben (L5340) and follow the signs to the castle. Just beyond the entranceway is the castle's architectural centrepiece, a two-storey arcaded Renaissance courtyard

with magnificent terracotta arches and rich red-brown carvings.

Backtrack to the B33. Be careful here that you stay on the south side of the river. When you reach the corner of Abt-Karl-Strasse and Bahnhofstrasse, go right and right again at the river. Follow the B1 for 4km to **15** **Schloss Schönbühel**, a 12th-century castle standing high on a rock some 5km northeast of Melk. Continue along this lovely stretch of the B33 in the direction of Krems. About 10km from Schloss Schönbühel the ruins of **16** **Burg Aggstein** swing into view. This 12th-century hilltop castle was built by the Kuenringer family and now offers a grand vista of the Danube. The 'robber barons' of both Schloss Schönbühel and Burg Aggstein are said to have imprisoned their enemies on a ledge of rock (the Rosengärtlein), where the hapless captives faced starvation (unless they opted for a quicker demise by throwing themselves into the abyss below).

From the right bank of the Danube you now get a bird's-eye view of the towns and ruins you passed earlier. One of the exquisite pleasures of the region is its famous *Marillen* (apricots), and you'll see lots of orchards among the vineyards.

About 27km from Melk some pretty cliffs rise up above the road. From Mautern it's a detour of about 6km to **17** **Stift Göttweig**. To reach it, at the roundabout near the bridge follow the road right from the B33 to Mautern and right again immediately afterwards towards Fürth. Stift Göttweig is signposted at the next roundabout on the L7071. From there it's a short drive back to Krems.

This road trip can also be done from St Pölten, situated 36km south of Krems an der Donau. If you do set out from there, be sure to include Stift Herzogenburg.

office@wachau-touristik.at; per day €12); book ahead. A taxi (☎2222) to Burg Oberanna costs about €15.

Maria Taferl & Artstetten

☎07413 / POP 850

Located off the river on the northern side of the Danube in the Waldviertel, the small town of Maria Taferl is famous for its **Pfarr- und Wallfahrtskirche Maria Taferl** (Parish & Pilgrimage Church; www.basilika.at, in German; Maria Taferl 1; ⊗7am-8pm) high above the Danube Valley. Created by Jakob Prandtauer (of Melk fame), this baroque church has two onion domes and dark dome-frescoes. Its altar is a complex array of figures in gold. You'll find lots of hotels and B&Bs if you decide to stay in town, and some of the most spectacular views across the Danube are from here.

About 6km east of Maria Taferl and about the same distance off the Danube is **Artstetten**, with its castle. This was created out of a 13th-century medieval castle and has seen modifications over the past 700 years, including Renaissance features. It gained fame and glory after passing into the hands of the Habsburgs in the early 19th century, winding up in the hands of Archduke Franz Ferdinand. Inside is a museum (Artstetten 1; adult/child/family €7.30/4.50/17; ⊗9am-5.30pm Apr-Nov; P) devoted to the luckless heir, displaying photos and stories of his and his wife's time at the castle and their fateful trip to Sarajevo where his murder triggered WWI. Their tomb is in the church.

You are better off with your own wheels to visit Maria Taferl and Artstetten as no trains and very few buses go there.

Melk & Around

☎02752 / POP 5200

With its sparkling and majestic abbey-fortress, Melk is a highlight of any visit to the Danube Valley. Many visitors cycle here for the day – wearily pushing their bikes through the cobblestone streets. While here, try to visit the Renaissance Schloss Schallaburg, 6km south of town, which has fantastic contemporary exhibitions.

☉ Sights

TOP CHOICE Stift Melk   ABBEY

(Benedictine Abbey of Melk; ☎5550; www.stiftmelk.at; Abt Berthold Dietmayr Strasse 1; adult/child/family €7.70/4.50/15.40, incl guided tour €9.50/6.30/19; ⊗9am-5.30pm) Of the many abbeys in Austria, Stift Melk is the most famous. Historically, Melk was of great importance to the Romans and later to the Babenbergs, who built a castle here. In 1089 the Babenberg margrave Leopold II donated the castle to Benedictine monks, who converted it into a fortified abbey. Fire destroyed the original edifice, which was completely rebuilt between 1702 and 1738 according to plans by Jakob Prandtauer and his disciple, Josef Munggenast.

The huge monastery **church** is enclosed by the buildings, but dominates the complex with its twin spires and high octagonal dome. The interior is baroque gone barmy, with endless prancing angels and gold twirls. The theatrical high-altar scene, depicting St Peter and St Paul (the two patron saints of the church), is by Peter Widerin. Johann Michael Rottmayr did most of the ceiling paintings, including those in the dome.

Other highlights include the **bibliothek** (library) and the **Marmorsaal** (Marble Hall); both have *trompe l'oeil*–painted tiers on the ceiling (by Paul Troger) to give the illusion of greater height, and ceilings are slightly curved to aid the effect. Eleven of the imperial rooms, where dignitaries (including Napoleon) stayed, are now used to house a **museum**.

From around November to March, the monastery can only be visited by guided tour (11am and 2pm daily). Always phone ahead, even in summer, to ensure you get an English-language tour.

TOP CHOICE Schloss Schallaburg   PALACE

(☎02754-6317; www.schallaburg.at; Schallaburg 1; adult/child/family €9/3.50/18; ⊗9am-5pm Mon-Fri, to 6pm Sat & Sun May-Nov) This Renaissance palace set in lovely gardens is famous not only for its stunning architecture but also for the innovative exhibitions it houses. Architecturally, it boasts some 400 terracotta images, completed between 1572 and 1573, the largest of which support the upper-storey arches of the palace. It hosts a prestigious annual exhibition based on a chosen cultural theme. A popular exhibition in recent years was on the 1960s, called 'The Beatles, the Pill and Revolt'. Combined tickets with Stift Melk cost €15.

🛏 Sleeping & Eating

There is no shortage of hotels, but you're better off taking in the Stift Melk and Schloss

Schallaburg on a day trip and staying in more attractive Dürnstein, Spitz or Krems.

Hotel Restaurant zur Post
HOTEL **€€**

(☎523 45; www.post-melk.at, in German; Linzer Strasse 1; s €61-71, d €98-112, apt €155-210; P@🖤🌐) A bright and pleasant hotel in the heart of town, it has the attraction of large, comfortable rooms in plush colours, with additional touches such as brass bed lamps. There's a sauna, facilities for massages and free bike use for guests (€12 per day for non-guests). The restaurant is also a very decent choice for Austrian classics.

Hotel Wachau
HOTEL **€€**

(☎525 31; www.hotel-wachau.at; Am Wachberg 3; s €65, d €95-125; ⊘dinner Mon-Sat; P⊜🌐@🖤🌐) Situated about 2km southeast of the train station – take Abt-Karl-Strasse and Wiener Strasse – this hotel offers comfortable, modern rooms tailored especially to business and seminar guests. Some rooms have air-con and there's a lift. The Austrian regional and international cuisine served in the restaurant (mains €12 to €20, gourmet menu €45) is among the best in town, and organic ingredients are often used.

ℹ️ Information

Tourist office (☎523 07-410; www.niederoesterreich.at/melk; Babenbergerstrasse 1; ⊘9am-noon & 2-6pm Mon-Fri, 10am-noon Sat & Sun) East of Rathausplatz, with maps and plenty of useful information.

ℹ️ Getting There & Away

BICYCLE Wachau Touristik Bernhardt (☎02713-2222; office@wachau-touristik.at; train station in Spitz; €12 per day) rents out bicycles from the ferry station in Melk and from the train station in Spitz. Reserve ahead if picking up from Spitz.

BOAT Boats leave from the canal by Pionierstrasse, 400m north of the abbey; see p111 for details.

TAXI Taxi Türke (☎523 16) runs a minibus from the Melk train station to Schloss Schallaburg (€4 one way, leaving 10.40am, 1.15pm and 4.45pm daily). A standard taxi trip to Schallaburg costs €17.

Tulln

☎02272 / POP 14,700

Tulln, the home town of painter Egon Schiele and situated 30km northwest of Vienna on the Danube, has a couple of interesting mu-

seums and can be easily visited on a day trip from Vienna or Krems.

🔴 Sights

Egon Schiele Museum
MUSEUM

(Donaulände 28; adult/child €5/3; ⊘10am-noon & 1-5pm Tue-Sun Apr-Oct) The Egon Schiele Museum, housed in a former jail near the Danube, vividly presents the story of the life of the Tulln-born artist. It contains 100 of his paintings and sketches, and a mock-up of the cell he was briefly imprisoned in (he was jailed in Neulengbach, however). He fell foul of the law in 1912 when 125 of his erotic drawings were seized; some were of pubescent girls, and Schiele was also in trouble for allowing children to view his explicit works. Schiele fans should also plan a visit to Vienna's Leopold Museum (p69).

Museum im Minoritenkloster
MUSEUM

(Minoritenplatz 1) This city-promoted museum space features some excellent changing exhibitions based around mostly Austrian artists. Recent ones have included Schiele, Wilhelm Kaufmann and in 2011 the Klosterneuburg artist Karl Paschek. It adjoins the Minorite church.

Minoritenkirche
CHURCH

(Minoritenplatz 1; ⊘8am-7pm) Alongside the tourist office, the rococo Minorite church from 1739 is decorated with magnificent ceiling frescoes dedicated to St Johannes Nepomuk.

Pfarrkirche St Stephan
CHURCH

(Wiener Strasse 20; ⊘7.30am-7.30pm) This parish church combines Gothic and baroque elements, along with the wonderful 13th-century frescoed Romanesque funerary chapel.

🍴 Sleeping & Eating

The tourist office keeps accommodation lists (including private rooms) and also stocks a free map of town.

TOP CHOICE Hotel Nibelungenhof
HOTEL **€€**

(☎626 58; www.nibelungenhof.info; Donaulände 34; s €48-86, d €98-138, f €160; ⊘lunch & dinner; P⊜🌐🖤) Situated alongside the Danube River with a lovely terrace garden and cafe-restaurant (mains €6.50 to €13) downstairs, this hotel has individually furnished rooms in bright and attractive colours. The most expensive doubles are larger and some rooms have pine furnishing. The terrace cafe is open in fine weather from April to October.

Junges Hotel Tulln
HOSTEL €

(☑651 65 10; www.tulln.noejhw.at; Marc-Aurel-Park 1; dm/s/d €20/30/50; ℙ☺) Youth hostel near the Danube catering for seminar guests as well as tourists. The building has a lift.

Donaupark Camping
CAMPGROUND €

(☑652 00; www.campingtulln.at; Hafenstrasse 4; camp sites per adult/child/tent & car €7/3.50/4.50; ☺Apr-Oct; ℙ) Campground located just east of the centre on the river and alongside a pretty forest.

Gasthaus zur Sonne
AUSTRIAN €€

(☑646 16; Bahnhofstrasse 48; mains €9-25; ☺Tue-Sat; ☺) This traditional restaurant serves excellent dishes such as goulash (€9) and veal liver in a balsamic vinegar (€18). Reserve ahead as it's popular.

❶ Information

Tourist office (☑675 66; www.tullner-donauraum.at; Minoritenplatz 2; ☺9am-7pm Mon-Fri, 10am-7pm Sat & Sun, closed Sat & Sun Oct-Apr) One block north of Hauptplatz from the fountain end.

❶ Getting There & Around

Bicycle

Tulln and its tourist office are well set up for cyclists, as the Danube cycleway runs alongside the river on the town's northern border. Tulln has numerous Leihradl stations where you can hire a bicycle (see p111).

Train

Tulln has two train stations, Bahnhof Stadt Tulln and Bahnhof Tulln. At the time of research, the situation regarding which trains would stop where was undecided (check your ticket or ask). Bahnhof Stadt Tulln is in the centre. From Bahnhof Tulln the centre is reached via Bahnweg (turn right on exiting the station) and Bahnhofstrasse, about 15 minutes on foot. Several regional and S-Bahn trains each hour connect Tulln with Vienna's Franz-Josefs-Bahnhof (€7.20, 30 to 45 minutes) and hourly trains go to Krems (€9.20, 35 minutes).

WALDVIERTEL & WEINVIERTEL

Forming a broad swath across Lower Austria north of the Danube, the Waldviertel (Woods Quarter) begins near Krems and the Kamptal in the east (the latter borders the largely agricultural and winemaking region, the Weinviertel or 'Wine Quarter') and ends at the Czech border in the north and west. The Waldviertel is a picturesque region of rolling hills and rural villages, and while there isn't actually much forest to speak of, there are a number of fine attractions and retreats. The Kamptal in particular is a great place for escaping the crowds.

The Waldviertel's central **tourist office** (☑02822-54109-0; www.waldviertel.at; Sparkasseplatz 4, Zwettl; ☺8am-4pm Mon-Fri) can help with information and planning.

❶ Getting There & Away

BUS Zwettl is best reached by bus from Krems (€10, 45 minutes to 1½ hours). Services are frequent but only a couple run on Sunday. From Horn, very irregular buses run to Altenburg (€2.40, 10 minutes).

TRAIN Several direct trains run from Krems to Horn daily (€9.20, 70 minutes), stopping at Rosenburg (€7.20, one hour). Eggenburg has plenty of daily train connections to Tulln (€9.20, 45 minutes).

Drosendorf

☑02915 / POP 1200

Situated on the extreme northern fringe of the Waldviertel, hard on the Czech border, the lovely fortressed town of Drosendorf is often overlooked by the Viennese – it's simply too far-flung. Yet, with a completely intact town wall, it is a unique and beautiful town.

An **information service** (☑232 10; ☺8am-4.30pm Mon-Thu, to 12.30pm Fri) is located inside the castle, and an information stand with a useful walk-by-numbers brochure (in German) as well as an accommodation list is situated on Hauptplatz, inside the walls. The fortress walk also begins here; it passes the **castle**, a mostly baroque structure on top of Romanesque foundations, and exits through the **Hornertor**, the main gate in the southeast dating from the 13th to 15th centuries. Cross the moat and follow the wall clockwise.

For overnight stays, the best option is **Schloss Drosendorf** (☑232 10; www.schloss-drosendorf.at, in German; Schlossplatz 1; s/d €39/64; ℙ☺@). Poppies – or rather poppy-seed specialities – are a big local industry in the Waldviertel. **MOKA** (☑22 27; www.moka.at, in German; Hauptplatz 5; cake & coffee €6; ☺9am-6pm Thu-Mon Apr-Oct) does a delicious poppy-seed cake and coffee, and also has a few comfortable rooms right on Hauptplatz (singles and doubles €70 to €120).

WALDVIERTEL ROAD TRIP

The Kamptal, immediately northeast of Krems towards Langenlois, is a major centre of winegrowing and one of the most picturesque entry points into the Waldviertel. This route, which can be done by train between Krems (or Hadersdorf) train station and Schloss Rosenburg (€5.40, one hour, four to six times daily), combines traditional *Heurigen* with a castle, top-class dining, wellness and wine.

From Krems the Weinstrasse Kremstal (Krems Valley Wine Rd; B35) leads northeast. About 2km past Gedersdorf – just before Hadersdorf train station – veer right under the railway line and immediately left to Diendorf, where you find **Hofkäserei Robert Paget** (www.mozzaundjazz.at; Kirchenweg 2, Diendorf am Kamp; ⊘10am-6pm Fri & Sat; P). Here Robert Paget (see p127) produces Austria's finest buffalo mozzarella cheese, as well as goat's cheese. You can buy from the shop. Cyclists and walkers can continue along the tiny Diendorfer Weg about another 1.5km to Hadersdorf's Hauptplatz, the magnificent central town square with Renaissance and baroque buildings, some of them *Heurigen* (by car take the B43).

In Hadersdorf, visit **Eat Art** (www.spoerri.at, in German; Hauptlatz 23; mains €9-17; ⊘5-10pm Thu, 11am-10pm Fri & Sat, 10am-5pm Sun; ☺✎), part of the food and museum concept by Romanian-born Swiss artist Daniel Spoerri, **Eat Art & Ab Art** (www.spoerri.at, in German; Hauptlatz 23; adult/child €7/free; ⊘11am-6pm Thu-Sun Easter-Oct, closed Thu Easter-May).

About 6km south of Diendorf is **Schloss Grafenegg** (see p115), the castle with the look and feel of an ornate Tudor mansion set in English woods.

Continuing north, the wine-focused **Loisium Hotel** (☎02734-77 100-0; www.loisium hotel.at; Loisium Allee 2, Langenlois; s €134-144, d €188-198, mains €15-30, 4-course menu €47; ⊘lunch & dinner; P☺@☎☲) is a useful stopover. Highlights are massages and wine treatments (some using sparkling wine or grape-seed oil), large spa facilities and the 20m heated outdoor pool that's open all year (wi-fi is in the foyer, cable LAN in the rooms). Alongside the hotel is the **Loisium Weinwelt** (www.loisium.at; Loisium Allee 1; 90min audio tour adult/child €11.50/6.30; ⊘10am-7pm; P), an aluminium cube designed by the New York architect Steven Holl that slopes to the south. Multilingual audio tours here set off every 30 minutes and lead you through the 1.5km network of ancient tunnels. Bring a pullover as it's chilly. You can also taste vintages.

Further north from Langelois, the B34 passes through the picturesque Naturpark Kamptal-Schönberg to **Schloss Rosenburg** (www.rosenburg.at, in German; Rosenburg am Kamp; tours & falconry adult/child/family €10/8.50/24; ⊘9.30am-4.30pm Mar-Oct, closed Mon Mar Apr & Oct; P), a Renaissance castle 50km north of Krems where falconry shows take place at 11am and 3pm (extra €3 to include falconry with pageantry).

From Rosenburg, the B34 and later B2 lead on an 18km detour east to the quaint town of **Eggenburg**. It's still surrounded by much of its original defensive walls.

Back in Rosenburg, follow the L53 and B38 5km to the Benedictine **Stift Altenburg** (www.stift-altenburg.at, in German; Stift 1; adult/child/family €9/4.50/18; audio guide €2; ⊘10am-5pm Apr-Oct), which can trace its foundations back to 1144. The **abbey library** (which has ceiling frescoes by Paul Troger) and the crypt (with frescoes by Troger's pupils) are highlights.

By continuing along the B38 you pass Peygarten-Ottenstein on the **Ottensteiner Stausee**, one of several dams in the Waldviertel, and finish the tour near Zwettl at the baroque Cistercian abbey **Stift Zwettl** (www.stift-zwettl.at, in German; Stift Zwettl 1; admission & audio guide adult/child/family €9/4/18; ⊘10am-4pm Easter-Oct; P). The B36 leads you 25km south back to the Danube Valley.

To reach Drosendorf from Vienna (Praterstern station), take the frequent train to Retz (€15.70, 70 minutes), making sure it connects with one of several buses weekdays (€6.40, one hour).

Nationalpark Thayatal

Straddling the border of Austria and the Czech Republic in the northwestern reaches of the Weinviertel is Austria's smallest

ℹ CYCLING THE KAMPTAL

The Waldviertel road trip can be easily done by bicycle on a slightly different route if you use the **Kamptalradweg** (Kamp Valley Bicycle Path; 107km one way from Krems to Zwettl) and other bike paths in the network. The route runs slightly northwest of the B35 from Krems, but from **Gobelsburg** you can pick up another trail to Hadersdorf, Diendorf and Schloss Grafenegg. It also leaves the Kamp for a while north of Rosenburg, but joins it again for the **Ottensteiner Stausee**. If you do the route, pick up the free *Freizeitkarte Kamptal* from Krems' tourist office showing routes.

national park, Thayatal. This unique stretch of land is actually two parks; its other half, Podyjí National Park, is located across the border. Of the 3000 plant species found in Austria, about 1300 occur in Thayatal. The landscape consists of a deep canyon cut by the Thaya river, numerous rock formations and steep slopes. Walking is the most popular activity in the park.

The **Nationalparkhaus** (☏02949-7005-0; www.np-thayatal.at; exhibition adult/child €3.80/2.20; ☉9am-6pm Apr-Sep, 10am-4pm Mar, Oct & Nov), near Hardegg, has loads of information and an exhibition on the park's ecology. Hardegg, the natural jump-off point for the park, is not easy to get to without your own transport; it's best approached by train from Vienna to Retz (€15.70, one hour), from where the occasional bus runs to the town (€4, 20 minutes).

ST PÖLTEN

☏02742 / POP 51,700

A destination few may even notice as they scream through on their way from Vienna to Salzburg, St Pölten may be Lower Austria's capital but it retains a very sleepy atmosphere. Though no beauty, it has a nice *Altstadt* (old town) contrasted by a new Landhaus Viertel (Landhaus Quarter).

History

The borders of Lower Austria were drawn by the Babenberg rulers in the 13th century, but in 1278 the region and empire-to-be fell to the Habsburgs. In a strange twist of fate – an ailing economy in the 1920s stalled the decision to give Lower Austria its own capital, and later the Nazis favoured making Krems the capital – St Pölten became capital of Lower Austria only in 1986, ending a long-running situation in which Lower Austria was administered geographically from Vienna, but was in fact a separate province. Ironically, it happens to have the oldest known municipal charter – granted in 1159. The *Altstadt* is noted for its baroque buildings: baroque master Jakob Prandtauer lived and died in the city.

◉ Sights

TOP CHOICE **Rathausplatz**   TOWN SQUARE

Situated in the heart of St Pölten, Rathausplatz is a pretty town square lined with cafes and eye-catching pastel-coloured buildings. It is dominated by the **Rathaus** on its southern side, which has a baroque facade (1727) designed by Joseph Munggenast. On the northern fringe is the **Franziskanerkirche** (Rathausplatz 12; ☉dawn-dusk), completed in 1770 with a grandiose altar offset by side altar paintings by Kremser Schmidt. Between the two is the tall **Dreifaltigkeitssäule** (Trinity Column) dating from 1782, a captivating white, oversized swirl of motifs, built partly as a religious vow following the passing of the plague.

TOP CHOICE **Stadtmuseum**   MUSEUM

(www.stadtmuseum-stpoelten.at; Prandtauerstrasse 2; adult/concession & child €5/2; ☉10am-5pm Wed-Sun) Although it obviously can't compete with the best of the bunch in Vienna, the City Museum is excellent and well worth a visit. Its permanent collection focusing on art nouveau in St Pölten is on the 1st floor, and a section on the ground floor is devoted to local archaeological treasures. Admission includes excellent temporary exhibitions.

Landesmuseum   MUSEUM

(Franz-Schubert-Platz 5; adult/child/family €8/3.50/16; ☉9am-5pm Tue-Sun) The Lower Austria State Museum houses an interesting collection on the history, art and environment of the region. A wave made from glass, frozen in movement above the entrance, sets the mood, and indeed water is a theme throughout. The highlight of the art collection spanning the Middle Ages to the present is the 13th-century Lion of Schöngrabern. The museum is situated in the **Landhausviertel** (State Parliament Quarter) of town, a modern conflux of state buildings alongside

St Pölten

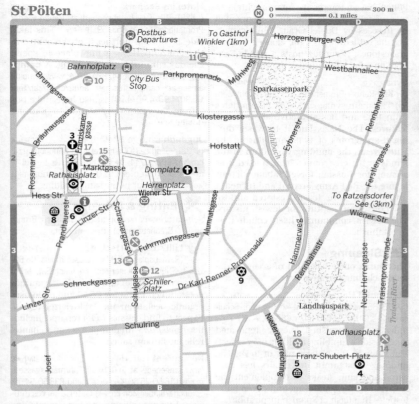

St Pölten

the river. For a bird's-eye view of the quarter take the lift to the top of the **Klangturm** (Landhausplatz; admission to platform free; ⊙8am-7pm Mon-Sat, 9am-5pm Sun), which often stages temporary art exhibitions.

Dom CATHEDRAL
(Domplatz 1; ⊙dawn-dusk) Jakob Prandtauer was one of the most important architects of the baroque epoch, and the cathedral, his masterpiece of baroque rebuilding in St

Pölten, has an impressive interior with lashings of fake marble and gold, augmented by frescoes by Daniel Gran. While exploring the cathedral, visit the cloister with its gravestones. Domplatz hosts a **market** every Thursday and Saturday morning.

Synagoge
SYNAGOGUE

(Dr-Karl-Renner-Promenade 22; ☺9am-3pm Mon-Fri) The main synagogue of St Pölten dates from 1912 and has attractive art nouveau features. The Nazis laid it to waste during the pogroms of 1938, and during the Hitler years the building wound up in the hands of the city council, which used it as a camp for Russian forced labour victims before the Red Army arrived and turned it into a grain store. It was restored and today houses an institute for Jewish history. The Jewish community itself couldn't be re-established.

🛏 Sleeping

The tourist office has a list of accommodation, including private rooms.

Stadthotel Hauser Eck
HOTEL €€

(☎733 36; www.hausereck.at, in German; Schulgasse 2; s €41-65, d €70-84, tr €87-99; ⊜🛜) This individually furnished, newly renovated hotel inside a rambling building offers excellent value in the historic part of town. The midrange restaurant downstairs has kangaroo and emu steaks to complement the Austrian classics, and sometimes even bull's testicles in a flash of Spanish inspiration.

Gasthof Graf
GUESTHOUSE €€

(☎352 757; www.hotel-graf.at; Bahnhofplatz 7; s €58-68, d €88-95; P@🛜) This pleasant *Gasthöfe* directly across from the *Hauptbahnhof* is very good value, with clean, modern rooms. Furnishings, though veneer, include a coffee table and desk. Cheaper rooms are slightly smaller.

Metropol
HOTEL €€€

(☎707 00-0; www.austria-trend.at/met; Schillerplatz 1; s €200-220, d €250-270, ste €300; P⊜@🛜📶) Cosy, upmarket and aimed at a business and culture clientele, the Metropol is not cheap (low season prices are 20% less), but for these prices you do get free use of the sauna, steam bath and infrared lamps. Its restaurant (mains €14 to €22) serves up steak and good business-type meals. Breakfast costs an extra €14.50; children under 12 years can occupy an extra bed or cot in the room for free.

Hotel im Seepark
B&B €€

(☎251 510; www.hotel-seepark.at; Bimbo Binder Promenade 15; s/d €53/59; P⊜🛜) This lakeside B&B, 3km northeast of the centre in the Freizeitpark, is a fine place to spend the day sunning and swimming. A **camping ground** (☎0664/88413014; www.camping amsee.at; camp sites per adult/child/car/tent €6.90/4.90/4.90/4.90) is also here. Take bus 7 from the main train station to 'Ratzersdorfer See'.

Jugendherberge St Pölton
HOSTEL €

(☎321 96; office3100@hostel.or.at; Bahnhofplatz 1; dm/s/d €22/31/44; @🛜) The youth hostel is about as convenient to the train station as it gets – it's all but in the same building.

🍴 Eating & Drinking

Self-caterers can shop at the **Billa** (cnr Brunngasse & Bräuhausgasse) supermarket.

Lilli's Gastwirtschaft
AUSTRIAN €

(Rathausplatz 15/Marktgasse; mains €8.50-12.50; ☺lunch & dinner Mon-Fri, lunch Sat; ⊜🍴) This comfortable and homely restaurant does a lunch menu for €6.50 and often uses organic beef from the Waldviertel region. Expect to find classics well prepared, including *Tafelspitz* with dumplings and a chanterelle mushroom sauce.

Restaurant Galerie
AUSTRIAN €€

(www.langeneder.at, in German; Fuhrmannsgasse 1; mains €16.50-25.50, 4-course menu €33.50-54.50; ☺lunch & dinner Mon-Fri; ⊜) Galerie serves delicious Viennese cuisine and has a great wine list, especially for Italian and French vintages. Although Wiener schnitzel isn't on the menu, it's always available for the asking.

Gasthof Winkler
AUSTRIAN €€

(☎364 944; www.gasthofwinkler.at, in German; Mühlweg 64; mains €9-22; ☺lunch & dinner Tue-Sat, dinner Sun; ⊜) This upmarket restaurant has been serving delicious local and Austrian seasonal specialities for over a century. You'll find it about 1km north of the *Hauptbahnhof*. Reserve ahead.

Landhaus Stüberl
AUSTRIAN €

(www.landhausstueberl.at, in German; Landhausboulevard 27; breakfast €3.60-5.80, lunch menu €5.90, mains €8.50-12; ☺Mon-Fri) Aimed at office workers in the quarter, Landhaus has good, cheap lunchtime dishes, including pasta. A terrace overlooks the Traisen River.

Cinema Paradiso
CAFE €

(www.cinema-paradiso.at, in German; Rathausplatz 14; Sat & Sun breakfast buffet €7.20; ☺9am-1am)

This is one of the best centrally located places in town for a coffee or drink. It also does an all-you-can eat breakfast buffet on weekends until 1pm and, true to its name, is an art-house cinema.

☆ Entertainment

FestSpielHaus CONCERT HALL
(☑90 80 80-222; www.festspielhaus.at, in German; Franz-Schubert-Platz 2) FestSpielHaus is a modern theatre which features an impressive array of music, theatre and dance performances from both Austria and abroad.

❶ Information

Tourist office (☑353 354; www.st-poelten. gv.at; Rathausplatz 1; ⊙8am-5pm Mon-Fri, 9am-5pm Sat, 10am-5pm Sun) Ask for the *Übernachten in St Pölten* booklet (in German, but with useful listings).

Post office (Wiener Strasse 12) Main post office.

❶ Getting There & Away

CAR St Pölten has good road connections: the east–west A1/E60 passes a few kilometres south of the city and the S33 branches north from there, bypassing St Pölten to the east, and continuing to Krems.

TRAIN Trains run every half-hour from Vienna to St Pölten (€11, 40 to 75 minutes), continuing on to Linz (€22, one hour) and Salzburg (€38, 2½ hours). Hourly direct trains run to Krems (€7.20,

45 minutes) and several each day to Mariazell (€15.70, 2½ hours).

Herzogenburg

Although the region around Lower Austria's capital won't bowl you over, the baroque Augustinian abbey **Stift Herzogenburg** (☑02782-831 12; Herzogenburg; adult/child €7/3; ⊙tours 9.30am, 11am, 1.30pm, 3pm & 4.30pm Apr-Oct) is a highlight. Admission is with a guided tour (in English at 9.30am and 11am Tue, Thu & Fri), which includes the **Stiftskirche** and a late-Gothic collection of paintings by the Danube school of artists.

Herzogenburg lies on the main train line between Krems (€3.60, 25 minutes) and St Pölten (€4.40, 15 minutes); at least a dozen trains pass through the town's train station (which is 10 minutes' walk from the abbey) daily.

MOSTVIERTEL

The Mostviertel, in Lower Austria's southwestern corner, takes its name from apple cider which is produced and consumed in the area. By Lower Austrian standards, the landscape is spectacular, with the eastern Alps ever-present in its southern reaches.

LOCAL KNOWLEDGE

ROBERT PAGET: ORGANIC CHEESE PRODUCER

The Philosophy

In the 1970s I studied biology, and moved onto the land looking for an independent lifestyle. From the very beginning we've been producing goat's cheese, and since 2002 we've added buffalo to the property. I worked for about 15 years on social projects in the Kach region of India and it was in India that I became familiar with buffalo. Parallel to this, I developed an interest in slow food. A feature of small-scale farming in Romania, for instance, is to keep several different types of animals, resulting in cheeses made from different types and cuvées of milk according to season.

The Cheeses

Buffalo milk is very high in fat and has a sweetish taste, resulting in a cheese with a rounded finish. If I blend in one-third goat's milk to two-thirds buffalo milk, I arrive at a cheese with additional pep and a longer shelf life. All cheeses we produce are organic.

Eat Art

In nearby Hadersdorf, Robert Paget's daughter co-manages **Eat Art** (www.spoerri.at, in German; Hauptlatz 23; mains €9-17; ⊙5-10pm Thu, 11am-10pm Fri & Sat, 10am-5pm Sun; ☻☑) with chef Benjamin Schwaighofer, part of the food and museum concept by Romanian-born Swiss artist Daniel Spoerri.

ⓘ TAKING IN THE ROMANS

Getting from one Roman site to the next in Carnuntum can be difficult during the week. Here are some tips:

» **Cycling from Vienna** If you feel very energetic, your best option is to hire a bike in Vienna and ride the roughly 65km along the Danube. The Danube path runs along the northern bank of the river through the Nationalpark Donau-Auen (Danube Lea National Park). This section on asphalt and gravel goes through mature forest, occasionally crossing backwaters of the Danube, and crossing the river to the south side on a bridge between Bad Deutsch-Altenburg and Hainburg.

» **Bike hire** You'll find Leihradl stations in Petronell-Carnuntum at the train station (only a few bikes) and also at the open-air museum; in Bad Deutsch-Altenburg at the Museum Carnuntinum, the train station and Pension Riedmüller; and in Hainburg at the Kulturfabrik and the Frachtenbahnhof.

» **Bus** On weekends from mid-March to October a free bus meets the Vienna train every two hours from 9.13am to 3.13pm and does the circuit of sites (the last bus from Museum Carnuntum is 4.50pm).

It's largely ignored by international tourists and is certainly an area off the beaten track.

One town not to be missed is **Waidhofen an der Ybbs**, with historic gabled houses, arcaded courtyards and dramatic onion domes. Staff at its **tourist office** (☎07442-511 255; www.waidhofen.at; Schlossweg 2; ☺9am-6pm) have information on the town and the numerous **mountain bike trails** of varying degrees of difficulty around Waidhofen. The tourist office rents road bicycles and mountain bikes for €1.50 per day for a maximum of one week. It also has useful maps of the region and can point you towards the mountain-bike trails.

From Gstadt, Bundesstrasse 31 leads through some lovely mountainous country and a string of pretty little villages such as **Göstling**, **Lunz am See** and **Gaming**.

In the eastern fringes of the Mostviertel, and only 23km south of St Pölten, is the

Cistercian monastery (www.stift-lilienfeld. at; Klosterrotte 1; adult/child €3/1, incl tour €7/4; ☺8am-noon & 1-5pm, tours 10am & 2pm Mon-Sat, 2pm Sun) of Lilienfeld. Founded in 1202, the foundations of the monastery are Romanesque, but have received Gothic and baroque makeovers.

ⓘ Getting There & Away

From St Pölten frequent daily trains go to Waidhofen an der Ybbs (€15.70, one hour, change at Amstetten) and to Lilienfeld (€5.40, 40 minutes). You are better off leaving a car or bicycle for Göstling, Lunz and for Gaming, which is 30km from Waidhofen.

MARCH-DONAULAND

The March-Donauland, stretching from the eastern border of Vienna to the Slovakian border, is dominated by the Danube and its natural flood plains. Carnuntum, an important Roman camp during the days of the Roman Empire, and the Nationalpark Donau-Auen are found here.

Carnuntum

The Roman town of Carnuntum was the most important political and military centre in the empire's northeast; with a population of 50,000 people at its peak, it made Vienna look like a village in comparison. The town developed around AD 40 and was abandoned some 400 years later. Today it exists as a relic of Roman civilisation in Upper Pannonia. The main sights are spread between the modern-day settlement Petronell-Carnuntum, the larger spa town of Bad Deutsch-Altenburg about 4km away, and Hainburg, another 4km east of this.

⊙ Sights

All four Roman attractions are covered by the one ticket (adult/child €9/3, tours extra €3), including transport in the archaeological park bus on weekends. Note that the months open change slightly each year (check the website).

Freilichtmuseum Petronell

MUSEUM, ROMAN RUINS
(www.carnuntum.co.at; Hauptstrasse 1a, Petronell-Carnuntum; ☺9am-5pm mid-Mar–Oct, tours 10am, 11.30am, 2pm & 3.30pm; P🚻) The open-air museum is the major attraction in Petronell-Carnuntum itself and lies on the site of the

old civilian town. It includes ruins of the public baths and a reconstructed temple of Diana. Hunky young actors lead tours in kitsch tunics and togas, and you can buy replicas of Roman sandals and clothing here for your next toga party. The museum is enclosed and very touristy, but nevertheless interesting and good fun; descriptions everywhere are in English. The **Heidentor** (Heathen Gate) was once the southwest entrance to the city and now stands as an isolated anachronism amid fields of grain.

Ampitheatre
ROMAN RUINS

(Wienerstrasse 52, Petronell-Carnuntum; ⊙9am-5pm mid-Mar–Oct) Situated about 2km on from the park towards Bad Deutsch-Altenburg, the grass-covered amphitheatre formerly seated 15,000. It now hosts a theatre festival over summer.

Museum Carnuntinum
MUSEUM

(Badgasse 40-46, Bad Deutsch-Altenburg; ⊙10am-5pm mid-Mar–Oct, tours 2pm & 3.30pm Sat & Sun) Situated in Bad Deutsch-Altenburg, this museum with archaeological displays is the largest of its kind in Austria, having amassed over 3300 Roman treasures in its 100-year existence. The museum's highlight, *Tanzende Mänade* (Dancing Maenad), a marble figure with a perfect bum, is usually displayed here. While in Bad Deutsch-Altenburg, take a stroll around the *Kurpark* (spa gardens), situated alongside the Danube.

TOP CHOICE Kulturfabrik
MUSEUM

(www.kulturfabrik-hainburg.at; Kulturplatz 1; adult/child €5/3; ⊙10am-5pm Tue-Sun) Situated 3.8km east of Bad Deutsch-Altenburg, this 'Culture Factory' is a museum depot for the archaeological riches of the region. It stages changing exhibitions mostly based around its own collection; see the website for details about what's currently on show. Combined tickets are often available (ask when buying your ticket at one of the museums).

The building in which the depot is housed is an interesting landmark in itself. It dates back to 1847 and was erected on the Danube to manufacture cigarettes and cigars, doing so until the local industry took its last draw here in the 1990s. Today it has been refurbished with a glass wall fronting the river, offering magnificent views. Entry is via a glass and mirrored lift from street level. The **fenestra** cafe offers fantastic views over the river, best enjoyed sipping coffee or nibbling a snack.

🛏 Sleeping & Eating

All of the following places are in Bad Deutsch-Altenburg, which with its pretty *Kurpark,* spa facilities and location near the Danube is far more appealing than Petronell-Carnuntum.

Gasthof Hotel zum Amphitheater
HOTEL €

(📞02165-627 37; www.zum-amphitheater.at; Wienerstrasse 51; s/d/tr €32/54/72; P@🌐🛜) Rising up opposite the amphitheatre, this friendly, family-run hotel is packed with local atmosphere; rooms are spacious and some have views over the fields or amphitheatre. Wi-fi is in the restaurant downstairs, but all rooms have power LAN from the socket.

Pension Riedmüller
HOTEL €

(📞02165-62473-0; www.tiscover.at/riedmueller. hotels; Badgasse 28; s/d €30/60; P) This hotel has massage facilities, free bike use for guests and organises tours or helps with bike tours to Bratislava (€50 each way). The rooms are fine, but the delicious apple strudel downstairs in the cafe is even better.

Hotel-Gasthof Stöckl
HOTEL €

(📞02165-623 37; Hauptplatz 3; s/d €33/56; P🏊) Comfortable, centrally located hotel with a solar-heated outdoor pool, and a sauna and steam bath.

Gasthaus Durkowitsch
AUSTRIAN €€

(Wiener Strasse 7; mains €9-18; ⊙Fri-Tue; 🍴) Family inn serving classics for under €15, along with more-expensive seasonal or game dishes such as venison ragout or duck. A room for smokers has a rustic, hunter atmosphere.

Wirtshaus an der Donau
AUSTRIAN €€

(Kurpark; mains €9-16; ⊙10am-11pm) Situated right alongside the Danube River in the *Kurpark,* this restaurant is especially popular for chilling out over a drink in the beer garden.

ℹ Information

Bad Deutsch-Altenburg tourist office
(📞02165-629 00-11; www.baddeutsch-altenburg.at, in German; Erhardgasse 2; ⊙8am-noon & 1-7pm Mon, 8am-noon & 1-4pm Tue-Thu, 8am-1pm Fri) Useful for information on all sights.

Petronell-Carnuntum tourist office
(📞02163-337 70; www.carnuntum.co.at; Hauptstrasse 1a; ⊙9am-5pm mid-Mar–Oct) At the open-air museum.

Regionalbüro Auland-Carnuntum (📞02163-3555-10; www.aulandcarnuntum.com; Hauptstrasse 3; ⊙9am-4.30pm Mon-Thu,

MOVING ON?

For tips, recommendations and reviews, head to shop.lonelyplanet.com to purchase a downloadable PDF of the Bratislava and West Slovakia chapter from Lonely Planet's *Czech & Slovak Republics* guide.

9am-2.30pm Fri) Information on the region, situated next to the open-air museum.

ℹ️ Getting There & Around

BICYCLE The cycle path from Vienna goes along the north bank of the Danube, crosses to the south near Bad Deutsch-Altenburg, and continues into Slovakia.

TRAIN There are hourly departures from Wien-Mitte for Petronell-Carnuntum, Bad Deutsch-Altenburg (both €9.20, one hour) and Hainburg (€11, 70 minutes).

Nationalpark Donau-Auen

Nationalpark Donau-Auen is a thin strip of natural flood plain on either side of the Danube, running from Vienna to the Slovakian border. Established as a national park in 1997, it was the culmination of 13 years of protest and environmentalist action against the building of a hydroelectric power station in Hainburg. You'll find plentiful flora and fauna, including 700 species of fern and flowering plants, and a high density of king-fishers (feeding off the 50 species of fish). Guided tours by foot or boat are available; for more information contact **Nationalpark Donau-Auen** (www.donauauen.at; Schlossplatz 1, Orth an der Donau; ⊙9am-6pm mid-Mar–Oct).

From Vienna, the Nationalpark Donau-Auen is best explored either by bicycle or on one of the Nationalpark-run 4½-hour summer **tours** (☑01-4000 494-80; adult/child €10/4; ⊙9am May-Oct) leaving from the Salztorbrücke (bookings are necessary).

WIENERWALD

The Wienerwald encompasses gentle wooded hills to the west and southwest of Vienna, and the wine-growing region directly south of the capital. For the Viennese, it's a place for walking, climbing and mountain biking. Numerous walking and cycling trails in the area are covered in the *Wienerwald Wan-*

der- und Radkarte, available free from local tourist offices and the region's main office, **Wienerwald Tourismus** (☑02231-621 76; www.wienerwald.info; Hauptplatz 11, 3002 Purkersdorf; ⊙9am-5pm Mon-Fri).

Attractive settlements, such as the grape-growing towns of **Perchtoldsdorf** and **Gumpoldskirchen**, speckle the Wienerwald. Picturesque **Mödling**, only 15km south of Vienna, was once favoured by the artistically inclined: Beethoven's itchy feet took him to Hauptstrasse 79 from 1818 to 1820, and Arnold Schönberg stayed at Bernhardgasse 6 from 1918 to 1925. More information is available from the **Tourismus Information Mödling** (☑02236-267 27; tourismus@moedling.at; Elisabethstrasse 2; ⊙9am-5pm Mon-Fri).

About 20km from Mödling is **Heiligenkreuz** and the 12th-century Cistercian abbey **Stift Heiligenkreuz** (☑02258-8703; www.stift-heiligenkreuz.at; Heiligenkreuz 1; adult/child €7/3.50; ⊙tours 10am, 11am, 2pm, 3pm & 4pm Mon-Sat, 11am, 2pm, 3pm & 4pm Sun). The chapter house is the final resting place of most of the Babenberg dynasty, which ruled Austria until 1246. The abbey museum contains 150 clay models by Giovanni Giuliani (1663–1744), a Venetian sculptor who also created the Trinity column in the courtyard. Note that tours in English are by advance request only.

Mayerling, which lies 6km southwest of Heiligenkreuz, has little to show now, but the bloody event that occurred here in 1889 still draws visitors to the site. The **Carmelite convent** (http://karmel-mayerling. org, in German; Mayerling 1; admission €2.20; ⊙9am-6pm) can be visited if you want to get a feel for events and see a few mementos. The altar in the chapel was built exactly where the bodies of Archduke Rudolf and Maria were found.

Between Mayerling and Weissenbach-Neuhaus, situated about 5km from both on the L4004 and accessible from the Schwarzensee parking area and bus stop, is **Peilstein** (716m), with rock climbing on the **Peilstein Klettersteig**. This is one of the most picturesque climbs in the region and a favourite among the Viennese. **Peilsteinhaus** (www.peilsteinhaus.gebirgsverein.at, in German; Schwarzensee 15; ⊙Wed-Sun; ♿), a hut and restaurant with a kids' playground, can be reached by hiking trails (01/06) via Mayerling from Heiligenkreuz (16km, 4½ hours to Peilstein). From the Schwarzensee/Peilstein bus stop, it's a half-hour hike and from Weisenbach it takes 1½ hours.

ℹ Getting There & Away

To really explore this region, it's best with your own bicycle or car, but trains and buses will get you to the main centres.

BUS Connections are from Baden bei Wien to Heiligenkreuz (€1.80, 20 to 30 minutes, seven daily weekdays) or from Baden to Schwarzensee (€5.40, one hour, six daily Monday to Saturday).

CAR The main road through the area is the A21 that loops down from Vienna, passes by Heiligenkreuz, then curves north to join the A1 just east of Altlengbach.

TRAIN Take the S9 from Wien-Meidling via Perchtoldsdorf (€2, eight minutes, four times each hour) to Gumpoldskirchen (€3.60, 30 minutes, hourly) and the S50 from Wien-Meidling to Purkersdorf (€3.60, 20 minutes, hourly). Indirect trains from Baden bei Wien to Weissenbach-Neuhaus (€5.40, 50 minutes, seven daily Monday to Saturday) require a change in Leobersdorf.

Baden bei Wien

📞 02252 / POP 25,100

With its sulphurous mineral springs (lending it an egglike smell in parts) and its lush green parks, gardens and woods, this spa town on the eastern fringes of the Wienerwald is a picturesque anomaly. Baden has a long history of receiving notable visitors; the Romans came here to wallow in the medicinal waters, Beethoven blew into town in the hope of a cure for his deafness, and in the early 19th century it flourished as the favourite summer retreat of the Habsburgs. Much of the town centre is in the 19th-century Biedermeier style. Note that Baden goes into hibernation between October and March.

The centre is about 15 minutes by foot from the train station. Follow Kaiser-Franz-Joseph-Ring west and turn right into Wassergasse.

◎ Sights & Activities

Mineral Spas & Springs   SPAS
Baden's prime attraction is its 14 hot springs that emerge at a temperature of 36°C and are enriched with sulphates. Its largest pool complex, the **Thermalstrandbad**, is actually dedicated to good old-fashioned fun. The **Römertherme** (Roman baths; 📞450 30; www.roemertherme.at; Brusattiplatz 4; 2hr/all-day entry €11.20/15.70, 3hr family card €23.50-34; ⊙10am-

10pm) is all about health and relaxation. Admission weekdays is slightly cheaper.

Arnulf Rainer Museum   MUSEUM
(www.arnulf-rainer-museum.at; Josefsplatz 5; adult/child €6/3; ⊙10am-6pm Thu-Mon, to 8pm Wed) Located inside the former Frauenbad (Women's Bathhouse), this interesting museum showcases the work of its namesake Arnulf Rainer, who was born in Baden in 1929 and studied for one day at the School of Applied Arts in Vienna. He also went to the Academy of the Fine Arts but left after three days, only to return as a respected artist and become a professor there. He began painting in a surrealist style before developing his characteristic multimedia works, some of them (like painting with chimpanzees) idiosyncratic and bizarre. The museum has retained the delightful marble features of the Biedermeier bathhouse from 1815, making it all the more worth a visit. Exhibitions change twice a year.

Kurpark   PARK
The *Kurpark* is a magnificent setting for a stroll or as a place to repose on the benches in front of the **bandstand**, where free concerts are held from May to September. The tourist office can tell you about these and others held in winter in the **Haus der Kunst** (prices and exhibitions vary); an operetta festival takes place from June to September. Attractive flower beds complement monuments to famous artists (Mozart, Beethoven, Strauss, Grillparzer etc). Near the southern entrance to the park, the **Undine-Brunnen** (fountain) is a fine amalgam of human and fish images.

Rollett Museum   MUSEUM
(Weikersdorfer Platz 1; adult/child €3/1.50; ⊙3-6pm Wed-Mon) The Rollett Museum, southwest of the town centre and just off Weilburgstrasse (a five-minute walk southeast of the Thermalstrandbad), covers important aspects of the town's history. The most unusual exhibit is the collection of skulls, busts and death masks amassed by the founder of phrenology, Josef Gall (1752–1828), who sparked the craze of inferring criminal characteristics from the shape of one's cranium. Keep your hat on.

Beethovenhaus   MUSEUM
(Rathausgasse 10; adult/child €3/1.50; ⊙4-6pm Tue-Fri, 10am-noon & 2-4pm Sat & Sun) Small museum but little to actually see inside.

MYSTERY AT MAYERLING

It's the stuff of lurid pulp fiction: the heir to the throne found dead in a hunting lodge with his teenage mistress. It became fact in Mayerling on 30 January 1889, yet for years the details of the case were shrouded in secrecy and denial. Even now a definitive picture has yet to be established – the 100th anniversary of the tragedy saw a flurry of books published on the subject, and Empress Zita claimed publicly that the heir had actually been murdered.

The heir was Archduke Rudolf, 30-year-old son of Emperor Franz Josef, husband of Stephanie of Coburg, and something of a libertine who was fond of drinking and womanising. Rudolf's marriage was little more than a public facade by the time he met the 17-year-old Baroness Maria Vetsera in the autumn of 1888. The attraction was immediate, but it wasn't until 13 January the following year that the affair was consummated, an event commemorated by an inscribed cigarette case, a gift from Maria to Rudolf.

On 28 January, Rudolf secretly took Maria with him on a shooting trip to his hunting lodge in Mayerling. His other guests arrived a day later; Maria's presence, however, remained unknown to them. On the night of 29 January, the valet, Loschek, heard the couple talking until the early hours, and at about 5.30am a fully dressed Rudolf appeared and instructed him to get a horse and carriage ready. As he was doing his master's bidding, Loschek reportedly heard two gun shots; racing back, he discovered Rudolf lifeless on his bed, with a revolver by his side. Maria was on her bed, also fully clothed, also dead. Just two days earlier Rudolf had discussed a suicide pact with his long-term mistress Mizzi Caspar. Apparently he hadn't been joking.

The official line was proffered by Empress Elisabeth, who claimed Rudolf died of heart failure. The newspapers swallowed the heart failure story, though a few speculated about a hunting accident. Then the rumours began: some believed Maria had poisoned her lover, that Rudolf had contracted an incurable venereal disease, or that he had been assassinated by Austrian secret police because of his liberal politics. Even as late as 1982, Empress Zita claimed the heir to the throne had been killed by French secret agents. Numerous books have been written on the subject, but no one can say what exactly occurred on that ill-fated morning.

Through all the intrigue, the real victim remains Maria. How much of a willing party she was to the apparent suicide will never be known. What has become clear is that Maria, after her death, represented not a tragically curtailed young life but an embarrassing scandal that had to be discreetly disposed of. Her body was left untouched for 38 hours, after which it was loaded into a carriage in such a manner as to imply that it was a living person being aided rather than a corpse beyond help. Her subsequent burial was a rude, secretive affair, during which she was consigned to the ground in an unmarked grave (her body was later moved to Heiligenkreuz). Today the hunting lodge is no more – a Carmelite nunnery stands in its place.

Dreifaltig-keitssäule   MONUMENT
Monument on Hauptplatz to the Holy Trinity, dating from 1714.

Kronprinz-Rudolf-Weg   CYCLING
Though interesting, the museums won't knock you over if you have seen those in Vienna, so cycling or hiking the 12-km long Kronprinz-Rudolf-Weg along the Schwechat River to Mayerling is a good summer alternative. The tourist office has a free trail description (in German) and bikes can be hired in town. The trail can be combined with a 6km return northern branch trail to Heiligenkreuz.

🛏 Sleeping

It's possible to visit Baden on a day trip from Vienna, and in summer the hotels can get very full. The tourist office has a good accommodation brochure.

TOP CHOICE Hotel Schloss Weikersdorf   HOTEL €€
(☎48 301-0; www.hotelschlossweikersdorf .at; Schlossgasse 9-11; s €90-140, d €140-180; P@🖥🏊) For a weekend of pampering, look no further. This hotel with modern rooms has massage services, relaxation coves and lounges and other wellness facilities; it's also set in beautiful gardens. Wi-fi is in the foyer and cable LAN in the rooms.

Villa Inge PENSION €

(☑431 71; Weilburgstrasse 24-26; s/d €42/62; ☺Apr-Oct; P@⚑) This large villa is set alongside the river and close to the Thermalstrandbad. Rooms are spacious and the breakfast room is lovely and bright, looking out to the garden. It offers good value for Baden, especially for its family apartment (from €85). Cable LAN is available in the rooms. Bus 362 stops nearby.

Hotel Kurpark HOTEL €€

(☑891 04; www.hotel-kurpark.at; Welzergasse 29; s €56-60, d 78-87, apt from €108; P🄿🛏⚑) This small hotel backing onto the *Kurpark* has a large garden, indoor and outdoor pools and bright, spacious, rooms. Children get discounts, and a third adult in the apartment pays €18. Walk north for about 10 minutes from Kaiser-Franz-Joseph-Ring.

Hotel Herzoghof HOTEL €€

(☑872 97; www.hotel-herzoghof.at; Kaiser-Franz-Ring 10; s €80-130, d €120-170, ste €140-210; P🄿) This central hotel opposite the *Kurpark* has recently been renovated and offers good value, not least for its suites, which have leadlight windows in the living area. There's a sauna and steam bath on-site, and it can be significantly cheaper in the low season. Wi-fi is in the foyer.

✖ Eating & Drinking

Baden is no great shakes when it comes to eating and drinking; nor is it really a town where the nightlife has a wild call. A few practical or very decent places can be found, however.

TOP CHOICE **Restaurant VillaNova**

INTERNATIONAL €€

(☑209 74 5; Helenenstrasse 19; mains €17-25; ☺5.30-11pm Tue-Sun) Veal roulade with carrot, ginger and polenta or tuna sashimi on carrot and ginger salad are dishes that might feature on the menu in this fine restaurant near the Thermalstrandbad. The menu is changing, but the standard is consistently high. Reserve ahead.

Café Central CAFE €

(Hauptplatz 19; coffee €3.50-7.50; ☺7am-9pm Tue-Sat, 8am-9pm Sun) Central takes pride of place on the Hauptplatz. It's a 1960s-style cafe that's a bit on the dark side but dripping with character.

Weinkult WINE BAR €€

(www.weinkult.at, in German; Pfarrgasse 7; antipasto €10; ☺11.30am-8pm Tue-Fri, 10.30am-5pm Sat) This wine shop sells almost 150 Austrian wines and serves 10 (mostly) Austrian wines by the glass, rotating the selection on a weekly basis. Antipasto is served to prime the palate.

Neumann im Josefsbad CAFE €

(www.neumann-baden.at; Josefsplatz 2; salads & schnitzel €5-7; ☺10am-1am Sun-Thu, to 2am Fri & Sat) An all-rounder serving light dishes such as chicken wings, but better known as a cafe and the hub of nightlife in town, with a DJ spinning on Friday and Saturday.

ⓘ Information

Baden Tourismus (☑226 00-600; www.baden.at; Brusattiplatz 3; ☺9am-6pm Mon-Fri, to 2pm Sat) Pick up some hiking and town maps.

Hit Mobil (Josefsplatz 3; per hr €3; ☺10am-9pm Mon-Sat, noon-9pm Sun) Internet access.

ⓘ Getting There & Around

BICYCLE **Bike 2 Train** (☑820 751; www.bike2train.at, in German; Bahnhof Baden; per 24hr €6.50-14; ☺9.30am-noon & 3-6.30pm Tue-Fri, to 1pm Sat) Useful mountain and city bike rental at the main train station.

BUS Buses depart every 30 to 60 minutes (€6, 40 minutes) from the Oper in Vienna. In Baden bus 362 runs between the Thermalstrandbad and Bahnhof via the centre.

EGGS BENEDICT IN THE BATH

Because of the sulphur content in its healing waters, Baden bei Wien has a distinctive 'poached egg' smell in parts of town. All the more unusual, therefore, when an outdoor swimming pool used for recreation and fun has this ubiquitous 'eggy' scent. If you've got a finely tuned nose, the egg smell is very in your face at the **Thermalstrandbad** (Helenenstrasse 19-21; all-day entry with locker or cabin €5.80-8.60, child/student €4.10; ☺8.30am-6.30pm May–mid-Sep). With its dubious brownish stretch of sand backed by a functionalist building from 1926, the pool complex is a sulphurous Hades-meets-Majorca. Originally, the designers wanted to import sand from the Adriatic (not exactly known for sandy beaches, but anyway); in the end they settled for sand from Melk in the Danube Valley.

CAR The north–south road routes, Hwy 17 and the A2, pass a few kilometres to the east of the town.

TRAIN Regional and S-Bahn trains connect Baden with Wien-Meidling (€5.40, 20 to 30 minutes, three times hourly) and with Wiener Neustadt (€5.40, 20 to 30 minutes).

TRAM A *Lokalbahn* tram (€5.40, one hour, every 15 minutes, one hour) connects the Oper in Vienna with Josefsplatz in Baden.

SÜD-ALPIN

This southern corner of Lower Austria, known as the Süd-Alpin (Southern Alps), has some of the province's most spectacular landscapes. Here the hills rise to meet the Alps, peaking at Schneeberg (2076m), a mountain popular among the Viennese for its skiing and hiking possibilities. Nearby Semmering has long been a favourite of the capital's burghers, due mainly to its crisp alpine air. One of the greatest highlights of the area though is the journey there; the winding railway over the Semmering Pass has been designated a Unesco World Heritage site.

Wiener Neustadt

♫ 02622 / POP 40,700

Wiener Neustadt used to be known simply as Neustadt (New Town) or Nova Civitas and was built by the Babenbergs in 1194 with the help of King Richard the Lionheart's ransom payment. It became a Habsburg residence in the 15th century during the reign of Friedrich III. His famous AEIOU (*Alles Erdreich Ist Österreich Untertan;* Everything in the world is subservient to Austria) engraving can be found throughout the city. The town was severely damaged in WWII (only 18 homes were left unscathed), so the historic buildings of Wiener Neustadt needed careful reconstruction.

◎ Sights

Hauptplatz TOWN SQUARE
The large town square is flanked by the **Rathaus**, which is something of a hybrid in styles. It began life as a Gothic building, was given some Renaissance flourishes from the late 16th century, and then when imitations came into vogue from the early 19th century a neo-Gothic spire was tacked onto it. In the centre of the square is the **Mariensäule** (Column of Mary) from 1678.

Neukloster CHURCH
(Ungargasse; ◎dawn-dusk) This 14th-century Gothic church is another hybrid. Architecturally, it is fairly straight up and down Gothic, with a vaulted ceiling and high windows, but the interior was later refurbished with baroque decorative elements, such as the altar. The clash of styles leaves a little to be desired, and the most attractive feature is the cloister, reached by the door on the right (facing the altar).

Dom CATHEDRAL
(Domplatz; ◎dawn-dusk) This cathedral runs an architectural gauntlet from the Romanesque (it dates from the late 13th century) to the Gothic and beyond to the baroque. The simplicity of the facade and clear lines are striking from the outside, but inside it will drive those who love the symmetry of the Romanesque style to despair. Fifteenth-century wooden apostles peer down from pillars and there's a baroque high altar and pulpit. To visit the **Turmmuseum**, a free-standing tower that provides grand views over the city's rooftops, you need to ask inside the Stadtmuseum. Someone will take you up there, but only in good weather.

Stadtmuseum MUSEUM
(♫373-950; Petergasse 2a; adult/student & child €3/1.50; ◎10am-4pm, to 8pm Thu) Partly housed in the former St Peter's monastery, the city museum has artefacts from the Dom and other displays on town history. Its prize item is the 15th-century Corvinus Cup that, according to legend, was a present from the Hungarian king Matthias Corvinus.

FREE Militärakademie CASTLE
(Military Academy; Burgplatz 1) Dating from the 13th century, this former castle was turned into a military academy in the mid-18th century (founded by Empress Maria Theresia) and was even commanded by the young Rommel from his pre-'desert fox' days. The academy had to be completely rebuilt after WWII, and its real highlight is **St-Georgs-Kathedrale** (◎10am-5pm), with a fine late-Gothic interior. Maximilian I, who was born in the castle, is buried under the altar. The eastern wall of the church is packed with heraldic coats of arms dating from 1453 and was the only part of the building to survive WWII unscathed. The relief depicts a genealogy of Austrian rulers. Only 19 of the heraldic arms are real – the rest were invented by Peter von Pusica, the

artisan who created it. Entry to the church is on the south side (register with the guard).

Wasserturm
WATER TOWER

(Burgplatz) Just south of the academy, rising between the convergence of two busy roads, is the town's water tower from 1910. Its shape intentionally apes the gilded goblet donated to the townsfolk by King Matthias Corvinus of Hungary after he took the town in 1487. It's still in operation today, so for reasons of hygiene you can't enter.

🛏 Sleeping

Hotel Corvinus
HOTEL €€

(☎24 134; www.hotel-corvinus.at; Bahngasse 29-33; s/d/tr €79/122/156; 🅿@🛜🍴) Catering to business and seminar guests as well as tourists, the Corvinus has bright rooms sweetened with extras such as a wellness area, a bar and a leafy terrace. The cube-like exterior may not appeal to all, but this four-star hotel is very comfortable inside. There's wi-fi in the foyer and some rooms (€1.50 per 15 minutes) and it has adjoining rooms suitable for families (cots provided).

Jugendherberge
HOSTEL €

(☎296 95; oejhv-noe@oejhv.or.at; Promenade 1; dm/s/d €17/20/40; 🅿🍴) This HI hostel is situated in the *Stadtpark,* near the *Wasserturm.* Phone ahead as reception is not always open and it's often full.

Hotel Zentral
HOTEL €

(☎23 169; www.hotel-zentral.tos.at; Hauptplatz 27; s €40-47, d €75-85, tr €98, q €115; 🍴@🛜) Situated right in the heart of town, Zentral has a historic foyer and comfortable rooms decked out with modern furnishings. Some front Hauptplatz.

🍴 Eating & Drinking

Billa supermarkets can be found on Bahngasse and Hauptplatz; the latter has **food stands** selling regional specialities each Friday from 12.30pm to 6pm. Herrengasse, just north of Hauptplatz, has a few drinking options.

TOP
CHOICE
Brod
AUSTRIAN €€€

(☎281 07; Bahngasse 1; mains €18-24, 4-6 course menus €40-60; ☉Tue-Sat; 🍴🍴) Situated in a lovely baroque house, this quality restaurant has the attraction of courtyard seating for warm summer nights. Austrian wines, especially those from Burgenland, feature prominently on its long wine list. Upmarket renditions of Austrian classics such as *Tafelspitz* share a place with delicious new cuisine. Most mains come in small and large portions.

Zum Weissen Rössl
BEISL €

(Hauptplatz 3; mains €7-11; ☉7am-8pm Mon-Sat; 🍴) This *Gasthaus* may look a little dusty from the outside, but it's cosy and welcoming and serves solid Austrian food, including a choice of a small or large goulash. There's outdoor seating on Hauptplatz.

Hartig's
AUSTRIAN €

(Domplatz 2; mains €8.50-14; ☉lunch & dinner) This *Gasthöfe* serves a range of Austrian classics (but not a true Wiener schnitzel from veal, unfortunately) in a *Beisl*-like atmosphere. The beer garden out the back is one of the most pleasant in town and this is also what makes it so popular among the locals.

ℹ Information

Tourist office (☎373-311; Hauptplatz 3; ☉8am-5pm Mon-Fri, to noon Sat) Stocks a free English-language booklet, *Cultural Promenade,* describing the central sights and giving their locations on a map.

ℹ Getting There & Away

Several trains each hour connect Wiener Neustadt with Wien-Meidling (€9.20, 25 to 45 minutes). Postbus services depart from the northern end of Wiener Neustadt train station.

Semmering
☎02664 / POP 600

With its clean air and grandiose peaks rising out of deeply folded valleys, Semmering is a popular alpine resort for the Viennese, especially among a slightly older crowd who come to this spa town in summer for peaceful walks or to ride the railway; a younger set hits the ski pistes. There's no real centre to the resort: it's mostly ranged along Hochstrasse, which forms an arc behind the train station.

🏃 Activities

Hiking
HIKING

Towering over Semmering to the south is the **Hirschenkogel** ('Zauberberg'; 1340m), where a modern cable car whisks walkers (one way/return €10/13.50) or skiers to the top. The tourist office and Infostelle have maps and brochures on walks.

Two fairly easy trails follow the scenic route of the Semmeringbahn, starting behind the train station. One follows the line

SEMMERING PASS BY TRAIN

For its time, it was an incredible feat of engineering and it took more than 20,000 workers' years to complete. Even today, it never fails to impress with its switchbacks, 15 tunnels and 16 viaducts. This is the **Semmeringbahn** (Semmering Railway; www.semmering-bahn.at, in German), a 42km stretch of track that begins at Gloggnitz and rises 455m to its highest point of 896m at Semmering Bahnhof.

Completed in 1854 by Karl Ritter von Ghega, the Semmering line was Europe's first alpine railway; due to its engineering genius, it gained Unesco World Heritage status in 1998. It passes through some impressive scenery of precipitous cliffs and forested hills en route; the most scenic section is the 30-minute stretch between Semmering and Payerbach.

From Vienna, most EC services stop at Mürzzuschlag, from where you take a regional train to Semmering (€25, 1¾ hours) or take regional trains and change at Payerbach-Reichenau (€21, two hours).

LOWER AUSTRIA SÜD-ALPIN

for 17km to Mürzzuschlag in Styria, where frequent trains chug you back to Semmering, and a second leads to Breitenstein and Klamm (Lower Austria), 9.5km and 15km respectively from the start. At Klamm the trail divides and one route leads to Payerbach (21km from the start) and another to Gloggnitz (23km from the start).

Skiing
SKIING

The tourist office can provide information on ski schools. A winter skiing day pass for the Hirschenkogel cable car costs €31.50. Regional skiing day passes are also available for €34.50.

Cycling
CYCLING

If the hills don't kill you, they'll make you stronger. The tourist office rents bicycles per 24 hours €10.

Hotel Panhans
SPA

(☑818 10; www.panhans.at; Hochstrasse 32) The four-star Hotel Panhans has a swimming pool and wellness area that can be used by nonguests (day cards weekdays/weekends €9/13).

Sleeping & Eating

Most sleeping options are situated on Hochstrasse. Many have their own restaurants, which means there's only a short hobble between table and bed. There is a **Billa** supermarket opposite the tourist office.

TOP CHOICE Panorama Hotel Wagner HOTEL €€

(☑2512-0; www.panoramahotel-wagner.at, in German; Hochstrasse 267; s/d/ste €69/138/158; P❄@🐾♨) Body and mind are catered for in this ecofriendly hotel: rooms have wood furniture, natural cotton bedding and grand views of the valley. Wi-fi is in the library. You can chill out with sauna, spa and massage facilities. Its highly rated restaurant (mains €10 to €20) uses organic products.

Pension-Restaurant Löffler PENSION €

(☑23 04; www.hotel-loeffler.at; Hochstrasse 174; s/d €43/80; P) Löffler is a fresh, colourful and modern B&B with a restaurant (mains €9 to €18) serving classic meat and fish dishes, including baby lamb, pepper steaks and trout.

Hotel-Restaurant Belvedere HOTEL €€

(☑22 70; www.belvedere-semmering.at; Hochstrasse 60; s/d €41/96; P♨🐾) The family-run Belvedere has alpine decor, rooms with balconies, and features such as a swimming pool, sauna and large garden and patio area. Doubles with connecting doors are suitable for families.

ℹ Information

Infostelle Bahnhof (www.semmeringbahn. at, in German; ⊙9-11.30am & 2-5pm May-Oct) Run by railway enthusiasts, with material on the Semmeringbahn. Good stock of the town's brochures. The *Semmering* booklet has useful addresses and a handy sketch map of town.

Tourismusbüro Semmering (☑200 25; www. semmering.at, in German; Passhöhe 248; ⊙8am-noon & 1-4pm Mon-Fri, 9am-noon Sat) A bank is located next door and shops are across the road.

ℹ Getting There & Around

CAR Consider taking the small back road northwest of Semmering to Höllental via Breitenstein; the road winds its way down the mountain, passing under the railway line a number of times and taking in the spectacular scenery you see on the train trip.

TAXI A **taxi** (☎8047) costs about €10 from the train station to the Hauptstrasse guesthouses.

TRAIN Semmering has frequent daily connections with Breitenstein (€2, 10 minutes), Klamm, (€3.60, 15 minutes), Payerbach (€5.40, 30 minutes) and Gloggnitz (change in Payerbach; €5.40, 40 minutes). At least once-daily direct EC/IC trains between Graz (€18, 1½ hours) and Vienna (€21, 1¼ hours) stop at Semmering.

Schneeberg, Raxalpe & Höllental

To the north of Semmering are two of Lower Austria's highest peaks, Schneeberg (2076m) and the Raxalpe (2007m). The area is easily reached by train from Vienna, making it popular for hiking.

The trailhead for hiking or taking the cogwheel railway is **Puchberg am Schneeberg**, where the **tourist office** (☎02636-2256; www.puchberg.at; Sticklergasse 3; ⊙9am-noon & 1-5pm Mon-Thu, 9am-noon & 3-5pm Fri) can tell you about hiking conditions on Schneeberg. The **Schneebergbahn** (☎02636-3661-20; www.schneebergbahn.at, in German; Salamander one way/return €22.60/32; ⊙late Apr-Oct) leaves from Puchberg am Schneeberg and takes about an hour on the Salamander and around 1¼ hours on the steam train; check the website for the train timetable.

Several huts are situated on the mountain for sustenance, accommodation or shelter. **Hengsthütte** (www.hengsthuette.at; Hoch schneeberg 1; ⊙Tue-Sun Apr-Oct, Sat & Sun Nov-Mar) and **Baumgartenhütte** (Hochschneeberg 5; light mains €6-8; ⊙daily when train runs) are situated along the railway line; **Berghaus Hochschneeberg** (☎02636-2257; berghaus. hochschneeberg@aon.at; Hochschneeberg 7; s/d €36/72) is at the mountain railway station and **Damböckhaus** (☎02636-2259; www.

damboeckhaus.at; Hochschneeberg 8; mattresses/beds €17/23; ⊙May-Oct) is on the plateau.

In Puchberg itself **Gasthof Pension Schmirl** (☎02636-2277; www.schmirl.at, in German; Muthenhofer Strasse 8; s/d €27/62; P⊗★) has comfortable rooms on the edge of town near the railway. Some have balconies; in others you can psyche yourself for the stiff climb ahead with window views of Schneeberg.

On the southern side of Schneeberg is the scenic **Höllental** (Hell's Valley), a deep, narrow gorge created by the Schwarza River. Rising to the south of Höllental is the **Raxalpe**, another place for walkers; from Hirschwang, a small village in Höllental, the **Raxseilbahn** (☎02666-524 97; www.raxseilbahn.at, in German; return adult/child/family €19.30/11.50/30.70) cable car ascends to 1547m and hiking trails. The Raxseilbahn is the site of Austria's first cable car, built in 1926.

In Höllental, the **Hotel Marienhof** (☎02666-529 95; www.marienhof.at, in German; Hauptstrasse 71-73, Reichenau; s/d €86/124; P⊗★), a grand old dame with a restaurant (mains €11 to €14), is not far from the Raxseilbahn. Suites cost €89 per person, and an extra bed is another €25 for children between six and 15 years for families. It also has bicycle hire.

❶ Getting There & Away

There are hourly direct trains daily from Vienna to Puchberg am Schneeberg (€13.90, 1½ hours), going via Wiener Neustadt (€9.20, 25 to 45 minutes). Hirschwang (€17.50, two hours) is only a little harder to get to from Vienna; a train must first be taken to Payerbach, from where hourly to two-hourly buses run up the Höllental valley (€1.80, 15 minutes) every morning.

Burgenland

Best Places to Eat

» Mooslechners Bürgerhaus (p144)

» Weingut Gabriel (p145)

» Zur Dankbarkeit (p148)

» Burg Güssing (p149)

Best Places to Stay

» Mooslechners Bürgerhaus (p144)

» Weingut & Weingasthof Kloster am Spitz (p146)

» St Martins Therme & Lodge (p147)

» Hotel-Restaurant Pannonia (p147)

» Burg Bernstein (p149)

Why Go?

Burgenland is all but the typical Austria you hear of or read about, as soaring mountains, glacial lakes and bombastic architecture are *not* the reasons for coming here. Even the jewel in its crown – Neusiedler See – has dried up and disappeared several times in its natural history, most recently in the mid-19th century.

What Burgenland does have is wine – wine in abundance – and the aquatic outdoors, especially around the reedy shores of the Neusiedler See (Europe's second-largest steppe lake). Around the Neusiedler See-Seewinkel National Park, a bike path takes you along this shore through a landscape humming and buzzing with birdlife, and even through Hungary before you re-emerge in Austria. In the south of the province, where you find a few interesting castles and museums, a car is useful. Burgenland is very low-key, but a place where you can relax lakeside or in rolling landscapes.

When to Go

Burgenland, especially the Neusiedler See region in the north, is only worth visiting during the main April to October period. At other times of year much of the province goes into winter hibernation and its prime attraction – the outdoors – becomes cold, grey and windswept. Two exceptions to this are St Martins Therme (St Martin's Spa) in Frauenkirchen, with its sauna, thermal pool and other spa facilities; and the capital Eisenstadt, which has a cultural focus.

Burgenland Highlights

1 Sipping wines and supping in one of the pretty **Heurigen** (wine tavern; p145) in Rust, or one of the other towns dotted across Burgenland

2 Swimming, splashing or sailing in the **Neusiedler See** (p143), Austria's slurping steppe lake

3 Cycling at a leisurely pace through the **Neusiedler See-Seewinkel National Park** (p148), a haven for bird life

4 Revelling in the views from Eisenstadt's **Bergkirche** (p141) after completing the Stations of the Cross

5 Taking in the thermal waters at Frauenkirchen's **St Martins Therme & Lodge** (p147)

6 Exploring the castles set in rolling hills in and around **Lockenhaus** (p149)

History

Burgenland is the youngest of Austria's provinces, arising after the collapse of the Austrian empire at the end of WWI. It's named for the 'burg' suffix of the four western Hungarian district names at that time – Pressburg (Bratislava), Wieselburg (Moson), Ödenburg (Soporn) and Eisenburg (Vasvär).

In the 10th century it fell into the hands of Hungary, but German-speaking peasants gradually settled land between the Hungarian villages. The arrival of marauding Turks in the 16th century quashed both the Hungarians and the Austrian-Germans, and devastated the local population. Landlords, without anyone to tend their farms, invited substantial numbers of Croats to settle, laying the foundations for the area's Hungarian and Croatian influences today – around 10% of the population is Croatian, and Croatian (along with Hungarian) is a recognised local language; a few small towns in middle Burgenland bear Croat signs.

With the demise of the Habsburg empire after WWI, Austria lost control of Hungary, but it eventually managed to retain the German-speaking western region of Hungary under the Treaty of St Germain. The new province of Burgenland was born, but Hungary was loath to lose Ödenburg (Sopron) to Austria, and a plebiscite held in December 1921 (under controversial circumstances) resulted in the people of Ödenburg opting to stay in Hungary. Burgenland lost its natural capital, and Eisenstadt became the new *Hauptstadt* (capital).

ℹ Getting There & Around

See the boxed text for more on cycling, and p144 for more on ferry services. Lower and middle Burgenland are mostly served by buses, but Sunday services are patchy or nonexistent. The A2 autobahn, heading south from Vienna towards Graz and Carinthia, runs parallel to the western border of Burgenland. Its many off-ramps provide quick, easy access to much of the province. The A4 leads to Neusiedl am See. Eisenstadt and the northern extension of Neusiedler See are easily reached by train from Vienna and Lower Austria.

EISENSTADT

📞 02682 / POP 12,900

The small capital of Burgenland is best known for its most famous former resident, 18th-century musician and composer, Joseph Haydn. Although it doesn't have a large number of attractions for visitors, it does have a wonderful palace, a couple of good museums and a rather bizarre church. Its nightlife hums rather than buzzes, but taking in its sights can easily be done on a day trip from Vienna or as an excursion from pretty, lakeside Rust.

◉ Sights

TOP CHOICE **Schloss Esterházy**　　　PALACE

(www.schloss-esterhazy.at; adult/child/family palace tour €7.50/6.50/16, 'Haydn Explosive' €8/6/17, combined ticket €9.90/8.50/19; ⊙tours hourly 10am-6pm, limited hr or closed mid-Nov–Mar; ℗) Schloss Esterházy, a giant, Schönbrunn-yellow castle-palace that dominates Esterházyplatz, is Eisenstadt's most important attraction. Dating from the 14th century, the *Schloss* (castle) received one makeover in baroque and a later one in the neoclassical style. Many of the 256 rooms are occupied by the provincial government, but 25 can be viewed on tours.

The regular tour covers about seven rooms, giving you an insight into the history of the palace and the lives of the people who lived in it. The highlight is the frescoed

ℹ HIRING BIKES

Burgenland is a cyclist's dream. Much of the landscape is flat or has gently rolling hills and is crisscrossed with well-marked cycle paths. Local tourist offices can supply cycle maps. From Neusiedl am See the 135-km Neusiedler See bike trail leads south, crossing into Hungary (bring your passport) for 38km before the path re-emerges in Austria just south of Mörbisch on the western side of the lake.

» **Nextbike** (📞01-319 0254 to pick up or return a bike; http://nextbike.at) Has over 16 stations around the Neusiedler See and in Eisenstadt where you can hire and drop off a rented bicycle. The website explains the steps and how to register (which you need to do in advance on the website).

» **Fahrräder Bucsis** (📞02167-207 90; www.fahrraeder-bucsis.at, in German; train station, Neusiedl am See; per day €15; ⊙8.30am-7pm Mar–mid-Oct) Located at the train station in Neusiedl am See. The bike path begins at the door.

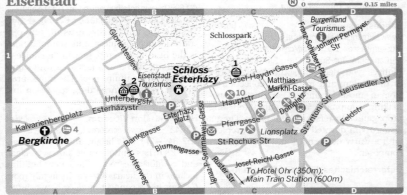

Haydn Hall, where during Haydn's employment by the Esterházys from 1761 to 1790 the composer conducted an orchestra on a nearnightly basis.

The **Haydn Explosive exhibition** across the palace courtyard offers an interesting conflux of history and the new: Haydn's music accompanies you as you walk past exhibitions on the life and work of the great composer, a nifty holograph depicts a string quartet, period furniture is projected onto the ceiling and a minuscule hole in the floor has an odd projection of a bare-breasted woman shouting abuse while burning in hell. To get the most out of the palace and Haydn, do the tour, then the Haydn exhibition.

Shortly after Joseph Haydn died in 1809, his skull was stolen from his grave in Vienna. The headless cadaver was returned to Eisenstadt in 1920, but it wasn't until 1954 that the skull rejoined it in the Bergkirche.

Bergkirche CHURCH
(www.haydnkirche.at, in German; Haydnplatz 1; admission €3; ⊙9am-5pm Apr-Oct) This unusual church contains the white-marble tomb with Haydn's reunited parts. It began life as a small chapel and in 1701 was transformed into a bizarre representation of Calvary, the mountain outside Jerusalem upon which Christ is thought to have been crucified. Manage all the dungeon-like rooms and you'll be feeling the Stations of the Cross in your feet; get to the top of the 'mountain', though, and awaiting you is not a gaggle of stone-throwing sinners but a fantastic view over town.

Haydn-Haus MUSEUM
(www.haydnhaus.at, in German; Josef-Haydn-Gasse 21; adult/child/family €4/3.50/9; ⊙9am-5pm Apr–mid-Nov) Situated in a house dating from the early 18th century, this museum dedicated to Haydn was where the great composer lived from 1766 to 1778. Although the museum won't knock your socks off unless you are an avid fan of Haydn, the collection offers an insight into his private life and has reconstructed rooms with furniture from the era to round off the Haydn experience. Original portraits cover the walls, and there are some rare exhibits such as a fortepiano that was made in Eisenstadt and a letter

from Haydn's lover to the son that he is generally believed to have sired.

Landesmuseum
MUSEUM

(www.burgenland.at/landesmuseum, in German; Museumgasse 1-5; adult/child/family €5/4/9; ☺10am-5pm Tue-Sun) The Landesmuseum plunges you deep into the local history of the region, and includes a collection of Roman mosaics, ancient artefacts, wine-making equipment and some interesting propaganda posters from the 1920s. There's also a room devoted to Franz Liszt, replete with a warty death mask of the Hungarian composer.

Österreichisches Jüdisches Museum
MUSEUM

(www.ojm.at, in German; Unterbergstrasse 6; adult/child/family €4/3/6; ☺10am-5pm Tue-Sun May-Oct) Situated in the former Judengasse, the street where Eisenstadt's Jewish population mostly lived in the Middle Ages, this museum has a permanent exhibition illustrating the rituals and lifestyle of Eisenstadt's Jews. Descriptions are in German and Hebrew. Part of the museum is the historic private synagogue of Samson Wertheimer, who was born in Worms in Germany in 1658 and rose to the position of rabbi in Hungary. He financed the synagogue, and it was one of the few to survive the pogroms of 1938.

★☆ Festivals & Events

Internationale Haydntage
CLASSICAL CONCERT

A 10-day series of concerts held in September, attracting excellent local acts and top international performers. It features everything from chamber pieces to full-scale orchestral performances. Most events take place in the Haydn Hall or the Bergkirche; for more information contact the **Haydnfestspiele Büro** (☎618 66-0; www.haydnfestival.at). Expect to pay from €20 to €80, depending on the performance and quality of seat.

Fest der 1000 Weine
WINE FESTIVAL

Schlosspark becomes the setting for wine tasting in late August, when you can try 1000 Burgenland wines and some local nibbles to scores of music.

🛏 Sleeping

Staff at the tourist office have a complete list of accommodation. While the offerings are fine, splurging is better done on Neusiedler See rather than in Burgenland's capital.

Hotel Burgenland
HOTEL €€

(☎6960; www.hotelburgenland.at; Franz-Schubert-Platz 1; s €85-110, d €160, ste from €220; ℗@🖥📶⛱) Despite the unflattering exterior, this centrally located business and seminar hotel is the best of the crop, offering a choice of restaurants and a wellness area with sauna and indoor swimming pool. The fitness area, though, is small. According to season and demand, prices can be lower.

Hotel-Pension Vicedom
PENSION €€

(☎642 22; www.vicedom.at; Vicedom 5; s/d €52/84; ☺🖥) This bright and breezy three-star B&B has quite simple but very clean and comfortable rooms in a new building located in the heart of town. Its family room for four has a connecting door between two bedrooms and staff can also set up a double and a single bed in the one room. If checking in early, you can pay €7 for breakfast on the day of arrival. Cable LAN costs €2 per 30 minutes.

Hotel Ohr
HOTEL €€

(☎624 60; www.hotelohr.at; Ruster Strasse 51; s €65-115, d €95-145, tr €140, q €160; ℗☺) The Ohr is a family-run hotel with nicely styled modern rooms and within walking distance of the centre. Its rustic restaurant (mains €8 to €16; closed Monday October to May) is one of the best around: there's leafy outdoor/undercover seating on decking and it serves seasonal dishes often on a theme, such as goose around St Martin's Day (11 November). Cable LAN is available.

Haus der Begegnung
HOSTEL €

(☎632 90; www.hdb-eisenstadt.at; Kalvarienbergplatz 11; s/d €46/76; ℗☺) This church-affiliated pension is spotless, very quiet and well run. Rooms are simple but comfortable and it has its own grassed cafe area. It's open to everyone, but obviously not the place to stay if you want to party all night.

✖ Eating

Mangoo
TEX-MEX €€

(www.mangoo-bar.at, in German; Domplatz 4 48; burgers €6, grills €15-25; ☺10am-4am Tue-Sat; ☺) This lively crossover eatery and lounge serves everything from hamburgers to the full range of Tex-Mex, like burritos, chicken wings, fajitas and good old-fashioned steak. There's a small outdoor area out the back and on Friday and Saturday a DJ works the crowd.

Haydnbräu   AUSTRIAN €

(www.haydnbraeu.at, in German; Pfarrgasse 22; mains €6.50-16; ⊗8am-11pm; ☻⊞) Duck into this microbrewery and restaurant for some of the best-value eating in town: culinary classics like schnitzel and goulash complemented by some seasonal dishes. The lunch menu is an affordable €6 and the snack menu has small portions suitable for kids.

Kredenz   INTERNATIONAL, BAR €€

(www.kredenz.at, in German; Pfarrgasse 33; mains €15-17, light mains €6.90-8.70; ⊗10am-10pm Mon-Thu, to midnight Fri & Sat; ☻) This small cafe and bistro-style eatery serves a small range of dishes but it does them superbly – steak, chicken breast in a teriyaki sauce, or a lunch menu (€6.90) that might be cream of celery soup with chicken breast and risotto with chanterelle mushrooms.

Spar   SUPERMARKET

(Hauptstrasse 13) Located on the main street.

ⓘ Information

Burgenland Tourismus (☏0633 84-0; www.burgenland.info; Johann-Permayer-Strasse 13; ⊗8.30am-5pm Mon-Fri)

Eisenstadt Tourismus (☏673 90; www.eisenstadt.at, in German; Glorietteallee 1; ⊗8am-5pm Mon-Fri, 9am-1pm Sat & Sun Apr-Oct, closed Fri from 1pm & Sat & Sun Nov-Mar) Located alongside the palace; provides a useful brochure listing hotels, private rooms, restaurants, festivals and details of museums.

Hospital and pharmacy (☏601; Esterházystrasse 26)

Main Post Office (☏62 27 10; Ignaz-P-Semmelweis-Gasse 7)

Ricky's Cafe (Pfarrgasse 18; per 25 min €2; ⊗9.30-2am) Internet access.

ⓘ Getting There & Away

BUS About 30 direct buses leave from Vienna's Südtiroler Platz daily (€7.20, 1¼ hours).

TRAIN Direct trains leave from Südbahnhof (Ostbahn)/Hauptbahnhof (€14.60, 1¼ hours, eight daily); frequent indirect trains leave from Wien-Meidling.

AROUND EISENSTADT

Burg Forchtenstein

Straddling a dolomite spur some 20km southwest of Eisenstadt, **Burg Forchtenstein** (www.burg-forchtenstein.at, in German;

Melinda Esterházy-Platz 1; guided tour of castle & arsenal adult/child/family €8/7/21; ⊗10am-6pm Apr-Oct) is one of Burgenland's imposing castles. This stronghold was built in the 14th century and enlarged by the Esterházys (who still own it today) in 1635. Apart from a grand view from its ramparts, the castle's highlights include an impressive collection of armour and weapons, portraits of regal Esterházys in the **Ahnengalerie** (Ancestral Gallery; guided tour of castle & Ancestral Gallery adult/child/family €13.50/12/35) and spoils from the Turkish wars (the castle curators will proudly tell you Forchtenstein was the only castle in the area not to fall to the Turks). Its **Schatzkammer** (treasury; guided tour of castle & treasury adult/child/family €15/13.50/42) contains a rich collection of jewellery and porcelain.

ⓘ Getting There & Away

On weekdays three buses run direct from Eisenstadt (€5.60, 40 minutes) and two from Wiener Neustadt (€4.70, 30 minutes) to Forchtenstein. Frequent indirect buses do the Eisenstadt route, and there's a train and bus (change to bus in Wiesen-Siegless) from Wiener Neustadt.

Wiesen

About 5km north of Forchtenstein lies the small town of Wiesen which, during summer, morphs into Austria's version of Glastonbury or Woodstock. The series of summer festivals hosted here is the biggest in the country and ranges from jazz to reggae. For more information, log on to www.wiesen.at.

Trains to Wiesen leave Vienna's Wien-Meidling station at least every two hours (€11, 50 to 80 minutes).

NEUSIEDLER SEE

Neusiedler See, Europe's second-largest steppe lake, is the lowest point in Austria. But what it lacks in height, it makes up for in other areas. Ringed by a wetland area of reed beds, it's an ideal breeding ground for nearly 300 bird species – its Seewinkel area is a favourite for bird-watching. The lake's average depth is 1.5m, which means the water warms quickly in summer. Add to this the prevailing warm winds from the northwest and you have a water enthusiast's dream come true. Thousands of tourists flock to the lake for windsurfing and sailing during the summer months. The best swimming beaches are on the eastern side of the

ℹ DISCOUNT CARD

If you are staying overnight in Eisenstadt or in towns on the Neusiedler See, make sure you get the **Neusiedler See Card**, which gives you free transport on buses and trains around the lake and on town buses, as well as free or discount admission to many sights. Take the registration form given to you by your host to an issuing office (tourist offices are the easiest) and you'll be given the card free for the duration of your stay.

lake, as the western shore is thick with reed beds.

The area is also perfect for cycling: a flat cycle track winds all the way round the reed beds, the ferries crisscrossing the lake carry bikes, and most hotels and pensions cater well to cyclists. It's possible to do a full circuit of the lake but, as the southern section stretches into Hungary, remember to bring your passport.

To top it all off there are acres of vineyards, making some of Austria's best wines. Rust, on the western shore of the lake, is a perfect place to sample wine in a *Heuriger*.

ℹ Information

Neusiedler See Tourismus (☎02167-8600; www.neusiedlersee.com; Obere Hauptstrasse 24, Neusiedl am See; ⊙8am-5pm Mon-Fri) The information centre for the lake region for telephone, post and email enquiries.

ℹ Getting Around

From late spring to early autumn ferries connect Illmitz with Mörbisch, Rust and Fertörákos in Hungary; Rust with Podersdorf, Breitenbrunn and Fertörákos; and Breitenbrunn with Podersdorf. See www.neusiedlersee.com/de (under Reiseführer/Fahrradfähren) for current schedules. Prices are €5 to €6.50 for adults and €3 to €4.50 for children.

For more on bike hire, see the boxed text, p140.

Bus connections are frequent; see the separate towns below for specific details.

Rust

02685 / POP 1700

Rust, 14km east of Eisenstadt, is one of the nicest towns along the Neusiedler See. Its reed seashore and hidden boatsheds give it a

sleepy, swampy feel on a steamy day, and in the summer months storks glide lazily overhead, make out with each other, and clack their beaks from rooftop roosts. Dozens of storks make their homes on chimneys in town, although it's wine, not storks, that has made Rust prosperous. In 1524 the emperor granted local vintners the right to display the letter 'R' (a distinctive insignia as a mark of origin from Rust) on their wine barrels and today the corks still bear this insignia. It's best to sample this history in one of the town's many *Heurigen*.

⊙ Sights & Activities

Katholische Kirche   CHURCH
(Haydengasse; ⊙10.30-noon & 2.30-5pm, closed Sun morning) This church's tower is a good vantage point for observing storks. It's at the southern end of Rathausplatz.

Fischerkirche   CHURCH
(Rathausplatz 16; ⊙dawn-dusk Apr-Oct) At the opposite end of Rathausplatz, this is the oldest church in Rust, built between the 12th and 16th centuries.

Burgher houses   HISTORIC BUILDINGS
Rust's affluent past has left a legacy of attractive burgher houses on and around the main squares. Storks, which descend on the town from the end of March to rear their young, take full advantage of these houses (and their kindly owners, who have erected metal platforms on chimneys to entice the storks). The clacking of expectant parents can be heard till late August.

Seebad Rust   SWIMMING
(www.seebadrust.at; adult €4; ⊙9am-7pm, May–mid-Sep) Access to the lake and bathing facilities is 1km down the reed-fringed Seepromenade. The swimming is very reedy but refreshing.

🛏 Sleeping

TOP CHOICE **Mooslechners Bürgerhaus**
                    HOTEL €€€
(☎6162; www.hotelbuergerhaus-rust.at; Hauptstrasse 1; ste €212-254; 3-/4-/5-course menus €49/59/69; P🐾🛜🍴) Popular for honeymoon nights and weddings, this exquisite hotel has spiral staircases inside a 1537 building. Rooms are in Biedermeier style, some with vaulted ceilings and drapes around the bed. It caters superbly for children, with cots on hand, and the option of an extra bed at a discount. The restaurant downstairs (closed Monday) is top class and has a magnificent

garden setting. Cable (LAN) internet costs €10 per day.

Hotel Sifkovits
HOTEL €€

(☑276; www.sifkovits.at; Am Seekanal 8; r €130; mains €10-18; [P][⊖][🛜][♿]) Close to the centre of town, Sifkovits is a fine family-run hotel with large rooms, a lift and extras like its downstairs lounge with a bowl of fruit and a refrigerator stocked with free mineral water. It also has a good restaurant. Cots are available and extra beds for kids at a discount.

Alexander
PENSION €€

(☑301; www.pension-alexander.at, in German; Dorfmeistergasse 21; s €57, d 76-114, ste €130; [P][❄][♿]) Though situated on the northern outskirts of town and more suitable if you have your own bike or car, Alexander is a great deal for comfortable three- and four-star rooms; take advantage of its sauna, garden and outdoor swimming pool. Cots and children's beds are available.

Storchencamp
CAMPING €

(☑595; office@gmeiner.co.at; Ruster Bucht; camp sites per adult/tent/car €5.60/4.50/4.50; ⊙Apr-Oct; [P][❄][♿]) With a large children's playground, cheap bike rental, close proximity to the lake and free access to the bathing area, this camp site is a great place for families.

Ruster Jugendgästehaus & Pension
HOSTEL €

(☑591; www.seebadrust.at; Ruster Bucht 2; dm/s/d €17/36/60; ⊙Jan-Dec; [⊖][♿]) This HI hostel is right on the harbour, forms part of the bathing complex and has modern, clean rooms.

✗ Eating & Drinking

When in Rust, do as the locals do and head for one of the many *Heurigen*. They're easy to spot – just look for the *Buschen* (small wreath) hanging in front of doorways. Some operate under restaurant licences and are therefore open throughout the summer. For some of the finest formal eating in town, see Mooslechners Bürgerhaus.

[TOP CHOICE] Weingut Gabriel
HEURIGER €€

(www.weingut-gabriel.at, in German; Hauptstrasse 25; cold platters about €12; ⊙from 4pm Thu & Fri, from 2pm Sat & Sun Apr-Oct; [♿]) Not only is the pay-by-weight buffet brimming with delicious sausage and cold cuts, the wine is a treat, and in season the idyllic cobblestone courtyard is a wonderful vantage point for observing storks.

Peter Schandl
AUSTRIAN €

(Hauptstrasse 20; mains €6-12; ⊙4pm-midnight Mon & Wed-Fri, from 11am Sat & Sun Apr-Oct) With more of a restaurant feel, here you can enjoy game goulash and other warm dishes just off Rathausplatz.

ℹ Information

Tourist office (☑502; www.rust.at; Conradplatz 1, Rathaus; ⊙9am-noon & 1-4pm Mon-Fri, 9am-6pm Sat, 9am-noon Sun) Has a list of wine growers offering tastings, plus hotels and private rooms in the town.

ℹ Getting There & Away

One to two hourly buses connect Eisenstadt and Rust (€3.60, 25 minutes). For Neusiedl am See (€3.60, 40 minutes, every one to two hours), change to the train at Schützen am Gebirge train station. Ferries cross the lake to Podersdorf, Breitenbrunn and Fertörákos.

Mörbisch am See

☑02685 / POP 2350

Mörbisch am See is a quiet town 6km south of Rust and only a couple of kilometres from the Hungarian border. It's pleasant for soaking up a relaxed atmosphere and taking in quaint whitewashed houses with hanging corn and flower-strewn balconies.

The town's sleepy mood changes dramatically during the evening from mid-July to August with the **Seefestspiele** (www.seefestspiele-moerbisch.at), a summer operetta festival that attracts some 200,000 people each year. Its biggest competitor is the **Opern Festspiele** (www.ofs.at, in German; ⊙early Jul-late Aug), an opera festival held in an old Roman quarry near St Margareten, around 7km northwest of Mörbisch.

The local **tourist office** (☑8430; www.moerbisch.com; Hauptstrasse 23; ⊙9am-5pm Mon-Fri, to noon Sat & Sun) can advise on accommodation and what's available, the festivals, and lakeside facilities, and give you a list of *Heurigen*.

Frequent buses go to Mörbisch via Rust from Eisenstadt (€3.60, 40 minutes). A foot- and cycle-only **border crossing** into Hungary, 2km south of Mörbisch, is handy for those circumnavigating the lake. There are no border controls, but you do need to be able to show your passport on demand. Alternatively, jump on the ferry across the lake to keep within Austria.

Purbach am See

📞 02683 / POP 2700

Purbach am See, 17km north of Rust, is another pretty town along the lake. Its small, compact centre is filled with squat houses and it is still protected by bastions and three gates – reminders of the Turkish wars. While there isn't a lot to see in the town – nor has it direct access to Neusiedler See – it's nice to soak up the slow pace of life and wander from one **wine cellar** (⊙from 4pm 1st Sat in month Apr-Oct) to the next along historic Kellergasse and Kellerplatz, both outside the town's walls.

The **tourist office** (📞5920; www.purbach. at, in German; Hauptgasse 38; ⊙9am-noon & 3-6pm Mon-Sat May-Oct, closed Sat Nov-Apr) has information on accommodation and wine. If you need a place to stay, look no further than **Camping Purbach & Jugendherberge** (📞51 70; office@gmeiner.co.at; Türkenhain; camp sites per adult/child/tent/car €4.90/3.40/2.90/2.90, dm €20; ⊙Apr-Oct; 🅓) on the edge of the reed beds, or **Gasthof zum Türkentor** (📞3400; www.foltin.at; Hauptgasse 2; s/d €58/116; 🅿🛜), situated right alongside the old city wall in the historic part of town.

TOP CHOICE **Weingut & Weingasthof Kloster am Spitz** (📞5519; www. klosteramspitz.at, in German; Waldsiedlung 2; s €75, d €120-140, q €300; 6-course menus incl wine €78, mains €13-26; ⊙lunch & dinner Thu-Sun & lunch Wed Mar-Dec; 🅿🍽), on the northwestern fringe of town among vineyards (follow Fellnergasse), is a small former monastery with a modern hotel. Wines from the vineyard are produced organically and served in its very highly rated restaurant.

ℹ Getting There & Away

Purbach has direct train connections with Neusiedl am See (€3.60, 11 minutes, 18 daily), Eisenstadt (€3.60, 15 minutes, 18 daily) and Vienna Südbahnhof (Ostbahn)/Hauptbahnhof (€12.40, 50 minutes, 11 daily), and direct bus connections with Eisenstadt (€3.60, 20 minutes, 14 daily). From Rust, get off in Schützen am Gebirge (centre) and walk 300m to the train station to change to a regional train.

Neusiedl am See

📞 02167 / POP 5900

Neusiedl am See is the region's largest town, the most accessible from Vienna, and a good springboard into the region.

Neusiedl's city **tourist office** (📞2229; www. neusiedlamsee.at; Untere Hauptstrasse 7; ⊙8am-6pm Mon-Fri, 8am-noon & 2-6pm Sat, 9am-noon Sun, closed from noon Fri-Sun Nov-Apr) has a map of the town and the lake, as well as information on other towns. If you do stay in town, **Rathausstüberl** (📞2883; www.rathausstueberl. at; Kirchengasse 2; s €44-75, d €108-118; 🅿🛜) has bright rooms. **Mole West** (📞20205; www.mole-est.at; Strandbad Westmole; mains €15-27; ⊙9am-10pm Jan–mid-Nov, closed Mon-Wed Jan-Mar; 🅿) is Burgenland's hottest lakeside drinking spot, situated over the water. It serves food, but the location is the draw. The Viennese roar down here to chill out.

ℹ Getting There & Around

BUS Daily buses leave hourly or two-hourly and travel down the eastern side of the lake, passing through Podersdorf (€3.60, 15 minutes) and Illmitz (€5.40, 30 minutes).

CITY BUS Fairly regular city buses (€1.10) run to town from the train station, or call a **taxi** (📞5959). For bike hire, see p140.

WORTH A TRIP

REED EXPLORATIONS

Although Purbach isn't located directly on the lake shore, it's inside a nature reserve and has reed banks that invite exploration on a bicycle ride or an easy walk. Kirchengasse/Gartengasse one block north of the tourist office leads down to the reeds, and from there a 2.5km path follows a canal out to the lake. An alternative ride or walk is to follow the Kirschblutenradweg (B12) north along the reeds to Breitenbrunn (about 4.5km), turn right onto the Schilflehrpfad (Reed Educational Path) and follow that out to the lake (about 3km), where there's lake swimming. Places to **hire bicycles** include the **Apotheke** (📞02683-2020; Hauptgasse 20; per day €9.50; ⊙8.30am-6pm Mon-Fri, to noon Sat) or the camping ground. **Canoe Excursions** (📞0664 382 8540; www.natur-neusiedlersee.com; 2hr adult/child €20/15; ⊙10am-noon Fri Apr-Sep) takes you out into the reeds and is also suitable for kids. Book at least one day ahead.

SPA & SWIMMING IN FRAUENKIRCHEN

In Frauenkirchen, 8km southeast from Podersdorf, you can take the cure at modern **St Martins Therme & Lodge** (☑02172-20 500; www.stmartins.at; Im Seewinkel 1, Frauenkirchen; d per person €128-226; P❄@🛜), a **spa resort** (day tickets adult/child under 15 €20/14, overnight guests visit free; ⊙9am-10pm) fed by hot springs. Wi-fi is in the lobby, but cable LAN is available in rooms. The area around the spa has been landscaped, and it's possible for day or overnight guests of the spa and hotel to swim outdoors in the lake fed by mineral springs. The hotel has lifts.

Book ahead at the hotel for free pick-up from Frauenkirchen train station if arriving by rail or bus, but St Martins can also be easily reached by bike on a detour from the main bike path (there's a Nextbike station at the spa and others at the train station and the basilica in Frauenkirchen).

TRAIN Three regional trains hourly connect Wien-Südbahnhof (Ostbahn)/Hauptbahnhof with Neusiedl am See (€11, 45 minutes). Hourly trains to Eisenstadt (€5.40, 30 minutes) pass through Purbach (€3.60, 15 minutes). For Rust, change to the bus in Schützen.

Podersdorf am See
☑02177 / POP 2100

Podersdorf am See, on the eastern shore, is the only town which can truly claim to be *Am See* (on the lake). It's the most popular holiday destination in the Neusiedler See region (and Burgenland), largely due to good wind conditions and a reed-free location.

🏃 Activities

Swimming & Windsurfing
SWIMMING, WATER SPORTS

Podersdorf offers bathing on Neusiedler See, with a long grassy **beach** (adult/child €4/2; ⊙7.30am-5pm Apr-Oct) for swimming, boating and windsurfing. Windsurfing costs an extra €3.50, even with your own board, and paddle/electric boat hire is €7/12 per day. Wind and water enthusiasts can head for the Südstrand, where **Fun & Sail** (☑0676-407 23 44; www.fun-and-sail.at, in German; boards per hr/day €10/50) has equipment for hire and offers kite-surfing courses (€199). **Surf & Segelschule Nordstrand** (☑23 20; www.nordstrand.at, in German; Seeufergasse 17; boat hire per hr €15) rents sailing boats and holds weekday sailing courses (from €160).

Bicycle Touring
CYCLING

If you haven't already picked up a bicycle – the perfect way to see the Seewinkel wetlands, which start about 5km south of town – five places around town rent for between €7 and €15 per day.

🛏 Sleeping & Eating

Book ahead for July and August. Seestrasse, the street leading from the tourist office to the lake, has many small places to stay.

TOP CHOICE Hotel-Restaurant Pannonia
HOTEL €€

(☑2245; www.pannonia-hotel.at, in German; Seezeile 20; s €49-70, d €97-137; P❄@🛒🐕) Set back from the waterfront, this recently renovated hotel has a New World feel, ultra-modern furnishings (including glass doors to the bathroom) and a large grassed area where children can play. The owners run a second hotel across the road with family rooms. The restaurant (meals €15 to €25, open lunch and dinner) has an enormous wine list and seasonal dishes such as venison carpaccio served on wild-garlic pesto with tomatoes.

Seewirt
HOTEL €€

(☑2415; www.seewirtkarner.at; Strandplatz 1; s €70-89, d €86-198; P❄🛜) Four-star Seewirt is especially popular because it occupies a prime spot right next to the ferry terminal and beach. Its restaurant (dishes €12 to €15, open lunch and dinner) serves straight-forward Austrian cuisine.

Strandcamping
CAMPGROUND €

(☑2279; Strandplatz 19; camp sites per adult/child/tent/car €7.10/5/5.70/4.80; ⊙late-Mar–Oct; P) Right by the beach, this popular camping ground is one of the largest around and has plenty of shade from sweltering heat.

Steiner
GUESTHOUSE €

(☑2790; www.steinergg.at, in German; Seestrasse 33; s/d €32.50/65; P❄🐕) This central *Gästehaus* has friendly staff, a quiet, homey atmosphere and super-clean rooms with modern bathrooms and balcony.

THE WINES OF BURGENLAND

The wine produced throughout this province is some of the best in Austria, due in no small part to the 300 days of sunshine per year, rich soil and excellent drainage. Although classic white varieties have a higher profile, the area's reds are more unusual, and the finest of the local wines is arguably the red Blaufränkisch, whose 18th-century pedigree here predates its arrival in the Danube region and Germany.

Sweet dessert wines are currently enjoying a renaissance in Austria. *Eiswein* (wine made from grapes picked late and shrivelled by frost) and selected late-picking sweet or dessert wines are being complemented by *Schilfwein*, made by placing the grapes on reed (*Schilf*) matting so they shrivel in the heat. The guru of *Schilfwein* is Gerhard Nekowitsch from **Weingut Gerhard Nekowitsch** (☎02175-2039; www.nekowitsch.at; Urbanusgasse 2, Illmitz).

Middle Burgenland, especially around the villages of Horitschon and Deutschkreutz, has a long tradition of Blaufränkisch, which is also at home in southern Burgenland (although this area is better known for Uhudler, a wine with a distinctly fruity taste).

One of the easiest ways to experience wine in the Neusiedler See region is to hire a bicycle in Neusiedl am See and pedal south through the vineyards towards the national park. Along the way you'll pass vineyards and places where you can taste the local wine.

Zur Dankbarkeit AUSTRIAN, PANNONIAN €€
(☎22 23; www.dankbarkeit.at; Hauptstrasse 39; Podersdorf; mains €9-20; ☺Fri-Tue Apr-Nov, Fri-Sun Jan-Mar, closed Dec; ☻) Zur Dankbarkeit is a lovely old restaurant that serves some of the best regional cooking around. The inner garden, with its trees and country ambience, is perfectly complemented by a glass of wine.

Weinklub 21 WINE BAR
(www.weinclub21.at; Seestrasse 37; tastings about €10; ☺9am-noon & 4-9pm May-Sep, 2-7pm Fri-Sun Oct-Apr, closed mid-Dec–mid-Feb) This excellent *Vinothek* represents 21 wine producers in town and the region; it holds regular tastings and events.

❶ Information

Tourist office (☎2227; www.podersdorfam-see.at; Hauptstrasse 2; ☺8am-4.30pm Mon-Fri, 9am-4.30pm Sat, 9am-noon Apr-Oct, closed from noon Fri & Sat & Sun Nov-Mar) Helpful for finding accommodation.

❶ Getting There & Away

Buses leave hourly or two-hourly connecting Neusiedl and Podersdorf (€3.60, 15 minutes). Ferries connect Podersdorf with Rust and Breitenbrunn on the western shore.

Seewinkel

☎02175
Seewinkel is the heart of the Neusiedler See-Seewinkel National Park, and a grassland and wetland of immense importance

to birds and other wildlife. The vineyards, reed beds, shimmering waters and constant birdsong make this an enchanting region for an excursion. This is an excellent area for **bird-watching** and explorations on foot or by bicycle.

The protected areas cannot be directly accessed by visitors, so to really get into the bird-watching you need a pair of binoculars. There are viewing stands along the way.

The park has its own information centre on the northern fringes of Illmitz, the **Nationalparkhaus** (www.nationalpark-neusiedlersee-seewinkel.at; ☺8am-5pm Mon-Fri, 10am-5pm Sat & Sun, closed Sat & Sun Nov-Mar). It has a small display on the ecology and staff can tell you the best places to spot local wildlife.

The town of **Illmitz**, 4km from the lake, is surrounded by the national park and makes for a good base. Staff at its **tourist office** (☎2383; www.illmitz.co.at; Obere Hauptplatz 2-4; ☺8am-noon & 1-5pm Mon-Fri, 9am-noon & 1-5pm Sat, 9am-noon Sun, closed Sat & Sun Nov-Jun) can provide information on the region. **Arkadenweingut-Gästehaus** (☎3345; www.tiscover.at/arkadenweingut-fam.heiss; Obere Hauptstrasse 20; s/d €29/50; P☻) is a lovely arcaded homestead in the centre of Illmitz.

Illmitz is connected with Möbisch, Rust, and Fertörákos in Hungary by ferry and Neusiedl am See by one- to two-hourly buses (€5.40, 30 minutes).

MIDDLE & SOUTHERN BURGENLAND

Heading south, the flat expanse of the Neusiedler See is soon forgotten as you enter an undulating landscape replete with lush hills, forested glens and castles that rise up in the distance. It's a region often overlooked by visitors and a place where life is still very much connected to the land; the influence of long-resident Hungarian and Croatian settlers can be felt here.

Lockenhaus & Around

Lockenhaus, in the centre of Burgenland, is famous for its castle (☑02616-23 94; www. ritterburg.at, in German; adult/child €5/2.50; ⊘9am-5pm Mar-late Dec), or more accurately, for its former resident Elizabeth Báthory. Better known as the 'Blood Countess', she has gone down in history for her reign of terror early in the 17th century, when she reputedly tortured and murdered over 600 mainly peasant women for her own sadistic pleasure. The castle has long been cleansed of such gruesome horrors but still contains an impressive torture chamber, complete with an iron maiden.

If you want to sleep inside a castle, the Burghotel Lockenhaus (☑02616-23 94; www. ritterburg.at; s/d €66/102; Ⓟⓢ) has antique-furnished rooms and a sauna.

Some 13km east of Lockenhaus is the tiny village of Klostermarienberg, home to a now-defunct monastery housing the only dog museum in Europe, the Europäisches Hundemuseum (www.kulturimkloster.at, in German; Klostermarienberg; adult/child/family €4/2/8; ⊘2-5pm Sun May-Aug; Ⓟ). The odd collection of dog paraphernalia includes paintings, statues and intriguing photos of dogs dressed for war during WWI and WWII, complete with gas masks. Take a few minutes to visit the monastery's crypt, a chamber containing archaeological finds dating from the 13th and 14th centuries.

Bernstein, 15km west of Lockenhaus, is dominated by the impressive Burg Bernstein (Bernstein Castle; ☑03354-63 82; www. burgbernstein.at; s €110-140, d €150-190; ⊘late Apr–mid-Oct; Ⓟⓢ). Thirteen of the castle's rooms, all tastefully decorated with period furniture, are now used to accommodate guests. The castle foundations date from 1199, creating the historic setting for a delightful retreat from the stress of modern-day living. In the town centre is a small Felsenmuseum (www.felsenmuseum.at, in German; Hauptplatz 5; adult/child €5/2.50; ⊘9am-6pm daily Mar-late Dec), which focuses on the gemstone serpentine and local mining (this was first mined in the town in the mid-19th century).

If your body needs some TLC, stop in at the spa town of Bad Tatzmannsdorf, 15km south of Bernstein. Aside from taking the waters at the Burgenland Therme (☑03353-89 90; www.burgenlandtherme.at; Am Thermenplatz 1; day card adult/child €18.50/11; ⊘9am-10pm Mon-Thu & Sun, to 12.30am Fri, to 11pm Sat; Ⓟ), you can visit the Südburgenländisches Freilichtmuseum (www. freilichtmuseum-badtatzmannsdorf.at, in German; Josef Hölzel-Allee; admission €1; ⊘9am-6pm; Ⓟ), a small but rewarding open-air museum filled with thatched buildings from 19th-century Burgenland. The local tourist office (☑03353-70 15; www.bad.tatzmannsdorf. at; Joseph-Haydn-Platz 3; ⊘8am-5.30pm Mon-Fri, 9.30am-2.30pm Sat, 9.30-11.30am Sun, closed Sun Nov-Mar) helps with accommodation.

ⓘ Getting There & Away

You're better off with your own transport in this region as bus connections can be thin. Three direct weekday buses connect Lockenhaus and Eisenstadt (€13.70, 1½ hours). On weekdays hourly and on Saturday two-hourly direct buses go north from Oberwart (where there's a train station) to Bad Tatzmannsdorf (€2.20, five minutes); from Oberwart to Bernstein (€4.70, 30 minutes, every one to three hours) or Lockenhaus (€6.40, one hour, twice each weekday) is also manageable.

Güssing & Around

If you're not castled out by this stage, head 40km south of Bad Tatzmannsdorf to Güssing, a peaceful town on the banks of the Strembach River. Here the arresting Burg Güssing (www.burgguessing.info, in German; adult/child/family €5.60/3.50/13; ⊘10am-5pm Tue-Sun Easter-Oct; Ⓟ) rises dramatically over the river and town. The castle, which is a mix of ruins and renovations, contains plenty of weapons from the Turks and Hungarians, striking portraits from the 16th century and a tower with 360-degree views. A modern 100m funicular railway (tickets €1; ⊘same hr as castle) helps those with weary legs reach the castle.

A visit to the Auswanderer Museum (Stremtalstrasse 2; adult/child €2/1; ⊘2-6pm Sat

& Sun May-Oct; **P**), to the north of the castle, is also worthwhile. It relays the story of the mass exodus of Burgenlanders (including Fred Astaire's father) to America before and after WWI – most emigrated due to lack of work or poor living conditions.

If you missed the open-air museum in Bad Tatzmannsdorf, head 5km west of Güssing to the **Freilichtmuseum** (Gerersdorf bei Güssing 66; adult/child/family €4.50/2/10; 9am-5pm Mon-Fri, 10am-6pm Apr–mid-Nov; **P**) at **Gerersdorf**. An hour or two could easily slip by while you explore the 30-odd buildings and their traditional furniture and fittings, which capture the rural culture of Burgenland in the 18th and 19th centuries.

The **tourist office** (03322-440 03; www.suedburgenland.info, in German; Hauptplatz 7;

9am-noon Mon-Fri, closed 3 weeks each yr) in Güssing can help with private rooms, otherwise try **Landgasthof Kedl** (03322-42 40 30; www.tiscover.at/gasthof.kedl; Urbersdorf 33; s/d €32/64; **P**), 3km north of Güssing in Urbersdorf. The castle's restaurant, **Burg Güssing** (03322-42 579; www.burgrestaurant.net; mains €9.50-14.50, 6-course menus €25; 10am-10pm Tue-Sun Mar-Dec), has a filling six-course Knight's menu and a terrace with extensive views over the countryside.

❶ Getting There & Away

Every one to two hours daily direct buses connect Güssing (€7.10, 45 to 70 minutes) with Oberwart. On weekdays and Saturday several direct buses connect Güssing and Geresdorf (€1.80, 10 minutes).

Upper Austria

Best Places to Eat

» k.u.k. Hofbäckerei (p159)

» Herberstein (p159)

» Knapp am Eck (p165)

» Löwenkeller (p168)

» Orangerie im Schlosspark (p165)

Best Places to Stay

» Spitz Hotel (p158)

» Schlossbrauerei Weinberg (p170)

» Gästehaus Stift St Florian (p163)

» Hotel Christkindlwirt (p165)

» Gangl (p167)

Why Go?

Upper Austria may not have the in-your-face splendour of the Tyrolean Alps or Vienna's imperial palaces. But, as locals delight in telling you, it has a taste of all that is great about Austria. For starters, the mighty Danube and a rich musical heritage, old-world coffee houses and castle-topped medieval towns, resplendent Augustinian abbeys and spas. And the best bit, they whisper, is that nobody really knows it.

It's true. Beyond the high-tech museums and avant-garde galleries of Linz lies a land in miniature waiting to be unwrapped. Each layer reveals new surprises: from rustic farmhouses serving home-grown *Most* (cider) to the limestone pinnacles of the Kalkalpen where the elusive lynx roams. Be it the mist-enshrouded hills rippling towards the Czech Republic or wheat fields fading into a watercolour distance at dusk – these landscapes have a quiet, lingering beauty all of their own.

When to Go

Upper Austria has a temperate climate, with milder winters than many other parts of Austria. Visit in spring to see the orchards in blossom and for a celebration of Schubert in Steyr, the town that inspired his sprightly *Trout Quintet*. Summer is a fine time to cycle along the Danube and through the countryside. Come in September for cutting-edge technology festivals and free riverside concerts in Linz. In winter there are glittering Christmas markets galore, as well as cross-country skiing in the Nationalpark Kalkalpen.

Upper Austria Highlights

① Play with pixels and converse with intelligent robots at **Ars Electronica Center** (p153) in Linz

② Be smitten by the storybook lanes and fast-flowing rivers of **Steyr** (p164)

③ Walk and sleep high above the treetops at the **Baumkronenweg** (p171) in Kopfing

④ Hike through the rugged limestone wilderness of **Nationalpark Kalkalpen** (p166), Austria's second-biggest national park

⑤ Drift away in a Caribbean lagoon, daiquiri in hand, at **Therme Geinberg** (p171)

⑥ Be amazed by the grace of St Florian's **Augustinian abbey** (p163)

⑦ Journey to the darkest depths of Austria's past at **KZ Mauthausen** (p164) concentration camp

Getting There & Around

AIR

Austrian Airlines, Lufthansa, Ryanair and Air Berlin are the main airlines servicing the **Blue Danube Airport** (www.linz-airport.at). There are flights to Vienna, Salzburg and Graz, as well as Berlin, Frankfurt, Düsseldorf, Stuttgart and Zürich. Ryanair has daily flights to London Stansted.

CAR & MOTORCYCLE

The A1 autobahn runs east–west to Vienna and Salzburg, the A8 heads north to Passau and the rest of Germany, and the A9 runs south into Styria.

PUBLIC TRANSPORT

Upper Austria's bus and train services are covered by the **Oberösterreichischer Verkehrsverbund** (www.ooevv.at). Prices depend on the number of zones you travel (one zone is €1.80). As well as single tickets, daily, weekly, monthly and yearly passes are available. Express trains between Vienna and Salzburg pass through Linz and much of southern Upper Austria, and there are also express trains heading south from Linz to St Michael in Styria, from where connections to Klagenfurt and Graz are possible.

LINZ

♪ 0732 / POP 189,000

It took a long time coming, but since Linz seized the reins as European Capital of Culture 2009, the world it seems is finally waking up to the charms of Austria's third city. Sitting prettily astride the Danube, Linz rewards visitors who look beyond its less-than-loveable industrial outskirts.

This dynamic city is on the move. Here, daring public art installations, a burgeoning cultural scene and flagship museums that look fresh-minted for a sci-fi movie all signal tomorrow's Austria. This is also a historic city, with a castle, a well-preserved *Altstadt* (old town) and grand cafes serving up *Linzer Torte* and tales of the Empire. This is a city both interesting and beautiful – albeit in an unconventional way.

History

Linz was a fortified Celtic village when the Romans took over and named it Lentia. By the 8th century, when the town came under Bavaria's rule, its name had changed to Linze, and by the 13th century it was an important trading town for raw materials out of Styria. In 1489 Linz became the imperial capital under Friedrich III until his death in 1493.

Like much of Upper Austria, Linz was at the forefront of the Protestant movement in the 16th and 17th centuries. However, with the Counter-Reformation, Catholicism made a spectacular comeback. The city's resurgence in the 19th century was largely due to the development of the railway, when Linz became an important junction.

Adolf Hitler may have been born in Braunau am Inn, but Linz was his favourite (he spent his school days here), and his largely unrealised plans for the city were grand. His Nazi movement built massive iron and steel works, which still employ many locals. After WWII Linz was at the border between the Soviet- and US- administered zones. Since 1955, Linz has flourished into an important industrial city, port and provincial capital.

◉ Sights & Activities

TOP CHOICE **Ars Electronica Center**   MUSEUM
(www.aec.at; Ars Electronica Strasse 1; adult/child €7/4; ⊙9am-5pm Wed & Fri, to 9pm Thu, 10am-6pm Sat & Sun; ⊕) The technology, science and digital media of the future are in the spotlight at Linz' biggest crowd-puller, the Ars Electronica Centre. Opened in 2009, the new Treusch-designed centre resembles a futuristic ship by the Danube after dark, when its LED glass skin kaleidoscopically changes colour.

The open-plan interior focuses on themed labs. Head down to **Funky Pixels** to create light drawings and **RoboLab** to interact with cutting-edge robots. Other hands-on highlights include the **BioLab** where you can clone plants and analyse DNA, the **FabLab** where you can animate digital objects and the **GeoCity** where you can take a virtual round-the-world trip.

Lentos   ART GALLERY
(www.lentos.at; Ernst-Koref-Promenade 1; adult/child/family €6.50/4.50/13; ⊙10am-6pm Wed & Fri-Mon,

ℹ CITY SAVER

The **Linz Card** (1-/3-day €15/25) gives unlimited use of public transport; entry to major museums including the Ars Electronica Center, Schlossmuseum, Lentos and the Landesgalerie; plus discounts on other sights, city tours and river cruises. The three-day card also includes a round trip on the Pöstlingbergbahn. Buy the Linz Card at the tourist office, airport, museums and some hotels.

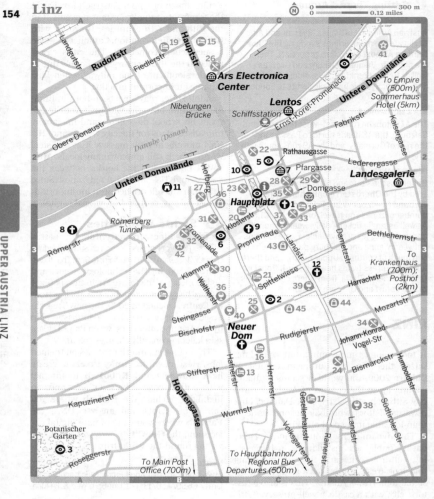

to 9pm Thu) Ars Electronica's rival icon across the Danube is the crystalline Lentos Kunst-museum, which also dazzles by night. Defined by razor-sharp lines, this glass-and-steel rectangle with a gap was designed by Zurich architects Weber & Hofer. The gallery guards one of Austria's finest collections of 20th- and 21st-century art, comprising works by Warhol, Schiele, Klimt and Kokoschka that are sometimes the focus of large-scale exhibitions.

Hauptplatz HISTORIC SITE
Street performers entertain the crowds, trams rumble past and locals relax in pavement cafes on this bustling square, framed by ornate baroque and pastel-coloured Renaissance houses. The centrepiece **Drei-faltigkeitssäule** (trinity column) – a 20m pillar of Salzburg marble carved in 1723 to commemorate the town's deliverance from war, fire and plague – glints when it catches the sunlight.

Landesgalerie ART GALLERY
(State Museum; www.landesgalerie.at; Museum-strasse 14; adult/child/family €6.50/4.50/13; ☉9am-6pm Tue, Wed & Fri, to 9pm Thu, 10am-5pm Sat & Sun) Housed in a sumptuous late 19th-century building, the Landesgalerie focuses on 20th- and 21st-century paintings,

photography and installations. The rotating exhibitions often zoom in on works by Upper Austrian artists, such as Alfred Kubin's expressionist fantasies and Valie Export's shocking Viennese actionist–inspired pieces. The open-air **sculpture park** contrasts modern sculpture with the gallery's neoclassical architecture.

Neuer Dom CATHEDRAL
(New Cathedral; Herrenstrasse 26; ⊙8am-7pm) This neo-Gothic giant of a cathedral lifts your gaze to its intricate stonework and riot of filigree spires. Designed in the mid-19th century by Vinzenz Statz of Cologne Dom fame, the cathedral sports a tower whose height was restricted to 134m, so as not to outshine Stephansdom in Vienna. The interior is lit by veritable curtains of stained glass, including the **Linzer Fenster** depicting scenes from Linz' history.

Schlossmuseum MUSEUM
(Castle Museum; www.schlossmuseum.at; Schlossberg 1; adult/child/family €6.50/4.50/13; ⊙9am-6pm Tue, Wed & Fri, to 9pm Thu, 10am-5pm Sat & Sun; ⊞) Romans, Hapsburg emperors, fire – Linz' hilltop **castle** has seen the lot. Enjoy the panoramic city views before delving into the museum's trove of treasures, gathered from abbeys and palaces over the centuries. The collection skips through art, archaeology, historical weapons and instruments,

technology and folklore. The Gothic ecclesiastical paintings are a real highlight.

Alter Dom
CATHEDRAL

(Old Cathedral; Domgasse 3; ⊘7am-7pm) The twin towers of this late-17th-century cathedral dominate Linz' skyline. With its stuccowork, pink marble altar and gilt pillars, the interior is remarkably ornate. Famous local lad Anton Bruckner served as organist here from 1856 to 1868.

Donaupark
PARK

(Danube Park; [⌖]) Next to Lentos on the southern bank of the Danube is the Donaupark, the city's green escape vault. Modern sculptures rise above the bushes in the well-tended gardens, which are a magnet to walkers, joggers, skaters, picnickers and city workers seeking fresh air in summer.

Pöstlingberg
SCENIC AREA

Linz spreads out beneath you atop Pöstlingberg (537m), which affords bird's-eye views over the city and the snaking Danube. It's a precipitous 30-minute ride aboard the narrow-gauge **Pöstlingbergbahn** (adult/child €5.60/2.80; ⊘every 30min 6am-10pm Mon-Sat, from 7.30am Sun) from the Hauptplatz. This gondola features in the Guinness Book of Records as the world's steepest mountain railway – quite some feat for such a low-lying city!

At the summit is the turn-of-the-century **Grottenbahn** (Am Pöstlingberg 16; adult/child €4.50/2.30; ⊘10am-5pm, to 6pm Jul & Aug; [⌖]), where families – and anyone who loves a bit of cult kitsch – can board the dragon train to trundle past gnomes, glittering stalactites and scenes from Grimms' fairytales.

Botanischer Garten
GARDEN

(Botanical Gardens; Roseggerstrasse 20-22; adult/child €3/2; ⊘8am-dusk) These peaceful botanical gardens, south of the centre, nurture 10,000 species, from native alpine plants to orchids, rhododendrons, tropical palms and one of Europe's largest cacti collections.

Bischofshof
HISTORICAL BUILDING

(Bichofstrasse) An ornate baroque bishop's residence built by Michael Pruckmayer following designs by Jakob Prandtauer, who also made his mark on the abbeys in St Florian and Melk.

Minoritenkirche
CHURCH

(Church of the Minor Friars; Klosterstrasse 7; ⊘8am-4pm) Founded in 1236 and redesigned in rococo style, this church contains altar paintings by Bartolomeo Altomonte.

Landhaus
HISTORICAL BUILDING

(Promenade) This striking Renaissance building with a trio of interlinking courtyards is now the seat of Upper Austrian parliament and government. The bronze Planet Fountain dates from 1582.

Martinskirche
CHURCH

(Römerstrasse; ⊘7.30am-6pm) One of Austria's oldest churches, first mentioned in 799. Notice the Roman inscriptions and oven through the window.

Ursulinenkirche
CHURCH

(Landstrasse 31; ⊘7.30am-6pm) This baroque, twin-domed former nunnery church features altar paintings by the prolific Martin Altomonte.

DON'T MISS

STARS IN OUR EYES

Romantic composer Anton Bruckner was the organist at the Alter Dom from 1856 to 1868. Today his symphonies still resound at cathedral concerts from July to September and at the annual Brucknerfest. His music is also the focus of the free **Linz-Genesis** (Hauptplatz 1; ⊘9am-1pm & 2-6pm Mon-Fri) museum in the 17th-century old town hall.

Not to be eclipsed in Linz' hall of fame is great astronomer, mathematician and astrologer Johannes Kepler, who lived and completed the groundbreaking Rudolphine Tables at Rathausgasse 5. The house now harbours the **Kepler Salon** (www.kepler-salon.at, in German), which hosts science-themed events. The genius is also commemorated by the university named after him and the Planet Fountain at the Landhaus, where he taught from 1612 to 1626.

A bust of Mozart graces the entrance to the grand Renaissance townhouse on Theatergasse, where he stayed as a guest of the Count of Thun in 1783 and is said to have bashed out the *Linzer Symphony* (No 36) in just four days.

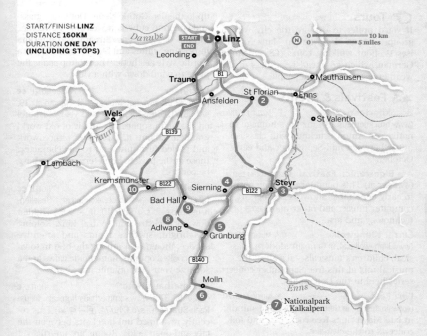

Danube
START ① **Linz**
Leonding ●

Traun ●
B1
● Mauthausen
St Florian ● Enns
Ansfelden ②
● St Valentin

Wels
Traun
B139

Kremsmünster ⑩ B122
● Lambach
Sierning ④ B122 **Steyr**
Bad Hall ⑨ ③
⑧
Adlwang ⑤
Grünburg

B140

Molln
⑥
Enns
⑦ Nationalpark
Kalkalpen

0 ──── 10 km
0 ──── 5 miles

Driving Tour
Upper Austria Highlights

❯ This off-the-beaten-track drive meanders
through Upper Austria's bucolic landscapes to resplendent abbeys, rustic villages,
spa towns and limestone mountains. It's
particularly beautiful on an autumn day,
when the apple trees are heavy with fruit and
the forests in the south of the province are a
vibrant palette of russet and gold. Tailor this
drive to suit yourself: stopping as often and
driving as far as you choose.

Heading south of ① **Linz**, the city's industrial fringes soon taper out and give way to
low-rise hills and meadows. Take the B1 to
② **St Florian** to explore its majestic Augustinian abbey, a masterpiece of baroque art and
the final resting place of Romantic composer
Anton Bruckner. Now continue south on minor roads through patchwork fields studded
with *Vierkanterhof*, huge square farmhouses
with inner courtyards. The rolling countryside
brings you to riverside ③ **Steyr**, the picture-
book town that inspired Schubert's *Trout
Quintet* and a relaxed place for lunch. Follow
the emerald-tinted Steyr River west along

the B122 to ④ **Sierning**, dominated by its
Renaissance Schloss Sierning. From here, the
B140 shadows the river south to the pretty
church-topped town of ⑤ **Grünburg**, nestled
in wooded hills. It's just a 15-minute drive
south to ⑥ **Molln**, the northern gateway to
the spectacular limestone peaks, waterfalls
and wilderness of ⑦ **Nationalpark Kalkalpen**. Find information on local walks at Molln's
national park visitor centre. Refreshed by the
mountain air, head north, passing Grünburg
and swinging west along a country road to tiny
⑧ **Adlwang**. Here Gangl farmhouse is a good
stop for home-grown apple juice and *Most*
(cider). Five minutes north sits the spa town of
⑨ **Bad Hall**, fabled for the healing powers of
its iodine-laced waters, which you can bathe
in at Mediterrana Therme and inhale (for free)
in the sculpture-dotted park. It's just a short
drive west along the B122 now to ⑩ **Kremsmünster**, whose opulent Benedictine abbey
harbours an incredible library and observatory. Drive back to Linz via the scenic church-
dotted villages lining the B139.

☞ Tours

If you'd prefer to explore the city with a group, Tourist Information Linz organises 1½-hour **walking tours** (€8; ⊙11am) in German, which go ahead regardless of the weather or the number of people.

✯✯ Festivals & Events

Brucknerfest MUSIC FESTIVAL
(www.brucknerhaus.at) Linz pays homage to native son Anton Bruckner with classical music between mid-September and early October.

Ars Electronica Festival TECHNOLOGY FESTIVAL
(www.aec.at) This boundary-crossing event in early September showcases cyber-art, computer music, and other marriages of technology and art.

Linzer Klangwolke MUSIC FESTIVAL
(www.klangwolke.at, in German) Modern, classical, children's musicals – it's all in the musical mix at this free September concert series held in the Donaupark.

Linz Fest MUSIC FESTIVAL
(www.linzfest.at, in German) This huge shindig in late May brings free rock, jazz and folk concerts to the city.

Pflasterspektakel STREET FESTIVAL
(www.pflasterspektakel.at) Musicians, jugglers, actors, poets and acrobats from across Europe descend on Linz for this three-day street festival in late July.

🛏 Sleeping

Nondescript chain hotels abound in Linz, but you'll also find some charming pensions and modestly priced boutique-chic hotels. Tourist Information Linz offers a free accommodation booking service, but only face-to-face and not over the phone.

TOP CHOICE Spitz Hotel HOTEL €€€
(☎73 37 33; www.spitzhotel.at; Fiedlerstrasse 6; r €130-250; 🅿🌐@📶) Much-lauded Austrian architect Isa Stein has left her avant-garde imprint on the Spitz. The lobby's moulded furnishings and UFO-style lighting set the tone. Each of the hotel's rooms spotlights an aspect of Linz' burgeoning arts scene, featuring bespoke pieces by local creatives. Minimalism rules here, with clean lines, open-plan bathrooms and hardwood floors.

Hotel am Domplatz HOTEL €€
(☎77 30 00; www.hotelamdomplatz.at; Stifterstrasse 4; s €120-140, d €150-180; 🅿🌐❄@) Sidling up to the neo-Gothic Neuer Dom, this glass-and-concrete cube is a welcome newcomer to Linz' design scene. Streamlined interiors in pristine whites and blonde wood reveal a Nordic-style aesthetic. The rooftop spa is the place to wind down with a view.

Wolfinger HISTORIC HOTEL €€
(☎77 32 91; www.hotelwolfinger.at; Hauptplatz 19; s/d €85/126; 🅿🌐@) This 500-year-old hotel on the main square has an air of old-world grandeur about it. Archways, stuccowork and period furniture lend rooms character; those at the back are quieter and some have balconies.

Hotel Kolping HOTEL €€
(☎66 16 90; www.hotel-kolping.at; Gesellenhausstrasse 7; s/d €85/110; 🅿🌐❄📶) Hidden down a backstreet in central Linz, Kolping has bright, spotless rooms and attentive service. Breakfast is among the best in town with cooked options, homemade cakes and a squeeze-your-own organic juice bar.

Sommerhaus Hotel HOTEL €
(☎24 57 376; www.sommerhaus-hotel.at; Julius-Raab-Strasse 10; s/d €49/74; 🅿🌐@🏊) This recently revamped uni hotel sits between the city and open fields. Rooms are no-frills yet comfy, breakfast is filling and there's a big indoor pool for swimming proper laps. Take tram 1 or 2 to Schumpeterstrasse and walk five minutes.

Zum Schwarzen Bären HOTEL €€
(☎77 24 77; www.linz-hotel.at; Herrenstrasse 9-11; s/d €70/98, ste €190-300; 🅿🌐❄📶♿) The birthplace of acclaimed tenor Richard Tauber, this 15th-century hotel is run by the friendly Nell family. Overlooking a courtyard, the rooms have recently been madeover in monochrome hues and parquet; some even sport waterbeds! The wood-panelled restaurant dishes up Austrian classics (mains €7 to €10).

Hotel Mühlviertlerhof HOTEL €€
(☎77 26 26-0; www.hotel-muehlviertlerhof.at; Promenade 17; s €67-81, d €97-111; 🌐📶) So do you fancy sleeping in a medieval castle guarded by a knight in shining armour? No, well how about in a hay-wagon bed in the countryside? Or, perhaps, in the Kama Sutra room complete with four-poster and *imaginative* Indian art? Fun is the name of the game at this friendly themed hotel.

Hotel & Loft Landgraf HOTEL €€
(☎700 712 400; http://hotellandgraf.com; Hauptstrasse 12; s/d €80/90; 🅿🌐📶) Occupying an

FRITZ RATH: LINZ BAKER

I've known the secret of the *Linzer Torte* since I was knee-high, and I bake mine to an age-old family recipe. For me, baking holds a mirror up to culture: Austria is the king of cakes, Germany rye bread, France baguettes...

The Secret Ingredient

I've met people who insist *Linzer Torte* is made with raspberry jam. My God, raspberry! It's redcurrant! But they are right in a way. The tart is world famous and each country interprets the recipe differently. It just tastes better in Linz because that's where it comes from.

In the Mix

You need the right balance of ingredients – almonds, flour, butter, spices (cinnamon, nutmeg, cloves) and redcurrant jam – and I usually add a dash of milk to the dough to achieve that perfect golden crust. But honestly, a lot boils down to instinct.

Baking is...

Like playing music: if you take the same piano, sheet of music and 10 musicians, the mixture is the same but each one produces a slightly different result.

art-nouveau apartment block, Landgraf is just steps from Ars Electronica and the Danube. Rooms are modern and massive, though furnishings are spartan and bathrooms on the poky side of small. Modern art punctuates the uberchic public spaces.

Herberge Linz   HOSTEL €
(☑0699-1180 7003; herberge.linz@aon.at; Kapuzinerstrasse 14; dm/s/d €17/25/40; ☻) Within staggering distance of the sights, this canary-yellow hostel has a sociable vibe and leafy garden. The spacious dorms all have lockers, fridges and showers.

Goldenes Dachl   GUESTHOUSE €€
(☑77 58 97; Hafnerstrasse 27; s/d €50/82) Few places can beat this guesthouse for price and centrality. Rooms aren't flash but they're comfortable, with wooden floors, sofas and loads of space. There's a restaurant and beer garden downstairs.

✖ Eating

Linz takes its innovative spirit to the kitchen and its flair for design to the dining room. Besides Austrian fare, you'll find fusion cuisine, organic produce and world flavours on many menus. Old-style cafes are the place to try the classic *Linzer Torte*. Made to a 17th-century recipe with almonds, spices and tangy redcurrant jam, the tart is the greatest rival to Vienna's own *Sacher Torte*.

The tourist office's *Linz Geniessen* booklet lists most restaurants in town.

k.u.k. Hofbäckerei `TOP CHOICE`   CAFE €
(Pfarrgasse 17; coffee & cake €3-6; ☺6.30am-6pm Mon-Fri, 7am-12.30pm Sat) The Empire lives on at this gloriously stuck-in-time cafe (first mentioned in 1371), where the wood-panelled walls are smothered in Sisi portraits and Habsburg curios. Fritz Rath pours years of experience and passion into baking *the* best *Linzer Torte* in town.

Herberstein   FUSION €€€
(☑78 61 61; www.herberstein-linz.at, in German; Altstadt 10; mains €18-26; ☺4pm-4am Mon-Sat; ☻) Oh-so-chic Herberstein comprises an oriental-style lounge, ivy-draped garden, well-stocked wine cellar and glamorous restaurant. Exposed stone and backlighting set the scene for fusion flavours like beautifully crisp pork-belly confit on curried sauerkraut, and scallop maki on black risotto.

Cubus   FUSION €€
(Ars-Electronica-Strasse 1; mains €8.50-14.50; ☺9am-1am Mon-Sat, to 6pm Sun; ☻☏) On the 3rd floor of the Ars Electronica Center, this glass cube has stellar views over the Danube to the south bank and glows purple after dark. The menu is strictly fusion – think veal osso bucco and minty Indian chickpea salad. The two-course lunch is a snip at €7.

Alte Welt   AUSTRIAN €€
(☑77 00 53; www.altewelt.at, in German; Hauptplatz 4; mains €9-16; ☺lunch Mon-Sat, dinner daily) Set around an arcaded inner courtyard, Alte Welt serves hearty fare, such as roast pork

and beef ragout, and a good-value two-course lunch (€6.50). By night, the cellar hosting jam sessions, live jazz and plays attracts students and arty types.

Spirali
CAFE €

(www.spirali.at, in German; Graben 32b; mains €5-7; ⊙10am-7pm Mon-Sat; ☑) Peter keeps the good vibes and groovy music coming at this ethnic-flavoured cafe. The accent is on regional produce, with great-value lunch specials from pasta to curries. Give the homemade cakes, teas and syrups a whirl.

Restaurant Verdi-Einkehr
AUSTRIAN €€

(☑73 30 05; www.verdi.at; Pachmayrstrasse 137; mains €10-25; ⊙dinner Tue-Sat; ☻) Linz spreads out picturesquely before you from this gastro duo, a short taxi ride from town. Erich Lukas prepares specialities like suckling-pig ravioli and slow-roasted Waldviertel lamb in ultra-chic Verdi. Wood-beamed Einkehr is an altogether cosier affair and serves Austrian comfort food. It's 5km north of the city centre.

Cafe Jindrak
CAFE €

(☑77 92 58; Herrenstrasse 22; lunch menus €5-7; ⊙8am-6pm Mon-Sat; ☻🖬) Join the cake-loving locals at this celebrated cafe. You'd need a huge fork (and appetite) to tackle the *Linzer Torte* that set a Guinness World Record in 1999, measuring 4m high and weighing 650kg. Bake your own (perhaps not quite as big) at one of the regular cookery workshops.

Tom Yam
THAI €€

(☑94 69 69; Johann-Konrad-Vogel-Strasse 11; mains €7-15; ⊙lunch Mon-Sat, dinner Sun) The King of Thailand beams down from the wall and Thai pop plays at Tom Yam. Spice things up with a green papaya salad or the house special: tom yam prawn soup. The all-you-can-eat lunch buffet is a bargain at €7.

Niu
FUSION €€

(☑78 67 78; Klammstrasse 1; mains €11-13; ⊙Tue-Fri; ☻) Asian fusion cuisine is served in Zen-style minimalist surrounds at Niu. The aromatic yellow porcini mushroom curry and palate-awakening chilli-mango salad come recommended.

Promenadenhof
AUSTRIAN €

(☑77 76 61; Promenade 39; www.promenadenhof.at, in German; mains €8-16; ⊙Mon-Sat; 🖬) Promenadenhof enjoys a loyal following for its Austrian soul food, served in a warren of different rooms, from a vaulted *Stube* (parlour) to a beer garden with a

kids' playground. The *Tafelspitz* (Austrian-style boiled beef) is spot-on, as is the Styrian-style chicken salad.

Wagnerei
ITALIAN €€€

(☑91 89 89; Pfarrgasse 18; mains €16.50-26.50; ⊙Tue-Sun) Chunky wood tables and vaults create a backdrop for clean Italian flavours like porcini risotto and venison carpaccio at this central foodie haunt. The handwritten menu changes daily.

Mia Cara
ITALIAN €€

(☑78 57 28; Pfarrplatz 13; mains €8-16; ⊙Mon-Sat) Mario cooks fresh, simple Italian fare at this *osteria*. Sample antipasti from the counter or homemade pasta with a nice glass of Chianti. The patio is popular in summer.

🌿 Gragger
CAFE €

(www.gragger.at, in German; Hofgasse 3; snacks €3-5; ⊙Mon-Sat; ☻☑) Antipasti, wholesome soups and delicious organic breads are served at wooden tables in this vaulted cafe.

p'aa
FUSION €€

(www.paa.cx, in German; Altstadt 28; mains €8.50-12.50; ⊙Mon-Sat; ☻☑) p'aa serves up vegan and organic dishes, from feisty curries to pumpkin schnitzel, in a trendy lounge setting with low seating and mellow music.

Bauernmarkt
MARKET

(Farmers' Market; Hauptplatz; 9am-2pm Tue & Fri) Twice-weekly market for picnic fixings and fresh local produce.

Billa
SUPERMARKET

(Landstrasse 60; ⊙7.15am-7.30pm Mon-Fri, to 6pm Sat) A supermarket for self-caterers.

🍺 Drinking

Linz' student population keeps the scene young and upbeat. Your best bet for a bar crawl is the area west of the Hauptplatz nicknamed the 'Bermuda Triangle'; Altstadt and Hofberg are peppered with pubs, cafes and wine bars.

Strom
BAR

(Kirchengasse 4; ⊙2pm-2am Sun-Thu, to 4am Fri & Sat) DJs spin hip hop, electro and funk at this upbeat bar, where partygoers spill out onto Kirchengasse in summer. Upstairs is rough 'n' ready Stadtwerk, which hosts clubbing events, gigs and party nights.

Cubus Terrace
COCKTAIL BAR

(Ars-Electronica-Strasse 1; ⊙5pm-midnight) There's no finer spot to see Linz light up than this glass-walled cafe on the top floor of the Ars

Electronica Center. Pick out the landmarks over a sunset cocktail.

Stiegelbräu zum Klosterhof   BEER GARDEN
(Landstrasse 30; ☺9am-midnight) Pass on the mediocre food and go straight for the freshly tapped Stiegl beer at the cavernous Klosterhof. The chestnut tree–shaded beer garden has space for 1500 thirsty punters.

Thüsen Tak   PUB
(Walterstrasse 21; ☺5pm-4am) This down-to-earth pub is pure rock 'n' roll, with loud music and walls smothered in posters of Led Zeppelin, Thin Lizzy and Deep Purple. Enjoy a beer and chat with Mike at the bar, or surf the web for free.

Madame Wu   TEA ROOM
(Altstadt 13; ☺11am-9pm Mon-Wed, to midnight Thu-Sat, 2-8pm Sun; ☻) Oriental-style tearoom full of cosy nooks, with a terrific selection of teas. There's a Chinese tea ceremony (€15) at 5pm on Saturdays.

Cheeese   BAR
(Waltherstrasse 11; ☺7pm-6am Wed-Sat) A party-loving bar attracting a young crowd, especially on Wednesday (cocktail night) and at the weekends when DJs play.

Divino   WINE BAR
(Domgasse 20; ☺2-11pm Mon-Sat) Pillar-box red walls, tapas and flamenco music set the scene in this Spanish *vinoteca*, with 200 different wines to choose from.

Jam's   BAR
(www.jams.at, in German; Landstrasse 71-75; ☺7pm-4am Wed-Fri) There's live jazz every Wednesday at this slinky backlit bar on Linz' main thoroughfare.

☆ Entertainment

Brucknerhaus   LIVE MUSIC
(☎76 12-0; www.brucknerhaus.linz.at; Untere Donaulände 7; ⏵) Linz' premier music venue stages top-drawer classical and jazz concerts. There is a dedicated program for kids of different ages ('mini' and 'midi' music).

Posthof   MUSIC, THEATRE
(☎77 05 48-0; www.posthof.at, in German; Posthofstrasse 43) Dockside Posthof covers everything from blues, funk and rock gigs to cutting-edge theatre and dance. Festivals are occasionally held here. Take bus 27 or 270 to Hafen/Posthofstrasse.

Landestheater   THEATRE
(☎76 11-0; www.landestheater-linz.at, in German; Promenade 39; ⏵) Opera, ballet and musicals take to the stage of Linz' main theatre, which hosts largely classic productions. The u\hof team keeps kids amused with plays aimed at a young audience.

Empire   CLUB
(www.empire-club.at, in German; Holzstrasse 3; ☺9pm-5am Thu-Sat) Such deck-spinning royalty as David Guetta and Paul van Dyk have played this voguish club. See the website for the weekly line-up. The club is close to Donaupark, 500m north of the Brucknerhaus.

🛍 Shopping

The main thoroughfare is Landstrasse, home to high-street stores and malls. Antique shops, galleries and secondhand bookshops line Bischofstrasse; this is a great street to rummage for handcrafted jewellery and crafts.

At the other end of the scale, the city's *Flohmärkte* (flea markets) spring forth in front of the Neues Rathaus Saturday mornings from November to March, and on the Hauptplatz Saturday mornings from March to October.

Glas Galerie   GLASSWARE
(Bischofstrasse 11; ☺11am-5pm Tue-Fri, 10am-1pm Sat) A gallery specialising in imaginative, contemporary glassware, from decorative objects to candy-coloured jewellery.

Arkade   MALL
(Landstrasse 12) This elegant mall shelters names like Augarten Porzellan, Redl Glass and Hugo Boss under one glass roof.

Confiserie Isabella   CONFECTIONERY
(Landstrasse 33) A nostalgic sweet shop for pralines, bonbons, jellies, marshmallows and other tooth-rotting delights.

Imkerhof   FOOD
(Altstadt 15) Honey you can eat, drink and bathe in (including chestnut and acacia varieties) fills the shelves here.

ℹ Information

Internet Access

Atlas Media (Graben 17; per hr €2.50; ☺9.30am-11pm Mon-Sat, from 1pm Sun) Internet access, discount international calls, Skype and copying available.

Hotspot Linz (www.hotspotlinz.at, in German) Offers free wi-fi at 120 hot spots in the city centre, including the Ars Electronica Center and Lentos.

Internet Resources

e-linz.at (http://e-linz.at, in German) The low-down on nightlife, culture and events.

Linz Termine (www.linztermine.at) Listings of cultural events and exhibitions throughout the year.

Lonely Planet (www.lonelyplanet.com/austria/the-danube-valley/linz) Planning advice, author recommendations, traveller reviews and insider tips.

Medical Services

Krankenhaus der Stadt Linz (☑78 06-0; Krankenhausstrasse 9) The main hospital, 1km east of the centre.

Unfallkrankenhaus Linz (☑69 20-0; Garnisonstrasse 7) Emergency hospital.

Money

There are a number of banks with ATMs in the *Innenstadt;* the *Hauptbahnhof* also has a **bank** (⊙9am-6pm Mon-Thu, 9am-4pm Fri).

Post

Main post office (Bahnhofplatz 11-13; ⊙7am-8pm Mon-Fri, 9am-6pm Sat, 9am-1pm Sun) Near the *Hauptbahnhof;* has an ATM.

Post office (Domgasse 1; ⊙8am-6pm Mon-Fri, 9am-noon Sat) Handier to the centre.

Tourist Information

Tourist Information Linz (☑7070 2009; www.linz.at; Hauptplatz 1; ⊙9am-7pm Mon-Sat, from 10am Sun) Brochures, accommodation listings, free room reservation service and a separate Upper Austria information desk can be found here. Hands out a free map, with an enlargement of the *Altstadt.*

Travel Agencies

STA Travel (Herrenstrasse 7; ⊙9am-7pm Mon-Fri)

❶ Getting There & Away

Boat

The **Schiffsstation** (Untere Donaulände 1) is on the south bank next to the Lentos Kunstmuseum. **Wurm + Köck** (www.donauschiffahrt.de, in German) sends boats westwards to Passau (one way/return €23/26, six to seven hours, 9.30am and 2.20pm Tuesday to Sunday May to October) and east to Vienna (€56, 11½ hours, 9am Saturday May to October).

Bus

Regional buses depart from stands at the main bus station adjacent to the *Hauptbahnhof.* Information can be obtained from the **bus information counter** (⊙6am-8pm).

Train

Linz is on the main rail route between Vienna (€31.20, 1½ hours) and Salzburg (€22, 1¼ hours), and express trains run twice hourly in both directions. Several trains depart daily for Prague (€42.80, 5½ hours). Aside from the obligatory **information desk** (⊙7am-7.30pm Mon-Fri, to 4pm Sat, 11am-8pm Sun), there are also some snack bars and an ATM at the *Hauptbahnhof.*

❶ Getting Around

To/From the Airport

Linz airport is 13km southwest of town. A direct shuttle bus service connects the *Hauptbahnhof* (€2.60, 20 minutes) with the airport hourly from Monday to Saturday.

Bicycle

Linz is a major stop on the Danube Trail and has some 200km of bicycle routes. Bikes are available for hire at **Donau Touristik** (Lederergasse 4-12; per day/week €15/70; ⊙8am-5pm Mon-Fri, plus 9am-4pm Sat & Sun May-Sep).

Car & Motorcycle

One-way systems, congested roads and pricey parking make public transport preferable to driving in central Linz, although a car is a definite plus if you're keen to explore more of Upper Austria. There are some free car parks along Obere Donaulände. Major car hire firms include **Avis** (www.avis.com) at the airport and **Hertz** (www.hertz.com; Bürgerstrasse 19).

Public Transport

Linz AG (www.linzag.at) Linz has an extensive bus and tram network, but by early evening services become infrequent. Single tickets (€1.80), day passes (€3.60) and weekly passes (€11.70) are available from pavement dispensers and *Tabak* (tobacconist) shops. Drivers don't sell tickets – buy and validate your tickets before you board.

AROUND LINZ

St Florian

☑07224 / POP 5650

Unassuming St Florian, a market town 18km southeast of Linz, hides one of Austria's finest Augustinian abbeys. Supposedly buried under the abbey, St Florian was a Roman officer who converted to Christianity and was subsequently tortured and drowned in the Enns River in the year 304 for his pains. In many Austrian churches,

HEAVENLY MUSIC

Famous Austrian Romantic composer Anton Bruckner was born 8km from St Florian in the village of Ansfelden in 1824. A choirboy in St Florian and church organist from 1850 to 1855, he was buried in the crypt below his beloved organ in 1896. Indeed the abbey has a long musical tradition, associated with names such as Schubert and Michael Haydn, and world famous for its resident boys' choir, the St Florianer Sängerknaben; see www.florianer.at (in German) for concert dates.

the patron saint of fire-fighters and Upper Austria is depicted as a Roman warrior dousing flames with a bucket of water.

◉ Sights & Activities

Augustiner Chorherrenstift　　　ABBEY
(www.stift-st-florian.at; Stiftstrasse 1; tours adult/child €8/5; ⊙11am, 1pm & 3pm May-Sep) Rising like a vision above St Florian, this abbey dates at least to 819 and has been occupied by the canons regular, living under Augustinian rule, since 1071. Today its imposing yellow and white facade is overwhelmingly baroque.

You can only visit the abbey's interior by guided tour, which takes in the resplendent apartments adorned with rich stuccowork and frescoes. They include 16 emperors' rooms (once occupied by visiting popes and royalty) and a galleried library housing 150,000 volumes. The opulent **Marble Hall** pays homage to Prince Eugene of Savoy, a Frenchman who frequently led the Habsburg army to victory over the Turks. Prince Eugene's Room contains an amusing bed featuring carved Turks, which gives a whole new meaning to the idea of sleeping with the enemy!

A high point of the tour is the **Altdorfer Gallery**, displaying 14 paintings by Albrecht Altdorfer (1480–1538) of the Danube School. The sombre and dramatic scenes of Christ and St Sebastian reveal a skilful use of chiaroscuro. Altdorfer cleverly tapped into contemporary issues to depict his biblical scenes (for example, one of Christ's tormentors is clearly a Turk).

The **Stiftskirche** (⊙7am-10pm) is an exuberant affair: its altar is carved from 700 tonnes of pink Salzburg marble and the huge 18th-century organ, which is literally dripping with gold, was Europe's largest at the time it was built. To hear the organ in full swing, time your visit to see one of the concerts (adult/child with tour €10.50/9.50; ⊙2.30pm Mon, Wed-Fri & Sun mid-May–mid-Oct).

Alongside Anton Bruckner's simple tomb in the **crypt** are the remains of some 6000 people believed to be Roman, which were unearthed in the 13th century. Stacked in neat rows behind a wrought-iron gate, their bones and skulls create a spine-tingling work of art.

OÖ Feuerwehrmuseum　　　MUSEUM
(Fire Brigade Museum; www.feuerwehrmuseum stflorian.at, in German; Stiftstrasse 2; adult/child €3/2.50; ⊙10am-noon & 2-5pm Tue-Sun May-Oct;) Opposite the Stiftskirche, this is a little boy's dream of a museum and an ode to St Florian, patron saint of fire-fighters. The collection comprises historic fire engines, hoses and other paraphernalia.

🛏 Sleeping & Eating

The tourist office hands out a useful accommodation booklet listing hotels and private rooms in and around St Florian.

Gästehaus Stift St Florian　　GUESTHOUSE €
(☎0664-1358 243; Stiftstrasse 1; s/d €48/76) It's oh-so-quiet in this guesthouse within the abbey's walls, overlooking the cloisters and manicured gardens. Antique furniture, solid wood floors and candles add character to the fittingly spartan rooms, which are flooded with natural light.

Landgasthof zur Kanne　　GUESTHOUSE €€
(☎42 88; www.gasthof-koppler.at, in German; Marktplatz 7; s/d €54/88; P) This yellow-fronted 14th-century guesthouse on the main square scores points for its clean, snug rooms and restaurant serving fresh produce from the Koppler family's farm.

Zum Goldenen Löwe　　AUSTRIAN €€
(☎89 30; Speiserberg 9; mains €7-13; ⊙Thu-Tue) The sound of the chef pounding humungous schnitzels welcomes you to this wood-panelled restaurant opposite the abbey gates. The sunny terrace out the back overlooks rolling countryside.

Information

The small **tourist office** (☑56 90; Marktplatz 2; ⊙9am-1pm Mon-Fri) is in the centre of town on Marktplatz, just below the abbey, where you'll also find a few guesthouses and the post office.

ⓘ Getting There & Away

St Florian (officially Markt St Florian) is not accessible by train. Buses depart frequently from the main bus station at Linz' *Hauptbahnhof* (€2.60, 22 minutes); there is a reduced service on Sunday.

Mauthausen

☑07238 / POP 4850

Today Mauthausen is an attractive small town on the north bank of the Danube, east of Linz, but its historic status as a quarrying centre prompted the Nazis to site the KZ Mauthausen concentration camp here. Prisoners were forced into slave labour in the granite quarry and many died on the so-called *Todesstiege* (stairway of death) leading from the quarry to the camp. Some 100,000 prisoners died or were executed in the camp between 1938 and 1945.

The camp, which is undergoing gradual renovation until 2012, has been turned into the emotive **Mauthausen Memorial** (www.mauthausen-memorial.at; Erinnerungsstrasse 1; adult/child/family €2/1/4.80; ⊙9am-5.30pm) museum that tells its history, and that of other camps such as those at Ebensee and Melk. Visitors can walk through the remaining living quarters (each designed for 200, but housing up to 500) and see the cramped and disturbing gas chambers. The former Sick Quarters now shelters most of the camp's harrowing material – charts, artefacts and many photos of both prisoners and their SS guards. It is a stark and incredibly moving reminder of human cruelty.

ⓘ Getting There & Away

From Linz, the quickest way to Mauthausen is by train (€7.20, 30 minutes, hourly). Mauthausen Memorial (follow the KZ Mauthausen signs) is around 3km northwest of the centre; it's a 40-minute walk or a short taxi ride.

THE TRAUNVIERTEL

The pleasantly green and rolling Traunviertel is a great place to abandon the map for a few days. This stretch of Upper Austria is less about sightseeing and more about easing into country life – whether hiking in the hills, sampling homemade *Most* in the apple orchards or bedding down on a rambling *Vierkanterhof* farmhouse.

Steyr

☑07252 / POP 38,350

Franz Schubert called Steyr 'inconceivably lovely' and was inspired to pen the sprightly *Die Forelle* (Trout Quintet) here. And lovely it is: on the confluence of the swiftly flowing Enns and Steyr Rivers, the postcard old town of cobbled lanes and candy-hued baroque houses is one of Upper Austria's most attractive. Every April, the town pays homage to the composer at the Schubert Festival.

⊙ Sights & Activities

Great for an aimless amble, Steyr's well-preserved old town centres on the Stadtplatz and its clutch of graceful Gothic, Renaissance and baroque houses.

Museum Arbeitswelt　　　　MUSEUM
(www.museum-steyr.at, in German; Wehrgrabengasse 7; adult/child/family €5/3.50/9; ⊙9am-5pm Tue-Sun Mar-Dec) Housed in a converted factory by the river, this excellent museum delves into Steyr's industrial past with exhibits on working-class history, forced labour during WWII and the rise of the Socialist party.

FREE **Stadtmuseum**　　　　MUSEUM
(Grünmarkt 26; ⊙10am-5pm Tue-Sun) Set in an early-17th-century granary with an eye-catching sgraffito mural facade, this museum spells out Steyr's culture and folklore in artefacts. The baroque and Biedermeier nativity figurines are the highlight of the permanent collection.

Schlosspark　　　　PARK
Footpaths through this quiet park lead to baroque **Schloss Lamberg**, sitting pretty between the confluence of the Enns and Steyr Rivers. A steep passageway next to the Bummerlhaus, with overhanging arches, squeezes through the old city walls and climbs up to cobbled Berggasse and the park.

Bummerlhaus　　　　HISTORICAL BUILDING
(Stadtplatz 32) This Gothic gabled house and former pub takes its name from the figurine of a golden lion, which punters, presumably after one too many, nicknamed *Bummerl* (small, fat dog).

UPPER AUSTRIA THE TRAUNVIERTEL

Franz Schubert's House — HISTORICAL BUILDING

(Stadtplatz 16) Look out for this fine house on the square, where Schubert apparently found inspiration to pen the *Trout Quintet*.

Stadtpfarrkirche — CHURCH

(Brucknerplatz 4; ⊙dawn-dusk) The spire of this Gothic church is one of Steyr's most visible landmarks. The church shares features with Stephansdom in Vienna and the same architect, Hans Puchsbaum.

Michaelerkirche — CHURCH

(Michaelerplatz; ⊙dawn-dusk) Just north of the Steyr River, this twin-towered baroque church is embellished with a fresco of St Michael and the fallen angels.

👉 Tours

The tourist office arranges several themed tours, including three-hour old town **walking tours** (in German; tickets €6; 2pm Sat Apr-Oct). Alternatively, you can explore at your own speed with a multilingual MP3 tour for €4.

🛏 Sleeping

The tourist office can help arrange private rooms, which are a good deal if you're willing and able to venture out of the centre.

Hotel Christkindlwirt — HOTEL €€

(☏521 84; www.christkindlwirt.at, in German; Christkindlweg 6; s €68-77, d €102-122; P🐾@🖧) Slip behind the pilgrimage church in Christkindl to this boutique newcomer. Many of the contemporary, warm-coloured rooms have balconies with river views. Candles create a restful feel in the grotto-like spa, with a sauna, steam room and treatments like shiatsu massage.

Stadthotel Styria — HISTORIC HOTEL €€

(☏515 51; www.stadthotel.at; Stadtplatz 40; s/d €87/132; P🐾🖧) Welcome to Steyr's most historic hotel. This 400-year-old townhouse has loads of original features, from period furnishings and beams to a frescoed breakfast room overlooking the rooftops. There's a sauna and hammam for guests' use.

Gasthof Bauer — PENSION €

(☏544 41; www.bauer-gasthof.at, in German; Josefgasse 7; s/d €35/62; P) Run by the same family since 1880, this homely pension sits on a little island in the Steyr River. The rooms are simple but comfy, and there's a leafy garden and a restaurant serving fresh, local fare. It's 10 minutes' walk northwest of Stadtplatz.

DON'T MISS

165

SANTA'S LETTERBOX

If you happen to arrive in Steyr over Christmas, head for the suburb of Christkindl, to the west of the old centre. During the festive season, a special **post office** (Schulweg; ⊙10am-5pm mid-Nov–6 Jan) is set up in the Christkindlkirche to handle the almost two million letters posted around the world.

Motel Maria — GUESTHOUSE €

(☏710 62; www.motel-maria.at, in German; Reindlgutstrasse 25; s/d €36/62; P🐾) Set in a lovingly converted *Vierkanthof* farmhouse, 2km west of town (bus 2B stops nearby), this peaceful guesthouse offers bright, country-style rooms dressed in wood furnishings.

Campingplatz Forelle — CAMPGROUND €

(☏780 08; www.forellesteyr.com, in German; Kematmüllerstrasse 1a; camp sites per adult/child/tent €5.50/2.40/3; 🐾) This leafy camp site on the banks of the Enns River has a playground and facilities for cyclists (take bus 1 from the centre).

🍴 Eating

Stadtplatz has lots to offer self-caterers; it hosts an open-air market on Thursday and Saturday mornings, and has snack stands as well as a **Billa Corso** (Stadtplatz 30) supermarket.

TOP CHOICE Knapp am Eck — EUROPEAN €€

(☏762 69; www.knappameck.at, in German; Wehrgrabengasse 15; mains €11-19; ⊙dinner Tue-Sat, lunch Sun; 🐾) A cobbled lane shadows the Steyr River to this boho-flavoured bistro. Dishes like tender lamb with polenta and sage-stuffed pork are inspired by local, seasonal produce. By night, candles and lanterns illuminate the ivy-covered walls, trailing roses and chestnut trees in the garden.

Orangerie im Schlosspark — EUROPEAN €€

(☏740 74; www.orangerie-steyr.at, in German; Blumauergasse 1; mains €16-24; 🐾) This beautifully converted 18th-century orangery opens onto a leafy terrace facing the Schlosspark. The chef cooks fresh, seasonal dishes from chanterelle tagliatelle to hearty beef broth with homemade dumplings.

Gasthof Mader — AUSTRIAN €€

(☏533 58; Stadtplatz 36; mains €8-18; ⊙8am-1am Mon-Sat; 🐾) With its Gothic vaults, frescoed

UPPER AUSTRIA STEYR

Schubertstüberl and arcaded inner courtyard, Mader is historic dining at its best. Specialities like crisp roast pork with dumplings or trout served with parsley potatoes figure on the thoroughly Austrian menu.

Cafe di Fiume CAFE €
(Michaelerplatz 11; lunch menu €5; ☉9am-7pm Tue-Sat, from 1pm Sun; ☻☒) Mismatching chairs, chipper staff and a terrace with views of the Enns create a laid-back atmosphere at this cafe. Try the excellent vegetarian dishes, organic coffee and freshly squeezed juices.

Bräuhof AUSTRIAN €€
(☒420 00; www.braeuhof.at, in German; Stadtplatz 35; mains €8-20; ☒) Dine by lantern light under 300-year-old vaults on the pavement terrace at the atmospheric Bräuhof. Regional numbers like Innviertel dumpling salad and pork filet with herby *Spätzle* (noodles) are matched with full-bodied Austrian wines.

China-Restaurant Xin Xin CHINESE €
(☒470 34; Enge Gasse 20; lunch menu €6, mains €7-12.50) A cheap and cheerful lunch spot, this Chinese restaurant has a peaceful, tree-shaded garden.

ⓘ Information

The **tourist office** (☒532 29-0; www.steyr.info; Stadtplatz 27; ☉8.30am-6pm Mon-Fri, 9am-noon Sat) is on the main square in the Rathaus.

Close to the *Hauptbahnhof* is the **main post office** (Dukartstrasse 13); the other **post office** (Grünmarkt 1) is more handy to the Stadtplatz.

ⓘ Getting There & Away

BUS Regional buses depart from the *Hauptbahnhof*, while city buses leave from outside the *Hauptbahnhof* to the north.

CAR & MOTORCYCLE Steyr is on the B115, the road branching from the A1 and running south to Leoben. There's free parking at the *Hauptbahnhof*.

TRAIN Some trains from Linz (€9.20, 50 minutes) require a change at St Valentin; there are fewer services on Sundays. Trains then continue south into Styria. Most trains for Wels (€12.40, 1¼ hours, hourly) also require a change in St Valentin.

Bad Hall
☒07258 / POP 4850

A sleepy spa town 18km west of Steyr, Bad Hall's big draw is the new **Mediterrana Therme** (www.eurothermen.at; Kurhausstrasse 10; adult/child €15.50/11; ☉9am-midnight;). The

iodine-rich waters that gush from its thermal springs are hailed for their therapeutic properties. Outside there are massage jets and mountain views, while inside an iodine steam room, a columned Roman bath and whirlpools pummel you into a blissfully relaxed state. A splash pool keeps tots amused.

After drifting (or possibly dropping) off in the spa, a walk in the sculpture-dotted **Kurpark** (☉dawn-dusk) opposite is invigorating. Kids love to bash away at the *Klangskulpturen*, larger-than-life musical instruments that include a glockenspiel and wind harp. To inhale the iodized salt for free, head for the central pavilion, where 1000L of the stuff filters through twig walls every hour.

Several family-run farmhouses and guesthouses offer rooms for around €15 to €20 per person. Pick up a list at the **tourist office** (☒72 00-0; www.badhall.at; Kurpromenade 1; ☉8am-5.30pm Mon-Fri, 9am-noon Sat).

From Steyr, there are frequent buses to Bad Hall (€4.30, 38 minutes).

Nationalpark Kalkalpen

This little-known, almost untouched wilderness of rugged limestone mountains, high moors and mixed forest, is home to the elusive golden eagle and lynx. Bordering Styria, this is Austria's second-largest national park after Hohe Tauern. Its valleys and gorges cut through classic alpine landscapes, dominated by **Hoher Nock** (1963m). It's particularly popular with hikers, cyclists and rock climbers in summer and cross-country skiers in winter. Kompass map 70 (1:50,000) covers the park and its trails in detail. For more information on activities, visit the ultramodern **ⓝNationalpark Zentrum Molln** (☒07584-36 51; www.kalkalpen.at; Nationalpark Allee 1; ☉8am-5pm Mon-Fri, 9am-5pm Sat & Sun) near the northern entrance to the park. Staff can arrange guided tours in English and help with accommodation, including the 15 mountain huts within the park. Regular direct buses from Steyr to Molln (€5.30, one hour) normally only run on weekdays.

Kremsmünster
☒07583 / POP 6420

Looming large above the fertile Krems Valley, Kremsmünster's majestic **Benedictine abbey** (www.stift-kremsmuenster.at, in German; adult/child/family €7/3/14; ☉tours 10am, 11am, 2pm, 3pm & 4pm May-Oct, 11am, 2pm & 3.30pm

SMALL PLEASURES

Village-hopping through Upper Austria's countryside reveals some little-known treasures. In the Traunviertel, take a detour to the orchards in **Adlwang** near Bad Hall, where apples go into making juice, *Most* (cider) and schnapps. Leopold Höllhuber sells award-winning potent stuff at Gangl (07258-40 18; Mandorferstrasse 28; d/apt €32/38; [⊞]), a *Vierkanterhof* farmhouse where you can also spend a very comfortable night.

Wending through the fields of the Mühlviertel, pause in **Hirschbach** to follow a steep 13km trail up to a high-altitude herb garden, which grows 150 different types of herbs, some famed for their healing properties. Organic peppermint and melissa are among hundreds of varieties for sale at Bergkräuter-Genossenschaft (www.bergkraeuter.at, in German; Thierberg 32; ⊘8am-5pm Mon-Fri).

Further west, while exploring the misty hills and moor lakes of the Böhmerwald (Bohemian Forest), you can stop off in sweet-toothed **Bad Leonfelden** for homemade gingerbread. Kastner (www.kastner-austria.at; Lebzelterstrasse 243; ⊘8.30am-6pm Mon-Fri, 9am-5pm Sat, 1-3pm Sun) has guarded a secret recipe since 1599; sample freshly baked fruit, nut, honey and chocolate varieties at the factory shop.

Nov-Apr) dates from 777, but was given a baroque facelift in the 18th century. Elaborate stuccowork and frescoes shape the long, low **Bibliothek** (library), where shelves creak under 160,000 volumes, and the **Kaisersaal** (Emperor's Hall). The most prized piece in the **Schatzkammer** (treasury) is the gold Tassilo Chalice, which the Duke of Bavaria donated to the monks in about 780. You can visit all three on a one-hour guided tour.

The other star attraction is the 50m-high Sternwarte (observatory tower; adult/child €8/3; ⊘tours 10am & 2pm May-Oct), dedicated to numerous schools of natural history. Spanning seven floors, the mind-boggling collection steps from fossilised starfish to the skeleton of an ice age cave bear. It's a giddy climb up a spiral staircase to the top floor, which displays the Keppler sextant and affords a bird's-eye perspective of Kremsmünster and the gently rolling countryside.

What can be seen without greasing the palms of the abbey with silver is the Stiftskirche (⊘dawn-dusk), a baroque church extravagantly adorned with lacy stucco, Flemish tapestries and frescoes. The 17th-century cloisters contain the Fischbehälter (Fish Basin; ⊘10am-4pm) containing five fish ponds, each centred on a mythological statue. The trickling of water is calming and you can feed the carp for €0.20.

ℹ Getting There & Away

Kremsmünster is on the rail line between Linz and Graz (from Linz €7.20, 40 minutes, hourly). Buses to/from Wels (€3.60, 30 minutes) and Steyr (€6.10, 1¼ hours) run regularly.

Wels

☎07242 / POP 58,600

Roman-rooted Wels is the largest town in the Traunviertel. While there are few real sights, this is a handy base for exploring rural Upper Austria. The centre is a pleasure to stroll through, with a clutch of Renaissance and baroque townhouses hiding inner courtyards and walled gardens. In summer the town springs to life with markets, open-air concerts and film festivals.

◉ Sights & Activities

Stadtplatz   HISTORIC SITE

Wels' main square is framed by slender townhouses, many of which conceal arcaded inner courtyards. Particularly attractive is the ivy-clad courtyard at No 18, nurturing palms, rhododendrons and Japanese umbrella trees. At the front, glance up to spy the 2000-year-old **Römermedallion** (Roman medallion) relief.

Nearby at No 24, the Renaissance **Haus der Salome Alt** sports a *trompe l'oeil* facade and takes its name from one-time occupant Salome Alt, mistress of Salzburg's most famous prince-archbishop, Wolf Dietrich von Raitenau. Opposite is the refreshingly simple Stadtpfarrkirche (⊘dawn-dusk), noteworthy for its Gothic stained glass.

The stout **Ledererturm** (Tanner's Tower), built in 1326, overshadows the western end of Stadtplatz and is the last remnant of the town's fortifications.

Burg Wels CASTLE

(Burggasse 13; adult/child €4.15/1.60; ⏲10am-5pm Tue-Fri, 2-5pm Sat, 10am-4pm Sun) Gathered around a quiet, flower-dotted garden, this castle is where Emperor Maximilian I drew his last breath in 1519. The folksy museum contains everything from cannon balls to Biedermeier costumes. Must-sees include the horse-drawn cider press and the circular room that's a shrine to baking, with walls smothered in animal-shaped pastries and gigantic pretzels.

Sleeping & Eating

The tourist office can help you find somewhere to stay. In summer, the Stadtplatz and its tributaries offer alfresco dining with a lively vibe.

Kremsmünstererhof HISTORIC HOTEL €

(☎466 23; Stadtplatz 62-63; s/d €48/68; P) Set in a 15th-century townhouse with an inner courtyard, this hotel on the main square has large light-filled rooms with parquet floors and sunny paint-jobs.

Hotel Ploberger HOTEL €€

(☎629 41; www.hotel-ploberger.at; Kaiser-Josef-Platz 21; s €75-112, d €100-140; P) In the heart of town, this Best Western has fresh, contemporary rooms in monochrome hues, some with comforts like Nespresso coffeemakers and DVD players. The sauna and open fire keep things cosy in winter.

Löwenkeller INTERNATIONAL €€

(☎797 85; www.loewenkeller.at; Hafergasse 1; mains €11-22; ⏲dinner Mon-Sat) With its exposed stone, starchy white linen and polished service, Löwenkeller is the most sophisticated restaurant in town. Mediterranean-inspired dishes like scallop gratin and roast sea bass with eggplant risotto are expertly matched with Austrian wines from the cellar.

Olivi ITALIAN €€

(☎911 900; Hafergasse 3; mains €6.50-16; ⏲Mon-Sat) This buzzy pizzeria rustles up tasty antipasti, wood-fired pizza and fresh pasta.

Snaxx CAFE €

(Stadtplatz 52; snacks €1-5; ⏲10am-4am) Next to party-loving bar Jaxx, Snaxx does a mean open sandwich. Our personal favourite: prosciutto with garlicky crème fraîche and chives.

Cafe Urban CAFE €

(Schmidtgasse 20; cakes €2-3) A convivial cafe with great pralines and pastries.

Information

Information, maps and audio guides (€4) of the city are available from **Tourismusverband Wels** (☎434 95; www.stadtmarketing-wels.at; Kaiser-Josef-Platz 22; ⏲9am-6pm Mon-Fri), two blocks north of the main square, Stadtplatz.

Getting There & Away

Trains and buses arrive at the *Hauptbahnhof*, 1.25km north of Stadtplatz. The town is on the InterCity (IC) and EuroCity (EC) express rail route between Linz (€5.40, several hourly), just 15 minutes away, and Salzburg (€20.10, one hour, hourly). There's also an hourly service to Passau (€15.70, 1¼ hours, hourly) on the German border.

THE MÜHLVIERTEL

The Mühlviertel is a remote, beautiful region of mist-enshrouded hills, thick woodlands and valleys speckled with chalk-white *Steinbloass* farmhouses. The scenery (as well as the beer and goulash!) is redolent of the not-so-distant Czech Republic. This offbeat corner of Upper Austria is known for its Gothic architecture, warm-hearted locals, and total peace and quiet.

Freistadt

☎07942 / POP 7400

Just 10km from the Czech border as the bird flies, Freistadt has some of the best-preserved medieval fortifications in Austria, and the beer isn't bad either; indeed locals are so passionate about *Freistädter* brews that they avoid places where it isn't on tap. Beer aside, pleasure can be had by strolling through the town's narrow streets to gate towers and the gardens that have taken root in the original moat.

Sights & Activities

Pick up the handy *City Walk* brochure from the tourist office, which pinpoints Freistadt's key attractions.

Stadtmauern HISTORIC SITE

Topping the must-see list are the sturdy 14th-century city walls complete with gate towers like the medieval **Linzertor** and skeletal **Böhmertor**, which reflect Freistadt's past need for strong defences as an important staging point on the salt route to Bohemia. The moat encircling the town is now given over to gardens and allotments.

BUYING INTO YOUR FAVOURITE BEER

Freistadt is a *Braucommune*, a town where the citizens actually own their brewery – buy a house and you automatically buy a share of your favourite tipple. Ownership is limited to the 149 households within the town walls, but if you have the spare change and *really* like your beer, properties sell for around €350,000. Realistically, the brewery cannot be taken over, as the business would have to buy the whole town in order to take control.

The arrangement started way back in 1777 when the brewery opened. In the ensuing centuries the lucky owners would receive their share of the profits in liquid form, which would be distributed in *Eimer Bier* containers holding 56L. Each owner might get up to 130 containers! Nowadays, for better or worse, owners get a cash payment of equivalent value (which, on Friday and Saturday nights, often goes straight back to the brewery).

Practically every bar in town serves the local brew, so it's not hard to see why the brewery remains a profitable business. If you'd like to learn more about Freistadt beer, there are **tours** (☏757 77; www.freistaedter-bier.at, in German; Promenade 7; tours €8; ⊘2pm Wed Jun-Sep) of the brewery; three small beers are thrown in with the price of the tour. Call ahead if you'd like to take a tour.

UPPER AUSTRIA FREISTADT

Hauptplatz
HISTORIC SITE

Freistadt's focal point is the elongated Hauptplatz, jammed between the old city walls. The square has some ornate buildings and a Gothic **Stadtpfarrkirche** (Parish Church; ⊘dawn-dusk) capped with a baroque tower. Some of the houses along Waaggasse, just west of the Hauptplatz, are embellished with sgraffito mural designs.

Schlossmuseum
MUSEUM

(Schlosshof 2; adult/child €3/1; ⊘9am-noon & 2-5pm Mon-Fri, 2-5pm Sat) The city's 14th-century castle, with a square tower topped by a tapering red-tiled roof, harbours this museum, exhibiting 600 works of engraved painted glass. Climb the 50m Bergfried tower for far-reaching views over Freistadt.

🛌 Sleeping & Eating

The following recommendations (apart from Camping Freistadt) are in the old town. Self-caterers can buy supplies at **Billa** (Eisengasse 14).

Pension Pirklbauer
PENSION €

(☏724 40; www.pension-pirklbauer.at; Höllgasse 2-4; s/d €30/50) Nudging up against medieval Linzertor is this charming pension. Christine is a dab hand at making her guests feel at home: from the rooftop terrace to country cottage-style rooms with pinewood, floral fabrics and squeaky-clean bathrooms.

Hotel Goldener Adler
HISTORIC HOTEL €€

(☏721 12; www.hotels-freistadt.at; Salzgasse 1; s/d/tr €49/78/99; P⊜@) Polished stone slabs, wrought-iron banisters and vaulted passages crammed with antique wagons and spinning wheels hint at this hotel's 700-year history. Unwind in the sauna and whirlpool, or tuck into the famous beer-marinated Bohemian pork shoulder in the beer garden (mains €6 to €16).

Camping Freistadt
CAMPGROUND €

(☏725 70; Eglsee 12; camp sites per adult/child/tent €5/2.50/4.50; ☀) This shady campground on the banks of the Feldaisth River is five minutes' walk northeast of the centre. The great facilities include table tennis and a sauna.

Vis à Vis
INTERNATIONAL €€

(☏742 93; Salzgasse 13; pizzas €7-17; ⊘9am-2am Tue-Fri, from 5pm Sat; 🍴) Pretzels dangle on racks at the bar at this cheery local haunt with a sunny conservatory. The kitchen whips up tasty pizzas (including vegetarian options), salads and generous portions of Austrian and international fare.

ⓘ Information

The **Mühlviertler Kernland tourist office** (☏757 00; www.oberoesterreich.at/kernland; Hauptplatz 14; ⊘8.30am-5pm Mon-Fri, 8am-noon Sat & Sun) provides information on the town and its surrounds.

ⓘ Getting There & Away

Freistadt is on a direct rail route from Linz (€11, one hour, hourly). This line then wriggles its way north to Prague; Czech rail fares are lower than those in Austria, so you can save money by waiting and buying (in Czech currency) your onward tickets once you've crossed the border.

NO F***ING JOKE

A tiny village with a big name, Fucking (pronounced 'fooking') in the far western corner of the Innviertel always has English speakers in fits of giggles. Indeed the Fucking signs were often stolen (no laughing matter, apparently), until 2005 when they were made theft-resistant. Word has it the new ones have attracted exhibitionists living up to the, erm, name as it were. In 2010 a brewery won the right to register a beer called Fucking Hell (*Hell* is German for light ale) here. Mayor Franz Meindl, though, is not amused: 'We don't find it funny. We just want to be left alone,' he said.

The B310, which connects to the A7 motorway to Linz, runs adjacent to the walled centre and then continues its way northwards towards Prague.

Kefermarkt

07947 / POP 2100

It's silent enough to hear a pin drop in the tiny village of Kefermarkt, home to the **Pfarrkirche St Wolfgang** (Oberer Markt 1; ⊙7am-8pm). The pilgrimage church's main claim to fame is its Gothic *Flügelaltar* (winged altar). A masterpiece of craftsmanship, the limewood altarpiece towers 13.5m, with latticework fronds rising towards the ceiling. At the centre are three expressive figures, carved with great skill (left to right as you face them): St Peter, St Wolfgang and St Christopher. The wings of the altar bear religious scenes in low relief.

Perched on a hill overlooking the forest and Schloss Weinberg's red turrets is microbrewery-cum-guesthouse **Schlossbrauerei Weinberg** (☑71 11; www.schlossbrauerei.at, in German; Weinberg 2; s/d €29/50; P), 10 minutes' walk from Kefermarkt. Homebrews are paired with hearty flavours like beer-drenched goulash, beer-battered schnitzel and fresh trout in the vaulted restaurant (mains €6 to €10), which opens onto a tree-shaded terrace. The quiet rooms have small windows with views of the castle.

Frequent trains travel between Kefermarkt and Freistadt (€2, 10 minutes). The church is about 1km north of the train station.

THE INNVIERTEL

Ping-ponged between Bavaria and Austria over the centuries, the Innviertel is a fertile farming region sliced in two by the Inn River, whose banks are a drawcard for cyclists in summer. As well as beautiful baroque and Gothic architecture in Schärding and Braunau, the region has a few other surprises worth sticking around for: from overnighting in a tree house to splashing around in a Caribbean lagoon.

Braunau am Inn

07722 / POP 16,250

A stone's throw from Germany, Braunau am Inn is a favourite pit stop for cyclists pedalling the Inn Radweg trail to or from Innsbruck. This border town has achieved unwanted attention as the birthplace of Hitler, though it would prefer to be described as *die gotische Stadt* (the Gothic city).

◉ Sights

Stadtplatz   HISTORIC SITE

This long main square is lined with elegant pastel-hued townhouses; its southern end narrows to the **Torturm**, a 16th-century gate tower. To the west of Stadtplatz rises the spire of the late-Gothic **Stadtpfarrkirche St Stephan** (Kirchenplatz; ⊙dawn-dusk). At almost 100m, it's one of the tallest in Austria.

Hitler's Geburtshaus   LANDMARK

(Hitler's Birthplace) Not far from the Torturm is the house where Hitler was born in 1889; he only spent two years of his life here before moving with his family to Linz. The inscription outside simply reads *Für Frieden Freiheit und Demokratie, nie wieder Faschismus, millionen Tote mahnen* (For peace, freedom and democracy, never again fascism, millions of dead admonish).

⊨ Sleeping & Eating

Hotel am Theaterpark   HOTEL €

(☑634 71; www.hotelamtheaterpark-neussl.at, in German; Linzerstrasse 21; s/d/tr €42/63/78; P ⊛) One of the best deals in town, this hotel has bright, well-kept rooms, bike storage and a little fitness room. You can wind down over a glass of wine in the Gothic cellar or in the tree-shaded garden.

Hotel Mayrbräu HOTEL €€
(☎633 87; www.mayrbraeu.at, in German; Linzer Strasse 13; s/d €45/84; P) This four-star hotel's large, warm rooms are a decent pick. A vaulted gallery full of contemporary art and a vine-clad inner courtyard lend character to the place.

Bogner AUSTRIAN €€
(☎683 43; Stadtplatz 47; mains €7-10; ☉10am-1am) Supposedly Austria's smallest brewery, Bogner is a rustic pub-restaurant with solid Austrian fare and several home-brewed beers to guzzle.

❶ Information
The **tourist office** (☎626 44; www.tourismus-braunau.at; Stadtplatz 2; ☉8.30am-noon & 1-6pm Mon-Fri, 9am-noon Sat) is at the northern end of the Stadtplatz.

❶ Getting There & Away
By train, at least one change is normally required from either Linz (€21, 2¼ hours) or Salzburg (€12.40, 1½ hours). From Wels, there are several daily direct trains (€17.60, 1½ hours).

Schärding
☎07712 / POP 5200
Schärding is an easygoing town on the Inn River, with peaceful riverfront walks and a baroque centre studded with merchants' houses in myriad pastel shades.

The **tourist office** (☎43 00-0; www.schaerding.at; Innbruckstrasse 29; ☉9am-6pm Mon-Fri, 11am-3pm Sat & Sun, closed weekends Oct-Mar), near the bridge spanning the river into Germany, has loads of information. Look to the **Silberziele** (silver row), a line of richly coloured houses with identically shaped gables, for accommodation and food.

Pension Lachinger (☎22 68; Silberzeile 13; s/d €30/76; P) has comfy, good-value

rooms. A more chic option is antique-meets-modern **Hotel Forstinger** (☎23 02-0; www.hotelforstinger.at; Unterer Stadtplatz 3; s/d €55/86; P❄✳🛜),whose tastefully appointed rooms have period features and DVD players.

If you have your own transport, the approach to Schärding from Linz, via Engelhartszell along the Danube, is beautiful and certainly off the beaten track. A more leisurely alternative is a **boat trip** (www.innschifffahrt.at, in German; Kaiserweg 1; adult/child €10/4; ☉Tue-Sun Apr-Oct) between Passau and Schärding. Trains connect Linz with Schärding (€17.60, 1¼ hours) roughly every hour.

Geinberg
☎07723 / POP 1350
A Caribbean-style lagoon fringed by palm trees is maybe not *quite* what you expect in the heart of the rural Innviertel, but that's precisely what you'll find at **Therme Geinberg** (www.therme-geinberg.at, in German; Thermenplatz 1; 4hr ticket adult/child/family €16.50/12.50/24.50; ☉9am-10pm Sat-Thu, to 11pm Fri; ⛲), one of Austria's top spas. St Lucia it isn't, but it is easy to forget quite where you are here: sipping a daiquiri on the beach, being massaged with coconut oil on a cabana bed and bathing in thermal, salt- and freshwater pools. The Vitalzentrum offers a huge array of pampering treatments, from goat's milk baths to stimulating Tui-Na massages to get the energy flowing. The massive complex also comprises a fitness centre, sauna area and a Mediterranean restaurant.

Geinberg is between Braunau am Inn and Schärding. Trains operate roughly every hour between Braunau am Inn and Geinberg on weekdays, less frequently at weekends (€3.60, 20 minutes). There are roughly hourly trains daily between Schärding and Geinberg (€11, 1½ hours).

WORTH A TRIP

HIGH ABOVE THE TREETOPS

Never has the phrase 'bird's-eye view' been more appropriate than at the **Baumkronenweg** (www.baumkronenweg.at, in German; Kopfing; adult/child €7.50/4.50; ☉10am-6pm Apr-Oct). At this canopy boardwalk in Kopfing, 21km east of Schärding, you can take a head-spinning walk above the treetops. The 2.5km trail is billed as one of the longest in the world and it's certainly a stunner – snaking high above misty spruce trees and comprising lookout towers, hanging bridges and platforms that afford exhilarating perspectives of the forest. For a peaceful room with a (very green) view, check into the 10m-high **Baumhotel** (07763-22 89; r €72), six pine-built tree houses elevated on stilts.

Styria

Best Places to Eat

» Aiola Upstairs (p181)

» Der Steirer (p181)

» Johanns (p192)

» Thomawirt (p181)

» Tom am Kochen (see the boxed text, p187)

» Stadt Meierei (p193)

Best Places to Stay

» Hotel Daniel (p179)

» Hotel Erzherzog Johann (p180)

» Burg Hotel (p186)

» Jugend- und Familiengästehaus Schloss Röthelstein (p196)

Why Go?

Austria's second-largest province is a perfect combination of culture, architecture, rolling hills, vine-covered slopes and, of course, mountains. Its capital, Graz, Austria's second-largest city, is attractive and has one of the highest standards of living in Europe. Head south from Graz and you're in wine country, dubbed the 'Styrian Tuscany'. This is also the land of *Kürbiskernöl* – the strong, dark pumpkin-seed oil ubiquitous in Styrian cooking.

The eastern stretch of Styria is dotted with rejuvenating thermal spas and centuries-old castles. If you're a fan of the former, Bad Blumau is a mandatory stop, not only to take the waters but also to appreciate its unusual architecture, designed by Friedensreich Hundertwasser. If you prefer castles, Schloss Riegersburg is one of Austria's best.

In the north and west, Styria's landscape changes to cold, fast-flowing alpine rivers, towering mountains and carved valleys. Two highlights are Admont Abbey and Erzberg's open-cast mine. Note that the northwestern reaches of Styria stretch into Salzkammergut.

When to Go

Unless you are here for the skiing, the best time to visit is during the main season from April to October. From November many of the sights and cultural events – such as Graz's best sight, Schloss Eggenberg – close or end for the season. Skiers usually hit Schladming from mid-December (or year round on the Dachstein Glacier), whereas the wine roads of southern Styria peak in September, when there are festivals, in October when the vineyards turn golden brown, and around St Martin's Day (11 November), when the young wine is released.

Planning your Itinerary

Styria mirrors Austria itself: broad in an east–west direction. Based in Graz, you can easily visit the wine regions of southern Styria on a day trip with your own wheels if time is at a premium. In northern Styria, Bruck an der Mur and Leoben can be combined into a long day, but if you want to visit Mariazell or Eisenerz, an overnight stop is unavoidable without a car. Murau (in the Mur River valley) is too far from Graz for a day trip and is a nice spot to spend a night. Admont in the Enns Valley combines well with Eisenerz, either with your own wheels or by bus. Once you are in the Enns Valley, trains, buses and roads connect Schladming and Admont. Exiting Styria to the Salzkammergut lakes region can easily be done by backtracking a short way from Schladming to the Steinach–Irdning rail junction.

DON'T MISS

High-profile **Graz** (p175), the capital of Styria, has Renaissance palace Schloss Eggenberg, replete with museums and lush gardens. The festivals of Graz fill the city's courtyards with music, and the Graz populace can stake a convincing claim to being the friendliest and most charming in Austria.

Low-key **Admont** (p195) attracts bus loads of visitors for its abbey, but beyond the car park Admont's attractions become sublime: the mountains of the Gesäuse region, gurgling rivers and streams, outdoor life and a relaxed feel.

The Great Outdoors

» **Cycling** is one of the best ways to enjoy the Styrian outdoors. Some of the best cycling on minor sealed roads is in southern Styria in the wine-growing region, especially southeast of Leutschach near the Slovenian border.

» **Skiing** is best in the Schladming region in the west of Styria; the Dachstein Glacier has year-round skiing.

» **Hiking** is a national pastime among Austrians, and the Styrians are no exception. The Gesäuse region, Schladming and the wine country in the south are places with good access to trails. Mariazell, Leoben, Bruck an der Mur and Eisenerz are others.

» **Mountain biking** has its mecca in Schladming, where some demanding trails wind through the mountains and there is no shortage of hire facilities.

» **Cable-car rides** are bountiful in Schladming, with the most spectacular of all gondolas leading up to the Dachstein mountains.

FAMOUS STYRIANS

Strongman, actor and governor of California Arnold Schwarzenegger, tennis champion Thomas Muster, and European and Hollywood actor Klaus Maria Brandauer all hail from Styria.

Where to Splurge

» **Graz** Splurge on a hotel, eat well and check out a wine bar and the small but rich cultural scene.

» **South Styrian wine roads** Stop at vineyards, taste the wines, eat and hike.

Getting Around Styria

Despite its remote valleys, Styria can be easily travelled by train and by bus. Plan ahead using the website www.mobilzentral.at (in German). Car-hire rates and choice are best in Graz.

Resources

» Overview of Steiermark (www.steiermark.com)

» Skiing and outdoors (www.bergfex.at/steiermark, in German)

» South Styrian wine roads (www.suedsteirischeweinstrasse.at, in German)

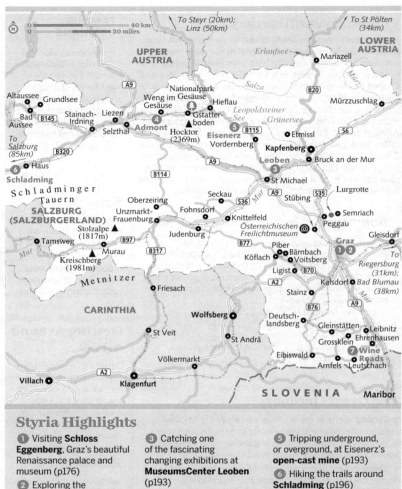

STYRIA

Styria Highlights

1 Visiting **Schloss Eggenberg**, Graz's beautiful Renaissance palace and museum (p176)

2 Exploring the restaurants and bars of **Graz** (p182), Styria's capital

3 Catching one of the fascinating changing exhibitions at **MuseumsCenter Leoben** (p193)

4 Visiting Admont's spectacular **abbey** (p195) and exploring its fascinating museums

5 Tripping underground, or overground, at Eisenerz's **open-cast mine** (p193)

6 Hiking the trails around **Schladming** (p196)

7 Cruising the **wine roads** of southern Styria (p187)

ⓘ Getting There & Away

BUS Postbus departures to Mariazell – not on the train line – are integrated with train arrivals at Bruck an der Mur; to Eisenerz, integrated bus services leave from Leoben, and for Admont and the Gesäuse the town of Liezen forms the main bus-transfer point.

CAR The A2, from Vienna to Villach in Carinthia, runs through southern Styria, passing just below Graz, while the A9 runs an almost north–south course through the middle of Styria, making it straightforward to travel from Linz and Salzburg to Graz. The A9 also connects Graz with Slovenia, 40km to the south.

TRAIN Styria's train lines are relatively sparse; the main line between Carinthia and Vienna passes well north of Graz through the region's main railhead, Bruck an der Mur. For Linz and Salzburg, a change is usually required at St Michael, 25km southwest of Bruck.

❶ Getting Around

Regional and city transport (☎050/678 910; www.verbundlinie.at) is based on a system of zones and time tickets. Tickets can be bought from machines for one to 22 zones; the price rises from a single trip in one zone (€1.90, valid for one hour), to 24-hour passes for one (€4.20) or multiple zones (eg €7.30 for four zones to Bärnbach). Weekly and monthly passes are also available.

In Graz, **Mobilzentral** (☎0316-82 06 06; www.mobilzentral.at, in German; Jakoministrasse 1; ⊙8am-6pm Mon-Fri, 9am-1pm Sat) is a useful store of information on Styrian regional buses. It also sells international train tickets. The website www.busbahnbim.at has timetable and price information.

GRAZ

☑0316 / POP 257,350

Austria's second-largest city is probably Austria's most relaxed, and after Vienna it is also Austria's liveliest for after-hours pursuits. It's an attractive place with bristling green parkland, red rooftops and a small, fast-flowing river gushing through its centre. Architecturally, it has Renaissance courtyards and provincial baroque palaces complemented by innovative modern designs. Styria's capital also has a very beautiful bluff connected to the centre by steps, a funicular and a glass lift. Last but not least, a large student population (some 50,000 in four universities) helps propel the nightlife and vibrant arts scene, creating a pleasant, lively and liveable city.

❍ Sights

HAUPTPLATZ & AROUND

TOP CHOICE Universalmuseum Joanneum

MUSEUM

(www.museum-joanneum.at; Raubergasse 10) Founded in 1811 by Archduke Johann, this ensemble of museums is Austria's oldest and with its 19 locations is the gardener of Graz's rich cultural landscape. The main building is situated off Raubergasse in the Joanneumsviertel (Joanneum Quarter), which at the time of publication was being developed and given a new visitor information centre. Until work is completed, some museums will be closed.

The **Naturkundemuseum** (Museum of Natural History; Joanneumsviertel; adult/child/family €8/3/16; ⊙10am-6pm Tue-Sun; ♿) houses Styria's premier collection on geology, palaeontology, minerals, zoology and botany

and should reopen in late 2012. Another, the **Neue Galerie Graz** (New Gallery; Joanneumsviertel; same hr & prices) should be open by late 2011 to showcase art from the 18th century to the present – this will be the most important historical and contemporary art collection in Styria.

FREE **Multimediale Sammlung** (Multimedia Collection; Joanneumsviertel; same hr) will focus on new art and multimedia when it opens in late 2011.

Landeszeughaus

ARMOURY

(Provincial Armoury; www.zeughaus.at; Herrengasse 16; adult/child/family €7/3/14; ⊙10am-6pm Apr-Oct, to 3pm Mon-Sat, to 4pm Sun Nov-Mar; ♿) If your passion is armour and weapons, don't miss this museum. It houses an astounding array of 30,000 gleaming exhibits, most from the 17th century when the original armoury was built.

FREE **Burg**

CASTLE

(Hofgasse) Graz's 15th-century Burg today houses government offices. At the far end of the courtyard, on the left under the arch, is an ingenious **double staircase** (1499) – the steps diverge and converge as they spiral. Adjoining it is the **Stadtpark**, the city's largest green space.

FREE **Domkirche**

CHURCH

(Burggasse 3; ⊙dawn-dusk) The Domkirche dates from the 15th century and became a cathedral in 1786. The interior combines Gothic and baroque elements, with reticulated vaulting on the ceiling; its highlight is the faded *Gottesplagenbild* fresco on the cathedral's exterior, which dates from 1485. It depicts life in the early 1480s, when Graz was besieged by its triple tragedy of Turks, the plague and locusts.

Mausoleum of Ferdinand II

MAUSOLEUM

(Burggasse 2; adult/child €4/2; ⊙10.30am-12.30pm & 1.30-4pm) The mannerist-baroque Mausoleum of Ferdinand II was designed by Italian architect Pietro de Pomis and was begun in 1614; after Pomis' death the mausoleum was completed by Pietro Valnegro, while Johann Bernhard Fischer von Erlach chipped in with the exuberant stuccowork and frescoes inside. Ferdinand (1578–1637), his wife and his son are interred in the crypt. The highlight is a red-marble sarcophagus of Ferdinand's parents, Karl II (1540–90) and Maria of Bavaria (1551–1608). Only Maria occupies the sarcophagus – Karl II lies in the Benedictine Abbey (p196) in Seckau.

ⓘ GRAZ' MUSEUMS

Most of Graz' museums are under the umbrella of the Universalmuseum Joanneum. Admission with a **24-hour ticket** (adult/child/family €11/4/22) allows you to visit the entire ensemble over two days (but within 24 hours). The major ones are **Schloss Eggenberg** and its museums, **Kunsthaus Graz**, **Landeszeughaus**, **Museum im Palais**, and **Naturkundemuseum** and the **Neue Galerie Graz** both in the Joanneumsviertel.

That's a tough schedule in 24 hours, but an alternative is a **48-hour ticket** (adult/child/family €17/7/34). The tickets can be purchased at any of the museums.

Museum im Palais   MUSEUM

(Sackstrasse 16; adult/child & student/family €8/3/16; ⊙10am-6pm Tue-Sun) Due to open in late 2011. Houses Styria's collection of treasures in a former baroque palace.

Stadtmuseum   MUSEUM

(Sackstrasse 18; adult/child & concession €4.50/2.50; ⊙10am-6pm Tue-Sun) Temporary exhibitions on local history.

FREE Stadtpfarrkirche   CHURCH

(Herrengasse 23; ⊙dawn-dusk) The stained-glass window of the town parish church has an interesting anomaly: the fourth panel from the bottom on the right (left of the high altar) clearly shows Hitler and Mussolini looking on as Christ is scourged.

Museum der Wahrnehmung   MUSEUM

(Museum of Perception; www.muwa.at, in German; Friedrichgasse 41; adult/child/family €3.50/1.80/8, samadhi bath €45; ⊙2-6pm Wed-Mon) Small but unusual collection that explores sensory illusions; the **samadhi** (meditative) bath is a therapeutic bath that deprives the body of all sensory input.

Volkskundemuseum   MUSEUM

(Paulustorgasse 11-13a; adult/child/family €7/3/14; ⊙9am-4pm Tue-Sun) Museum devoted to folk art and lifestyle; highlights include 2000 years of traditional clothing.

MUR RIVER & AROUND

Kunsthaus Graz   ART GALLERY

(www.kunsthausgraz.at; Lendkai 1; adult/child/family €7/3/14, tours €2.50; ⊙10am-6pm Tue-Sun, tours 2pm Tue-Fri, 11am & 4pm Sat & Sun) Designed by British architects Peter Cook and Colin Fournier, this world-class contemporary-art space is a bold creation which looks something like a space-age sea slug. Exhibitions change every three to four months, and tours cover not only the exhibitions but also the unusual building.

FREE Murinsel   BRIDGE

This artificial island-bridge of metal and plastic in the middle of the Mur contains a cafe (p182), a kids' playground with a safety net to prevent them climbing over the edge, and a small stage. In summer, further downstream a beach bar is set up and sometimes Graz' daring young lads and lasses do some **river surfing** in the rapids.

SCHLOSSBERG

Schlossberg   GARDEN

Rising to 473m, this is the site of the original fortress that gave Graz its name. Its wooded slopes can be reached by a number of paths, with the funicular **Schlossbergbahn** (Castle Hill Railway; 1hr ticket €1.90, with public-transport ticket free) from Kaiser-Franz-Josef-Kai, or by **glass lift** (1hr ticket €1.90, with public-transport ticket free) from Schlossbergplatz. Even Napoleon was hard-pressed to raze this fortress, but he did it. The area was later landscaped and today the **Kasematten** open-air theatre, a great restaurant-bar (see p181) and a small **Garnison Museum** (Garrison Museum; Schlossberg 5a; adult/child €1/free; ⊙10am-4pm Thu-Sun mid-May–Oct) are the legacy.

Uhrturm   CLOCK TOWER

Perched on the southern edge of Schlossberg is the Uhrturm, the city's symbol. In what must have been a good deal for Europe's modernising midget, the townsfolk paid Napoleon a ransom of 2987 florins and 11 farthings to save the tower during the 1809 invasion.

EGGENBERG

TOP CHOICE Schloss Eggenberg   PALACE

(Eggenberger Allee 90; adult/child €7/3; ⊙10am-5pm Tue-Sun Palm Sunday-Oct) Reached by tram 1 from Hauptplatz, this baroque palace was built on a Gothic predecessor (which explains an interesting Gothic chapel in one section of the palace viewed from a glass cube) and has numerous features of the Italian Renaissance, such as the attractive courtyard arcades. The palace was created for the Eggenberg dynasty in 1625 by Giovanni Pietro de Pomis (1565-1633) at the request of Johann Ulrich (1568-1634), who rose from ordinariness to become governor of Inner Austria in 1625. At the time, Inner Austria was a powerful province that included Carinthia and parts of Slovenia and northern Italy.

A highlight of the palace is the guided tour (incl with admission; ⊙10am-4pm on the hr except at 1pm) in English or German through the 24 **Prunkräume** (staterooms), which like everything else in the palace and gardens is based around astronomy, the zodiac and classical or religious mythology. The tour ends at Planet Hall, which is a riot of white stuccowork and baroque frescoes. Along the way you learn the idiosyncrasies of each room, the stories told by the frescoes and about the Eggenberg family itself.

Alte Galerie & Museums MUSEUM
(☑58 32 64-9770; adult/child €7/3; ⊙10am-6pm Tue-Sun Apr-Oct, to 5pm Tue-Sun Nov-Mar, closed 3 weeks in Jan) The second interesting aspect of any visit (the important one in winter months) is the remarkable works of art held in museums inside the palace and grounds. The **Alte Galerie** (Old Gallery) houses paintings from the Middle Ages to the baroque. In a clever touch, each room has been individually coloured to highlight and complement the dominant tones of the paintings displayed in them. In summer, admission to the Alte Galerie is included in the price of tours.

The palace houses three other excellent collections, which can be visited with admission to the Alte Galerie or Schloss itself. In the **Pre- and Early-History Collection** the prize exhibition is the exceptional Strettweg Chariot and a bronze mask, both dating from the 7th century BC. The same building contains a **Collection of Roman Provincial Antiquities** covering Roman finds in the province. Finally, there's a **Coin Collection**, with magnifying glasses on the cases so you can see the coins close up.

Schlossgarten GARDEN
(adult/child €1/free; ⊙8am-7pm Apr-Oct, to 5pm Nov-Mar) In summer, the mood and atmosphere of the palace gardens is set by the squawking of seemingly indignant peacocks and by deer roaming among Roman stone reliefs. The **Planetengarten** (Planet Garden; ⊙10am-6pm May-Oct, to 4pm Nov & Apr) is based on the same Renaissance theme of planets.

👉 Tours

The tourist office (Graztourismus; see p184) offers a walking tour (€9.50/3.50 per adult/child) in German and English at 2.30pm daily from April to October and at 2.30pm Saturday from November to March (none in December). Also ask about its theme tours, or weekend day trips outside Graz, or pick up its nifty multimedia (and multilingual) guide to sights, using a handheld computer (€7.50/8.50 for two/four hours).

🎊 Festivals & Events

Stadtfest MUSIC
Held in early July. Renaissance courtyards are transformed into raucous stages for rock and classical music for the weekend.

Styriarte CLASSICAL MUSIC
Classical festival featuring almost continuous concerts in June and July. Pick up information from **Styriarte Kartenbüro** (☑82 50 00; www.styriarte.com; Sackstrasse 17; tickets €21-115). Some concerts are held in Renaissance courtyards and are free.

Steirischer Herbst CLASSICAL MUSIC, PERFORMANCE
Held during October, includes performances in music, theatre and film, plus exhibitions and art installations. Contact **Steirischer Herbst Informationsbüro** (☑81 60 70; www.steirischerherbst.at; Sackstrasse 17; tickets €8-22) for more.

GRAZ FOR CHILDREN

With its green spaces, playgrounds and relaxed atmosphere, Graz is made for children. The creation of **FriDa & FreD** (www.fridaundfred.at; Friedrichgasse 34; adult & child over 6yr/under 6yr/family €4/1.50/11; ⊙9am-5pm Mon, Wed & Thu, 9am-7pm Fri, 10am-5pm Sat & Sun; 🚼), Graz's first museum devoted to children, makes it even better. This small but fun-packed museum is aimed at kids up to the age of 12, and hosts workshops, exhibitions and theatre. Like any good children's museum, it has loads of hands-on tasks and interactive displays.

The **Schlossberg Cave Railway** (Schlossbergplatz; rides 1 person €3.50, 2-4 people €6.50-10; ⊙10am-5pm; 🚼), the longest grotto railway in Europe, is another highlight for the little 'uns. The trip, taking about 20 minutes, winds its way around fairy-tale scenes through tunnels once used as a safe haven from Allied bombings during WWII.

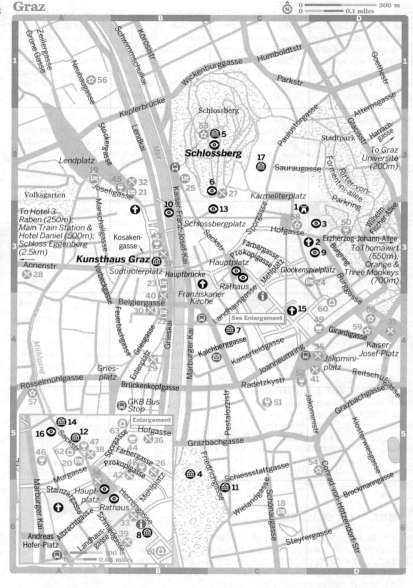

Jazz Sommer Graz JAZZ

(www.jazzsommergraz.at, in German) Free jazz concerts (often with an impressive international line-up) take place in Dom im Berg from early July to late August, with late-night shows at the club p.p.c. (see p183).

🛏 Sleeping

The tourist office books hotels without charge. Visit the Ibis (www.ibishotel.com), Mercure (www.mercure.com) and Etap (www.etaphotel.com) websites for central chain hotels.

GRAZ SLEEPING

TOP CHOICE **Hotel Daniel** HOTEL €€
(☎711 080; www.hoteldaniel.com; Europaplatz 1; r €59-79, breakfast per person €9; P❀❀@) Perched at the top of Annenstrasse and looking for all the world like a block of 1950s beachside holiday apartments that's lost its beach, the Daniel is an exclusive design hotel with two categories of rooms: 'Smart' and 'Loggia'. The former are smaller, though decent sized, and have queen-size beds. The Loggia category is larger and has balconies. All rooms have cable LAN; you can rent a Vespa (€15 per day) and there's a 24-hour espresso bar. The bathroom – but, thankfully, not the toilet – wall is transparent.

Hotel Strasser   HOTEL €€

(☎71 39 77; www.hotel-strasser.at; Eggenberger Gürtel 11; s/d/tr/apt €45/65/93/180; P@🛜📶) Strasser has some fascinating pseudo-neoclassical and Mediterranean touches, with Tuscan gold and ochre blending with mirrors and cast-iron balustrades. There are a couple of bar areas, and cots are available for toddlers in this option convenient to the train station.

Hotel zum Dom   HOTEL €€

(☎82 48 00; www.domhotel.co.at; Bürgergasse 14; s €83-93, d €170-220, ste €227-332; P😊🛜) Hotel zum Dom is a charming, graceful hotel with tasteful and individually furnished rooms. These come either with steam/power showers or whirlpools, and one suite even has a terrace whirlpool. Ceramic art throughout the hotel is crafted by a local artist.

Gasthof-Pension zur Steirer-Stub'n   GUESTHOUSE €

(☎71 68 55; www.pension-graz.at; Lendplatz 8; s/d €43/78, apt €110-160; 😊🛜) This guesthouse combines the best of a traditional atmosphere with a bright and breezy feel, complemented by features like tiled floors in the corridors, a potted plant in each room and patios outside many of the good-sized rooms overlooking Lendplatz. Wi-fi is in the restaurant.

Hotel Feichtinger Graz   HOTEL €€

(☎724 100; www.hotel-feichtinger.at; Lendplatz 1a; s/d/tr €53/100/132; P😊🛜) This modern seminar and business hotel offers some of the best-value beds in town. Rooms are spacious, and the furnishings are modern and have a light touch, which extends to the very large breakfast room.

Augarten Hotel   HOTEL €€

(☎20 800; www.augartenhotel.at; Schönaugasse 53; s/d €115-165, d €140-190; P😊✳🛜📶) Though it's not an 'art hotel', art plays an important role in the Augarten. It's decorated with the owner's private collection, which includes a great oil of the German crooning superstar Heino. All rooms are bright and modern, and the end rooms have windows on two walls. The pool and sauna round off an excellent option.

Hotel Erzherzog Johann   HOTEL €€

(☎81 16 16; www.erzherzog-johann.com; Sackstrasse 3-5; s €125-172, d €145-248, ste €265-370; P😊🛜) Weekend deals are the thing to watch out for here, but you could also throw caution to the wind and splurge in one of the ostentatious theme rooms. The Wanda-Sacher-Masoch-Suite is in white and has projections of classical statues in the bathroom, whereas Orientalists will love the Moroccan room. All have cable LAN.

Schlossberg Hotel   HOTEL €€€

(☎80 70-0; www.schlossberg-hotel.at; Kaiser-Franz-Josef-Kai 30; s €155-185, d €190-235, ste €311-375; P@🛜♨) Central but away from the city tumult, four-star Schlossberg is blessed with a prime location at the foot of its namesake. Rooms are well sized and decorated in the style of a country inn, but the fitness room is mediocre. The rooftop terrace with views is perfect for an evening glass of wine.

Hotel Wiesler   HOTEL €€

(☎70 66-0; www.hotelwiesler.com; Grieskai 4; r €79-169, ste €199-299; P@) This art-nouveau gem has reinvented itself as a hotel with an offbeat edge. It has four categories of rooms (small, medium, large and 'extra'), all with cable LAN. Top of the range is a fully-fledged grand suite. The foyer and abundance of bars and restaurants bear the hallmarks of the new-style Wiesler; the rooms are fairly old-style. Visit the breakfast room to check out Leopold Forstner's (1878–1936) art-nouveau mosaic depicting Venus stepping out of an oyster.

Camping Central   CAMPGROUND €

(☎0676/378 51 02; freizeit@netway.at; Martinhofstrasse 3; camp sites per adult/child/car & tent €8/5/16; ☉Apr-Oct; P@♨📶) Excellent camping ground with pool and playground 6km from the centre (take bus 32 from Jakominiplatz).

Jugend- und Familiengästehaus Graz   HOSTEL €

(☎70 83 210; graz@jufa.at; Idlhofgasse 74; dm €22, s €39-46.50, d €64-77; P😊🛜📶) Take bus 31, 32 or 33 from Jakominiplatz for this HI hostel about 800m south of the main train station.

Hotel 3 Raben   HOTEL €€

(☎71 26 86; www.dreiraben.at; Annenstrasse 43; s from €81, d from €121, f from €126; P😊🛜📶) Near the station and with rooms significantly cheaper than the official rates, even during trade-fair periods, when singles and doubles can cost €69/104. A family room holds up to five guests. Call or check the website.

Hotel Weitzer   HOTEL €

(☎7030; www.weitzer.com; Grieskai 12; r €69-149, breakfast per person €12; P@🛜) Furnishings in the budget 'Casual' rooms are older, while 'Classic', 'Comfort' and 'Rubin' rooms are modern. The price for these varies according to size (and demand or season, starting around €99). With sauna and fitness room.

✕ Eating

TOP CHOICE **Aiola Upstairs** INTERNATIONAL €€
(http://upstairs.aiola.at, in German; Schlossberg 2; pasta €9.50-15, mains €17.50-25; ☺9am-midnight Mon-Sat; ✐) Ask any local where to find the best outdoor dining experience in Graz, and they'll probably say Aiola. Whether it's king prawns with pasta or corn-fed chicken, this wonderful restaurant on Schlossberg has great views, delicious international flavours, a superb wine list, spot-on cocktails and very chilled music.

TOP CHOICE **Der Steirer** BEISL €€
(www.dersteirer.at, in German; Belgiergasse 1; mains €9-18.50, tapas €2, lunch menu €6.90; ☺11am-midnight) This Styrian *neo-Beisl* and wine bar has a small but fantastic selection of local dishes, which you can wash down with a large choice of wines, a true Wiener schnitzel from veal, and Austro-tapas if you just feel like nibbling. Its goulash with fried polenta is surely one of the best in the country.

Aiola City BAR, INTERNATIONAL €€
(http://city.aiola.at, in German; Mehlplatz 1; lunch menu €9.50, pasta €11-15.50, mains €18.50-25.50; ☺7.30-2am Mon-Sat, 9am-midnight Sun; ☻✐) In the centre, this Aiola has great food, low vaulting, a cool lounge feel and outdoor seating on Mehlplatz.

Yamamoto JAPANESE €€
(Prokopigasse 4; sushi & sashimi mains €12-18, udon €7.50-10; ☺Tue-Sat) Yamamoto is refreshingly authentic; it's Japanese-owned and run, and gets its sushi delivered throughout the week, so it's always fresh and, like the noodle dishes, delicious.

TOP CHOICE **Thomawirt** BEISL €€
(www.thomawirt.at, in German; Leonhardstrasse 40-42; lunch menu €7.50, mains €9.50-15.90; ☺11am-2am; ☻) This *neo-Beisl* and pub in the uni quarter serves lunch from 2pm (11am on weekends) and other excellent dishes ranging from Styrian classics to steaks until 1am. Chill out with occasional music in the bar; the place is divided up into cafe, restaurant and lounge-bar areas.

ⓘ SPOTS TO EAT, DRINK & SNACK

When in Graz, enjoy the restaurant scene. The traditional Styrian fare is delicious and there are also some excellent international options.

» Aside from these listings, there are plenty of cheap eateries near Universität Graz (tram 1 and 7), particularly on Halbärthgasse, Zinzendorfgasse and Harrachgasse. The freshest fruit and vegetables are at the **farmers markets** (☺4.30am-1pm Mon-Sat) on Kaiser-Josef-Platz and Lendplatz.

» For **fast-food stands**, head for Hauptplatz and Jakominiplatz. Supermarkets are plentiful throughout the city, among them **Billa** (Annenstrasse 23) and **Eurospar** (Sackstrasse 7-11); a **Spar** (☺6am-10pm) is located in the Hauptbahnhof.

» Most bars are concentrated in three areas: around the university, on Mehlplatz and Prokopigasse (dubbed the 'Bermuda Triangle'), and a third area near the Kunsthaus. Lines are often blurred, so don't dismiss a place for a good night out just because it serves food. Good examples include the two Aiola restaurants, iku and Thomawirt.

iku INTERNATIONAL €
(✆8017 9292; www.iku-graz.at, in German; Lendkai 1; lunch menu €7; ☺9am-1am; ▥) Inside the surrealistic Kunsthaus, this sleek bar and restaurant does weekday breakfasts, as well as a salad buffet and a vegetarian and meat menu weekdays between 11.30am and 3pm. The Sunday brunch with music is the highlight of the culinary calendar (reserve ahead); events, especially Latino nights, dominate the evenings. There's a small play area for kids.

Dainadoo TAMIL, SRI LANKAN €
(www.dainadoo.at, in German; Entenplatz 1a; curry of the day €9, lunch menu €7; ☺Mon-Sat; ☻ⓦ✐) Friendly, authentic but also with a foot in the cultural scene (musicians set up some nights), this excellent restaurant serves one delicious vegetarian or meat curry, a dhal (lentil curry) and other bites from a small menu.

Krebsenkeller

AUSTRIAN €€

(Sackstrasse 12; mains €6-12; ☺lunch & dinner; ☺) Krebsenkeller does inexpensive regional cuisine – which means lots of pumpkin oil – and appeals to locals and tourists alike, not only for its home-style cooking, but also for a lovely inner courtyard and traditional atmosphere.

Tramina

BEISL €€

(Klosterwiesgasse 2; mains €7.50-12; ☺6pm-2am daily; ☺☑) In the family for three generations, this organic traditional restaurant has earned a Grüne Küche (Green Kitchen) award for good ecological practice. It specialises in lamb, but you'll also find thin slices of beef served in vinegar and oil and half a dozen vegetarian dishes.

Hofkeller

WINE BAR €€

(www.hofkeller.at, in German; Hofgasse 8; pasta, salads & mains €10-23; ☺Mon-Sat) This authentic wine bar and restaurant is the perfect place for sipping from a large selection of Italian wines. Choose a pasta or main dish from the blackboard; expect anything from octopus salad to lamb from a small, changing menu. There's outdoor seating in summer.

Mangolds

VEGETARIAN €

(www.mangolds.at, in German; Griesgasse 11; meals €5-10; ☺11am-7pm Mon-Fri, 11am-4pm Sat; ☺☑) Tasty vegetarian patties, rice dishes and over 40 salads are served at this pay-by-weight vegetarian cafeteria.

Landhauskeller

AUSTRIAN €€

(www.landhauskeller.at, in German; Schmiedgasse 9; mains €12.50-21.50; ☺11.30am-midnight Mon-Sat; ☺☑) Traditional, with *Tafelspitz* (prime boiled beef) and other classics, in a courtyard ambience packed with historical punch.

Magnolia

INTERNATIONAL €€€

(☎82 38 35; www.augartenhotel.at, in German; Schönaugasse 53; 3-/4-course menu €49/62; ☺Mon-Fri; ℗) Stylish and part of the Augarten Hotel, with outdoor seating.

🍷 Drinking

The cafe and bar scene in Graz is propelled by a healthy student crowd. Some of the cafes we've listed here change into bars as the night wears on, but they tend not to stay open as late.

TOP CHOICE \ Operncafé

CAFE

(www.temmel.com/opernnew, in German; Opernring 22; coffee & cake from €4; ☺7.30am-9pm Mon-Sat, 9am-9pm Sun) Operncafé is a traditional cafe with good coffee, homemade pastries and pleasant, suited waiters who have found a calling in life.

TOP CHOICE La enoteca

WINE BAR

(www.laenoteca.at, in German; Sackstrasse 14; ☺5-11pm Mon, 11.30am-11pm Tue-Fri, 10am-11pm Sat) This small wine bar situated in a courtyard has an informal, relaxed atmosphere, making it an ideal place to enjoy a Schilcher Sekt (sparkling Schilcher rosé; €26) and mixed antipasti (€10).

Flan O'Brien

PUB

(www.flannobrien.at; Paradeisgasse 1; ☺10.30am-2am Mon-Sat, 2pm-1am Sun) Largest and liveliest Irish pub in town, with a courtyard, live music and inexpensive standards like burgers, Irish stew and very decent fish and chips.

Insel Café

CAFE

(Murinsel; ☺9.30-midnight; ☑) This cafe on the Murinsel offers a unique experience – here you can sip a drink as the Mur River splashes below your feet and the kids play on the rope net.

Edegger-Tax

CAFE

(Hofgasse 8; coffee & cakes €2-5; ☺6.30am-8pm Mon-Fri, to 3pm Sat) This modern cafe is perfectly complemented by its 1569 bakery (open 7am to 6pm Monday to Friday, to noon Saturday) next door. As well as yummy goodies baked on the premises, it has a stunning wood-carved facade.

Orange

BAR, CLUB

(www.cafe-bar-orange.at, in German; Elisabethstrasse 30; ☺8pm-3am) A young, fashionable student crowd gets down in this modern lounge bar and club, which has a patio perfect for warm summer evenings. DJs spin sounds regularly here. Admission is €2 to €3 from Wednesday to Saturday after 11pm. Minimum age is 19 years.

Kulturhauskeller

BAR

(Elisabethstrasse 30; ☺9pm-5am Tue-Sat; ☺) Next door to Orange, the Kulturhauskeller is a cavernous, relaxed cellar bar that heaves with raunchy students on weekends. Minimum age is 19 years. After 11pm admission is €3.

Cafe Centraal

BEISL, CAFE €

(Mariahilferstrasse 10; breakfast €3-7, salad & snacks €6-8; ☺8am-2am) This traditional bar and *Beisl* with a dark-wood interior and outside seating has an alternative feel.

Exil
BAR

(Josefigasse 1; ☺7.30pm-late Tue-Sat) If you like the Centraal, you'll probably like Exil – it's a laid-back alternative bar with outdoor seating and a couple of turntables for Friday and Saturday nights.

Stockwerk Jazz
JAZZ CLUB

(http://stockwerkjazz.mur.at, in German; Jakominiplatz 18; concerts €10-15; ☺4pm-1am Mon-Sat, to midnight Sun) Graz's premier jazz bar for home-grown artists and international acts has rustic wooden features and a summer rooftop terrace.

Three Monkeys
BAR

(www.three-monkeys.at, in German; Elisabethstrasse 31; ☺9pm-6am Mon-Thu, to 7am Fri & Sat, to 5am Sun) A young crowd flocks to this raunchy place, which is generally known as a pick-up joint.

Promenade
CAFE

(www.cafepromenade.at, in German; Erzherzog-Johann-Allee 1; snacks €7.40; ☺8am-11pm) Popular with all walks of life, the delightful Promenade is a Graz institution – styled along the lines of a Vienna coffee house on a tree-lined avenue in the Stadtpark.

M1
COCKTAIL BAR

(www.m1-bar.at, in German; 3rd fl, Färberplatz; ☺9am-2am Mon-Sat, to 5pm Sun) M1 is a modern three-storey cafe-bar replete with rooftop terrace attracting a mixed crowd. Its spiral staircase can cause a few problems after one or two of the 200 or so cocktails on offer.

Stargayte
GAY BAR

(www.stargayte.at, in German; Keesegasse 3; ☺9pm-4am Mon-Thu, 8pm-open end Fri & Sat) This gay cocktail bar and lounge near Jakominiplatz is Graz's main cruising bar. Out back is a darkened room with a sling and labyrinth.

☆ Entertainment

To find out what's on and where in the city, pick up a copy of *Megaphon* (€2.20, in German), a monthly magazine that combines entertainment listings with political and social commentary. It's sold on most street corners.

Cinemas

See the website www.uncut.at/graz (in German) for cinema listings. The main venue showing films in their original versions is KIZ RoyalKino (Conrad-von-Hötzendorf-Strasse 10).

Clubs

Dom im Berg
CLUB

(www.domimberg.at, in German; Schlossbergplatz) The tunnels under Schlossberg were once used as air-raid shelters. Today, some of them have been refashioned into a large art-clubbing venue. The sound system and light show are the best in Graz. See the website for opening times.

p.p.c.
CLUB

(www.popculture.at, in German; Neubaugasse 6; ☺from 10pm Thu-Sat) Electronic club nights with top-name DJs.

Postgarage
CLUB

(www.postgarage.at, in German; Dreihackengasse 42; ☺from 10pm Fri & Sat) Electronic, retro theme nights and everything between for 20-somethings.

Theatre & Opera

Graz is an important cultural centre, hosting musical events throughout the year. Theaterservice Graz (☎8008 1102; www.theater-graz.com, in German; Kaiser-Josef-Platz 10; ☺9am-6.30pm Mon-Fri, to 1pm Sat, closed mid-Jul–mid-Aug) is the ticket office for both venues listed below.

Opernhaus
OPERA

(www.theater-graz.com/oper, in German; Kaiser-Josef-Platz 10; ☺closed early Jul-late Aug) The main venue for opera.

Schauspielhaus
THEATRE

(www.schauspielhaus-graz.com, in German; Hofgasse 11; ☺closed early Jul-late Aug) Graz' main venue for theatre.

🛍 Shopping

Aside from its divine pumpkin-seed oil, Styria is known for painted pottery and printed linen. Good places to pick up quality handicrafts are Steirisches Heimatwerk (☎82 71 06; Sporgasse 23) or Kastner & Öhler (Sackstrasse 7-11), a department store north of Hauptplatz. Bookshops:

English Bookshop (☎82 62 66; Tummelplatz 7; ☺9am-6pm Mon-Fri, to 2pm Sat) Lots of English books, but expensive.

Freytag & Berndt (Fischer von Erlachgasse 1; ☺10am-6.30pm Mon-Fri, 9am-6pm Sat) The best source of maps and guidebooks.

ℹ Information

Internet Access

High Speed Internet-Selfstore (Herrengasse 3; per 30min €1; ☺7am-10pm) A coin-operated internet space inside the passage.

Speednet Cafe (www.speednet-cafe.com, in German; Europaplatz 4; per hr €2.60-4.20; ⊙8am-10pm Mon-Sat, 10am-10pm Sun) Located in the train station.

Internet Resources

Graz (www.graz.at) Provides a snapshot of most aspects of the city.

InfoGraz (www.info-graz.at, in German) Practical information on life in Graz.

Lonely Planet (www.lonelyplanet.com/austria/the-south/graz) Planning advice, author recommendations, traveller reviews and insider tips.

Welcome to Graz (www.graztourismus.at) The city's excellent tourist-information portal.

Left Luggage

Lockers (€2 to €4 for 24 hours) are inside the train station.

Medical Services

Unfallkrankenhaus (☎505-0; Göstinger Strasse 24) Emergency hospital at tram 1 terminus.

Post

Hauptbahnhof post office (Hauptbahnhof; ⊙7am-9pm Mon-Fri, 8am-6pm Sat, 1-8pm Sun) Located inside the station.

Main post office (Neutorgasse 46; ⊙8am-7pm Mon-Fri, 9am-noon Sat)

Tourist Information

Graztourismus (☎80 75-0; www.graztourismus.at; Herrengasse 16; ⊙10am-6pm) Graz' main tourist office, with loads of free information on the city. Inside the train station is an information stand and terminal and free hotline to the tourist office.

Travel Agencies

STA (☎82 62 62-0; graz@statravel.at; Raubergasse 20; ⊙9am-7pm Mon-Fri, 10am-3pm Sat) Nationwide travel agency specialising in student and discount travel.

Getting There & Away

Air

The **airport** (☎29 02-0; www.flughafen-graz.at) is 10km south of the town centre, just beyond the A2 and connected by train and bus from the Hauptbahnhof. Direct connections with Graz include to/from Berlin Tegel in Germany with **Air Berlin** (☎0820 737 800), Frankfurt am Main in Germany with **Lufthansa** (☎0810 1025 8080), and with many other German cities on **Austrian Airlines** (☎291 669); London Stansted with **Ryanair**, (www.ryanair.com) and London Heathrow with Lufthansa; inland flights to Innsbruck with **Welcome Air** (☎0512-295 296 300) and Vienna with Austrian Airlines. Facilities at the airport include an

information desk (☎29 02-172; departure hall; ⊙5am-10pm), free internet terminals and wi-fi inside the security zone, and a bank with an ATM in arrivals on the ground floor.

Bus

Postbus (☎050/678 910; www.verbundlinie.at) services depart from outside the Hauptbahnhof and from Andreas-Hofer-Platz to all parts of Styria. Indirect **GKB buses** (☎59 87-0; www.gkb.at) run to Bärnbach (€7.30, 1¼ hours) and Piber (€7.30, one hour) several times each day from Monday to Friday; more frequent services go to Deutschlandsberg (€9, two hours) Monday to Saturday. All leave from Griesplatz, though a few begin at the Hauptbahnhof. Six direct ÖBB buses daily (€35.50, two hours) leave for Klagenfurt from the Hauptbahnhof.

Car Rental

Companies include **Avis** (☎81 29 20; Reinighausstrasse 66), **Hertz** (☎82 50 07; Andreas-Hofer-Platz 1), which also has an office at the airport, and **MegaDrive** (DenzelDrive; ☎050/105 4130; www.denzeldrive.at; Kärntnerstrasse 164). See p417 for more on car hire.

Note that much of Graz is a *Kurzparkzone* (short-term parking zone); tickets are available from parking machines (€0.60 per 30 minutes).

Train

Trains to Vienna depart hourly (€34, 2½ hours), and six daily go to Salzburg (€48, four hours). All trains running north or west go via Bruck an der Mur (€11, 35 to 45 minutes, every 20 minutes), a main railway junction with more frequent services. Trains to Klagenfurt (€35, 2¾ to 3½ hours, seven daily) require a change either in Bruck or Leoben (check with the conductor).

International direct train connections from Graz include Zagreb (€35, 3½ hours), Ljubljana (€34, 3½ hours), Szentgotthárd (€14, 1½ hours) and Budapest (€46, 5½ hours).

Getting Around

TO/FROM THE AIRPORT Trains depart the Hauptbahnhof (€2) from 4.24am to 12.10am Monday to Friday, and from 5.50am to 12.10am Saturday and Sunday. Trains leave the airport from 4.48am to 10.48pm Monday to Friday, from 5.18am to 10.48pm Saturday and from 5.40am to 9.48pm Sunday at least hourly (18 minutes). An infrequent bus also runs to the airport from the Hauptbahnhof; it can be convenient between trains. Expect to pay about €17 for a taxi.

BICYCLE Rental available from **Bicycle** (☎68 86 45; Körösistrasse 5; per 24hr €10; ⊙7am-1pm & 2-6pm Mon-Fri). Mobilzentral (see p184) has a few city rental bicycles for €10 per day or €40 per week.

PUBLIC TRANSPORT Graz has one zone (zone 101). Single tickets (€1.90) for buses and trams are valid for one hour, but you're usually better off buying a 24-hour pass (€4.10). Ten one-zone tickets cost €15.80, and weekly/monthly passes cost €10.70/36.40. Hourly and 24-hour tickets can be purchased from the driver; other passes can be purchased from *Tabak* (tobacconist) shops, pavement ticket machines or the tourist office.

TAXI Call ☑2801, ☑878 or ☑889.

TRAM Trams 1, 3, 6 and 7 connect Jakominiplatz with the Hauptbahnhof every five to 20 minutes from 4.40am to 7pm Monday to Saturday. After that trams 1 and 7 do the run alone until services end just before midnight (€1.90).

AROUND GRAZ

The following sights are within easy distance of Graz and make for a pleasant excursion into the countryside.

Österreichischen Freilichtmuseum
OPEN-AIR MUSEUM
(www.freilichtmuseum.at; adult/child/family €8.50/4.50/24; ☺9am-5pm Tue-Sun Apr-Oct) Located some 15km northeast of Graz and consisting of about 100 Austrian farmstead buildings, the Austrian Open-Air Museum in Stübing is ideal for a family outing. All buildings are originals and on the last Sunday in September the **Erlebnistag**, a special fair with crafts, music and dancing, takes place here. Pick up a copy of the English-language guidebook (€2.20) at the entrance.

The museum is about a 20-minute walk from the Stübing train station; turn left out of the train station and pass over the tracks, then under them before reaching the entrance. Hourly trains make the journey from Graz (€3.60, 15 minutes).

Bundesgestüt Piber
HORSE STUD
(Piber Stud Farm; www.piber.com, in German; Piber 1; tours adult/child €12/7.50; ☺tours hourly 10am-4pm Apr-Oct, 11am & 3pm Nov-Mar; P🐴) Piber is home to the world-famous Lipizzaner stallion stud farm Bundesgestüt Piber. Originally the farm was based in Lipica (Slovenia) but was moved here when Slovenia was annexed after WWI. About 40 to 50 foals are born at the farm every year, but of these only about five stallions have the right stuff to be sent for training to the Spanische Hofreitschule (Spanish Riding School) in Vienna. In summer, you have the choice of a do-it-yourself tour using a sheet map of the stud or taking a fully fledged tour. For in-

formation, head to the **Tourismusverband Lipizzanerheimat** (☑03144-72 777-0; www.lipizzanerheimat.com, in German; An der Quelle 3; ☺9am-noon & 2-5pm Mon-Fri, 9am-noon Sat) in Köflach, 3km south of Piber.

To get to Piber from Graz, the most convenient option is to catch the **GKB** (www.gkb.at) morning bus at 8am from Graz' Griesplatz, arriving in Piber at 9.15am (you have to change to a connecting bus at Voitsberg Hauptplatz). The last bus leaves Piber at 2.45pm. This only works weekdays. Frequent trains also go to Köflach (€7.30, one hour), from where it's a 3.5km walk from Hauptplatz along Piberstrasse (follow the signs). A taxi (☑26 26; fares €6.50) from the train station to Piber is also an option.

Bärnbach
☑03142 / POP 4900
Otherwise unremarkable, Bärnbach is famous for its St Barbara Kirche, a church designed by Friedensreich Hundertwasser. The town is also a centre for exquisite glass-making, and has an interesting factory tour on the theme.

Tourist information is available from the glassmaking centre and **Bärnbach Information** (☑615 50; tourismus@baernbach.at; Hauptplatz 1; ☺8-11.30am Mon-Fri, 2-4.30pm Mon & Thu) inside the town hall. The church and glass centre are an equal distance west and east respectively from Hauptplatz.

FREE **St Barbara Kirche** (☑625 81; Piberstrasse; admission free, tours adult/child €2.50/1.20, call ahead; ☺dawn-dusk) – built after WWII – needed renovating in the late 1980s, and about 80% of the town population voted to commission maverick Viennese artist Friedensreich Hundertwasser to undertake the redesign. Work began in 1987 and was completed in 1988. This was a bold move: Hundertwasser was notorious for his unusual designs, particularly those based on spiritual ecology. The gamble paid off: the church is a visual treat. Leave a donation and pick up the explanation card in English, which reveals the symbolism behind the architectural features. Tours are run by appointment only.

Bärnbach has been a glassmaking centre for three centuries and is home to the **Stölzle Glas Center** (☑629 50; www.glasmuseum.at; Hochregisterstrasse 1; adult/child/family €6.50/4/15; ☺9am-5pm Mon-Fri, to 1pm Sat Mar-Dec), a working glass-blowing factory and museum. Try to get here in the morning, as the entrance fee includes a guided tour (11am Monday to Friday May to October) of the glassmaking facilities and the small museum filled with delicate pieces. In the afternoon the factory is off-limits.

❶ Getting There & Away

Hourly trains run from Graz (€7.20, 50 minutes), but the train station is 2km south of the town centre; a bike is useful here. Cross the railway line, follow the road around until you reach the main highway and then take this right. A taxi (☑0664/3402247) to the centre of town costs about €6. Bundesgestüt Piber (Piber Stud Farm) is close to Bärnbach (€4 by taxi); from the church, head west on Piberstrasse for 2km and after about 30 minutes you'll reach it.

SOUTHERN STYRIA

Southern Styria is known as *Steirische Toskana* (Styrian Tuscany), and for good reason. Not only is this wine country, but the landscape is reminiscent of Chianti; gentle rolling hills cultivated with vineyards or patchwork farmland, and capped by clusters of trees. It's also famous for *Kürbiskernöl*, the rich pumpkin-seed oil generously used in Styrian cooking.

Region Süd und West Steiermark (☑03462-43152; www.sws.st, in German; Hauptplatz 36, Deutschlandsberg) handles telephone, email and postal enquiries for western and southern Styria.

Styrian Wine Roads

The *Weinstrassen* (wine roads) of southern Styria comprise an idyllic bundle of winding roads crisscrossing a picturesque landscape that is reminiscent of Tuscany. The region is at its best about two weeks after the grape harvest (usually September), when *Sturm* (young wine) is sold. The **Weinlesefest** (Wine Harvest Festival) takes place in Leutschach on the last weekend in September, with lots of wine and song.

On weekends in September and October accommodation is usually booked out. During the week and at other times it's usually fine if you're flexible.

The tourist office in Leutschach rents e-bikes (€10 per day), and the BP petrol station Skotschnigg (☑03454-282-6; Schlossberg 144; ⊙6am-8pm Mon-Sat, 7.30am-8pm Sun) rents touring bikes for €10. If you're without

your own wheels, take a train from Graz to Leibnitz. A bus runs five to eight times from Monday to Saturday via Grossklein from Leibnitz to Leutschach (€7.40, 40 minutes), where there's bike hire, easy access to hiking trails and numerous wine and panorama roads. Car hire is in Graz (p184).

To explore further, from Leutschach a road veers left at the top of the main street at Rebenlandhof restaurant. This leads to Eichberg-Trautenstein, a pretty region with *Buschenschänke (Heurigen)* and narrow sealed roads. A walking trail (560) goes through forest, across meadows and partly alongside the road. Regions along and south of the Alte Weinstrasse are more remote, with lesser-used wine and panorama roads but fewer vineyards.

Deutschlandsberg

☑03462 / POP 8000

In the heart of the Schilcher wine region, Deutschlandsberg is a bustling little town dominated by a well-restored castle, some 25 minutes' walk uphill from the town centre. Inside the castle is a museum (www.burgmuseum.at, in German; Burgplatz 2; adult/child €9/4; ⊙10am-7pm Mar–mid-Nov) with exhibits on ancient history, the Celts, historical weapons and antique jewellery. The extensive collection, whose highlights include a delicate gold necklace from the 5th century BC, takes about 1½ hours to see. As with any good castle, there's a torture chamber in the underground vaults.

The tourist office (☑75 20; www.schilcherheimat.at, in German; Hauptplatz 34; ⊙9am-1pm & 2-5pm Mon-Fri, 9am-noon Sat, closed 2-5pm & Sat Nov-Feb) is a good source of information on the town and environs.

For sleeping arrangements, look no further than the Burg Hotel (☑56 56-0; www.burghotel-dl.at, in German; Burgplatz 1; s €65-90, d €98-118, ste €150-310; [P][⊙][@][❄]), which is located in the castle. Its crowning glory is the tower suite, with complimentary champagne and a fruit basket; rooms are large and quiet and have views of the woods.

If Burg is out of your budget, the Jugend- und Familiengästehaus Deutschlandsberg (☑05/7083-260; deutschlandsberg@jufa.at; Burg 5; s/d €41/68; [P][@][❄]) is a good option. It's set in a vineyard at the foot of the castle. Wi-fi is in the foyer only.

At least hourly trains (€9.20, one hour) connect Graz and Deutschlandsberg.

THE WINE ROADS OF SOUTHERN STYRIA

This 50km circuit takes you from Ehrenhausen to Leutschach and back to Gamlitz, along the wine roads of Southern Styria, traversing some of the most attractive areas. Along the way you will find lookouts where you can leave the main road and enjoy broad panoramas.

From the Hauptstrasse (B69) in **Ehrenhausen** veer left on the southern edge of town at the **Südsteirische Weinstrasse** (L613) signpost. Almost immediately you see vineyards and *Buschenschänke* where you can taste wines. After **Berghausen** and **Grassnitzberg** the road reaches the Slovenian border (the left of the road is Slovenia, the right Austria) and veers west, where about 2km from Berghausen settlement you reach Gästehaus & Atelier Sonnenberg (☎03453-5219; manfred@msonnenberg.at; Wielitsch 34, Berghausen; holiday houses per person €40), situated across the road from Slovenia. Here the Hannover-born artist Manfred Sonnenberg has holiday flats sleeping two to six and offers landscape-painting courses (about €350 per person over several days, including accommodation). Just before an outlying part of Ratsch an der Weinstrasse, a road leads right for about 500m to the Bärengehege Berghausen (Berghausen-Ratsch an der Weinstrasse; ☺8am-6pm), a refuge for bears no longer able to live in the wild. The was established in 1980 for maltreated circus bears and today has enclosures where injured or 'problem' bears are housed.

Continuing along the L613, you reach Rebenhof (☎03453-25 750; www.rebenhof.at; Ottenberg 38, Ratsch an der Weinstrasse; light dishes €6-12; ☺Easter-Nov). This *Buschenschank* has wine, platters and small servings of fine food prepared and conserved in jars by the region's top chef, Tom Riedere. At the junction settlement of Eckberg, a road leads north 5km to Gamlitz. If doing the complete circuit, turn left at the junction (away from Gamlitz), and continue along the L613 to Schlossberg and **Leutschach**, where you will need to reserve ahead for a table at the gourmet restaurant Tom am Kochen (☎03454-700 99; www.trac.at, in German; Arnsfelder Strasse 2, Leutschach; 4-/5-course menu €45-55; ☺lunch Wed-Fri, dinner Tue-Sat; Ⓟ☺), run by Tom Riedere. He also conducts cooking courses (see p393). Other eating and drinking options are on the pretty main street of Leutschach, including Tscheppes Lang-Gasthof (☎03454-246; www.langgasthof-tscheppe.at, in German; Hauptplatz 6; s/d/f €63/94/108, mains €14-23; Ⓟ☺), a four-star hotel with a sauna and a herbal bath filled with hops (this is also a big hop-growing district). Leutschach's tourist office (☎03454-70 70 10; www.rebenland.at, in German; ☺9am-noon & 2-5pm Mon-Fri, to noon Sat) has a free **Freizeitkarte** with hiking trails and *Buschenschänke* (with opening times) marked. Brochures and maps are on racks outside, even when the office is closed.

From Leutschach backtrack to Schlossberg and follow the **Alte Weinstrasse** east to **Langegg**. This wine road has mostly fallen into disuse, partly following the course of a small river before it swings north at Langegg to join the Südsteirische Weinstrasse at Gasthof Mahorko. Turn right and follow the signs to Gamlitz.

Grossklein

Southern Styria was once a stomping ground of the Celts, and this legacy has gradually been unearthed by archaeologists. Some of their finds are housed in the four exhibition rooms of the Hallstattzeitliches Museum (Hallstatt Period Museum; www.archaeo-grossklein.com; adult/child/family €4/2/9; ☺10am-noon & 2-5pm Wed-Sun Apr-Oct; ♿) in the small town of Grossklein, 26km southeast of Deutschlandsberg. Most of the exhibits are from the nearby grave mounds and include coins, pottery and tools, and a copy of a bronze mask dating from 600 BC (the original is housed in Graz' Schloss Eggenberg. The museum has a children's playroom where you can leave the kids. If this fails to get the adrenalin pumping, then a 9km archaeology trail heading northwest from the town towards Kleinklein should – it takes in approximately 700 Celtic grave mounds.

Five to eight buses (€3.80, 25 minutes) connect Leibnitz and Grossklein from Monday to Saturday. Weekdays, a train-bus connection (€10.70, 1¼ hours) from Graz via Leibnitz works well.

Ehrenhausen

☑ 03453 / POP 1200

The picturesque town of Ehrenhausen, near the A9 that connects Graz with the Slovenian border, makes a fine base for exploring the vineyards of southern Styria.

The town is little more than one street of pastel-coloured houses dominated by the baroque **Pfarrkirche** (Hauptplatz; admission free; ☉dawn-dusk). Before setting off for the wine country, follow the path (three minutes' walk) on the right of the Rathaus up to the **mausoleum** (☉groups of 10 or more only) of Ruprecht von Eggenberg (1546–1611), hero of the Battle of Sisak against the Turks. Towering above Hauptplatz, this white-and-yellow building is guarded by two Roman-like bruisers.

Hourly trains (€9.20, 45 minutes) run from Graz to Ehrenhausen. The train station is about four minutes' walk east of Hauptplatz.

Riegersburg

☑ 03153 / POP 2560

Located 50km southeast of Graz at Riegersburg and perched on a 200m-high rocky outcrop, **Schloss Riegersburg** (http://riegersburg.com, in German; adult/child/family €10/7/26; ☉10am-5pm Apr & Oct, 9am-5pm May-Sep) is a hugely impressive 13th-century castle built against invading Hungarians and Turks; today it houses a **Hexenmuseum** on witchcraft and the **Burgmuseum** featuring the history of the Liechtenstein family, who acquired it in 1822. A **war memorial** is a reminder of fierce fighting in 1945, when Germans occupying the castle were attacked by Russian troops.

A cable car on the north side whisks you up in 90 seconds (one-way €2).

For more information on the Schloss or activities, contact the **tourist office** (☑86 70; tourismus@riegersburg.com; Riegersburg 4; ☉10am-4pm, closed Tue & Thu).

If you have your own transport, consider stopping in at **Schloss Kapfenstein** (☑03157-300 30-0; www.schloss-kapfenstein.at, in German; Kapfenstein 1; s €91-113, d €132-184; mains €13-20; P @), a hotel-restaurant 17km south of Riegersburg. Weekdays rooms cost significantly less and can be booked for one night or more, but on weekends only Friday-to-Sunday packages are possible. The restaurant serves delightful Styrian cuisine in its outer courtyard overlooking the valley; a four-course meal as half-board costs €32.

Frequent trains run from Graz to nearby Feldbach and from there seven weekday buses head for Riegersburg (€1.90, 20 minutes). The last bus back is at around 6pm (check before setting out).

NORTHERN STYRIA

Heading north from Graz the landscape of Styria begins to change; gentle hills and flat pastures are replaced by jagged mountains, virgin forests, deep valleys and cold, clear mountain streams. This is also the region's industrial heartland, home to the *Steirische Eisenstrasse* (Styrian Iron Rd), where for centuries iron mining was the backbone of the economy and, in places such as Eisenerz, left the landscape scarred.

Huddled beneath the soaring peaks are the towns of northern Styria, home to impressive churches; the best are the pilgrimage church of Mariazell and the abbey of Admont.

Mariazell

☑ 03882 / POP 1530

Situated on the slopes of the eastern Alps' lower reaches, the pretty town of Mariazell is one of Austria's icons. It offers opportunities for hiking, mountain biking and skiing, but

---

HUNDERTWASSER SPA

East Styria is well known throughout Austria for its thermal activity, and in particular the spa centres that have sprung up around its thermal springs. Fans of the architectural style of Friedensreich Hundertwasser won't want to miss the unusual spa **Rogner-Bad Blumau** (☑03383-51 00-0; www.blumau.com; s €170-191, d €280-322; P ⊖ ✖), near the town of Bad Blumau, 50km east of Graz. The spa has all the characteristics of his art, including uneven floors, grass on the roof, colourful ceramics and golden spires. Overnight accommodation includes entry to the spa.

what makes Mariazell so well known is its status as Austria's most important pilgrimage site. Its basilica, founded in 1157, holds a sacred statue of the Virgin, and busloads of Austrians flock to the site on weekends and on 15 August (Assumption) and 8 September (Mary's name day).

◉ Sights

FREE Basilika CHURCH
(Kardinal Eugen Tisserant Platz 1; ☺7am-8pm) Originally Romanesque, the basilica underwent a Gothic conversion in the 14th century and then received a massive baroque facelift in the 17th century. The result from the outside is a strange clash of styles, with the original Gothic steeple bursting like a wayward skeletal limb from between two baroque onion domes. The interior works better, with Gothic ribs on the ceiling combining well with baroque frescoes and lavish stuccowork. Both Johann Bernhard Fischer von Erlach and his son Josef Emmanuel had a hand in the baroque features; the crucifixion group sculpture (1715) on the high altar is by Lorenzo Mattielli.

Unusually, the church is centred on a small but exquisite chapel, known as the **Gnadenkapelle** (Chapel of Grace). This gold and silver edifice houses the Romanesque statue of the Madonna, whose healing powers reputedly helped King Louis of Hungary defeat the Turks in 1377. In the upper galleries, the **Schatzkammer** (treasury; adult/child €3/0.50; ☺10am-3pm Tue-Sat, 11am-3pm Sun May-Oct) contains votive offerings spanning six centuries, mainly naive-style paintings.

Europeum SPA
(www.europeum.at, in German; Wiener Strasse 9; adult/child exhibition €4/1, 4hr in wellness & spa €7/5.90; ☺exhibition 10am-5pm Thu-Sun, wellness & spa 2-10pm Tue-Sun) This modern complex combines a multimedia exhibition space dedicated to living together in the EU with a section reserved for the good old body and soul: a wellness area with sauna, pool and chill-out areas (on Thursday the sauna is for women only).

Erlebniswelt Holzknechtland MUSEUM
(Erlebniswelt Holzknechtland; entry & cable car adult/child €14.90/8.80; ☺9am-5pm Mar-Oct) The mountain above town, **Bürgeralpe** (1270m), has a couple of restaurants and a small museum devoted to wood and all its wonderful uses.

Mariazell

◉ **Top Sights**
Basilika...B2

◉ **Sights**
1 Europeum..A2

Activities, Courses & Tours
2 Bürgeralpe Cable Car........................A1

Sleeping
3 Goldene Krone A2
4 Hotel Drei Hasen................................A2

Eating
5 Billa...B2
6 Brauhaus Mariazell............................A2

🏃 Activities

Bürgeralpe HIKING, SKIING
The mountain is a great starting or finishing point for hiking in the summer months, and also has skiing in winter. The **cable car** (www.mariazell-buergeralpe.at; adult/child return €11.90/7.50) operates year-round. It has an artificial lake used as a setting for special events. During winter, adult daily/weekly ski passes cost around €28/135.

Erlaufsee   SWIMMING, WATER SPORTS, WALKING

This small lake a few kilometres to the northwest of the town reaches about 22°C in summer and, apart from swimming, it offers good opportunities for windsurfing and scuba diving; contact addresses for water sports are listed in the booklet *Mariazellerland von A-Z*, available at the tourist office. An easy four-hour *Rundwanderweg* (circuit trail) runs past the lake and south through forest back into Mariazell; alternatively, you can take the steam **Museumstramway** (one-way/return €5/8), which runs at weekends and holidays between July and September. It leaves from the Museumstramway Bahnhof.

Sleeping & Eating

The only problem times for finding a room in Mariazell are around the pilgrim days. Aside from hotels and pensions, there is a smattering of private rooms. You'll find a **Billa supermarket** just north of the tourist office.

TOP CHOICE **Hotel Drei Hasen**   HOTEL €€

(☎2410; www.dreihasen.at; Wiener Strasse 11; s €69, d €160, ste €160; mains €9-15; ⊙closed mid-Mar–mid-Apr & Nov; P🐾) This hotel has a direct passage to the wellness facilities of the Europeum – an added benefit to what is a very good hotel with a first-class restaurant (specialising in seasonal game dishes). Some rooms have wi-fi, others cable LAN.

Goldene Krone   HOTEL €

(☎2583; www.mariazell.at/krone, in German; Grazer Strasse 1; s €48, d €76; mains €9-15; 🖐) Goldene Krone has a homely feel in its big and bright rooms, complemented by a Finnish sauna. The ground floor has an excellent restaurant, with traditional Austrian cuisine, toys for the kids and street-side seating.

Campingplatz Erlaufsee   CAMPGROUND €

(☎49 37; www.st-sebastian.at; camp sites per adult/child/tent/car €4.20/2/3.20/2.90; ⊙May–mid-Sep; P) A small camping ground in St Sebastian on the Erlaufsee, flanked by pine trees. Regular buses run to St Sebastian from the bus station.

Jugend- und Familiengästedorf HOSTEL €

(☎26 69; stsebastian@jfgh.at; Erlaufseestrasse 49; s/d €36.50/72; P🐾@🖐) Located halfway between Mariazell and Erlaufsee, this hostel has a sauna, solarium and fitness room. Some rooms have two bedrooms for families.

Brauhaus Mariazell   BREWERY €€

(☎25 23-0; Wiener Strasse 5; mains €11-16.50; ⊙10am-11pm Mon-Wed, to midnight Fri & Sat,

lunch Sun; 🖐) This lovely, rustic microbrewery has some of the best Styrian cuisine in these parts; there's a garden out back and a few rooms upstairs (rooms from €60 per person, suites €109).

ℹ Information

Tourist office (☎23 66; www.mariazell.at; Hauptplatz 13; ⊙9am-5.30pm Mon-Fri, to 4pm Sat, to 12.30pm Sun, closed Sat & Sun Nov-Apr) Has a town map-brochure with walking trails marked; doesn't book rooms but has accommodation listings.

ℹ Getting There & Away

A narrow-gauge train departs from St Pölten, 77km to the north, every two to three hours. It's a slow trip (€16, 2½ hours), but the scenery is good for the last hour approaching Mariazell. Bus is the only option for further travel into Styria; four daily direct buses run to/from Bruck an der Mur (€11, 1½ hours), where trains travel to/from Graz (€22, 2¼ hours). There is also one direct early-morning bus daily from Vienna (€21, three hours).

Bruck an der Mur

☎03862 / POP 13,400

Bruck, at the confluence of the Mur and Mürz rivers, is the Mur valley's first real town and an important railway junction for Styria. Although its attractions are limited, it's quite a pleasant town once you let it work on you, and you may find yourself enjoying an extended stopover here between trains and buses.

⊙ Sights

Schloss Landskron   CASTLE RUINS

Several paths wind up to this castle, where local nobility ruled the roost until fire ravaged it along with the rest of the town in 1792. The population helped itself to the stone to rebuild their houses, and today all that remains is a clock tower and a couple of canons captured from the French. On the way, drop by the 15th-century Gothic **Pfarrkirche** (Kirchplatz; ⊙dawn-dusk).

Koloman-Wallisch-Platz   TOWN SQUARE

The **Rathaus** on the town square has an attractive arcaded courtyard, whereas the **Kornmesserhaus** (1499) brings together Gothic and some Renaissance features and was based on the design of a Venetian palace. Other historic highlights on the square include the **art-nouveau facade** above

Bruck an der Mur

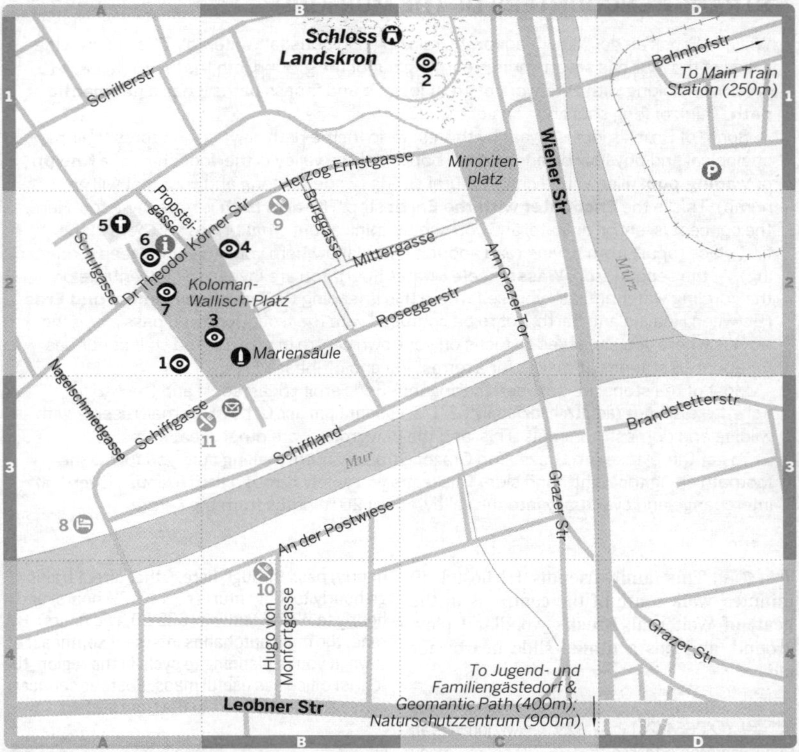

the ice-cream shop at No 10 and the fine Renaissance-style **wrought-iron well** created by Hans Prasser in 1626. Twice weekly, a **food and flower market** (Wed & Sat) takes place on the main square.

Sleeping & Eating

For provisions, head for the **Billa** (Herzog Ernstgasse 6) supermarket.

Landskron HOTEL €€
(58 458; www.hotel-landskron.at, in German; Am Schiffertor 3; s/d €75/104, ste per person €65; P@) Value is best on weekends in this business hotel directly on the Mur River. Here you can loll about in large, tastefully furnished rooms, and in some you can even hear the river gurgling below the window. It has a sauna and a good midrange restaurant.

Jugend- und Familiengästedorf HOSTEL €
(05/7083-370; www.jufa.at/bruck.php; Stadtwaldstrasse 1; dm/s/d €28.30/41.30/62.60;

Bruck an der Mur

Top Sights
- Schloss Landskron ... B1

Sights
1. Art-Nouveau Facade ... A2
2. Clock Tower ... C1
3. Food & Flower Market ... B2
4. Kornmesserhaus ... B2
5. Pfarrkirche ... A2
6. Rathaus ... A2
7. Wrought-Iron Well ... A2

Sleeping
8. Landskron ... A3

Eating
9. Billa ... B2
10. Johanns ... B4
11. Restaurant Riegler Schmankerlwirtshaus ... B3

STRANGE ENCOUNTERS OF THE MUR KIND

While in Bruck an der Mur, head for the relaxing and unusual Weitental. This narrow side valley of the Mur has seven springs gurgling out of the ground into the Weitentalbach (a creek), and along with a network of great jogging and fitness paths it has a **geomantic path**. Think of feng shui and you get the idea.

Some of Bruck's locals swear by this esoteric theme path, saying it restores their psychological and physical balance. At the bottom of the valley is the 'foot chakra', a **Kneipp** or **wading pool** filled with a chilly natural spring (wade too long and your feet will go numb). This is the **Encounter with the Earth** stop. The **arm bath** is refreshing too. Here, the concept is 'entry' or 'gate' and you should think about what brings you here in the first place (apart from having read about it here), and where you are going (keep reading). At the second stop, **Wasserseele** (Water Soul), you are invited to concentrate on the gurgling water and ask yourself where this is leading to. **Zwischen Himmel und Erde** (Between Heaven and Earth, not to be confused with the trout pond you pass along the way) is where you are asked to focus on your own centre of gravity. And so it continues for about 18 stations. It makes for a refreshing and off-beat walk.

Most of the stops are between the Jugend- und Familiengästedorf and the **Naturschutzzentrum** (adult/child/family €2/1/3; ⊙9am-6pm Apr-Oct; 👪), a small reserve with wildlife and domestic animals. This, and the playground, are other great stops.

To get there, take Am Grazer Tor/Grazer Strasse south, making sure you follow the footpath along the right-hand side. This leads you safely through the hideous clover-leaf interchange and eventually into the valley, about 20 minutes from the centre.

ⓟⓢ@👪) This family-friendly HI hostel, 10 minutes' walk south of the centre, is in the heart of Weitental, Bruck's woodland playground, and has a tunnel slide nearby for kids.

TOP CHOICE Johanns AUSTRIAN €€€
(☎0664/241 31 29; www.johanns.at; Hugo von Monfortgasse 2; 4-/6-/10-course menu €44/64/98; ⊙Mon-Fri) Reserve several months ahead for a Friday table, or a week or two ahead on other days for a meal in this celebrated restaurant. The focus is on finely prepared seasonal dishes based on fresh fish and meats.

Restaurant Riegler Schmankerlwirtshaus
AUSTRIAN €€
(Koloman-Wallisch-Platz 11; mains €7-14; ⊙9am-midnight Tue-Sun) There's something for everyone – not least a terrace overlooking the Mur – in this traditional restaurant serving good-quality classics.

ⓘ Information

Tourist office (☎890-121; www.bruckmur-tourismus.at, in German; Koloman-Wallisch-Platz 1; ⊙9am-4pm Mon-Fri) Reached by taking Bahnhofstrasse to the town's main square.

ⓘ Getting There & Away

Along with Leoben, Bruck is the region's main rail hub; all fast trains to Graz (€11, 45 minutes, hourly) pass through here. Other direct trains go hourly to Klagenfurt (€28.10, 2¼ hours) and hourly to Wien-Meidling (€25.60, two hours). By road, the main autobahns intersect southeast of town. If you're planning to cycle in the region, the tourist office has useful maps. Postbus services arrive and depart next to the train station.

Leoben

☎03842 / POP 25,800

Leoben is another of those unprepossessing towns that reveal a few surprises once you dig down into their modest urban souls. A revamped museum quarter is one very good reason to prolong a flying visit here between trains. The town is also a centre for metallurgical industries and home to Gösser beer, and achieved ultimate fame with the peace treaty signed here in 1797 by Napoleon and Emperor Franz II.

⊙ Sights & Activities

Hauptplatz TOWN SQUARE
Dating from the 13th century, this long, rectangular square has a **Pestsäule** (Plague Column; 1717); at the northern end is a fountain from 1794 with an angel holding the town's heraldic shield, and at the opposite end is a fountain dedicated to miners (1799). Many of the elegant facades lining the square were created in the 17th century, including the

baroque **Hacklhaus** (Hauptplatz 9) from 1660. Leoben's connection with the iron industry is seen in the curious town motif displayed on the **Altes Rathaus** (Hauptplatz 1) facade, which shows an ostrich eating horseshoes.

Pfarrkirche St Xaver
CHURCH
(Kirchplatz 1; ⊙8am-7pm) The simple exterior of this early baroque church belies a complex interior of white walls and black-and-gold baroque altars. It was built in 1665 as a Jesuit church and today has a small **Museum Sacrum** (⊙10am-5pm) with religious relics, linked by a walkway to the MuseumsCenter Leoben.

Kunsthalle
MUSEUM
(www.kunsthalle-leoben.at, in German; Kirchgasse 6; ⊙9am-6pm) This new museum complex stages some of Austria's best temporary exhibitions outside the capital. Its permanent *Schienen der Vergangenheit* (Tracks of the Past) in the **MuseumsCenter Leoben** (adult/child/family €5/3.50/11; ⊙9am-6pm Tue-Sun) tells the history of Leoben and the town's industries. The standard is very high; check the website for information on current exhibitions and prices. Combined tickets are available.

Stiftkirche & Gösser Brewery
CHURCH
Tourismusverband Leoben can help arrange tours into the early-Romanesque crypt of this church or visits to the brewery, both about 4km south of the centre in the suburb of Göss.

Asia Spa
SPA
(☎245 00; www.asiaspa.at, in German; In der Au 3; 4hr in spa adult/under 16 yr €7/3, 4hr sauna card adult €18) Leoben's new spa centre with massages and treatments. Note that children under 16 may not enter the sauna.

🛏 Sleeping & Eating

Falkensteiner Hotel
HOTEL **€€**
(☎40 50; www.leoben.falkensteiner.com; In der Au 1-3; s €85-175, d €105-235; P ♣ @ 🛜 🖪) This new seminar and business hotel is part of the Asia Spa complex and offers quality, stylish rooms with high-speed cable or wi-fi for €8 per day. Tones are warm and attractive, and one wall of the shower cubicle is glass and fronts the double bed (but has a curtain for the discreet). A night here includes use of the Asia Spa.

Pension Jahrbacher
PENSION **€**
(☎436 00; jahrbacher.gmbh@gmx.at; Kirchgasse 14; s/d €44/79) This small, centrally located

pension has comfortable rooms and is associated with **Cafe am Schwammerlturm** (☎43 600; Homanngasse 11; ⊙11am-6pm), a tiny cafe with wonderful outdoor seating on top of the circular city tower. From here you have breathtaking views over the town and countryside. Book ahead for the pension, and if no one answers the door, drop by the antique shop next door or the cafe.

 Stadt Meierei
AUSTRIAN, INTERNATIONAL **€€**
(☎446 03; www.stadt-meierei.at, in German; Homanngasse 1; lunch menu €8, mains €12.50-20; ⊙Tue-Sat, lunch Sun; ♠) Run by chef Martin Neuretter and *chef de rang* and sommelier Isabella Pichler, this restaurant offers quality cuisine from a menu featuring lamb, beef, poultry and fish specialities.

ℹ Information

Tourismusverband Leoben (☎481 48; Peter Tunner-Strasse 2; ⊙9am-5pm Mon-Fri) Main information centre for Leoben; stocks a *Gast in Leoben* booklet with useful listings. Its Leoben map also includes a great environs map with hiking trails.

Stadt Information Leoben (☎440 18; www. leoben.at; Hauptplatz 12; ⊙8am-6pm Mon-Thu, to 1pm Fri, 9am-12.30pm Sat) Community and tourist-information centre with brochures.

ℹ Getting There & Away

Leoben is 16km west of Bruck (€3.60, 15 minutes, hourly) and is on the main rail route from there to Klagenfurt or Linz. The town centre is 10 minutes' walk from Leoben Hauptbahnhof: cross the Mur River and bear right.

Eisenerz
📞03848 / POP 6430
Eisenerz is one of the important stops along the **Steirische Eisenstrasse** (Styrian Iron Rd), and lies at the foot of the extraordinary Erzberg (Iron Mountain), a mine that chomps spectacularly into the mountains. While the town has certainly seen better days, it's still an interesting place to visit if you like low-key places with a long industrial heritage; narrow, cobblestone streets, solid houses and the gurgle of alpine streams create a relaxed mood.

👁 Sights & Activities

Erzberg
INDUSTRIAL MUSEUM
(☎32 00; www.abenteuer-erzberg.at, in German; Erzberg 1; adult/child separate tour €14/7.50,

TRANSPORT CONNECTIONS IN NORTHERN STYRIA

Travelling in northern Styria requires bus travel between some towns. Plan your arrivals and getaways using www.verbundlinie.at, www.postbus.at or www.oebb.at. Some useful direct connections:

» Leoben–Eisenerz: €7.20, one hour, six to 10 daily.

» Eisenerz–Hieflau: €3.80, 25 minutes, three to four daily; another four on weekdays during school term.

» Hieflau–Admont: €3.80, 30 minutes, three to eight daily.

» Admont–Liezen–Schladming: €12.40, 80 minutes to 1¾ hours, six to 12 daily. Change to train in Liezen.

» Admont–Gesäuse: €3.80, 12 minutes, five to nine daily.

» Schladming–Graz: €34, 2½ hours, daily every two hours. Trains run via Stainach-Irdning (the main transfer point for trains north to the Hallstätter See and elsewhere in the Salzkammergut) and Liezen (the transfer point for buses to Admont and the Gesäuse).

combined tour €22/12.50; ☉tours 10am-3pm May-Oct, advance booking required; P⊕) Your first impression of Eisenerz is likely to be this peak, which has been completely denuded by open-cast stope mining and now resembles a step pyramid. The outcome is eerie and surprisingly beautiful, with its orange and purple shades contrasting with the lush greenery and grey crags of surrounding mountains. The ironworks can be seen up close and personal in two ways: with a 90-minute 'Schaubergwerk' tour which burrows into the mountain to the underground mines, abandoned in 1986, or with a 60-minute 'Hauly Abenteuerfahrt' tour, which explores the surface works aboard an enormous truck, with fine views along the way. Both tours are usually in German, with English-language notes available. The departure point is a 10-minute walk from the centre, following the course of the river.

FREE Wehrkirche St Oswald   CHURCH
(Kirchenstiege 4; ☉9am-7pm Apr-Oct)
More a fortress than a Gothic church, this soaring bastion gained its heavy walls in 1532 as protection against the Turks.

Hiking Trails   HIKING
The town is surrounded by hiking trails. The tourist office has a free town map with trails marked, including to the idyllic **Leopoldsteiner See**, only 3km north on the road towards Admont. This small lake has a wall of granite rising to 1649m as a backdrop; you can hire boats in summer – it's a very chilly swim, though.

🛏 Sleeping & Eating
There are several good pensions and hotels in the old town, but not so many good eating options.

Jugend- und Familiengästehaus   HOSTEL €
(☎605 60; eisenerz@jufa.at; Ramsau 1; s/d €34.50/67; P⊕@🛜🐾) This lovely HI hostel is 5km south of Eisenerz; it's situated at an altitude of 1000m and has a sauna and indoor and outdoor climbing walls as well as hiking trails going off into the mountains. Children aged up to 11 receive a 50% discount. Each room has its own bathroom and there's a restaurant on-site. You need a car to reach it (a taxi costs about €13).

Gästehaus Tegelhofer   GUESTHOUSE €
(☎20 86; www.gaestehaus-tegelhofer.at; Lindmoserstrasse 8; s/d €29/48; P⊕🛜🐾) This modern guesthouse is great value, with spacious and clean rooms spiced with a free sauna and fitness room; there's also an inexpensive apartment for two to six people.

Gästehaus Weninger   GUESTHOUSE €
(☎22 580; www.gaestehaus-weninger.at; Krumpentalerstrasse 8; s €39, d €60; P⊕) Another very decent guesthouse with fitness room and sauna, Weninger aims at those staying for a few days, but does take guests for one night at very short notice. Some bathrooms are cramped but rooms are a good size.

Gasthof zu Post   AUSTRIAN €
(Flutergasse 5; mains €7-10; ☉closed dinner Sun & Mon; P) This traditional place serves some local classics like *Beuschel* (lung and heart) or inexpensive goulash and venison ragout, mostly with dumplings. It's the kind of place where Willy Loman–type travelling salesmen are found alongside lumberjacks.

Barbarastub'n   CAFE
(Bergmannplatz 2; apple strudel €2.50; ☉8am-7pm Mon-Sat, 2-7pm Sun) If the tourist office is closed when you visit, consider the delicious apple strudel here or simply relax on

the comfy chairs out back. Sometimes it has brochures and maps of town.

ℹ️ Information

Tourist office (📞37 00; www.eisenerz-heute. at, in German; Dr Thedor Körner Platz 1; 🕙9am-noon & 3-5pm Mon-Fri) Helpful and in the centre of the town. Good maps for hiking.

ℹ️ Getting There & Away

Direct buses run hourly from Leoben to Eisenerz (€7.20, one hour), less frequently on Sunday. Several daily connect Eisenerz and Hieflau (€3.80, 25 minutes), where you can pick up buses and the occasional train to Selzthal and Liezen.

Trains no longer operate to Eisenerz, except for the special Vordernberg–Eisenerz **Nostalgie** (nostalgic train; 📞03849-832; www. erzbergbahn.at, in German; adult/child/family €10.50/5.50/25.50), which leaves Vordernberg 'Markt' at 10.30am and 3pm Sunday from July to mid-September and takes 70 minutes to reach Eisenerz. For a taxi, call 📞4636.

Nationalpark Gesäuse

Established in 2003, Gesäuse is Austria's newest national park in a pristine region of jagged mountain ridges, rock towers, deep valleys, alpine pastures and dense spruce forests. Traditional farming is still allowed on selected meadows.

Dividing the park into two uneven halves is the Enns, a fast-flowing alpine river that eventually spills into the Danube near Mauthausen in Upper Austria. It's a favourite of rafting connoisseurs, and a number of companies offer rafting trips during the summer months. Hiking and mountain climbing, and to a lesser extent mountain biking, also feature among the park's outdoor activities; of the six peaks over 2000m within the park, Hocktor (2369m) rises above them all and is the destination of many hikers. The occasional spelunking excursion is also available; around 150 caves burrow under the high limestone mountains, the deepest of which descends 600m below the surface.

The staffed national park pavilion (📞03611-21101-20; Gstatterboden 25; 🕙10am-6pm May-Oct) is a useful source of information, and the tourist office in Admont also has information on accommodation and activities in the park.

The bus from Hieflau to Admont stops in Gstatterboden (€1.90, eight minutes, three to eight daily) and Gesäuse (Bachbrücke/

Weidendom), the bridge at the turn-off about 5km from Johnsbach (€1.90, 30 minutes). Ask the driver for the Johnsbach turn-off.

Admont

📞03613 / POP 2770

Admont, nestled in a broad section of the Enns valley, is a low-key town that revs up during the day when groups arrive in buses to see its spectacular abbey. Each night it all but sinks back into pleasant oblivion. The town makes a good base for kicking off deeper into the region.

Admont's **Benedictine Abbey** (www. stiftadmont.at; Admont 1; adult/child/family €9.50/6.50/22; 🕙10am-5pm, by arrangement Nov-Mar) is arguably Austria's most elegant and exciting baroque abbey. It brings together museums, religious and modern art and architecture in a delightful whole – which is why a few years back it won an award for Austria's best museum.

The centrepiece of the abbey is its **Stiftsbibliothek** (abbey library), the largest abbey library in the world. Survivor of a fire in 1865 that severely damaged the rest of the abbey, it displays about 70,000 volumes of the abbey's 200,000-strong collection, and is decorated with heavenly ceiling frescoes by Bartolomeo Altomonte (1694–1783) and statues (in wood, but painted to look like bronze) by Josef Stammel (1695–1765).

The abbey is also home to the **Kunsthistorisches Museum** (Art History Museum), featuring some unusual and rare pieces, such as its tiny portable altar from 1375, made from amethyst quartz and edged with gilt-silver plates, some Gerhard Mercator globes from 1541 and 1551, and monstrances from the 15th and 16th centuries. Each year innovative temporary exhibitions complement the permanent ones. A recent piece was an industrial robot in the centre of the baroque library that transcribed the New Testament onto a scroll in elegant script, reflecting the work earlier carried out by monks.

Another museum, the **Museum für Gegenwartkunst** (Museum for Contemporary Art), contains works by about 100 mainly Austrian artists, and has pieces you can explore with your hands. The **Naturhistorisches Museum** (Natural History Museum) began in 1674 with a small collection and today includes rooms devoted to flying insects (one of the largest collections in the world), butterflies, stuffed animals, wax fruits (bizarrely) and reptiles. From the **glass stairway** and **Herb Garden** there are views to the Gesäuse National Park.

The tourist office (☑21160; www.gesaeuse. at, in German; Hauptstrasse 35; ☉8am-6pm Mon-Fri, 10am-4pm Sat & Sun May-Oct, 8am-5pm Mon-Fri Nov-Apr) is opposite the *Rathaus* and near the abbey church. It doubles as a national-park office.

Admont has several central guesthouses, some with restaurants. Jugendgästehaus Admont (☑05/7083-310; admont@jufa.at; Schulstrasse 446; dm €24, d €48; ☉closed Dec; P☺) is situated on the edge of town, a few minutes' walk from the centre. Jugend- und Familiengästehaus Schloss Röthelstein (☑05/7083-320; roethelstein@jufa.at; Aigen 32; s/d/tr/q €44/88/132/176; P☺☎) is where the monks from the abbey used to stay in summer. It's located in a baroque castle from the 17th century, about 5km southwest of the centre off Aignerstrasse. Hotel Gasthof Traube (☑24 400; www.hotel-traube.info; Hauptstrasse 3; s/d/tr €42/68/78; P☎) is one of the best places in town, with modern rooms a notch above the others on Hauptstrasse.

Admont is 15km to the east of Selzthal, but served by only very limited train services. Hieflau (€3.80, 30 minutes, three to eight daily) and Liezen (or Selzthal) are the two main hubs for Admont.

WEST STYRIA

Like northern Styria, west Styria is a mountainous region divided by jagged ranges and alpine streams. It's an area for enjoying Austria's natural splendour and escaping crowds.

Murau, high up in the Mur valley, is a picturesque town well placed for hikes and cycle trips into the surrounding forests. If you're heading this way from Graz, consider a detour to Seckau or Oberzeiring. The former is famous for its Benedictine Abbey (Seckau 1; basilica free, tours adult/child €5/3.50; ☉8am-8pm, tours 11am & 2pm May-Oct), a stunning Romanesque basilica and the mausoleum of Karl II, while the latter is known for its old silver mine (www.silbergruben.at, in German; adult/child/family €8/4.50/16; ☉tours 11am, 1.45pm & 3pm May-Oct, 4pm Wed Nov-Apr), now resurrected as a small health resort for sufferers of respiratory diseases.

Schladming

☑03687 / POP 4500

Situated deep in the Ennstal (Enns valley) in western Styria at the foot of the glacial Dachsteingebirge (Dachstein mountains), Schladming is a winter ski resort that in summer also offers glacier skiing and snowboarding, easy access to hiking trails, white-water rafting on the Enns River and excellent mountain biking. On Hoher Dachstein (2996m), don't miss the opportunity to walk through a glacier crevice in the Eispalast or to admire views over the Enns valley from the Skywalk high-altitude panorama platform.

◉ Sights

Dachstein Eispalast   GLACIER
(www.dachsteingletscher.at; Ramsau am Dachstein; adult/child €9/5.50; ☉8.30am-4.30pm) It's difficult to know what to make of this 'Ice Palace' situated in a crevice of the Dachstein Glacier at the sheer cliff face of the mountains. Walking through the crevice is a bit like getting lost inside an enormous, hollow ice cube. You are completely surrounded by ice (including on the floor, so wear sensible shoes), which is lit up and given an accompaniment of music to create an effect, but then suddenly you reach the Simpsons – yes, that's right, from the US TV series. You can sit on the laps of carved ice figures of Homer or Marge while your friends take a snapshot. Some like this; others find it inappropriate for a natural feature such as this.

A less contentious highlight of the region is the **gondola** (return adult/child €30/16.50; ☉every 20min 7.50am-5.10pm) that runs up there and becomes near-vertical at the rock face of the summit. It is indisputably one of the world's most spectacular cable-car rides

STYRIA WEST STYRIA

SCHLADMING NIGHT RACE

Schladming's most famous skiing event is the men's **Nachtslalon** (Night Race), a cult race held on the floodlit Planai ski piste in January that attracts the world's top slalom skiers. Schladming high kicks, sips and swills for the weekend as 50,000 people descend on the town. To be part of it, contact the tourist office, which will arrange accommodation in the area for you. In 2013 the Planai run will also be the stage for the **Alpine Ski World Cup** (4 to 17 February 2013). A new **Planet Planai** stadium is being built for the event at the base station.

and terminates at the **Skywalk** – a viewing platform offering fantastic views back into the valley on a clear day. About 10 buses daily (€8.10, 45 minutes) leave Lendplatz or Rathausplatz in Schladming for the base station near Ramsau.

🏃 Activities

The area around Schladming has over 900km of mountain-bike trails, divided among 20 routes shown on the excellent, free mountain-bike map from the tourist office. Hiking trails begin almost from the centre of town – the tourist office's town map has trails marked.

Schladming Ski Fields   SKIING, SNOWBOARDING
The winter ski period from December to March is the peak season in Schladming, when the area's 223km of downhill ski pistes and over 100 ski lifts rev into action. Adults/children can expect to pay €42/34 for a day pass and for downhill ski hire about €30 per day (a medium-quality snowboard costs €14 and snow-hiking shoes €15). Most of the **cross-country skiing** is done across the valley in Ramsau (about €14 for ski hire). Skiing and **snowboarding** on the Dachstein Glacier can be done year-round (but not all lifts are open in summer). Prices are similar.

Riesachfälle waterfalls   HIKING
Start from Talbachgasse in Schladming and follow the stream for about 40 minutes along a shared mountain-bike and walking trail to Untertal. From there it's about another 3½ hours to the waterfalls. Alternatively, catch a bus to the popular valley restaurant **Gasthof zu Riesachfall** and walk the forest trail or the gravel forestry road to the falls and beyond to the Riesachsee (Lake Riesach).

[pi:tu] Bikecenter   MOUNTAIN-BIKE RENTAL
(☑0650/4130 321; www.pi-tu.at, in German; Coburgstrasse 52) At the Planai Stadium rents mountain bikes from €15 to €60 per day.

Trittscher   MOUNTAIN-BIKE & SKI RENTAL
(☑226 47-11; www.tritscher.at, in German; Salzburgerstrasse 24) In summer Trittscher rents mountain bikes for €15; in winter it hires out ski equipment.

🛏 Sleeping & Eating

Book ahead during the ski season to be sure of a room. The tourist office can help place you.

TOP CHOICE **Post Hotel**   HOTEL €€
(☑225 71; www.posthotel-schladming.at; Hauptplatz 10; r €89-127, apt €95-135; P ⊕ ☺ @ ☎ ⊕)
This four-star hotel has spacious, modern rooms decorated in tasteful tones. Some of its doubles have connecting doors for families, and its family apartment is in fact a fully fledged suite with a separate living room. There's wi-fi in the lobby and in a separate eating area reserved for guests with full or half board. Expect to pay €12 to €24 for mains in the restaurant next door. It also has sauna and issues the Sommercard.

Jugendgästehaus Schladming   HOSTEL €
(☑05/7083-330; www.jufa.at/schladming; Coburgstrasse 253; dm/s/d €34/41/62; ⊜☎) Situated in the pedestrian zone close to the Planai base station, this excellent hostel has maisonette rooms with upstairs and downstairs beds, doubles with beds you can shift together as well as standard rooms. It issues the Sommercard.

Hotel Landgraf   HOTEL €€
(☑223 95; www.landgraf.cc, in German; Hauptplatz 37; s/d/tr/q €55/110/120/160; P ⊕ ☎ ⊕) This clean and comfortable hotel is situated right in the centre and, as well as standard rooms, has some spacious apartments suitable for families (it doesn't issue the Sommercard).

Maria's Mexican   TEX-MEX €€
(Steirergasse 3; light mains & salads €7.90-17, mains €10-18; ⊙dinner, closed Mon & Tue Apr-Oct) This Tex-Mex joint in the centre has a good range

of salads served with meat accompaniments, as well as burgers, steaks, spare ribs and chicken wings. When the snow's on the slopes, it kicks on late.

Bio Chi
HEALTH FOOD €

(Martin Luther-Strasse 32; breakfasts €4.50-9, buffet lunch mains €6-8.50; ⊙breakfast & lunch; ⊜🌿) This health-food shop (open standard shop hours as well as for breakfast and lunch) whips up healthy salads and vegetarian mains using organic ingredients, which you can wash down with freshly squeezed juices.

Hohenhaus Tenne
BAR

(www.tenne.com/schladming, in German; Coburgstrasse 512; ⊙11am-4am) Finding aprés ski in Schladming in the ski season isn't a problem – the revamped Hohenhaus Tenne promises to be the hottest.

❶ Information

Tourismusverband Schladming-Rohrmoos
(☎22 777 22; www.schladming.at; Rohrmoosstrasse 234; ⊙9am-6pm Mon-Sat, 9am-noon Sun, closed Sat Apr & Nov, closed Sun Apr-Nov) Stocks mountain-bike-trail and hiking maps, has lots of tips on the region and will organise accommodation if you call ahead. A useful accommodation board and free telephone are situated outside.

❶ Getting There & Around

Every two hours trains pass through on their way to Graz (€34, 2½ hours) and at least five times daily to Salzburg (€18, 1½ hours). The Dachsteinstrasse toll road to the gondola costs €5/2.50 per adult/child.

Five buses daily leave from Rathausplatz and Lendplatz to Riesachfall Wilde Wasser (€5.60, 35 minutes), the access point to the Riesachfälle waterfall and the lake.

For a taxi, call ☎222 22. For bicycle hire, see p197.

Murau
📞03532 / POP 2100

Murau, in the western reaches of the Mur valley on the banks of the river, is an attractive town filled with pastel-coloured houses and surrounded by forested hills and alpine meadows. Its close proximity to Stolzalpe to the north and the Metnitzer mountains to the south makes it an excellent base for hiking and cycling during the summer months.

◉ Sights & Activities

Schloss Obermurau
CASTLE

(Schlossberg 1; tours adult/child €3/2; ⊙2pm Wed & Fri mid-Jun–Sep) Built in 1250 by the Liechtenstein family, which once ruled the region, Schloss Obermurau took its present Renaissance form in the 17th century. Tours take you through seven rooms, including the chapel and the **Rittersaal** (Knight's Room), where concerts are often held. The altar in the chapel dates from 1655 and was created by masters from the town of Judenberg.

Stadtpfarrkirche St Matthäus
CHURCH

(St Matthew's Church; Schlossberg 8; ⊙dawn-dusk) Just below the castle is this restored church. Its Gothic and baroque elements work surprisingly well together, especially in the combination of the Gothic crucifixion group (1500) and the baroque high altar (1655). The beautiful frescoes date from the 14th to the 16th centuries.

Brewery Museum
MUSEUM

(Raffaltplatz 19-23; adult/child €3/free; ⊙3-5pm Fri May, Jun & Oct, 3-5pm Wed & Fri Jul-Sep) Murau is also famous for its Brauerei Murau, which has a brewery museum. Entry includes a glass of the local brew. In 2005 the brewery won a pan-European environmental-management award for its environmental practices.

🛏 Sleeping & Eating

TOP CHOICE Hotel Ferner's Rosenhof
HOTEL €€

(☎23 18; www.hotel-ferner.at; Rosseggerstr 9; s €48-65, d €96-130; ⊙lunch & dinner; ℗@🌐🍴) With lovely rooms, sauna and herbal steam bath, and an attractive restaurant terrace (mains €9 to €16), Hotel Ferner's Rosenhof has style and cosiness that even extends to a piano in the downstairs guest area. The more expensive rooms have a balcony and are larger, and some have connecting doors for families.

Hotel Lercher
HOTEL €€

(☎24 31; ww.meisterstrasse.at/hotel.lercher; Schwarzenbergstrasse 10; s €46-78, d €92-156; ℗@🌐) The more expensive rooms in the comfortable four-star Hotel Lercher have been recently renovated and are away from the street, but even the cheaper ones are very comfortable. It has two restaurants: the small and highly rated Panorama (mains €20 to €30, open Tuesday to Saturday, reservation required), and the Wirtshaus (mains €12 to €18, open lunch and dinner) for simpler cuisine.

Almost a dozen cycling tracks and mountain-bike trails can be accessed from Murau. The granddaddy of them all is the 450km-long Murradweg following the course of the Mur River. Trails are numbered and routes marked on the Murau tourist office's useful *Rad & Mountainbike* booklet (in German but easy to decode if you don't speak German).

Hiking trails also branch out into the region from here, some beginning from the train station, the Billa supermarket (near the tourist office) and the tourist office itself. A strenuous nine-hour return hike to the Stolzalpen peak (1817m) begins at Billa. The tourist office has a useful booklet on hikes.

Intersport Pintar (☑23 97; www.sportpintar.at, in German; Bundesstrasse 7a; per day €11), near the tourist office, rents bikes, including ones for kids.

Jugend- und Familiengästehaus   HOSTEL €
(☑05/7083-280; murau@jufa.at; St Leonhard Platz 4; dm €32.50, s €44.50, d €69) This HI hostel is situated in four buildings near the train station and has bike hire, a sauna and a peaceful inner courtyard. Call ahead in September or October, when it closes for one month.

ℹ Information
Tourist office (☑27 20-0; www.murau-kreisch berg.at; Bundesstrasse 13a; ☺8.30am-5pm Mon-Fri) Has loads of brochures on the town and its surrounds, including hiking trails and bicycle ways.

ℹ Getting There & Away
If you're coming from Salzburgerland, the most pleasant mode of transport is the **Murtalbahn** (www.stlb.at, in German; return €17), a steam train that chugs its way between Tamsweg and Murau once every Tuesday and Wednesday from late June to late September on a narrow-gauge line.

Every two hours direct ÖBB trains connect Murau with Tamsweg (€7.30, one hour). Trains to Leoben (€18.50, 1½ hours, every two hours) require a change in Unzmarkt, also the junction for trains from Murau to Klagenfurt (€22, 2¼ hours, every two hours).

STYRIA MURAU

The Salzkammergut

Best Places to Eat

» Goldenes Schiff (p203)

» Balthazar im Rudolfsturm (p206)

» Restaurant-Pizzeria Simmer (p208)

» Balthazar (p209)

» Landhotel Grünberg am See (p212)

Best Places to Stay

» Seehotel Grüner Baum (p205)

» Heritage.Hotel Hallstatt (p205)

» Schlosshotel Freisitz Roith (p212)

» Im Weissen Rössl (p214)

» Gjaid Alm (p207)

Why Go?

The Salzkammergut is a spectacular region of alpine and subalpine lakes, picturesque valleys, rolling hills and rugged, steep mountain ranges rising to almost 3000m. Much of the region is remote wilderness, and even in those heavily visited parts such as the Wolfgangsee and Mondsee, you'll always find isolated areas where peaceful, glassy waters provide limitless opportunities for boating, swimming, fishing or just sitting on the shore and chucking stones into the water. The popular Hallstätter See, flanked by soaring mountains that offer great hiking, is arguably the most spectacular of the lakes. Salt is the 'white gold' of the Salzkammergut, and the mines that made it famous now make for an interesting journey back in time to the settlers of the Iron Age Hallstatt culture, and to the Celts and Romans.

When to Go

The mountain lakes can be chilly or cold outside July to early September, so go during those months if lake swimming is your passion. The Wolfgangsee and Mondsee are warmer. The shoulder season (spring and autumn) has changeable weather, and in midsummer short, sudden rain showers are not unusual. There's good skiing on the Dachstein Mountains once the snow settles, from December to March, and with the experience, right equipment and maps you can ski to the Schladming side of the range on a cross-country trail.

Salzkammergut Highlights

1 Reeling from views at the **5Fingers platform** (p207) in the Dachstein Mountains

2 Hiking around the **Hallstätter See** (p204) from Obertraun to Hallstatt and cooling off in the crystal waters between trails

3 Exploring the Wolfgangsee and the remarkable pilgrimage church in **St Wolfgang** (p214), filled with priceless works of art

4 Strolling through the **Kaiservilla** (p202), Franz Josef's summer residence in Bad Ischl

5 Plunging into the chilling depths to masterfully illuminated towers of ice in the **Dachstein Caves** (p206)

6 Finding the toilet in Gmunden's **K-Hof museum** (p210) – a museum with a sanitary objects section for whenever nature calls

7 Winter skiing on the 11km downhill piste from **Krippenstein** in the Dachstein Mountains (p207)

ⓘ Getting There & Away

To reach the Salzkammergut from Salzburg by car or motorcycle, take the A1 to reach the north of the region, or Hwy 158 to Bad Ischl. Travelling north–south, the main road is Hwy 145 (the Salzkammergut Bundesstrasse), which follows the train line for most of its length. By rail, the main routes into the province are from Salzburg or Linz, with a change at Attnang-Puchheim onto the regional north–south railway line. From Styria, change at Stainach-Irdning.

ⓘ Getting Around

BOAT Ply the waters of the Attersee, Traunsee, Mondsee, Hallstätter See and Wolfgangsee.

BUS Regular bus services connect all towns and villages in the area, though less frequently or not at all on weekends. Hourly buses depart Salzburg for various towns in the region, including Bad Ischl, Mondsee and St Wolfgang (see p240); for services from Styria, see www.busbahnbim.at.

TRAIN The Salzkammergut is crossed by regional trains on a north–south route, passing through Attnang-Puchheim on the Salzburg–Linz line and Stainach-Irdning on the Bischofshofen–Graz line. Hourly trains take 2½ hours to complete the journey. Smaller stations are *unbesetzter Bahnhof* (unattended train station); at these you'll have to use a platform ticket machine or pay on the train. Attersee is also accessible by rail.

BAD ISCHL

☏06132 / POP 14,050

This spa town's reputation snowballed after the Habsburg Princess Sophie took a treatment here to cure her infertility in 1828. Within two years she had given birth to Emperor Franz Josef I; two other sons followed and were nicknamed the Salzprinzen (Salt Princes). Rather in the manner of a salmon returning to its place of birth, Franz Josef made an annual pilgrimage to Bad Ischl, making it his summer home for the next 60 years and hauling much of the European aristocracy in his wake. The fateful letter he signed declaring war on Serbia and sparking off WWI bore a Bad Ischl postmark.

Today's Bad Ischl is a handsome town that makes a handy base for visiting the region's five main lakes.

◎ Sights & Activities

Kaiservilla PALACE
(Jainzen 38; www.kaiservilla.com; adult/child/family €12/7.50/26, grounds only €4.50/3.50/10.50; ☺9.30am-4.45pm, closed Nov & Thu-Tue Jan-Mar) Franz Josef's summer residence was the Kaiservilla, an Italianate building that was bought by his mother, the Princess Sophie, as an engagement present for her son and Princess Elisabeth of Bavaria. Elisabeth, who loathed the villa and her husband in equal measure, spent little time here, but the emperor came to love it and it became his permanent summer residence for over 60 years. In a kinky twist, his mistress, Katharina Schratt, lived nearby in a house chosen for her by the empress.

The interior of the villa can only be seen by guided tours (which leave every half-hour in summer), with English information sheets. You'll learn of the emperor's habit of rising at 3.30am each morning to take a bath before beginning his day's work punctually at 4am, and that the only recreation he allowed himself was hunting. You can see the stuffed corpse of the 2000th chamois he shot. There are various other exhibits, including a bust of the Empress Elisabeth, made when she was in her mid-40s (a grandmother and still an internationally famous beauty), and a death mask made after she was killed by a knife-wielding madman at the age of 60. The parkland surrounding the villa contains a small **Photomuseum** (adult/child/family €2/1.50/4; ☺9.30am-5pm Apr-Oct).

Stadtmuseum MUSEUM
(Esplanade 10; adult/child €4.70/2.30; ☺2-7pm Wed, 1-5pm Fri, 10am-5pm Thu, Sat & Sun, closed Nov) The City Museum showcases the history of Bad Ischl and stages changing exhibitions inside the building where

---

SALZKAMMERGUT REGION

The Salzkammergut, a cultural region whose centre is around Bad Ischl and the Hallstätter See, falls within three provinces: Upper Austria, which takes the lion's share; Styria, comprising the small area around Bad Aussee; and Salzburg province. For general information, check out www.salzkammergut.at. The nontransferable **Salzkammergut Erlebnis Card**, available from tourist offices and hotels, costs €4.90 and offers significant discounts for 21 days between 1 May and 31 October.

Franz Josef and Elisabeth were engaged (the day after they met at a ball).

Katrin Seilbahn CABLE CAR

(www.katrinseilbahn.com; return adult/child €17.50/11.50; ⊙closed Apr–mid-May & Nov–mid-Dec) The local mountain Mt Katrin (1542m), with walking trails and limited skiing in winter, is served by a cable car.

Kaiser Therme SPA

(☎204-0; www.eurothermen.co.at; Bahnhofstrasse 1; adult/child €13.50/9.50; ⊙9am-midnight) If you'd like to follow in Princess Sophie's footprints, check out treatments at this spa.

✯✯ Festivals & Events

The home of operetta composer Franz Lehár, Bad Ischl hosts the **Lehár Festival** (www.leharfestival.at) in July and August, with the staging of works by Lehár and other composers.

🛏 Sleeping

Hotel Garni Sonnhof HOTEL €€

TOP CHOICE (☎230 78; www.sonnhof.at; Bahnhofstrasse 4; s €65-95, d €90-150; P⊛🐾📶) Nestled in a leafy glade of maple trees next to the station, this lovely hotel has cosy, traditional decor, a beautiful garden (complete with pond), grazing chickens that deliver low-cholesterol breakfast eggs, a sunny conservatory and large bedrooms with interesting old furniture. There's also a sauna and a steam bath on-site.

Goldenes Schiff HOTEL €€

(☎242 41; www.goldenes-schiff.at; Adalbert Stifter-kai 3; s €98-109, d €144-176, apt €192; P⊛@📶) Most doubles in this four-star hotel have bath-tubs, and the best rooms (junior suites) have large windows overlooking the river. There's also a wellness centre with solarium and sauna, and an excellent restaurant (mains €14 to €18) that serves fine Austrian cuisine using local ingredients.

Goldener Ochs Hotel HOTEL €€

(☎235 29; www.goldenerochs.at; Grazer Strasse 4; s €61-78, d €98-194; P⊛📶🏊) This large hotel just across the Traun caters mostly to business customers and guests on packages. It offers a variety of health and massage treatments to complement its excellent wellness area.

Jugendgästehaus HOSTEL €

(☎265 77; jgh.badischl@oejhv.or.at; Am Rechensteg 5; dm/s/d €16.50/31/47; @⊛) The characterless but clean HI guesthouse is in the town centre behind Kreuzplatz.

🍴 Eating & Drinking

Supermarkets include **Billa** on Pfarrgasse and **Eurospar** on Götzstrasse.

Café Sissy CAFE €€

(www.cafe-sissy.at, in German; Pfarrgasse 2; mains €11-18.50; ⊙8am-midnight) Sissy was the nickname of the Kaiserin Elisabeth, unhappy wife of Emperor Franz Josef, and her pictures hang on the walls of this popular riverside bar-cafe. You can breakfast here, lunch or dine on a Wiener schnitzel and other simple fare, or simply nighthawk at the front-room bar till the midnight hour.

Weinhaus Attwenger AUSTRIAN €€

(☎233 27; www.weinhaus-attwenger.com, in German; Lehárkai 12; mains €14-22; ⊙Tue-Sun, closed Tue Nov-Apr; ⊛) This quaint chalet with a garden next to the river serves prime-quality Austrian cuisine from a seasonal menu, with wines to match.

Grand Café & Restaurant Zauner Esplanade AUSTRIAN €€

(Hasner Allee 2; mains €10-18.50; ⊙10am-10pm; ⊛) This offshoot of Café Zauner, the famous pastry shop at Pfarrgasse 7, serves quite decent Austrian staples, some using organic local meats, in a pleasant location beside the river. The Pfarrgasse pastry shop (open 8.30am to 6pm) was founded in 1832; Franz Josef's mistress ordered pastries for their breakfast here every morning when the emperor was in residence.

Rettenbachmühle AUSTRIAN €€

(☎235 86; Hinterstein 6; mains €11-16; ⊙11am-10pm Wed-Sun; P⊛🐾) Situated 2.5km southeast of the centre in the lush Rettenbach Valley, this restaurant in a former mill alongside a gurgling stream is a relaxing place to enjoy some regional and Austrian classics on a warm day in the garden. To get here, take Grazer Strasse from the Goldener Ochs Hotel and after the B145 turn left into Rosenkranzgasse/Rettenbachtalbezirksstrasse. A taxi is easiest if you don't have your own wheels.

K.u.K. Hofbeisl BEISL €

(Wirerstrasse 4; food €8-20; ⊙8am-3.30am) This *Beisl* is the scene of some of the liveliest late-night partying in Bad Ischl, but it also does a delicious plate of food. It has two separate drinking areas to choose from, DJs get the floors writhing regularly during events, and the drinks list would do a Russian novelist proud – about 150 cocktails in all.

ⓘ TRANSPORT ON & AROUND THE LAKE

As well as excursions, **Hemetsberger** (☑06134-8228; Am Hof 126; 80min excursions €9.50; mid-Jul–mid-Sep) does a scheduled run between Obertraun and Hallstatt-Markt (€5, 25 minutes, three or four daily) during summer. It also operates the all-important year-round service between Hallstatt-Markt and Hallstatt train station (€2.20, 10 minutes, 10 to 12 daily), situated across the lake, connecting with trains in both directions on the main railway line. The last boat leaves Hallstatt-Markt at 6.15pm; going to Hallstatt-Markt from Hallstatt station, the last boat is at 6.55pm. Between Obertraun and Hallstatt town, a **taxi** (☑06131-542) costs about €12. Reserve ahead. Eight to 10 daily buses connect Hallstatt (Lahn) town with Obertraun (€1.90, eight minutes).

ⓘ Information

Post office (Bahnhofstrasse; ⊙8am-6pm Mon-Fri, 9am-noon Sat)

Salzkammergut Info-Center (☑240 00-0; www.salzkammergut.co.at; Götzstrasse 12; ⊙9am-8pm, closed Sun Oct-Mar) A helpful private regional agency with bike rental (per 24 hours €13) and internet (per 10 minutes €1.10).

Tourist office (☑277 57-0; www.badischl.at; Auböckplatz 5; ⊙8am-6pm Mon-Fri, 9am-6pm Sat, 10am-1pm Sun) A telephone service (8am to 10pm) for rooms and information complements this office.

ⓘ Getting There & Away

BUS Postbus services depart from outside the train station, with hourly buses to Salzburg (€9.10, 1½ hours) via St Gilgen (€4.80, 40 minutes). Buses to St Wolfgang (€3.60, 30 minutes) go via Strobl.

CAR Most major roads in the Salzkammergut go to or near Bad Ischl. Hwy 158 from Salzburg and the north–south Hwy 145 intersect just north of the town centre.

TRAIN Hourly trains to Hallstatt (€3.60, 25 minutes) go via Steeg/Hallstätter See and continue on to Obertraun (€4.30, 30 minutes). There are also frequent trains to Gmunden (€7.20, 40 minutes), as well as to Salzburg (€21, two hours) via Attnang-Puchheim.

SOUTHERN SALZKAMMERGUT

The Dachstein mountain range provides a stunning 3000m backdrop to the lakes in the south. Transport routes go round rather than over these jagged peaks.

Hallstätter See

The Hallstätter See, set among sharply rising mountains at an altitude of 508m in the Southern Salzkammergut, is one of the prettiest and most accessible lakes in the region. It offers some of the best hiking and swimming in summer, good skiing in winter, and a fascinating insight into the cultural history of the region any time of year. Just 5km round the lake lies Obertraun, the closest resort to the Dachstein ice caves. The whole Hallstatt-Dachstein region became a Unesco World Heritage site in 1997.

Hallstatt

☑06134 / POP 840

With pastel-coloured houses casting shimmering reflections onto the glassy waters of the lake, and towering mountains on all sides, Hallstatt's beauty alone would be enough to guarantee it fame. Boats chug tranquilly across the lake from the train station to the village, situated precariously on a narrow stretch of land between mountain and shore. So small is the patch of land occupied by the village that its annual Corpus Christi procession takes place largely in small boats on the lake.

Salt in the hills above the town made it a centre of salt mining. The Hallstatt Period (800 to 400 BC) refers to the early Iron Age in Europe, named after the village and the Iron Age settlers and Celts who worked the salt mines here. Today the sheer volume of visitors can get annoying at times, and makes finding a hotel room difficult in midsummer. Consider staying in Obertraun, which retains its sleepy feel.

The train station is across the lake from Hallstatt; to get into town you have to take the ferry.

⊙ Sights & Activities

Salzbergwerk MUSEUM

(salt mine; return funicular & tour adult/child/family €24/12/50, tour only €12/6/25; ⊙9.30am-4.30pm May–mid-Oct) The region's major cultural attraction is situated high above Hallstatt on Salzberg (Salt Mountain). Visitors travel down an underground railway and miner's slides (a photo is taken of you while sliding) to an illuminated subterranean salt lake. In 1734 the fully preserved body of a prehistoric miner was found; today he is known as the 'Man in Salt' and the standard tour (in English and German) revolves around his fate. An audio guide (€2, bring photo ID) is available from the base station of the funicular, leading you through 35 numbered stations of the Hallstätter Hochtal (Hallstatt High Valley), explaining excavation sites and early history.

The easiest way to reach the mine is by funicular railway (one-way adult/child/family €7/3.50/15) to the mountain station, from where the mine is 15 minutes' walk; a switchback trail takes about 40 minutes to walk. Another option is to take the steps behind the Beinhaus and follow the trail until it joins the picturesque Soleleitungsweg; go left and follow the very steep trail past the waterfall and up steps. It's a tough climb, and not really for children.

Beinhaus   CHURCH
(Kirchenweg 40; admission €1; ☉10am-6pm May-Oct) Don't miss the macabre yet beautiful Beinhaus behind Hallstatt's parish church. This small charnel house contains rows of neatly stacked skulls, painted with flowery designs and the names of their former owners. Bones have been exhumed from the overcrowded graveyard since 1600 and the last skull in the collection was added in 1995. The Beinhaus stands in the grounds of the 15th-century Pfarrkirche (Kirchenweg 40) and has Gothic frescoes and three winged altars; arguably the best one, on the right, dates from 1510 and shows saints Barbara and Katharina, with Mary in the middle.

Weltkulturerbe Museum   MUSEUM
(☎8206; www.museum-hallstatt.at; Seestrasse 56; adult/child/family €7.50/4/18; ☉10am-6pm, closed Mon & Tue Nov-Mar) The high-tech Stadtmuseum covers the region's history of Iron Age/Celtic occupation and salt mining. All explanations are in German, but pick up the Museum Hallstatt booklet (€2; in English) which explains the exhibits. Not to be missed is the room re-enacting the fatal rockslides that may have led to the area being abandoned.

Celtic and Roman excavations can be seen downstairs in Dachsteinsport Janu (Seestrasse 50; admission free; ☉8am-6pm), a

shop opposite the tourist office, or near the Salzbergwerk, where excavation continues.

Hallstätter See   WATER SPORTS
You can hire boats and kayaks (per hour from €11) on the lake, go swimming or scuba dive with Tauchclub Dachstein (☎0676/644 99 89; www.zauner-online.at; 2-3hr course from €35).

🛏 Sleeping
Rooms fill quickly in summer, so book ahead or arrive early. The tourist office can help you if you arrive without a booking. All of the following places provide free parking for guests within the town limits.

🔝 Seehotel Grüner Baum   HOTEL €€
CHOICE (☎8263; Marktplatz 104; s €80, d without view €140, d or ste with lake view €170-210; P@🛜) The quality of this hotel is higher than its three stars suggest, and because it has its own pontoon and lakeside seating area you feel like you are right on the lake the whole time. Rooms are tastefully furnished and retain the historic features of the building; three suites have enormous patios to the lake, and all except the cheaper doubles have large balconies. A complimentary bottle of mineral water arrives each day, and staff will deliver breakfast to your bedside to accompany those sweeping views of the lake.

🔝 Heritage.Hotel Hallstatt   HOTEL €€
CHOICE (☎200 36-0; www.heritagehotel.at; Landungsplatz 102; s/d €140/200, tr €300-350, ste €350-450; 🛜🛜) Rooms in this luxury hotel are spread across three buildings, with prime position in the main building at the landing stage on the lake. Most rooms offer stunning views and all have modern decor, though compared to the equally luxurious Grüner Baum they have a slightly less lakeside feel.

Bräugasthof am Hallstätter See
                                       GUESTHOUSE €€
(☎8221; www.brauhaus-lobisser.com; Seestrasse 120; s €49-55, d €98, tr €130-135) A friendly guesthouse beside the lake in the centre of town – like most places in Hallstatt it's small, so book ahead. It also has a good lakeside restaurant.

Gasthof Zauner   GUESTHOUSE €€
(☎8246; www.zauner.hallstatt.net; Marktplatz 51; s/d €60/120; ☉closed mid-Nov–mid-Dec; P🛜) This quaint, ivy-covered guesthouse has very tasteful, pine-embellished rooms, some with a balcony and a view of the lake. The restaurant (mains €15 to €20) is excellent, not just for fish.

Campingplatz Klausner-Höll CAMPGROUND €
(☑8322; www.camping.hallstatt.net, in German; Lahnstrasse 7; camp sites per adult/child/tent/car €7/4/4/3; ☺mid-Apr–mid-Oct; P) Conveniently located south of the centre.

Gasthaus Mühle HOSTEL €
(☑8318; www.hallstatturlaub.at, in German; Kirchenweg 36; dm €23; ☺Wed-Mon, closed Nov) This lively hostel is handily situated on the way up to the church.

✖ Eating

For self-caterers, there's a **Konsum** (Kernmagazinplatz 23) supermarket between Hallstatt and Lahn.

TOP CHOICE Balthazar im Rudolfsturm
AUSTRIAN €
(Rudolfsturm; mains €10-13.50; ☺9am-6pm May-Oct; ☺) With the most spectacular terrace seating in the region, Balthazar is situated 855m above Hallstatt with views over the lake. The food is excellent, and the building was originally the tower occupied by the head of the salt mine; today you can pop upstairs and check out a small exhibition about it.

Restaurant zum Salzbaron EUROPEAN €€
(Marktplatz 104; mains €15-22; ☺lunch & dinner, closed Nov; ☺☑) One of the best gourmet acts in town, the Salzbaron is perched alongside the lake inside the Seehotel Grüner Baum and serves a seasonal pan-European menu; local trout features strongly in summer.

Bräugasthof AUSTRIAN €
(Seestrasse 120; mains €14-19; ☺May-Oct) Meats of all descriptions are an excellent choice here, but you can also enjoy a few salads, trout and other local specialities in this restaurant with a lovely lakeside terrace.

ℹ Information

For internet access, try the **umbrella bar** (Seestrasse 145; per 15min €1; ☺9.30am-10pm May–mid-Oct). To reach the **tourist office** (☑8208; www.dachstein-salzkammergut.at; Seestrasse 169; ☺9am-6pm Mon-Fri, to 4pm Sat, to noon Sun, closed Sat & Sun Sep-Jun), turn left from the ferry. It stocks the free leisure map of lakeside towns and hiking and cycling trails.

ℹ Getting There & Around

BOAT Ferry excursions do the Hallstatt Lahn via Hallstatt Markt, Obersee, Untersee and Steeg circuit (€9.50, 90 minutes, three daily) from mid-July to August.

BUS Eight to 10 daily buses connect Hallstatt (Lahn) town with Obertraun (€1.90, eight minutes).

CAR Access into the village is restricted from early May to late October: electronic gates are activated during the day. Staying overnight in town gives free parking and a pass to open the gates.

TRAIN About a dozen trains daily connect Hallstatt and Bad Ischl (€3.60, 22 minutes), and Hallstatt with Bad Aussee (€3.60, 15 minutes). Hallstatt train station is across the lake, and boat services to the village coincide with train arrivals (€2.20, 10 minutes, last ferry 6.55pm).

Obertraun

☑06131 / POP 740

Quieter, more low-key than Hallstatt, this broad settlement offers great access to the Dachstein caves. It's also a good starting point for hikes around the lake or more strenuous treks up to the caves themselves and beyond through alpine meadows. Signs from the train station point the way to the cable-car station and ice caves. The trail (No 16) to the caves is a stiff 2½-hour hike from the valley station. Obertraun has a free grassy beach area with a small waterslide, a children's play area and boat rental.

◎ Sights & Activities

Dachsteinhöhlen CAVES
(www.dachsteinwelterbe.at; 1/2 caves adult €10.80/15.80, child €6/10, cable car return plus 1/2 caves adult €27/32, child €15/19; ☺May–mid-Oct) Climb to the Dachstein caves and you'll find yourself in a strange world of ice and subterranean hollows extending 80km in places. The two caves take about 15 minutes to reach by foot in different directions from the Schönbergalm cable-car station at 1350m. Tours of each cave last an hour.

The ice in the **Rieseneishöhle** (Giant Ice Cave; ☺tours 9.20am-4pm) is no more than 500 years old, forming an 'ice mountain' 8m high – twice as high now as it was when the caves were first explored in 1910. The formations here are illuminated with coloured light and the shapes they take are eerie and surreal. This cave can only be seen on a guided tour; if you let the tour guide know, they will do the tour with English as well as German commentaries.

The **Mammuthöhle** (Mammoth Cave; ☺tours 10.15am-2.30pm) is among the 30 or so deepest and longest caves in the world and is free of ice. Tours offer an insight into the formation of the cave, which also has installations and artworks based on light and shadow to heighten the experience.

Also part of the Dachstein cave system, the water-filled **Koppenbrüllerhöhlen** (adult/child €10/6; ⊙tours 9am-4pm) caves are situated down the valley towards Bad Aussee. A trail leads off towards them from behind the Dachsteinhof hotel.

Cable Car
SCENIC AREA

(⊙closed mid-Oct–Nov & Easter–mid-May) A highlight in itself, the cable car departs about every 15 minutes from the valley station and has several stages, becoming more low-key and remote the further you go. After the middle station (for the caves), **Schönbergalm** (return adult/child €16.20/9), it continues to the highest point (2109m) of **Krippenstein** (return adult/child €23/14), with the eerie **5Fingers viewing platform** dangling over the precipice. The final stretch is to **Gjaid Alm** (return from Krippenstein adult/child €7.60/3.90), taking you away from the crowds to an area where walking trails wind across the rocky meadows or lead higher into the mountains. Some of these trails begin at the simple Gjaid Alm guesthouse and working organic farm situated 10 minutes by foot from the cable-car station.

🛏 Sleeping & Eating

Obertraun has many private rooms (from €19) and holiday apartments, plus several hotels. The **Konsum** supermarket near the tourist office is convenient for hiking supplies.

GETTING THE MOST OUT OF THE CAVES & MOUNTAINS

Planning the Day

To view the caves in **one day**, take the cable car up to the first stop (Schönbergalm) by noon or earlier. Do the Mammuthöhle first, allowing 30 to 45 minutes to reach the Rieseneishöhle from the Mammuthöhle. To view one or both caves and the 5Fingers viewing platform (about 15 minutes by foot from the Krippenstein station), allow a whole day, setting off from the valley cable-car station around 10am. Over **two days** you can view one or both of the caves (the Rieseneishöhle is the best) and the 5Fingers viewing platform, take the final section of the cable car to Gjaid Alm station, drop by the Gjaid Alm hut and explore the area on walks or hike back down to the valley.

Discounts

There are various combined tickets and deals, including a ticket for all sections of the cable car and the caves in summer (return adult/child €33/20). Check them out at the valley station.

Winter Skiing

In winter Krippenstein is also a ski and snowboard free-riding area (day pass €32). The cable car begins service again in December, depending on completion of maintenance and snow conditions; it usually ends around Easter. Advanced cross-country ski hiking is also possible on the mountain. For downhill skiers, the best piste is an 11km downhill run beginning at Krippenstein and going via Gjaid Alm station to the valley station. Hold onto your hat!

Staying & Eating on the Peaks

Lodge am Krippenstein (☎0664/38040 54; www.lodge.at, in German; dm/s/d €28.50/33.50/67; ⊜) is a modern alpine guesthouse and restaurant open all year. It has great views to the mountains but gets busy with Krippenstein visitors during the day.

Gjaid Alm (☎596; www.gjaid.at, in German; s/d incl half board €46/92; ⊜☑) is set in a rocky hollow replete with grazing cattle and horses, an easy 10-minute walk from the cable-car station. All dishes in the restaurant (daily mains €10) are prepared with organic ingredients. Regular meditation, climbing and Qi Gong courses are held here.

Etiquette

In many places (such as Gjaid Alm or the youth hostel in Obertraun), the done thing is to remove your shoes at the door.

Gasthof-Pension Dachsteinhof GUESTHOUSE €
(☎393; www.dachsteinhof.at, in German; Winkl 22; s/d €36/72; P) This simple, traditional pension has an idyllic setting by the river on the way to the ice caves. The good-sized rooms are clean and functional, with the sound of rushing water to lull you to sleep at night. There's also a midrange restaurant here serving classics like schnitzel and steak, and also local trout.

Seehotel am Hallstätter See HOTEL €
(☎462; www.hallstatt-blick.at; Seestrasse 152; s/d €40/76; P🌐🍽️♿) This large hotel is another comfortable option near the lake. Its large garden area out front and around the pool makes it ideal for kids; families can take advantage of rooms with connecting doors.

Hotel Haus am See HOTEL €€
(☎26777; www.hotel-hausamsee.at; Obertraun 169; s/d €44/88; P😊🌐) Situated conveniently alongside the boat station and swimming area, this hotel has rooms with views over the lake. While they lack frills, the rooms are very clean and comfortable, and you can throw open the balcony door at night and sleep with a lakeside breeze.

Campingplatz Hinterer CAMPGROUND €
(☎265; camping.am.see@chello.at; Winkl 77; camp sites per adult/child/tent/car €10/6/6.50/3; ⏰May-Oct; P🌐) This informal, grassy campground is by the lake south of the river.

Restaurant-Pizzeria Simmer
AUSTRIAN, ITALIAN €
(Seestrasse 178; mains €9-12, pizza €5-8.50; ⏰10am-10pm Tue-Sun) Easily the most atmospheric of all the budget restaurants in the region, this Italo-Austrian place has cosy indoor seating and outdoor tables alongside a gurgling brook; the pizza is great, and there's ten-pin bowling out the back.

ℹ️ Information

The very helpful **tourist office** (☎351; www.dachstein-salzkammergut.at; ⏰8am-noon & 2-5pm Mon-Fri, 8am-noon Sat, closed Sun Nov-Apr) has a free lake and hiking trail map. It's on the way to the Dachstein cable car from the train station (an ATM is next door).

ℹ️ Getting There & Away

Buses run from Bad Ischl to the car park at the cable-car station (€4.30, one hour, five to nine daily). A ferry runs from Hallstatt Markt via Hallstatt Lahn to Obertraun (€5, 25 minutes, five daily). Obertraun-Dachsteinhöhlen is the train station for Obertraun settlement. There are trains to Bad Ischl (€5.40, 30 minutes, 17 daily) via Hallstatt (€3.60, three minutes).

A **taxi** (☎542) to the cable-car valley station or between Hallstatt and Obertraun costs about €12.

Gosausee
☎06136 / ELEV 923M
This small lake is flanked by the impressively precipitous peaks of the Gosaukamm range (2459m). The view is good from the shoreline, and it takes a little over an hour to walk around the entire lake. The **Gosaukammbahn** (return adult/child €11.70/7.30) cable car goes up to 1475m, where there are spectacular views and walking trails. One- to two-hourly Postbus services run to the lake from Bad Ischl (€6.10, one hour) via Steeg.

Before reaching the lake you pass through the village of **Gosau**, which has its own **tourist office** (☎8295; www.dachstein-salzkammergut.at; ⏰8am-noon & 1-5pm Mon-Fri, 9am-noon Sat, closed Sat Sep-Apr), with an accommodation board outside. Gosau is at the junction of the only road to the lake and can be reached by Hwy 166 from Hallstätter See.

Bad Aussee
☎03622 / POP 4900
Quiet, staid Bad Aussee is the largest Styrian town in the southern Salzkammergut. It is close to two lakes, and convenient by rail and a walking trail to a third, the Hallstätter See. If it's nightlife you're after, look further – such as to Bad Ischl – this is not a high-kicking sort of place, and a stroll in the pretty Kurpark must suffice.

The train station is 1.5km south of the town centre. After getting off the train, dash to the bus stop out front to raise your chances of catching one of the one- to two-hourly buses.

◎ Sights & Activities

Altaussee Salzbergwerk MUSEUM
(www.salzwelten.at; adult/child/family €15/7.50/32; ⏰tours hourly 9am-4pm Jun-Sep, 9am, 11am, 1pm & 3pm Oct-May; P♿) Situated near the Altaussee about 6km north of Bad Aussee, this is still a working salt mine and was the secret hiding place of art treasures stolen by the Nazis during WWII. Tours include the treasure chambers, an underground lake and a chapel made of blocks of salt and dedicated to St Barbara, the patron saint of miners. All tours are bilingual in German and English.

Hourly buses run to Altaussee from the post office (€1.90, 10 minutes).

Kammerhof Museum
MUSEUM
(www.badaussee.at/kammerhofmuseum; Chlumeckyplatz 1; adult/child/family €4/2/6; ⊙10am-noon & 3-6pm May-Oct) Kammerhof Museum, housed in a beautiful 17th-century building, covers local history and salt production. There are also some portraits of Anna Plöchl, the local postmaster's daughter who scandalously married a Habsburg prince. All explanations are in German but there's an English sheet available.

Grundlsee
WATER SPORTS
Five kilometres northeast of Bad Aussee, Grundlsee has a good lookout at its western end as well as water sports (including a sailing school) and walking trails. Extending from the eastern tip of the lake are two smaller lakes, **Toplitzsee** and **Kammersee**. Between May and October, boat tours (☑03622 8613; www.3-seen-tour.at, in German; adult/child €18/9) take you through all three. Buses leave hourly from the post office (€1.90, 10 minutes).

FREE Ausseer Lebkuchen
BAKERY
(Gingerbread Bakery; www.lebkuchen. at, in German; Pötschenstrasse 146; ⊙8am-noon & 1-6pm Tue-Sat, 1-6pm Sun; P) Tours of a working gingerbread factory. A cafe is on the premises.

Panoramastrasse
SCENIC AREA
(toll per car €15) A scenic road climbing most of the way up **Loser** (1838m), the main peak overlooking the Altausseer See. Snow chains are required in winter.

Koppentalweg
HIKING
A picturesque 10km hiking trail, the Koppentalweg runs west through the lush Traun River valley, connecting via the Koppenbrüllerhöhlen (caves) with the Ostuferwanderweg running along the Hallstätter See. The trail begins at the train station.

🛏 Sleeping
There's a 24-hour information touch screen and free phone to contact hotels outside the office. The tourist office has a listings brochure.

TOP CHOICE Erzherzog Johann
HOTEL €€
(☑525 07; www.erzherzogjohann.at; Kurhausplatz 62; r per person €109-119, ste per person €176; P) Bad Aussee's four-star hotel has rooms with comforts, but the facilities are what really catapult you into seventh heaven: a wonderfully large sauna and wellness area, a 30m salt-water swimming pool (public, with direct access for guests) and excellent bikes free for guests. The hotel caters to kids with a program of special activities. The restaurant (mains €18 to €22) is quite good, but wines are best of all. You can try these in the bar, too, where there is wi-fi.

Pension Stocker
PENSION €
(☑524 84; www.zimmer-ausseerland.at/stocker; Altausseer Strasse 245; s/d €30/60; P) Located 500m northwest of Kurhausplatz, this is a very pretty pension with wooden balconies and flower-filled window boxes. It has clean rooms and a large garden overlooking tennis courts.

HI Jugendgästehaus
HOSTEL €
(☑0570 83 520; www.jfgh.at/bad-aussee.php; Jugendherbergsstrasse 148; dm/s/d €33/46/72; P) Recently upgraded. It's 15 minutes' walk by road, but there are shorter (unlit) footpaths.

Josefinum
HOSTEL €
(☑521 24; www.tiscover.at/josefinum; Gartengasse 13; s/d €30/60; P) Peaceful retreat in the centre, run by nuns. Telephone ahead for evening arrival.

Gasthof Blaue Traube
GUESTHOUSE €€
(☑523 63-0; www.blauetraube.at; Kirchengasse 165; s/d €55/96) Historic guesthouse in the centre with modern and well-sized but somewhat bland rooms.

🍴 Eating & Drinking
Bad Aussee is no great shakes when it comes to eating and drinking, so you're better off splurging elsewhere. The restaurant at Erzherzog Johann, however, has a very strong wine list, some good dishes and service with character.

TOP CHOICE Balthazar
INTERNATIONAL €
(☑545 20; Kirchengasse 28; mains €10-14; ⊙4pm-midnight Tue-Sat, 11am-10pm Sun) With its small but eclectic menu of dishes ranging from baked potatoes (€4.90 to €8.20) to wok or Asian-inspired mains, Balthazar offers a greater variety of flavours than most places in town.

Konditerei Lewandofsky-Temmel
CAFE €
(Kurhausplatz 144; cake €2.90; ⊙8am-10pm Mon-Sat, from 9am Sun) The favoured place in town for coffee and cake or a postwork tipple on the terrace alongside the Kurpark.

Zum Lebzelter
CAFE

(☎524 26; www.zumlebzelter.at, in German; mains €11-17; ⊙Tue-Sun; P🐾🏠) Next door to the gingerbread factory. Many ingredients used in this Austrian cafe are organic.

Vinothek Annamax
WINE BAR

(www.annamax.at; Meranplatz 39; ⊙9am-12.30pm & 2.30-6.30pm Mon-Fri, 9am-1pm Sat) Small wine bar with a great selection of wine and a mixed antipasto (about €7).

ℹ Information

Post office (Ischlerstrasse 94; ⊙8am-noon & 2-5.30pm Mon-Fri) The tourist office is inside and the main bus stop with timetable information is outside this multifunctional post office.

Tourist office (☎523 23; www.ausseerland. at, in German; Ischlerstrasse 94; ⊙9am-6pm Mon-Fri, 9am-noon Sat) Excellent tourist office with helpful staff. Pick up the town map, with hiking trails marked for the region.

ℹ Getting There & Around

Bad Aussee is on the rail route between Bad Ischl (€6.10, 35 minutes) and Stainach-Irdning (€5.60, 35 minutes), with trains running hourly in both directions. Buses run every one to two hours from the post office to both the Altaussee and the Grundlsee (€1.90, 10 minutes). A **taxi**

ℹ TRANSPORT AROUND THE TRAUNSEE

Train

The resorts are strung along the western shore and are connected by rail. Trains run between Gmunden and Traunkirchen (€2, 10 minutes, hourly) and Ebensee (€3.60, 20 minutes, hourly), continuing to Bad Ischl (€7.20, 40 minutes).

Boat

Traunsee Schiffahrt (www.traunsee schiffahrt.at, in German; Rathausplatz, Gmunden) vessels tour the shoreline between late April and mid-October. There are connections from Gmunden's Rathausplatz to Gasthof Grünberg (adult/child €2.50/2, seven minutes, twice daily), Traunkirchen (€7/5, 55 minutes, five daily) and Ebensee (€8.50/6, 70 minutes, five daily). A boat does a round trip of the lake (€17/12, 130 minutes, five daily).

(☎540 08, 521 75) from the train station to the centre costs about €6.

NORTHERN SALZKAMMERGUT

The two most popular of the northern lakes are Traunsee – with the three resorts of Gmunden, Traunkirchen and Ebensee on its shores – and Wolfgangsee, home to the villages of St Wolfgang and St Gilgen (the latter provides access to Schafberg mountain).

Traunsee

Traunsee is the deepest lake in Austria, going down to a cool 192m. The eastern flank is dominated by rocky crags, the tallest of which is the imposing **Traunstein** (1691m).

Gmunden
☎07612 / POP 13,100

With its yacht marina, lakeside square and promenades, Gmunden exudes a breezy, Riviera feel. It was formerly known for its castles and ceramics, and also doubled as an administration centre for both the Habsburgs and the salt trade. Today it makes for an attractive stopover in the lakes region.

◉ Sights & Activities

K-Hof
MUSEUM

(www.k-hof.at, in German; Kammerhofgasse 8; adult/child €6/2; ⊙10am-5pm Tue-Sun, closed Tue Sep-May) Recently revamped and combined with one of Austria's most unusual and refreshing museums, the **Museum for Sanitary Objects**, the K-Hof museum complex gives a fascinating insight into the history of the region. The exhibition covers ceramics manufacture (for which Gmunden was famous in its early years), fossils and the life of the 15th-century astronomer Johannes von Gmunden, whose theories influenced Copernicus. It is an eclectic museum, and it integrates the Gothic St Jakob's, Gmunden's first church. After these, you reach a section dedicated to sanitary objects – mostly toilets, urinals and basins. The collection is monumental and intriguing. About 80 examples are on display, including a toilet regularly mounted by the royal *Po* (bottom) of Kaiser Franz Josef in his hunting lodge near Ebensee. Descriptions throughout most of the museum are in German and English.

Gmunden

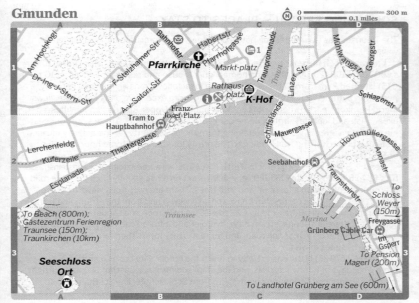

Toscana Park & Seeschloss Ort

PARK, CASTLE

(www.schlossorth.com; Orth 1; admission free) Flanking the lake on the eastern side, a pretty nature reserve known as Toscana Park forms a backdrop to Seeschloss Ort. This castle on the lake is believed to have been built on the ruins of a Roman fortress. It dates from 909 or earlier (rebuilt in the 17th century after a fire) and has a picturesque courtyard, a late-Gothic external staircase and sgraffito from 1578. The **Bummelzug** (adult/child €4.50/2.50; ⊙10am-6pm, from 1pm Tue), an electric train on wheels, runs to Seeschloss Ort from the Rathausplatz every 30 minutes from May to October.

Pfarrkirche

CHURCH

(Kirchplatz) North of the Rathausplatz is the 12th-century Pfarrkirche, a Gothic church later remodelled in baroque style and with an altar (dating from 1678) by the sculptor Thomas Schwanthaler (1634–1707).

Schloss Weyer

PALACE

(Freygasse 27; admission €8.50; ⊙10am-noon & 2-5.30pm Tue-Fri, 10am-1pm Sat Jun-Sep) Palace containing a good collection of porcelain, silver and jewellery.

Grünberg Lookout

SCENIC AREA

(cable car return adult/child/family €12.50/6.50/26.70) A cable car whisks visitors 984m up to the local mountain, Grünberg. Trails also lead up there on an easy walk from the base station.

🛏 Sleeping & Eating

Private rooms are the best deal for budget travellers – ask the excellent tourist office to help you find one.

Keramikhotel Goldener Brunnen HOTEL **€€**
(☑644 310; www.goldenerbrunnen.at; Traungasse 10; s €68, d €108-140; ℗🐕🐾) This excellent boutique hotel in the centre has very tastefully appointed rooms with modern fittings. Ceramic art adds a decorative touch and its restaurant (lunch menu €7, mains €7 to €13)

SOMETHING SPECIAL – PLACES TO STAY

The Traunsee has two interesting hotels on its eastern shore, both unique in different ways.

Landhotel Grünberg am See (☑777 00; www.gruenberg.at; Traunsteinstrasse 109; s €60-70, d €100-120; ℗☺@☎) is a homely guesthouse and restaurant (mains €10 to €15) situated 2km from Rathausplatz, with a loyal following as an informal getaway, especially in summer. Rooms are modern and the more expensive ones have lake views. Ingrid Pernkopf, part-owner, writes cooking books on Upper Austrian specialities, so expect fish and local favourites, some using organic ingredients. There's outdoor seating with lake views as well as waterskiing from the private jetty for the actively inclined. A section of the walking trail leading to the pretty Laudachsee (three hours) begins behind the building.

Nearby, **Schlosshotel Freisitz Roith** (☑649 05; www.freisitzroith.at; Traunsteinstrasse 87; s €84-96, d €95-115, ste €135-160; ℗☺@☎) is set on a rise slightly back from the road in grounds replete with a fountain and fruit trees. There are rapturous views from the rooms (less expensive rooms don't have the lake views) and from the atrium and terrace restaurant (lunch menu €19, mains €22 to €28). A bath robe and slippers await you in your room; there is a sauna, steam bath, hydrojet and infrared cabin to pick you up after a swim at the beach across the road; and for real luxury lovers there are two neobaroque (ie modern) suites in white.

A **taxi** (☑679 09) is the easiest way to reach the hotels. City buses 4 and 5 run out there weekdays at hourly intervals, and the ship landing stage Gasthof Grünberg is right in front of Landhotel Grünberg, about 350m from Schlosshotel Freisitz Roith.

is a plus, with Austrian dishes such as Styrian chicken and some international favourites. The hotel also has sauna and wellness facilities.

Pension Magerl   PENSION €€
(☑636 75; www.pension-magerl.at, in German; Ackerweg 18; s €50-60, d €84-94; ℗☎) This rambling pension is spread over three buildings near the cable-car station. From the outside the main building looks very drab, but rooms are clean and modern. The other buildings are newer.

Café Brandl   CAFE €
(Rathausplatz 1; light dishes €2-5) This smart cafe-bar has bright yellow walls, black leather sofas and cubist artworks spiking its interior. It serves breakfast, cakes and light meals during the day, and turns into a drinking venue (with snacks) at night.

ⓘ Information

Gästezentrum Ferienregion Traunsee (☑643 05; www.traunsee.at; Toscanapark 1; ☺8am-8pm Mon-Fri, 10am-7pm Sat & Sun) Regional tourist office for the lake, with accommodation booking service.

Tourist office (☑657 520; www.traunsee.at/gmunden; Rathausplatz 1; ☺9am-5pm Mon-Fri, 10am-4pm Sat) Information and maps of

town and the lake. Helps with accommodation bookings.

ⓘ Getting There & Around

The Gmunden *Hauptbahnhof* on the Salzkammergut Attnang-Puchheim to Stainach-Irdning line is the main train station for the town. The Bad Ischl–Gmunden train fare (€6.10, 45 minutes, 14 daily) includes the connecting tram to Gmunden's centre. The Seebahnhof, near the marina, services the slow, private train line from Vorchdorf-Eggenburg.

The main train station is 2km northwest of the town centre: tram G (€1.70) runs to Franz-Josef-Platz after every train arrival. Bus tickets in town cost €1.70.

Traunkirchen

☑07617 / POP 1775

The attractive hamlet of Traunkirchen sits on a spit of land about halfway along the western shore of the Traunsee. It's chiefly famous for the wooden **Fischerkanzel** (Fisherman's Pulpit; Klosterplatz 1; ☺8am-5pm) in the Pfarrkirche. This was carved in 1753 and depicts the miracle of the fishes, with the Apostles standing in a tub-shaped boat and hauling in fish-laden nets. The composition, colours (mostly silver and gold) and detail (even down to wriggling, bug-eyed fish) create a vivid impression.

For information on accommodation, contact the **tourist office** (☑2234; www.traunsee. at; Ortsplatz 1; ☺8am-6pm Mon-Fri, 9am-noon & 2-5pm Sat, closed Sat Sep-Jun).

Trains run hourly to Traunkirchen from Gmunden (€2, 10 minutes).

Ebensee

☑06133 / POP 7950

Ebensee is an unlikely town to achieve film fame, but in 2006 it achieved renown as the setting for the Salzkammergut's unusual teenage splatter film, *In 3 Tagen bist du Tod* (In Three Days You're Dead). In 1968 it was also the setting for the film *Where Eagles Dare*, staring Richard Burton and Clint Eastwood.

The town lies on the southern shore of the Traunsee, with a cable car (adult/child €18/€9, hourly) running up to **Feuerkogel** (1592m), where you find walking trails leading across a flattish plateau. Within an hour's walk is **Alberfeldkogel** (1708m), with an excellent view over the two Langbath lakes, a nature reserve popular for hiking and for cross-country skiing in winter. Feuerkogel also provides access to winter **skiing** (day pass €30) with easy to medium slopes.

In early January every year, the men of Ebensee don giant illuminated headdresses made of tissue paper in a bizarre ritual known as the Glöcklerlauf.

For details on accommodation and especially for activities like hiking and mountain-bike hire and trails, the local **tourist office** (☑8016; www.ebensee.com; Hauptstrasse 34; ☺8am-6pm Mon-Fri, 9am-noon & 2-6pm Sat, closed Sat Sep-Jun) by the Landungsplatz train station can help.

Ebensee-Landungsplatz, rather than the larger Ebensee station, is the train station for the centre and the boat landing stage.

Attersee

☑07566 / POP 1500

The largest lake in the Salzkammergut is flanked mostly by hills, with mountains in the south. It's one of the less scenic and less visited of the Salzkammergut's lakes, but a few resorts cling to the shoreline, offering the usual water-leisure activities. The main resort is Attersee, which has a museum

and a couple of churches. Its **tourist office** (☑7719; www.attersee.at; Nussdorferstrasse 15; ☺9am-6pm Mon-Fri, 9am-noon Sat, 9-11am Sun, closed Sat & Sun Oct-Apr) can help with accommodation.

Attersee-Schifffahrt (www.atterseeschiff fahrt.at) does mostly alternating boat circuits of the north (adult/child €9/4.50, 1¼ hours) and south (€14/7, 2¼ hours) regions of the lake several times most days from early May to late September. It also does a daily full circuit (adult/child €17/8.50, 3¾ hours) in July and August.

ℹ Getting There & Away

The two lakeside towns of Attersee and Schörfling are each connected to the rail network by a line branching from the main Linz–Salzburg route (only regional trains stop): for Kammer-Schörfling change at Vöcklabruck, and for Attersee change at Vöcklamarkt.

Wolfgangsee

Named after a local saint, this lake has two very popular resorts, St Wolfgang and St Gilgen, of which St Wolfgang is the most appealing. The third town on the lake, **Strobl** (population 2750), is a less remarkable but pleasant place at the start of a scenic toll road (per car and per person €3) to Postalm (1400m).

A **ferry** (www.wolfgangseeschifffahrt.at; ☺May-Oct) runs between Strobl and St Gilgen (adult/child €8.80/4.40, 75 minutes), stopping at points en route. Services are most frequent from June to early September. Boats run from St Wolfgang to St Gilgen almost hourly during the day (adult/child €6.50, 50 minutes). The free *Eintauchen & Aufsteigen* timetable from local tourist offices gives exact times that will help with planning day trips and connecting with buses or the Schafbergbahn cogwheel railway.

The Wolfgangsee is dominated by the 1783m Schafberg mountain on its northern shore. At the summit you'll find a hotel, restaurant and phenomenal views over mountains and lakes (especially Mondsee, Attersee and, of course, Wolfgangsee). If you don't fancy the three- to four-hour walk from St Wolfgang (early tourists were carried up in sedan chairs), ride the **Schafbergbahn** (adult/child €19.60/9.80, return €28.60/14.30; ☺May-Oct), which takes 45 minutes one way. Departures are approximately hourly between 9.15am and 4pm, but the trip is so popular that you probably won't be able to get on the next train. Queue early, purchase a ticket for a specific train and then go for a wander along the lake or around St Wolfgang until your time comes to depart.

St Wolfgang

📞 06138 / POP 2830

St Wolfgang is a charming town situated on the steep banks of the Wolfgangsee. Although its streets can get clogged with visitors during the day, things usually settle down by early evening, which is the best time for a tranquil stroll along the forested lakeshore past the gently creaking wooden boathouses.

The village's main fame came as a place of pilgrimage and today's visitors still come to see the 14th-century pilgrimage church, packed with art treasures.

👁 Sights & Activities

Wallfahrtskirche   CHURCH

(Pilgrimage Church; Markt; donation €1; ⊙9am-6pm) St Wolfgang's impressive Wallfahrtskirche is a spectacular gallery of religious art, with glittering altars (from Gothic to baroque), an extravagant pulpit, a fine organ and countless statues and paintings. The most impressive piece is the winged high altar, created by celebrated religious artist Michael Pacher between 1471 and 1481 – it's a perfect example of the German Gothic style, enhanced with the technical achievements of Renaissance Italy.

Wolfgangsee   SWIMMING

Many hotels have jetties for swimming and a tourist office booklet details the many water sports on offer. A nice thing to do is to walk or cycle to Strobl, 6km away, or around 1.5 hours on foot, ending the excursion with a swim.

🛏 Sleeping

St Wolfgang has some good private rooms in village homes or in farmhouses in the surrounding hills. Lists are available from the tourist office, which will phone places on your behalf.

TOP CHOICE **Im Weissen Rössl**   HISTORIC HOTEL €€€
(📞2306-0; www.weissesroessl.at; Im Stöckl 74; s €130-160, d €190-280, ste per person €170-200; P❄@🛜☷) St Wolfgang's most famous hotel was the setting for Ralph Bena-

tzky's operetta *The White Horse,* and a bed from the operetta today takes pride of place on one floor. Rooms are individually styled and somewhat idiosyncratic, but the more expensive ones have a balcony and view over the lake. There's a large wellness area, and two pools – one pool literally floats on the lake (heated to 30°C), and another is indoors. It also has several good junior suites.

Hotel Peter   HOTEL €€
(📞2304; www.tiscover.at/hotel-peter; s/d €83/136, ste per person €83; P❄@🛜) The generous-sized rooms at this four-star hotel have balconies looking onto the lake, large bathrooms and tasteful decor. The restaurant (most mains €11 to €15) has a terrace overlooking the lake, with pasta and a good fish platter filled with poached, fried and baked local fish. The restaurant has wi-fi.

Haus am See   PENSION €
(📞2224; Michael Pacher Strasse 98; s/d without bathroom €30/50; P) This is a remarkable pension with features ripe for a Wolfgangsee mystery novel: it's run by a retired professor and his wife, and evokes earlier decades. The owners also rent out four rooms in their boatshed down on the water (same price). Guests get free use of a boat and bike. It's conveniently opposite the Au bus stop.

🍴 Eating & Drinking

Kraftstoff-Bar   MEXICAN €
(Markt 128; mains €10-20; ⊙Wed-Mon) Decked out like a petrol station, this chilled-out bar and restaurant is an unusual place to curl your fingers around a drink, accompanied by wings and potato wedges, pasta, salads or grills; check out the charming balcony.

Im Weissen Rössl   AUSTRIAN €€
(Im Stöckl 74) There are two restaurants and a lovely wine cellar in this highly respected hotel. The Seerestaurant (kitchen open all day, mains €12.50 to €19) tempts with regional and international dishes, while the Romantik has à la carte dining (dinner only, mains €25 to €31) and an exceptional six-course menu for €56.50.

ℹ Information

Tourist office (📞8003; www.wolfgangsee.at; Au 140; ⊙9am-8pm Mon-Fri, 9am-6pm Sat, 10am-5pm Sun) At the eastern tunnel entrance.

Pilgerstrasse branch (Michael-Pacher-Haus, Pilgerstrasse; ⊙9am-noon & 2-5pm Jun-Sep) At the other end of town, near the road tunnel.

Getting There & Around

The only road to St Wolfgang approaches from Strobl in the east. Boats run to St Gilgen roughly hourly (adult/child €6.50, 50 minutes). A Postbus service from St Wolfgang via Strobl to St Gilgen (€3.90, 50 minutes) is frequent out of season, but tails off somewhat in summer when the ships run. For buses to Salzburg (€6.40, 1¾ hours) you need to connect in St Gilgen or Strobl (€2.10, 12 minutes).

Wolfgangsee ferries stop at the village centre (Markt stop) and at the Schafberg railway. **Pro Travel** (🖉25 25; www.protravel.at, in German; Markt 152; mountain bike per day €16; ☺8.30am-6pm) hires bikes.

St Gilgen
🖉06227 / POP 3680

The ease of access to St Gilgen, 29km from Salzburg, makes this town very popular for day trippers, but it has also grown in recent years because of its very scenic setting. Along with quieter Strobl, it's a good base for lake water sports, and is not quite as crowded as St Wolfgang.

☉ Sights

Muzikinstumente-Museum der Völker
MUSEUM

(Folk Music Instrument Museum; Aberseestrasse 11; adult/child €4/2.50; ☺9-11am & 3-7pm Tue-Sun) The cosy little Muzikinstumente-Museum der Völker is home to 1500 musical instruments from all over the world, all of them collected by one family of music teachers. The son of the family, Askold zum Eck, can play them all and will happily demonstrate for hours. Visitors are welcome to have a go at anything from an African drum to an Indian sitar.

Heimatkundliches Museum
MUSEUM

(Pichlerplatz 6; adult/child €3.50/2; ☺10am-noon & 3-6pm Tue-Sun Jun-Sep) The town museum won an award a few years back for its eclectic collection ranging from embroidery (originally manufactured in the building) to 4700 animal specimens and religious objects.

🏃 Activities

Water sports such as windsurfing, waterskiing and sailing are popular activities in St Gilgen. There's a town swimming pool and a small free beach with a grassy area beyond the yacht marina.

The mountain rising over the resort is 1520m **Zwölferhorn** (return cable car adult/child €20/14.50), from where there are good views and two trails (two to 2½ hours) leading back to St Gilgen. Skiers ascend in winter.

🛌 Sleeping & Eating

Gasthof Zur Post
GUESTHOUSE €€

(🖉2157; www.gasthofzurpost.at; Mozartplatz 8; s €86, d €120-160, f €152; 🅿☺🛜📶) The 'Post-Geschichten' rooms at this old inn

---

WORTH A TRIP

LOW-KEY STROBL

While high-profile towns like St Wolfgang and St Gilgen justifiably attract large numbers of visitors, the lesser known and more low-key Strobl at the eastern end of the Wolfgangsee is well worth a visit.

From the shoreline in Strobl you can walk northeast along the lake for about five to 10 minutes towards Bürglstein, the high bluff rising above the lake. Just over the bridge, a trail (also a bike trail, though you'll need to dismount at a few sections) leads to St Wolfgang (6km, 1.5 hours, easy) along the shore. This follows a path and boardwalks around the bluff (the nicest stretch) to the settlement of Schwarzenbach (also a ferry stop). From Schwarzenbach the road runs near the trail, so it's not as secluded or tranquil. Locals who are reasonably strong swimmers sometimes enter the water near the bridge and even swim part or all of the way to Schwarzenbach. Joggers, cyclists and hikers can also walk around Bürglstein (9km, 1.5 hours, easy) or join other trails going away from the Wolfgangsee.

Strobler Hof (🖉06137-7308; www.stroblerhof.at, in German; Ischler Strasse 16; s/d €68/€136, mains €18-22; ☺lunch & dinner; 🅿☺@🛜), an upmarket hotel and restaurant set in its own grounds, is a great place to stay or eat in Strobl. Reserve ahead for an outside table in summer; some ingredients are organic.

In Strobl, **Sport Girbl** (🖉0664/221 79 85; Bahnstrasse 300; 7-gear bicycles per day €10; ☺8am-noon & 2.30-6pm) hires bicycles.

KIDS' PLAYGROUND

St Gilgen has one of the lake's best kid's playgrounds, situated at the shore near the ferry landing. As well as swings, there's a nifty flying fox and slides, and things to climb or hang around on. It's partly shaded.

are beautifully designed in a cosily rustic style with shades of minimalism. There are heavy wooden beds, interesting colour schemes and wooden floors. One family room or apartment sleeps four people. The restaurant (mains €15 to €20) serves national and regional specialities in a low-ceilinged, whitewashed dining room or outside on the elegant terrace.

Pension Rosam PENSION €
(☎2591; www.tiscover.at/rosam; Frontfestgasse 2-4; s/d €28/60, f per person €35; ☺Easter-Oct; **P@☎**) Situated down near the lake, this family-run pension is well managed and refreshing, with clean rooms that are very good value for the location.

Pension Falkensteiner PENSION €
(☎2395; www.pension-falkensteiner.at; Salzburgerstrasse 13; s/d €40/56; **P☺@**) Some of the rooms have balconies and all are large in this no-frills but spotless pension with helpful management.

Jugendgästehaus Schafbergblick HOSTEL €
(☎2365; jgh.stgilgen@oejhv.or.at; Mondseer Strasse 7; dm/s/d €21/32/25; ☺reception 8am-1pm & 5-7pm Mon-Fri, 8-7pm Sat & Sun; **P☺@**) This upmarket youth hostel has a good location near the town beach.

Restaurant Timbale AUSTRIAN €€€
(☎7587; Salzburger Strasse 2; mains €25-28, 6-course menu €62; ☺lunch & dinner Aug, closed Thu & lunch Fri Sep-Jul) Reserve ahead for a table in one of the finest restaurants on the Wolfgangsee. The atmosphere is informal and it specialises in seasonal regional dishes.

Fischer-Wirt Restaurant FISH €€
(www.fischer-wirt.at; Ischlerstrasse 21; mains €9-15; ☺lunch & dinner, closed Mon mid-Sep–May) Situated on the water's edge, this popular seafood restaurant does a well-priced fish platter for two people; some meat dishes also feature on the menu.

San Giorgio PIZZA €
(www.marvins-gastro.com, in German; Ischler Strasse 18; pizza €8-10; ☺lunch & dinner Wed-Sun, closed lunch Nov-Apr) This Italian restaurant by the lake has eat-in (inside or in the garden) and takeaway food. The bar-disco downstairs, the Zwolfer Alm Bar (open from 9pm), claims to be the oldest nightclub in Austria (it was founded in 1930) and hosts lots of sponsored events.

ℹ Information

The **tourist office** (☎2348; www.wolfgangsee.at; Mondsee Bundesstrasse 1a; ☺9am-8pm Mon-Fri, 9am-6pm Sat, 10am-5pm Sun) helps find rooms. Brochures are also available inside the *Rathaus* on Mozartplatz.

ℹ Getting There & Away

St Gilgen is 50 minutes from Salzburg by Postbus (€5.40), with hourly departures until early evening; some buses continue on to Stobl and Bad Ischl (€4.80, 34 minutes). The bus station is near the base station of the cable car. Highway 154 provides a scenic route north to Mondsee. Boats run to St Wolfgang roughly hourly (€6.50, 50 minutes).

Mondsee
☎06232 / POP 3280

The town of Mondsee extends along the northern tip of this crescent-shaped lake, noted for its warm water. Coupled with its closeness to Salzburg (30km away), this makes it a highly developed, popular lake for weekending Salzburgers.

◉ Sights & Activities

Parish Church CHURCH
(☺8am-7pm) If you're allergic to the film *The Sound of Music,* there's just one piece of advice: blow town. Even the lemon-yellow baroque facade (added in 1740, incidentally) of the 15th-century parish church achieved notoriety by featuring in those highly emotional Von Trapp wedding scenes in the film.

Museum Mondseeland und Pfahlbaumuseum MUSEUM
(Wrede Platz; adult/child & student €3/1.50; ☺10am-5pm Tue-Sun May-Sep) Next door to the church, the museum has displays on Stone Age finds and the monastic culture of the region (Mondsee is a very old monastery site).

Segelschule Mondsee   WATER SPORTS

(☑3548-200; www.segelschule-mondsee.at, in German; Robert Baum Promenade 3; 1-week courses €225, plus €19 exam fee) The largest sailing school in Austria, offering sailing and windsurfing courses.

🛏 Sleeping & Eating

As well as the hotel restaurants listed here, other eating and drinking options are located along Marktplatz. For lists of hotels and restaurants, ask at the tourist office. Book ahead in summer.

TOP CHOICE Seegasthof-Hotel Lackner   HOTEL €€

(☑2359; www.seehotel-lackner.at; Mondseestrasse 1; s €65, d €180-250, ste €490-510; P⊕) Situated 15 minutes by foot from the centre (turn right heading towards the lake from the tourist office) on the shore of the Mondsee, the four-star Lackner offers rooms with balconies and lake views. It has a private beach among the reeds and an excellent terrace restaurant (mains €17 to €28, six-course menu €75, open Friday to Wednesday) serving venison and lamb dishes as well as fish, complemented by a *Vinothek* (wine bar). There is cable internet access (LAN) in the rooms. It's situated on the main road but all rooms are away from the street.

Iris Porsche Hotel & Restaurant   HOTEL €€€

(☑2237; www.irisporsche.at; Marktplatz 1; s €130-240, d €180-290; P⊕❄☀🛜) Rooms in this modern, upmarket tourist and business hotel with lovely wooden floors are priced according to size and are cheaper during the low season. There's a lift, wellness area, bath-tubs and steam showers, and a writing desk in all rooms. A laptop can be borrowed from reception. The restaurant (mains €10 to €16) serves well-prepared fish and Austrian dishes from a small menu.

Hotel Krone   HOTEL €€

(☑2236; www.hotelkrone.org; Rainerstrasse 1; s €58, d €84-104; P⊕🛜🛏) The more-expensive rooms in this attractive and comfortable hotel have a balcony and are larger in this three-star hotel situated in the centre. Some doubles have a connecting door that families will find useful, and there's a restaurant (mains €10 to €13, open for lunch and dinner Wednesday to Monday).

Jugendgästehaus   HOSTEL €

(☑2418; jgh.mondsee@oejhv.or.at; Krankenhausstrasse 9; dm/s/d €21/31/47; P) This recently renovated HI hostel is a few minutes' walk from the centre of town.

❶ Information

The **tourist office** (☑2270; www.mondsee.at; Dr Franz Müller Strasse 3; ⊙8am-6pm Mon-Fri, 9am-6pm Sat & Sun, closed Sat & Sun Oct-May) can help with accommodation.

❶ Getting There & Away

Hourly Postbus services connect Mondsee with Salzburg (€5.70, 55 minutes), but only three direct buses a day go to St Gilgen (€3, 20 minutes). Expect to pay €25 for a ride to St Gilgen by **taxi** (☑0664-22000 22).

Salzburg & Salzburgerland

Best Places to Eat

» Obauer (p245)
» Alter Fuchs (p234)
» Afro Café (p235)
» Riedenburg (p235)
» Bistro Barock (p243)

Best Places to Stay

» Haus Reichl (p231)
» Villa Trapp (p233)
» Arte Vida (p231)
» Haus Wartenberg (p232)
» Bio-Hotel Hammerhof (p246)

Why Go?

One of Austria's smallest provinces, Salzburgerland is proof that size really doesn't matter. Well, not when you have Mozart, Maria von Trapp and the 600-year legacy of the prince-archbishops behind you. This is the land that grabbed the world spotlight and shouted 'visit Austria!' with Julie Andrews skipping joyously down the mountainsides. This is indeed the land of crisp apple strudel, dancing marionettes and high-on-a-hilltop castles. This is the Austria of your wildest childhood dreams.

Salzburg is every bit as grand as you imagine it: a baroque masterpiece, a classical music legend and Austria's spiritual heartland. But it is just the prelude to the region's sensational natural beauty. Just outside of the city, the landscape is etched with deep ravines, glinting ice caves, karst plateaux and mountains of myth – in short, the kind of alpine gorgeousness that no well-orchestrated symphony or yodelling nun could ever quite capture.

When to Go

In January orchestras strike up at Mozartwoche in Salzburg and hot-air balloons glide colourfully above Filzmoos' summits. Providing you've booked tickets months ahead, you can partake in the colossal feast of opera, classical music and drama that is the Salzburg Festival from late July to August. Beds are like gold dust at this time. Come in winter for fine downhill skiing in the south of the province, and in summer for trekking in the limestone pinnacles of the Tennengebirge and Dachstein ranges.

Alpine Escapades

Julie Andrews was wrong – these aren't hills, they're mountains; and they aren't alive with the sound of music, but with the sound of footsteps, bicycle bells and swishing skis.

A little preplanning helps whether you plan to freewheel along the **Salzach River** (p228) in Salzburg, mountain bike the challenging 182km **Dachstein Tour** (p245) through Salzburgerland, or flirt with mountaineering in the otherworldly limestone peaks of the **Tennengebirge**. Visit www.salzburgerland.com or local tourist offices for details on activities, equipment rental and maps.

Come winter, the Southern Salzburg Province becomes a skiing wonderland, with resorts like Filzmoos and Radstadt forming part of the gargantuan **Salzburger Sportwelt** (www.salzburgersportwelt.com); see the website for piste maps and details on lift passes, and to order brochures online.

MUSICAL LEGENDS

Salzburg is a force to rival Vienna when it comes to classical music and musical classics. This is, after all, the birthplace of such musical royalty as Mozart and Herbert von Karajan; the city that inspired the carol 'Silent Night' and Julie Andrews' high-octave vocals.

While you'll need to book tickets months ahead for the venerable **Salzburg Festival** (www.salzburger festspiele.at) in summer, music fills this city 365 days a year – and we're not talking second-rate stuff. Beyond the obvious, you can watch marionettes perform opera, dine to Mozart's symphonies and attend a chamber concert in Schloss Mirabell's exquisite baroque Marble Hall. See p238 for the low-down and find ticket agency details on www.salzburg.info.

Less high-brow is Salzburg's *Sound of Music* obsession. Twirl in Maria's footsteps on a guided tour (see p228), fine-tune your own tour of the film locations (p231), or even stay the night at *the* **Villa Trapp** (p233) for the all-singing truth behind the Hollywood legend.

Top Cultural Highs

» The palatial state apartments and Old Master paintings at the Residenz (p223), once home to Salzburg's powerful prince-archbishops

» The Keltenmuseum (p242) in Hallein, tracing regional heritage through Celtic artefacts and the history of salt extraction

» Salzburg's *Altstadt* (p221), an early baroque masterpiece and Unesco World Heritage site, often hailed the 'Rome of the North'

» The avant-garde art and architecture of Museum der Moderne (p223) atop Mönchsberg's cliffs

» Salzwelten (p243) near Hallein, a cavernous salt mine that once filled Salzburg's princely coffers with 'white gold'

ROCK ME, AMADEUS

Nobody ever rocked Salzburg quite like Mozart. See where the city's most famous son lived, loved and composed on our Mozart walking tour (p229).

Natural Icons

» The jaw-dropping Liechtensteinklamm (p245)

» Filzmoos' distinctive Bischofsmütze (p245) peaks

» The frozen sculptures of Eisriesenwelt (p244)

Three Fairytale Castles

» Salzburg's cliff-top Festung Hohensalzburg (p222), an archetypal fortress with a turbulent 900-year history

» Medieval Burg Hohenwerfen (p244) on its fairy-tale perch above Werfen

» The whimsically turreted 13th-century Burg Mauterndorf (p247), a favourite of the prince-archbishops

Resources

» Salzburgerland (www.salzburgerland.com) Accommodation, regional activities and events, up-to-date weather reports.

» Salzburger Verkehrsverbund (SVV; www.svv-info.at) Travel planning.

» Lonely Planet.com (www.lonelyplanet.com/austria/salzburg) Planning advice, author recommendations, traveller reviews and insider tips.

Salzburg & Salzburgerland Highlights

1 Survey Salzburg's baroque cityscape from the heights of 900-year-old **Festung Hohensalzburg** (p222)

2 Go subzero in the frozen depths of **Eisriesenwelt** (p244) in Werfen,

3 Tune into the life of a genius at **Mozart-Wohnhaus** (p223) in Salzburg

4 Get drenched like a drunken prince-archbishop by fountains at **Schloss Hellbrunn** (p241)

5 Do a Julie singing 'Do-Re-Mi' in the fountain-dotted gardens of Salzburg's **Schloss Mirabell** (p227)

6 Marvel at puppetry magic at the exquisite **Salzburg Marionettentheater** (p238)

7 Don a boiler suit for a slippery-when-waxed ride at the **Salzwelten** (p243) salt mine in Bad Dürrnberg

8 Ski or trek in the alpine splendour of **Filzmoos** (p245)

9 Thank heaven for small breweries and brimful steins at Salzburg's monastery-run **Augustiner Bräustübl** (p237)

History

Salzburg has had a tight grip on the region as far back as 15 BC, when the Roman town Iuvavum stood on the site of the present-day city. This Roman stronghold came under constant attack from warlike Celtic tribes and was ultimately destroyed or abandoned due to disease.

St Rupert established the first Christian kingdom and founded St Peter's church and monastery in around 700. As centuries passed, the successive archbishops of Salzburg gradually increased their power and eventually were given the grandiose titles of princes of the Holy Roman Empire.

Wolf Dietrich von Raitenau, Salzburg's most influential prince-archbishop from 1587 to 1612, spearheaded the total baroque makeover of the city, commissioning many of its most beautiful churches, palaces and gardens. He fell from power after losing a fierce dispute over the salt trade with the powerful rulers of Bavaria, and died a prisoner.

Another of the city's archbishops, Paris Lodron (1619–53), managed to keep the principality out of the Europe-wide Thirty Years' War. Salzburg also remained neutral during the War of the Austrian Succession a century later, but bit by bit the province's power gradually waned and Salzburg came under the thumb of France and Bavaria during the Napoleonic Wars. In 1816 Salzburg became part of the Austrian Empire and was on the gradual road to economic recovery.

The early 20th century saw population growth and the founding of the prestigious Salzburg Festival in 1920. Austria was annexed to Nazi Germany in 1938 and during WWII some 40% of the city's buildings were destroyed by Allied bombings. These were restored to their former glory, and in 1997 Salzburg's historic *Altstadt* (old town) became a Unesco World Heritage site.

ⓘ Getting There & Around

AIR

Both scheduled and no-frills flights from Europe and the USA serve **Salzburg airport** (www. salzburg-airport.com), a 20-minute bus ride from the city.

BUS

Salzburg's efficient bus network, run by **Salzburger Verkehrsverbund** (SVV; www.svv-info. at), makes it easy to reach the province's smaller villages. Available online and at tourist offices in the province, the **Salzburgerland Card** (www. salzburgerlandcard.com) provides discounts on attractions in the province. A six-day card costs €43/21.50 for an adult/child.

CAR & MOTORCYCLE

By road, the main routes into the region are the A8/E52 from Munich and the A1/E60 from Linz. To enter the province from Carinthia and the south, you can use the A10 from Spittal an der Drau or the Autoschleuse Tauernbahn south of Bad Gastein.

TRAIN

Salzburg is well connected to the rest of Austria by public transport, with excellent rail connections to Hohe Tauern National Park and neighbouring Salzkammergut. Salzburg's *Hauptbahnhof* has good connections to Germany, Italy and the Czech Republic.

SALZBURG

🕿 0662 / POP 147,600 / ELEV 430M

Salzburg is storybook Austria. Standing beside the fast-flowing Salzach River, your gaze is raised inch by inch to the *Altstadt*'s mosaic of graceful domes and spires, the formidable cliff-top fortress and the mountains beyond. It's a view that never palls. It's a backdrop that did the lordly prince-archbishops and home-grown genius Mozart proud.

Tempting as it is to spend every minute in the Unesco-listed *Altstadt* drifting from one baroque church and monumental square to the next in a daze of grandeur, Salzburg rewards those who venture further. Give Getreidegasse's throngs the slip, meander side streets where classical music wafts from open windows, linger decadently over coffee and cake, and let Salzburg slowly, slowly work its magic.

Beyond Salzburg's two biggest money-spinners – Mozart and *The Sound of Music* – hides a city with a burgeoning arts scene, wonderful food, manicured parks and concert halls that uphold musical tradition 365 days a year. Everywhere you go, the scenery, the skyline, the music, the history sends your spirits soaring higher than Julie Andrews octave-leaping vocals.

⊙ Sights

Salzburg's trophy sights huddle in the pedestrianised *Altstadt,* which straddles both banks of the Salzach River but centres largely on the left bank. Here the tangled lanes are made for a serendipitous wander, leading to hidden courtyards, medieval squares framed by burgher houses and baroque fountains.

SALZBURG IN...

Two Days

Get up early to see **Mozart's birthplace** and boutique-dotted **Getreidegasse** before the crowds arrive. Take in the baroque grandeur of **Residenzplatz** and the stately prince-archbishop's palace, **Residenz**. Divine chocolate *Annatorte* cake at **Demel** fuels an afternoon absorbing history at the hands-on **Salzburg Museum** or monastic heritage at **Stiftskirche St Peter**. Toast your first day with homebrews and banter in **Augustiner Bräustübl**'s beer garden.

Begin day two with postcard views from 900-year-old **Festung Hohensalzburg**'s ramparts, or cutting-edge art at **Museum der Moderne**. Have lunch at **M32** or bag goodies at the **Grüner Markt** for a picnic in **Schloss Mirabell**'s sculpture-strewn gardens. Chamber music in the palace's sublime **Marble Hall** or enchanting puppetry at **Salzburger Marionettentheater** rounds out the day nicely.

Four Days

With another couple of days to explore, you can join a Mozart or *Sound of Music* **tour**. Hire a bike to pedal along the Salzach's villa-studded banks to summer palace **Schloss Hellbrunn** and its trick fountains. Dine in old-world Austrian style at **Alter Fuchs** before testing the **right-bank nightlife**.

The fun-packed salt mines of **Hallein** and the Goliath of ice caves, **Eisriesenwelt** in Werfen, both make terrific day trips for day four. Or grab your walking boots or skis to head up to Salzburg's twin peaks: **Untersberg** and **Gaisberg**.

Many of the places mentioned below close slightly earlier in winter and open longer – usually an hour or two – during the Salzburg Festival.

TOP CHOICE **Festung Hohensalzburg** FORTRESS
(www.salzburg-burgen.at; Mönchsberg 34; adult/child €7.40/4.20, with funicular €10.50/6; ☺9-7pm; 🖐) Salzburg's most visible icon is this mighty 900-year-old cliff-top fortress, one of the biggest and best preserved in Europe. It's easy to spend half a day up here, roaming the ramparts for far-reaching views over the city's spires, the Salzach River and mountains. The fortress is a steep 15-minute jaunt from the centre or a speedy ride in the glass **Festungsbahn funicular** (Festungsgasse 4; adult/child one way €3.60/1.80, return €6/3.20; ☺9am-8pm).

The fortress began life as a humble bailey, built in 1077 by Gebhard von Helffenstein at a time when the Holy Roman Empire was at loggerheads with the papacy. The present structure, however, owes its grandeur to spendthrift Leonard von Keutschach, prince-archbishop of Salzburg from 1495 to 1519 and the city's last feudal ruler. Highlights of a visit include the **Golden Hall** where lavish banquets were once held, with a gold-studded ceiling imitating a starry night sky. Your ticket also gets you into the **Marionette Museum** and the **Fortress Museum**; the latter showcases Roman artefacts, Gothic furniture, armour and some pretty gruesome torture instruments.

The Golden Hall is the backdrop for year-round **Festungskonzerte** (Fortress Concerts), which often focus on Mozart's works. See www.mozartfestival.at for times and prices.

TOP CHOICE **Salzburg Museum** MUSEUM
(www.smca.at; Mozartplatz 1; adult/child/family €7/3/14; ☺9am-5pm Tue-Sun, to 8pm Thu; 🖐) Housed in the baroque Neue Residenz palace, this flagship museum takes you on a fascinating romp through Salzburg's past. A visit starts beneath the courtyard in the strikingly illuminated **Kunsthalle**, presenting rotating exhibitions of modern art. On the 1st floor, **Salzburg Persönlich** spotlights the characters that have shaped Salzburg's history, including 16th-century alchemist and astrologer Paracelsus. Upstairs, prince-archbishops glower down from the walls at **Mythos Salzburg**, which celebrates the city as a source of artistic and poetic inspiration. Be sure to see Carl Spitzweg's renowned *Sonntagsspaziergang* (Sunday Stroll; 1841) painting and the home videos of Asian tourists giving their unique take on Salzburg.

Salzburg's famous 35-bell **glockenspiel**, which chimes daily at 7am, 11am and 6pm, is on the western flank of the Neue Residenz.

A passage showing the remnants of Salzburg's Roman walls leads through to the **Panorama Museum** (Residenzplatz 9; adult/child €2/1; ⊙9am-5pm Fri-Wed, to 8pm Thu), Johann Michael Sattler's 360-degree painting of Salzburg as it was in 1829.

Dom
CATHEDRAL

(Cathedral; Domplatz; ⊙8am-7pm Mon-Sat, from 1pm Sun) Gracefully crowned by a bulbous copper dome and twin spires, the Dom stands out as a masterpiece of baroque art. Italian architect Santino Solari redesigned the cathedral during the Thirty Years' War and it was consecrated in 1628. Its origins, though, date to an earlier cathedral founded by Bishop Virgil in 767. Bronze portals symbolising faith, hope and charity lead into the cathedral, where intricate stucco and ceiling frescoes guide the eye to the polychrome dome.

The adjacent **Dommuseum** (adult/child €6/2; ⊙10am-5pm Mon-Sat, 11am-6pm Sun) is a treasure trove of sacred art. Star pieces include a gem-encrusted monstrance, a Eucharistic dove, goldwork and carved ivory.

Residenz
PALACE

(www.residenzgalerie.at; Residenzplatz 1; adult/child €8.50/2.70; ⊙10am-5pm Tue-Sun) Nowhere is the pomp and circumstance of Salzburg more tangible than at the regal Residenz. A man of grand designs, Wolf Dietrich von Raitenau, prince-archbishop of Salzburg from 1587 to 1612, gave the go-ahead to build this baroque palace on the site of an 11th-century bishop's residence. The prince-archbishops held court here until Salzburg became part of the Hapsburg Empire in the 19th century.

An audio-guide tour takes in the exuberant **state apartments**, a hotchpotch of baroque and neoclassical styles, which are lavishly adorned with tapestries, stucco and frescoes by Johann Michael Rottmayr.

Admission also covers the **Residenz Galerie**. Here the focus is on Flemish and Dutch masters, with must-sees such as Rubens' *Allegory on Emperor Charles V* and Rembrandt's chiaroscuro *Old Woman Praying*. Thomas Ender's alpine landscapes and Heinrich Bürkel's Salzburg scenes are among the 19th-century standouts.

Museum der Moderne
ART GALLERY

(www.museumdermoderne.at; Mönchsberg 32; adult/child €8/6, incl Rupertinum €12/8; ⊙10am-6pm Thu-Tue, to 8pm Wed) Straddling Mönchsberg's cliffs, this contemporary glass-and-marble oblong of a gallery stands in stark contrast to the fortress. The gallery shows first-rate temporary exhibitions of 20th- and 21st-century art. The works of Gerhard Richter, Max Ernst and Hiroshi Sugimoto have previously featured. The **Mönchsberg Lift** (Gstättengasse 13; return €1.70, incl gallery ticket €2.90; ⊙8am-7pm Thu-Tue, to 9pm Wed) whizzes up to the gallery year-round.

While you're up here, take in the far-reaching views over Salzburg over coffee or lunch at M32. Also take in the nearby **art installations** such as Mario Merz' neon-lit *Numbers in the Woods* and James Turrell's elliptical *Sky Space;* both are best seen at dusk.

Mozarts Geburtshaus
MUSEUM

(Mozart's Birthplace; www.mozarteum.at; Getreidegasse 9; adult/child/family €7/2.50/16.50; ⊙9am-5.30pm) Wolfgang Amadeus Mozart, Salzburg's most famous son, was born in this bright yellow townhouse in 1756 and spent the first 17 years of his life here. Today's museum harbours a collection of instruments, documents and portraits. Highlights include the mini-violin he played as a toddler, plus a lock of his hair and buttons from his jacket. In one room, Mozart is shown as a holy babe beneath a neon blue halo – we'll leave you to draw your own analogies...

Mozart-Wohnhaus
MUSEUM

(Mozart's Residence; www.mozarteum.at; Makartplatz 8; adult/child/family €7/2.50/16.50; ⊙9am-5.30pm) Tired of the cramped living conditions on Getreidegasse, the Mozart family moved to this more spacious abode

---

DON'T MISS

THE ROOT OF THE PROBLEM

While exploring Festung Hohensalzburg, keep your eyes peeled for turnips – there are 58 in total. Rumour has it that Prince-Archbishop Leonard von Keutschach was a spendthrift, so his miserly uncle flung a turnip at his head to (literally) knock some sense into him. Ironically the turnip became a symbol for Leonard's new-found wisdom and features prominently on the family coat of arms.

Salzburg

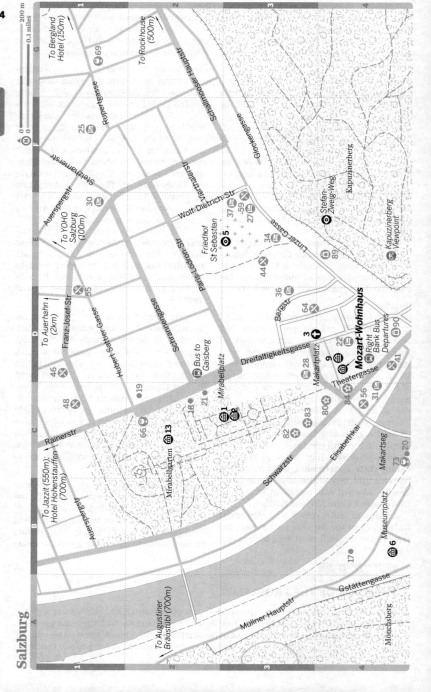

0 200 m
0 0.1 miles

To Bergland Hotel (150m)

69

To Rockhouse (500m)

Rupertgasse

25

Stelzhamerstr

To YOHO Salzburg (100m)

Auerspergstr

30

Wolf-Dietrich-Str

37

59

27

34

Linzer Gasse

Glockengasse

Stefan-Zweig-Weg

Kapuzinerberg

89

Kapuzinerberg Viewpoint

5

Friedhof St Sebastian

Paris-Lodron-Str

Schrannengasse

55

44

36

Bergstr

64

Mozart-Wohnhaus

3

22

Right Bank Bus Departures

90

Franz-Josef-Str

Hubert Sattler Gasse

To Auerhahn (2km)

46

Bus to Gaisberg

Dreifaltigkeitsgasse

Makartplatz

28

9

Theatergasse

41

56

31

48

19

18

21

1

2

66

13

Mirabellplatz

Mirabellgarten

83

80

34

82

Schwarzstr

Elisabethkai

Makartsteg

73

20

Rainerstr

To Jazzit (550m); Hotel Hohenstauffen (700m)

Auerspergstr

To Augustiner Bräustübl (700m)

Müllner Hauptstr

17

6

Museumplatz

Gstättengasse

Mönchsberg

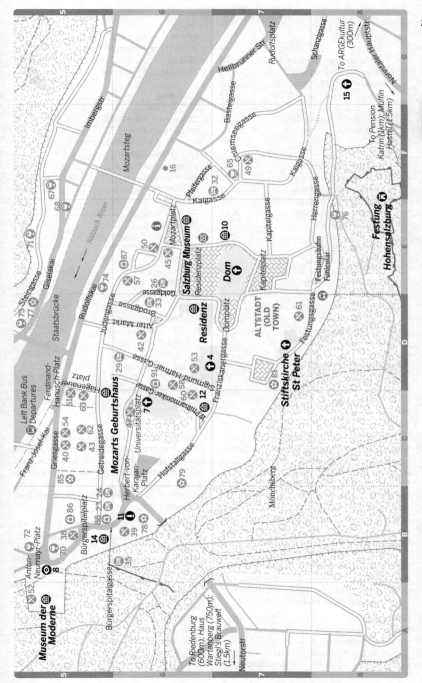

To ARGEkultur (300m)

To Pension Katrin (1km); Muffin Hostel (1.5km)

Festung Hohensalzburg

15

Nonnberg Hauptstr

Schanzlgasse

Rudolfsplatz

Hellbrunner Str

Bastergasse

Kaigasse

Pfeifergasse

16

65 Chiemseegasse

49

32

Herrengasse

Kaigasse

6

76

Festungsbahn Funicular

Kapitelgasse

Kapitelplatz

Mozartsteg

Imbergstr

Mozartplatz

Salzburg Museum

10

Dom

Residenzplatz

ALTSTADT (OLD TOWN)

61

Festungsgasse

i

50

45

87

57

26

33 Goldgasse

Residenz

Domplatz

Steingasse

75

77

67

68

71

Giselakai

Sulzach River

Staatsbrücke

Rudolfskai

74

Judengasse

Brodgasse

Alter Markt

42

29

53

4

91

Franziskanergasse

Sigmund-Haffner-Gasse

60

58

12

Stiftskirche St Peter

83

81

Mönchsberg

79

Hofstallgasse

7

W Philharmonikergasse

Universitätsplatz

Herbert-von-Karajan-Platz

Mozarts Geburtshaus

Hagenauerplatz

Ferdinand-Hanusch-Platz

Left Bank Bus Departures

Franz-Josef-Kai

Griesgasse

Getreidegasse

51

63

85

40

54

43 62

Anton-Neumayr-Platz

Museum der Moderne

52

72

70

38

86

88

24

21

Bürgerspitalplatz

14

11

35

39

78

8

Bürgerspitalgasse

To Riedenburg (600m); Haus Wartenberg (750m); Stiegl's Brauwelt (1.5km)

Neutorstr

in 1773, where a prolific Mozart composed works such as the *Shepherd King* (K208) and *Idomeneo* (K366). Emanuel Schikaneder, a close friend of Mozart and the librettist of *The Magic Flute,* was a regular guest here. An audio guide accompanies your visit, serenading you with opera excerpts. Alongside family portraits and documents, you'll find Mozart's original fortepiano.

Under the same roof is the free **Mozart Ton-und Filmmuseum** (⊙9am-1pm Mon, Tue & Fri, 1-5pm Wed & Thu), a film and music archive of interest to the ultra-enthusiast, with some 25,000 audiovisual recordings.

Residenzplatz   HISTORIC SITE
With its horse-drawn carriages, palace and street entertainers, this stately baroque square is the Salzburg of a thousand postcards. Its centrepiece is the **Residenzbrunnen**, an enormous marble fountain ringed by four water-spouting horses and topped by a conch shell–bearing Triton. The plaza is the late-16th-century vision of Prince-Archbishop Wolf Dietrich von Raitenau who, inspired by Rome, enlisted Italian architect Vincenzo Scamozzi.

Stiftskirche St Peter   CHURCH
(St Peter's Abbey Church; St Peter Bezirk 1-2; ⊙8.30am-noon & 2.30-6.30pm) A Frankish missionary named Rupert founded this abbey church and monastery in around 700, making it the oldest in the German-speaking world. Though a vaulted Romanesque portal remains, today's church is overwhelmingly baroque, with rococo stucco, statues – including one of archangel Michael shoving a crucifix through the throat of a goaty demon – and striking altar paintings by Martin Johann Schmidt.

Take a stroll around the **cemetery** (☺6.30am-7pm), where the graves are mini works of art with their intricate stonework and filigree crosses. Composer Michael Haydn (1737–1806), opera singer Richard Mayr (1877–1935) and renowned Salzburg confectioner Paul Fürst (1856–1941) lie buried here; the last is watched over by skull-bearing cherubs.

The cemetery is home to the **catacombs** (adult/child €1/0.60; ☺10.30am-5pm Tue-Sun), cavelike chapels and crypts hewn out of the Mönchsberg cliff face.

Schloss Mirabell   PALACE, GARDEN
(☺dawn-dusk) Prince-Archbishop Wolf Dietrich built this splendid palace in 1606 to impress his beloved mistress Salome Alt. It must have done the trick because she went on to bear the archbishop some 15 children; sources disagree on the exact number – poor Wolf was presumably too distracted by spiritual matters to keep count himself. Johann Lukas von Hildebrandt, of Schloss Belvedere fame, remodelled the palace in baroque style in 1721. The only way to see the interior is by attending an evening concert in the sublime **Marmorsaal** (Marble Hall).

It's free to visit the manicured **Mirabellgarten** (Mirabell Gardens). The flowery parterres, rose gardens and leafy arbours are less overrun first thing in the morning and early evening. The lithe *Tänzerin* (dancer) sculpture is a great spot to photograph the gardens with the fortress as a backdrop. *Sound of Music* fans will of course recognise the Pegasus statue, the steps and the gnomes of the **Zwerglgarten** (Dwarf Garden), where the mini von Trapps practised 'Do-Re-Mi'.

Rupertinum   ART GALLERY
(www.museumdermoderne.at, in German; Wiener-Philharmoniker-Gasse 9; adult/child/family €6/4/8; ☺10am-6pm Tue & Thu-Sun, to 8pm Wed) In the

ℹ SALZBURG CARD

If you're planning on doing lots of sight-seeing, save by buying the **Salzburg Card** (1-/2-/3-day card €25/33/38). The card gets you entry to all of the major sights and attractions, a free river cruise, unlimited use of public transport (including cable cars) plus numerous discounts on tours and events. The card is half-price for children and €3 cheaper in the low season.

heart of the *Altstadt*, the Rupertinum is the sister gallery of the Museum der Moderne and is devoted to rotating exhibitions of modern art. There is a strong emphasis on graphic works and photography.

Friedhof St Sebastian   CEMETERY
(Nonnberggasse 2; ⊙7am-dusk) Tucked behind the baroque **Sebastianskirche** (St Sebastian's Church), this peaceful cemetery and its cloisters were designed by Andrea Berteleto in Italianate style in 1600. Mozart family members and well-known 16th-century physician Paracelsus are buried here, but out-pomping them all is Prince-Archbishop Wolf Dietrich von Raitenau's mosaic-tiled mausoleum, an elaborate memorial to himself.

Stift Nonnberg   CHURCH
(Nonnberg Convent; Nonnberggasse 2; ⊙7am-dusk) A short climb up the Nonnbergstiege staircase from Kaigasse or along Festungsgasse brings you to this Benedictine convent, founded 1300 years ago and made famous as *the* nunnery in *The Sound of Music*. You can visit the beautiful rib-vaulted church, but the rest of the convent is off-limits.

Steingasse   HISTORIC SITE
On the right bank of the Salzach River, this narrow, cobbled lane was, incredibly, the main trade route to Italy in medieval times. Look out for the 13th-century **Steintor** gate and the house of **Joseph Mohr**, who wrote the lyrics to that all-time classic of a carol 'Silent Night'. The street is at its most photogenic in the late morning when sunlight illuminates its pastel-coloured townhouses.

Kollegienkirche   CHURCH
(Universitätsplatz; ⊙8am-6pm) Johann Bernhard Fischer von Erlach's grandest baroque design is this late-17th-century university church, with a striking bowed facade. The high altar's columns symbolise the Seven Pillars of Wisdom.

Pferdeschwemme   LANDMARK
(Horse Trough; Herbert-von-Karajan-Platz) Designed by Fischer von Erlach in 1693, this is a horse-lover's delight, with rearing equine pin-ups surrounding Michael Bernhard Mandl's statue of a horse tamer.

Franziskanerkirche   CHURCH
(Franziskanergasse 5; ⊙6.30am-7.30pm) A real architectural hotchpotch, Salzburg's Franciscan church has a Romanesque nave, a Gothic choir with rib vaulting and a baroque marble altar (another of Fischer von Erlach's creations).

Dreifältigkeitskirche   CHURCH
(Church of the Holy Trinity; Dreifaltigkeitsgasse 14; ⊙6.30am-6.30pm) Baroque master Johann Bernhard Fischer von Erlach designed this graceful right-bank church, famous for Johann Michael Rottmayr's dome fresco of the Holy Trinity.

Baroque Museum   MUSEUM
(Mirabellplatz 3; adult/child €4.50/free; ⊙10am-5pm Wed-Sun) Worthwhile baroque art collection, including sketches, paintings and designs from the likes of Rubens, Paul Troger and Johann Michael Rottmayr.

🏃 Activities

Salzburg's rival mountains are 540m Mönchsberg and 640m Kapuzinerberg – Julie Andrews and locals used to bigger things call them 'hills'. Both are thickly wooded and criss-crossed by walking trails, with photogenic views of the *Altstadt* on the right bank and left bank respectively.

There's also an extensive network of cycling routes to explore: from a gentle 20-minute trundle along the Salzach River to Hellbrunn, to the highly scenic 450km Mozart Radweg through Salzburgerland and Bavaria.

👉 Tours

Both the horse-drawn carriages *(Fiaker)* and the colourful rickshaws that pull up in front of Residenz will take you on a guided tour of the *Altstadt;* prices depend on your itinerary.

One-hour guided tours (in German and English; €9) of the historic centre depart daily at 12.15pm and 2pm from Mozartplatz. If you'd rather go it alone, borrow an iGuide from the tourist office for two hours (€7.50) to take in the sights at your own speed.

Fräulein Maria's Bicycle Tours   BICYCLE TOURS
(www.mariasbicycletours.com; adult/child €24/15; ⊙9.30am May-Sep) Maria looked a little

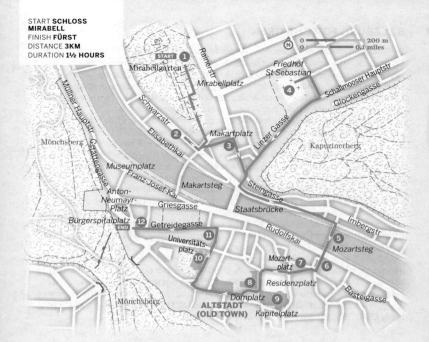

START **SCHLOSS MIRABELL**
FINISH **FÜRST**
DISTANCE **3KM**
DURATION **1½ HOURS**

Walking Tour
In Mozart's Footsteps

❯ Mozart was the ultimate musical prodigy: he identified a pig's squeal as G sharp aged two, began to compose when he was five and first performed for Empress Maria Theresia at the age of six. When not writing music, he is said to have enjoyed heavy drinking sessions and teaching his pet starling to sing operettas (one presumably led to the other). Follow in his footsteps on this classic walking tour.

Begin at baroque **1** **Schloss Mirabell**, where the exquisite *Marmorsaal* is often the backdrop for chamber concerts of Mozart's music. Stroll south through the fountain-dotted gardens, passing the strikingly angular **2** **Mozarteum**, a foundation honouring Mozart's life and works, and the host of the renowned Mozartwoche festival in January. Just around the corner on Makartplatz is the 17th-century **3** **Mozart-Wohnhaus**, where you can see how the Mozart family lived and listen to rare recordings of Mozart's symphonies at the **Mozart Ton-und Filmmuseum**. Amble north along Linzer Gasse to **4** **Friedhof St Sebastian**, the atmospheric cemetery where Wolfgang's father Leopold and wife Constanze lie buried. Now retrace your steps towards the Salzach River, turning left onto medieval Steingasse and crossing the art-nouveau **5** **Mozartsteg** (Mozart Bridge). Look out for the **6** **memorial plaque** at No 8, the house where Mozart's beloved Constanze died, as you approach **7** **Mozartplatz**. On this elegant square, Mozart is literally and metaphorically put on a pedestal. Across the way is the grand **8** **Residenz** palace where Mozart gave his first court concert at the ripe old age of six. Beside it rests the baroque **9** **Dom**, where Mozart's parents were married in 1747 and little Mozart was baptised in 1756. Mozart later composed sacred music here and was cathedral organist. Follow Franziskanergasse to reach the **10** **Kollegienkirche** on Universitätsplatz, where Mozart's D Minor Mass, K65, premiered in 1769. On parallel Getreidegasse, stop to contemplate the birthplace of a genius at **11** **Mozarts Geburtshaus** and buy some of **12** **Fürst**'s famous chocolate *Mozartkugeln* (Mozart balls).

SALZBURG FOR CHILDREN

With dancing marionettes, chocolate galore and a *big* fairy-tale-like fortress, Salzburg is kid nirvana. If the crowds prove unbearable with tots in tow, take them to the city's adventure **playgrounds** (there are 80 to pick from); the one on Franz-Josef-Kai is a central choice. In summer, children love to race down the slides at Austria's largest outdoor pool, **Leopoldskron** (Leopoldskronstrasse 50; adult/child €4.10/2.10; ⊙9am-7pm May-Sep), just 1km south of the centre (take bus 21 or 22 to Nussdorferstrasse).

Salzburg's sights are usually half-price for children and most are free for under-six-year-olds. Many galleries, museums and theatres also have dedicated programs for kids and families. These include the **Museum der Moderne**, which has Sunday art workshops for children (€2), and the matinée performances at the enchanting **Salzburger Marionettentheater**. The **Salzburg Museum** has lots of hands-on displays, from glockenspiel-ringing to puzzles and a kids-only Biedermeier room.

Kids will love the **Haus der Natur** (www.hausdernatur.at; Museumsplatz 5; adult/child €6/4; ⊙9am-5pm), comprising an interactive science museum, a reptile enclosure teeming with snakes and crocs, and an impressive aquarium with Nemo-style clownfish and coral reefs. Shark-feeding time is 10.30am on Mondays and Thursdays. The nostalgic **Spielzeugmuseum** (Toy Museum; Bürgerspitalgasse 2; adult/child €1/3; ⊙9am-5pm Tue-Sun) nearby puts on a Punch and Judy show at 3pm on Tuesdays and Wednesdays.

Outside Salzburg, near Untersberg, the open-air **Freilichtmuseum** (www.freilicht museum.com; Hasenweg; adult/child/family €8.50/4/17; ⊙9am-6pm Tue-Sun late Mar-Oct) harbours 70 archetypal Austrian farmhouses and has tractors to clamber over, goats to feed and a huge adventure playground. Kids can come face to face with lions, flamingos and alpine ibex at **Salzburg Zoo** (www.salzburg-zoo.at; Anifer Landesstrasse 1; adult/child/family €9/4/20.50; ⊙9am-5pm) near Schloss Hellbrunn.

subdued the last time we saw her, but these freewheeling bike tours, taking in the main *Sound of Music* locations, are usually pretty jovial. No advance booking is necessary; just turn up at the meeting point on Mirabellplatz.

Salzburg Schifffahrt RIVER CRUISES
(www.salzburgschifffahrt.at; adult/child €13/7; ⊙Apr-Oct) A boat ride along the Salzach is a leisurely way to pick out Salzburg's sights. Hour-long cruises depart from Makartsteg bridge, with some of them chugging on to Schloss Hellbrunn (adult/child €16/10, not including entry to the palace).

Stiegl's Brauwelt BREWERY
(www.stiegl.at; Bräuhausstrasse 9; adult/child €9/4; ⊙10am-5pm) Brewing and bottling since 1492, Stiegl is Austria's largest private brewery. A tour takes in the different stages of the brewing process and (woohoo!) the world's tallest beer tower. A free Stiegl beer and pretzel are thrown in for the price of a ticket. The brewery is 1.5km southwest of the *Altstadt*; take bus 1 or 8 to Bräuhausstrasse.

Bob's Special Tours COACH TOURS
(☑84 95 11; www.bobstours.com; Rudolfskai 38; ⊙office 10am-3pm Mon-Fri, noon-2pm Sat & Sun) Minibus tours to *Sound of Music* locations

(€40), the Bavarian Alps (€40) and Grossglockner (€80). Prices include a free hotel pick-up for morning tours starting at 9am. Reservations essential.

Salzburg Panorama Tours COACH TOURS
(☑87 40 29; www.panoramatours.com; Mirabellplatz; ⊙office 8am-6pm) Boasts the 'original *Sound of Music* Tour' (€37) as well as a huge range of others, including city tours, Mozart tours and excursions to the Bavarian Alps.

Salzburg Sightseeing Tours COACH TOURS
(☑88 16 16; www.salzburg-sightseeingtours. at; Mirabellplatz 2; ⊙office 8am-6pm) Sells a 24-hour ticket (adult/child €20/7) for a multilingual hop-on hop-off bus tour of the city's key sights and *Sound of Music* locations.

✹ Festivals & Events

Mozartwoche MUSIC FESTIVAL
(Mozart Week; www.mozarteum.at) World-renowned orchestras, conductors and soloists celebrate Mozart's birthday with a feast of his music in late January.

Osterfestspiele MUSIC FESTIVAL
(Easter Festival; www.osterfestspiele-salzburg.at) This springtime classical-music shindig

draws the Berliner Philharmonic, under Sir Simon Rattle's sprightly baton, to the Festspielhaus in March/April.

SommerSzene CULTURAL FESTIVAL
(www.sommerszene.net) Boundary-crossing performing arts are the focus of this event in July.

Jazz & the City JAZZ FESTIVAL
(www.salzburgjazz.com, in German) Salzburg gets its groove on at some 100 free concerts in the *Altstadt* in late October.

Christkindlmarkt CHRISTMAS MARKET
(www.christkindlmarkt.co.at) Salzburg is at its storybook best during Advent, when Christmas markets bring festive sparkle to Domplatz and Residenzplatz.

🛏 Sleeping

Salzburg's accommodation is pricey by Austrian standards, but you can get a good deal if you're willing to go the extra mile or two. Ask the tourist office for a list of private rooms and pensions. Medieval guesthouses oozing history, avant-garde design hotels with river

views and chilled-out hostels all huddle in the *Altstadt,* where booking ahead is advisable.

Bear in mind that the high-season prices below are jacked up another 10% to 20% during the Salzburg Festival. If Salzburg is booked solid, consider staying in Hallein or just across the border in Bavaria.

TOP CHOICE **Haus Reichl** PENSION €
(☎82 62 48; www.privatzimmer.at; Reiterweg 52; s €30-35, d 48-52, tr €66-72; P♿) The welcome couldn't be more genuine at this superb little pension, surrounded by meadows and mountains. Nothing is too much trouble for the kindly Reichls – a pick-up from the station, free bicycle hire, sightseeing tips, you name it. Buttery smells drift from the kitchen, where Frau Reichl uses home-grown fruit in the delicious pastries and jams served at breakfast. Bus 21 often trundles into the *Altstadt,* 5km away.

Arte Vida GUESTHOUSE €€
(☎87 31 85; www.artevida.at; Dreifaltigkeitsgasse 9; s €50-110, d €70-120; ♿🛜) Arte Vida has the boho-chic feel of a Marrakech riad, with its

---

DON'T MISS

DIY SOUND OF MUSIC TOUR

Do a Julie with a yodel-ee-hee-hee self-guided tour of *The Sound of Music* film locations. OK, let's start at the very beginning:

» **The hills are alive** Cut! Make that *proper* mountains. The opening scenes were filmed around the jewel-coloured Salzkammergut lakes. Maria makes her twirling entrance on alpine pastures just across the border in Bavaria.

» **A problem like Maria** Nuns waltzing on their way to mass at Benedictine Stift Nonnberg is fiction, but it's fact that the real Maria von Trapp intended to become a nun here before romance struck.

» **Have confidence** Residenzplatz is where Maria belts out 'I Have Confidence' and playfully splashes the spouting horses of the Residenzbrunnen fountain.

» **So long, farewell** The grand rococo palace of Schloss Leopoldskron, a 15-minute walk from Festung Hohensalzburg, is where the lake scene was filmed. Its Venetian Room was the blueprint for the Trapp's lavish ballroom, where the children bid their farewells.

» **Do-Re-Mi** Oh the Pegasus fountain, the steps with fortress views, the gnomes...the Mirabellgarten might inspire a rendition of 'Do-Re-Mi', especially if there's a drop of golden sun.

» **Sixteen going on seventeen** The loved-up pavilion of the century hides out in Hellbrunn Park, where you can act out those 'oh Liesl', 'oh Rolf' fantasies.

» **Edelweiss and adieu** The Felsenreitschule (Summer Riding School) is the dramatic backdrop for the Salzburg Festival in the movie, where the Trapp Family Singers win the audience over with 'Edelweiss' and give the Nazis the slip with 'So Long, Farewell'.

» **Climb every mountain** To, erm, Switzerland. Or content yourself with alpine views from Untersberg, which appears briefly at the end of the movie when the family flees the country.

DON'T MISS

FESTIVAL TIME

In 1920, dream trio Hugo von Hofmannsthal, Max Reinhardt and Richard Strauss combined creative forces and the Salzburg Festival (www.salzburgfestival.at) was born. Now, as then, one of the highlights is the staging of Hofmannsthal's morality play *Jedermann* (Everyman) on Domplatz. A trilogy of opera, drama and classical concerts of the highest calibre have since propelled the five-week summer festival to international renown, attracting some of the world's best conductors, directors, orchestras and singers.

Come festival time, late July and August, Salzburg crackles with excitement, as a quarter of a million visitors descend on the city for some 200 productions. Theatre premieres, avant-garde works and the summer-resident Vienna Philharmonic performing Mozart works are all in the mix. The Festival District on Hofstallgasse has a spectacular backdrop, framed by Mönchsberg's cliffs. Most performances are held in the cavernous **Grosses Festspielhaus** accommodating 2179 theatre-goers, the **Haus für Mozart** in the former royal stables and the baroque **Felsenreitschule**.

If you're planning on visiting during the festival, don't leave *anything* to chance – book your flights, hotel and tickets months in advance. Sometimes last-minute tickets are available at the ticket office (📞80 45-500; info@salzburgfestival.at; Herbert-von-Karajan-Platz 11; ⏰10am-6pm during the festival), but they're like gold dust. Ticket prices range from €5 to €370.

lantern-lit salon, communal kitchen and serene garden. Inspired by his travels in Asia and Africa, Markus has brought the rich colours, fabrics and art of those distant lands to individually designed rooms, all with DVD players and iPod docks. He gives invaluable tips on Salzburg, and arranges yoga sessions and outdoor activities.

Haus Wartenberg PENSION €€
(📞84 84 00; www.hauswartenberg.com; Riedenburgerstrasse 2; s/d €65/95; P@) This welcoming family-run pension is just a 15-minute stroll southwest of the *Altstadt*. It's set in vine-strewn gardens and housed in a gorgeous 17th-century chalet full of creaky floors and family heirlooms. The chunky pinewood and florals in the country-style rooms are in keeping with the character of the place. Take bus 1, 4 or 5 to Moosstrasse.

Hotel am Dom HOTEL €€
(📞842 765; www.hotelamdom.at; Goldgasse 17; s €90-180, d €140-260; ❄@🌐) Antique meets boutique at this *Altstadt* hotel, where the original vaults and beams of the 800-year-old building contrast with razor-sharp design features. Artworks inspired by the musical legends of the Salzburg Festival grace the rooms, which sport caramel-champagne colour schemes, funky lighting, velvet throws and ultra-glam bathrooms.

Hotel & Villa Auersperg HOTEL €€
(📞88 94 40; www.auersperg.at; Auerspergstrasse 61; s €109-139, d €145-188, ste 205; P@🌐🏠)

This charismatic villa and hotel duo fuse late-19th-century flair with contemporary design. Guests can relax by the lily pond in the vine-strewn garden or in the rooftop wellness area with a sauna, tea bar and mountain views. Free bike hire is a bonus.

Hotel Schloss Mönchstein HOTEL €€€
(📞84 85 55-0; www.monchstein.at; Mönchsberg Park 26; d €335-445, ste €595-1450; P❄❄🌐) On a fairy-tale perch atop Mönchsberg and set in hectares of wooded grounds, this 16th-century castle is honeymoon (and second mortgage) material. Persian rugs, oil paintings and Calcutta marble finish the rooms to beautiful effect. A massage in the spa, a candlelit tower dinner for two with Salzburg views, a helicopter ride – just say the word.

Wolf Dietrich HOTEL €€
(📞87 12 75; www.salzburg-hotel.at; Wolf-Dietrich-Strasse 7; s/d/f €130/190/255; P❄@🌊) For old-fashioned elegance you can't beat this central hotel, where rooms are dressed in polished wood furnishings and floral fabrics. There's even a suite based on Mozart's *Magic Flute,* with a star-studded ceiling and freestanding bath-tub. By contrast, the spa and indoor pool are ultramodern. Organic produce is served at breakfast.

Weisse Taube HISTORIC HOTEL €€
(📞84 24 04; www.weissetaube.at; Kaigasse 9; s €85-98, d €135-148; 🌐) Housed in a listed 14th-century building in a quiet corner

of the *Altstadt*, the 'white dove' is a solid choice. Staff go out of their way to help and the warm-coloured rooms are large and well kept (some have fortress views). Breakfast is a generous spread.

YOHO Salzburg
HOSTEL €

(☑87 96 49; www.yoho.at; Paracelsusstrasse 9; dm €19-21, d €50; ☺@🛜) This fun-loving hostel has got it sussed. Free wi-fi, secure lockers, comfy bunks, plenty of cheap beer and good-value schnitzels – what more could a backpacker ask for? Except, perhaps, a merry sing-along with *The Sound of Music* screened at 10.30am daily (yes, *every* day). The friendly crew can arrange tours, adventure sports like rafting and canyoning and bike hire.

Pension Katrin
PENSION €€

(☑83 08 60; www.pensionkatrin.at; Nonntaler Hauptstrasse 49b; s/d €58/99; P☺🛜) With its flowery garden, bright and cheerful rooms and homemade cakes at breakfast, this pension is one of the homiest in Salzburg. The affable Terler family keep everything spick and span. Be prepared to lug your bags as there's no lift. The pension is 1km south of the *Altstadt;* take bus 5 to Wäschergasse.

Arthotel Blaue Gans
HOTEL €€

(☑84 24 91-50; www.hotel-blaue-gans-salzburg.at; Getreidegasse 43; s €119-139, d €139-199; ☺✳🛜) Contemporary design blends harmoniously with the original vaulting and beams of this 650-year-old hotel. Rooms are pure and simple, with clean lines, lots of white and streamlined furnishings. The restaurant is well worth a visit.

Hotel Elefant
HOTEL €€

(☑84 33 97; www.bestwestern.at/elefant; Sigmund-Haffner-Gasse 4; s €95, d €130-150; ☺✳🛜) Occupying a 700-year-old building and run by the good-natured Mayr family, this central Best Western hotel has loads of charm. Bright colours add a modern touch to the spacious, elegantly furnished rooms. A generous breakfast is available.

Hotel Sacher
HOTEL €€€

(☑88 97 70; www.sacher.com; Schwarzstrasse 5-7; s €325, d €385-625; P☺✳@🛜) Tom Hanks, the Dalai Lama and Julie Andrews have all stayed at this 19th-century pile on the banks of the Salzach. Scattered with oil paintings and antiques, the rooms have gleaming marble bathrooms, and fortress or river views. Compensate for indulging on chocolate *Sacher Torte* in the health club.

Hotel Mozart
HISTORIC HOTEL €€

(☑87 22 74; www.hotel-mozart.at; Franz-Josef-Strasse 27; s/d/tr/q €95/140/160/180; P☺🛜🛏) An antique-filled lobby gives way to spotless rooms with comfy beds and sizeable bathrooms at the Mozart. You'll have to fork out an extra €10 for breakfast, but it's a good spread with fresh fruit, boiled eggs, cold cuts and pastries.

Goldener Hirsch
HOTEL €€€

(☑80 84-0; www.goldenerhirschsalzburg.com; Getreidegasse 37; s €204-376, d €274-538; P☺✳@🛜) A skylight illuminates the arcaded inner courtyard of this 600-year-old *Altstadt* pile, where famous past guests include Queen Elizabeth and Pavarotti. Countess Harriet Walderdorff tastefully scattered the opulent rooms with objets d'art and

---

DON'T MISS

NO TOURIST TRAPP

Did you know that there were 10, not seven Trapp children, the eldest of whom was Rupert (so long Liesl)? Or that the captain was a gentle, family-loving man and Maria no soft touch? Or, perhaps, that in 1938 the Trapp family left quietly for the United States instead of climbing every mountain to Switzerland? For the truth behind the Hollywood legend, stay the night at **Villa Trapp** (☑63 08 60; www.villa-trapp.com; Traunstrasse 34; d €109-500; ☺), tucked away in Salzburg's biggest private park in the Aigen district, 3km east of the *Altstadt*.

Marianne and Christopher have transformed the original von Trapp family home into a beautiful guesthouse (for guests only, we might add). The 19th-century villa is elegant, if not as palatial as in the movie, with tasteful wood-floored rooms and a balustrade for sweeping down á la Baroness Schräder. Family snapshots and heirlooms, including the baron's model ships and a photo of guest Pink Floyd guitarist David Gilmour strumming 'Edelweiss', grace the dining room. From the main station, take a train or bus 160 to Aigen.

hand-printed fabrics. Downstairs are two restaurants: beamed s'Herzl and vaulted Restaurant Goldener Hirsch.

Bergland Hotel
HOTEL €€

(☑87 23 18; www.berglandhotel.at; Rupertgasse 15; s €68, d €90-108, tr €125; P🅿😊🛜) Don't be fooled by the nondescript exterior. In the Kuhn family since 1912, the Bergland is ever so homely inside, with art (courtesy of the owner) on the walls, touches like traditional Austrian hats and painted furnishings in the rooms, and a handsome piano room.

Hotel Amadeus
HISTORIC HOTEL €€

(☑87 14 01; www.hotelamadeus.at; Linzer Gasse 43-45; s/d €92/180; 😊🛜) Centrally situated on the right bank, this 500-year-old hotel has a boutique feel, with bespoke touches such as chandeliers and four-poster beds in the vibrantly coloured rooms. Guests are treated to free afternoon tea.

Hotel Bristol
HOTEL €€€

(☑87 35 57; www.bristol-salzburg.at; Makartplatz 4; s/d/ste €289/340/581; P🅿😊❄🛜) The Bristol transports you back to a more decadent era. Chandelier-lit salons, champagne at breakfast, exquisitely crafted furniture, service as polished as the marble – this is pure class. Even Emperor Franz Josef and Sigmund Freud felt at home here.

Hotel Hohenstauffen
HOTEL €€

(☑87 21 93; www.hotel-hohenstauffen.at; Elisabethstrasse 19; s/d €90/140; P🅿😊@) Granted, it's not in the nicest part of town (erotica shops and all), but don't be put off. This genuinely friendly family-run place has comfy old-style rooms and is geared up for cyclists, as the bicycle bell at reception confirms.

Hotel Wolf
HISTORIC HOTEL €€

(☑84 34 53-0; www.hotelwolf.com; Kaigasse 7; s €80-120, d €110-210;@) Tucked in a quiet corner of the *Altstadt*, Hotel Wolf occupies a lovingly converted 15th-century building. Uneven stone staircases and antique furnishings are a nod to its past, while the light, parquet-floored rooms range from modern to rustic.

Hotel Zur Goldenen Ente
HISTORIC HOTEL €€

(☑84 56 22; www.ente.at; Goldgasse 10; s/d/apt €85/160/280; 😊❄@) Bang in the heart of the *Altstadt*, this 700-year-old townhouse has oodles of charm – some rooms have four-poster beds, while Emperor Franz Josef guards over others. The sunny terrace overlooks the rooftops of the old town.

Muffin Hostel
HOSTEL €

(☑0664-63 67 635; www.salzburghostel.com; Hegigasse 9; 3-bed dm €22-26, d €52-70; P🅿😊@) This summer-only hostel is 15 minutes' walk from the centre. Affable staff, neat-and-tidy dorms, bike hire, a communal kitchen and a volleyball court in the garden make it a fine budget choice. From the train station, take bus 1 to Moosstrasse and walk five minutes. The hostel is open from mid-July to early September.

Camping Schloss Aigen
CAMPGROUND €

(☑62 20 79; www.campingparadies.at; Weberbartlweg 20; camp sites per adult/child/tent €5/3/4.60; �8May-Sep; 🐾) Overlooking meadows and Gaisberg mountain, this tree-shaded campground has a playground, minimarket, laundry and restaurant. The campground is 5km east of the *Altstadt;* you can cycle into town or take bus 7 from the stop 700m away.

Stadtalm
HOSTEL €

(☑84 17 29; www.diestadtalm.com; dm €19) A recently revamped hostel atop Mönchsberg, where the big draw is the incredible view over Salzburg. There's a good-value restaurant on-site.

Trumer Stube
PENSION €€

(☑87 47 76; www.trumer-stube.at; Bergstrasse 6; s €56-89, d €89-103; 😊@) Marianne runs this charming little pension. Rooms are borderline twee (think pastels, ruching and floral fabrics) but immaculate and homey.

Institut St Sebastian
GUESTHOUSE €

(☑87 13 86; Linzer Gasse 41; www.st-sebastian-salzburg.at; dm/s/d €21/42/67; 🛜) A peaceful guesthouse behind Sebastianskirche with monastic charm. Vaulted corridors lead to well-kept dorms and rooms. Ring the bell if reception is unstaffed.

✗ Eating

Salzburg's eclectic dining scene skips from the traditional to the super-trendy to the downright touristy. This is a city where schnitzel is served with a slice of history in vaulted taverns, where you can dine in Michelin-starred finery or be serenaded by a warbling Maria wannabe. Save euros by taking advantage of the lunchtime *Tagesmenü* (fixed menu) served at most places.

⬛TOP CHOICE Alter Fuchs
AUSTRIAN €

(☑88 20 22; Linzer Gasse 47-49; mains €9-16; �8Mon-Sat; 🍴🐾) This sly old fox prides itself on witty service and old-fashioned Austrian fare – both rarities in the *Altstadt*.

Go for a schnitzel fried to golden perfection or pumpkin seed–coated cordon bleu. Bandana-clad foxes guard the bar in the vaulted interior and there's a courtyard for good-weather dining. In the cosy *Stube* out back, scribbling on the walls (chalk only, please) is positively encouraged.

Afro Café
AFRICAN €€

(☎84 48 88; www.afrocoffee.com; Bürgerspitalplatz 5; lunch €6.90, mains €10-14; ⊙10am-midnight Mon-Sat; ➋) Hot-pink walls, butterfly chairs, artworks made from beach junk and *big* hair...this afro-chic cafe is totally groovy. Staff keep the good vibes and food coming – think grilled chicken with honey-lime glaze and barracuda with couscous. See the website for events from afro beats to speed dating.

Riedenburg
AUSTRIAN €€€

(☎83 08 15; www.riedenburg.at, in German; Neutorstrasse 31; lunch €18, mains €26-35; ⊙Tue-Sat; ➋) Richard Brunnauer serves art on a plate at this Michelin-starred restaurant, with a romantic garden pavilion. His creative Austrian signatures, such as venison and guinea fowl crêpes with wild herbs, are expertly matched with top wines. The €18 lunch is a bargain. Riedenburg is a 10-minute walk southwest of the *Altstadt* along Neutorstrasse; take bus 1, 4 or 5 to Moosstrasse.

zum Fidelen Affen
AUSTRIAN €€

(☎87 73 61; Priesterhausgasse 8; mains €10.50-16.50; ⊙dinner Mon-Sat) The jovial monkey lives up to its name with a sociable vibe. Presuming you've booked ahead, you'll dine heartily under vaults or on the terrace on well-prepared Austrian classics like goulash, *Schlutzkrapfen* (Tyrolean ravioli) and sweet curd dumplings.

M32
FUSION €€

(☎84 10 00; www.m32.at, in German; Mönchsberg 32; mains €14-26; ⊙9am-1am Tue-Sun; ➏➍) Bold colours and a veritable forest of stag antlers reveal architect Matteo Thun's imprint at Museum der Moderne's ultra-sleek restaurant. The seasonal food is superb – think fragrant orange-fennel soup and tortellini of organic local beef on pumpkin purée. Whether in the glass-walled restaurant or on the terrace, the view of Salzburg's skyline is remarkable.

Wilder Mann
AUSTRIAN €€

(☎84 17 87; Getreidegasse 20; mains €9-12.50; ⊙Mon-Sat) *Dirndl*-clad waitresses bring goulash with dumplings, schnitzels and other light and airy fare to the table at this old-world Austrian tavern in the *Altstadt*.

Ikarus
GOURMET €€€

(☎21 97 77; www.hangar-7.com; set menu €85-110; ➋) At the space-age Hangar-7 complex at the airport, this glamorous restaurant is the epitome of culinary globetrotting. Each month, Eckart Witzigmann invites a world-famous chef to cook for a serious foodie crowd.

Triangel
AUSTRIAN €€

(☎84 22 29; www.triangel-salzburg.at; Wiener-Philharmoniker-Gasse 7; mains €9-20) The menu is market-fresh at this arty bistro, where the picture-clad walls pay tribute to Salzburg Festival luminaries. It does gourmet salads such as saddle of veal with rocket and parmesan, a mean Hungarian goulash with organic beef, and delicious homemade ice cream.

Saran Essbar
INDIAN, AUSTRIAN €€

(☎84 66 28; Judengasse 10; mains €10-14) Eat under the vaults or on the pocket-sized terrace at this Austro-Indian restaurant, run by the smiley Mr Saran. This is the only place in Salzburg where you'll find Bengali fish curry, schnitzel and strudel on the same menu.

Spicy Spices
INDIAN €

(☎87 07 12; Wolf-Dietrich-Strasse 1; mains €6.50; ➋➍) 'Healthy heart, lovely soul' is the mantra of this all-organic, all-vegetarian haunt. Service is slow but friendly. It's worth the wait for the good-value thali (appetisers) and curries mopped up with paratha (flat bread).

Spoon
ASIAN €€

(Wiener-Philharmoniker-Gasse 9; mains €8.50-18.50; ⊙10am-1am Tue-Sat, to 6pm Mon; ➋➎➍) Colourful stained glass illuminates this vaulted place at the Rupertinum, opening on to a courtyard. Expect Asian food such as crispy duck and red Thai curry, which is especially good value at lunchtime (two courses €6.50).

Blaue Gans Restaurant
AUSTRIAN €€

(☎84 24 91-50; www.blauegans.at; Getreidegasse 43; mains €13-25; ⊙noon-1am Mon-Sat) In the 650-year-old vaults of Arthotel Blaue Gans, this restaurant is a refined setting for regional cuisine, like roast saddle of Hohe Tauern venison, and full-bodied wines. The curd dumplings polish off a meal nicely. The terrace at the foot of Mönchsberg is popular in summer.

DON'T MISS

CAFE CULTURE

Who says only the Viennese have great coffee houses? You can make yourself pretty *gemütlich* (comfy) over coffee and people-watching in Salzburg's grand cafes. Expect to pay around €4 for a slice of cake and €8 for a day special. Here are our five favourites:

Demel
CAFE

(www.demel.at; Mozartplatz 2; ⊗9am-8pm; ⊜🗟) Demel's chocolate-lilac interior is sugary chic and its 1st-floor balcony has a prime view of Mozartplatz. The must-try is *Annatorte*: moist chocolate sponge with a splash of orange liqueur, topped with a chocolate-nougat swirl. Nip down to the shop for a tin of the famous candied violets.

Café Tomaselli
CAFE

(www.tomaselli.at, in German; Alter Markt 9; ⊗7am-9pm) Going strong since 1705, this marble and wood-panelled cafe is a former Mozart haunt. It's famous for having Salzburg's flakiest strudels, best *Einspänner* (coffee with whipped cream) and grumpiest waiters.

Sacher
CAFE

(www.sacher.com; Schwarzstrasse 5-7; ⊗7.30am-midnight; ⊜) Nowhere is the chocolate richer, the apricot jam tangier and cream lighter than at the home of the legendary *Sacher Torte*. The cafe is pure old-world grandeur, with its picture-lined walls and ruby-red banquettes. Sit on the terrace by the Salzach for fortress views.

Fingerlos
CAFE

(Franz-Josef-Strasse 9; ⊗7.30am-7.30pm Tue-Sun; ⊜) Salzburgers rave about the dainty petits fours, crumbly pastries and creamy tortes served at this high-ceilinged cafe. Join a well-dressed crowd for breakfast or a lazy afternoon of coffee and newspapers.

Café Bazar
CAFE

(www.cafe-bazar.at; Schwarzstrasse 3; ⊗7.30am-11pm Mon-Sat, 9am-6pm Sat) All chandeliers and polished wood, Bazar is Sacher's glamorous neighbour. Over breakfast, cake and intelligent conversation, locals enjoy the same river views today as Marlene Dietrich did in 1936.

Scio's Specereyen
AUSTRIAN €

(Sigmund-Haffner-Gasse 16; mains €5.50-11, snacks €2.20-4.90; ⊗10am-8pm Tue-Sat) Snag a table at this pint-sized bistro for day specials like goulash, blinis with trout caviar, or oysters in season. The naughty-but-nice *Venusbrüstchen* (Venus nipples) are chestnut-nougat treats that have been around since Mozart's day.

Alt Salzburg
AUSTRIAN €€

(📞84 14 76; Bürgerspitalgasse 2; mains €14-28; ⊗lunch & dinner Tue-Sat, dinner Mon) Tucked into a courtyard at the base of Mönchsberg, this supremely cosy restaurant has attentive service, hearty regional specialities like venison and veal knuckle, and fine Austrian wines.

Auerhahn
AUSTRIAN €€

(📞45 10 52; Bahnhofstrasse 15; mains €15-22; ⊗lunch & dinner Tue-Sat, lunch Sun; ⊜) The chef cooks fresh and seasonal fare at this restaurant, with a tree-shaded garden. Wood beams, crisp linen and candlelight create the backdrop for flavours like herb-crusted rack of lamb and fluffy *Topfenknödel* (sweet dumplings). Auerhahn is 2km north of town; bus 23 stops nearby.

Schloss Restaurant
GOURMET €€€

(📞84 85 55-0; Mönchsberg Park 26; mains €25-32; ⊜) Oh the castle setting, the dreamy Salzburg views, the food! Seasonally changing dishes might include rack of rabbit with mushroom polenta, fresh lake trout and wild boar – all beautifully served in regal surrounds.

K+K
AUSTRIAN €€

(📞84 21 56; Waagplatz 2; mains €10-22; 🖼) This buzzy restaurant on the square is a warren of vaulted and wood-panelled rooms. Whether you go for crayfish tails, saddle of venison in morel sauce or good old bratwurst with lashings of potatoes and cabbage – the food here is spot on.

zum Eulenspiegel
AUSTRIAN €€

(📞84 31 80; Hagenauerplatz 2; mains €11-23) All fairy lights, centuries-old beams and hidden nooks – 15th-century zum Eulenspiegel is very Brothers Grimm. The food (fried trout, beef stroganoff and the like) was rather average on our last visit, though, and genuine smiles are reserved for good tippers.

Nagano
JAPANESE €€

(☑84 94 88; Griesgasse 19; mains €10-18; ☺) Hidden in the cobbled Artis Hof courtyard. Serves freshly prepared sushi, maki and tempura.

Mensa Toskana
INTERNATIONAL €

(Sigmund-Haffner-Gasse 11; lunch €4.20-5.10; ☺lunch Mon-Fri) Atmospheric *Mensa* (university cafe) in the *Altstadt,* with a sunny terrace and decent lunches.

Heart of Joy
CAFE €

(Franz-Josef-Strasse 3; lunch €6.50, snacks €3-6; ☺8am-6pm Sun-Fri; ☺☺☺) Ayurveda-inspired cafe with an all-vegetarian, mostly organic menu. It does great bagels, salads, homemade cakes and juices. Vegan options available.

Pescheria Backi
FISH €€

(Franz-Josef-Strasse 16b; mains €9-15; ☺Mon-Fri) A fishmonger-cum-bistro with shipshape decor and a faithful local following. Check out the fish dish of the day.

IceZeit
ICE CREAM €

(Chiemseegasse 1; scoop €1-1.30; ☺10am-10pm) Cool down with flavours like passionfruit, tiramisu and poppy seed at this hole-in-the-wall ice-cream parlour in the *Altstadt.*

Cafe Würfel Zucker
CAFE €

(Getreidegasse 36; ☺Tue-Sun; ☺) Squirreled away in the courtyard of Sternbräu and housed in its former malting house. Nice spot for strudel and coffee.

Cappomio
CAFE €

(Linzer Gasse 39; snacks €3-9, lunch €6.90-7.30; ☺8am-11pm; ☺☺) Laid-back right-bank choice, with moreish *tramezzini* (small Italian sandwiches), a big terrace and free wi-fi.

Self-Catering

There are several supermarkets for self-caterers, including Billa (Griesgasse 19).

Grüner Markt
FOOD MARKET

(Green Market; Universitätsplatz; ☺Mon-Sat) On one of Salzburg's grandest squares, this market is great for picnic goodies like Salzburgerland ham, cheese, fresh fruit, bread and gigantic pretzels.

Kaslöchl
CHEESE

(Hagenauerplatz 2) A mouse-sized shop for Austrian cheeses, from creamy alpine varieties to holey Emmental and fresh cheese with basil.

Stiftsbäckerei St Peter
BAKERY

(Mühlenhof; ☺8am-5.30pm Mon, Tue, Thu & Fri, 7am-1pm Sat) Next to the monastery where the watermill turns, this 700-year-old bakery still bakes Salzburg's best sourdough loaves (€2.95 per kilogram) in a wood-fired oven.

🍷 Drinking

A stein-swinging beer hall, a sundowner on the Salzach, an intimate wine bar for appreciating the subtle nuances of Grüner Veltiner wines – all possible ideas for a good night out in Salzburg. Nobody's pretending this is rave city, but the days of lights out by 11pm are long gone. You'll find the biggest concentration of bars along both banks of the Salzach and some of the hippest around Gstättengasse.

TOP CHOICE Augustiner Bräustübl
BREWERY

(Augustinergasse 4-6; ☺3-11pm Mon-Fri, 2.30-11pm Sat & Sun) Who says monks can't enjoy themselves? This cheery monastery-run brewery serves potent homebrews in traditional ceramic *Stein* mugs. Fill yours from the pump in the foyer, visit the snack stands and take a pew in the vaulted hall or beneath the chestnut trees in the 1000-seat beer garden.

Republic
BAR

(www.republic-cafe.at, in German; Anton-Neumayr-Platz 2; ☺8am-1am Sun-Thu, to 4am Fri & Sat) One of Salzburg's most happening haunts, this backlit lounge-bar opens onto a popular terrace on the square. By night, DJs spin to a 20-something, cocktail-sipping crowd in the club. Check the website for free events from jazz, Latin and swing breakfasts to weekly tango (9pm on Sundays) and salsa nights (9pm on Tuesdays).

StieglKeller
BEER HALL

(Festungsgasse 10; ☺11am-11pm) For a 365-day taste of Oktoberfest, try this cavernous Munich-style beer hall, which shares the same architect as Munich's Hofbräuhaus. It has an enormous garden above the city's rooftops. Beer is cheapest from the self-service taps outside.

Steinterrasse
COCKTAIL BAR

(Giselakai 3; ☺noon-midnight) Hotel Stein's chichi 7th-floor terrace attracts Salzburg's Moët-sipping socialites and anyone who loves a good view. It isn't cheap, but it is the best spot to see the *Altstadt* light up against the theatrical backdrop of the fortress.

Humboldt Stub'n
BAR

(Gstättengasse 4-6; ⊙10am-4pm) Cartoons deck the walls and a nail-studded Mozart punk guards this upbeat bar opposite Republic. Try a Mozart cocktail, a sickly composition of liqueur, cherry juice, cream and chocolate. Wednesday is student night, with beers a snip at €2.50.

Köchelverzeichnis
WINE BAR

(Steingasse 27; ⊙3-10pm Tue-Fri, from 11am Sat) This is a real neighbourhood bar with jazzy music, antipasti and great selection of wines. Taste citrusy Grüner Veltliners and Rieslings from the family's vineyards in the Wachau.

Threesixty Bar
COCKTAIL BAR

(www.hangar-7.com; ⊙7pm-2am Sun-Thu, noon-3am Fri & Sat; 🖐) Peer down at Flying Bulls' aircraft through the glass floor at this crystalline bar, part of the airport's futuristic Hangar-7 complex. Strikingly illuminated by night, it's a unique place for a fresh fruit cocktail.

Cave le Robinet
WINE BAR

(Steingasse 43, ⊙3-7pm Thu & Fri, to 6pm Sat) This historic vaulted cellar has an excellent range of Austrian and European wines, including pinots from the owner's vineyard in Burgundy. Open wines start at €2.50 a glass.

Die Weisse
PUB

(☎87 22 46; Rupertgasse 10; ⊙10.30am-midnight Mon-Sat) The cavernous brewpub of the Salzburger Weissbierbrauerei, this is the place to guzzle cloudy wheat beers in the wood-floored pub, the industrial-style bar or the shady beer garden out back.

City Wintergarten
COCKTAIL BAR

(Imbergstrasse 2a; ⊙10am-1am Mon-Thu & Sun, to 4am Fri & Sat) On the banks of the Salzach, this virginal white, champagne-kissed lounge has superb fortress views from its garden terrace. Try a ginger prosecco or a minty Wintergarten mojito. DJs play house and lounge on Friday nights.

220 Grad
CAFE

(Chiemseegasse 5; ⊙Tue-Sat; 🖐) Famous for freshly ground coffee, this retro-chic cafe serves probably the best espresso in town.

Shamrock
PUB

(Rudolfskai 12) Always good for the *craic*, this Irish pub has daily live music, snooker, Guinness on tap and a lively vibe.

Salzach-Insel-Bar
BAR

(Hanuschplatz; ⊙May-Sep) This bar on a boat moored in the Salzach River is a novel spot for taking in Salzburg's skyline over a sundowner.

Bellini's
BAR

(Mirabellplatz 4; ⊙8am-1am Mon-Sat, from 11am Sun) Buzzy Italian bar next to the Mirabellgarten, with a terrace, good cocktails and *tramezzini* sandwiches.

☆ Entertainment

TOP CHOICE Salzburger Marionettentheater
THEATRE

(☎87 24 06; www.marionetten.at; Schwarzstrasse 24; ⊙May-Sep, Christmas, Easter; 🖐) The red curtain goes up on a miniature stage at this marionette theatre, a lavish stucco, cherub and chandelier-lit affair. The repertoire star is *The Sound of Music*, with a life-sized Mother Superior and a marionette-packed finale. Other enchanting productions include Mozart's *The Magic Flute*, Tchaikovsky's *The Nutcracker* and Strauss' *Die Fledermaus*. All have multilingual surtitles.

Landestheater
THEATER

(☎87 15 12-0; www.theater.co.at, in German; Schwarzstrasse 22; 🖐) Opera, operetta, ballet and musicals dominate the stage at this elegant 18th-century playhouse. There's a strong emphasis on Mozart's music, with the Mozarteum Salzburg Orchestra often in the pit. There are dedicated performances for kids.

Schlosskonzerte
CLASSICAL MUSIC

(☎84 85 86; www.salzburger-schlosskonzerte. at; box office Theatergasse 2; ⊙8pm) A fantasy of coloured marble, stucco and frescoes, Schloss Mirabell's baroque *Marmorsaal* (Marble Hall) is the exquisite setting for chamber music concerts. Internationally renowned soloists and ensembles perform works by Mozart and other well-known composers such as Haydn and Chopin.

Mozarteum
CLASSICAL MUSIC

(☎88 94 0-0; www.mozarteum.at; Schwarzstrasse 26-28) Opened in 1880 and revered for its supreme acoustics, the Mozarteum highlights the life and works of Mozart through chamber music (October to June), concerts and opera. The annual highlight is Mozart Week in January.

ARGEkultur
CONCERT VENUE

(www.argekultur.at, in German; Josef-Preis-Allee 16) This alternative cultural venue was born out of protests against the Salzburg Festival in the 1980s. Today it's a bar and performing-arts hybrid. Traversing the entire arts spec-

LOCAL KNOWLEDGE

GRETL AICHER, PUPPETEER

My grandfather started the marionette theatre in a gym in 1913 and in 1926 he gave it as a wedding present to my father, who expanded the repertoire to include Mozart operas and fairy tales. I grew up in this theatre and puppetry is my profession, my passion, my home.

Puppetry is...

Perfecting the art of illusion. To breathe life into a marionette, you must be a dancer, an actor, a singer. After a while, the techniques are second nature and each character becomes an alter ego. I love the fact you can make marionettes fly, take them apart, even swap their heads – tricks actors can only achieve with complex special effects.

Inspired by Mozart

No composer can make marionettes come alive like Mozart. His joyful, playful operas are perfectly suited to puppetry. Like Mozart, the marionette theatre is as much a part of Salzburg as the Salzburgers themselves.

The Sound of Music

The Sound of Music is the first musical we've ever staged and it's simply magical. The effect it has upon audiences both in Salzburg and worldwide is hypnotic. The production has special meaning for me as my family were travelling performers in the 1950s, rather like the von Trapps.

trum, the line-up features concerts, cabaret, DJ nights, dance, poetry slams and world music. It's a five-minute walk east of the *Altstadt*.

Rockhouse LIVE MUSIC VENUE
(www.rockhouse.at, in German; Schallmooser Hauptstrasse 46) Salzburg's hottest live music venue, Rockhouse presents first-rate rock, pop, jazz, folk, metal and reggae concerts – see the website for details. There's also a tunnel-shaped bar that has DJs (usually free) and bands. Rockhouse is 1km northeast of the *Altstadt;* take bus 4 or 151 to Canavalstrasse.

Jazzit JAZZ CLUB
(☎88 32 64; www.jazzit.at, in German; Elisabeth-strasse 11; ☻Tue-Sat) Hosts regular concerts from tango to electro alongside workshops and club nights. Don't miss the free Tuesday-night jam sessions in Jazzit:Bar. It's 600m north of the Mirabellgarten along Elisabethstrasse.

Salzburg Arena CONCERT VENUE
(☎24 04-0; www.salzburgarena.at; Am Messezentrum 1) Under a domed wooden roof, this is Salzburg's premier stage for sporting events, musicals and big-name concerts (Santana and Bob Dylan have played here). The arena is 3km north of town; take bus 1 to Messe.

Das Kino CINEMA
(www.daskino.at, in German; Giselakai 11) Shows independent and art-house films from Austria and across the globe in their original language. The Latin American Film Festival takes place here in April.

Sound of Salzburg Show SHOW
(☎82 66 17; www.soundofsalzburgshow.com; Griesgasse 23; ☻7.30pm May-Oct) This all-singing show at Sternbräu is a triple bill of Mozart, *The Sound of Music* and operetta faves performed in traditional costume. Kitsch but fun.

Mozart Dinner Concert SHOW
(☎84 12 68-0; www.haslauer.at; Stiftskeller St Peter, Sankt-Peter-Bezirk 1; ☻8.30pm) You'll love or hate this themed dinner, with Mozart music, costumed performers and (mediocre) 18th-century-style food. It's held in Stiftskeller St Peter's lavish baroque hall.

 Shopping

Whether you're after a bottle of Mozart eau de toilette or a pair of yodelling *Lederhosen,* Getreidegasse is your street. Traditional wrought-iron signs hang above the shops, which sell everything from designer fashion to hats. Goldgasse, where goldsmiths once plied their trade, has accessories, antiques and porcelain. A popular street for a shop and stroll is Linzer Gasse.

TOP CHOICE **Fürst** CONFECTIONERY
(www.original-mozartkugel.com; Getreidegasse 47; ☺10am-6.30pm Mon-Sat, 11am-5pm Sun) Pistachio, nougat and dark chocolate dreams, the *Mozartkugeln* (Mozart balls) here are still handmade to Paul Fürst's original 1890 recipe and cost €0.90 per mouthful. Other specialities include cube-shaped Bach Würfel – coffee, nut and marzipan truffles dedicated to yet another great composer.

Johann Nagy & Söhne GIFTS
(Linzer Gasse 32) Since it opened in 1870, this family-run store has been doing a brisk trade in hand-painted candles, wax figurines and gingerbread; there are around 40 different kinds of gingerbread to choose from.

Musikhaus Katholnigg MUSIC
(Sigmund-Haffner-Gasse 16) Housed in a 16th-century townhouse and a music shop since 1847, this is the place to pick up high-quality recordings of the Salzburg Festival. There's a huge selection of classical, jazz, chanson and folk CDs and DVDs.

Christmas in Salzburg GIFTS
(Judengasse 11) It really *is* Christmas every day in this five-floor Santa's grotto of a shop. Spangly baubles, gold cherubs, stockings and plenty of festive kitsch are what you'll find.

Lanz Trachten CLOTHING
(Schwarzstrasse 4; www.lanztrachten.at) Just the place if it's a tight-fitting *Dirndl* or a snazzy felt hat you're after.

Salzburg Salz GIFTS
(Wiener-Philharmoniker-Gasse 6) Pure salt from Salzburgerland and the Himalaya, herbal salts and rock-salt tea lights are among the high-sodium wonders here.

Drechslerei Lackner GIFTS
(Badergasse 2) The hand-carved nutcrackers, nativity figurines and filigree Christmas stars are the real deal at this traditional craft shop.

Schmuq ACCESSORIES
(Goldgasse 19) Stocks fun beads, bright bangles and shell rings to glam up any outfit.

Spirituosen Sporer WINE
(Getreidegasse 39) In Getreidegasse's narrowest house, family-run Sporer sells Austrian wines, herbal liqueurs and famous *Vogelbeer* (rowan berry) schnapps.

ℹ️ Information

Emergency

Hospital (☎44 82; Müllner Hauptstrasse 48) Just north of Mönchsberg.
Police headquarters (☎63 83; Alpenstrasse 90)

Internet Access

There are several cheap internet cafes near the train station, including **International Telephone Discount** (Kaiserschützenstrasse 8; per hr €2; ☺9am-8pm Mon-Sat, from 1pm Sun), also offering discount calls.

Money

Bankomaten (ATMs) are all over the place. Many hotels, bars and cafes offer free wi-fi. Exchange booths are open all day every day at the airport. There are also plenty of exchange offices downtown, but beware of potentially high commission rates.
Western Union (☺8am-8.30pm Mon-Fri, 8am-2pm Sat, 1-6pm Sun) Changes money at its branch in the station post office.

Post

Main post office (Residenzplatz 9)
Station post office (Südtiroler Platz 1)

Tourist Information

The main **tourist office** (☎889 87-330; www.salzburg.info; Mozartplatz 5; ☺9am-7pm) has plenty of information about the city and its immediate surrounds. There's a ticket booking agency in the same building. For information on the rest of the province, visit **Salzburgerland Tourismus** (www.salzburgerland.com).

Travel Agencies

STA Travel (www.statravel.at; Rainerstrasse 2) Student and budget travel agency.

ℹ️ Getting There & Away

Air

Salzburg airport (www.salzburg-airport.com), a 20-minute bus ride from the centre, has regular scheduled flights to destinations all over Austria and Europe. Low-cost flights from the UK are provided by **Ryanair** (www.ryanair.com) and **EasyJet** (www.easyjet.com). Other airlines include **British Airways** (www.britishairways.com) and **KLM** (www.klm.com).

Bus

Buses depart from just outside the *Hauptbahnhof* on Südtiroler Platz, where timetables are displayed. Bus information and tickets are available from the information points on the main concourse. For more information on buses in Salzburgerland and the Salzkammergut and an online timetable see www.svv.at.

Hourly buses leave for the Salzkammergut:

Bad Ischl €9.10, 1½ hours

Mondsee €5.70, 50 minutes

St Gilgen €5.70, 50 minutes

St Wolfgang €8.40, 1¾ hours

Car & Motorcycle

Three motorways converge on Salzburg to form a loop around the city: the A1/E60 from Linz, Vienna and the east; the A8/E52 from Munich and the west; and the A10/E55 from Villach and the south. The quickest way to Tyrol is to take the road to Bad Reichenhall in Germany and continue to Lofer (B178) and St Johann in Tyrol.

Train

Salzburg has excellent rail connections with the rest of Austria, though the *Hauptbahnhof* was undergoing extensive renovation at the time of writing. Tickets (no commission) and train information are available from **Salzburger Landesreisebüro** (☎87 34 03; Schwarzstrasse 11).

Trains leave frequently for Vienna (€47.50, three hours) and Linz (€22, 1¼ hours). There is a two-hourly express service to Klagenfurt (€35.50, three hours).

The quickest way to Innsbruck is by the 'corridor' train through Germany; trains depart at least every two hours (€37.80, two hours) and stop at Kufstein. Trains to Munich take about two hours and run every 30 to 60 minutes (€34); some of these continue to Karlsruhe via Stuttgart.

There are also several trains daily to Berlin (€129, eight hours), Budapest (€76, 5¾ hours), Prague (€63.20, seven hours) and Venice (€49, 6½ to nine hours).

ⓘ Getting Around

To/From the Airport

Salzburg airport is around 5.5km west of the centre along Innsbrucker Bundesstrasse. Bus 2 (€2.10, 19 minutes) departs from outside the terminal roughly every 10 minutes and terminates at the *Hauptbahnhof*. This service operates from 5.30am to 11pm and doesn't go via the *Altstadt*, so you'll have to take a local bus from the *Hauptbahnhof* once you arrive, or walk (15 to 20 minutes). A taxi between the airport and the centre costs €15 to €20.

Bicycle

Salzburg is one of Austria's most bike-friendly cities, with an extensive network of scenic cycling trails heading off in all directions, including along the banks of the Salzach River. See www.movelo.com (in German) for a list of places renting out electric bikes.

A Velo (Mozartplatz; 1hr/half-/full day €4.50/10/16; ☉mid-Apr–Oct) Just across the way from the tourist office.

Top Bike (www.topbike.at; Staatsbrücke, Franz-Josef-Kai; ☉10am-5pm) Rents bikes for around €15 per day (half-price for kids). The Salzburg Card yields a 20% discount.

Bus

Bus drivers sell single (€2.10), 24-hour (€5) and weekly tickets (€12.80). Single tickets bought in advance from machines are slightly cheaper. If you're planning on making several trips, *Tabak* (tobacconist) shops sell tickets even cheaper still (€1.60 each), but only in units of five. Under-six-year-olds travel free, while all other children pay half-price.

Bus routes are shown at bus stops and on some city maps; buses 1 and 4 start from the *Hauptbahnhof* and skirt the pedestrian-only *Altstadt*.

Bus Taxi

'Bus taxis' operate from 11.30pm to 1.30am (3am on weekends) on fixed routes, dropping off and picking up along the way, for a cost of €4.50. Ferdinand-Hanusch-Platz is the departure point for suburban routes on the left bank, and Theatergasse for routes on the right bank.

Car & Motorcycle

Parking places are limited and much of the *Altstadt* is only accessible on foot, so it's easier to leave your car at one of three park-and-ride points to the west, north and south of the city. The largest car park in the centre is the Altstadt Garage under Mönchsberg (€14 per day); some restaurants in the centre will stamp your ticket for a reduction. Rates are lower on streets with automatic ticket machines (blue zones); a three-hour maximum applies (€3, or €0.50 for 30 minutes) from 9am to 7pm on weekdays.

Avis (www.avis.com; Ferdinand-Porsche-Strasse 7)

Europcar (www.europcar.com; Gniglerstrasse 12)

Hertz (www.hertz.com; Ferdinand-Porsche-Strasse 7)

Fiaker

A *Fiaker* (horse-drawn carriage) for up to four people costs €36 for 25 minutes. The drivers line up on Residenzplatz. Not all speak English, so don't expect a guided tour.

AROUND SALZBURG

Hellbrunn

A prince-archbishop with a wicked sense of humour, Markus Sittikus built **Schloss Hellbrunn** (www.hellbrunn.at; Fürstenweg 37; adult/child/family €9.50/4.50/24; ☉9am-5.30pm, to 9pm Jul & Aug; 🎫) in the early 17th century as a summer palace and an escape from his functions at the Residenz. The Italianate villa became a beloved retreat for rulers of state who flocked here to eat, drink and make merry. It was a Garden of Eden to all who beheld its exotic fauna, citrus trees and trick fountains – designed to sober up the clergy without dampening their spirits. Domenico Gisberti, poet to the court of Munich, once gushed: 'I see the epitome of Venice in these waters, Rome reduced to a brief outline.'

While the whimsical palace interior – especially the oriental-style Chinese Room and frescoed Festsaal – is worth a peek, the eccentric **Wasserspiele** (trick fountains) are the big draw in summer. Be prepared to get soaked in the mock Roman theatre, the shell-clad Neptune Grotto and the twittering Bird Grotto. No statue here is quite as it seems, including the emblematic tongue-poking-out Germaul mask (Sittikus' answer to his critics). The tour rounds out at the 18th-century water-powered Mechanical Theatre, where 200 limewood figurines depict life in a baroque city. Tours run every 30 minutes.

Studded with ponds, sculptures and leafy avenues, the palace **gardens** are free and open until dusk year-round. Here you'll find the fabled *Sound of Music* pavilion of 'Sixteen Going on Seventeen' fame.

❶ Getting There & Away

Hellbrunn is 4.5km south of Salzburg, a scenic 20-minute bike ride (mostly along the Salzach River) or a 12-minute ride on bus 25 (€2.10, every 20 minutes) from Mozartsteg/Rudolfskai in the *Altstadt*.

Untersberg

Rising above Salzburg and straddling the German border, the rugged 1853m peak of Untersberg affords a spectacular panorama of the city and the Tyrolean, Salzburg and Bavarian alpine ranges. The mountain is a magnet to local skiers in winter, and hikers, climbers and paragliders in summer. A cable car to the top (up/down/return €12.50/11/20) runs every half-hour year-round; closed from 1 November to mid-December. Take bus 25 from Salzburg's *Hauptbahnhof* to St Leonhard and the valley station.

Gaisberg

A road snakes up to 1287m Gaisberg, where stellar views of the Salzburg Valley, Salzkammergut lakes, the limestone Tennengebirge range and neighbouring Bavaria await. The best way to appreciate all this is on the 5km around-the-mountain circuit trail. Salzburgers also head up here for outdoor pursuits from mountain biking to cross-country skiing. Bus 151 (€4, 40 minutes, hourly) runs from Mirabellplatz to Gaisberg in summer. From November to March the bus only goes as far as Zistelalpe, 1.5km short of the summit.

Hallein

📞 06245 / POP 18,900 / ELEV 460M

Too few people visit Hallein in their dash north to Bavaria or south to Salzburg, but those who do are pleasantly surprised. Beyond its industrial outskirts lies a pristine late-medieval town, where narrow lanes are punctuated by courtyards, art galleries and boho cafes. Hotels are cheaper and less sought-after here than in Salzburg, a 25-minute train ride away – a point worth considering during the Salzburg Festival.

◎ Sights

TOP CHOICE Keltenmuseum　　　　　　MUSEUM
(Celtic Museum; www.keltenmuseum.at, in German; Pflegerplatz 5; adult/child €6/2.50; ⊙9am-5pm) Overlooking the Salzach, the

---

SILENT NIGHT

Hallein's festive claim to fame is as the one-time home of Franz Xaver Gruber (1787–1863) who, together with Joseph Mohr, composed the carol 'Stille Nacht' (Silent Night). Mohr penned the poem in 1816 and Gruber, a schoolteacher at the time, came up with the melody on his guitar. You can see that fabled guitar in Gruber's former residence, now the **Stille Nacht Museum** (www.stillenachthallein.at; Gruberplatz 1; adult/child €2/0.70; ⊙3-5pm) next to Hallein's parish church. The museum tells the story of the carol through documents and personal belongings.

glass-fronted Keltenmuseum runs chronologically through the region's heritage in a series of beautiful vaulted rooms. It begins with Celtic artefacts, including Asterix-style helmets, an impressively reconstructed chariot and a selection of bronze brooches, pendants and buckles. The 1st floor traces the history of salt extraction in Hallein, featuring high points such as a miniature slide and the mummified Mannes im Salz (man in salt) unearthed in 1577. There is a pamphlet with English explanations (€2.50).

Salzwelten
SALT MINE

(www.salzwelten.at Ramsaustrasse 3, Bad Dürrnberg; adult/child/family €18/9/38; ⊙9am-5pm; 🏃) The sale of salt filled Salzburg's coffers during its princely heyday. At Austria's biggest show mine, you can slip into a boiler suit to descend to the bowels of the earth. The tour aboard a rickety train passes through a maze of claustrophobic passageways, over the border to Germany and down a 27m slide – don't brake, lift your legs and ask the guide to wax for extra speed! After crossing a salt lake on a wooden raft, a 42m slide brings you to the lowest point (210m underground) and back to good old Austria. Guided tours depart every half-hour. Bus 41 (€2.10, 11 minutes) runs from Hallein train station hourly on weekdays, less often at weekends.

Keltenblitz
TOBOGGAN RUN

(Bad Dürrnberg; adult/child €8.80/6; ⊙10am-6pm, closed Nov-Apr; 🏃) In summer, families pick up speed on this toboggan run close to Salzwelten. A chairlift takes passengers up to the top of Zinken mountain, where they board little wheeled bobsleds to race 2.2km down hairpin bends. The ride is over in a flash and affords fleeting views of the Salzach Valley.

🎊 Festivals & Events

First-rate musicians and artists draw crowds to the two-week **Halleiner Stadtfestwoche** in June and July. The festival is one of the headliners on the summer events program in Salzburgerland, with everything from classical concerts to live jazz, theatre, comedy acts, readings and exhibitions. For more details, see www.forum-hallein.at (in German).

🛏 Sleeping & Eating

Hallein can be visited on a day trip from Salzburg, but there are lots of value-for-money places to stay if you'd rather base

All train stations in the region sell the money-saving **Salz Erlebnis Ticket**, which covers a return train journey to Hallein, a bus transfer to Bad Dürrnberg, plus entry to Salzwelten, the Keltenmuseum and the Stille Nacht Museum. From Salzburg, the ticket costs €41.70/21.70 for adults/children.

yourself here. The tourist office helps book private rooms.

Pension Sommerauer
PENSION €

(☎800 30; www.pension-hallein.at; Tschusistrasse 71; s/d €39/61; P🅿️🏃) Housed in a 300-year-old farmhouse, the rustic rooms at this guesthouse are a bargain. There's a heated pool and conservatory as well as kiddie stuff including a playroom, sandpit and swings.

Pension Hochdürrnberg
PENSION €

(☎751 83; Rumpelgasse 14, Bad Dürrnberg; d/tr €50/63; P🏃) Surrounded by meadows, this farmhouse in Bad Dürrnberg has countrified rooms with warm pine furnishings and downy bedding. The furry residents (rabbits, sheep and cows) keep children amused.

Hotel Auwirt
HOTEL €€

(☎804 17; www.auwirt.com; Salzburgerstrasse 42; camp sites per adult/child/tent €6/4.30/3.80, s/d/f €55/90/140; P🅿️🛜🏃) Auwirt's light-filled rooms are a tad dated but comfy (ask for one with a balcony). The hotel is a good family base with its tree-shaded garden and playground. You can also pitch a tent here.

Bistro Barock
ITALIAN €€

(Gollinger-Tor-Gasse 1; lunch €6.90, mains €7-16; ⊙Mon-Sat; 🖋) Hidden down an old-town backstreet, the cobbled terrace at this art-strewn bistro is a magnet to lunching locals. The menu is inspired by light, herby Italian flavours – think grilled sea bass with lemon salsa, and homemade spaghetti with scampi, sundried tomatoes and rocket.

Koi
CAFE €

(Schantzplatz 2; lunch €6.90-7.90; ⊙9am-11pm Mon-Sat; 🖋) A Buddha welcomes you to this industrial-style cafe with Asian overtones. The menu tempts with fresh-from-the-wok noodles and crunchy beansprout salads, washed down with organic juices. There's a cool breeze to be had on the raised terrace by the stream.

Pur
CAFE €€

(Schiemerstrasse 2; breakfast €5.10-12.90; ⊗8am-8pm; ⊛⌀) Opposite the Keltenmuseum and with a terrace by the Salzach, this relaxed cafe is done out in zesty colours and fruit-themed artworks. The organic breakfasts are great, as are the baguettes, ice creams and the coffee (roasted in Hallein).

Stadtkrug Hallein
AUSTRIAN €€

(Bayrhamerplatz 10; lunch €7, mains €8-12; ⊗lunch & dinner Mon-Fri, dinner Sun; ⌀) Tables fill quickly at midday at this bustling, wood-beamed *Gasthaus*. If it's warm, pull up a chair beside the trickling fountain on the square for an enormous schnitzel or plate of goulash.

ℹ Information

The post office is opposite the train station. The **tourist office** (☑853 94; www.hallein.com; Mauttorpromenade 6; ⊗8.30am-5.30pm Mon-Fri) is on the narrow Pernerinsel island adjoining the Stadtbrücke.

ℹ Getting There & Away

Hallein is close to the German border, 18km south of Salzburg via the B150 and A10/E55 direction Graz/Villach. It's a 25-minute bus or train journey, with departures roughly every 30 minutes (€3.60).

Werfen

☑06468 / POP 3020 / ELEV 525M

The world's largest accessible ice caves, the soaring limestone turrets of the Tennengebirge range and a formidable medieval fortress are but the tip of the superlative iceberg in Werfen. Such salacious natural beauty hasn't escaped Hollywood producers – Werfen stars in WWII action film *Where Eagles Dare* (1968) and makes a cameo appearance in the picnic scene of *The Sound of Music*.

⦿ Sights & Activities

TOP CHOICE Eisriesenwelt
ICE CAVE

(www.eisriesenwelt.at; adult/child €8.50/4.50, with cable car €19/9.50; ⊗9am-3.30pm May-Oct; ⛟) Billed as the world's largest accessible ice caves, Eisriesenwelt is a glittering ice empire spanning 30,000 sq metres and 42km of narrow passages burrowing deep into the heart of the mountains. Even if it's hot outside, entering the caves in any season is like stepping into a deep freeze – bring warm clothing and sturdy footwear.

A tour through these Narnia-esque chambers of blue ice is a unique experience. As you climb up wooden steps and down pitch-black passages, with carbide lamps aglow, otherworldly ice sculptures shaped like polar bears and elephants, frozen columns and lakes emerge from the shadows. A highlight is the cavernous **Eispalast** (ice palace), where the frost crystals twinkle when a magnesium flare is held up to them. A womblike tunnel leads to a flight of 700 steps, which descends back to the entrance.

In summer, minibuses (single/return €2.90/5.80) operate every 25 minutes between Eisriesenstrasse in Werfen and the car park, which is a 20-minute walk from the bottom station of the cable car. The last bus departs at around 6pm. Allow roughly three hours for the return trip (including tour). You can walk the whole route, but it's a challenging four-hour ascent, rising 1100m above the village.

Burg Hohenwerfen
CASTLE

(adult/child/family €14/7.50/32; ⊗9am-5pm Apr-Oct; ⛟) Slung high on a wooded cliff top and cowering beneath the majestic peaks of the Tennengebirge range, Burg Hohenwerfen is visible from afar. For 900 years this fortress has kept watch over the Salzach Valley, its current appearance dating to 1570. The big draw is the far-reaching view over Werfen from the 16th-century belfry, though the dungeons (displaying the usual nasties such as the iron maiden and thumb screw) are also worth a look. The entry fee also covers a **falconry show** in the grounds (11am and 3pm), where falconers in medieval costume release eagles, owls, falcons and vultures to wheel in front of the ramparts. There is commentary in English and German.

Both the fortress and the ice caves can be squeezed into a day trip from Salzburg; start early, visit the caves first and be at the fortress for the last falconry show. The brisk walk up from the village takes 20 minutes.

🛏 Sleeping & Eating

Pension Obauer
PENSION €

(☑52 24-0; www.obauer.at; Markt 36; s/d €40/70; ⓟ) Not to be confused with the smart restaurant of the same name, this pension has spotless wood-floored rooms with comfy beds and scatter rugs. The family runs the deli next door, so you'll sample their cheese and homemade sausages at breakfast.

Camping Vierthaler

CAMPGROUND €

(☑56 57; www.camping-vierthaler.at; Reitsam 8, Pfarrwerfen; camp sites per adult/child/tent €5/2/5.50, bungalows d/tr/q €25/33/41; ☺mid-Apr–mid-Sep; ⓦ) This lovely campground on the bank of the Salzach River has a back-to-nature feel. Facilities include a snack bar and playground. Bungalows with kitchenettes, patios and barbecue areas are also available.

Weisses Rössl

PENSION €

(☑52 68; Markt 39; s/d €30/52) In the village centre, this good-value pension has great views of the fortress and the Tennengebirge from its rooftop terrace. Rooms are a blast from the 1970s, but all are large and cosy with sofas and cable TV.

TOP CHOICE Obauer

MODERN AUSTRIAN €€€

(☑52 12-0; www.obauer.com; Markt 46; mains €15-45, set lunch €35-40, dinner €58-98) Culinary dream duo Karl and Rudi Obauer run the show at this Michelin-starred restaurant, making use of fresh local produce. Sit in the rustic-chic restaurant or the garden, where most of the fruit and herbs are grown. Signatures like meltingly tender Werfen lamb and flaky trout strudel are matched with the finest of Austrian wines.

ℹ Information

The **tourist office** (☑53 88; www.werfen.at; Markt 24; ☺9am-noon & 2-5pm Mon-Fri) hands out information and maps, and makes hotel bookings free of charge.

ℹ Getting There & Away

Werfen is 45km south of Salzburg on the A10/E55 motorway. Trains run frequently to Salzburg (€9.20, 40 minutes).

SOUTHERN SALZBURG PROVINCE

Much of the ravishing lake and mountain scenery in the Southern Salzburg Province is covered in the Hohe Tauern National Park and Salzkammergut chapters. If you're driving to Radstadt or Mauterndorf in the remote Lungau region, look out for the Roman milestones along the Tauern pass road.

Filzmoos

☑06453 / POP 1450 / ELEV 1055M

Theatrically set amid the jagged limestone spires of the Dachstein massif, rolling pastures and the aptly named Bischofsmütze (Bishop's Mitre) peaks – Filzmoos is quite the alpine idyll. Despite some wonderful hiking and skiing, the resort's out-of-the-way location deters the masses and the village has kept its rural charm and family-friendly atmosphere.

🏃 Activities

Overshadowed by the iconic Bischofsmütze (2454m), the village shares 32km of downhill slopes with neighbouring Neuberg and is criss-crossed with 50km of serene winter **walking trails**.

Queues are practically unheard of on Filzmoos' ski slopes, which mostly suit beginners. The resort's nursery slopes, central ski schools and floodlit toboggan run appeal to families. A day ski pass costs €36.50, and free ski buses shuttle between lifts. On a grander scale, Filzmoos is part of the huge Ski Amadé (www.skiamade.com) arena, covering 860km of varied terrain in five regions.

WORTH A TRIP

LIECHTENSTEINKLAMM

One of the deepest and longest ravines in the Alps, the Liechtensteinklamm (Liechtenstein Gorge; www.liechtensteinklamm.at; adult/child €4/2.50; ☺8am-6pm May-Sep, 9am-4pm Oct; ⓦ) is well worth a detour. The jaw-dropping chasm was carved out during the last ice age and takes its name from Johann II, Prince of Liechtenstein, who dipped into the royal coffers to render the gorge accessible in the 19th century.

Today, a footpath burrows into the gorge, past swirling ultramarine waters, glistening boulders and 300m-high cliffs, and through tunnels gouged into slate cliffs veined with white granite. The ravine is at its loveliest in the late afternoon when the light turns the water opal blue. The trail culminates at a 50m-high waterfall. Allow at least an hour to explore the ravine.

Trains run frequently between Werfen and St Johann im Pongau (€3.60, 18 minutes), a 4km walk from the gorge, where free parking is available.

Hiking and rock climbing are Filzmoos' main raisons d'être in summer. A network of well-graded, colour-coded trails takes walkers to the glaciated peaks and bizarre limestone formations of the Dachstein range. The two-day **Gosaukamm circuit** via Hofalm provides a fantastic overview of the area, as does the eight-day **Dachstein circuit**. The tourist office has trail maps and information on family hikes, like the marmot-dotted Bachalm Trail, and can arrange guided hikes.

Other popular activities include Nordic walking in the surrounding hills and mountain biking the challenging 182km **Dachsteinrunde** (Dachstein Tour) through Salzburgerland, Upper Austria and Styria. Pick up a map (€2.90) of the latter at the tourist office.

Mountain bikes, skis, snowshoes, sledges and cross-country equipment are available for hire at Intersport Flory (www.flory.at; Filzmoos 103).

⚜ Festivals & Events

Thanks to its central alpine location and stiff winds, Filzmoos has become something of a ballooning mecca. In mid-January the village hosts the spectacular International Hot Air Balloon Week. The highlight is the magical Night of Balloons, when 40 balloons illuminate the night sky.

🛏 Sleeping & Eating

Filzmoos is scattered with characterful, modestly priced chalets, private rooms and hotels, though rates can be up to double those quoted below in the high winter season.

TOP CHOICE Bio-Hotel Hammerhof   HOTEL €€
(✆82 45; www.hammerhof.at, in German; Filzmoos 6; s/d €77/138; P👶🐾) Set in a beautifully converted 400-year-old farmhouse, this ecofriendly hotel is a find. Bathed in soft light, the rooms are decorated with natural wood and country touches; some have balconies and tiled ovens. The restaurant serves home-grown organic produce. Unwind in a herbal bath at the beauty centre or saddle a horse to canter off into the hills (the owner, Matthias, is a riding instructor and arranges tours).

Haus Obermoos   GUESTHOUSE €€
(✆0664-1261 403; www.hausobermoos.com; Neuberg 190; d €76, apt €80-100; P👶🐾📶🍴) Adrian and Michelle bid Ireland farewell to fulfil their dream of living in the Austrian Alps. Their love for this guesthouse shows in bright, immaculate rooms and apartments, tastefully done out in wood, marble and earthy hues. A heated ski room and a spa area are welcome touches. Haus Obermoos is near the ski lifts, a 10-minute walk from the centre.

Jugendgästehaus Aumühle   HOSTEL €
(✆82 46; Filzmoos 26; dm €22; P) Backing onto forest, this 17th-century farmhouse turned hostel has spacious four-bed dorms, easy access to the slopes, a common room and garden. It's five minutes' walk from town.

Fiakerwirt   AUSTRIAN €
(✆82 09; Filzmoos 23; mains €5.50-11; 🍴) This rambling farmhouse and beer garden serves meaty fare such as schnitzel, goulash and pork roast. Kids love the pet goats, ducks and ponies. In winter, horse-drawn sleighs depart from here (€15 to €17 per person).

ℹ Information

The centrally located **tourist office** (✆82 35; www.filzmoos.at; Filzmoos 50; ⊙8.30am-6pm Mon-Fri) provides stacks of information on activities in the region and will also help book accommodation.

ℹ Getting There & Away

Filzmoos is a 10km detour from the A10/E55 Tauern-Autobahn motorway. Several buses operate daily between Salzburg *Hauptbahnhof* and Filzmoos (€12.30, 1¾ hours), but most require a change at Bischofshofen.

Radstadt

✆06452 / POP 4800 / ELEV 856M

Low-key Radstadt has an attractively walled town centre, with round turrets and a Stadtpfarrkirche (town parish church) that is a pot-pourri of Gothic and Romanesque elements. Most people, however, come for the varied skiing and snowboarding. The resort is part of the vast Ski Amadé arena, covered by a single ski pass and interconnected by ultramodern lifts and free ski buses.

The same mountains attract active types in summer, too, with more than 1000km of walking trails and opportunities for canyoning, climbing, white-water rafting and mountain biking. For information, contact the Salzburger Sportwelt Tourist Office (www.salzburgersportwelt.com).

ℹ Getting There & Away

Radstadt is on the route of two-hourly IC trains running between Innsbruck and Graz (both €35.40, three hours). Zell am See (€13.90, 80 minutes) and Bruck an der Mur (€26.70, two hours) are on this route. From Radstadt, the B99 climbs to the dramatic Radstädter Tauern Pass (1739m), then over to Carinthia. Just to the west is the A10/E55, which avoids the high parts by going through a 6km tunnel.

Mauterndorf

☏ 06472 / POP 1750 / ELEV 1122M

Sleepy little Mauterndorf has fairy-tale appeal, its narrow streets dotted with candy-coloured houses and fountains. While the surrounding high moors and exposed bluffs are set up for walking and skiing, its remote setting in the Lungau region keeps things quiet.

The village centrepiece is medieval Burg Mauterndorf (adult/child €8.20/5.10; ⏱10am-6pm May-Oct). Dominating a rocky outcrop, this 13th-century castle was built by the prince-archbishops of Salzburg on the site of a Roman fort. The castle now houses a regional museum and provides the backdrop for various cultural events. It is believed that in the Middle Ages the main road passed directly through the castle courtyard and tolls were extracted from road users.

ℹ Getting There & Away

Mauterndorf is on Hwy 99. Bus 780 runs from Radstadt to the Mauterndorf post office (€7.50, 50 minutes, three times daily).

Carinthia

Includes »

Best Places to Stay

» Arcotel Moser Verdino (p252)

» Hotel Palais Porcia (p254)

» Hotel Mosser (p258)

» Holiday Inn (p259)

» Villa Verdin (p269)

Best Places to Eat

» Restaurant Maria Loretto (p254)

» Sushi Rolls (p254)

» Dolce Vita (p254)

» Lagana (p259)

» Stern (p259)

Why Go?

Few regions in Europe match the rugged beauty of Carinthia, and you'll find that travelling through it is often a serpentine journey in valleys and natural conduits. Carinthia can also, at times, seem larger than life: the spectacularly high peaks, the gouged valleys and the glistening lakes, not to forget the flamboyant show of opulence in the capital, Klagenfurt, and the popular resorts around the more famous of its 1270 pristine mountain lakes. The most popular of these lakes, like the large Wörthersee, have waters warmed to a comfortable swimming temperature by thermal springs.

Carinthia's deep medieval heritage is another attraction – celebrated in picturesque walled villages such as Friesach and Gmünd, and impressive castles like the hilltop fortress of Hochosterwitz. Many of the towns and villages nestled in Carinthia's rolling hills hold an annual summer festival, with roving performers coming from neighbouring Italy and Slovenia to take part alongside the locals.

When to Go

If you want to make the most of Carinthia's lakes and excellent mountain hiking, head to Carinthia in mid-summer. Not to be forgotten, though, is that in winter the province morphs into one of Austria's best ski regions. Because it gets more sunshine than elsewhere in Austria, lake temperatures are warmer and the ski season shorter. The shoulder season periods are less interesting here except for valley hiking or cycling. Despite a couple of gems, the museum landscape is fairly limited in Carinthia – the activities seasons are therefore the time to hit Carinthia.

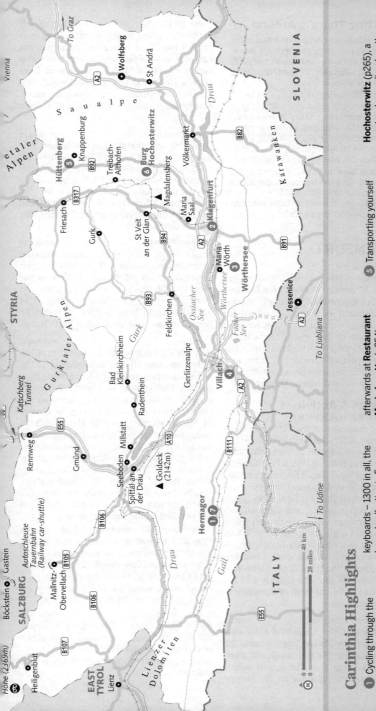

Carinthia Highlights

1 Cycling through the mountainous wilds around **Hermagor** (p262)

2 Visiting the **Eboard Museum** (p250) in Klagenfurt and playing vintage pre-digital keyboards – 1300 in all, the largest collection in Europe

3 Swimming the shores of the **Wörthersee** (p251) and enjoying a lakeside meal afterwards at **Restaurant Maria Loretto** (p254)

4 Stopping over in **Villach** (p258) for skiing in winter, splashy fun in summer in the lakes, or hiking in the mountains

5 Transporting yourself to the tranquil ambience of Tibet at the **Heinrich Harrer Museum** (p264) in Hüttenberg

6 Admiring the views from the top of **Burg**

Hochosterwitz (p265), a spectacular medieval castle

7 Winter skiing on Nassfeld at the top of the 6-km long **Millennium-Express cable car** (p262)

ℹ️ Getting There & Around

Klagenfurt airport has cheap connections with the UK (www.ryanair.com) and Germany (www.airberlin.com). For more information, see p256. Klagenfurt and Villach are the main hubs for trains from elsewhere in Europe.

Carinthia is divided into regional zones for public transport, with either single tickets or passes that are valid for one day or longer. Ask what's cheapest when buying a ticket, or contact **Kärntner Linien** (☎0463-5461821; www.kaerntner-linien.at) in Klagenfurt. Many of the lakes are served by boat services in summer.

The **Kärnten Card** (www.kaerntencard.at; 1-/2-week card €34/42) gives free or cheaper access to the province's major sights and 50% discounts on buses and trains. It's sold at hotels and tourist offices from mid-April to early October.

KLAGENFURT

☎0463 / POP 94,000

Not an urban centre comparable with Graz or Vienna, Klagenfurt walks a very fine line between being Austria's boondocks capital and a playground for a partying set. It's an enjoyable, sunny city that offers easy access to lakeside villages on and around the beautiful Wörthersee. At the town's western limit is the wide green space of Europapark, home to a couple of children's attractions including the bizarre world-in-miniature of Minimundus.

⦿ Sights & Activities

CENTRAL KLAGENFURT

TOP CHOICE **Landesmuseum Rudolfinum** MUSEUM (Map p252; www.landesmuseum-ktn.at, in German; Museumgasse 2; adult/child/family €7/5/15; ⏰10am-6pm Tue, Wed & Fri, 10am-8pm Thu, 10am-5pm Sat & Sun) This museum has lots on natural and cultural history, often organised around themes; Celtic and classical objects and jewellery, and the multimedia 'Glocknerrama' – an acoustic and visual simulation that leads you to the peak of Austria's highest mountain – are highlights. Its *Lindwurmschädel* (dragon skull; located in the room next to the relief of the Hohe Tauern) was found in the 14th century and became the model for the head of Klagenfurt's central fountain.

TOP CHOICE **Eboard Museum** MUSEUM (off Map p252; ☎0699/1914 4180; www.eboardmuseum.com; Florian Gröger Strasse 20; adult/family €10/20; ⏰2-7pm Sun-Fri, call ahead Sat, closed Jul & Aug) With the largest collection of keyboard instruments in Europe (over 1300), this quirky new museum will definitely appeal to anyone who loves music. It's literally a 'fingers-on' museum: you can play most of the organs, which includes rare items like a Model A Hammond from 1934, a Hohner Clavinet model, which Stevie Wonder still uses today, and many more. Live bands perform on Friday nights at 8pm. See p255.

Stadtgalerie ART GALLERY (Map p252; www.stadtgalerie.net, in German; Theatergasse 4; adult/child €5/free; ⏰10am-6pm Tue-Sun) Some excellent rolling art exhibitions are held here, which has a main venue on Theaterstrasse and a second nearby in the **Alpen-Adria-Galerie im Stadthaus** (Map p252; Theaterplatz 3; adult/child €2.20/free; ⏰10am-6pm Tue-Sun).

Dragon Fountain MONUMENT Neuer Platz, Klagenfurt's central square, is dominated by the 16th-century **Dragon Fountain** (Map p252), the emblem of the city. The blank-eyed, wriggling statue is modelled on the *Lindwurm* (dragon) of legend, said to have resided in a swamp here long ago, devouring cattle and virgins.

Landhaus PARLIAMENT (Map p252; Landhaushof 1; adult/child €3/2; ⏰9am-5pm Apr-Oct) The Renaissance *Landhaus* (state parliament) building dates from the late 16th century and is still the centre of political power today. The stairs on the right (facing the portico) lead up the **Grosser Wappensaal** (Heraldic Hall), with its magnificent *trompe l'oeil* gallery painted by Carinthian artist Josef Ferdinand Fromiller (1693–1760) depicting landowners paying homage to Charles VI. Part of a (real) Doric stone classical column, the **Fürstenstein**, stands at one end of the hall, and above this is a painting by Fromiller that shows a peasant perched on the same column.

Stadthauptpfarrkirche St Egyd CHURCH (Map p252; http://st-egid-klagenfurt.at, in German; Pfarrplatz; church free, tower adult/child €1/0.50; ⏰tower: 10am-5.30pm Mon-Fri, 10am-12.30pm Sat Easter–mid-Oct) Climb the 225 steps of its 45m-high tower for a bird's-eye view of town and the surrounding mountains.

Dom CATHEDRAL (Map p252; Domplatz 1; ⏰dawn-dusk) A monolith with an ornate marble pulpit, sugary pink-and-white stuccoed ceiling, and an altar painting by Paul Troger in one of the chapels.

MMKK ART GALLERY

(Museum für moderne Kunst Kärnten; Map p252; www.mmkk.at; Burggasse 8; adult/child €5/2.50; ☉10am-6pm, to 8pm Thu, closed Mon) State gallery for modern art.

FREE Botanischer Garten GARDEN

(admission free; ☉9am-6pm daily May, 9am-4pm Mon-Thu Oct-Apr) Small botanical garden. Adjoining it is the Kreuzbergl-kirche, perched on a hillock with some pretty mosaics of the Stations of the Cross on the path leading up to it. Take bus 60 or 61 from Heiligengeistplatz to Keuzbergl.

Bergbaumuseum INDUSTRIAL MUSEUM

(Mining Museum; www.bergbaumuseum.at, in German; Prof-Dr.-Kahler-Platz 1; adult/child €5/free; ☉9am-6pm Apr-Oct) Exhibits including tools and drilling equipment are housed in tunnels that lead from the grounds of the botanical gardens deep into the hill. Take bus 60 or 61 from Heiligengeistplatz to Keuzbergl.

EUROPAPARK

Minimundus MUSEUM

(Map p251; www.minimundus.at; Villacher Strasse 241; adult/child €12/7; ☉9am-6pm; P) This 'miniature world' has around 140 replicas of some of the world's architectural icons, downsized to a scale of 1:25. By lying on the ground with a camera, you can later impress your friends at parties with great snaps of the Taj Mahal, Eiffel Tower or Arc de Triomphe.

TOP CHOICE Strandbad SWIMMING

(Map p251; www.stw.at/inhalt/Strand-baeder.htm; Metnitzstrand 2; day card adult/child €3.70/1.60, 1hr before closing €1/free; ☉8am-8pm

early May-late Sep; P) Klagenfurt's wonderful lakeside beach has cabins, restaurants and piers for basking like a seal. You can also plough a satisfying circuit 100m offshore for about 500m along the buoys. *Kästchen* (lockers large enough for day packs) in the *Strandbad* cost €1 plus €20 deposit. There's also good swimming outside the buoys further south, past the Maria Loretto beach. Those lounge lizards for whom all this might sound a tad too strenuous will enjoy indulging in **paddle or electric boat** (per 30 min €2.50-7) escapades alongside the *Strandbad*.

Happ's Reptilienzoo ZOO

(Map p251; ☎234 25; www.reptilienzoo.at, in German; Villacher Strasse 237; adult/child €11/6.50; ☉8am-5pm winter, 8am-6pm summer, closed

Europapark Vicinity

◎ Top Sights

Strandbad.............................A1

◎ Sights

1 Happ's Reptilienzoo.......................C1
2 Minimundus..............................C1

Sleeping

3 Camping Klagenfurt am
  Wörthersee........................B2
4 Jugendgästehaus Klagenfurt............D2

Eating

5 Restaurant Maria Loretto................A2
6 Villa Lido...............................A1

Entertainment

7 Lakeside Stage.........................A2

Europapark Vicinity

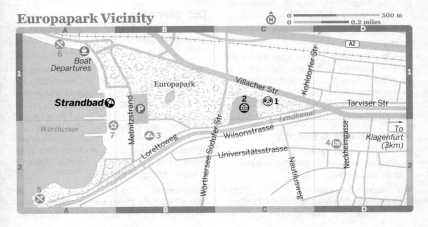

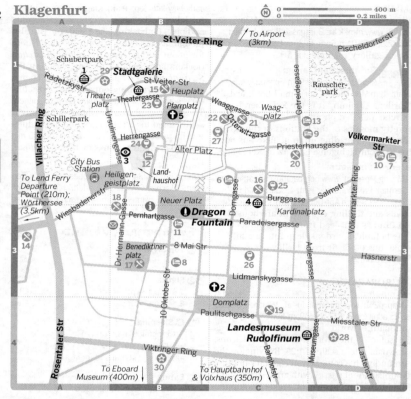

Nov; **P**🛏) Lounge lizards can also nip down the road to check out real-life role models at Happ's Reptilienzoo; there are crocodiles plus all manner of creepers, crawlers and slitherers here for kids and adults to admire. Some signs are in English.

Walks

To take a walking tour of Klagenfurt, pick up the brochure in English from the tourist office. It has a map and descriptions of monuments, historic buildings and hidden courtyards. Free guided tours depart from the tourist office at 10am in July and August.

🎊 Festivals & Events

Klagenfurter Stadtfest   SUMMER FESTIVAL
Two-day music and theatre festival every year in late August.

Wörthersee Festspiele   CONCERT
(www.klagenfurt-tourismus.at; tickets €45-80) Every summer between late June and mid-August, with operas, ballets and pop concerts taking place on an offshore stage on the Wörthersee.

🛏 Sleeping

When you check into accommodation in Klagenfurt, ask for a *Gästekarte* (guest card), entitling you to discounts.

TOP
CHOICE **Arcotel Moser Verdino**   HOTEL €€
(Map p252; ☑578 78; www.arcotel.at/moserverdino; Domgasse 2; s €80-144, d €104-256, ste €128-180, apt from €148; ☻@🛜🛏) Prices in this excellent four-star hotel vary by demand, making it always worth a phone call, even if your budget is tight. What you get are high-quality, modern rooms with flair, very helpful staff and a free stay for kids under 12 in higher-category rooms.

Hotel Geyer   HOTEL €€
(Map p252; ☑578 86; www.hotelgeyer.com; Priesterhausgasse 5; s €70-88, d €102-135, tr €135-145,

KLAGENFURT SLEEPING

q €156; (P ⊖ @ 🛜) This three-star hotel has modern and quite spacious rooms (singles have queen-sized beds) either with wi-fi or a modem available from reception and plugged into the TV antenna. Frequent surfers will find the connections too slow (log off each time or you will quickly use up your €10 credit for 24 hours online), but other aspects of the hotel, such as the tasteful breakfast room and summer patio and a garage for bicycles make up for this.

Pension Zlami   PENSION €€
(Map p252; 📞554 16; www.pension-zlami.at; Getreidegasse 16; s/d/tr €55/100/144; P ⊖ @ 🛜) Some of the rooms in this place have been renovated and create a chirpy feel, while others are still awaiting their chance for a makeover and have blonde wood panelling that jars by today's tastes (and are perhaps a tad overpriced for their size and decor); all are clean and share the same colourful, modern foyer, where you can surf on wi-fi. Cable LAN is available in the rooms.

Hotel Liebetegger   HOTEL €€
(Map p252; 📞569 35; www.liebetegger.com, in German; Völkermarkter Strasse 8; s €60, d €85-95, apt €110-200; P ⊖ @ 🛜 ♿) Though not an art hotel, the floors are decorated with original artwork in this three-star option. The apart-

ments can sleep up to four guests and it offers free use of bikes.

Camping Klagenfurt am Wörthersee
                                  CAMPGROUND €
(Map p251; 📞287 810; www.camping-woerthersee.at, in German; Metnitzstrand 5; site per adult/child/tent €8.40/4.90/6.50; ☺May-Sep; P 🛜 ♿) This shady camping ground offers free use of the *Strandbad*.

> ℹ️ **REACHING EUROPAPARK**
>
> The large, green expanse of Europapark and the *Strandbad* (beach) on the shores of Wörthersee are centres for splashy fun, and especially good for kids. Boating and swimming are usually possible from May to September. To get there, take bus 10, 11, 12 or 22 from Heiligengeistplatz via Minimundus to *Strandbad*. To get to the Wörthersee by bicycle, avoid Villacher Strasse and take the bicycle path running along the northern side of Lendl Canal. You can access it from the small streets running west from the junction of Villacher Ring and Villacher Strasse.

Hotel Palais Porcia
HOTEL €€

(Map p252; ☎51 15 90-0; www.palais-porcia.at; Neuer Platz 13; s €84-182, d €113-197, ste €197-349; P😊✱@🛜) This marvellously ornate and old-fashioned hotel has gilt, mirrors and red-velvet couches, with pink marble and gold taps in the bathrooms. It also has a private beach guests can use near its other hotel in Pörtschach.

Palais Hotel Landhaushof
HOTEL €€€

(Map p252; ☎59 09 59; www.landhaushof.at; Landhaushof 3; s €135, d €165-300, ste €390; 😊@🏠) Klagenfurt's grandest hotel is housed in a converted Renaissance palace. Rooms range from elegant and traditional to kitsch and funky, with original baroque furniture given a new lease of life with new fabrics and colours. Cable LAN is in the rooms and a connecting door makes two of the doubles suitable for families.

Jugendgästehaus Klagenfurt
HOSTEL €

(Map p251; ☎23 00 20; www.oejhv.or.at; Neckheimgasse 6; dm/s/d €21/29/49; P😊@) The modern HI hostel near Europapark is reached by bus 10, 12, 13 or 22. Get off at Jugendgästehaus or (depending on the bus route) Neckheimgasse.

Hotel Garni Blumenstöckl
HOTEL €

(Map p252; ☎577 93; www.blumenstoeckl.at; 10 Oktober Strasse 11; s €47, d €76; 😊) Rooms are arranged around a plant-filled courtyard in this two-star, family-run place in a 400-year-old building. The traditionally furnished ones aren't terribly grand, but its location and very friendly owners make up for this.

Cityhotel Ratheiser
HOTEL €€

(Map p252; ☎512 994; www.cityhotel-ratheiser.at, in German; Völkermarkter Strasse 10; s €58, d €83, ste €95-130; P) This quirky hotel has two extraordinary suites (8 and 10) with upstairs and downstairs sections joined by a spiral staircase. This hotel is not bright and modern, but it is central and comfortable.

✖ Eating

A **fruit and vegetable market** (Map p252) as well as a flower market come to life on Benediktinerplatz on Thursday and Saturday mornings. There are several tiny restaurants on the market square, making it a very cheap and atmospheric place to pick up a lunch of sausages, stew or cheese. Self-caterers can stock up at the **Spar Supermarket** (Map p252) on Dr-Hermann-Gasse. There is another **Spar Supermarket** (Map p252) on Bahnhofstrasse, plus one in the station itself.

TOP CHOICE Restaurant Maria Loretto
AUSTRIAN €€

(Map p251; ☎244 65; Lorettoweg 54; mains €15-25; ⊙lunch & dinner Mar-Dec; P😊🍽) Situated on a headland above Wörthersee, this wonderful restaurant is easily reached by foot from the *Strandbad*. You might also hire a bicycle and make a day of it, perhaps taking a dip from reedy banks or the lakeside beach. It is the sheer character of the place that makes it a wonderful choice for food and casual drinks. Reserve for evenings or an outside table.

TOP CHOICE Zauberhutt'n
AUSTRIAN, ITALIAN €€

(Map p252; Osterwitzgasse 6; mains €10-17; ⊙Mon-Sat, closed lunch Sat; 😊) Pasta, pizza, delicious grilled squid and classic meat dishes all feature on the menu of this inexpensive, family-run restaurant. It's the headquarters of the local Magic Club (with a very unexpected visiting card).

Der Franzos
FRENCH, WINE BAR €€€

(Map p252; ☎0664/466 55 00; Villacher Strasse 11; 3-4 course menu €30-36; ⊙dinner Mon-Fri; 😊) Set just outside the ring road on Villacher Strasse, this French wine bar and top-quality restaurant has outdoor seating away from the street and serves a handful of seasonal dishes.

Sushi Rolls
JAPANESE €

(Map p252; ☎515 100; www.sushirolls.at, in German; Getreidegasse 7; bento box €10, noodle soups €5.50-10, mains €7-11, 15-piece sashimi €17; ⊙Mon-Fri; 😊) Although the *udon* and *ramen* (noodle) soups have been adapted to Austrian tastes, they taste very good in this small eat-in and take-away place popular among lunchtime workers. Sushi and sashimi portions are generous and the staff relaxed.

Dolce Vita
ITALIAN €€€

(Map p252; ☎554 99; www.dolce-vita.at, in German; Heuplatz 2; lunch menu €11-28, dinner mains €24-28, 6-10 course menu €65-99; ⊙Mon-Fri) In a region strongly influenced by northern Italian cuisine, this restaurant is something of a local flagship. Inexpensive it is not, but it builds a seasonal menu mostly around fresh local produce and game, while also offering a lunchtime Venetian *Sarde in saor* (sardines in a marinade). Expect to pay about €14 for a pasta entree.

Firenze
ITALIAN

(Map p252; Bahnhofstrasse 8; pizza & pasta €6-11, mains €14-17; ⊙lunch & dinner; 😊) Large Italian restaurant and pizzeria with a continuous kitchen and take-away.

Wirtshaus zum Heiligen Josef AUSTRIAN €€
(Map p252; Osterwitzgasse 7; mains €7-18; ⊗Mon-Sat; ⊜) Austrian classics and seafood opposite Zauberhutt'n.

Villa Lido INTERNATIONAL €€
(Map p251; ☑21 07 02; Friedelstrand 1; pasta €9-13.50, mains €16-23; ⊗lunch & dinner; ⊜) The lakeside location is the highlight here. Aims at a broad beach crowd that often dresses up a little, especially in the evening. The unaffiliated upstairs lounge is open from 5pm till late.

Drinking

Winter nights in Klagenfurt are the liveliest; in summer many locals decamp to the bars and nightclubs in the Wörthersee resorts of Pörtschach (p256) or Velden (p257). Herrengasse has lots of bars but can be a bit of a teenage drinking dive; there are alternatives.

TOP CHOICE RAJ BAR, INTERNATIONAL €€
(Map p252; www.innenhofkultur.at, in German; Badgasse 7; ⊗5pm-midnight Tue-Thu, 5pm-2am Fri & Sat; ⊜) Raj means 'paradise' in Slovenian. This piece of eclectic heaven is an unusual combination of gourmet restaurant (excellent light dishes and mains cost between €8 and €18), creative and performance arts and music, wine bar and what it calls 'inner-courtyard culture'. The food is good too.

Kamot JAZZ BAR
(Map p252; www.kamot.at, in German; Bahnhofstrasse 9; ⊗8pm-2am) This jazz joint has a warm pub atmosphere. It hosts some of the top national jazz names on the pub circuit, but it's a nice place for a drink anytime.

Bierhaus zum Augustin BEISL
(Map p252; Pfarrhofgasse 2; ⊗11am-midnight Mon-Sat) Traditional in character, this place has an attractive, copper-plated bar and wooden floorboards. There's a cobbled courtyard at the back for cheap alfresco eating.

Checkpoint Charlie BAR
(Map p252; Herrengasse 3; ⊗9am-2am Mon-Sat) This downbeat, low-life bar has an alternative feel and sometimes hosts live rock and blues outfits.

Pankraz BAR
(Map p252; www.pankraz.at, in German; 8 Mai Strasse 16; ⊗9am-4am Mon-Sat, 1pm-4am Sun; ⊜) This favourite among students and electronic music fans is funkily decorated and sometimes features DJs and live acts. There's a shop selling house and electronica CDs here, too.

☆ Entertainment

Klagenfurt is somewhat limited, but you can catch plays, musicals and operas at the **Stadttheater** (Map p252; ☑540 64; www.stadttheater-klagenfurt.at, in German; Theaterplatz 4; ⊗box office 9am-6pm Mon-Fri, 1 hr prior show Sat & Sun, closed mid-Aug–Sep), and the **Konzerthaus** (Map p252; ☑542 72; www.konzerthaus-klagenfurt.

KLAGENFURT DRINKING

LOCAL KNOWLEDGE

GERT PRIX: MUSICIAN & CURATOR OF THE EBOARD MUSEUM

'I started collecting instruments in the late 1980s when digital instruments were making inroads and the analogue instruments had a low standing. A few years later that changed. The digital instruments are fantastic and have huge advantages, but the gentler tones that are more compatible with the human ear come from analogue instruments. There was enormous interest in these after I had the idea of opening up a museum, and this interest continues to this day. My favourite instruments are the old Hammonds, and the Yamaha CP80, which I use when I play live.

'I've only ever sold one instrument in my life – and regret it to this day. In 1979 I exchanged my Eko Sensor piano for a newer model. It will go down in music history as a totally worthless instrument, but I'd pay 40 million to get back the Eko Sensor with the serial number 0549 – okay, maybe a little less.'

Gert Prix's top live venues in Klagenfurt:

» Eboard Museum ('Of course!' – stages live gigs on Friday nights; p250)

» Kamot (p255)

» Stereo (p256)

» Volxhaus (p256)

at, in German; Miesstaler Strasse 8) stages a mixed bag of opera and popular music. An events booklet from the tourist office is useful. In summer, the **lakeside stage** (Map p251) by the Europapark is a great experience.

The two most interesting clubs in town are **Stereo** (Map p252; www.stereoclub.at, in German; Viktringer Ring 37-39; ☺Mon-Sat), which does a mixed bag from theatre or *Kabarett* (cabaret) to parties, and **Volxhaus** (www.volxhaus.at; Südbahngürtel 24), with a broad but interesting cultural program – sometimes it rocks in a big way with independent bands. It's located near the train station.

Information

INTERNET Café-bar G@tes (Map p252; Waagplatz 7; per 10 min €1; ☺9am-1am Mon-Fri, 7pm-1am Sat & Sun) Wi-fi free if you buy a drink.

POST Main Post Office (Map p252; Dr-Herrmann-Gasse 4)

TOURIST INFORMATION Tourist office (Map p252; ☑53 722 23; www.info.klagenfurt.at; Rathaus, Neuer Platz 1; ☺8am-6pm Mon-Fri, 10am-5pm Sat, 10am-3pm Sun) Sells Kärnten cards and books accommodation.

Getting There & Away

AIR Klagenfurt's **airport** (☑415 00-0; www.klagenfurt-airport.com; Flughafenstrasse 60-66) is 3km north of town. Ryanair connects Klagenfurt with London Stansted and Frankfurt (Hahn), Air Berlin services Berlin, Hamburg and Cologne, and Austrian Airlines flies to Vienna (p413).

BOAT The departure point for boat cruises on the lake is a few hundred metres north of *Strandbad*. See p258 for information on timetables and lakeside resorts.

BUS Postbus services depart outside the *Hauptbahnhof*, where there's an **information office** (☑543 40; ☺7am-5pm Mon-Fri) with a timetable board outside. See p261 for information on buses going to lake resorts. Direct two-hourly ÖBB buses connect Klagenfurt with Graz (€45.50, two hours)

CAR & MOTORCYCLE The A2/E66 between Villach and Graz skirts the north of Klagenfurt. **Avis** (☑559 38; Klagenfurt Airport) and **Megadrive** (Denzeldrive; ☑5 01 05 41 40; Klagenfurt Airport) are among the car-rental companies at the airport.

TRAIN Two-hourly direct IC/EC (InterCity/EuroCity) trains run from Klagenfurt station to Vienna (€48, 3¾ hours) and Salzburg (€35.50, three hours). Trains to Graz depart every two to three hours (€35.50, 2¾ hours); these go via Leoben (€26, two hours). Trains to western

Austria, Italy, Slovenia and Germany go via Villach (€7.20, 30 to 40 minutes, two to four per hour). See p260 for more information.

Getting Around

TO/FROM THE AIRPORT Take bus 40 from the *Hauptbahnhof* or Heiligengeistplatz to Annabichl (€1.80, 25 minutes, four times hourly), then change to bus 45 (10 minutes). A taxi costs about €7.

BICYCLE In summer the tourist office co-operates with a hire company for **bicycles** (per 24 hr €10-19), which can also be picked up and dropped off at various points around the lake. The tourist office has a brochure with the points.

BOAT A **motor ferry** (one-way adult/child €5/3) chugs along the Lendkanal between the centre of Klagenfurt, through Europapark and up to the shore of the Wörthersee (50 minutes, two to three times daily from May to September).

BUS Single bus tickets (which you buy from the driver) cost €1.10 for two or three stops or €1.80 for one hour. Drivers also sell 24-hour passes for €4.20. An **STW Verkehrsbetriebe office** (Map p252; ☑521 542; Heiligengeistplatz 4; ☺7.30am-2.30pm Mon-Fri) is near the city bus station. Validate your advance tickets after boarding.

TAXI Call ☑311 11 or ☑27 11. A taxi between the Wörthersee and the city costs about €10.

CENTRAL CARINTHIA

Wörthersee

Owing to thermal springs, the picturesque Wörthersee is one of the warmer lakes in the region and among the best for swimming, frolicking on the lakeshore or whizzing across the waters in pursuit of sport. The average water temperature between June and September is 21°C, but in a hot year it can climb to 27°C. The lake stretches from west to east between Velden and Klagenfurt. The southern shore is the most picturesque, but the northern shore has the best transport access and is the busiest section. The website for lakeside towns is www.woerthersee.com.

PÖRTSCHACH
☑04272 / POP 2650

Tiny Pörtschach is the most exclusive of all Wörthersee resorts, with a distinctive tree-lined peninsula and a sumptuously curving

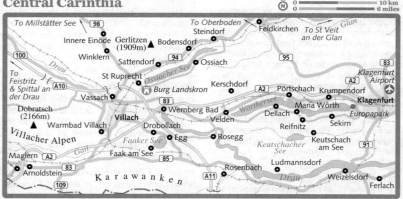

bay on either side where society figures live it up.

Contact **Pörtschach Information** (☎04272-23 54; www.poertschach.at; Hauptstrasse 153; ⊙8am-6pm Mon-Fri, 10am-1pm & 4-6pm Sat & Sun, closed Sat & Sun Oct-Apr) for information on (often expensive) hotels and activities.

The cheapest rooms at the four-star **Seehotel Dr Jilly** (☎04272-2258; www.jilly.at, in German; Alfredweg 5-7; s €165, d €212-278; P❄@🔒🐾) have no balconies, but at the top end you get lake views and a terrace. This quiet hotel situated on the lake has modern furnishing, wellness facilities, free use of bicycles and its own beach. Wi-fi (and the cable LAN in rooms) costs €6.50 per hour.

The most celebrated nightclub on the lake is **Fabrik** (☎0463-57 186 75; www.fabrik.at, in German; Saag 10), in the tiny village of Saag between Pörtschach and Velden. Shuttle buses run to here from both places.

VELDEN
☎04274 / POP 8850

Velden enjoys a reputation as the Wörthersee's top nightlife resort and is also the venue of various high-adrenaline sports events on summer weekends. It's a brash, lively place packed with a strange combination of young and beautiful people nursing cocktails, and parties of old-age pensioners nibbling ice cream.

Veldener Tourismus (tourist office; ☎21 03-0; www.velden.at; Villacher Strasse 19; ⊙8am-8pm Mon-Thu, 8am-10pm Fri & Sat, 9am-5pm Sun, closed Sun Nov-Apr) can advise on accommodation and information.

Five kilometres south of Velden is Rosegg, with its **Tierpark** (animal park; ☎04274-523 57; www.rosegg.at; adult/child €7.50/4.60; ⊙9am-6pm Mar-Oct) and a **Schloss** (palace; ☎04274-30 09; www.rosegg.at; adult/child €6/4; ⊙10am-6pm May-Sep, closed Mon Sep, May & Jun).

MARIA WÖRTH
☎04273 / POP 1500

Maria Wörth is a small resort on the southern shore dominated by two medieval churches. The larger **Pfarrkirche** (parish church) combines Gothic, baroque and Romanesque elements, while the smaller 12th-century **Winterkirche** (Winter Church) has frescoes of the Apostles.

On the hill southwest of Maria Wörth is the **Pyramidenkogel** (☎04273-2443; adult/child/family €6/3/16; ⊙10am-6pm Apr & Oct, 9am-7pm May & Sep, 9am-8pm Jun, 9am-9pm Jul & Aug, closed Nov-Mar), a hill topped by a rather avant-garde tower that provides fine views of Wörthersee. Further information is available from the Maria Wörth **tourist office** (☎04273-22400; www.maria-woerth.at; Seepromenade 5; ⊙8am-6pm Mon-Fri, 10am-12.30pm & 1.30-5pm Sat & Sun).

❶ Getting There & Around

BICYCLE

A circuit of the lake is about 50km, and enjoyable with an overnight stop. In summer a *Fahrrad Verleih* (rent-a-bike) scheme allows you to take a standard bicycle from one of many outlets around the lake and return it to any other (three hours/24 hours/one week/two weeks €6/10/40/70). Mountain bikes (€12/19/85/160) are also available. The tourist office in Klagenfurt is one convenient outlet.

BOAT

WSG (☎0463-211 55; www.energieklagenfurt. at/schifffahrt.html, in German) runs motorboats and steamers on the lake two to five times daily from mid-April to October. Boats call at both sides, stopping at Klagenfurt, Krumpendorf, Reifnitz, Maria Wörth, Pörtschach, Dellach, Weisses Rössl and Velden. They return by the same route (departing from Klagenfurt at 8.30am, 10am, noon, 2pm and 4pm daily).

A **Tagesticket** (adult/child/family €13/8.50/32) is valid all day and allows as many stops as you like. The longest trip (Klagenfurt to Velden) takes 1¾ hours on a steamer, but motorboats are quicker (80 minutes).

BUS

For Postbus information, call ☎0463-543 40. Three to four buses run between Klagenfurt and Maria Wörth weekdays, but few on Saturday (€3.30, 20 minutes). Three to seven run from Monday to Saturday via the north shore to Velden (€5.20, one hour).

CAR & MOTORCYCLE

The A2/E66 and Hwy 83, which runs closer to the shore, are on the northern side of the lake. On the southern side, the route is classified as a main road, but it's much smaller.

TRAIN

Several trains run each hour between Klagenfurt and Villach along the northern shore of the lake (€7.20, 40 minutes). Regional trains from Klagenfurt stop at Krumpendorf (€2, six minutes), Pörtschach (€3.60, 15 minutes) and Velden (€5.40, 20 minutes); express trains only stop at Velden.

Villach

☎04242 / POP 59,100

Although there are more picturesque cities in the region, Villach is arguably the most dynamic, partly because of its role as an important transport hub for routes into Italy and Slovenia. It attracts an international bunch of visitors and is a very lively and liveable city, despite having no big-hitting sights. Consider using it as a base for activities and exploring the region.

◉ Sights

Pick up a copy of the tourist office's free walking booklet in English with descriptions of buildings and sights.

Stadtpfarrkirche St Jakob   CHURCH
(Oberer Kirchenplatz 8; ⊙10am-6pm Mon-Sat) The Stadtpfarrkirche St Jakob dominates the old town and has frescoes, a stuccoed ceiling and a vast rococo altar in gold leaf, arrayed with fresh cream flowers. The walls are studded with the ornate memorial plaques of the region's noble families. Each summer a pair of falcons nests in the **Stadtpfarrturm** (steeple; adult/child & student €2/free; ⊙same times as church).

Relief Von Kärnten   MUSEUM
(Peraustrasse; ⊙10am-6pm Mon-Sat) Relief Von Kärnten is a huge relief model of Carinthia housed in Schillerpark, south of the old town. It covers 182 sq metres and depicts the province at a scale of 1:10,000 (1:5000 vertically, to exaggerate the mountains).

Villacher Fahrzeugmuseum   MUSEUM
(www.oldtimermuseum.at, in German; Ferdinand-Wedenig-Strasse 9; adult/child €6.50/4.50; ⊙10am-6pm) Located 3km outside town, the Villach Automobile Museum focuses on icons of everyday motoring such as the Fiat Topolino, BMW Isetta and about 250 others. Take bus 5179 from the train station towards Zauchen.

Museum der Stadt Villach   MUSEUM
(☎Widmanngasse 38; adult/under 8yr €3/free; ⊙10am-6pm Mon-Sat) Back in town, the Museum der Stadt Villach is a fairly unexciting museum covering local history, archaeology and medieval art.

✦ Festivals & Events

On the first Saturday in August, the pedestrian centre is taken over by the **Kirchtag** (☎205 66 00; www.villacherkirchtag. at, in German), a folk-music festival featuring national and local musicians, as well as international acts from Italy, Latvia, Slovenia and elsewhere. There are plenty of costumes, food stalls and fireworks. Many events begin during the preceding week, culminating on the Saturday.

🛏 Sleeping

The tourist office can help with finding accommodation in town.

TOP CHOICE **Hotel Mosser**   HOTEL €€
(☎241 15; Bahnhofstrasse 9; s €55-75, d €90-180, ste €180-250, apt €140-190; P@⊛) Despite a bomb-drop during WWII, this hotel retains genuine historic charm (look for the collection of old room keys in the cabinet downstairs). Some rooms have angled mirrors above the head boards, or whirlpools for romantic interludes, whereas cheaper singles are functional and unremarkable. Staff are friendly and helpful, there's a lift

and the breakfast room is spacious and airy; choose your partner and the room carefully and you could even spend a good honeymoon or silver anniversary in some of the doubles.

TOP CHOICE Holiday Inn
HOTEL €€€

(☎225 220; www.hi-villach.at; Europaplatz 1-2; s €128-135, d €168-175, ste €255-490; P❄🐾🏠) All rooms in this chain hotel have partial stone tiling, are strong on burgundy tones and have a nifty toilet and shower section with a smart use of doors to create privacy; the best have views to the Drau River and include extras like a free drink, and a bathrobe for the sauna and wellness area. Prices vary according to demand, so always check out the website. The restaurant, Lagana, is excellent.

Romantik Hotel Post
HOTEL €€

(☎261 01-0; www.romantik-hotel.com; Hauptplatz 26; s €75-150, d €90-170, tr €117-197, ste €200-280; P❄🐾@🏠🏡) The corridors of this smart hotel offer a foretaste of its charms, with chandeliers and oriental rugs. The wooden furnishings have a light and breezy feel, and the lift and some of the doubles joined by doors make it ideal for families; there's a very good restaurant downstairs.

Kramer Hotel-Gasthof
HOTEL €€

(☎249 53; www.hotelgasthofkramer.at; Italiener Strasse 14; s €48-75, d €87-104, tr €127, f €208; P❄🐾@🏡) You'll find very good value among contemporary furnishings in rooms at this hotel just up the road from the Stadtpfarrkirche. They're spacious and are priced by size and how recently they were renovated. Family rooms consist of two doubles with a connecting door.

Jugendherberge
HOSTEL €

(☎563 68; www.oejhv.or.at; Dinzlweg 34; dm/s/d €23/31/53; P❄@🏡) Located 1km west of the centre, off Sankt-Martiner-Weg. Sauna facilities and a children's playground are on-site.

Gasthof Kasino
HOTEL €€

(☎244 49; www.hotel-kasino.at; Kaiser Josef Platz 4; s/d €55/84; P❄🐾@) Drab corridors but quite modern rooms. Bathrooms are rather pokey.

Hotel Goldenes Lamm
HOTEL €€

(☎241 05; www.goldeneslamm.at; Hauptplatz 1; s €55-75, d €90-120, tr €120-150, q €158; P❄🐾🐾) A great location but uneven aesthetics. Ask for something nice or check out a couple of rooms before choosing.

✖ Eating & Drinking

For self-caterers, there's a Billa supermarket opposite the train station, with various snack places close by. The main area for bars extends from Hauptplatz to Kaiser-Joseph-Platz and north towards the river.

TOP CHOICE Lagana
AUSTRIAN, MEDITERRANEAN €€€

(☎225 220; Europaplatz 1-2; 3-6-course menu €46-69, mains €18-32; ⊙Tue-Sat; 🐾) Located inside the Holiday Inn, Lagana is arguably the top restaurant in town. The views from the terrace (heated in winter) to the river and to the distant mountains are superb, and this is matched by the cuisine, which includes a delicious octopus served with polenta, along with classics such as *Tafelspitz* (boiled beef with radish sauce) and an eclectic gourmet selection.

Stern
INTERNATIONAL, STEAK €€

(☎247 55; www.stern-villach.com; Kaiser Josef Platz 5; mains €9-13.50; ⊙7am-midnight Mon-Thu, 7-2am Fri, 9-2am Sat) This lounge and restaurant gets a clientele from the very young hanging out on the psychologist's couches and postmodern sofas during the day to a mixed crowd that comes here to feed on steak – its speciality (although Stern also does wok and salad dishes). These are quite good, and to get one you fill out a lengthy check-list on type of steak, sauce, accompaniment and how it's prepared.

Trastavere
ITALIAN €€

(☎21 56 65; www.trastavere.at, in German; Widmanngasse 30; mains €11-16, pizza €7-10; ⊙lunch & dinner; 🐾) Book ahead for an outdoor table on weekend summer evenings in this trattoria situated in a lovely courtyard. It has a broad range of seafood dishes, such as calamari, but it doubles as an excellent pizza restaurant.

Café Konditerei Rainer
CAFE €

(Oberer Kirchenplatz 5; cakes €2.70; ⊙7am-7pm Mon-Sat, 10am-7pm Sun 🐾🏡) Villach's oldest cafe offers a sumptuous array of more than 50 different cakes and lunch snacks, and has a kids' play area.

Romantik Restaurant Post
AUSTRIAN €€

(Hauptplatz 26; mains €15.50-24.50; ⊙Mon-Sat; 🐾🎵) The restaurant of the Romantik Hotel Post serves acclaimed regional specialities in a cosy and intimate atmosphere. The midday meat or veg *Menü* (set menu) is good value and there's also a healthy selection of salads.

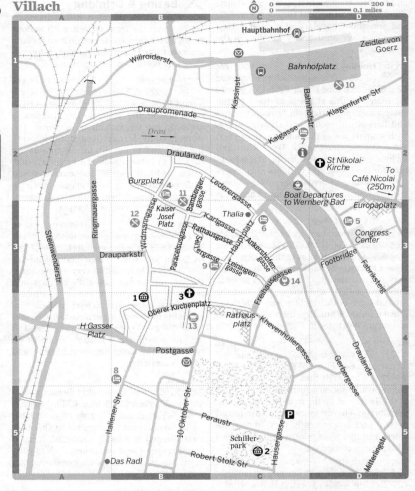

CARINTHIA CENTRAL CARINTHIA

Soho   BAR
(☏0664-14 54 222; Freihausgasse 13; ⏰10pm-late)
This is Villach's fashionable bar-cum-club,
with a resident team of DJs and plenty of
sponsored events.

❶ Information

BOOKSHOP Thalia (☏23 434 38; Hauptplatz
4) A large bookshop with guidebooks, hiking
maps and some English-language books.

INTERNET ACCESS Café Nicolai (☏22 511;
Nikolaigasse 16; per 10 min €1; ⏰7am-9pm
Mon-Fri, 7am-2pm Sat) Fast but expensive,
whereas **Bouhia Internet Callshop** (☏22 511;

Bahnhofplatz; per hr €2; ⏰9am-10pm) is a
cheaper call shop.

**TOURIST OFFICE Tourismusinformation
Villach-Stadt** (☏205-2900; www.villach.at;
Bahnhofstrasse 3; ⏰9am-5pm Mon-Fri, 10am-
6pm Sat, 10am-1pm Sun, closed Sun Sep-Jun)
City tourist office, helps with accommodation
and maps. Free internet terminal.

❶ Getting There & Around

BICYCLE Das Radl (☏269 54; www.das-radl.
at, in German; Italiener Strasse 25; per day city
bike & mountain bike €10) rents bikes in Villach
(ring ahead) and also from Bodendorf and Faak

Villach

train stations on the Ossiaker and Faaker lakes respectively.

BUS Call ☎44410-1510 or ☎0810 222 33 39 for Postbus information. The bus station is opposite the *Hauptbahnhof*. At least four InterCity buses go to Venice daily (€25, 3½ hours). For information about other bus services to the Wörthersee resorts, see p261.)

TRAIN Villach is situated on three Austrian IC/EC rail routes, which serve Salzburg (€31, 2½ hours, every two hours), Lienz (€20, 1¾ hours, hourly) and Klagenfurt (€7.20, 30 to 40 minutes, two to four per hour). Direct services run to seemingly everywhere: Munich (€67, 4½ hours, four daily) in Germany, Ljubljana (€20, 1¾ hours, five daily) in Slovenia, Zagreb (€38, four hours, five daily) in Croatia, and Belgrade (€82, 11 hours, three daily) in Yugoslavia.

Around Villach

FAAKER SEE & OSSIACHER SEE

Villach is blessed with two major lakes nearby with low-key summer resorts. Both the **Faaker See**, situated 6km east of Villach and close to the Karawanken Range, and the **Ossiacher See**, 4km to the northeast, provide plenty of camping, boating and swimming opportunities. Above Annenheim and providing a backdrop to the Ossiacher See is **Gerlitzen** (1909m), a popular **ski area**. Expect to pay about €35 for a **ski pass** here.

Browse through the region-wide accommodation brochure obtainable from the Villach tourist office, or contact the **regional tourist office** (☎04242-420 00; www.da-lacht-das-herz.at; Töbringer Strasse 1, Villach; 9am-7pm Mon-Fri, noon-4pm Sat, 10am-2pm Sun) for more on the lakes and skiing.

On the Ossiacher See, **boats** (www.schiffahrt.at/drau, in German) complete a crisscross circuit between St Andrä and Steindorf (adult/child €12/6, 2½ hours, approximately hourly from May to October). Boats run by the same company also navigate the Drau River from Villach Congress-Center to Wernberg Bad (one way adult/child €7/3.50, 50 minutes) via St Niklas an der Drau (about 2km northeast of the Faaker See) up to four times a day between late April and early October.

Regular train and Postbus services leave from the bus station and Villach train station, running along the northern shore of Ossiacher See via Annenheim (€1.90, 12 minutes) and Bodensdorf (€3.30, 20 minutes). Regular trains run to Faak am See (€3.30, 30 minutes), and regular buses run to Drobollach (€3.30, 20 minutes), both on the Faaker See.

You can also explore the region by **bicycle**. These can be hired in Villach if you ring ahead, and at the Bodensdorf (Ossiaker See) and Faak (Faaker See) train stations; hotels and camp sites in the region hire them out, too.

BURG LANDSKRON

Situated between Villach and the Ossiacher See, the castle ruins of Burg Landskron are home to the impressive **Adler Flugschau** (falconry show; ☎04242-428 88; www.adlerflugschau.com; Burgruine Landskron, Schlossweg; adult/child €9/4.50; ⊙core times 11am & 2.30pm May-Oct, closed Nov-Apr), a 40-minute spectacle featuring these birds of prey.

Five to 11 buses (€1.90, nine minutes) daily leave from alongside Villach's train station stop in St Andrä, below the castle.

DREILÄNDERECK

Walkers and mountain bikers will find much to do in the **Dobratsch** (2166m) area, in the Villacher Alpen about 12km west of Villach. Just south of here, hiking trails go from the small town of Arnoldstein to the Dreiländereck – the point where Austria, Italy and Slovenia meet. At 1500m there's an **Alpine garden** (www.alpengarten-villach.at; adult/child €2.50/1; ⊙9am-6pm Jun-early Sep) with flora

ℹ MOUNTAIN BIKING

Mountain bikers should pick up a copy of *The Best Bicycle & Bike Tours* from the tourist office in Hermagor. This gives an overview of trails, including an 11.7km downhill trail from the top of the Millennium-Express cable car to the Gmanberg station. Bikes are carried free of charge but can also be hired at the valley and mountain station.

from the southern Alps. To reach the garden, follow the Villacher Alpenstrasse from town. This is a toll road (€13 per car), but it's free from about mid-November to mid-April, or free in summer if all occupants have the Kärnten Card. Dobratsch is popular with cross-country skiers.

From early July to early October, a bus leaves Villach's main train station at 8.50am and 12.50pm on Wednesday, Saturday and Sunday to Villacher Alpe Rosstratte in the **Naturpark Dobratsch** (www.naturparkdobratsch.info, in German), via the Alpenstrasse and the alpine garden (adult/child €5/3, 70 minutes). The bus returns at 11.50am and 4.30pm from Rosstratte. Frequent trains connect Villach and Arnoldstein (€3.60, 25 minutes).

Hermagor

📞 04282 / POP 7150

Situated about 50km west of Villach, Hermagor is popular as a base for skiing in the nearby Nassfeld ski pistes, where you can zip around 110km of pistes (day pass €36) and explore Nordic skiing trails and snowboarding runs; in summer it morphs into a low-key spot for hikers and mountain bikers. Hermagor is also the starting point for hiking the spectacular **Garnitzenklamm**, a narrow gorge some 2.5km west of town. Ask at the tourist office for advice.

Facilities such as banks, supermarkets and a post office are all central or near the tourist office.

The **tourist office** (📞2043; www.hermagor.info; Göseringlände 7; ⏰8.30am-7pm Mon-Fri, 8.30am-1pm & 2-4pm Sat & Sun) is about 400m west of the train station on the B111. It has well-informed staff with information on skiing, guided and unguided hiking, and mountain biking in the area.

The **Millennium-Express cable car** (adult/child €15/5 return) climbs 6km up to Nassfeld (mountain station: Madritsche), making it Austria's longest. The valley station is in Tröpolach, 8km west of town along the B111 and then B90, or also reached by train.

Hotel Bürgerbräu (250 85; www.buergerbrau.at; Gasserplatz 1; s/d €60/92; 🅿🛜) has clean, modern rooms and a helpful owner, free bicycle use for guests and facilities catering to skiers in winter – a free bus to the Millennium-Express picks you up here. Wi-fi is in the lobby but not in all rooms.

ℹ Getting There & Around

Trains run to Hermagor from Villach (€9.20, 70 minutes) every one to two hours, some continuing to Tröpolach (€2, 10 minutes), complemented by bus services from Hermagor to Tröpolach. **Bike Paradies** (📞2010; hermagor@bikeparadies.at; Obervellach 48), at the Rudolf service station 1km towards Villach on the B111, rents mountain/trek/child bicycles for €15/13/8 per day.

EASTERN CARINTHIA

Eastern Carinthia's prettiest medieval towns and most impressive castles lie north of Klagenfurt, on or close to Hwy 83 and the rail route between Klagenfurt and Bruck an der Mur, with mountain ranges on either side: the Seetaler Alpen and Saualpe to the east and the Gurktaler Alpen to the west.

Friesach

📞 04268 / POP 5200

Once a key staging post on the Vienna–Venice trade route, Friesach is Carinthia's oldest town. The hills on either side of town bristle with ruined fortifications and the centre is surrounded by a moat (it's the only town in Austria that still has one) and a set of imposing, grey-stone walls. Once a year Friesach's gates are locked, everyone in town dresses up in medieval costumes and Friesach re-enacts its history. Picturesque Hauptplatz is a few minutes' walk from the train station along Bahnhofstrasse. Turn left on leaving the station.

⦿ Sights

Friesach was long known for its contemporary 'Die Spur des Einhorns' (The Trail of the Unicorn) exhibition, blending medieval themes with ultra-modern installations. There were plans to dismantle this sometime after 2010, but at the time of writing it was still unclear what (if anything) would take its place in the building. The tourist office can tell you more.

Erlebnis Burgbau in Friesach CASTLE
(www.burg-friesach.at, in German; ☺Apr-Oct) Situated about 1km south of Hauptplatz (off St Veiter Strasse), this display of castle construction set in the forest should move into full swing in summer 2011 (exact opening times and prices were still being decided). This, says Friesach's tourist office, will consist of a bevy of local men and women in historic attire reconstructing a castle using original techniques. Apparently you'll be able to engage the workers in conversation. In about 20 years the result will be another castle under Friesach's medieval belt.

Medieval Fortifications & Churches
CHURCH, FORTRESS
An excellent free map of town (available from the tourist office) has a detailed **Burgenwanderweg** (Castle Trail) plan that helps you explore the fortifications and churches. There are four medieval fortress ruins ranged along the hills rising above Hauptplatz to the west, all offering excellent views. The northernmost is **Burg Geyersberg**; the furthest south are the **Virgilienberg** ruins. The middle two (**Rotturm** and **Petersberg**) are the most easily visited from the centre, with lovely views from **Peterskirche** (☺11am-5pm Tue-Sun May-Sep), accessible by paths ascending from the front of the Romanesque **Stadtpfarrkirche** (☺dawn-dusk), dating from AD 927.

Stadtmuseum MUSEUM
(adult/child & student €3/1; ☺11am-5pm Tue-Sun May-Sep) Behind Peterskirche, Petersberg also houses the small town museum with exhibits covering the town's medieval history and religious art.

✯✦ Festivals & Events

Spectaculum MEDIEVAL FESTIVAL
On the last Saturday in July: electric lights are extinguished and the town closed off and lit by torches and flares as jesters, princesses and armoured knights stroll around juggling, fire-eating and staging jousting tournaments and duels. Friesach reverts to the currency that made it famous, with medieval meals from street stalls being paid for with Friesach pen-

nies. Contact the tourist office for event information.

Petersberg Fortress OPEN-AIR THEATRE
The site for open-air theatre performing anything from Shakespeare to Brecht in summer. Obtain details and tickets (prices ranging from about €13 to €23) from the tourist office.

🛏 Sleeping & Eating

Several hotels and eating options are on Hauptplatz and around.

Metnitztalerhof HOTEL €€
(☑25 10-0; www.metnitztalerhof.at; Hauptplatz 11; s €57, d €96-108; mains €15.50-23.50; ☺lunch & dinner; P✿🐾@🛜) This pastel-pink edifice at the far end of the town square is the only four-star hotel in Friesach; rooms are modern and comfortable and have small balconies. There's a sauna, jacuzzi and steam room onsite, plus a restaurant that serves Austrian and Carinthian dishes.

Zum Goldenen Anker GUESTHOUSE €
(☑23 13; www.goldeneranker-friesach.at; Bahnhofstrasse 3; s €33, d €56, f per person €28; P✿🛜📶) Some of the rooms in this small guesthouse have antique furniture and traditional ceramic stoves, and family rooms have separate bedrooms (children under 14 years pay €15). Reception is in the restaurant next door.

ℹ Information

Tourist Office (☑43 00; www.friesach.at; Fürstenhofplatz 1; ☺10am-4pm daily May-Sep, 10am-noon Mon-Fri Oct-Apr) Located a couple of minutes by foot north of Hauptplatz.

ℹ Getting There & Away

Friesach has direct connections with Vienna's Meidling (€39, 3¼ hours, three daily), Villach (€16, 1½ hours, 12 daily), Bruck an der Mur (€22, 1¾ hours, 12 daily), St Veit (€7.20, 30 minutes, 14 daily) and Klagenfurt (€11, 60 minutes, 12 daily).

Gurk
📞04266 / POP 1300
This small town (Krka in Slovenian), some 18km west of the Friesach–Klagenfurt road, is famous for its former **Dom** (cathedral; ☑Domplatz 11; ☺closed during services), which was built between 1140 and 1200, and still operates as a church. With its harmonious pillared crypt, this is Austria's foremost

church from the Romanesque epoch. Inside you will also find Gothic reticulated vaulting, and most of the church fittings are either baroque or rococo. The early-baroque high altar has a startling 72 statues and 82 angel heads.

The frescoes in the **Bischofskapelle** (episcopal chapel; adult/child €3.70/2.90; ☺guided tours 11.20pm, 2.20pm & 3.50pm), dating from around 1200, are all the more beautiful for the use of raw colours.

❶ Getting There & Away

Go on a weekday if using public transport – a morning train from Klagenfurt to Treibach-Althofen connects with a bus (€12, 1¾ hours). With your own transport, take Hwy 93.

Hüttenberg

☑04263 / POP 1570

Step off the bus in the tiny mining village of Hüttenberg and you might be forgiven for thinking you've stumbled into Tibet, for here you see fluttering prayer flags rising up the cliff. Hüttenberg is the birthplace of Heinrich Harrer, who famously spent Seven Years in Tibet and was immortalised by Brad Pitt in film.

Outside the **Heinrich Harrer Museum** (☑8108; Bahnhofstrasse 12; adult/child €13.50/8; ☺10am-5pm May-Oct) you can sip on a bowl of butter tea and listen to the rush of water through wooden prayer wheels, before going inside the beautiful stone and wood building to see the huge collection of objects and photographs Harrer brought back from his world travels. Opposite the museum is the Lingkor, a metal walkway built up the cliff face. The colourful prayer wheels made from oil drums are testament to Hüttenberg's history of being a site for heavy industry (this is an iron-ore mining area). The steep admission price to the Heinrich Harrer Museum includes the inconveniently located **Puppenmuseum** (Doll Museum) and the **Mineralienschaubergwerk** (Mineral Mining Museum) 3km away in Knappenberg.

❶ Getting There & Away

Three direct buses run to Hüttenberg weekdays from St Veit an der Glan, two on Saturday and none leave Sunday (€8.70, 1½ hours). Three direct buses daily leave from Klagenfurt (€10.50, 1¼ hours); a few indirect bus services from both cities add to frequency but Sunday travel is difficult. Buses continue on to Knappenberg. A train and bus connecting service works on weekdays via Treibach-Althofen (€12, one hour).

St Veit an der Glan

☑04212 / POP 12,800

St Veit was historically important as the seat of the dukes of Carinthia from 1170 until 1518. These days it's a mildly interesting, midsized town that makes an agreeable base for explorations of the medieval towns and other attractions further north. To get to the pedestrian-only town centre from the *Hauptbahnhof,* walk left down Bahnhofstrasse for 600m and then go one block right.

◉ Sight & Activities

Hauptplatz   TOWN SQUARE

The centrepiece of St Veit's Hauptplatz at No 1 is the **Rathaus**; its baroque stuccowork was pasted onto the building in 1754 and features a double-headed eagle on the pediment with St Veit (the saint, not the town) standing between the eagle's wings. After walking through the Gothic vaulted passage you arrive at an arcaded courtyard bedecked with sgraffito (a mural or decoration in which the top layer is scratched off to reveal the original underneath).

Hauptplatz itself has a fountain at both ends and a central column erected in 1715 as a memorial to plague victims. The north-eastern fountain, the **Schüsselbrunnen**, is surmounted by a bronze statue, created in 1566. This figure is the town mascot: its hand is raised as if in greeting, while a jet of water spits forth from its mouth. The south-western fountain bears a statue of the local medieval poet, Walther von der Vogelweide.

Rogner Hotel Ernst Fuchs Palast
                                          NOTABLE BUILDING

A surrealist structure designed by mystical artist Ernst Fuchs. The outside of the building is studded with blue and red glass tiles in fantastical and astrological designs. It operates as a hotel.

Verkehrsmuseum   MUSEUM

(Hauptplatz 29; adult/child €5/2; ☺9am-6pm, closed noon-2pm Sep-Jun) The Transport Museum has a virtual locomotive you can drive between Maria Saal and Friesach.

🛏 Sleeping & Eating

Rogner Hotel Ernst Fuchs Palast
TOP CHOICE
                                            HOTEL €€

(☑4660-0; www.hotel-fuchspalast.at; Friesacher Strasse 1; s/d €70/90; ⓟ@☏) Blue and red glass tiles in amazing, surreal designs decorate the outside. Inside, surrealism gives way to fluted columns and jewel-like mosaics. The rooms are a little bland but that's how the artist Ernst Fuchs designed them. There's a sauna on-site.

Hotel Garni Mosser HOTEL €
(✆3223; www.hotel-mosser.at; Spitalgasse 6; s €39-52, d €74; mains €9.50-16; restaurant: ⊗Mon-Sat; ⊛⊚) This budget hotel is excellent value – the rooms are extremely comfortable, it's bang in the centre of town and there's a generous breakfast buffet. The downstairs **Suppenkasper** restaurant serves inexpensive classics.

La Torre ITALIAN €€
(✆39250; www.latorre.at; Grabenstrasse 39; mains €15.50-26, 6-course menu €66; ⊗Tue-Sat) This magnificent Italian restaurant is set in one of the towers of the 14th-century town wall. As well as the smart, romantic interior, there's a beautiful, walled garden and terrace, and an Italian owner who exudes bonhomie.

ℹ Information

Tourist office (✆288 806 911; www.stveit. carinthia.at, in German; Hauptplatz 23; ⊗9am-6pm Mon-Fri, 10am-4pm Sat & Sun, closed Sat & Sun Oct-Apr) Sells maps of the town (€0.50). There's also an information screen in the *Rathaus*.

ℹ Getting There & Away

St Veit is 33km south of Friesach and 20km north of Klagenfurt. Two-hourly express trains run to Villach (€9.20, 35 minutes), stopping at Klagenfurt (€3.60, 12 minutes). There are no left-luggage lockers at the station.

Burg Hochosterwitz

This fairytale fortress (it claims to be the inspiration for the castle in *Sleeping Beauty*) drapes itself around the slopes of a hill, with 14 gate towers on the path up to the final bastion. These were built between 1570 and 1586 by its former owner, Georg Khevenhüller, to ward off invading Turks. A *Burgführer* (castle guide; information booklet (in English; €4) outlines the different challenges presented to attackers by each gate – some have spikes embedded in them, which could be dropped straight through unwary invaders passing underneath. The **castle** (www.burg-hochosterwitz.at, in German; adult/child incl tour €7.50/4.50; ⊗9am-6pm Palm Sunday-Oct; Ⓟ⚐) has a museum featuring the suit of ar-

mour of one Burghauptmann Schenk, who measured 225cm at the tender age of 16.

ℹ Getting There & Away

Regional trains on the St Veit–Friesach route stop at Launsdorf Hochosterwitz station, a 3km walk from the car park and the first gate, where a lift (€5) ascends to the castle.

Maria Saal

✆04223 / POP 3900

Maria Saal, a small town perched on a fortified hill 10km north of Klagenfurt, is easily visited on an excursion from Klagenfurt or St Veit. Its **Pilgrimage Church** (Domplatz 1; ⊗dawn-dusk) was built in the early 15th century from volcanic stone, some of it filched from a nearby Roman ruin. The exterior south wall is embedded with relief panels and ancient gravestones.

The **tourist office** (✆22 14-25; www.maria. saal.at, in German; Am Platzl 7; ⊗7.30am-12.30pm & 1-4pm Mon-Fri) is just off Hauptplatz.

There are no left-luggage facilities in the small train station, but if you're just passing through on the way somewhere else, the ticket clerk might watch your bags. Regional trains run from St Veit (€3.60, nine minutes, every one to two hours) and Klagenfurt (€2.90, nine minutes, every one to two hours).

WESTERN CARINTHIA

Besides Hohe Tauern National Park (p271), the main attractions of Western Carinthia are Millstatt with its serene and pretty lake for swimming and boating, its abbey and famous music festival (p269), and Spittal an der Drau, with its stately Renaissance palace and pretty, floral park (p266).

Both Millstatt and Spittal an der Drau are close to the primary road route north from Villach, the A10/E55 that leads to Salzburg. It has a special vehicle toll section (€9.50 on top of the normal Autobahn toll) covering the two long tunnel sections north of Rennweg – the Tauerntunnel and Katschbergtunnel. Traffic jams are common.

Gmünd

✆04732 / POP 2600

Gmünd is an attractive 11th-century village with a delightful walled centre and a 13th-century hilltop castle, **Alte Burg**. From 1480,

UNEXPECTED GMÜND

Gmünd probably has more artist ateliers per square metre than any other town in the world. These complement magnificently an attractive medieval centre. It's most unusual attraction, though, is the **Pankratium** (www.pankratium.at; Hintere Gasse 60; 1hr tour adult/child/family €8/4.50/19; ⊙10am-6pm May-Oct). This extraordinary space brings together water, light and sound (ie vibration) in hands-on pieces to lure the visitor into what is literally a 'vibrant' world of the senses. While doing a tour you can play various harps (and have a quick jam session with your fellow visitors if you feel inclined), create music on water-filled copper and bronze bowls by rubbing the handles, play a mechanical violin driven by a pendulum, explore other sound machines or create visual impressions of musical notes by using your voice to vibrate sand on a surface. The tour ends with some good old-fashioned bubble-blowing in the yard.

Hungarians conducted a seven-year siege of the city, breaking through and partially destroying the castle; a fire in 1886 brought its ultimate demise. Today it's the setting for plays and musical events.

Of an entirely different era is the excellent, privately owned **Porsche Museum Helmut Pfeifhofer** (www.auto-museum.at, in German; Riesertratte 4a; adult/child €7/3.50; ⊙9am-6pm mid-May–mid-Oct, 10am-4pm mid-Oct–mid-May). A Porsche factory operated in Gmünd from 1944 to 1950, and the first car to bear that famous name (a 356) was handmade here. There's a film (in German and English) on Ferdinand Porsche's life and work.

Gmünd has a range of inexpensive accommodation options, including hotels with child-minding geared towards families with young children. Staff at the **tourist office** (☑22 1514; www.familiental.com; Hauptplatz 20; ⊙8am-5pm Mon-Fri, 9am-3pm Sat, closed Sat Sep-Jun) can outline options. It also has an excellent sheet map of town in English, German and Italian with sights and galleries numbered and briefly explained.

Gasthof Kohlmayr (☑2149; www.gasthof-kohlmayr.at, in German; Hauptplatz 7; s/d/q €38/62/96; ℗) has an eclectic mix of historic and modern rooms in a 400-year-old building right in the heart of Gmünd and a restaurant (€8.50 to €13.50) serving tasty local fare. **Vinothek Bacchus** (Kirchgasse 48; ⊙from 6pm; ⊜) is one of two wine bars in town where you can sip the nectar of the gods.

❶ Getting There & Away

Gmünd is not on a rail route; one to two hourly buses connect it with Spittal an der Drau (€4.30, 30 minutes) Monday to Saturday.

Spittal an der Drau

☑04762 / POP 15,800

Spittal is an important economic and administrative centre in upper Carinthia. Its name comes from a 12th-century hospital and refuge that once succoured travellers on this site. Today it's a town with an impressive Italianate palace at its centre and a small, but attractive, park with splashing fountains and bright flowerbeds. To get into town from the station, walk straight up the road, then cut through the Stadtpark on your right.

◉ Sights & Activities

Schloss Porcia & Museum für Volkskultur   PALACE, MUSEUM

(Local Heritage Museum; www.museum-spittal.com, in German; adult/child & student €7/3.50; ⊙9am-6pm daily mid-Apr–mid-Oct, 9am-1pm Mon-Thu mid-Oct–mid-Apr; ⅶ) Boasting an eye-catching Renaissance edifice, Schloss Porcia was built between 1533 and 1597 by the fabulously named Graf von Salamanca-Ortenburg. Inside, Italianate arcades run around a central courtyard used for summer theatre performances. The top floors contain the enormous **Local Heritage Museum**. This has lots of exhibits of interest to children and adults alike. The display begins with an enormous map of Carinthia, which you walk over in felt slippers (a commentary in English and German explains more about the province), then continues with 3-D projections, such as a virtual navigation through the Hohe Tauern National Park: you stand at a joystick and navigate a virtual flight through the park between altitudes of 100m and 10,000m while changing the angle of flight. You will also find lots of applied arts and objects of everyday life in the region.

Goldeck

Spittal's nearest mountain, offering inspiring views, is Goldeck (2142m) to the southwest. In summertime, the peak can be reached by cable car (one-way/return €11/16.50) or by the Goldeckstrasse toll road (cars/motorbikes €12/6, free with the Kärnten Card). The road stops 260m short of the summit. In winter, the peak is popular for skiing (lift pass adult/child €32/16). The cable car doesn't operate from mid-April to mid-June or from mid-September to mid-December.

🛏 Sleeping

Staff at the tourist office help with accommodation free of charge.

Haus Hübner PENSION €

(☑2112; www.huebner-spittal.com; Schillerstrasse 20; s €31-42, d €62-70, 2-person apt €80, 4-person apt €75; 🅿🖨🛜🍴) This central, peaceful pension near Schloss Porcia has a lovely garden and modern and comfortable rooms. The apartments are good alternatives for families but the minimum stay for these is five days.

TOP CHOICE **Hotel Erlebnis Post** HOTEL €€

(☑22 17 0; www.erlebnis-post.at; Hauptplatz 13; s €58, d €99, tr €122; 🅿🖨🛜) Situated in the centre, this hotel has recently reinvented itself in a highly unusual way. Rooms are comfortable and many are individually designed on a particular theme, usually with the sponsor's name in the room itself, in a kind of *room-vertisement*. One room decked out in light woods, for instance, has the timber merchant's name plastered on the wall. The hotel is a favourite among skiers, and a bonus is the ski room and transfers to the pistes.

Hotel Ertl HOTEL €€

(☑204 80; www.hotel-ertl.at; Bahnhofstrasse 26; s/d €65/110; 🅿🖨🛜🏊) Spittal's second hotel (Hotel Erlebnis Post is the other one in town) is also reinventing itself, with the ochre colours of its Tex-Mex restaurant downstairs trickling into the interior design. The result is refreshing. Comfortable rooms and close proximity to the station make it an excellent choice for day trips out of town. The pool is about 25m and outdoors.

Goldeck Sportakademie HOSTEL €

(☑0699-144 144 60; www.sportsacademy.at, in German; Zur Seilbahn 2; d & dm per person €24) This former youth hostel at the base of the Goldeck cable car is today a sports academy aimed at young skiers and snowboarders

(there's ski hire and a ski school). It also has summer activities. It's usually booked out by groups between January and March.

Drautluss Camping CAMPGROUND €

(☑24 66; www.drauwirt.com; Schwaig 10; camp site per adult/child/tent/car €5/3/3.50/3.50; ⏰Jun-Sep). This camping ground is about 3.5km from the town centre on the southern bank of the Drau River.

🍴 Eating & Drinking

The tourist office has a good *Gastronomieführer* (Gastronomy Guide), with restaurants and bar listings (in German). Just off Bahnhofstrasse is a **Eurospar** supermarket. The main nightlife area is on Brückenstrasse and Bogengasse. It's a thin and eclectic line of low-life bars and regular pubs. Occasionally, strays from the local army barracks get tanked and aggro there, though.

Restaurant Zellot AUSTRIAN €€

(Hauptplatz 12; mains €10-17; ⏰lunch & dinner Mon-Sat) This is possibly the most important address in town: it's a funky and rather eccentric restaurant that does a good steak as well as Austrian staples. On top of this, it has the Glashaus bar and bistro (open 9am to 1am Monday to Saturday), and the Garage, a space for live acts and DJs that is decked out like a garage – its features become even more intriguing after your second drink. It's open 9.30pm to 4am Friday and Saturday.

Schloss Café CAFE €€

(Burgplatz 1; cakes €2.80, mains €9-16; ⏰7.30am-8pm Mon-Sat, 2-8pm Sun; @) This bakery–cafe occupies one end of Schloss Porcia, with a terrace overlooking the fountains and greenery of the Stadtpark. It does some classic dishes, and for €2 per 30 minutes you get a laptop and can surf the internet at your table.

Mettnitzer AUSTRIAN €€

(☑358 99; Neuerplatz 17; mains €16-24; ⏰Wed-Sun) Zellot is a hard act to beat all round, but Mettnitzer – the finest eatery in town – does it from the purely culinary standpoint in a formal atmosphere.

ℹ Information

Post office (SüdTyrolerplatz 3) Near the train station. A second one is located off Tiroler Strasse.

Tourist Office (☑56 50 220; www.spittaldrau.at, in German; Burgplatz 1; ⏰9am-noon & 1-6pm Mon-Fri, 9am-noon Sat, closed Sat Sep-Jun) On one side of Schloss Porcia.

ⓘ Getting There & Around

BICYCLE More (📞2555-0; service@more-der
-spezialist.at; Bahnhofstrasse 11) rents city
and mountain bikes for €12/60 per day/week
(top mountain bikes €20 per day) and electric
bicycles (€19 per day, range 60km, 120km
with auxiliary battery). Pick up the tourist
office's free city/regional map, which has paths
marked.

BUS One- to two-hourly Postbuses leave from
outside the train station and Neuer Platz to
Gmünd (€4.30, 30 minutes) Monday to Saturday,
but none on Sunday. Call 📞39 16 or
📞0180 222 33 39 for schedule information.

TRAIN Spittal-Millstättersee is an important
rail junction: two-hourly IC/EC services run
north to Bad Gastein (€11, 40 minutes); at
least hourly regional services run west to Lienz
(€12.50, one hour) and to Villach (€7.20, 35
minutes), 37km to the southeast. The railway
line north via Mallnitz-Obervellach clings spectacularly
to the valley walls.

TAXI Call 📞5580 or 📞2422. Expect to pay
€20 to get to Millstatt.

Millstätter See

Stretching out 12km and just 1.5km wide,
the Millstätter See is second in size in Carinthia
after the Wörthersee. It was gouged
out during the ice age about 30,000 years
ago, and today is studded with a handful of
small towns. Millstatt on the north shore
and Seeboden at the western end are the
most important. The warm waters of the
lake (about 22°C to 26°C in summer) lend
themselves to sailing, kayaking and open-water
swimming.

The central information office, **Infocenter Millstätter See** (📞04766-3700-0;
www.millstaettersee.at;   Thomas-Morgenstern-

ⓘ ACCESS TO JETTIES & THE LAKE

The public bathing foreshore in Millstatt
is a bustling place in midsummer.
If you're after some tranquillity, hire a
boat or kayak and head for the leafy
shore opposite. For swimming, private
jetties belonging to the hotels are the
nicest options. All places we list here
have a private jetty or offer lake access.
Seeboden is in a reedy cove with hotels
on the shore and, though quite pleasant,
is a little too developed for some
people's taste.

Platz 1; ⏰9am-6pm Mon-Fri, 10am-noon & 2-5pm
Sat), is situated in a modern building in
Seeboden with an unusual 'curtain' of water
that parts as you enter. This symbolises
'touching the lake' (the curtain is tap water,
though), a theme to bring people close
to water. The Infocenter doubles as a call
centre with English- and Italian-speaking
staff, and there's a supermarket, cafe and
ATM, as well as toilets, in or near the building.
The centre is very useful for organising
activities in advance, but Seeboden itself is
the least attractive of the towns on the lake.

The bus to Millstatt stops near the Infocenter
in Seeboden (ask the driver to let you
off there).

MILLSTATT
📞04766 / POP 3400

The genteel lakeside village of Millstatt lies
10km east of Spittal an der Drau on the
northern shore. It got its name from Emperor
Domition, an early Christian convert who
tossed *mille statuae* (1000 heathen statues)
into the lake. A gaunt and crazed-looking
sculpture of the emperor stands in the lake,
portrayed in the act of consigning a Venus to
a watery grave.

The town has three main parallel streets:
the B98 (Kaiser-Franz-Joseph-Strasse) and
square Georgsritterplatz, Marktplatz north
(uphill) from this, and the beach road on
the lake. Stiftsgasse/Seemühlgasse, near Full
House, connects all three.

⊙ Sights & Activities

Stift Millstatt ABBEY
(tours in German adult/child €5/2.50; ⏰tours
10.30am Wed & Fri, no tours conducted mid-Sep–
May) Apart from the lake itself, Millstatt's
main attraction is its Romanesque Benedictine
abbey, founded in 1070. This pretty
complex consists of the 11th-century abbey,
a graveyard that invites a stroll, and foundation
buildings south of the abbey, with lovely
yards and arcades. If you walk downhill
along Stiftsgasse from the abbey, you see on
the left a **1000-year-old lime tree**.

Stiftsmuseum MUSEUM
(Abbey Museum; 📞06246-750 35; Stiftsgasse 1;
adult/child €2.50/1.50; ⏰10am-noon & 2-6pm early
May-Sep) The Stiftsmuseum contains everything
from documentation of the town's history
to reliquaries and a geology collection.

Wassersport Strobl WATER SPORTS
(📞22 63; Seemühlgasse 56a) Windsurfing
boards costing €9 to €14 per hour are hired

Among the interesting tours and events on the Millstätter See, several are clustered around the idea of 'touching the lake' – designed to bring people close to the water. For example, you can have your own romantic dinner for two out on the water. A boat chugs you to a raft, the food is delivered in all its courses, and later it returns at some point to bring you back to digest it all – or file for divorce, as the case may be (this one costs €155 per person). If the kids get sick of watching from the shore with mum and dad bob about stuffing their faces, they can be placated with pirate hunts (€20) in costume and make-up, or everyone can mellow out by bobbing in the waves of the lake – colourfully called a 'Massage of 1000 Hands' – or at a yoga session. The helpful Infocenter Millstätter See can arrange the 1000 Hands, the dinner and other goodies for you.

out from three locations in Millstatt by Wassersport Strobl, along with electric boats (€11 to €13 per hour) and kayaks (€5 per hour). One is alongside Villa Verdin. East of Millstatt is **Bad Kleinkirchheim**, a spa resort and large winter skiing centre with 26 lifts and cable cars (see Information).

⚡ Festivals & Events
If two Carinthians meet, they start a choir, according to a local saying. If two Millstätters get together, they start a music festival, and one that's put this small place firmly on the classical music map is the **Musikwochen Millstatt** (Millstatt music weeks; ☎20 22-35; www.musikwochen.com, in German; tickets €13-35). It happens every year from May to September, with most performances taking place in the Abbey.

🛏 Sleeping & Eating
High season is June to September. Check availability with tourist offices outside these months as some places go into winter hibernation. Most hotels and pensions are south of the B98. The cheapest are back from the lake.

TOP CHOICE Villa Verdin   HOTEL €€
(☎374 74; www.villaverdin.at, in German; Seestrasse 69; s €50-70, d €100-140; P@) This converted 19th-century villa-hotel mixes contemporary design style with antiques and interesting junk to create a comfortable, informal yet stylish atmosphere. The rooms are all different, some with funky, red furniture and zebra-print accessories, some with Buddhas and Japanese screens. Several have enclosed verandas or balconies with views of the lake. It's gay-friendly and there's also a retro beach cafe for daytime snacks, and a private jetty.

Hotel See-Villa   HOTEL €€
(☎21 02; www.see-villa-tacoli.com; Seestrasse 68; s €59-82, d €112-172, ste €164-192; P@🐕) Next

door to Villa Verdin, this staid, old-fashioned hotel is a complete contrast: it's a handsome old building right on the lake, with a huge terrace restaurant, a private sauna and a swimming jetty. The rooms are wooden floored, creaky and quaint, with a variety of different styles and colour schemes, all very traditional. Its restaurant (mains €14.50 to €20) is open daily for lunch and dinner.

Die Forelle   HOTEL €€€
(☎2050-0; www.hotel-forelle.at; Fischergasse 65; s €97, d €166-259, 2-4 person apt per person €112-160; P@🏊) Some guests like its lakeside bar, others gravitate towards this large lakeside hotel for its wellness facilities, including whirlpool and baths, plus a Hawaiian massage or cosmetic treatment. Rooms are well sized, the more expensive doubles have a balcony to the lake, and prices fall significantly during the shoulder season or with special deals. Check out the website for details. Its midpriced restaurant opens for lunch and dinner, and offers a reduced menu between meal times and half-board (€20 extra).

Frühstuckspension Strobl   PENSION €
(☎3142; pension-hansstrobl@aon.at; Kaiser-Franz-Josef-Strasse 59; s €38, d €66; 🐕) This budget hotel is back from the lake but has views across it from most of the rooms; it's in a 400-year old Gothic building that once belonged to the monastery; all rooms have balconies.

Pizzeria Peppino   PIZZA €
(Seemühlgasse 57; pizza €5.50-8.90; ⏰4pm-midnight) This pizza joint in town is convenient for eat-in or take-away.

Full House   BAR
(Kaiser-Franz-Josef-Strasse; ⏰7pm-2am) For pub entertainment, Full House, near the Volksbank, is the place to hang out.

THE AUTOSCHLEUSE TAUERNBAHN

If you're driving to Bad Gastein from Spittal an der Drau, you'll need to use the *Autoschleuse Tauernbahn* (railway car-shuttle service; www.gasteinertal.com/autoschleuse, in German) through the tunnel from Mallnitz to Böckstein. The fare for cars is €17 one way or €30 return (valid for two months). For motorcycles, the price is €15/26. For information, call ☑05 717. Departures are every 60 minutes, or 30 minutes on busy weekend periods, with the last train departing at 10.20pm heading south, and 9.50pm going north. The journey takes 13 minutes.

ⓘ Information

Tourist Office – Millstatt (☑20 23; www.millstaettersee.com; Marktplatz 8; 8am-6pm Mon-Fri, to noon Sat & Sun) Located inside Millstatt's *Rathaus*, with useful information on the town.

Tourist Office – Bad Kleinkirchheim (☑04240-82 12; www.badkleinkirchheim.at; Dorfstrasse 30) Helpful for ski information.

ⓘ Getting There & Around

Postbus services to Millstatt depart from outside Spittal train station (€3.30, 20 minutes, two hourly), with some continuing to Bad Kleinkirchheim (from Spittal €7, one hour). **Mountainbike Station Thomas Graf** (☑0650, 3563 181; Kaiser-Franz-Josef-Strasse 59; 9am-6pm Mon-Fri, 9am-1pm Sat & Sun May–mid-Oct) rents mountain bikes for €22.50 per 24 hours.

Hohe Tauern National Park

Best Places to Eat

» Mayer's (p276)
» Kirchenwirt (p290)
» Lutter & Wegner (p285)
» Steinerwirt (p276)
» Dolomitenhütte (p290)

Best Places to Stay

» Hotel Haidenhof (p289)
» Pension Hubertus (p275)
» Hotel Miramonte (p284)
» Chalet-Hotel Senger (p281)
» Burgeck Panorama Hotel (p282)

Why Go?

If you thought Mother Nature pulled out all the stops in the Austrian Alps, Hohe Tauern National Park was her magnum opus. Welcome to Austria's outdoor wonderland and one of Europe's biggest nature reserves (1786 sq km), straddling Tyrol, Carinthia and Salzburgerland. Try as we might, no amount of hyperbole about towering snow-clad peaks, shimmering glaciers, impossibly turquoise lakes and raging waterfalls can quite do this place justice.

The poetry of such landscapes is set in motion on high-altitude roads twisting to elegant spa towns, Roman ruins and the 3798m hump of Grossglockner. But to really appreciate Hohe Tauern, you must strike out into its wilderness. Grab your boots or skis, slip into a bicycle saddle or launch yourself off a mountain to send your spirits soaring from peak to glorious peak, and commit every last inch of loveliness to memory.

When to Go

Each season has its own flavour in the Hohe Tauern National Park. Summer brings festivals and fireworks to the shores of Zell am See. This is also the best time to do high-altitude hikes and climbs, and adventure along the dizzying Grossglockner Road. A wintry dusting of snow brings skiing to Zell am See-Kaprun, the Kitzsteinhorn Glacier and spa town Bad Gastein. Everything starts to bud in late spring, while in autumn the slopes are beautifully cloaked in golden larch trees.

GERMANY

To Salzburg

SALZBURG
(SALZBURGERLAND)

TYROL

Kitzbüheler Alpen

0 ——— 20 km
0 ——— 12 miles

Bischofshofen

Saalfelden

St Johann
im Pongau

Hopfgarten
Kitzbühel
To
Innsbruck

Saalbach
Hinterglemm
161

Schmittenhöhe
(1965m)
Prielau
Thumersbach

Pinzgauer
Spaziergang 4
Zell
am See
Zeller See

311

Thurn Pass

Mittersill
168
Bruck

311

Salzach

Kaprun
Fusch

Gerlos Pass
165
Neukirchen

Krimml
2
Gerlos

Obersulzbachtal

Hohe

Volvo Ice
Camp 5
Kitzsteinhorn
(3203m)

Tauern

Ferleiten
Toll

Wildpark
Ferleiten

Grossglockner
Road

1

Gasteiner Tal
167

Bad
Hofgastein

Felbertauerntunnel

Felber-Tauern-Str.

Edelweiss Spitze
(2571m)

Böckstein

Bad
Gastein
3
Kötschachtal

Grossvenediger
(3674m)

Matreier
Tauernhaus

Fuscher Törl
(2428m)

Pasterze Glacier

Grossglockner
(3798m)

Stubnerkogel
(2246m)

Hochtor

Sportgestein

Graukogel
(2492m)

Railway car-shuttle
Tauernbahn
Autoschleuse

Guttal

Hinterbichl

Matrei
in Osttirol

Kals

Kaiser-Franz-
Josefs-Höhe
(2369m)

Heiligenblut Toll

Mallnitz

107

Isel

108

Defereggen

St Jakob

Schwarzach

EAST TYROL
(OSTTIROL)

Grosskirchheim

Obervellach

106

To Spittal-
Millstättersee
(30km)

ITALY

Defereggengebirge

Isel

Winklern

Möll

CARINTHIA

Sillian

100

Lienz
7 8

Drau

Lienzer
Dolomiten

Oberdrauburg

100

Karnische

111

Obertilliach

Alpen

Gail

110

Kötschach

Hohe Tauern National Park Highlights

1 Buckle up for a
rollercoaster ride of Alps and
glaciers on the **Grossglockner
Road** (p279), one of Austria's
greatest drives

2 Hear the thunder of the
Krimmler Wasserfälle (p281),
Europe's highest waterfall

3 Feel 10 years younger
bathing in the radon-laced

waters of **Bad Gastein** (p283),
hailed for healing properties

4 Be elevated by evocative
alpine views while hiking
the high-altitude **Pinzgauer
Spaziergang** (p277)

5 Discover your inner Inuit
sleeping in an igloo at the
Volvo Ice Camp (p278) at the
Kitzsteinhorn Glacier

6 Take a walk on the wild
side of Hohe Tauern with a
guided **ranger tour** (p279)

7 Be moved by the sombre
works of Albin Egger-Lienz
at medieval castle **Schloss
Bruck** (p286) in Lienz

8 Let llamas lead the way
through the Dolomites from
Lienz (p288)

HIKING & CLIMBING IN HOHE TAUERN NATIONAL PARK

Hohe Tauern's deep valleys, towering peaks and plateaux are a mecca to hikers and climbers. The reserve has treks to suit every level of ability, from gentle day walks to extreme expeditions to inaccessible peaks and ridges.

Freytag & Berndt produce detailed 1:50,000 walking maps covering the national park and surrounding areas. When planning a major trek, it's worth booking overnight stops in advance, as accommodation can be sparse the higher you go; local tourist offices can advise.

Popular hikes include the ascent of the eternally ice-capped **Grossvenediger** (3674m), flanked by glaciers. The closest you can get by road is the 1512m-high **Matreier Tauernhaus** (☑04875-88 11; www.matreier-tauernhaus.at, in German; Matrei in Osttirol; dm €26, d €24-32) at the southern entrance to the Felbertauerntunnel. You can park here and within an hour's walk gain fine views of the mountain.

Anyone with climbing experience and a reasonable level of fitness can climb the mighty **Grossglockner** (3798m) via the 'normal' route, though a guide is recommended. The main trail begins at the **Erzherzog-Johann-Hütte** (☑04876-85 00; dm/r €21/35), a four- to five-hour hike from Heiligenblut. From here, the roughly two-hour route crosses ice and rocks, following a steel cable over a narrow snow ridge, to the cross at the summit. It's essential to have the proper equipment (maps, ropes, crampons etc) and to check weather conditions before setting out. For guides, contact the tourist office in Heiligenblut or visit www.glocknerfuehrer.at (in German).

History

The Austrian Alps once formed the boundary between the more-established southern Roman territories and their newer, less stable conquests to the north. The main trade route for pack animals ran along the pass at the end of the Tauern Valley, but few settlements were established due to the Romans' distrust of the treacherous climate (tales of malevolent snowy spirits abounded) and difficult mountainous topography.

In 1971 the provinces of Carinthia, Salzburg and Tyrol agreed to the creation of a national park; regions were added in stages between 1981 and 1991 until it became Europe's largest national park. Today Hohe Tauern is widely regarded as one of Europe's biggest conservation success stories, an example of an approach where the needs of the local population are addressed right from the start.

ℹ Getting There & Around

BUS Getting around by bus is made more attractive by special passes; such deals change periodically, so make enquiries upon arrival. Buying zoned day or week passes should work out significantly cheaper than buying single tickets.

CAR & MOTORCYCLE To limit traffic through the park, many of the roads have toll sections and some are closed in winter. The main north–south road routes are the year-round Felber-Tauern-Strasse (B108) between Mittersill and Lienz, and the spectacular Grossglockner Road (open May to October). The 5.5km-long Felbertauerntunnel is on the East Tyrol–Salzburgerland border; the toll is €10 for cars and €8 for motorcycles. Buses on the Lienz–Kitzbühel route operate along this road.

TRAIN The main hubs for train services are Zell am See (for services to Salzburg and points north via St Johann im Pongau) and Lienz (for trains east and west into Tyrol and Carinthia).

Zell am See

☑06542 / POP 10,000 / ELEV 757M

Zell am See is an instant heart-stealer. From its bluer than blue lake (Zeller See) and pocket-sized centre studded with brightly painted chalets, the snowcapped peaks of the Hohe Tauern lift your gaze to postcard heaven. You can dive into that lake and cycle its leafy shores, hike and ski in those mountains and drive high, high on the Grossglockner Road. Every year, more than one million visitors – from American families to Saudi playboys in souped-up Mustangs – do just that, all in search of the Austrian dream.

🏃 Activities

Downhill Skiing

SKIING

(2-day lift pass adult/child €80/40) Together with neighbouring Kaprun, Zell am See has 138km of downhill skiing in its mountainous backyard. The two must-ski

Zell am See

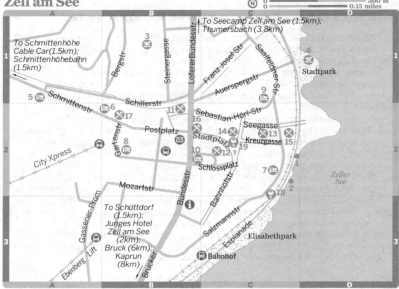

Zell am See

biggies are **Schmittenhöhe** (1965m) and the **Kitzsteinhorn Glacier** (3203m); the latter also offers cross-country skiing, year-round glacier skiing on a variety of pistes, and a half-pipe, rails, kickers and boxes for boarders at the **Mellow Park**. The terrain is more tree-lined and scenic than hair-raising, but there are a couple of steep black pistes for experts. Expect fairly long lift queues in the high winter season.

Combined lift passes for the region are for a minimum two-day period; ski buses are free for ski-pass holders. The most convenient way to reach the slopes is by taking the **City Xpress** gondola from central Zell am See. About 1.5km west of town and served by bus, the **Schmittenhöhe cable car** takes you even higher – to the summit of Schmittenhöhe.

Guided Walks   WALKING
From mid-June to September, the tourist office arranges free guided walks on Schmittenhöhe and Kitzsteinhorn, including glacier hikes, herb walks and five-hour treks to 2995m Maurerkogel. The staff can also advise you on family-friendly **llama treks** in the Kaprun area, and have maps and GPS devices to help you plan your route.

The **hiking** around Zell am See is among the finest in the Alps. Almost everywhere, you're rewarded with staggering views of the Hohe Tauern range – whether you opt for a gentle walk through alpine pastures tinkling with cow bells or a high-altitude day hike. For the 'greatest hits' of regional scenery, consider walking the **Pinzgauer Spaziergang**, accessed by the Schmittenhöhebahn and the Schattberg X-Press gondolas.

Zeller See
SWIMMING

The Zeller See may be on the cold side of refreshing, but the views are marvellous. There's also loads of high-speed action on the water in summer, from waterskiing to wakeboarding. If you'd rather not grit your teeth as you swim, there are several **lidos** (adult/child €5.90/3.90) dotted around the lake, including those at Zell am See, Thumersbach and Schüttdorf. They all feature sunbathing lawns, solar-heated pools and children's splash areas. Entry is free with the Zell am See-Kaprun Card or Mountain & Swimming Ticket.

Freizeitzentrum
LEISURE CENTRE

(Steinergasse 3-5; pool adult/child €8.50/6.10; ◷10am-10pm) Preferable to a dip in the icy Zeller See in winter, this leisure centre shelters a 25m pool, whirlpool and saunas. There's also a bowling alley, ice rink and (in summer) a lido here.

Boat Trips
BOAT TOURS

(adult/child €9.50/4.70; ◷10am-5pm May-Oct) Laid-back boat tours leave from Zell am See Esplanade for a 45-minute spin on the lake. Boats occasionally stop at Seecamp Zell am See (one way/return €2.90/4.80). If you'd prefer to go it alone, a number of places along the promenade hire out pedalos/motorboats for around €11.50/14.50 per hour from April to October.

Barbecue Donut
BOAT HIRE

(☑0664-992 73 29; Esplanade 2) If the idea of drifting gently across Zeller See with a drink in hand and a barbecue on the go appeals, consider renting the Barbecue Donut, a giant battery-powered ringo complete with charcoal grill. Call ahead for times and prices.

Adventure Service
ADVENTURE SPORTS

(☑735 25; www.adventureservice.at; Steinergasse 7; ◷office 8.30am-12.30pm) From May to September, Adventure Service takes the daring tandem paragliding (€100), white-water rafting (€44), canyoning (€51 to €69), climbing (€41) and mountain biking (€22 to €29). It also rents out bikes (half-/full day €11/16).

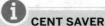

ℹ️ CENT SAVER

If you're in town in summer, ask your host for the free **Zell am See-Kaprun Card** (◷mid-May–mid-Oct). The card gets you free entry to all major sights and activities in the region, including the swimming pools around the lake, Wildpark Ferleiten and the Krimmler Wasserfälle (Krimml Falls). It also gives you one free ride per day on the cable cars that ascend to Schmittenhöhe and Kitzsteinhorn.

For unlimited use of all mountain transport, consider purchasing a good-value, six-day **Mountain & Swimming Ticket** (adult/child €67/32.50).

Windsurfcenter Zell am See
WINDSURFING

(☑0664-644 36 95; Seespitzstrasse 13; 2hr intro course €29.50; ◷9am-5pm May-Sep) Stiff mountain breezes create the ideal conditions for windsurfing on Zeller See. This reputable windsurfing centre is 2.5km south of town. Call for more information on its wide range of courses.

⭐ Festivals & Events

Zell am See swings into summer with live music, fireworks and sports events at its two **lake festivals**, held in mid-July and early August. The free **Zell Summer Night** festival draws Dixie bands, street entertainers and improvised theatre to streets and squares every Wednesday night from July to August.

🛏️ Sleeping

Winter prices are roughly 50% higher than the summer rates quoted below. Note that many places close between seasons – usually from October to November and April to May.

TOP CHOICE Pension Hubertus
PENSION €€

(☑724 27; www.hubertus-pension.at; Gartenstrasse 4; s €43-52, d €72-90; [P]☻) Beate and Bernd extend a warm welcome at their eco-savvy chalet. Opposite the ski lifts, the pension uses 100% renewable energy (solar and wind power), and organic produce and fair-trade coffee are served at breakfast. The bright, airy rooms are decked out country-style, with lots of pine, floral drapes and downy bedding.

Schloss Prielau HISTORIC HOTEL €€€
(☎729 11-0; www.schloss-prielau.at; Hofmannsthalstrasse; s €145, d €180-260; P ⊖ @) A once-upon-a-dream fairy tale of a hotel, this 16th-century castle set in mature grounds was once the haunt of Bavarian prince-bishops. Wood panelling and antiques add a touch of romance to the rustic-chic rooms, many with lake and mountain views. With its private beach, mini spa and Michelin-starred restaurant, Mayer's, this is luxury all the way. Schloss Prielau is 2.5km northeast of the centre along the lakefront promenade.

Steinerwirt HOTEL €€
(☎725 02; www.steinerwirt.com; Dreifaltigkeitsgasse 2; s/d €55/110; P ⊖ @ ᯤ) A 500-year-old chalet turned boutique hotel, Steinerwirt has bright rooms tastefully done out in muted tones and untreated pinewood. The rooftop whirlpool, mountain-facing sauna and meditation room invite relaxation. There's an excellent restaurant on-site (mains €9 to €20).

Haus Haffner GUESTHOUSE €
(☎723 96-0; www.haffner.at; Schmittenstrasse 29; s €24-32, d €44-58, apt €65-82; P ⊖ ᯤ 👪) Tucked down a quiet backstreet near the ski lift, Haffner's spacious rooms all sport balconies, cable TV and kettles. The family apartments have kitchenettes and chunky wood furniture (the owner is a cabinet maker).

Romantik Hotel Zell am See HISTORIC HOTEL €€
(☎725 20; www.romantik-hotel.at; Sebastian-Hörl-Strasse 11; incl half board s €88-118, d €136-184; P ⊖ @ ᯤ ≋) This dark wood chalet, ablaze with geraniums in summer, looks back on a 500-year history. Antique wood furnishings in the cosy rooms, a solar-heated pool with mountain views and a small spa with pampering treatments like chocolate baths create an ambience of discreet luxury.

Junge Hotel Zell am See HOSTEL €
(☎571 85; www.hostel-zell.at, in German; Seespitzstrasse 13; dm/s/d €22/30/48; ⊖) Right on the lake and beach, a 15-minute walk south of town, this hostel is a great budget deal. Dorms are well kept, the mountain views dreamy and there's always plenty going on – from volleyball matches to weekly barbecues. Half board costs an extra €7.50 per day.

Hotel Seehof HOTEL €€
(☎726 66; www.seehof.at; Salzmannstrasse 3; s/d/apt €55/94/95; P ⊖ ᯤ 👪) This lemon-fronted chalet is just steps from the lake. Rooms are cosy, if a tad small, with good beds and pine trappings. Light sleepers may hear the trains; rooms at the back are quieter but sacrifice the fine lake views. The family puts on a generous breakfast spread.

Haus Wilhelmina PENSION €
(☎726 07; www.haus-wilhelmina.at; Schmittenstrasse 14; r €74-80, apt €74-149; P ᯤ 👪) Just a joyous skip from the ski lift and centre, this friendly pension has simple but homey rooms with lots of pine, floral prints and balconies. There are also family-sized apartments.

Seecamp Zell am See CAMPGROUND €
(☎721 15; www.seecamp.at; Thumersbacherstrasse 34; camp sites per adult/child/tent €8.50/5.30/5.20; ᯤ) If waking up to views of the snowcapped Kitzsteinhorn mountains appeals, camp out at this tree-shaded site on the lakeshore. Facilities include a shop, restaurant, mini market and kids club. Guided mountain-bike and hiking tours are available.

Eating

The cafes and restaurants lining the lakefront and the old town serve up everything from Middle Eastern snacks to Michelin-starred finery. Many places close in shoulder seasons.

TOP CHOICE **Mayer's** FRENCH €€€
(☎729 11-0; Hofmannsthalstrasse; tasting menus €69-99; ⏲dinner Mon-Fri, lunch & dinner Sat & Sun; ⊖) Andreas Mayer, Austria's chef of the year in 2007 and holder of two Michelin stars, mans the stove at Schloss Prielau's refined restaurant. Freshness is key, with home-grown vegetables and organic produce shining through in French-infused specialities like *pot au feu* of crustaceans, and chocolate soufflé with Burgundy cherries – all totally divine and creatively presented. Advance reservations are recommended.

Steinerwirt AUSTRIAN €€
(☎725 02; Dreifaltigkeitsgasse 2; mains €8.50-20) Whether you dine in the contemporary bistro or in the old-world ambience of the wood-panelled Salzburger Stube, you get the same great food and service at Steinerwirt. The Austrian menu emphasises locally sourced meat and fresh lake fish, accompanied by wines drawn from the 600-year-old cellar.

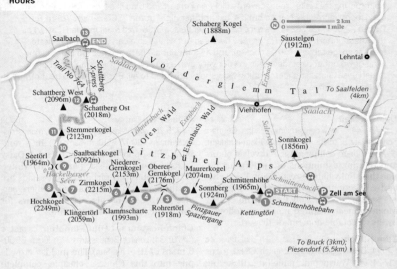

START **ZELL AM SEE**
FINISH **SAALBACH**
DISTANCE **19KM**
DURATION **FIVE TO SIX HOURS**

Schaberg Kogel
(1888m) ▲

Saalbach ⑬ END

Schattberg
X-press

Saustelgen
(1912m) ▲

Lehntal ○

0 — 2 km
0 — 1 mile

V o r d e r g l e m m   T a l

To Saalfelden
(4km)

Schattberg West
(2096m) ⑫ ▲ Schattberg Ost
(2018m)

Viehhofen ●

Saalach

Löhnersbach

Ofen Wald

Exenbach Wald

Sötersbach

Erlbach

⑪ Stemmerkogel
(2123m)

K i t z b ü h e l   A l p s

Sonnkogel
(1856m) ▲

Seetörl
(1964m) ⑩ Saalbachkogel
(2092m)
⑨

Niederer-
Gernkogel
(2153m)

Oberer-
Gernkogel
(2176m)

Maurerkogel
(2074m)

Schmittenhöhe
(1965m)

Schmittenbach

⑧ Hochkogel
(2249m) ⑦ Zirmkogel
(2215m) ⑥ ⑤ ④ ③ ② Sonnberg
(1924m)

START ① Zell am See ℗

Hackelberger
Seen

Klingertörl
(2059m) Klammscharte
(1993m) Rohrertörl
(1918m) Pinzgauer
Spaziergang

Kettingtörl

Schmittenhöhebahn

To Bruck (3km);
Piesendorf (5.5km)

Walking Tour
Pinzgauer Spaziergang

❯ Stretching 32km from Zell am See to Mittersill, this is one of Austria's greatest alpine walks. The moderately challenging 'best of' day hike affords magnificent views of the Kitzbühel Alps and Hohe Tauern range. Bring supplies and consider buying Kompass 1:35,000 map No 30 *Zell am See-Kaprun*.

At ① **Schmittenhöhebahn** (1965m) top station, begin a gradual descent from Saalbach/Pinzgauer Spaziergang, enjoying views of Zeller See and the glaciated Hohe Tauern range. The ever-narrowing path continues up an incline and passes through tarn-studded forest, occasionally drawing your gaze to shimmering Grossglockner (3798m) and the Kitzsteinhorn Glacier (3203m) to the south.

The landscape soon opens up as you wend through wildflower-streaked meadows and, after roughly an hour, contour the rounded summit of ② **Maurerkogel** (2074m). Make a short, painless ascent to ③ **Rohrertörl** (1918m) saddle, where you can contrast the limestone Kaisergebirge to the north with the icy Hohe Tauern peaks to the south.

Passing two junctions, follow a balcony trail that contours the base of ④ **Oberer-Gernkogel** (2176m) and gently mounts ⑤ **Niederer-Gernkogel** (2153m). You'll soon reach the foot of ⑥ **Zirmkogel** (2215m), which, with will and expertise, can be climbed in little over an hour.

The rocky trail runs through high meadows and mottled mountains, passing a small hut near a stream. Around four hours from the trailhead, the path ascends a steepish incline to the ⑦ **Klingertörl** saddle (2059m), where a sign shows the way to Saalbach. Traverse the base of cliffs that sweep down from ⑧ **Hochkogel** (2249m) and make a short descent to the grassy col of ⑨ **Seetörl**.

Walk north from here, either climbing over the ⑩ **Saalbachkogel** (2092m) or skirting its western slopes. The same option is repeated for ⑪ **Stemmerkogel** (2123m). Descend then and continue towards Schattberg, making a final ascent to the ⑫ **Schattberg X-Press** gondola and then down to ⑬ **Saalbach**.

A FROSTY WELCOME

Shimmering ice walls, frosty caverns flickering green and blue like Northern Lights – it may sound incredibly Nordic but it's just another night at the 2500m-high **Volvo Ice Camp** (☎0699 131 382 41; www.ice-camp.at; per person €168; Wed & Sat mid-Jan–Easter) at the Kitzsteinhorn Glacier. Rates may be steep but where else can you have a raclette feast at an ice table, a frozen cocktail and a starlit bubble bath in a hot tub before snuggling down under a reindeer skin in your very own igloo? By day, the camp's ice bar, freestyle sessions and ice-climbing workshops are open to all. Book ahead to beat other would-be Eskimos to it.

Deins & Meins
FUSION €€

(☎472 44; www.deins-meins.at, in German; Schlossplatz 5; mains €9-20; ⊙8.30am-midnight; 🛜🖐) Floor-to-ceiling glass, red velvet chairs and rotating exhibitions of modern art define this slinky lounge-restaurant. Local chef and confectioner David Fischböck has put his stamp on the slow-food menu: herby Mediterranean-inspired mains are followed by his delectable homemade desserts.

Zum Hirschen
AUSTRIAN €€

(☎774; Dreifaltigkeitsgasse 1; lunch €8.80, mains €17-24; 🖐) Warm pine panelling, flickering candles and friendly yet discreet service create an intimate feel in this smart restaurant. Specialities like Pinzgauer *Kasnocken* (cheese noodles) and crispy pork drenched in beer sauce figure on the thoroughly Austrian menu.

Feinkost Lumpi
DELI €

(Seegasse 6; ⊙8.30am-6pm) This deli is picnic central. Stop by for dense rye bread, Pinzgauer ham and cheese and homemade *Knödel* (dumplings). The farm-fresh ice cream is superb, too.

Ristorante Giuseppe
ITALIAN €€

(☎723 73; Kirchengasse 1; pizza €6.50-10, mains €10-24) Large and crisp, the pizzas tend to be a better choice than pasta at this upbeat Italian place in the pedestrian-only centre. Choose between the pavement terrace and rustic wood-panelled restaurant. Lunch is good value at €7.20.

Zur Einkehr
INTERNATIONAL €€

(☎723 63; Schmittenstrasse 12; mains €9.50-19; ⊙lunch & dinner winter, dinner Mon-Sat summer) Near the slopes, this barn-style bistro is a local favourite. Dishes like sticky spare ribs and seafood lasagne are polished off nicely with pear schnapps at the crescent-shaped bar.

Villa Crazy Daisy
FUSION

(☎725 26; www.villa-crazydaisy.at; Salzmannstrasse 8; mains €10-17; ⊙10am-6am; 🖐) In a rambling villa opposite the Grand Hotel, Daisy hosts full-on après-ski parties in winter. Pizza, gambas piri-piri and giant salads are on the menu in the restaurant, where service can be hit-or-miss. Head upstairs for live music, DJs and slapstick fun.

China-Restaurant Fünf Planeten
CHINESE €

(☎701 34; Loferer Bundesstrasse 3; lunch €5.50-6, mains €7-11; ⊙Tue-Sun) The midday crowds pile into this Chinese cheapie, complete with mini fish pond, for well-heaped plates of spring rolls, noodles and beef with bean sprouts.

🍷 Drinking

Zell am See's nightlife gathers momentum in winter when skiers descend on the town and many restaurants and bars double as après-ski haunts.

B17
BAR

(Salzmannstrasse; 2; ⊙4pm-3am Mon-Sat) This funky little shack re-creates a B17 bomber, festooned with engines, army combats and fighter-plane pictures. The cheery barman mixes excellent fresh fruit cocktails and the measures are generous. You can head up to the roof terrace in summer.

Insider
BAR

(Kreuzgasse 1; ⊙6pm-late) Join the cocktail sippers for a daiquiri or Cuba libre at this upbeat, backlit lounge bar. There's live music on Fridays and guest DJs spinning everything from house to salsa on Saturdays.

ℹ️ Information

Tourist office (☎770; www.zellamsee-kaprun. com; Brucker Bundesstrasse 1a; ⊙8am-6pm Mon-Fri, 9am-6pm Sat, 9am-1pm Sun) Staff at this office will help find rooms; there's also an accommodation board in the foyer with a free 24-hour telephone.

ℹ Getting There & Away

BICYCLE You can hire bikes to pedal around the lake at any of the sports shops in town.

BUS Buses leave from outside the *Hauptbahnhof* and from the bus station behind the post office. They run to Kaprun (€3, 13 minutes, twice hourly), Krimml (€8.40, 1¼ hours, hourly) and in summer twice daily to Lienz (€21, 2½ hours) via Kaiser-Franz-Josefs-Höhe.

CAR & MOTORCYCLE Zell am See is on the B311 running north to Lofer, where it joins the B178, which connects St Johann in Tyrol with Salzburg (passing through Germany). It's also just a few kilometres north of the east–west highway linking St Johann im Pongau with Tyrol (via the Gerlos Alpine Rd).

TRAIN Hourly trains run from Zell am See to destinations including Salzburg (€20.10, 1½ hours), Kitzbühel (€11, 55 minutes) and Innsbruck (€25.60, 2½ hours).

Grossglockner Road

A stupendous feat of 1930s engineering, the 48km **Grossglockner Road** (www.grossglockner.at; toll per car/motorcycle €28/18; ⊘6am-8pm May-Oct, to 9.30pm mid-Jun–mid-Sep) swings giddily around 36 switchbacks, passing jewel-coloured lakes, forested slopes and above-the-clouds glaciers from Bruck in Salzburgerland to Heiligenblut in Carinthia. The super-fit can bike it: it's worth the backbreaking uphill for the exhilarating downhill, some say.

Between toll gates, all attractions are free. Begin your drive bright and early to beat the crowds, as the road is often bumper-to-bumper by midday, especially in July and August. It's also worth checking the forecast before you hit the road, as the drive is not much fun in snow or a storm. Variations of the following route include overnighting in Heiligenblut or continuing on to Lienz.

The route is doable by bus, albe[...] consuming option. Bus 5002 runs f[...] between Lienz and Heiligenblut o[...] days (€7.90, one hour), less frequ[...] weekends. From late June to late Sep[...] four buses run from Monday to Friday, and three at weekends between Heiligenblut and Kaiser-Franz-Josefs-Höhe (€4.30, 30 minutes). From June to September, bus 651 runs twice daily between Kaiser-Franz-Josefs-Höhe and Zell am See (€10.70, 1½ hours).

Heiligenblut

📞 04824 / POP 1200 / ELEV 1301M

One of the single-most striking images on the Grossglockner Rd is Heiligenblut, the needle-thin spire of its pilgrimage church framed by the glaciated summit of Grossglockner. The village's iconic scenery and easily accessible mountains lure skiers, hikers and camera-toting tourists. The compact centre is stacked with wooden chalets and, despite an overload of yodelling kitsch souvenirs, retains some traditional charm.

◎ Sights & Activities

Wallfahrtskirche St Vinzenz CHURCH
(Hof 2; ⊘dawn-dusk) As though cupped in celestial hands and held up to the mighty Alps, this 15th-century pilgrimage church lifts spirits and gazes. Inside is a tabernacle which purportedly contains a tiny phial of Christ's blood; hence the village name (*Heiligenblut* means 'holy blood'). Legend has it that the phial was discovered by a saint named Briccius, who was buried in an avalanche on this spot more than a thousand years ago.

Schareck & Gjaidtroghöhe SKIING
(1-day lift pass €36.50) Skiers can play on 55km of snow-sure slopes in the shadow of Grossglockner in Heiligenblut. This is perfect cruising terrain for beginners and easygoing intermediates, while families often choose the resort for its Bobo's Kids' Club.

DON'T MISS

ROAM RANGER

If you want to get out and stride in the Hohe Tauern National Park, consider [...] for one of the back-to-nature **guided tours** led by a team of well-informed [...] July to September, Hohe Tauern offers 26 hikes, several of which are free w[...] card. The broad spectrum covers everything from herb discovery trails to h[...] hikes, around-the-glacier tours, gorge climbing and wildlife spotting. For th[...] program and price list, visit www.nationalpark.at.

Salzach

Zell am See

START
Bruck

Grossglockner Rd

0 — 4 km
0 — 2 miles

Ferleiten Toll

2

Grosses
Wiesbachhorn
▲(3564m)

Hohe Tauern
National
Park

3

4

▲ Edelweiss
Spitze
5 (2571m)

Kaiser-
Franz-Josefs-
Höhe
(2369m)

6
7

8 ○ Hochtor

Grossglockner
(3798m)
▲ **END** **10**

9

Driving Tour
Grossglockner Road

❯ Buckle up and prepare for one of Europe's greatest Alpine drives – the Grossglockner Road, 48 head-spinning, glacier-gawping, wow-what-a-mountain kilometres.

Leaving **1** **Bruck** behind, you enter the wild, mountainous Fuschertal (Fuscher Valley), passing Fusch and **2** **Wildpark Ferleiten**, an alpine wildlife park. Once through the tollgate, the road climbs steeply up to the **3** **Hochmais** (1850m), where glaciated peaks including 3564m Grosses Wiesbachhorn crowd the horizon. The road zigzags up to the **4** **Haus Alpine Naturschau** (2260m), spotlighting local flora and fauna. A little further along, a 2km side road (no coaches allowed) corkscrews up to **5** **Edelweiss Spitze** (2571m), the road's highest viewpoint – climb the tower for staggering 360-degree views of more than 30 peaks of 3000m. You can refuel with coffee and strudel on the terrace at the hut.

You'll soon want your camera handy for **Fuscher Törl** (2428m), commanding super on both sides of the ridge, and the gemstone of a lake **7** **Fuscher Lacke** (2262m) nearby. Here a small exhibition documents the construction of the road, built by 3000 men over five years during the Great Depression.

The road wriggles on through high meadows to **8** **Hochtor** (2504m), the top of the pass, after which there is a steady descent to **9** **Schöneck**. Branch off west onto the 9km Gletscherstrasse, passing waterfalls and *Achtung Murmeltiere* (beware of marmots) signs – you may well spot one of the burrowing rodents.

The Grossglockner massif slides into view on the approach to flag-dotted **10** **Kaiser-Franz-Josefs-Höhe** (2369m), affording memorable views of the bell-shaped Grossglockner (3798m) and the rapidly retreating Pasterze Glacier. The 8km swirl of fissured ice is best appreciated on the short and easy **Gamsgrubenweg** and **Gletscherweg** trails. Allow time to see the glacier-themed exhibition at the visitor centre and the crystalline **Wilhelm-Swarovski** observatory before driving back to Bruck.

Most of the skiing takes place on Schareck (2604m) and Gjaidtroghöhe (2969m) peaks.

In summer, serious **mountaineers** head here to bag peaks in the Hohe Tauern National Park. Enquire at the tourist office for details on mountain-bike trails in the park.

Sleeping & Eating

Heiligenblut has a handful of places to stay and eat, most clustered around the village centre. The tourist office can book private rooms. Rates jump between 20% and 30% in winter.

Chalet-Hotel Senger
TOP CHOICE   HOTEL €€

(☎22 15; www.romantic.at, in German; Hof 23; s €46, d €104-144; P🌐) Colourful prayer flags flutter at this farmhouse, a tribute to the Tibetan monks who once stayed here. All cosy nooks, warm wood and open fireplaces, this is just the spot for a little mountain hibernation and soul-searching. Most of the snug rooms have balconies; room 24 offers Grossglockner views instead.

Jugendherberge   HOSTEL €

(☎22 59; www.oejhv.or.at; Hof 36; dm/s/d €20/28/48; P) Near the church, this chalet-style HI hostel has light, spacious dorms, ski storage and a common room. It's next to the public swimming pool, sauna and climbing wall.

Camping Grossglockner   CAMPGROUND €

(☎20 48; Hadergasse 11; camp sites per adult/child/tent €6.90/3/2.50; P) Open year-round, this tree-shaded campground on the village outskirts features a restaurant and has great views of Grossglockner.

Di Casa   AUSTRIAN €€

(Hof 9; mains €8-14; ☉closed Nov) Walls festooned with rams' heads, ploughs and leather boots recount the 400-year history of this woodsy hut. The first mountaineers to climb Grossglockner ate here, so expect wholesome fare (the grill platter and zander fish fillet are favourites). Retreat to the patio for wonderful views.

Café Dorfstüberl   AUSTRIAN €€

(Hof 5; mains €7-12) Opening onto a tiny terrace, this is a real local haunt with hearty, sensibly priced food. The *halbes Hendl* (half a roasted chicken) with a mound of potato salad goes down well.

Information

National park information office (☎27 00; www.hohetauern.at; ☉10am-5pm Jun-Sep,

5-7pm Oct-May) In the Gästehaus Schober; has some museum exhibits. From 4pm to 5pm Monday to Friday someone from the Bergführer-informationsbüro (mountain guides office) gives advice on climbing and walking.

Tourist office (☎20 01; www.heiligenblut.at, in German; Hof 4; ☉9am-6pm Mon-Fri, 9am-noon & 4-6pm Sat) On the main street, close to the Hotel Post bus stop. Books mountain guides.

Getting There & Away

As well as buses running to/from Kaiser-Franz-Josefs-Höhe from late June to September, there is a year-round service to/from Lienz.

Krimml

☎06564 / POP 850 / ELEV 1076M

A real crash-bang spectacle, the 380m-high, three-tier Krimmler Wasserfälle, Europe's highest waterfall, is the thunderous centrepiece of this tiny village. Those who look beyond the falls find even more to like about Krimml – gorgeous alpine scenery, fine mountain walks and farmstays that are great for tiptoeing back to nature for a few days.

Sights

Krimmler Wasserfälle   WATERFALL
TOP CHOICE

(Krimml Falls; www.wasserfaelle-krimml.at; adult/child €2/0.50, Dec-Apr free; ☉ticket office 8am-6pm mid-Apr–late Oct) Enshrouded in mist, arched by a rainbow, frozen solid – no matter the time of year, this waterfall always look extraordinary. The **Wasserfallweg** (Waterfall Trail), which starts at the ticket office and weaves gently uphill through mixed forest, has numerous viewpoints with photogenic close-ups of the falls.

It's about a two-hour round-trip walk, or double that if you want to continue along the glacial Achental valley, which shadows a burbling brook to **Hölzlahneralm**. Up here, you'll have fantastic views of boulder-strewn pastures and 3000m-high peaks – you can even stay the night if you're too tired to head back down to Krimml.

WasserWunderWelt   ADVENTURE PARK

(adult/child €7/3.50; ☉9.30am-5pm May-Oct) Near the entrance to the falls, thi~~~~ater-related park has loads of hands-on ~~~~ from physics experiments to ar~~~~ tions and outdoor games where th~~~~ get completely and utterly soake~~~~

🏃 Activities

The tourist office has details on activities for kids, from pony riding to climbing.

Zillertal Arena
SKIING

(www.zillertalarena.at; 1-/3-/6-day ski pass €41/80.50/199) Krimml is part of the Zillertal Arena, covering 166km of pistes that are mostly geared towards intermediates. Krimml also appeals to families and non-skiers in winter, with low-key activities like tobogganing, snowshoeing and horse-drawn sleigh rides.

Tauernradweg
CYCLING

(www.tauernradweg.com) Well-marked cycling and hiking trails fan out into the surrounding Alps, including the Tauernradweg, a 310km bike route through the mind-blowing scenery of the Hohe Tauern National Park to Salzburg and then on to Passau. The route covers some high-altitude stretches and demands a good level of fitness. The Wasserfallweg walking trail begins near the Tauernradweg's starting point.

🛏 Sleeping

Krimml makes an easy day trip from Zell am See or Mayrhofen in Tyrol, but it's a shame not to stay the night as the village has pensions and farmstays with bags of character. Winter prices are roughly a third higher than those given below.

TOP CHOICE Burgeck Panorama Hotel
GUESTHOUSE €

(☏72 49; www.burgeck.com, in German; Oberkrimml 79; s/d/apt €42/70/75; P🅿️🛜📶) Scenically perched above the village and next to forest, this guesthouse is run by the kindly Bachmaier family and has terrific waterfall views. The recently renovated rooms are modern, while others are done out in rustic alpine style. Kids are well catered for with a playground and, in winter, an illuminated toboggan track right on the doorstep.

🍃 Hölzlahneralm
MOUNTAIN HUT €

(☏0664-402 68 78; www.hoelzlahner.at, in German; dm adult/child €20/14; ⊙May-Oct) High above the falls, this wood-shingled farmhouse has comfy bunks for weary walkers and hearty mountain fodder like *Kaspressknödel* (dumplings in gooey Pinzgauer cheese). The ecofriendly chalet generates its own electricity and uses natural spring water.

Hotel Klockerhaus
HOTEL €€

(☏72 08-0; www.klockerhaus.com; Oberkrimml 10; ···l half board €49/98; P🅿️🛜🏊📶) Plenty of pine keeps things cosy in the rooms with waterfall views and the lounge with an open fire at Klockerhaus. The untreated outdoor pool and free-roaming guinea pigs and goats have the wow factor for kids. There's a small spa with a sauna, saline steam bath and treatments like Tibetan massage.

ℹ️ Information

The **tourist office** (☏72 39; www.krimml.at; Oberkrimml 37; ⊙8am-noon & 2.30-6pm Mon-Fri, 8.30-10.30am & 4.30-6pm Sat) is in the village centre next to the church. The post office is next door.

ℹ️ Getting There & Away

BUS Buses run year-round from Krimml to Zell am See (€8.40, 1¼ hours, hourly).

CAR & MOTORCYCLE The village is about 500m north of the falls, on a side turning from the B165. There are parking spaces (€4 per day) near the path to the falls, which branches to the right just before the toll booths for the Gerlos Alpine Rd to Mayrhofen.

Gerlos Alpine Road

Open year-round, the highly scenic **Gerlos Alpine Road** (www.gerlosstrasse.at; toll per car/motorcycle €7.50/4) links the Zillertal in Tyrol to Krimml in Salzburgerland, winding 12km through high moor and spruce forest, and reaching a maximum elevation of 1630m. The lookout above the turquoise *Stausee* (reservoir) is a great picnic stop, with a tremendous vista of the Alps. On the approach to Krimml near Schönmoosalm, there are bird's-eye views of the Krimml Falls.

Buses make the trip between Krimml and Zell am Ziller (one way including toll €8.70, 1½ hours) in Tyrol from 1 July to 30 September. By car, you can avoid using the toll road by following the (easy-to-miss) signs to Wald im Pinzgau, 6km north of Krimml.

Bad Gastein

☏06434 / POP 4460 / ELEV 1000M

Spiritually somewhere between Brighton and St Moritz, Bad Gastein runs hot and cold, with therapeutic spas year-round and first-class skiing in winter. Though the damp is rising in places, the resort has kept some of the grandeur of its 19th-century heyday, when Empress Elisabeth came to bathe and pen poetry here. And the backdrop is timeless: belle-époque villas cling to forest-

TAKING THE WATERS

Bad Gastein is famous for its **radon-laced waters**, which trickle down from the mountains, heat up to temperatures of 44°C to 47°C around 2000m underground, then gush forth at 18 different springs in the area. Renowned since Roman times for their healing properties and described by 16th-century physician Paracelsus as 'God's own composita', the therapeutic waters are said to boost potency, alleviate rheumatism and respiratory ailments, stop inflammation, stimulate circulation and (phew!), stabilise the immune system. Strauss and Empress Elisabeth (Sisi) both put the waters' benefits to the test; the empress was so impressed that she penned a poem beginning: 'Only sick bones I thought of bringing, where mystically your hot water springs...'

The product of 3000 years of geological forces, the radon is absorbed through the skin and retained in the body for nearly three hours, but vapour tunnels burrowed deep in the rock and emitting radon gases are used for more intensive treatments.

A glass elevator zooms up to **Felsentherme Gastein** (www.felsentherme.com; Bahnhofplatz 5; 3hr/day ticket adult €19/22.50, child €10.50/14; ☉9am-9pm, sauna to 10pm), where you can splash around in the rejuvenating waters. The spa shelters grottolike pools and an outdoor thermal bath with pummelling massage jets and stellar mountain views. For those prepared to bare all, there are panoramic saunas and salty steam baths to test out. Curative massages, radon baths and electrotherapy are available next door in the **Thermalkurhaus** (Bahnhofplatz 7; ☉8am-noon & 2-5pm Mon-Fri, 8am-noon Sat).

To feel the water's benefits without tapping into your euros, fill your bottle at one of the town's **Thermalwasser Trinkbrunnen** (thermal water drinking fountains), such as those on Kongressplatz and Mozartplatz. Two to six cups per day are recommended for glowing health.

cloaked cliffs that rise above the falls and springs still hailed for their miraculous healing properties.

⊙ Sights

TOP CHOICE **Gasteiner Wasserfall** WATERFALL
Bad Gastein's star attraction is this 341m waterfall, which rages over rugged cliff faces and through thick forest to tumble into three turquoise pools. The waterfall's wispy, ethereal beauty captured the imagination of Klimt, Max Liebermann, Schubert and Empress Elisabeth. The stone **Wasserfallbrücke** (waterfall bridge) is the best vantage point and the trailhead for the **Wasserfallweg** (waterfall path) that shadows the magnificent cataract and provides some great photo ops.

Nikolauskirche CHURCH
(Bismarckstrasse; ☉dawn-dusk) A statue of 16th-century physician Paracelsus guards the entrance to this early-Gothic church. Built in 1389, the church is tiled with wood shingles and built around a central pillar. Its interior is simple yet beautiful, with an uneven flagstone floor, baroque altar and rudimentary frescoes fading with age.

Gasteiner Museum MUSEUM
(www.gasteinermuseum.at; Grand Hotel de l'Europe, Kaiser-Franz-Josef-Strasse 14) This eclectic little museum spans everything from minerals to Stone Age artefacts and vintage tourism billboards. The museum was closed at the time of research and is expected to reopen at this new address in summer 2011; see the website for times and prices.

🏃 Activities

Sportwelt Amadé SKIING
(1-day ski pass €42) Bad Gastein's slopes and spas are a match made in heaven in winter. The resort's 200km of varied pistes challenge confident beginners and intermediates, with attractive wooded runs and some great carving opportunities. Mountain transport is not brilliant, and reaching the slopes in neighbouring resorts can be time-consuming unless you have your own wheels.

The resort is part of the expansive Sportwelt Amadé arena, comprising 865km of slopes, with skiing and snowboarding centred on **Stubnerkogel** (2246m) and **Graukogel** (2492m). Cross-country skiing is also big in Bad Gastein, with 90km of prepared *Loipe* (tracks) including a floodlit trail at **Böckstein** (3.5km south of Bad Gastein).

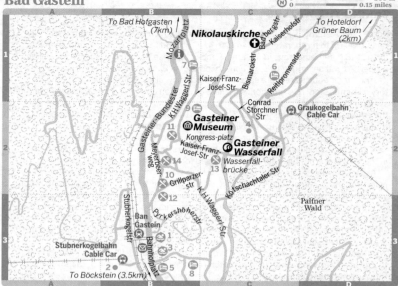

At **Sport Schober** (http://sport-schober.at; Stubnerkogel; ⊗8am-6pm) you can rent skis for €20, snowboards for €24 and cross-country sets for €12 per day.

Stubnerkogel & Graukogel　　　　WALKING
Both Stubnerkogel and Graukogel are excellent for summertime walking, with high-altitude trails traversing alpine pastures and craggy peaks, and taking you up to authentic mountain huts. The two-section **Stubnerkogelbahn** cable car near Bad Gastein's train station costs €20.50 return. The **Graukogelbahn** cable car is 300m northeast of the centre and also costs €20.50 return.

GASTEINCARD

Pick up the free GasteinCard from your host for some great freebies, including guided hikes and bike tours, spa concerts and history walks; the tourist office has full details. The card also yields substantial discounts on cable cars, buses, spas and activities. The winter card offers similar reductions plus free use of all buses, the ice-skating rink, toboggan rental and guided ski safaris.

From mid-May to mid-September, the tourist office organises daily guided walks that range from half-day hikes to herb trails and dairy visits.

🛏 Sleeping

Some of the resort's hotels feature their own spas and offer special packages. Expect rates in the high winter season to be roughly 30% higher than those given in the listings below.

TOP CHOICE　**Hotel Miramonte**　　　　HOTEL €€
(☏25 77; www.hotelmiramonte.com; Reitl-promenade 3; s €108-130, d €145-188; ⊜🛜) This hilltop hotel impressed the likes of *Vanity Fair* with its retro-chic design and phenomenal mountain backdrop. A terrace overlooking forested peaks, a thermal spa with pampering Aveda treatments and a yoga instructor (Andrea) draw a style-conscious crowd here. The studio-style rooms are all about pared-down glamour, with bare wood floors, cowskin rugs and flat-screen TVs mounted on tripods.

Hoteldorf Grüner Baum　　　　HOTEL €€€
(☏25 16; www.hoteldorf.com; Kötschachtal 25; s €124-150, d €248-300; 🅿🛜♨) The Shah of Persia, Princess Margaret of Holland, Jude Law – they've all stayed at this mountain retreat set in 30-hectare grounds. More of

Bad Gastein

a hamlet than a hotel, the Grüner Baum's cluster of alpine chalets shelter rooms beautifully furnished with antiques. A spa and thermal pools, delicious food and polished service justify the hefty price tag.

Villa Solitude   HOTEL €€
(✆51 01; www.villasolitude.com; Kaiser-Franz-Josef-Strasse 16; ste €110-150; P☺@) Once home to an Austrian countess, this belle-époque villa shelters six suites crammed with oil paintings and antiques. The intimate piano room downstairs is the place to slip into your role as lord or lady of the manor. Lutter & Wegner restaurant is next door.

Pension Charlotte   PENSION €
(✆24 26; Paracelsusstrasse 6; s/d €25/50) Expect a warm welcome from the Weghofer family and a slobbery one from their Great Dane, Aramis, at this tucked-away pension. You can make yourself at home in the garden and in the lounge, decked out with curios from hand-carved *Krampus* masks to mountain crystals. The bright, spotless rooms have balconies overlooking the forest and mountains.

Hotel Mozart   HISTORIC HOTEL €€
(✆268 60; www.hotelmozart.at; Kaiser-Franz-Josef-Strasse 25; s/d 46/84; P☺) Done out in cherry

wood and chandeliers, the breakfast room at this family-run place is adorned with portraits of Mozart, whose mother, Anna Maria, visited Bad Gastein in 1750. Rooms are old-style but comfy and some have fine views. There's a whirlpool, sauna and steam room on-site.

Euro Youth Hotel   HOSTEL €
(✆233 00; www.euro-youth-hotel.at; Bahnhofplatz 8; dm/s/d €17/29/58; ☺closed Apr & Oct-Nov; P@☂) With its well-kept, high-ceilinged rooms, this century-old manor has more charm than your average hostel. Backpackers praise the facilities, which include a restaurant, TV lounge and barbecue area. Staff can arrange adventure sports like rafting and canyoning (around €35). Bike hire costs €10 per day.

Kur-Camping Erlengrund   CAMPGROUND €
(✆27 90; www.kurcamping-gastein.at; Erlengrundstrasse 6; camp sites per adult/child/tent €7.40/4.25/5.35; P☂☷) Close to a lake, this campground has shady pitches and a heated outdoor pool. It's an hour's walk following the waterfall north of Bad Gastein to Kötschachdorf; buses run from the train station.

✖ Eating & Drinking

Most of Bad Gastein's eating options line up along Kaiser-Franz-Josef-Strasse. Many places close or have shorter opening hours in the shoulder seasons.

Lutter & Wegner   FUSION €€
(✆510 11; Kaiser-Franz-Josef-Strasse 16; mains €15-24; ☺dinner) Big on atmosphere, this smart restaurant at Villa Solitude has a fairy-tale tower setting, award-winning fusion cuisine and a terrace overlooking the falls. Fine wines (choose from 180 bottles) accompany flavours such as porcini risotto and Creole lamb curry.

Jägerhäusl   AUSTRIAN €€
(✆202 54; Kaiser-Franz-Josef-Strasse 9; mains €9-16) Modern Austrian dishes like pike perch in an apple-celeriac crust are served at this galleried villa. Sit on the maple-shaded terrace when the sun's out. There's live Tyrolean music on Thursdays in summer.

Hofkeller   AUSTRIAN €€
(✆203 70; Grillparzerstrasse 1; mains €16-20; ☺dinner Mon-Sat) In winter, there's no place like this stone cellar beneath the Salzburger Hof hotel for warming up over fondue, a raclette cheese fest or hot stone specialities.

Silver Bullet Bar
INTERNATIONAL €€

(www.silverbulletbar.com; Grillparzerstrasse 1; mains €7.50-10) Wagon wheels, a stuffed buffalo head and cow-print benches give this barn-style restaurant a mock Wild West look. Finger-lickin' snacks like 100% Austrian beefburgers are accompanied by a party vibe and regular live music.

Revolution
SNACK BAR €

(Grillparzerstrasse 14; snacks €3-5.50; 🛜) Crimson walls and cushion-filled nooks create a warm, relaxed setting for drinks or a bite to eat at Revolution. The day's snacks, such as tortilla wraps, are scrawled on a blackboard.

Sancho's
MEXICAN €€

(📞217 62; Kaiser-Franz-Josef-Strasse 1; mains €9-21; ⊙dinner) Sombreros, stuffed cockatoos, Mayan murals and other colourful kitsch glam up this lively Mexican place. The jalapeno peppers and burritos are tasty, but the steaks are the stars of the menu – thick, juicy and drenched in salsa.

ⓘ Information

Post office (Bahnhofplatz 9) Next to the train station.

Tourist office (📞06432-3393 560; www.gastein.com; Kaiser-Franz-Josef-Strasse 27; ⊙8am-6pm Mon-Fri, 3-6pm Sat, 9am-noon Sun) To get here, go left from the train station exit and walk down the hill. Staff will find you accommodation free of charge. There's information on the national park in the foyer.

ⓘ Getting There & Away

CAR & MOTORCYCLE Driving south, you'll need to use the Autoschleuse Tauernbahn (railway car-shuttle service) through the tunnel that starts at Böckstein (one-way/return €17/30). On the A10 Tauern-Autobahn from the north (Salzburg), take the Gasteinertal exit near Bischofshofen, then the B167.

TRAIN Trains trundle through Bad Gastein's station every two hours, connecting the town to points north and south including Spittal-Millstättersee (€11, 40 minutes), Salzburg (€17.60, 1¼ hours) and Innsbruck (€33.70, 3½ hours). When travelling north from Bad Gastein to Bad Hofgastein, sit on the right side of the train for the best views.

Around Bad Gastein

Stepping 3.5km south of Bad Gastein, you reach the unassuming village of Böckstein, whose medieval gold mine has been reinvented as a much-celebrated health centre, the **Gasteiner Heilstollen** (📞375 30; www.gasteiner-heilstollen.com; ⊙8am-5pm Mon-Fri, to noon Sat mid-Jan–mid Nov). Visitors board a small train at the Gasteiner Heilstollen that chugs 2km into the depths of Radhausberg mountain, where you absorb the healing radon vapours. The trial session costs €28, while the full three-week cure will set you back €520 (includes 10 entries to the tunnel).

Seven kilometres north of Bad Gastein is the sibling spa town of **Bad Hofgastein** (858m), home to the architecturally innovative **Alpen Therme** (www.alpentherme.com; 4hr/day ticket adult €22/26.50, child €13.50/15.50; ⊙9am-9pm Sun-Wed, to 10pm Thu-Sat). This mammoth spa is split into seven different worlds, where experiences stretch from relaxing in radon-rich thermal baths to racing down white-knuckle flumes. The sauna village comprises brine grottos, loft saunas, red-hot Finnish saunas and an ice-cold plunge pool. For some pampering, pop over to the beauty centre for treatments like goat's-milk wraps and hot-chocolate massages.

Bad Gastein, Bad Hofgastein and Böckstein are linked by both bus and rail. The scenic 7km Gastein Alpine Rd (per person €4; price included in the ski pass) links Böckstein to Sportgastein via tunnels and galleries.

Lienz

📞04852 / POP 11,950 / ELEV 673M

The Dolomites rise like an amphitheatre around Lienz, straddling the Isel and Drau Rivers, and just 40km north of Italy. Those same arresting river and mountain views welcomed the Romans, who settled here some 2000 years ago and whose legacy is explored at medieval castle Schloss Bruck and archaeological site Aguntum. Looking up to the blushing Dolomites at sunset, it's easy to see why they were so taken with this little corner of East Tyrol.

⊙ Sights

TOP CHOICE **Schloss Bruck**
CASTLE

(Schlossberg 1; adult/child/family €7.50/2.50/15; ⊙10am-6pm mid-May–late Oct) Lienz' trophy sight is this medieval fortress, a 15-minute walk west of town. Once the seat of the counts of Görtz, the hilltop castle now houses a **heritage museum**, which

HOHE TAUERN NATIONAL PARK

Lienz

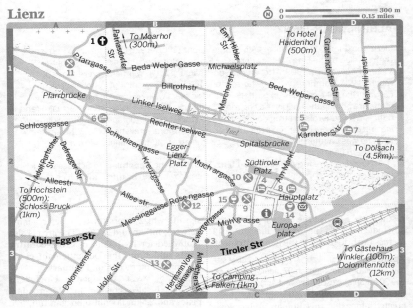

takes a chronological spin through regional history. The permanent collection brings together Roman artefacts, Gothic winged altars, traditional Tyrolean costumes and Cold War memorabilia. The **tower** hosts temporary exhibitions and is worth climbing for exhilarating views over Lienz. For art enthusiasts, the real highlight is the **gallery** devoted to the emotive works of Albin Egger-Lienz, with masterpieces such as the *Totentanz* (Dance of Death) and *Das Kreuz* (The Cross).

Stadtpfarrkirche St Andrä　　　CHURCH
(St Andrew's church; Pfarrgasse; ☉dawn-dusk) Sitting just north of the Isel River, this atmospheric Gothic church was reconstructed on the site of an earlier Romanesque chapel in the 15th century by the counts of Görtz. The frescoed, rib-vaulted interior houses a pair of tombs sculpted in red Salzburg marble, where the last two counts lay buried. The undoubted highlight is the **Kriegergedächtniskapelle** (War Memorial Chapel), where you can see Albin Egger-Lienz's highly emotive antiwar frescoes, paying homage to the dead of WWI. The sculpture of the risen Christ – emaciated and wearing nothing but a skimpy loincloth – outraged the Vatican when it was unveiled to the public in 1925. This is also Egger-Lienz' final

DON'T MISS

ALBIN EGGER-LIENZ

Lienz' most famous son is artist Albin Egger-Lienz (1868–1926), who grew up here and then studied at the Fine Arts Academy in Munich before becoming a member of the Vienna Secession in 1909. After a brief spell teaching art in Weimer, Egger-Lienz spent much of WWI capturing wartime horrors and the pervading spirit of hopelessness on canvas. Ghostlike corpses on battlefields and soldiers walking hand in hand with skeletons are among the deeply moving motifs that won the artist international acclaim (and criticism). The Tyrolean struggle for liberation (1809), the hardship and anguish of rural life and destiny are other recurring themes in his sombre, fatalistic works. When asked what he was painting shortly before he died, the artist bluntly replied, 'Ich bin fertig' (I have or am finished).

The new seven-stop **Albin Egger-Lienz Trail**, from the Hauptplatz to Schloss Bruck, takes you in the footsteps of the artist in his hometown; stop by the tourist office for more details.

resting place. To visit the chapel, pick up the key that hangs on the door at Pfarrgasse 13 (across the bridge facing the main entrance).

Aguntum ARCHAEOLOGICAL SITE
(www.aguntum.info; Stribach 97; adult/child €5/3; 9.30am-6pm, closed Nov–mid-Apr) An ultra-modern glass-walled museum has been erected alongside this Roman archaeological site, which is unique in these parts. Excavations are constantly under way to piece together this 2000-year-old *municipium* (a Roman city of the second-highest rank), which flourished as a centre of trade under Emperor Claudius. A stroll outside takes in the remains of a spa and artisan quarter and a reconstructed villa. The **museum** spells out Lienz' Roman history, with interactive stuff for the kids, including a virtual tour through Aguntum and dress-up costumes. There's also an exhibition on traditional Roman recipes – sow's udder with sea urchins, anyone? The site is 1.5km east of the centre.

Galitzenklamm SCENIC AREA
(Leisach; adult/child €3.20/2; 10am-5pm Jun-Sep) This vertiginous walkway clings to the sheer cliffs of a gorge that rises above the swirling waters of the Drau River. To get there, take bus 4421 to Leisach, 3km from Lienz.

🏃 Activities

Zettersfeld SKIING
(www.topski.at; 1-day ski pass €36) Beginners and intermediates should find enough of a challenge on Lienz' 40km of pistes, which afford seductive views of the rugged Dolomites. Most of the action takes place around Zettersfeld, where a cable car and

six lifts whizz skiers up to slopes reaching between 1660m and 2278m. The area is also renowned for its 100km of **cross-country trails** and hosts the Dolomitenlauf cross-country skiing race in mid-January.

Slightly west of Lienz, **Hochstein** (2057m) is also popular for its groomed pistes and 2.5km floodlit toboggan run; free buses link the train station to the cable-car valley stations in summer and winter high seasons.

One-day ski passes cover both mountains and the ski lifts run from 1 December to Easter, depending on snow. Multiday passes (eg two days for €72) cover all of East Tyrol's ski lifts.

Dolomites Trails WALKING
The tourist office sells walking (€4) and via ferrate (€1) maps and can advise on the high-altitude trails that thread through the steely peaks of the Dolomites. The cable cars spring back to life from June to September. The ride up to Hochstein costs €13 return, while Zettersfeld costs €10 (€17 including the chairlift to 2214m). Family and child fares are also available. If you're planning on making several trips, it's worth investing in the Osttirol Card.

Dolomiten Lamatrekking GUIDED WALKS
(680 87; www.dolomitenlama.at; in German; Oberlienz 36;) Nope, you're not in the Andes; yep, those really are llamas. Nothing motivates kids to walk quite like these gentle-natured camelids. The llamas lug the packs, leaving you free to enjoy the magnificent mountains and valleys of Hohe Tauern National Park. Tours range from two-hour

rambles to two-week treks to Mariazell. Call Karl-Peter ahead for times and prices.

Drau Radweg
CYCLING

(www.drauradweg.com) A network of well-signposted mountain-bike trails radiates from Lienz, taking in the striking landscape of the Dolomites. The scenic 366km Drau Radweg passes through Lienz en route to Maribor in Slovenia. Ask the tourist office for the map *Rad und Mountainbike Karte Osttirol,* which details cycling routes.

Probike Lienz (Amlacherstrasse 1a; half-/full day €13/18; ⏱9am-noon & 2-6pm Mon-Fri, 9am-noon Sat) is the most central place to hire your own set of wheels.

La Ola
ADVENTURE SPORTS

(☎611 99; www.laola.at, in German; Mühlgasse 15; ⏱9.45am-12.30pm & 2-6pm Mon-Fri, 9.45am-noon Sat) The fast-flowing rivers, narrow gorges and forests of the Dolomites around Lienz are the perfect place for adrenalin-pumping sports. Thomas Zimmermann at La Ola organises the whole gamut – from canyoning, kayaking and climbing in summer to ski touring, snowshoeing and ice-climbing in winter. Call for times and prices.

Osttirol Adventures
ADVENTURE SPORTS

(☎0664-356 0450; www.osttirol-adventures.at; Ainet 108) Specialises in rafting (from €25 to €59) among other outdoor pursuits. Call ahead for times and prices.

go! Eddy
ADVENTURE SPORTS

(☎0664-897 8259; www.raftcompany.at; Ainet 41) Outdoor camp in Ainet, offering rafting (€19 to €65), including family rafting, and canyoning (€49 to €110).

✵ Festivals & Events

Lienz hosts the testosterone-fuelled **Dolomiten Mann** (www.dolomitenmann.com) in September, a Red Bull–sponsored iron-man competition billed as the world's toughest team challenge. Headlining the program is the cross-country relay race, where teams of runners, paragliders, kayakers and mountain bikers battle it out for the title. Lively open-air concerts and parties complement the line-up.

In late July, a free street festival draws top circus and theatre acts from around the world. Summer also welcomes a series of events celebrating Tyrolean culture, plus free concerts on Hauptplatz and in other squares (8pm on Wednesdays and Sundays June to September).

🛏 Sleeping

The tourist office hands out a free brochure listing inexpensive private rooms; expect to pay around €15 to €25 per person per night. Wherever you stay, ask your host for the *Gästekarte* (guest card) for discounts on local sights and transport.

TOP CHOICE Hotel Haidenhof
HOTEL €€

(☎624 40; www.haidenhof.at, in German; Grafendorferstrasse 12; s/d €86/142; P 🅿 🐾 🛜) This glorious country escape sits high in the orchards above Lienz and has a dress-circle view of the Dolomites. Decked out in blond wood, the rooms are light and spacious, many with balconies overlooking the town and mountains. The roof terrace is a fine place to snuggle in a blanket and enjoy the panorama. In the South Tyrolean–style restaurant (mains €7 to €20), nearly everything that lands on your plate is home-grown: the herbs, the trout and even the apples in the strudel!

Grand Hotel Lienz
HOTEL €€€

(☎640 70; www.grandhotel-lienz.com; Fanny-Wibmer-Peditsstrasse 2; ste €230-280; P 🅿 🐾 🛜 🏊) This hotel designed in fin de siècle style is a classy new addition to Lienz. Every imaginable luxury comes with the price tag: impeccable service, a first-rate spa and pool, fine dining on a terrace overlooking the Isel River and Dolomites – you name it. The bright suites with canopy beds are rather grand, too.

Romantik Hotel Traube
HISTORIC HOTEL €€

(☎644 44; www.hoteltraube.at; Hauptplatz 14; s €68, d €128-152; P 🅿 @ 🏊) Right on the main square, this hotel races you back to the Biedermeier era with its high ceilings and wrought-iron balconies. The recently revamped rooms are dressed in Italian antique furnishings. Step up to the 6th-floor pool for views over Lienz to the Dolomites.

OSTTIROL CARD

Lienz' best summer deal is the seven-day **Osttirol Card** (adult/child €43/17.50), which is sold at the tourist office. The card is available from June to September and covers all of Lienz' major sights, including Schloss Bruck and Aguntum, as well as activities like Galitzenklamm, local swimming pools and cable cars.

Moarhof HOTEL €€
(📮675 67; www.hotel-moarhof.at; Moarfeldweg 18; s/d incl half board €78/154; P) Set in serene gardens, 10 minutes' stroll from the centre, this chalet-style hotel has big, modern rooms with mountain views. In the restaurant you'll dine heartily on farm-fresh produce, locally reared meat and fish. The stone-clad spa is the hotel's showpiece, with assorted saunas, whirlpools and relaxation rooms.

Goldener Stern PENSION €
(📮621 92; www.goldener-stern-lienz.at; Schweizergasse 40; s/d €39/72; P) Framed by neat gardens, this 600-year-old pension with rooms that are spacious and bright, if a little old fashioned. Breakfast is served in the tiny courtyard in summer.

Goldener Fisch HOTEL €€
(📮621 32; www.goldener-fisch.at; Kärntnerstrasse 9; s/d €53/92; P🛜🖶) The chestnut tree–shaded beer garden is a big draw at this family-friendly hotel. The rooms are light and modern – if not fancy – and you can wind down in the sauna and herbal steam baths. The beamed restaurant (mains €8 to €14) does a mean *Tafelspitz* (boiled beef with apple and horseradish sauce).

Altstadthotel Eck HOTEL €
(📮647 85; Hauptplatz 20; s/d €42/74) Sure, it could do with a makeover, but for some that's part of this hotel's old-world appeal. Wood-panelled corridors lead to rooms that are a little tired but comfortable, all with tea-making facilities. Take in Lienz views over breakfast in the conservatory.

Camping Falken CAMPGROUND €
(📮0664-4107973; www.camping-falken.com; Eichholz 7; camp sites per adult/child/tent €6.50/4/8.50; ⏱mid-Dec–mid-Oct; 🛜) Wake up to Dolomite views at this leafy campground, a 20-minute walk south of the centre. There's a minimarket, restaurant and play-

ground on-site, and guests get free access to swimming pools in Lienz.

Gästehaus Winkler PENSION €
(📮705 18; Roter Turmweg 5; s/d €22/42; P🖶) Handy for the cycling and cross-country trails that are on its doorstep, this convivial pension is a 20-minute walk south of town and has eight comfy rooms. There's a well-kept garden, playground and ski storage room.

✗ Eating

Italy is but a hop and over-the-mountain skip from Lienz and it shows: menus are often a fusion of East Tyrolean and Italian fare. When the sun's out, locals gather at gelatarias and pavement cafes on and around Hauptplatz.

For self-caterers, supermarkets include a **Spar** (Tiroler Strasse 23).

TOP CHOICE **Kirchenwirt** AUSTRIAN €€
(📮625 00; Pfarrgasse 7; mains €8.50-16; ⏱9am-1am) Opposite Stadtpfarrkirche St Andrä and housed in the 800-year-old Mesnerhaus, this newcomer is hands-down Lienz' most atmospheric restaurant. Dine under the vaults or on the streamside terrace on well-prepared local dishes – the *Tafelspitz* is flavoursome, as is the East Tyrolean milk-fed lamb.

Adlerstüberl Restaurant AUSTRIAN €€
(📮625 50; Andrä-Kranz-Gasse 7; mains €7.50-13.50) Attracting a loyal following, Adlerstüberl is where locals put the world to rights over beer, humungous schnitzels and plates of piping-hot goulash. Find a cosy nook in one of the vaulted rooms to join them.

La Taverna AUSTRIAN €€
(📮647 85; Hauptplatz 14; mains €8.50-16; ⏱Tue-Sun) A staircase twists down to this wood-panelled tavern in the bowels of Romantik

WORTH A TRIP

CLIFF-HANGER

Clinging to a 1600m clifftop like an eagle's nest and watched over by jagged peaks, the recently renovated **Dolomitenhütte** (📮0664 2253782; www.dolomitenhuette.at; Amlach 39; mains €7.50-16) is extraordinary. With the Dolomites and larch woods as its mesmerising backdrop, the cosy alpine hut is like something out of a fairy tale. In summer, walkers and cyclists make the 12km jaunt south of Lienz for the enticing views from the terrace and home cooking like *Kaspressknödel* (fried cheese dumpling) and *Schlipfkrapfen* (Tyrolean-style ravioli). Snowy winter's days up here are equally enchanting – bring your sled and you'll be able to race back down to Lienz on a scenic toboggan track.

Hotel Traube. Chefs whip up Italian and Tyrolean flavours in the show kitchen (try the rocket tagliatelle). The resident Bacchus gives an indication of the mind-boggling wine list – there are 800 bottles to choose from.

Gösser Bräu im Alten Rathaus
INTERNATIONAL €€

📞721 74; Johannesplatz 10; mains €8-22; ⊘9am-1am Mon-Fri, to 2am Sat, 9.30am-midnight Sun) Gathered around a horseshoe-shaped bar, this vaulted brewpub's draught Gösser Brau beers go well with meaty favourites like rump steak with oven-roasted potatoes. The vine-clad terrace is popular in summer.

Gasthaus Marinelli
AUSTRIAN €

(📞682 08; Dölsach 78; mains €5-10; ⊘Thu-Tue) Locals rave about the home-cooked local food at this tiny restaurant in the schnapps-making village of Dölsach, 4.5km east of Lienz. It's best to reserve in advance.

🍷 Drinking

Relaxed best describes Lienz' after-dark scene, with many locals whiling away an evening at a bar or pavement cafe on Hauptplatz.

Deep Blue
COCKTAIL BAR

(Hauptplatz 14) This groovy underground lounge harbours an aquarium that even Nemo would surely sacrifice the sea for; it's apparently East Tyrol's biggest. Plastic fish continue the aquatic theme, and one too many cocktail specials and you'll almost certainly see the room swim.

Petrocelli's
CAFE

(Hauptplatz 9; ⊘8am-11pm) Lively hang-out with a big terrace on the square. Good spot for an ice cream, beer or sundown Aperol spritzer.

Zeitlos
BAR

(Zwergergasse 3a; ⊘8am-2am Mon-Sat) A retro-glam, champagne-kissed lounge bar, with a decked terrace out front. Great for cocktails, fancy ice creams and fresh-pressed juices.

Joy
CLUB

(Hauptplatz 9; ⊘10pm-5am Thu-Sat) Party haunt downstairs from Petrocelli's, with DJs playing a mix of music.

ℹ️ Information

Bibliothek (Muchargasse 4; ⊘9am-noon & 3-6pm Tue-Fri, 9am-noon Sat) Free internet access at four terminals.

Main tourist office (📞050-212 400; www.stadt-lienz.at; Europaplatz 1; ⊘8am-6pm Mon-Fri, 9am-noon & 5-7pm Sat) Staff will help you find accommodation (even private rooms) free of charge.

Osttirol Werbung (📞050-212 212; www.osttirol.com) For information about the wider East Tyrol area. The office sends brochures, but isn't set up for visits.

ℹ️ Getting There & Away

Regional transport in Tyrol comes under the wing of the **Verkehrsverbund Tirol** (VVT; www.vvt.at). For information on VVT transport tickets, valid for travel between Tyrol and East Tyrol, see p325.

BUS Buses pull up in front of the train station, where you'll find the Postbus information office. There are bus connections to regional ski resorts and northwards to the Hohe Tauern National Park. Buses to Kitzbühel (€13.80, 1½ hours) are quicker and more direct than the train, but less frequent.

CAR & MOTORCYCLE To head south, you must first divert west or east along Hwy 100, as the Dolomites are an impregnable barrier. The main north–south road routes are the year-round Felber-Tauern-Strasse (B108) between Mittersill and Lienz, the spectacular Grossglockner Road (open May to October) and the 5.5km-long Felbertauerntunnel (cars/motorcycles €10/8). Hauptplatz has lots of parking in its Kurzparkzone, or park for free in front of Stadtpfarrkirche St Andrä.

TRAIN Most trains to the rest of Austria, including Salzburg (€33.70, 3½ hours, hourly), go east via Spittal-Millstättersee, where you usually have to change. The quickest and easiest route to Innsbruck (€31.20, four hours) is to go west via Sillian and Italy.

Tyrol

Includes »

Best Places to Eat

» Paznaunerstube (p328)

» Chez Nico (p303)

» Hosteria (p319)

» Batzenhäusl (p321)

» Museum Restaurant (p332)

Best Places to Stay

» Altes Thönihaus (p331)

» Auracher Löchl (p321)

» Nepomuks (p302)

» Enzianhof (p312)

» Nature Resort Ötztal (p323)

Why Go?

There's no place like Tyrol for the 'wow, I'm in Austria' feeling. Nowhere else in the country is the downhill skiing as exhilarating, the après ski as pumping, the wooden chalets as chocolate box, the food heartier. Whether you're schussing down the legendary slopes of Kitzbühel, cycling the Zillertal or hiking in the Alps with a big blue sky overhead – the scenery here makes you glad to be alive.

Alps aside, it's the locals that make Tyrol unique. Down-to-earth, notoriously proud and a touch rebellious, Tyroleans embrace both tradition and innovation. Welcome to a place where snowboarders brag about awesome descents under the low beams of a medieval tavern; where *Dirndls* and *Lederhosen* have street cred; and where *Volksmusik* (folk music) features on club playlists. Like its famous eagle, Tyrol will lift you high with its free spirit, party-loving soul and boundless natural beauty.

When to Go

Tyrol goes outdoors in summer with rafting on the Inn River, and paragliding and high-altitude hiking in the Alps. July and August are festival season in Innsbruck, while the Zillertal rocks to accordion-driven folk music. In winter Tyrol is like a snow-globe scene – all fairy-tale Christmas markets, snowbound villages and world-class skiing. Wildflowers carpet mountainsides in spring, a tranquil season. The golden silence of autumn, when the cows descend from the high pastures, can be beautiful too.

Legendary Skiing

Tyrol is powdery perfection. Even the tiniest speck of an alpine village has its own ski school and lift, so the question is not *if* but *how* you ski. **Kitzbühel** (p317) for purists and its world-class Hahnenkamm, **Mayrhofen** (p313) for its fantastic free-ride terrain and knee-trembling Harakiri, **St Anton am Arlberg** (p329) for glorious off-piste and après-ski...so many illustrious names, so many expectations. And Tyrol lives up to them all. Beyond downhill, you'll also find Olympic-level cross-country tracks in **Seefeld** (p309) and year-round skiing at **Stubai** (p309) and **Hintertux** (p313) glaciers.

Once you've got the destination sorted, you can start planning. Visit www.tirol.at for special ski packages, guide information, snow reports and the low-down on Tyrol's 110 ski resorts and 193 ski schools.

APRÈS-SKI ACTION

Singing oompah-pah in your salopettes, grooving to Europop in your ski boots, rounds of Jägermeister bombs, dancing polar bears – it's just another slopeside afternoon in Tyrol. Nowhere in Europe throws a better après-ski party. Save some energy and euros and remember what goes up, must come down – it's amazing how a few shots can ruin your snowplough!

The unrivalled après-ski king is, of course, **St Anton am Arlberg** (p332), where barns like Mooserwirt and Heustadl whip throngs into a frenzy with beer and live music. Rivals to the crown include wild child **Ischgl** (p328), dubbed the Ibiza of the Alps, with its go-go dancing bars, top DJs and clubs like Pacha. The pubs and igloo bars in **Mayrhofen** (p316) are buoyed by party-loving boarders, particularly during the Snowbombing festival in April.

Top Five Adrenalin Thrills

» Pinballing down Innsbruck's **Olympic bob run** (p301) at speeds of up to 100km/h – one minute of sheer madness

» Catapulting into the void on the **Harakiri** (p313), Austria's steepest piste with a 78% gradient

» Feeling your stomach drop as you nosedive off the 192m-high **Europabrücke** (p300) bridge, one of Europe's scariest bungee jumps

» Throwing yourself down a waterfall (canyoning) or along a foaming river (rafting) in **Landeck** (p326)

» Bombing downhill on your mountain bike on the **Nordkette Singletrail** (p300), with Innsbruck but a blur beneath you

BEST HIKE

Tyrol's rugged peaks and valleys become fantastic walking country in summer. A classic alpine day hike is the **Zillertal Circuit** (p315), starting at the jewel-coloured Schlegeis Reservoir near Ginzling.

Tastes of Tyrol

» Aromatic *Schlegeis-Speck* ham, cured at 1800m, from Metzgerei Kröll (p314) in Mayrhofen

» Apple and plum schnapps from the orchards of Stanz (p327)

» Flavoursome Tilsiter, Bergkäse and Graukäse cheese from Sennerei Zillertal (p314) in Mayrhofen

What a View!

» Innsbruck's skyline and the Nordkette range from **Bergisel** (p299) ski jump

» The Tyrolean and Bavarian Alps from 2962m **Zugspitze** (p325), Germany's highest peak

» Glacial panoramas from the 3250m sundeck at **Hintertux Glacier** (p313)

Resources

» Tyrol.com (www.tirol.at) Activities, accommodation, transport and weather.

» Verkehrsverbund Tirol (www.vvt.at) Timetables and tickets.

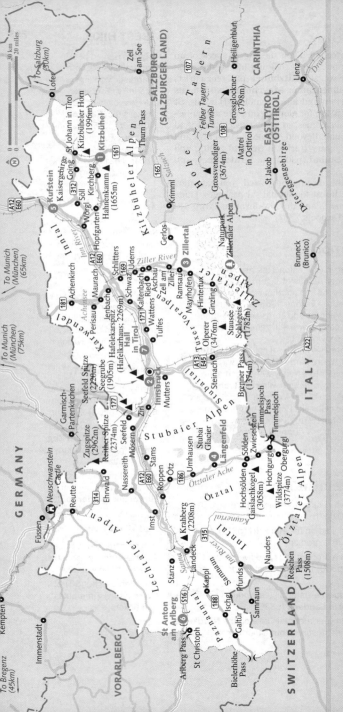

Tyrol Highlights

1 Save your best schuss (and snowsuit) for the legendary slopes of **Kitzbühel** (p317)

2 See the midday sun burnish Innsbruck's iconic **Goldenes Dachl** (p297), Emperor Maximilian's royal box

3 Get on your mountain bike for pulse-racing ascents and descents in the **Zillertal** (p312)

4 Bathe in out-of-this-world whirlpools and saunas at **Aqua Dome** (p322) in Längenfeld in the Ötztal

5 Glide above the treetops in Kufstein's retro

chairlift (p321) to the wild Kaisergebirge peaks

6 Take a snowy ride to dinner on St Anton am Arlberg's floodlit **toboggan run** (p332)

7 Slip back 500 years roaming the pristine medieval old town of **Hall in Tirol** (p307)

History

Despite its difficult alpine terrain, Tyrol has been settled since the Neolithic age, verified by the discovery of a 5400-year-old body of a man preserved in ice in the Ötztal Alps in 1991 (see p324). The Brenner Pass (1374m), crossing into Italy, allowed the region to develop as a north–south trade route.

Tyrol fell to the Habsburgs in 1363, but it wasn't until the rule of Emperor Maximilian I (1490–1519) that the province truly forged ahead. He boosted the region's status by transforming Innsbruck into the administrative capital and a cultural centre. In 1511 the emperor drew up the Landibell legislation, allowing Tyroleans to defend their own borders, thus creating the *Schützen* (marksmen militia) which still exists today. When the last Tyrolean Habsburg, Archduke Sigmund Franz, died in 1665 the duchy of Tyrol was directly ruled from Vienna.

In 1703 the Bavarians attempted to capture Tyrol in the War of the Spanish Succession. In alliance with the French, they reached the Brenner Pass before being beaten back by the *Schützen*. In 1805 Tyrol passed into Bavarian hands under Napoleon, a rule that was short-lived and troublesome. In 1809 South Tyrolean innkeeper Andreas Hofer led a successful fight for independence, winning a famous victory at Bergisel. The Habsburg monarchy did not support his heroic stance and Tyrol was returned to Bavaria later that year.

The Treaty of St Germain (1919) dealt a further blow to Tyrolean identity; prosperous South Tyrol was ceded to Italy and East Tyrol was isolated from the rest of the province.

A staunch ally of Mussolini, Hitler did not claim back South Tyrol when his troops invaded Austria in 1938. In the aftermath of WWII, Tyrol was divided into zones occupied by Allied forces until the country proclaimed its neutrality in 1955. Since then Tyrol has enjoyed peace and [...] tourism, particularly the ski [...] flourished.

ⓘ Getting There & Aroun[...]

AIR Lying 4km west of Innsbru[...] **Innsbruck Airport** (www.innsbru[...] com), caters to a handful of natio[...] (Vienna and Graz) and international flights (London, Amsterdam, Antwerp, Bern, Frankfurt and Hannover), handled mostly by Austrian Airlines, British Airways, EasyJet and Welcome Air.

CAR & MOTORCYCLE The main road and rail route in and out of Tyrol follows the Inntal (Inn River), with the east–west A12/E60 cutting the province into almost equal halves, entering from Germany near Kufstein and exiting west of St Anton in Vorarlberg. The A13 connects Tyrol with Italy, crossing the Brenner Pass directly south of Innsbruck.

PUBLIC TRANSPORT Regional transport, covering buses, trams and ÖBB (Austrian federal railway) trains, is run by the **Verkehrsverbund Tirol** (www.vvt.at). Ticket prices depend on the number of zones you travel through; a single ticket costs €1.80, a day pass €3.60. Additionally, Tyrol is divided into 12 overlapping transport regions. A Regio Ticket pass for individual regions costs €31.50/99.80 per week/month or €53/185.50 for the Tirol Ticket covering all 12 regions.

INNSBRUCK

☏ 0512 / POP 119,250 / ELEV 574M

One of the great things about Innsbruck is that almost every corner you turn affords spectacular views of the Nordkette Alps, the city's natural skyscrapers. Urban meets outdoors in the relaxed Tyrolean capital, where Zaha Hadid's space-age funicular speeds you from the centre to alpine pastures clanging with cowbells in a matter of minutes.

Innsbruck is a one-off. Where else can you spend the morning browsing Old

A HERO CALLED HOFER

Nobody epitomises the proud, resilient spirit of Tyrol quite like rabble-rousing hero Andreas Hofer. An innkeeper and horse dealer, Hofer was an imposing bearded figure of a man and a staunch patriot. In 1809 he led a local revolt against Napoleon's Franco-Bavarian forces and was initially successful, winning the Battle of Bergisel and reclaiming Innsbruck. But his victory was short-lived: in January 1810 Hofer's neighbour Franz Raffl was bribed to betray his hideout in the Passeiertal. That February, Hofer was shot by firing squad in Mantua and proved brave to the last, telling his executioner to 'shoot straight'. Today he lies buried in Innsbruck's Hofkirche, and the Tyrolean anthem *Zu Mantua in Banden* recounts his tragic fate.

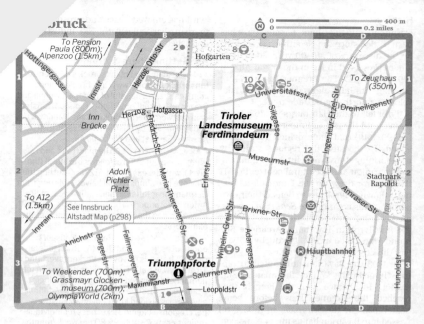

Innsbruck

Master paintings in Habsburg palaces, the afternoon skiing and the evening in a rollicking brewpub? With a late-medieval *Altstadt* (old town), vibrant cultural scene and adrenalin-fuelled pursuits of Olympic fame, Innsbruck is one of those rare places that really can say it has something for everyone without sounding clichéd.

History

Innsbruck dates from 1180, when the little market settlement on the north bank of the Inn River spread to the south bank via an eponymous new bridge – Ynsprugg.

In 1420 Innsbruck became the ducal seat of the Tyrolean Habsburgs, but it was under the reign of Emperor Maximilian I (1490–1519) that the city reached its pinnacle in power and prestige; many of the emperor's monuments, including the shimmering Goldenes Dachl, are still visible today. Maximilian was not the only Habsburg to influence the city's skyline: Archduke Ferdinand

II reconstructed the Schloss Ambras, and Empress Maria Theresia the Hofburg.

Two world wars aside, Innsbruck has enjoyed a fairly peaceful existence over the centuries. More recently, the city held the Winter Olympics in 1964 and 1976, and is gearing up to host the Youth Olympic Games in 2012.

⊙ Sights

Many of the sights listed below close an hour or two earlier in winter (generally from November to early May).

TOP CHOICE **Goldenes Dachl & Museum**
LANDMARK, MUSEUM
(Golden Roof; Map p298; Herzog-Friedrich-Strasse 15; adult/child €4/2; ⊙10am-5pm, closed Mon Oct-Apr) Innsbruck's golden wonder is this Gothic oriel, crowned by a roof embellished with 2657 fire-gilt copper tiles that glitter in the midday sun. The royal box was built for Emperor Maximilian I to watch tournaments on the square below. Maxi was a notorious bon vivant with an eye for the ladies, as revealed in the relief scenes that show the emperor with his two wives and disguised in a jester costume and donkey ears. An audioguide whizzes through the **museum** recounting the history of Maximilian; look for the grotesque tournament helmets designed to resemble the slit-eyed Turks of the rival Ottoman Empire. There's a jester-themed room with puppets and books for kids.

TOP CHOICE **Hofkirche & Volkskunst Museum**
CHURCH, MUSEUM
(Map p298; www.tiroler-landesmuseum.at; Universitätstrasse; combined ticket adult/child/family €8/4/16; ⊙10am-6pm Mon-Sat, from 12.30am Sun) Innsbruck's pride and joy is the Gothic Hofkirche, one of Europe's finest royal court churches. It was commissioned in 1553 by Ferdinand I, who enlisted top artists of the time such as Albrecht Dürer, Alexander Colin and Peter Vischer the Elder. Top billing goes to the empty **sarcophagus of Emperor Maximilian I** (1459–1519), a masterpiece of German Renaissance sculpture, elaborately carved from black marble. The tomb is embellished with Alexander Colins' white marble reliefs based on Dürer's *Ehrenpforte* (Triumphal Arch) woodcuts, depicting victorious scenes from Maximilian's life such as the Siege of Kufstein (1504). The twin rows of 28 giant bronze figures that guard the sarcophagus include Dürer's legendary King Arthur, who was apparently Emperor Maximilian's biggest idol. You're now forbidden to touch the statues, but numerous inquisitive hands have already polished parts of the dull bronze, including Kaiser Rudolf's codpiece!

Andreas Hofer (1767–1810), the Tyrolean patriot who led the rebellion against Napoleon's forces, is entombed in the church. In the **Silberkapelle**, a dazzling silver Madonna keeps watch over the marble tomb of Archduke Ferdinand II and his first wife, Philippine Welser.

Next door the **Volkskunst Museum** (Folk Art Museum; Map p298) presents a fascinating romp through Tyrolean folk art from handcarved sleighs and Christmas cribs to carnival masks and cow bells. On the 1st floor is a beautifully restored Gothic *Stube* (parlour) complete with low-ceiling, wood panelling and antique tiled oven.

Hofburg
PALACE
(Map p298; www.hofburg-innsbruck.at; Rennweg 1; adult/child €8/free; ⊙9am-5pm) Demanding attention with its imposing facade and cupolas, the Hofburg was built as a castle for Archduke Sigmund the Rich in the 15th century, expanded by Emperor Maximilian I in the 16th century and given a total baroque makeover by Empress Maria Theresia in the 18th century. The centrepiece of the lavish rococo state apartments is the 31m-long **Riesensaal** (Giant's Hall), adorned with frescoes and paintings of Maria Theresia and her 16 children (including Marie Antoinette), who look strangely identical – maybe the artist was intent on avoiding royal wrath arising from sibling rivalry in the beauty stakes.

CITY SAVERS

The money-saving **Innsbruck Card** allows one visit to Innsbruck's main sights and attractions, a return journey on all cable cars and unlimited use of public transport including the Sightseer tour bus. The card also yields numerous discounts on tours and activities. It's available at the tourist office and costs €29/34/39 for 24/48/72 hours (half-price for children).

Stay overnight in Innsbruck and you'll receive a **Club Innsbruck Card**, which gives discounts on transport and activities, and allows you to join the tourist office's free guided hikes in summer.

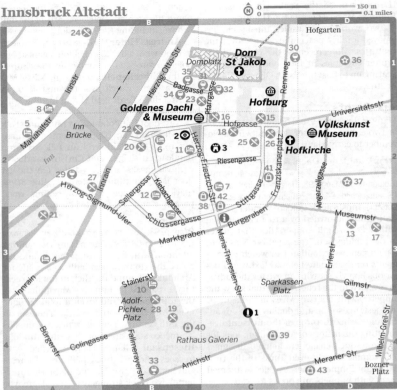

Tucked behind the palace is the **Hofgarten** (Map p296; admission free; ⊙dawn-dusk), an attractive garden for a stroll with its palm house and botanical species including an Indian bean tree.

Dom St Jakob CATHEDRAL
(St James' Cathedral; Map p298; Domplatz; ⊙7.30am-9.30pm Mon-Sat, from 8am Sun) Innsbruck's twin-towered 18th-century cathedral is a feast of over-the-top baroque. The Asam brothers from Munich completed much of the sumptuous art and stucco work, though the Madonna above the high altar is by German Renaissance painter Lukas Cranach the Elder.

Tiroler Landesmuseum Ferdinandeum ART GALLERY
(Map p296; www.tiroler-landesmuseum.at; Museumstrasse 15; adult/child/family €8/4/16; ⊙10am-6pm Tue-Sun) This treasure trove of Tyrolean history and art moves from Bronze Age arte-facts to the original reliefs used to design the Goldenes Dachl. Alongside brooding Dutch paintings of the Rembrandt ilk, the gallery displays an astounding collection of Austrian art including Gothic altarpieces, a handful of Kokoschka and Klimt paintings, and some shocking Viennese Actionist works. More specific to Tyrol are the late-baroque works by fresco master Paul Troger, Alfons Walde's Kitzbühel winterscapes and Albin Egger-Lienz' sombre depictions of rural life in postwar Tyrol.

Schloss Ambras PALACE
(www.khm.at/ambras; Schlossstrasse 20; adult/child/family €10/free/18; ⊙10am-5pm) Picturesquely perched on a hill, this Renaissance pile was acquired in 1564 by Archduke Ferdinand II, then ruler of Tyrol, who transformed it from a fortress into a palace. He was the mastermind behind the **Spanische Saal** (Spanish Hall), a 43m-long banquet hall with a wooden inlaid ceiling and Tyro-

◎ **Top Sights**

Dom St Jakob		C1
Goldenes Dachl & Museum		B2
Hofburg		C1
Hofkirche		C2
Volkskunst Museum		D2

◎ **Sights**

1	Annasäule	C4
2	Helblinghaus	B2
3	Stadtturm	C2

◎ **Sleeping**

4	Basic Hotel	A3
5	Cityhotel Schwarzer Bär	A2
6	Goldener Adler	B2
7	Hotel Weisses Kreuz	C2
8	Mondschein	A1
9	Nepomuks	B3
10	Penz Hotel	B3
11	Weinhaus Happ	B2
12	Weisses Rössl	B2

◎ **Eating**

13	Billa	D3
14	Cafe Central	D3
	Cafe Katzung	(see 11)
	Cafe Munding	(see 9)
15	Cafe Sacher	C2
16	Gasthaus Goldenes Dachl	C2
17	Hofer	D3
18	Kröll	C2

19	Lichtblick	B4
20	Mamma Mia	B2
21	Markthalle	A3
22	Ottoburg	B2
23	s'Culinarium	C1
24	Shere Punjab	A1
25	s'Speckladele	C2
26	Stiftskeller	C2
27	Tapabar	A2
28	Thai-Li-Ba	B4

◎ **Drinking**

	360°	(see 19)
29	Beach Club	A2
30	Das Stadtcafe	C1
31	Dom Cafe-Bar	C1
32	Elferhaus	C1
33	Krahvogel	B4
34	La Copa	B1
35	Moustache	B1

◎ **Entertainment**

36	Tiroler Landestheater	D1
37	Treibhaus	D2

◎ **Shopping**

38	Christmas & Easter in Innsbruck	C2
39	Kaufhaus Tyrol	C4
40	Rathaus Galerien	B4
41	Spezialitäten aus der Stiftsgasse	C2
42	Swarovski Crystal Gallery	C3
43	Tiroler Heimatwerk	D4

INNSBRUCK SIGHTS

lean nobles gazing from the walls. Also note the *grisaille* (grey relief) around the courtyard and the sunken bath-tub where his beloved Philippine used to bathe.

Ferdinand instigated the magnificent Ambras Collection, encompassing three elements. Highlights of the **Rüstkammer** (Armour Collection) include the archduke's wedding armour – specially shaped to fit his bulging midriff! – and the 2.6m suit created for giant Bartlmä Bon. The **Kunst und Wunderkammer** (Art and Wonders Collection) is crammed with fantastical objects, including a petrified shark, gravity-defying stilt shoes and the *Fangstuhl* – a chair designed to trap drunken guests at Ferdinand's raucous parties.

The **Portraitgalerie** features room upon room of Habsburg portraits, with paintings by Titian, Velázquez and van Dyck. Maria Anna of Spain (No 126, Room 22) wins the prize for the most ludicrous hairstyle. When Habsburg portraits begin to pall, you can stroll or picnic in the extensive **castle gardens** (admission free; ⊙6am-8pm), home to strutting peacocks.

Schloss Ambras is 4.5km southeast of the centre. Take bus 4134 from the *Hauptbahnhof* to the castle for discounted entry and a free return journey.

Bergisel　　　　　　　　　　SKI JUMP
(www.bergisel.info; adult/child/family €8.50/ 4/16.50; ⊙10am-6pm) Rising above Innsbruck like a celestial staircase, this glass-and-steel ski jump was designed by much-lauded Iraqi architect Zaha Hadid. From May to July, fans pile in to see athletes train, while preparations step up a gear in January for the World Cup Four Hills Tournament.

It's 455 steps or a two-minute funicular ride to the 50m-high **viewing platform**.

DON'T MISS

RING MY BELL

En route to Bergisel, consider stopping at the **Grassmayr Glockenmuseum** (Bell Museum; www.grassmayr.at; Leopoldstrasse 53; adult/child €4.50/2.50; ⊙9am-5pm Mon-Fri, plus 9am-5pm Sat May-Sep) to discover the Grassmayr family's 400 years of bell-making tradition. Besides exhibits including some formidable Romanesque and Gothic bells, you can watch the casting process and have a go at ringing the bells to achieve different notes.

Here, the panorama of the Nordkette range, Inn Valley and Innsbruck is breathtaking; the cemetery at the bottom has undoubtedly made a few ski-jumping pros quiver in their boots though, not least plucky Brit Eddie 'the Eagle' Edwards, who broke his jaw and collarbone here in a spectacular missed jump.

Next to the stadium at the bottom, the **museum** is a mini hall of fame, crammed with black-and-white photos of death-defying daredevils who used to jump in leather shoes and without helmets.

Bus 4143 and line TS run from the *Hauptbahnhof* to Bergisel, 2km south of the centre.

Alpenzoo   ZOO
(Weiherburggasse 37; adult/child €8/4; ⊙9am-6pm) Billing itself as a conservation-oriented zoo, this is where you can get close to alpine wildlife like golden eagles, chamois and ibex. To get there, walk up the hill from Rennweg or take bus W from the Marktplatz.

Zeughaus   MUSEUM
(Zeughausgasse; adult/child/family €8/4/16; ⊙10am-6pm Tue-Sun) Emperor Maximilian's former arsenal, the Zeughaus runs chronologically through Tyrol's cultural history. It kicks off with geological and mineral history, including the silver that made Hall and Schwaz medieval powerhouses, but mostly concentrates on Tyrol's greatest hero, Andreas Hofer.

Stadtturm   LANDMARK
(city tower; Map p298; Herzog-Friedrich-Strasse 21; adult/child €3/1.50; ⊙10am-8pm) Climb this tower's 148 steps for 360-degree views of the city's rooftops, spires and surrounding mountains.

Helblinghaus   LANDMARK
(Map p298; Herzog-Friedrich-Strasse) A late-Gothic-turned-rococo townhouse that is the architectural equivalent of a wedding cake, with its stucco-like piped icing, pastel colours and naturalistic ornament.

Annasäule   LANDMARK
(St Anne's Column; Map p298; Maria-Theresien-Strasse) Topped by a statue of the Virgin Mary, this column was erected in 1703 to mark the repulsing of a Bavarian attack.

Triumphpforte   LANDMARK
(Map p296; Salurnerstrasse) This triumphal arch was built in 1765 to commemorate the marriage of the then emperor-to-be Leopold II.

🏃 Activities

Anyone who loves the great outdoors will be just itching to head up into the Alps in Innsbruck. Aside from skiing and walking, rafting, mountain biking, paragliding and bobsledding tempt the daring.

Summer Activities

Guided Hikes   WALKING
From late May to October, Innsbruck Information arranges daily guided hikes with a professional mountain guide, free to those with a Club Innsbruck Card. Pop into the tourist office to register and browse the program, which includes highlights such as sunrise walks to Rangger Köpfl and lantern-lit strolls.

Nordketten Bahnen   FUNICULAR
(Map p296; www.nordkette.com; ⊙every 15min 8.30am-5.30pm) Designed by Zaha Hadid of Bergisel fame, this space-age funicular whisks you from the Congress Centre to the top of the Nordkette in 25 minutes. Tickets cost €14.10/23.40 one-way/return to Seegrube and €15.60/26 to Hafelekar. Both afford superb views of Innsbruck and the Alps, and are criss-crossed with walking trails such as the picturesque 1½-hour meadow hike from Seegrube and the high-alpine 4½-hour Goetheweg circuit from Hafelekar.

Innsbrucker Klettersteig   VIA FERRATA
(adult/child incl cable car €24/12; ⊙Jun-Sep) Hafelekar (2256m) is the starting point for Innsbruck's head-spinning, seven-hour via ferrata (fixed-rope route). The trail is not for

the fainthearted – it traverses seven peaks and affords tremendous views of the Stubaier, Zillertaler and Ötztaler Alps. You can rent equipment at the sports shop at Seegrube.

Nordkette Singletrail   MOUNTAIN BIKING
(http://nordkette-singletrail.at, in German; ⊙late May-early Nov) A magnet to hardcore downhill mountain bikers, this *very* steep, technically demanding track begins 200m below Seegrube. It's free to transport your bike on the cable car but make sure it is clean. There is a special half-/one-day ticket costing €20/27 in case you want to ride it more than once.

Die Boerse   ADVENTURE SPORTS
(Map p296; www.dieboerse.at; Leopoldstrasse 4; ⊙9am-6.30pm Mon-Fri, to 5pm Sat) Rents skis and snowboards (€17 to €29 per day) and mountain bikes (€20 per day).

Inntour   ADVENTURE SPORTS
(Map p296; www.inntour.com; Leopoldstrasse 4; ⊙9am-6.30pm Mon-Fri, to 5pm Sat) Check out Inntours, at the same address as Die Boerse, for adrenalin-based thrills, including canyoning (€75), tandem paragliding (€95), white-water rafting (€45) and bungee jumping from the 192m Europabrücke (Europe Bridge).

Winter Activities

Alpine Skiing   SKIING
Innsbruck is the gateway to a formidable ski arena, the Olympia SkiWorld Innsbruck (www.ski-innsbruck.at), covering nine surrounding resorts and 282km of slopes to test all abilities. The most central place to pound powder is the Nordpark (⊙cable cars every 15min 8am-7pm). At the top, boarders can pick up speed on the quarter-pipe, kickers and boxes at Nitro Skylinepark (www.skylinepark.at, in German), while daring skiers ride the Hafelekarrinne, one of Europe's steepest runs with a 70% gradient.

The Innsbruck Glacier Ski Pass (3-/7-day pass €105/200) covers all areas; ski buses

are free to anyone with an Innsbruck Card. Alternatively, there's the Innsbruck Super Ski Pass (4/5 out of 6 days €168/222), covering the above ski areas plus Kitzbühel and Arlberg.

☞ Tours

Innsbruck Information organises guided city walks, which meander through the historical centre for an hour or so. Tours leave at 11am and 2pm May to October and over Christmas, and cost €9.

To capture more than the *Altstadt* in a tour, jump on a bright-red Sightseer bus (www.sightseer.at), running between the Zeughaus and Schloss Ambras. Buses depart from Maria-Theresien-Strasse every 40 minutes between 10am and 5.30pm. A day pass costs €6/4.40 for adults/children. Innsbruck Information sells tickets.

✹✹ Festivals & Events

Vierschanzentournee   SPORTS EVENT
(Jack Wolfskin Four Hills Tournament; www.4schanzentournee.com) Innsbruck sees in the New Year by hosting one of four World Cup ski-jumping events at Bergisel.

Festwochen der Alten Musik   MUSIC FESTIVAL
(Festival of Early Music; www.altemusik.at) This festival brings baroque concerts to venues such as Schloss Ambras, the Landestheater and Dom St Jakob in July and August.

Tanzsommer   DANCE FESTIVAL
(www.tanzsommer.at, in German) From classical ballet to gravity-defying acrobatics, dance takes the stage by storm at this festival from mid-June to mid-July.

Christkindlmarkt   CHRISTMAS MARKET
(www.christkindlmarkt.cc) Innsbruck twinkles festively at Christmas markets in the *Altstadt*, Marktplatz and Maria-Theresien-Strasse from mid-November to Epiphany (6 January). Kids love the fairy-tale-themed Kiebachgasse and Köhleplatzl.

DON'T MISS

COOL RUNNINGS

For a minute in the life of an Olympic bobsleigh racer, you can't beat the Olympiabobbahn (☎377 160; www.olympiaworld.at; Heiligwasserwiese, Igls; tickets €30; ⊙Nov-early Mar & mid-Apr–mid-Oct), built for the 1976 Winter Olympics. Zipping around 10 curves and picking up speeds of up to 100km/h, the bob run is 800m of pure hair-raising action. You can join a professional bobsled driver in winter or summer; call ahead for the exact times. To reach it, take bus J from the Landesmuseum to Igls Olympiaexpress.

DEVIL IN DISGUISE

Every year on 5 December, the eve of St Nicholas, some 70 *Krampusse* in shaggy sheep-skins, goat horns and grotesque masks run riot through Igls, 6km south of Innsbruck. The aim of these guys is to scare people silly (the smaller the better...) with rusty chains, birch rods and baskets to carry naughty little children off to the pits of hell. Kids get to let out all that pre-Christmas excitement by screaming their hearts out. By nightfall, you may see *Krampus* slurring after one too many schnapps; after all, the devil is allowed to misbehave and leave the good-guy stuff to ol' St Nick.

🛏 Sleeping

Aside from the options below, Innsbruck and the villages of Igls and Mutters offer private rooms that cost between €20 and €40; Innsbruck Information can make bookings.

Nepomuks HOSTEL €
(Map p298; ☑584 118; www.nepomuks.at; Kiebachgasse 16; dm/d €22/54; 🖭🖥) Could this be backpacker heaven? Nepomuks comes close, with its prime *Altstadt* location, well-stocked kitchen and high-ceilinged dorms with homely touches like books and CD players. The delicious breakfast in attached Cafe Munding, with homemade bread, jam, pastries and freshly roasted coffee, gets your day off to a grand start.

Hotel Weisses Kreuz HISTORIC HOTEL €€
(Map p298; ☑594 79; www.weisseskreuz.at; Herzog-Friedrich-Strasse 31; s €36-72, d €100-132; 🅿🖭@🖥) Beneath the *Altstadt*'s arcades, this atmospheric 500-year-old hotel has played host to famous guests including a 13-year-old Mozart. Creaking stairs wind past a trickling fountain up to the antique-filled reception. The spotless rooms are country-style with chunky pinewood and floral trimmings.

Pension Paula PENSION €
(☑292 262; www.pensionpaula.at; Weiherburggasse 15; s/d €39/62; 🅿) Nestled in the hills above Innsbruck and with great city views, this family-run pension occupies an alpine chalet and has super-clean, homely rooms (most with balcony). It's in St Nikolaus district, 1.5km north of the *Altstadt* and near the Alpenzoo.

Romantik Hotel Schwarzer Adler HOTEL €€€
(Map p296; ☑587 109; www.deradler.com; Kaiserjägerstrasse 2; s €110-159, d €150-211, ste €295-480; 🅿🖭@🖥🖥) This boutique hotel is honeymoon material, particularly if your bank balance stretches to a spin in the white limo featured in Madonna's 'Material Girl' video. The fabulously over-the-top suites glitter with Swarovski crystals and one features the solid-marble bed Gianni Versace once slept in. Crystal fountains gush in the spa, which pampers with Asian-inspired treatments.

Pension Stoi PENSION €
(Map p296; ☑585 434; www.pensionstoi.at; in German; Salurnerstrasse 7; s/d/tr/q €44/69/85/98; 🅿🖭🖥🖥) Run by the kind, knowledgeable Lantschner family, this central yet quiet pension is housed in an art-nouveau villa. The high-ceilinged, parquet-floored rooms are large and bright, but you'll need to schlep your bags (there's no lift) and buy your own breakfast.

Goldener Adler HISTORIC HOTEL €€
(Map p298; ☑571 111; www.goldeneradler.com; Herzog-Friedrich-Strasse 6; s/d €92/135; 🅿🖭🖥🖥) Since opening in 1390, the grand Goldener Adler has welcomed kings, queens and Salzburg's two biggest exports: Mozart and Mrs von Trapp. Rooms are elegant with gold drapes and squeaky-clean marble bathrooms.

Penz Hotel HOTEL €€€
(Map p298; ☑575 657; www.the-penz.com; Adolf-Pichler-Platz 3; s €140-220, d €180-260, f €230-280; 🅿🖭🖥🖥🖥) Behind a sheer wall of glass, the Penz is a contemporary design hotel next to the Rathaus Galerien. The minimalist rooms in muted hues are spruced up with flat-screen TVs and shiny chrome fittings. At breakfast, a whole table is piled high with exotic fruits.

Mondschein HOTEL €€
(Map p298; ☑227 84; www.mondschein.at; Maria-hilfstrasse 6; s €87-105, d €105-180; 🅿🖭🖥🖥) The moon lights the way to this riverside hotel, set in a 15th-century fisherman's house. Rooms painted in blues and sunny yellows give way to Swarovski crystal–studded bathrooms glittering like a night sky.

Weisses Rössl
GUESTHOUSE €€

(Map p298; ☑583 057; www.roessl.at; Kiebachgasse 8; s/d/tr/q €80/120/135/160; 🅿🖭@🛜🐾) An antique rocking horse greets you at this 600-year-old guesthouse. The vaulted entrance leads up to spacious rooms with blond wood and crisp white linen. Mr Plank is a keen hunter, so it's no surprise that the restaurant (mains €7 to €18) has a meaty menu.

Camping Innsbruck Kranebitterhof
CAMPGROUND €

(☑279 558; www.camping-kranebitterhof.at; Kranebitterallee 216; camp sites €25; ☺Apr-Oct; 🛜) This modern campground west of town has alpine views and a rural feel. There's an on-site pizzeria and playground. Bus line O stops nearby or take the scenic cycle route along the River Inn into town, 5.5km away.

Weinhaus Happ
HISTORIC HOTEL €€

(Map p298; ☑582 980; www.weinhaus-happ.at; Herzog-Friedrich-Strasse 14; s/d €82/102; 🅿) Happ looks back on 600 years of history. The old-fashioned rooms are crying out for a makeover, but its plus points are many: prime views of the Goldenes Dachl, a cavernous wine cellar and a rustic restaurant (mains €9.50 to €22.50).

Cityhotel Schwarzer Bär
HOTEL €€

(Map p298; ☑294 900; www.cityhotel.cc; Mariahilfstrasse 16; s/d/tr/f €65/105/125/145; 🅿🖭🛜🐾) This family-run hotel is in a prime spot by the River Inn and just steps from the *Altstadt*. The bright, modern rooms – including family ones – sport parquet floors and flatscreen TVs; those facing the back are quieter but sacrifice the views.

Grand Hotel Europa
HOTEL €€€

(Map p296; ☑59 31; www.grandhoteleuropa.at; Südtiroler Platz 2; s €145-185, d €204-264, ste €324-424; 🅿@🛜) This luxurious pile opposite the station has been given a facelift. Pared-down chic now defines the rooms, though old-world grandeur lingers in the opulent Baroque Hall and wood-panelled restaurant. Mick Jagger and Queen Elizabeth II are famous past guests.

Basic Hotel
HOTEL €€

(Map p298; ☑586 385; www.basic-hotel.at; Innrain 16; s €60-75, d €90-100; 🖭🛜) This central newcomer to Innsbruck goes for streamlined, ultramodern design in its bright, open-plan rooms and bistro, and has 24-hour self check-in. Light sleepers take note: the hotel is on a main road.

✖ Eating

A mix of Austrian and international restaurants, bistros and pavement cafes cluster in the pedestrianised *Altstadt*. Self-caterers will find supermarkets like Hofer and Billa on Museumstrasse.

TOP CHOICE Chez Nico
VEGETARIAN €€

(Map p296; ☑586 398; www.chez-nico.at; Maria-Theresien-Strasse 49; lunch €12.50, 7-course menu €45; ☺lunch & dinner Tue-Fri, dinner Sat; 🖭🍴) Take a creative Parisian chef with an artistic eye and a passion for herbs, *et voilà* you get Chez Nico. At this intimate bistro, Nicolas Curtil (alias Nico) treats a handful of lucky, lucky guests to an all-vegetarian menu that changes daily – think along the lines of chanterelle-apricot goulash and porcini-sage ravioli.

Lichtblick
FUSION €€€

(Map p298; ☑566 550; Rathaus Galerien; www.restaurant-lichtblick.at; lunch €8-13, set menus €35-46; ☺10am-1am Mon-Sat; 🖭) On the 7th floor of the Rathaus Galerien, this chic glass-walled restaurant has sweeping views over Innsbruck to the Alps beyond. Backlighting and minimalist design create a sleek backdrop for Mediterranean-inspired cuisine like tuna in a sesame crust with couscous and grilled melon.

Cafe Munding
CAFE €

(Map p298; Kiebachgasse 16; cakes €2-4; ☺8am-8pm) Modern art hangs on the walls of this 200-year-old cafe. Besides whipping up delicious cakes – try the moist chocolate-raspberry *Haustorte* or the chocolate-marzipan *Mozarttorte* – the family roast their own coffee and make preserves with fruit freshly picked from local farms.

Romantik Hotel Schwarzer Adler Restaurant
FUSION €€€

(Map p296; ☑587 109; Kaiserjägerstrasse 2; menus €32-42; ☺Mon-Sat) Dine with a fine view of the *Altstadt* on the rooftop terrace at Schwarzer Adler. Flavours like rack of lamb with basil risotto star on the Mediterranean-inspired menu. Special occasion? Book the table in the chandelier-lit cable car.

Shere Punjab
INDIAN €€

(Map p296; ☑282 755; www.sherepunjab.eu; Innstrasse 19; mains €9-12; 🖭🍴) The aroma of spices fills this authentic Indian restaurant. Word has it even the Bollywood stars come here for a respectable shrimp biryani, lamb korma or flavoursome vegetarian dishes.

THE PERFECT PICNIC

With the Alps and River Inn as its backdrop, Innsbruck has some incredibly scenic spots for a picnic. Here's where you'll find goodies:

s'Speckladele
AUSTRIAN

(Map p298; Stiftsgasse 4; ⊗9am-1pm & 2-6pm Tue-Fri, 9am-3pm Sat) Two at a time please... This Lilliputian shop has been doing a brisk trade in quality regional sausages, hams and speck made from 'happy pigs' for the past 60 years. Mini *Teufel* sausages with a chilli kick are the must-try.

s'Culinarium
WINE

(Map p298; Pfarrgasse 1; ⊗10am-6pm Mon-Fri, 3-6pm Sat) The charming Herby Signor will help you pick an excellent bottle of Austrian wine at his shop-cum-bar. s'Culinarium also stocks other Tyrolean specialities from honey to schnapps.

Markthalle
MARKET

(Map p298; www.markthalle-innsbruck.at; Innrain; ⊗7am-6.30pm Mon-Fri, to 1pm Sat) Fresh-baked bread, Tyrolean cheese, organic fruit, smoked ham and salami – it's all under one roof at this riverside covered market.

Mamma Mia
PIZZA €

(Map p298; ☑562 902; Kiebachgasse 2; mains €5-8; 🖫) This no-frills Italian bistro has a great buzz, alongside huge pizzas, fresh salads and healthy pasta dishes. The shady terrace is a favourite spot in summer.

Cafe Sacher
CAFE €€

(Map p298; www.sacher.com; Rennweg 1; mains €9-17; ⊗8.30am-midnight; 🖫) Sidling up to the Hofburg, this grand chandelier-lit cafe is the place to linger over chocolate *Sacher Torte,* salads or lunch. There are free classical concerts in the courtyard in summer.

Ottoburg
AUSTRIAN €€

(Map p298; ☑584 338; www.ottoburg.at; Herzog-Friedrich-Strasse 1; lunch €6-9, mains €17-26; ⊗Tue-Sun; 🖫) Less of a tourist trap than it looks, this 12th-century castle hides a warren of wood-panelled *Stuben* (parlours), serving tournedos of venison, *Topfenknödel* (cottage-cheese dumplings) and similar hearty fare.

Cafe Katzung
CAFE €

(Map p298; ☑586 183; Herzog-Friedrich-Strasse 16; snacks €4-7; ⊗8am-midnight Mon-Sat, from 9am Sun) Expect lounge music, a lively vibe and the best hot chocolate in town at this cool cafe. Menu favourites include all-day breakfasts, toasted sandwiches and wholesome soups.

Gasthaus Goldenes Dachl
AUSTRIAN €€

(Map p298; ☑589 370; www.gasthaus-goldenes dachl.at; Hofgasse 1; mains €10-18) Portions are generous and the menu typically Tyrolean at this tavern, a cosy spot to try *Gröstl* (potatoes and bacon topped with a fried egg).

Cafe Central
CAFE €€

(Map p298; www.central.co.at; Gilmstrasse 5; mains €8-16; ⊗6.30am-10pm; 🖫) Little has changed since this old-world, Viennese-style cafe opened in 1889. Come to lunch on schnitzel or goulash or to browse the daily papers over a slice of torte. There's live piano music on Sunday evenings.

Solo Pasta
ITALIAN €€

(Map p296; ☑587 206; Universitätsstrasse 15b; mains €9-18; ⊗8am-midnight Tue-Sat) Fresh pasta is the mainstay at this minimalist-chic spaghetteria, with an alfresco terrace in summer. Next door, Solo Vino pairs Italian wines with antipasti and fresh fish.

Stiftskeller
AUSTRIAN €€

(Map p298; Hofgasse 6; mains €8-15; ⊗10am-midnight) A vaulted restaurant with a large beer garden for Augustiner Bräu beers and hearty fare like pork roast with beer sauce, dumplings and sauerkraut.

Kröll
STRUDEL €

(Map p298; Hofgasse 6; snacks €3-4.50; ⊗9am-midnight) Forget plain apple, this hole-in-the-wall cafe's strudels include rhubarb, poppy, feta and plum. The fresh juices pack a vitamin punch.

Thai-Li-Ba
THAI €€

(Map p298; ☑567 888; Rathaus Galerien; mains €12-18; ⊗9am-midnight Mon-Sat; 🖫) Stylish and buzzy Thai restaurant centred on an open kitchen. The noodle and curry dishes are garnished with orchids.

Tapabar
TAPAS €€

(Map p298; ✆586 398; Innrain 2; mixed tapas €11.20-15.80; ⊙8.30am-1am) A Spanish-themed place by the river, with flamenco music, appetising tapas and cocktails.

🍷 Drinking

Innsbruck's student population keeps the bar and clubbing scene upbeat. Besides a glut of bars in the *Altstadt,* a string of bars huddles under the railway arches on Ingenieur-Etzel-Strasse, otherwise known as the Viaduktbögen.

Moustache
BAR

(Map p298; www.cafe-moustache.at, in German; Herzog-Otto-Strasse 8; ⊙11am-2am Tue-Sun) Playing spot-the-moustache – look out for Einstein, Charlie Chaplin and co – is the preferred pastime at this retro newcomer, with a terrace on pretty Domplatz. Club Aftershave in the basement keeps the party going late and continues the facial hair (or lack of it) theme.

Hofgarten Café
BAR

(Map p296; Rennweg 6a; ⊙11am-2am Tue-Thu, to 4am Fri-Sun) A young crowd gathers in the chestnut tree–shaded beer garden of this trendy lounge-bar in the Hofgarten. Sip cocktails beneath the stars or gaze up at the star-studded ceiling in the pavilion. The happening events line-up skips from summer festivals to weekend house parties.

360°
COCKTAIL BAR

(Map p298; Rathaus Galerien; ⊙10am-1am Mon-Sat) There's no better place to see Innsbruck start to twinkle over cocktails and lounge beats. Grab a cushion and drink in 360-degree views of the city and Alps from the balcony that skirts the circular bar.

Sixty Twenty
BAR

(Map p296; Universitätsstrasse 15; ⊙11am-2am Mon-Thu, from 5pm Fri, from 7pm Sat & Sun) This retro-chic lounge is student central with its funky Innsbruck murals and outdoor seating. Come for half-price drinks on Mondays, hip hop on Thursdays and vodka-fuelled Saturdays.

Theresienbräu
BREWERY

(Map p296; Maria-Theresien-Strasse 53; ⊙10am-1am Mon-Wed, to 2am Thu-Sat, to midnight Sun) Copper vats gleam and rock plays at this lively microbrewery, opening onto a garden seating 120 beer guzzlers and pretzel munchers. The ceiling is studded with 10,000 dried roses.

Das Stadtcafe
BAR

(Map p298; Universitätsstrasse 1; ⊙10am-2am Tue-Sun, to 4am Fri & Sat) Das Stadtcafe sports a glam interior and a people-watching terrace facing the Hofburg. It can feel a bit *schickimiki* (self-consciously cool) at times, but there's a great events line-up: from Wednesday's salsa nights to funky house at Friday's City Club.

Elferhaus
PUB

(Map p298; Herzog-Friedrich-Strasse 11; ⊙10am-2am) Eleven is the magic number at Elferhaus, where you can nurse a beer beside Gothic gargoyles at the bar or take a church-like pew to hear live rock bands play.

Krahvogel
PUB

(Map p296; Anichstrasse 12; ⊙10am-2am Mon-Sat, 5pm-1am Sun) A big black crow guards the bar at this industrial-style pub. It doesn't make much noise, but the punters do after one drink too many. There are regular live bands and big-screen sports.

Dom Cafe-Bar
BAR

(Map p298; www.domcafe.at; Pfarrgasse 3; ⊙11am-2am) Chandeliers, vaulted ceilings and an HMV gramophone set the scene in this convivial Gothic-style bar.

La Copa
BAR

(Map p298; www.lacopa-cabana.com; Badgasse 4-6; ⊙Tue-Sat) Relaxed bodega with karaoke on Wednesday nights and flamenco with José Márquez and amigos on Thursdays.

Beach Club
BAR

(Map p298; Innrain; ⊙11am-11pm May-Sep) Complete with sand, river views and chilled tunes, this is a laid-back spot for quaffing a cold one in summer.

Jimmy's
BAR

(Map p296; Wilhelm-Greil-Strasse 19; ⊙Mon-Sat) Student mainstay with a party vibe, vodka shots and DJs spinning hip hop and funk.

☆ Entertainment

For more entertainment options, pick up a copy of *Innsider,* found in cafes across town, or visit www.innsider.at (in German). Schloss Ambras hosts a series of classical concerts in summer.

Weekender
CLUB

(www.weekenderclub.net, in German; Tschamlerstrasse 3; ⊙9pm-4am Mon, Fri & Sat) There's always a great buzz at this warehouse turned club, with an eclectic line-up of concerts, party nights and DJs spinning indie and electro. It's a 10-minute walk south of Maria-Theresien-Strasse along Leopoldstrasse.

Treibhaus   CLUB
(Map p298; www.treibhaus.at, in German; Anger-zellgasse 8; ☺10am-1am) Young Innsbruckers flock to this cultural complex for the big garden terrace, chilled atmosphere and regular DJs. There's free live music from rock to reggae on Friday evenings.

Tiroler Landestheater   THEATRE
(Map p298; ☑520 744; www.landestheater.at, in German; Rennweg 2) Innsbruck's imposing neoclassical theatre stages year-round performances of opera, dance, drama and comedy.

OlympiaWorld   CONCERT VENUE
(www.olympiaworld.at; Olympiastrasse 10) This cutting-edge venue hosts big-name concerts, musicals and sports events from football to ice-hockey matches. Take bus J from the Landestheater to Landessportcenter.

Cinematograph   CINEMA
(Map p296; www.cinematograph.at, in German; Museumstrasse 31) Independent films are screened in their original language here.

 ## Shopping
When in the *Altstadt,* try Seilergasse for jewellery and accessories by local creators, Herzog-Friedrich-Strasse for everything from chocolates to crystals, and Maria-Theresien-Strasse for high-street brands.

Spezialitäten aus der Stiftsgasse   FOOD
(Map p298; Stiftsgasse 2) An Aladdin's cave of homemade goodies, this vine-clad shop stocks all-Austrian honeys, oils, preserves, wines and spirits from gentian liqueur to hay schnapps.

Tiroler Heimatwerk   CRAFTS
(Map p296; Meraner Strasse 2) Great for traditional gifts, this place sells everything from *Dirndls* to hand-carved nativity figurines, stained glass and Tyrolean puppets.

Christmas & Easter in Innsbruck   SOUVENIRS
(Map p298; Herzog-Friedrich-Strasse 30; ☺9am-7pm Mon-Sat, to 6pm Sun) This marvellously kitsch shop brims with spangly decorations, painted eggs, crib figurines and nutcrackers.

Swarovski Crystal Gallery   GIFTS
(Map p298; Herzog-Friedrich-Strasse 39; ☺8am-6.30pm) Swarovski's flagship store in Innsbruck is this gallery-style boutique,

crammed with sparkling crystal trinkets, ornaments and jewellery.

Rathaus Galerien   MALL
(Map p296; www.rathausgalerien.at, in German; Maria-Theresien-Strasse 18; ☺9am-7pm Mon-Fri, to 6pm Sat) High-street shops, boutiques and cafes line this glass-roofed mall.

Kaufhaus Tyrol   MALL
(Map p296; http://kaufhaus-tyrol.at; Maria-Theresien-Strasse 31; ☺9am-7pm Mon-Wed, to 8pm Thu & Fri, to 6pm Sat) New shopping mall with big-name stores and eateries.

ℹ Information
The *Hauptbahnhof* and Innsbruck Information have exchange facilities and *Bankomaten* (ATMs) are ubiquitous in the *Altstadt.* See lonelyplanet.com/austria/tirol/innsbruck for planning advice, author recommendations, traveller reviews and insider tips.

Internet Access
Bubble Point (Brixner Strasse 1; per hr €6; ☺8am-9pm Mon-Fri, to 8pm Sat & Sun) Wash while you surf.

International Telephone Discount (Südtiroler-platz 1; per hr €2.50; ☺9am-9pm Mon-Sat, 10am-9pm Sun) Cheap phone calls as well.

Medical Services
Landeskrankenhaus (☑50 40; Anichstrasse 35) The *Universitätklinik* (University Clinic) at the city's main hospital has emergency services.

Post
Main post office (Maximilianstrasse 2)

Post office (Brunecker Strasse 1) This second post office is handy to the *Hauptbahnhof.*

Tourist Information
City Tourist Board (☑59 85-0; www.innsbruck.info; Burggraben 3; ☺8am-6pm Mon-Fri) Above Innsbruck Information, it mostly fields telephone enquiries.

Innsbruck Information (☑535 60; www.innsbruck.info; Burggraben 3; ☺9am-6pm) Main tourist office with truckloads of info on the city and surrounds, including skiing and walking. Sells ski passes, public-transport tickets and city maps (€1); will book accommodation (€3 commission); has an attached ticketing service; and has internet access (€1 for 10 minutes).

Travel Agencies
STA Travel (Wilhelm-Greil-Strasse 17; ☺9am-7pm Mon-Fri, 10am-2pm Sat) Friendly student-focused travel agency.

① Getting There & Away

Bus

The bus station is at the southern end of the *Hauptbahnhof;* its ticket office is located within the station.

Car & Motorcycle

The A12 and the parallel Hwy 171 are the main roads heading west and east. The B177, to the west of Innsbruck, continues north to Germany and Munich. The A13 is a toll road (€8) running south through the Brenner Pass to Italy and crossing the 192m Europabrücke, spanning the Sill River. Toll-free Hwy 182 follows the same route, passing under the bridge.

Train

The *Hauptbahnhof* is Innsbruck's most convenient station, though some local trains also pull up at the Westbahnhof (actually to the south) and at Hötting (to the west). Fast trains depart daily every two hours for Bregenz (€31.30, 2¾ hours) and Salzburg (€37.80, two hours). From Innsbruck to the Arlberg, the best views are on the right-hand side of the train. Two-hourly express trains serve Munich (€37, two hours) and Verona (€33.20, 3½ hours). Direct services to Kitzbühel also run every two hours (€17.60, 1¾ hours) while six daily trains head for Lienz (€31.20, three to five hours); some pass through Italy while others take the long way round via Salzburgerland.

① Getting Around

To/From the Airport

The airport is 4km west of the centre and served by bus F. Buses depart every 15 or 20 minutes from Maria-Theresien-Strasse (€1.80); taxis charge about €8 to €10 for the same trip.

Car & Motorcycle

Most of central Innsbruck has restricted parking, indicated by a blue line. You can park within these areas for a maximum of 1½ or three hours during set times (approximately shop hours). Parking garages (such as the one under the *Altstadt*) will set you back about €2.50/17 per hour/day.

Avis (www.avis.com; ⊘7.30am-6pm Mon-Fri) At the airport.

Hertz (www.hertz.com; Südtiroler Platz 1; ⊘7.30am-6pm Mon-Fri, 8am-1pm Sat)

Inntour (www.inntour.at; Leopoldstrasse 4; ⊘9am-6.30pm Mon-Fri, to 5pm Sat) Rents city, mountain, freeride and children's bikes for €19/24/35/12 per day respectively.

Public Transport

Single tickets on buses and trams cost €1.80 (from the driver; valid upon issue), but if you

MOVING ON?

For tips, recommendations and reviews, head to shop.lonelyplanet.com to purchase downloadable PDFs of the Trentino-Alto Adige chapter or the Friuli-Venezia Giulia chapter from Lonely Planet's *Italy* guide.

plan to use the city's public transport frequently you're better off buying a 24-hour ticket (€4.10). Weekly and monthly tickets are also available (€12.90 and €42.50, respectively). Tickets bought in advance, which are available from *Tabak* (tobacconist) shops, Innsbruck Information and the **IVB Kundenbüro** (Stainerstrasse 2; ⊘7.30am-6pm Mon-Fri), must be stamped in the machines at the start of the journey.

AROUND INNSBRUCK

Hall in Tirol

☑ 05223 / POP 12,400 / ELEV 574M

Nestled beneath the Alps, just 9km east of Innsbruck, Hall is a beautiful medieval town that grew fat on the riches of salt in the 13th century. The winding lanes, punctuated by pastel-coloured townhouses and lantern-lit after dark, are made for aimless ambling. If you're in town for the *Weinherbst* festival in September, watch as the water in the Wilden Mannes fountain miraculously turns to wine.

⊙ Sights & Activities

All streets in Hall lead to the medieval Obererstadt (Upper Town), which centres on the main square, Oberer Stadtplatz.

TOP⟍ **Burg Hasegg** CASTLE, MUSEUM
CHOICE⟋ (Burg Hasegg 6; adult/child €8/6; ⊘10am-5pm Tue-Sun) This turreted 14th-century castle sits just south of the Oberestadt. A spiral staircase twists up to the 5th floor for far-reaching views over Hall. The castle had a 300-year career as a mint for silver *Thalers* (coins, the root of the modern word 'dollar'), and this history is unravelled in the **Münze Hall** (mint), displaying water-driven and hammer-striking techniques. Kids will enjoy minting their own coins.

Pfarrkirche St Nikolaus — CHURCH
(St Nicholas Parish Church; ☉dawn-dusk) This graceful 13th-century church is best known for its **Waldaufkapelle**, home to Florian Waldauf's grisly collection of 45 skulls and 12 bones, picked from the remains of minor saints. Each rests on embroidered cushions, capped with veils and elaborate headdresses, reminiscent of spiked haloes; the whole effect is both repulsive and enthralling.

Bergbau Museum — MUSEUM
(Fürstengasse; adult/child €3.50/2; ☉tours 11.30am Mon, Thu & Sat Apr-Sep) This reconstructed salt mine, complete with galleries, tools and shafts, can only be visited by guided tour.

Rathaus — TOWN HALL
(Oberer Stadtplatz) Bordering the main square is Hall's 15th-century town hall, with its distinctive courtyard, complete with crenellated edges and mosaic crests.

Damenstift — CONVENT
(Stiftplatz) A convent founded in 1557 and topped by a baroque tower; unfortunately the convent's church is often locked.

🛏 Sleeping & Eating

Gasthof Badl — GUESTHOUSE €
(☎567 84; www.badl.at; Innbrücke 4; s/d €47/78; 🅿❧) A short dash across the Inn River, this gem of a guesthouse has immaculate rooms (most with river view) and a tavern that knocks up a great strudel. Children will love the playground and docile St Bernard, Max. Rent a bike here to pedal along the banks to Innsbruck.

Parkhotel — HOTEL €€
(☎537 69; www.parkhotel-hall.com; Thurnfeldgasse 1; s/d €96/154; 🅿❧@🛜) It's a surprise to find such an avant-garde design statement as this cylindrical hotel in tiny Hall. The mountains seem close enough to touch in the curvy glass-walled rooms, done out in minimalist style and earthy hues.

Rathaus Cafe — CAFE €€
(Oberer Stadtplatz 2; snacks €3-6.50) Part of Hall's vaulted town hall has been transformed into this modern cafe. There's a terrace for people-watching over breakfast, a baguette or drink.

Goldener Engel — AUSTRIAN €€
(☎546 21; Unterer Stadtplatz 5; mains €8-15; ☉9am-midnight) The ambience is cosy in the historic *Stuben* and vaulted Gothic cellar of this central tavern. Or join locals for filling Tyrolean fare and Augustiner Bräu brews in the beer garden.

ℹ Information
Staff at the **tourist office** (☎455 44; www.regionhall.at, in German; Wallpachgasse 5; ☉8.30am-6pm Mon-Fri, 9am-1pm Sat) can help you sort out accommodation. They also organise **guided tours** (adult/child €6/3.50; ☉10am Mon-Sat Apr-Sep).

ℹ Getting There & Away
The B171 goes almost through the town centre, unlike the A12/E45, which is over the Inn River to the south. The train station is about 1km southwest of the centre; it is on the main Innsbruck–Wörgl train line. Trains run frequently to/from Innsbruck (€2, eight minutes).

Wattens
The quaint village of Wattens has one claim to fame: it's the glittering heart of the Swarovski crystal empire. Call them kitsch or classy, but there is no doubting the pulling power of these crystals at the fantastical **Swarovski Kristallwelten** (Swarovski Crystal Worlds; http://kristallwelten.swarovski.com; Kristallweltenstrasse 1; adult/child €9.50/free; ☉9am-6.30pm), one of Austria's most-visited attractions. A giant's head spewing water into a pond greets you in the park. Inside you'll find Alexander McQueen's crystal winterscape, a kaleidoscopic crystal dome and even zebras drifting past on ruby slippers in a twinkling theatre. A play on light and dark, the Conran-designed shop is where, budget depending, you can buy a bejewelled pen for a few euros or spend thousands on a crystal-encrusted elephant. Decisions, decisions...

Trains run roughly half-hourly from Innsbruck to Fritzens-Wattens (€3.60, 16 minutes), 3km north of Swarovski Kristallwelten and on the opposite side of the river.

Schwaz
☎05242 / POP 12,900 / ELEV 545M
What is today a sleepy little town with pastel-washed houses and winding streets was once, believe it or not, Austria's second-largest city after Vienna. Schwaz wielded clout in the Middle Ages when its eyes shone brightly with silver, past glory that you can relive by going underground to the show silver mine.

⊙ Sights & Activities

Altstadt   HISTORIC SITE
Schwaz' biggest draw is its well-preserved *Altstadt*. Taking pride of place on pedestrianised Franz-Josef-Strasse, the Gothic **Pfarrkirche** (parish church; ⊘dawn-dusk) immediately catches your eye with its step-gabled roof bearing 14,000 copper tiles. The web-vaulted interior purportedly harbours the largest symphonic organ in Tyrol, which is put to use at 8.15pm every Monday.

Not far south is the Gothic-meets-baroque **Franziskanerkirche** (Gilmstrasse; ⊘dawn-dusk); Gothic windows and unfinished frescoes line its inner courtyard.

Haus der Völker   MUSEUM
(www.hausdervoelker.com, in German; St Martin; adult/child €6/4; ⊘10am-6pm) Local photographer Gert Chesi set up this museum, showcasing a rich collection of African and Asian ritual art. Rotating exhibitions home in on elements of the collection, such as spiritual Tanzania or African textile art.

Silberbergwerk Schwaz   SILVER MINE
(Silver Mine; www.silberbergwerk.at; Alte Landstrasse 3a; adult/child/family €15/8/34; ⊘9am-5pm) You almost feel like breaking out into a rendition of 'Heigh-Ho' at Silberbergwerk Schwaz, as you board a mini train and venture deep into the bowels of the silver mine for a 90-minute trundle through Schwaz' illustrious past. The mine is about 1.5km east of the centre.

🛏 Sleeping & Eating

Franz-Josef-Strasse has a handful of cafes and snack bars.

Gasthof Einhorn Schaller   GUESTHOUSE €
(⌨740 47; www.gasthof-schaller.at, in German; Innsbruckerstrasse 31; s/d/tr/q €39/60/75/90; ⊘🐾📶🍴) This super-central, family-friendly *Gasthof* combines modern rooms with a traditional restaurant dishing up regional fare like *Zillertaler Kasspätzle* (eggy pasta with cheese and onions).

Culinaria   CAFE €
(Burggasse 1; lunch €4.50, mains €6-7) Locals love this cafe for its cheap lunches and post-work drinks in the vine-strewn courtyard. The simple menu features various takes on pasta, bruschetta and salads.

ℹ Information

The helpful **tourist office** (⌨632 40; www.silberregionkarwendel.at; Franz-Josef-Strasse

2; ⊘8am-noon & 1-5pm Mon-Fri, 8am-noon Sat) provides information on sights and accommodation in Schwaz.

ℹ Getting There & Away

Schwaz is 30km east of Innsbruck and 10km west of the Zillertal on the A12 Inntal-Autobahn. There are frequent trains between Innsbruck and Schwaz (€5.40, 20 minutes).

Stubai Glacier

It's a bizarre feeling to slip out of sandals and into skis in midsummer, but that's precisely what draws people to the Stubai Glacier. Just 40km south of Innsbruck, the glacier is a year-round skiing magnet with more than 100km of wide, snow-sure pistes that are great for cruising and intermediate skiing. Summer skiing is limited to between 2900m and 3300m. Walkers are attracted to the network of trails lower down in the valley; a good hiking map for the area is Kompass' *Stubaier Alpen* (scale 1:50,000). The Stubaital branches off from the Brenner Pass route (A13/E45) a little south of the Europabrücke and runs southwest.

Stubaitalbahn (STB) buses from Innsbruck journey to the foot of the glacier (€8, 1½ hours) on an hourly basis.

If you're based in Innsbruck and want to go skiing for the day on the glacier, consider the package tour offered by Innsbruck Information. For €56, you get a return bus journey, ski or snowboard rental and a ski pass.

Seefeld

📞05212 / POP 3050 / ELEV 1180M
Seefeld sits high on a south-facing plateau, ringed by the rugged limestone peaks of the Wetterstein and Karwendel Alps. While most Tyrolean resorts are crazy about downhill, Seefeld's first love is *Langlauf* (cross-country skiing), and fans of oversized skis come here to skate and glide along 266km of prepared trails in winter. The resort is gearing up to host the biathlon events in the 2012 Youth Olympic Games.

⊙ Sights & Activities

Pfarrkirche St Oswald   CHURCH
(Dorfplatz; ⊘8am-7pm) Seefeld's trophy sight is this late-Gothic parish church, the supposed location of a miracle. The story goes that Oswald Milser gobbled a wafer reserved for the clergy at Easter communion here in 1384.

After almost being swallowed up by the floor, the greedy layman repented, but the wafer was streaked with blood – not from foolish Oswald but from Christ, naturally. You can view the **Blutskapelle** (Chapel of the Holy Blood), which held the original wafer, by climbing the stairway.

Strandbad
LIDO

(adult/child €4.50/2.90; ⏱9am-7pm late May-Sep) After following the 45-minute lakeside **walking trail** that wriggles around bottle-green, pine-fringed Wildsee, a short stroll from the centre in the Reither Moor conservation area, you can stop off for a refreshing dip at the Strandbad lido.

For longer, more challenging walks, cable cars ascend nearby Seefeld Spitze (2220m) and Reither Spitze (2374m); consult the tourist office for more information or join one of its regular guided walks.

Cross-Country Skiing
SKIING

Seefeld's raison d'être is cross-country skiing. Well-groomed *Loipen* (trails) criss-cross the sunny plateau to Mösern, 5km away, where there are fine views of the Inn River and the peaks beyond. The downhill skiing here suits beginners and intermediates.

Seefeld is linked to other ski resorts, including Garmisch-Partenkirchen and Ehrwald in Germany, all of which are covered by the three-day **Happy Ski Card** (adult/child €99/59.50). The two main areas are Gschwandtkopf (1500m) and Rosshütte (1800m); the latter connects to higher lifts and slopes on the Karwendel range.

🛏 Sleeping & Eating

Rates jump by around a third during the high winter season. Ask your host for a guest card for discounts on activities. Many places close in the shoulder seasons.

🌿 Central
HOTEL €€

(📞26 88; www.central-seefeld.at; Münchnerstrasse 41; d €92-116, half board €12; 🅿♿) Friendly service, an attractive spa and kids' play areas make the Central a good choice. The well-lit rooms with balconies are contemporary Tyrolean in style, with light birch wood and earthy hues. The food makes the most of local products and there are organic options at breakfast.

Pension Edelweiss
PENSION €

(📞23 04; www.seefeld-austria.com; Klosterstrasse 176; d €58-74; 🅿) This pension is as clean, bright and happy to meet you as the 'Edelweiss' song suggests. Mrs Kirchmair takes pride in keeping her pretty rooms with balconies spotless. There's a garden for quiet moments.

Hotel Garni Dorothea
HOTEL €€

(📞25 27; www.hotel-dorothea.at; Am Kirchwald 391; s/d €43/86; 🅿♨) Great views over Seefeld unfold as you trudge uphill to this hotel. The rooms in natural colours are spacious and modern. After carving up the slopes, the indoor pool and sauna are just the ticket.

Strandperle
INTERNATIONAL €€

(📞24 36; www.strandperle.at, in German; Innsbrückerstrasse 500; mains €9-18; ☺) Overlooking the calm waters of Wildsee, Strandperle is a funky glass-and-granite place. The menu delivers Med-inspired flavours like pepper-crusted tuna with lemon rice and saffron risotto. The decked terrace has the finest views of the Alps anywhere in Seefeld.

Restaurant Südtiroler Stube
AUSTRIAN €€

(📞504 46; www.suedtirolerstube.com; Reitherspitzstrasse 17; mains €9-26) This low-beamed South Tyrolean restaurant pips the competition with delicious specialities such as rosemary-infused rack of lamb and tender venison medallions.

ℹ Information

The central **tourist office** (📞05-088 00; www.seefeld.com; Klosterstrasse 43; ⏱8.30am-6.30pm Mon-Sat, 10am-12.30pm & 3-5pm Sun) has stacks of info on accommodation and outdoor activities.

ℹ Getting There & Away

Seefeld is 25km northwest of Innsbruck, just off the Germany-bound B177. The track starts climbing soon after departing Innsbruck, providing spectacular views across the whole valley. Trains run to/from Innsbruck (€5.40, 35 minutes) every two hours. There are hourly buses to Mittenwald (€7.20, 25 minutes) and Garmisch-Partenkirchen (€11, 55 minutes) in Germany.

NORTHEASTERN TYROL

The Zillertal

Sandwiched between the Tuxer Voralpen and the Kitzbüheler Alpen, the Zillertal (Ziller Valley) is storybook Tyrol. A steam train chugs through the broad valley, passing fertile farmland and wooded mountains, and affording snatched glimpses of snowy peaks and the fast-flowing Ziller River.

GET INTO THE ALPINE GROOVE

As well as skis or walking boots, the Zillertal is one place you'll be glad you packed that figure-hugging *Dirndl* or extra pair of *Lederhosen*. This valley is the Austrian Alps' land of song and thigh-slapping tradition, where down-to-earth locals tune into *Alpenrock* (alpine rock), every *Gasthaus* worth its weight swings to accordion-loaded *Volksmusik* (folk music) in summer, and names like the Zillertaler Hadelumpen (literally the Zillertal good-for-nothings) are sacrosanct. Go, enjoy!

🏃 Activities

Alpine Skiing
SKIING

While Mayrhofen is the prime spot for serious skiing, there is downhill and cross-country skiing elsewhere. The **Zillertaler Superskipass** (4 days/4 out of 6 days €138/153) covers all 166km of slopes in the valley. Ski buses connect the resorts.

Alpine Walks
WALKING

In summer, the alpine valley morphs into excellent walking territory, with high-altitude trekking in the Tuxer Voralpen and myriad trails fanning out from the resorts of Ried, Kaltenbach, Aschau, Zell am Ziller and Ramsau. Mountain huts at elevations of around 1800m beckon weary hikers; the handy *Hütten-, Ausflugs- & Erlebnisführer* booklet (German only) lists all the huts in the valley. A detailed walking map covering the entire region is the Kompass *Zillertaler Alpen-Tuxer Alpen* (scale 1:50,000).

If you're planning on spending a week or more in the valley between June and October, the value-for-money **Zillertal Activecard** (6/9/12 days €51/70/88) covers public transport, one journey per day on any of the Zillertal cable cars and entry to swimming pools.

Other adrenalin-based activities include rafting, rock climbing, paragliding and cycling. The Ziller and its tributaries are also good for fishing, but permits are only valid for certain stretches.

🎉 Festivals & Events

Zillertal Bike Challenge
BIKE RACE

(www.zillertal-bikechallenge.com) Hardcore mountain bikers with nerves of steel descend on the Zillertal for this three-day bike race in July.

Almabtriebe
HERITAGE EVENT

(www.almabtrieb.net, in German) Throughout September, the Zillertaler celebrate the coming home of the cows, which are adorned with elaborate floral headdresses and bells. The event is a valley-wide party with feasting, *Volksmusik* and schnapps before another harsh winter shovelling cow dung.

🛏 Sleeping & Eating

Four campgrounds are situated in the valley and there is the chalet-style **Finsinger-hof Hostel** (☑05288-620 10; www.finsingerhof.at; Finsingerhofweg 1; dm €18; P) at Uderns, 17km south of Jenbach. Local tourist offices will usually help you find pensions, private rooms, holiday apartments and farmhouses for free. Wherever you stay, enquire about the resort's *Gästekarte* (guest card).

Note that many hotels, restaurants and bars close in shoulder seasons: early April to late June and early November to mid-December.

ℹ Information

Practically every resort has its own tourist office, but the main **tourist office** (☑05288-871 87; www.zillertal.at; ⊙8.30am-noon & 1-5.30pm Mon-Fri, 8.30am-noon Sat) covering the whole valley is in Schlitters, 6km from Jenbach. It stocks plenty of information on outdoor activities, along with the *Zillertaler Gästezeitung* (partially in English) magazine.

ℹ Getting There & Away

The Zillertal is serviced by a private train line, the **Zillertalbahn** (www.zillertalbahn.at), which travels the 32km from Jenbach to Mayrhofen.

Those with a thirst for nostalgia can take a *Dampfzug* (steam train) along the valley; it runs twice daily year-round (10.35am and 3.35pm). It takes about 85 minutes to reach the last stop, Mayrhofen, and costs €12 one-way to either Zell or Mayrhofen. If you just want to get from A to B, it's better to take the ordinary train as it costs €6.30.

Zell am Ziller

☑05282 / POP 1750 / ELEV 575M

Scenically located at the foot of knife-edge Reichenspitze (3303m), Zell am Ziller is a former goldmining centre. There's now less

DON'T MISS

CYCLING THE ZILLERTAL

The Zillertal is cycling nirvana, particularly for serious mountain bikers, many of whom limber up here before taking part in the gruelling three-day **Zillertal Bike Challenge** in July. The wide, sunny valley and surrounding 3000m peaks are laced with 800km of well-marked routes that reach from easygoing two-hour jaunts along the valley floor to panoramic mountain passes, such as the notoriously tough 56km trail from Fügen to Kellerjoch, a test of stamina and condition.

You can access many of the high-altitude and downhill routes using the cable cars in the valley, and local trains will transport your bike for free. Bikes are available for hire at major stations throughout the Zillertal, including Zell am Ziller and Mayrhofen, for €8/12 per half-/full day. For free maps, detailed route descriptions and downloadable GPS bike tours, visit www.zillertal.at or www.best-of-zillertal.at.

sparkle and more swoosh about this rural and deeply traditional little village, with its fine skiing and thrilling 7.5km floodlit toboggan run. In summer, active types come to hike in the mountains or pedal up the Gerlos Pass to Krimml in the Hohe Tauern National Park.

◎ Sights & Activities

Pfarrkirche   CHURCH
(parish church; ☺dawn-dusk) The spire of this pink-and-white parish church dominates the village centre and is surrounded by a sea of filigree crosses. You can peek inside the church, but you do so at your own risk – a sign on the door issues a warning that it is *not* a museum!

Abenteuer Goldbergbau   GOLD MINE
(www.goldschaubergwerk.com, in German; Hainzenberg 73; adult/child €10/5; ☺9am-5pm) Abenteuer Goldbergbau is a two-hour tour of a gold mine, 2km east of Zell on the Gerlos road. The entry price covers a cheese-making demonstration and a visit to the animal enclosure with deer, emus and llamas.

Freizeitpark Zell   LEISURE CENTRE
(www.freizeitparkzell.at; Schwimmbadweg 7; ice rink adult/child €4/3, swimming pool €6/3.50; ☺9am-7pm) There's ice skating, tennis, football, bowling and a fun pool with plenty to amuse the kids at this riverside sports centre.

Aktivzentrum Zillertal   ADVENTURE SPORTS
(☎0664-87 25 913; www.aktivzentrum-zillertal.at, in German; Freizeitpark Zell) Craving a little adventure? This specialist takes you paragliding (€55 to €130), rafting on the Ziller (€35), climbing (€45) and llama – yep, llama – trekking (€20) in summer. Winter activities include snowshoe hikes (€40) and ice climbing (€70).

★☆ Festivals & Events

Gauderfest   BEER FESTIVAL
(www.gauderfest.at, in German) Over-strenuous activities are not recommended after a bellyful of super-strong Gauderbier (reputedly over 10% alcohol), brewed specially for this shindig on the first weekend in May. As well as eating, dancing and excessive drinking, there's a historical parade and alpine wrestling.

⊨ Sleeping & Eating

In winter, expect room rates to be roughly a third higher than those quoted below. There are several mediocre restaurants in the village centre and a **Billa** (Bahnhofstrasse 3) supermarket.

TOP CHOICE **Enzianhof**   FARMSTAY €
(☎22 37; www.enzianhof.eu, in German; Gerlosberg 23; s/d incl half board €38/64; P☺) High on a hilltop, this rustic farmhouse is perfectly located for hiking and skiing, and has warm, spacious rooms. The farmer makes his own gentian schnapps and smokes his own ham, and you can fill up on Zillertaler specialities like *Pressknödelsuppe* (Tyrolean dumpling soup) in the wood-beamed restaurant.

Gästehaus Brindlinger   PENSION €
(☎26 71; brindlinger.zell@aon.at; Gaudergasse 4; s/d €27/53; P@) Tucked down a quiet lane, this chalet has bright rooms with plenty of pine, rag rugs and balconies affording mountain views. Guests can wind down in the small sauna and Mrs Brindlinger lends out bikes free of charge.

Camping Hofer   CAMPGROUND €
(☎22 48; www.campingdorf.at; Gerlosstrasse 33; camp sites per adult/child/tent €6.90/4.60/8, s/d €21/42; P▨) This tree-shaded site's first-rate

facilities include a playground, barbecue area and heated pool. If you don't fancy roughing it, check out the well-kept rooms in the guesthouse.

ℹ Information

The **tourist office** (📞22 81; www.zell.at; Dorfplatz 3a; ⏰8.30am-12.30pm & 2.30-6pm Mon-Fri, 9am-noon & 4-6pm Sat) near the train tracks is a mine of information on walking, skiing and adventure activities in the area. At the other end of Dorfplatz is the post office, with bus stops at the rear.

ℹ Getting There & Away

Normal trains to Mayrhofen (€2.30, 11 minutes) and Jenbach (€5.50, 47 minutes) are cheaper than the steam train. Zell am Ziller is the start of the Gerlos Pass route to the Krimml Falls; buses tackle the pass from July to September twice daily (€10.70, 1½ hours).

Trains to and from Innsbruck (€12.60, 1½ hours, hourly) require a change at Jenbach.

Mayrhofen

📞05285 / POP 3850 / ELEV 630M

Mayrhofen is ever so traditional in summer, with its alpine dairies, trails twisting high into the mountains and stein-swinging *Volksmusik* pouring out of every *Gasthof*. But it dances to a different tune in winter. The skiing at Ahorn and Penken is some of the country's finest, a double whammy of cruising and kamikaze in the shadow of the glaciated Zillertal range, and the après ski is the hottest this side of the Tyrolean Alps.

🏃 Activities

Winter Activities

Alpine Skiing   SKIING

Snow-sure Mayrhofen has varied skiing on 166km of slopes, mostly geared towards confident intermediates, as well as some great off-piste opportunities. The skiing ranges

from scenic tree-lined runs for cruisers to knee-trembling black runs, including the infamous Harakiri, to challenge experts. The ski pass (1-day pass €41.50) is valid for all cable cars and lifts in Mayrhofen.

Hintertuxer Gletscher   SKIING

(Hintertux Glacier; www.hintertuxergletscher.at; day pass summer/winter €16/41.50) Mayrhofen provides easy access to year-round skiing on the Hintertuxer Gletscher; the cable car is an attraction in itself, gliding above sheer cliff faces and jagged peaks to the tip of the ice-blue glacier. The sundeck at 3250m affords phenomenal views of the Tuxer Alps and, on clear days, Grossglockner, the Dolomites and Zugspitze. From Christmas until early May, a free bus shuttles skiers from Mayrhofen to the glacier (included in the ski pass).

Vans Penken Park   SNOWBOARDING

(www.vans-penken-park.com) Snowboarders are in their freestyle element on the obstacles, boxes, rails and halfpipe at the Vans Penken Park in the Penken area, ranked one of Europe's best terrain parks.

Summer Activities

Alpine Walks   WALKING

Walking is the big deal in Mayrhofen in summer, particularly in the glorious alpine country of the Naturpark Zillertaler Alpen. The tourist office website, www.mayrhofen.at, has excellent information on walks, maps and GPS downloads. From the village itself, two cable cars (one-way/return €10.30/16) give walkers a head start to Ahorn (1965m) and Penken (1800m). If you know your karabiner from your crampons, Mayrhofen also has some prime rock climbing and via ferrate (fixed-rope routes) on its doorstep.

The new **Run & Walk Park** challenges Nordic walkers and joggers. The eight different routes, colour coded according to difficulty – yellow is easy, red moderate, black difficult – include the Harakiri, which is only slightly easier to run than it is to ski!

DON'T MISS

THE HARAKIRIIIIIIII...

With a 78% gradient, the Harakiri is Austria's steepest piste. This is half diving, half carving; a heart-stopping, hell-for-leather descent that leaves even accomplished skiers quaking in their ski boots. Only super-fit, experienced skiers with perfect (think Bond) body control should consider tackling this monster of a run. Test out slope 17 first to see if you're able, and check piste conditions before heading out as ice renders the slope treacherous. For bragging rights in the après-ski bars, you can pick up 'survivor' souvenirs in the shop at the base of the Ahornbahn.

Penken
MOUNTAIN BIKING

(day pass €22) Downhill mountain bikers are in heaven on Penken. The tourist office can point you in the direction of bike rental, routes and hotels, as can the website http://mayrhofen.mtbfreeride.tv (in German).

Sennerei Zillertal
SHOW DAIRY

(www.sennerei-zillertal.at; Hollenzen 116; with/without tasting €11.20/5.80; ⊙10am-3pm mid-Dec–Oct) For a fly-on-the-wall tour of a working dairy, head to Sennerei Zillertal. A tour takes you through the various cheese-making processes and rounds out with a tasting of the final products: Tilsiter, Bergkäse and Graukäse, a mouldy, virtually fat-free grey cheese.

Action Club Zillertal
ADVENTURE SPORTS

(☑629 77; www.actionclub-zillertal.com; Hauptstrasse 458; ⊙9am-noon & 3-6pm) A one-stop daredevil shop, offering everything from rafting on the Ziller River (€29) to canyoning (€29 to €59), tubing (€35), climbing (€35 to €65) and mountain-bike tours (€25 to €60).

Rocky Nature
ROCK CLIMBING

(www.rockynature.at, in German) Climbing-pro Gerhard Hörhager helps you come to grips with the Zillertal's granite wonderland. See the website for courses and prices, including the introductory two-hour *Schnupperklettern* (€25).

Faleva Mountain Shop
ROCK CLIMBING

(☑632 58; Hauptstrasse 412; ⊙8.30am-6pm Mon-Sat) Runs three-hour climbing tours costing €35/25 per adult/child and rents out climbing equipment (€10).

★☆ Festivals & Events

The self-proclaimed greatest show on snow, **Snowbombing** (www.snowbombing.com) in early April is Mayrhofen's biggest shindig. Some of the world's top boarders compete on the slopes, but most people are just here for the party – five solid days of drinking and dancing to a cracking line-up of bands and DJs.

🛏 Sleeping

The tourist office can help you trawl through the mountain of sleeping options in the village; rates are roughly 30% higher in winter. Bear in mind that many hotels and restaurants close between seasons.

Hotel Kramerwirt
HISTORIC HOTEL €€

(☑67 00; www.kramerwirt.at; Am Marienbrunnen 346; s/d €89/154; P❄≋🕾) Ablaze with gera-niums in summer, this rambling 500-year-old chalet has corridors full of family heirlooms, spacious rooms and a whirlpool. Twist your tongue in the restaurant (mains €8 to €21) asking for *Zillertaler Bauernschmaus* (farmers' platter with meat, dumplings and sauerkraut).

Hotel Garni Glockenstuhl
HOTEL €

(☑631 28; www.glockenstuhl.com, in German; Einfahrt Mitte 431; s/d/tr €45/78/113; P❄@) Good old-fashioned Austrian hospitality, dreamy alpine views and a spa make this chalet stand out. If you can drag yourself out of the comfiest of beds, you'll find a delicious breakfast with fresh eggs on the table.

Hotel Rose
HOTEL €€

(☑622 29; Brandbergstrasse 353; www.hotel-rose.at; s/d €50/88; P🕾) In the capable hands of the fourth-generation Kröll family, this place has spacious rooms with chunky pine furnishings and balconies. There's a little sauna and whirlpool for après-ski relaxing. The garden pumps to live *Volksmusik* daily in summer.

Pension Kumbichlhof
PENSION €

(☑624 58; www.kumbichlhof.com; Kumbichl 874; s/d €28/48; P) This family-run farmhouse is a great budget choice. The decor teeters on the old-fashioned, but rooms are immaculate and have their own balconies.

🍴 Eating

Self-caterers stock up at **Billa** (Am Marienplatz) and **Spar** (Hauptstrasse).

TOP CHOICE Metzgerei Kröll
BUTCHER €

(Scheulingstrasse 382; snacks €3-8; ⊙7.30am-12.30pm & 2.30-6pm Mon-Fri, 7am-noon Sat) This award-winning family-run butchery is famed for its *Schlegeis-Speck* ham, cured in a hut at 1800m for three months to achieve its aroma. There are a handful of tables where you can sample this speciality and delicious homemade sausages.

Wirtshaus zum Griena
AUSTRIAN €€

(☑67 67; Dorfhaus 768; mains €7-15) Set in high pastures, this woodsy 400-year-old chalet is the kind of place where you pray for a snow blizzard, just so you can huddle around the fire and gorge on *Schlutzkropf'n* (fresh pasta filled with cheese).

Schneekarhütte
AUSTRIAN €€

(www.schneekarhütte.com, in German; ⊙lunch) Upping the ante in slope-side dining, this sophisticated hut has terrific views and an enticing open fire. Regional organic produce

Walking Tour
Zillertal Circuit

❯ This high-level circuit provides tremendous views to the startlingly turquoise Schlegeisspeicher and snowcapped Zillertal Alps. Though the trek involves 850m of incline, the path is well graded and mostly gentle; however, use care in bad weather. Kompass 1:50,000 map No 37 *Zillertaler Alpen-Tuxer Alpen* covers the walk in detail. Begin at the ❶ **Schlegeisspeicher**, ringed by rugged 3000m-high peaks. From the northeast end of the car park, take the trail and follow signs towards the Dominikus Hütte, bearing right towards Friesenberghaus. The path ascends through shady forest and traverses a couple of streamlets to emerge at the tree line near ❷ **Friesenbergalm** after about 45 minutes. The trail flattens to cross tarn-dotted pastures. Sidle around a shoulder and enter a valley overshadowed by the bulk of Hoher Riffler.

Boulder-strewn meadows give way to scree patches and the ❸ **Lapenkarbach**. The trail winds uphill via long bends, then tight switchbacks, to the ❹ **Friesenberghaus** at the head of the valley around 1½ hours from Friesenbergalm. This is a scenic spot for a break, with views of the steely grey Grosser Grainer.

Retrace your steps for 50m, following the signs right towards the Olperer Hütte and the Berliner Höhenweg. The trail descends slightly, crossing the outlet stream of ❺ **Friesenbergsee**, then makes a short, steep ascent up the rocky slope on the other side. Turn left when you reach a junction and contour the mountainside ahead. The next 1½ hours follow an easygoing balcony trail, part of the multiday ❻ **Berliner Höhenweg** route. It leads under the glacier-capped peaks of the Gefrorene-Wand-Spitzen and affords memorable views of the Schlegeisspeicher and Zillertal Alps.

About two hours from Friesenberghaus, cross a stream to reach ❼ **Olperer Hütte**, a great place for a drink. Then it's a steady descent to the reservoir, winding gently over grassy hummocks before zigzagging down beside ❽ **Riepenbach** to the road (1½ hours from the Olperer Hütte). Turn left and follow the road for 1km to return to the parking area.

goes into dishes from schnitzels to *tarte flambée*. Reach it by taking the Horbergbahn cable car in Schwendau.

Mamma Mia
PIZZA €€

(☑67 68; Einfahrt Mitte 432; mains €7-9; ☺11am-midnight) This basement pizzeria is a snippet of Italy with its Florence murals and stone-oven pizzas that are thin, crisp and delicious.

Cafe-Konditorei Kostner
CAFE €

(Hauptstrasse 414; mains €7-12; ☺6.30am-6pm) Great wholemeal bread and homemade cakes, alongside salads and heart-warming dishes like goulash.

Drinking

Mayrhofen's après-ski scene rocks; most bars go with the snow and open from mid-December to early April.

White Lounge
BAR

(www.white-lounge.at; Ahorn; ☺10am-4.30pm) Kick your skis off and chill over cocktails at this 2000m ice bar, with a big sunny terrace for catching rays. Things heat up with DJs and night sledding at Tuesday's igloo party (begins 8pm).

Brück'n Stadl
LIVE MUSIC

(Gasthof Brücke, Ahornstrasse 850; ☺6pm-midnight Jun-Sep, 4pm-10pm Dec-Apr) For year-round *Spass* (fun), you can't beat this lively barn and marquee combi. *Lederhosen*-clad folk stars get beer glasses swingin' in summer, while plentiful schnapps and DJ Mütze fuel the après-ski party in winter.

Scotland Yard
PUB

(www.scotlandyard.at; Scheulingstrasse 372; ☺7pm-late) Scotland Yard is a British pub with all the trimmings: Guinness, darts and a red phone box where expats can pour their hearts out to folk back home after a pint or three.

Mo's
BAR

(Hauptstrasse 417; ☺noon-1am) An American-themed bar with an upbeat vibe, tasty finger food and live music at weekends.

Ice Bar
BAR

(Hotel Strass, Hauptstrasse 470; ☺3.30-9pm) A loud, lary, anything-goes après-ski haunt brimming with boot-stomping revellers and, occasionally, go-go polar bears (we kid you not!).

ℹ Information

The ultramodern **tourist office** (☑676 00; www.mayrhofen.at; Europahaus; ☺8am-6pm Mon-Fri, 9am-6pm Sat, 9am-noon Sun) stocks loads of information and maps on the resort. Look for the comprehensive *Info von A-Z;* it's free and written in English. There is a handy topographic model of the surrounding Alps, a 24-hour accommodation board and free wi-fi.

ℹ Getting There & Away

By normal train, it's €6.30 each way to Jenbach (55 minutes).

Ginzling

☑05286 / POP 400 / ELEV 999M

For a taste of what the Austrian Alps looked like before the dawn of tourism, head to Ginzling, an adorable little village 8km south of Mayrhofen.

The main draw for hikers is the **Naturpark Zillertaler Alpen** (www.naturpark-zillertal.at, in German), a 379-sq-km nature park and pristine alpine wilderness of deep valleys and glaciated peaks. The **tourist office** (☑52 18; www.ginzling.at; Naturparkhaus Zillertaler Alpen; ☺8am-6pm Mon-Fri, plus 10am-5pm Sat & Sun May-Oct) doubles as the park's information centre and runs excellent themed guided hikes, most costing around €5, from May to October. The extensive program includes everything from llama trekking to sunrise photo excursions. The office also has information on climbing, mountain biking and ski touring in the area.

The most charming place to stay is **Gasthof Alt-Ginzling** (☑52 01; www.altginzling.at; s/d €33/66, mains €7-16; ℗), once a wayside inn for smugglers travelling to Italy. The 18th-century farmhouse oozes history from every creaking beam and the low-ceilinged, pine-panelled rooms are supremely cosy. The restaurant serves local rainbow trout.

In winter, free ski buses run frequently to Mayrhofen; otherwise there is an hourly service (€2.30, 17 minutes). A road (toll €10) snakes on from Ginzling up the valley to the Schlegeisspeicher reservoir, the trailhead for the stunning Zillertal Circuit. Alternatively, buses run between Mayrhofen and the reservoir (one-way €5.50, one hour, seven daily).

Achensee

Around 6km north of Jenbach, the fjord-like Achensee is Tyrol's largest lake and one of its loveliest, flanked by thickly wooded mountains. The **Achenseebahn** (www.

achenseebahn.at; one way/return €22/29), a private cogwheel steam train, trundles to the lake from Jenbach between May and October, connecting with two-hour **boat tours** (www.tirol-schiffahrt.at, in German; adult/child €15/7.50) of the lake. Sweeping views over the lake and the surrounding peaks can be had from Erfurter (1831m), which is easily reached by the Rofanseilbahn (adult/child return €17/10; ⊙8.30am-5pm) from Maurach.

Kitzbühel

☑05356 / POP 8450 / ELEV 762M

Ask an Austrian to rattle off the top ski resorts in the country, and Kitzbühel will invariably make the grade. Kitzbühel began life in the 16th century as a silver and copper mining town, and today continues to preserve a charming medieval centre despite its other persona as a fashionable and prosperous winter resort. It's renowned for the white-knuckled Hahnenkamm downhill ski race in January and the excellence of its slopes.

⊙ Sights

It's a joy simply to stroll the cobbled lanes of Kitzbühel's late-medieval town, stopping to people-watch at one of the many pavement cafes.

Museum Kitzbühel   MUSEUM
(www.museum-kitzbuehel.at; Hinterstadt 32; adult/child €5.60/2.10; ⊙10am-5pm) This museum traces Kitzbühel's heritage from its humble Bronze Age beginnings to the present day. The big emphasis is on winter sports and the town's famous son, champion skier Toni Sailer.

Alpine Flower Garden   GARDEN
(cable car adult/child €16.70/9.20; ⊙8.30am-5pm May-Sep) Arnica, edelweiss, purple bellflowers and other fragile alpine blooms flourish at this quiet garden at the top of Kitzbüheler Horn. It's best reached by cable car. A road also twists up to the mountain (toll per car/motorcycle €6/3, plus €3 per person).

Pfarrkirche St Andreas   CHURCH
(Pfarrauweg) Slightly above the town is this Gothic-meets-baroque parish church, undergoing renovation at the time of writing.

Liebfrauenkirche   CHURCH
(Pfarrauweg; ⊙dawn-dusk) Next to Pfarrkirche St Andreas, this rococo church has a chunky 48m belfry and an elaborately frescoed interior.

Along with the activities listed below, Kitzbühel gets pulses racing with scenic flights, skydiving, ballooning, golf, water sports and even bungee jumping.

Kitzbüheler Horn   SKIING
The world-famous Hahnenkamm-Rennen ski race and its mind-bogglingly steep, breathtakingly fast Streif downhill course lure veteran skiers to Kitzbühel. Extending northeast, the Kitzbüheler Horn is much loved by freeriders for its boxes, rails and ramps, while beginners flock here for gentle cruising on sunny slopes.

Hahnenkamm   SKIING
Besides the downhill on the resort's 170km of well-groomed slopes, there's some first-rate cross-country trails and off-piste skiing. Spreading southwest, the Hahnenkamm (1712m) connects with some heart-stopping black runs in the **Pengelstein** (1938m) area.

Ski Safari   SKIING
Confident intermediates up for a challenge can tackle this incredibly scenic 35km route, linking the Hahnenkamm to Jochberg. The alpine tour is marked by elephant signs and is a good introduction to the entire ski area.

Kaiser Trail   WALKING
Kitzbühel makes a terrific base for walking in summer, with scores of well-marked trails, including the 15km Kaiser Trail with superlative views of the jagged Kaisergebirge massif. You can pick up a comprehensive *Wanderwegeplan* (hiking map) for €1 at the tourist office or visit www.kitzbuehel.com for themed walk suggestions. If you'd prefer some company, the tourist office organises **guided half-day hikes** with

---

TICKET TO GLIDE

One-/three-/six-day passes in the high winter season cost €41.50/112/196 and €36.50/97/170 at all other times. Passes cover lifts, cable cars and ski buses as far south as Thurn Pass. If you plan to cover a lot of terrain, the **Kitzbüheler Alpen AllStarCard** is your best bet; it spans the whole region, including Kitzbühel, Schneewinkel, Wilder Kaiser-Brixental and Zell am See-Kaprun (some 762km of runs) and costs €45/122/217 for one/three/six days.

TYROL KITZBÜHEL

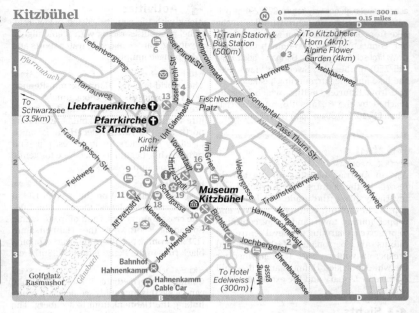

English-speaking Engelbert and Madeleine, daily at 8.45am (summer) or 9.45am (winter), which are free for *Gästekarte* holders.

The **Kitzbüheler Alpen Summer Card** (3-/7-day pass €36/50) covers 29 lifts and cable cars. Even better value if you hike only in the immediate Kitzbühel area is the **Flex-Ticket** (3 of 7 days without/with bus €34/43).

Bike Trail Tirol   CYCLING
(www.bike.tirol.at) As the trailhead for the epic 1000km, 32-stage Bike Trail Tirol, Kitzbühel is mountain-biking central. Whether you want to pedal gently through the valley or rattle downhill on the new **Gaisberg Trail**, the tourist office's *KitzAlpBike* cycling map (€3) is an excellent reference, showing all routes in the area. Bikes are transported for free on cable cars including Hahnenkammbahn, Kitzbüheler Hornbahn and Fleckalmbahn.

Mountain Edge   MOUNTAIN BIKING
(☑0650-720 3500; www.mountainedge.co.uk; Hotel Tyrol, Josef-Pirchl-Strasse 14; ☉9am-noon & 4-6pm May-Oct) Mountain-bike guru Rob Pearce arranges guided rides around Kitzbühel from €39 per day and rents top-quality bikes (€16 to €34 per day).

Intersport   BIKE RENTAL
(Jochbergerstrasse 7; www.kitzsport.at; ☉9am-12.30pm & 2-6.15pm Mon-Fri, 9am-1pm Sat)

Rents electro bikes (€20 per day) that take the uphill slog out of cycling.

Element 3   ADVENTURE SPORTS
(☑723 01; www.element3.at; Klostergasse 8; ☉10am-6pm) A ski school in winter, in summer this is a one-stop shop for adventure sports, including rafting, climbing, canyoning and paragliding.

Schwarzsee   LAKE
For a cool summer swim, venture 3km northwest of the centre to Kitzbühel's natural swimming hole, the tree-flanked Schwarzsee. There are two beach complexes, each costing about €3.50 per day.

✸ Festivals & Events

Hahnenkamm-Rennen   SKI RACE
(www.hahnenkamm.com) One of the highlights of the FIS Alpine World Cup, this is the mother of all downhill races, held on the third weekend in January.

Snow Arena Polo World Cup   SPORTS EVENT
(www.kitzbuehelpolo.com) International polo teams battle it out on ice at this glamorous event in mid-January.

Austrian Open   SPORTS EVENT
(www.austrianopentennis.com) In early August, tennis stars compete in the Austrian Open.

Kitzbühel

🛏 Sleeping

Budget digs are not Kitzbühel's forte, but the tourist office has a list of good-value private rooms and guesthouses. Rates leap up to 50% in the high winter season.

Villa Licht   HOTEL €€
(☎622 93; www.villa-licht.at; Franz-Reich-Strasse 8; s/d €85/150; P⏚⏛⏜⏝) Pretty gardens, warm-hued rooms with pine trappings, mountain views – this charming Tyrolean chalet has the lot. Kids love the tree house and outdoor pool.

Snowbunny's Hostel   HOSTEL €
(☎067-6794 0233; www.snowbunnys.co.uk; Bichlstrasse 30; dm/d €25/60; ⏛@⏝) This friendly, laid-back hostel is just a bunny hop from the ski lifts. Dorms are fine, if a tad dark, and breakfast is DIY-style in the kitchen. There's a TV lounge, ski storage room and a shop for backpacker staples (Vegemite, Jägermeister etc).

Pension Kometer   PENSION €€
(☎622 89; Gerbergasse 7; www.pension-kometer. com; s/d €57/94; P⏝) Make yourself at home in the bright, sparkling clean rooms at this family-run guesthouse. There's a relaxed lounge with games and DVDs. Breakfast is a treat with fresh breads, fruit and eggs.

Hotel Erika   HOTEL €€€
(☎648 85; www.erika-kitz.at; Josef-Pirchl-Strasse 21; d incl half board €194-238; P⏛⏝⏚⏜) This turreted art-nouveau villa has luxurious high-ceilinged rooms and polished service. The rose-strewn garden centres on a vine-clad pagoda and pond that are illuminated by night. Unwind with treatments from thalassotherapy to hay baths in the spa.

Hotel Edelweiss   HOTEL €€
(☎752 52; www.edelweiss-kitzbuehel.at; March-feldgasse 2; d incl half board €130; ⏝) Near the Hahnenkammbahn, Edelweiss oozes Tyrolean charm with its green surrounds, alpine views and cosy interiors. Food is fresh, and there's a relaxing garden and sauna.

🍴 Eating

For self-caterers there's a **Spar** (Bichlstrasse 22) supermarket.

Hosteria   ITALIAN €€
(☎753 02; Alf Petzoldweg 2; mains €8-16) Run like a well-oiled Vespa, this contemporary Italian is buzzy and stylish. Yet prices are modest for authentic antipasti and wood-fired pizzas, served with fine wines and genuine smiles.

Lois Stern   ASIAN €€
(☎748 82; www.loisstern.com, in German; Josef-Pirchl-Strasse 3; mains €17-25; ⏰Tue-Sat; ⏝) Lois works his wok in the show kitchen of this modern and intimate bistro. On the menu: Asian fusion cuisine from fiery tom-yam soup to stir-fried gambas. Reservations are recommended.

Metzgerei Huber   SNACK BAR €
(Bichlstrasse 14; snacks €3.50-7; ⏰8am-1pm & 3-6pm Mon-Fri, to 12.30pm Sat) Huber is a fantastic local butcher's for a meaty snack like *Schweinebauch* (belly of pork) and flavoursome sausages.

Chizzo   FUSION €€
(☎624 75; Josef-Herold-Strasse 2; mains €11-18; ⏝) A grandfather clock, white linen and fresh flowers create a refined ambience at Chizzo. The menu blends Austrian and world flavours, from well-spiced Thai red curry to homemade Tyrolean-style tagliatelle.

Huberbräu Stüberl AUSTRIAN €€
(☑656 77; Vorderstadt 18; mains €7-13) This vaulted tavern serves up large portions of Austrian classics, such as schnitzel and liver dumplings, cooked to perfection.

🍷 Drinking & Entertainment

Kitzbühel rocks with fun-seeking skiers during the winter season. If you can muster up the energy after a day on the slopes, check out the following places.

Stamperl BAR
(Jochbergerstrasse 62; ⊗3pm-2am) A funky little shack that's chilled in summer and a rollicking après-ski haunt in winter, with DJs, parties and champagne cocktails.

Londoner PUB
(Franz-Reisch-Strasse 4; ⊗6pm-late Wed-Sat) This raucous British den has great beer, crazy events and plenty of slapstick fun.

Bergsinn BAR
(Vorderstadt 21; ⊗9am-2am Mon-Sat, from 11am Sun; 🛜) Pop art glams up this slinky lounge with a cocktail happy hour (8pm to 9pm) and free wi-fi.

Club Take Five CLUB
(www.club-takefive.com; Hinterstadt 22; ⊗10pm-late) Chic and pricey club with a trio of bars, a VIP area and DJs spinning house, soul and funk.

ℹ️ Information

Surf online at **Kitz Video** (Schlossergasse 10; per hr €5; ⊗10am-9pm Mon-Sat, 2-8pm Sun). The **post office** (Josef-Pirchl-Strasse 11) is midway between the train station and tourist office.

The central **tourist office** (☑666 60; www.kitzbuehel.com; Hinterstadt 18; ⊗8.30am-6pm Mon-Wed, to 7.30pm Thu & Fri, 9am-6pm Sat, 10am-noon & 4-6pm Sun, closed Sun btwn seasons) has loads of info in English and a 24-hour accommodation board.

ℹ️ Getting There & Away

BUS It's far quicker and cheaper to reach Lienz by bus (€13.80, two hours, twice daily) than by train.

CAR & MOTORCYCLE Kitzbühel is on the B170, 30km east of Wörgl and the A12/E45 motorway.

TRAIN The main train station is 1km north of central Vorderstadt. Trains run frequently from Kitzbühel to Innsbruck (€17.60, 1½ hours) and Salzburg (€25.60, 2½ hours). For Kufstein (€9.20, one hour), change at Wörgl.

Kufstein

☑05372 / POP 17,150 / ELEV 499M

In the 1970s, Karl Ganzer sang the praises of Kufstein in his hit yodelling melody 'Perle Tirols' (The Pearl of Tyrol) and rightly so. Resting at the foot of the mighty limestone Kaisergebirge and crowned by a fortress, Kufstein's backdrop is picture-book stuff. Control of the town was hotly contested by Tyrol and Bavaria through the ages until it finally became Austrian property in 1814.

👁 Sights

TOP CHOICE **Festung Kufstein** FORTRESS
(Oberer Stadtplatz 6; adult/child €9.90/5.90; ⊗9am-5pm) For an insight into Kufstein's turbulent past, head up to cliff-top Festung Kufstein. The castle dates from 1205 (when Kufstein was part of Bavaria) and was a pivotal point of defence for both Bavaria and Tyrol during the struggles. The round **Kaiserturm** (Emperor's Tower) was added in 1522.

The lift to the top affords sweeping views over Kufstein and the surrounding peaks. Inside is the small but imaginatively presented **Heimatmuseum** (Heritage Museum), showcasing everything from Bronze Age urns to folk costumes and – drum roll please – Andreas Hofer's shoe. Below the Kaiserturm is the **Heldenorgel** (Heroes Organ) with 4307 pipes, 46 organ stops and a 100m gap between the keyboard and the tip of the pipes; the delay in the sounding of the notes making playing it a tricky business. Catch recitals at noon and, in July and August, 6pm.

When the fortress is closed in the evening you can walk up the path in under 15 minutes and roam the ramparts and grounds free of charge.

Römerhofgasse HISTORIC AREA
A classic saunter leads along gingerbready Römerhofgasse, a reconstructed medieval lane that looks fresh-minted for a Disney film set with its overhanging arches, lanterns and frescoed facades. Even the crowds and souvenir kitsch – marmot ointment, *Dirndls,* strapping *Lederhosen,* you name it – detract little from its appeal.

🏃 Activities

Kaisergebirge HIKING, SKIING
The Kaisergebirge range is a sheer wall of limestone to the east of Kufstein, rising to 2300m and stretching as far as St Johann in

RETRO RIDE

A real blast from the past, Kufstein's 1970s **chairlift** (one-way/return €8/11; ⊙9am-4.30pm May-Oct) to Wilder Kaiser has become a cult attraction. A sign says 'bouncing not permitted': not because of the speed (it's arthritically slow) but because only an itty-bitty bar prevents you from sudden death. Look out for wildlife as you glide above the treetops and bounce like a yo-yo above precipitous gorges. The magnificent limestone spires of the Kaisergebirge unfold at the top station, Brentenjoch; it's the trailhead for the **Kaisergebirge Circuit**, a scenic 18km hike back down to Kufstein via forest, alpine meadows and the dizzying Bettlersteig (Beggars' Climb).

Tirol. It attracts walkers, mountaineers and skiers alike. The Kaisergebirge is actually two ranges, split by the east–west Kaisertal valley. The northern range is the Zahmer Kaiser (Tame Emperor) and the southern is the Wilder Kaiser (Wild Emperor) – no medals for guessing which has the smoother slopes! Pick up a free *Wanderkarte* (walking map) from the tourist office.

Hechtsee & Stimmersee　　SWIMMING
(adult/child €3.70/1.50) The tree-fringed lakes around Kufstein are best explored on foot or by bike; the closest are in the wooded area west of the Inn River, where there's a network of walking trails. Hechtsee, 3km to the northwest, and Stimmersee, 2.5km to the southwest, both have swimming areas open from late May to September. A free city bus goes to Hechtsee in summer during fine weather (ask at the tourist office).

🛏 Sleeping & Eating

TOP CHOICE **Auracher Löchl**　　HISTORIC HOTEL €€
(☑621 38; www.auracher-loechl.at; Römerhofgasse 3-5; s/d €59/118; ⊜@🛜) Squeezed between Römerhofgasse and the Inn River, this hotel marries medieval charm with 21st-century comfort; river or fortress views cost a little extra. Cross the footbridge to the low-beamed restaurant (mains €9 to €18), one-time haunt of Andreas Hofer, where creaking floors and grinning badgers create a rustic feel. Austrian classics like *Schweinshaxe* (basically half a pig) are served in gut-busting portions.

Gasthof-Pension Felsenkeller
　　　　　　　　　　　GUESTHOUSE €€
(☑627 84; www.felsenkeller.at, in German; Kienbergstrasse 35; s/d/f €48/96/184; P) Snug against tree-clad cliffs, this quiet guesthouse has large country-style rooms with balconies. The cosy, wood-panelled restaurant serves freshly caught trout.

Camping Maier　　CAMPGROUND €
(☑583 52; www.camping-maier.com, in German; Egerbach 54, Schwoich; camp sites per adult/child/tent €4/2.70/6; 🛋) Bordering woodland, this friendly campground 5km south of Kufstein has tree-shaded pitches, plus a playground and an outdoor pool.

Batzenhäusl　　TYROLEAN €€
(☑624 33; Römerhofgasse 1; mains €9-14; ⊙Tue-Sat) Murals of merry wine-guzzlers welcome you to Tyrol's oldest wine tavern. Burrowing into cliffs below the fortress, this 530-year-old haunt is packed with curios like 16th-century cannon balls. The food is thoroughly Austrian: *Tafelspitz, Gröstl* and the fluffiest *Salzburger Nockerl* (Austrian soufflé) ever. Reserve ahead.

Villa Masianco　　FUSION €€
(☑636 33; Unterer Stadtplatz 18; mains €8-18) This is a perennially popular choice with a stylish vaulted interior and a big chestnut tree-shaded terrace. The globetrotting menu skips from Italian risotto to Thai curries.

Inn-Café Hell　　CAFE €
(Unterer Stadtplatz 3; snacks €3-7, lunch €8.50; ⊙8.30am-9pm) Sit on the riverside terrace for a good-value two-course lunch or a scrummy homemade strudel with ice cream.

ⓘ Information

At the **tourist office** (☑622 07; www.kufstein.com; Unterer Stadtplatz 8; ⊙8am-6pm Mon-Fri, 9am-1pm Sat), staff will hunt down accommodation without charging commission. If you stay overnight, ask for the *Gästekarte*, which has different benefits in summer and winter.

ⓘ Getting There & Away

The frequent train to Kitzbühel (€9.20, one hour) requires a change at Wörgl. The easiest road route is also via Wörgl.

Kufstein is on the main Innsbruck–Salzburg train route. Direct trains to Salzburg (€31.20, 1¼ hours) run at least every two hours; those to Innsbruck (€13.90, 50 minutes) are half-hourly. Buses leave from outside the train station.

Söll

📞 05333 / POP 3500 / ELEV 703M

Söll is a well-known ski resort 10km south of Kufstein. Once a favourite of boozy, boisterous visitors in the 1980s, the resort has successfully reinvented itself and is now a family-oriented place with myriad outdoor activities.

The **tourist office** (📞050 509-210; www.wilderkaiser.info; Dorf 84; ☺8am-noon & 1.30-6pm Mon-Fri, 3-6pm Sat, 9am-noon Sun), in the centre of the village, provides information on activities and will help you find accommodation.

The highest skiing area overlooking the resort is Hohe Salve at 1828m, though Söll has also combined with neighbouring resorts Itter, Brixen, Scheffau, Hopfgarten and Going to form the mammoth **Skiwelt** (www.skiwelt.at) area, comprising 279km of mostly red and blue pistes. Passes are €40 a day in the high season. Cross-country skiing is also popular, with trails running as far as St Johann in Tirol.

In summer, walkers are drawn to **Hohe Salve** (cable car one-way/return €10/12). At the first stop is **Hexenwasser**, a fun-loaded family walking trail with water obstacles, sundials, playgrounds, a working mill and bakery and an apiary. Throughout the summer you can see (and sample) bread, schnapps and cheese made the traditional way.

ℹ️ Getting There & Away

Söll is on the B178 between Wörgl and St Johann in Tirol. It's not on a train line, but there are plenty of buses from Kufstein (€3.90, 25 minutes).

WESTERN TYROL

Stams

📞 05263 / POP 1300 / ELEV 672M

One of Tyrol's true architectural highlights is the ochre-and-white **Zisterzienstift** (Cistercian abbey; Stiftshof 1; tours adult/child €4.70/2.50; ☺guided tours hourly 9-11am & 1-5pm) in Stams, founded in 1273 by Elizabeth of Bavaria,

the mother of Conradin, the last of the Hohenstaufens. Set in pristine grounds, the monumental facade is identified by its twin silver cupolas, which were added as a final flourish when the abbey was revamped in baroque style in the 17th century. The exuberant church interior is dominated by the high altar: the intertwining branches of this version of the 'tree of life' support 84 saintly figures surrounding an image of the Virgin. Near the entrance is the **Rose Grille**, an exquisite iron screen made in 1716. Crane your neck to admire the ceiling which swirls with rich stuccowork, gilding and elaborate frescoes by Georg Wolker.

Marmalade, juice and schnapps made on the premises can be bought from the **Kloster shop** (☺9am-noon & 1-5pm).

Stams is on the train route between Innsbruck and Landeck (both €7.20, 38 minutes). Both the A12 and B171 pass near the abbey.

The Ötztal

POP 12,000

Over millennia, the Ötztal (Ötz Valley) has been shaped into rugged splendour. No matter whether you've come to ski its snow-capped mountains, raft its white waters or hike to its summits, this valley is all about big wilderness. Guarding the Italian border and dominated by Tyrol's highest peak, Wildspitze (3774m), this is one of three river valleys running north from the Ötztaler Alpen to drain into the Inn River.

⊙ Sights & Activities

TOP CHOICE Aqua Dome   SPA

(📞05243-64 00; www.aqua-dome.at; Oberlängenfeld 140, Längenfeld; 3hr card adult/child Mon-Fri €16/8, Sat & Sun €19/10.50; ☺9am-11pm) Framed by the Ötztaler Alps, this crystalline spa looks otherworldly after dark when its trio of flying saucer–shaped pools are strikingly illuminated. And there's certainly something surreal about gazing up to the peaks and stars while floating in a brine bath, drifting around a lazy river or being pummelled by water jets.

The 'textile-free' **sauna world** (admission €10; ☺10am-11pm) is an adult-only wonderland, with a hay-barn sauna, steam dome and canyon sauna with the occasional thunderstorm. To cool off, there's an ice grotto and a rain temple where you can choose between mist, tropical rain and a raging waterfall – it's quite a Niagra, so stand back.

For full-on pampering, there are treatments from energising Ötztal stone massage to fango (volcanic mud) wraps.

Area 47
ADVENTURE PARK

(☑05266-876 76; www.area47.at; water park adult/child/family €18/10/39; ☺10am-7pm May–mid-Sep) Billing itself as the ultimate outdoor playground, this huge sports and adventure park is the Ötztal's new flagship attraction, dramatically set at the foot of the Alps and on the edge of a foaming river. The place heaves with families and flirty teenagers in summer.

Besides a water park with a natural lake and some pretty hairy diving boards and waterslides, there is a thrilling flying fox, climbing walls and an adventure centre offering canyoning and rafting. Events from party nights to concerts are held in summer and there's a tipi village for overnight stays (€22 per person). A free shuttle bus runs here from Ötztal Bahnhof.

Ötzi Dorf
OPEN-AIR MUSEUM

(www.oetzi-dorf.at; Umhausen; adult/child €6.30/3; ☺9.30am-5.30pm May-Oct; ⊞) This small open-air museum brings to life the Neolithic world of Ötzi the ice man. A visit takes in traditional thatched huts, herb gardens, craft displays and enclosures where wild boar and oxen roam. Multilingual audio guides are available.

Stuibenfall
SCENIC AREA

From Ötzi Dorf, it's a beautiful 20-minute forest walk to Tyrol's longest waterfall, the wispy Stuibenfall, cascading 159m over slate cliffs and moss-covered boulders. You can continue for another 40 minutes up to the top viewing platform and hanging bridge. A thrilling new 450m *Klettersteig* (via ferrata) takes you right over the waterfall; bring your own karabiner and helmet.

Sölden
SKI RESORT

(www.soelden.com; day ski pass €43.50) At 1377m, Sölden is a snow-sure ski resort with a high-speed lift network and fun-loving après-ski scene. The resort's 148km of slopes particularly appeal to confident intermediates and are complemented by glacier skiing at Rettenbach and Tiefenbach. For many, the highlight is the panoramic 50km **Big 3 Rally**, a four-hour downhill marathon which begins at Giggijoch gondola and takes in three 3000m peaks.

Obergurgl & Hochgurgl
SKI RESORTS

(day ski pass €42.50) Around 14km south of Sölden is family-friendly Obergurgl

You can save in summer by investing in the **Ötztal Card** (3/7/10 days €44/66/77), which is half-price for children. The pass covers public transport and cable cars in the valley, plus many activities from swimming pools to bike rental. The seven- and 10-day cards allow one free entry to Aqua Dome and Area 47.

(1930m), Austria's highest parish, with skiing largely aimed at beginners and intermediates. Obergurgl is actually at the head of the valley, but the road doubles back on itself and rises to Hochgurgl (2150m), where the pistes are steeper and the views equally impressive.

Sleeping & Eating

Nearly every village in the valley has a supermarket and camping ground. Room rates are 30% to 50% higher in winter. Many places close out of season (November and mid-April to mid-June).

Nature Resort Ötztal
HOTEL €€

(☑05252-603 50; www.nature-resort.at; Piburgerstrasse 6, Ötz; s/d/tr €78/130/169; P☺@🛜⊞) This riverside retreat has eco-chic chalet rooms, warmly decorated in sustainable pine. It's a solid family choice, with free activities like guided mountain hikes and bike tours, plus deals on rafting and canyoning. That's if you can tear yourself away from the saunas and open fire in the spa.

Hotel Garni Granat
GUESTHOUSE €€

(☑05254-20 62; www.hotel-granat.at; Gemeindestrasse 2, Sölden; s/d/tr €64/128/174; P☺@🛜⊞) This friendly pension in Sölden is near the ski lifts in winter and runs free guided hikes in summer. Many of the bright, traditional rooms have whirlpool bath-tubs. A playground and sandpit occupy kids, and guests have free use of the pool, sauna and tennis court at the nearby leisure centre.

Aqua Dome Hotel
HOTEL €€€

(☑05243-64 00; www.aqua-dome.at; Oberlängenfeld 140, Längenfeld; P☺@🛜♨⊞) There's direct access to the Aqua Dome spa at this sleek hotel, done out in wood, stone and earthy hues. Feng-shui principles rule in the contemporary rooms, most with balconies overlooking the mountains. There's a great on-site restaurant and wine bar.

TYROL THE ÖTZTAL

ICE MAN

In 1991 German hiker Helmut Simon came across the body of a man preserved within the Similaun Glacier in the Ötztaler Alpen, some 90m within Italy. Police and forensic scientists were summoned to the scene. Carbon dating revealed that the ice man, nicknamed 'Ötzi', was nearly 5400 years old, placing him in the late Stone Age and making him the oldest and best-preserved mummy in the world.

Ötzi became big news, more so because his state of preservation was remarkable; even the pores of his skin were visible. In addition, Ötzi had been found with 70 artefacts, including a copper axe, bow and arrows, charcoal and clothing. Physiologically he was found to be no different from modern humans. X-rays showed he had suffered from arthritis, frostbite and broken ribs.

Not everybody was worried about these finer points, however. Several Austrian and Italian women contacted Innsbruck University shortly after the discovery and asked to be impregnated with Ötzi's frozen sperm, but the all-important part of his body was missing.

Ötzi was relinquished to the Italians to become the centrepiece of a museum in Bolzano in 1998. In September 2010 the family of the late Helmut Simon were rewarded €175,000 for his groundbreaking discovery.

TYROL WESTERN TYROL

ℹ Information

The valley's main **tourist office** (☑057-200; www.oetztal.com; Gemeindestrasse 4, Sölden; ⊘8am-6pm Mon-Fri, to 4pm Sat, 9am-noon & 3-6pm Sun) is in Sölden, though there are others in villages like Ötz and Längenfeld. All can arrange accommodation and have brochures on activities in the area.

ℹ Getting There & Away

BUS From Ötztal Bahnhof, buses head south roughly hourly to destinations including Ötz (€2.30, 13 minutes), Umhausen (€3.90, 30 minutes) and Sölden (€8.50, 1¼ hours).

CAR & MOTORCYCLE With your own wheels you should be able to get at least as far as Hochgurgl all year, but the road beyond into Italy via the high-alpine 2509m **Timmelsjoch Pass** (car/motorbike €14/12; ⊘7am-8pm) is often blocked by snow in winter.

TRAIN Trains arrive at Ötztal Bahnhof at the head of the valley and run frequently to Innsbruck (€9.20, 30 minutes), Imst (€2, 10 minutes) and Landeck (€5.40, 25 minutes).

Imst

☑05412 / POP 9200

Beautifully situated in the wide Gurgltal (Gurgl Valley) and spreading towards a range of thickly wooded mountains, Imst is famous for its many springs. While the town itself won't keep you long, its surrounding meadows, rugged peaks and gorges might. Imst makes a fine base for hiking and skiing in the nearby Ötztal.

◉ Sights & Activities

The tourist office sells the good-value **Gletscherpark Card** (3/7 days €36/51), which covers all public transport and attractions in the region.

Fasnachthaus   MUSEUM
(Streleweg 6; adult/child €4/1; ⊘4-6pm Fri) Every four years, Imst plays host to a Shrovetide festival, the Unesco-listed **Schemenlaufen** (ghost dance); the next takes place on 12 February 2012. The highlight is the vibrant parade of characters, from hunchback *Hexen* (witches) to *Spritzer* that squirt water at spectators. This museum homes in on this centuries-old tradition and exhibits many of the hand-carved ghost masks.

Starkenberger Biermythos   BREWERY
(☑662 01; www.biermythos.at, in German; Griesegg 1; adult/child €7/6; ⊘10am-5pm May-Oct) Housed in a medieval castle, this 200-year-old brewery sits 3km north of Imst in Tarrenz. A visit dashes through the brewing process and includes a beer tasting. If you can't get enough of the stuff, you can even bathe in it by calling ahead – it does wonders for the complexion, apparently.

🛏 Sleeping & Eating

Hotel Hirschen   HOTEL €€
(☑69 01; www.hirschen-imst.com, in German; Thomas-Walch-Strasse 3; s/d €56/96; 🅿@🛜🏊) This central guesthouse has comfy rooms, an indoor pool and modern spa area. A plate of venison ragout is never far away in the

wood-panelled restaurant (mains €10 to €18), where stag heads stud the walls.

Camping Imst-West
CAMPGROUND €

(📞662 93; Langgasse 62; camp sites per adult/child/site €5.30/3.70/8.40) Perched above Imst, this quiet campground is flanked by cow-nibbled pastures – dairy goodness that goes into the *Milch Automat* (milk machine) at the neighbouring farm; bring your own bottle. There's also a snack bar and playground.

ℹ️ Information

The **tourist office** (📞69 10-0; www.imst.at; Johannesplatz 4; ⊘9am-6pm Mon-Fri, 10am-noon Sat) is highly informed on accommodation and activities in Imst and its surrounds; there's also a free internet terminal.

ℹ️ Getting There & Around

The town is slightly to the north of the main east–west roads (the A12 and B171), and is served by frequent buses and trains (from Innsbruck €11, 50 minutes).

Grown men may feel slightly silly boarding the Imster Bummelbär (€1.50, three daily) tourist train, but it's handy for reaching nearby sights like Starkenberger Biermythos.

The tourist office has a list of outfits with bike and electro-bike rental.

Ehrwald

📞05673 / POP 2660

Ehrwald's crowning glory is the glaciated 2962m **Zugspitze** (cable car one-way/return €23.50/34.50), Germany's highest peak, straddling the Austro-German border. From the crest there's a magnificent panorama of the main Tyrolean mountain ranges, as well as the Bavarian Alps and Mt Säntis in Switzerland. North of Zugspitze is Garmisch-Partenkirchen, Germany's most popular ski resort.

Ehrwald is linked with other resorts in Austria (including Seefeld) and Germany (including Garmisch-Partenkirchen) under the **Happy Ski Card** (2-day pass adult/child €69/41.50). For information on accommodation and activities, contact the **tourist office** (📞05673-2000 0208; www.ehrwald.com; Kirchplatz 1; ⊘8.30am-6pm Mon-Fri, from 9am Sat) in the heart of the town. Staff will help find rooms free of charge.

Trains from Seefeld (€9.80, 1¼ hours) and Innsbruck (€12.20, two hours) to Ehrwald pass through Germany; you must change at Garmisch-Partenkirchen. Austrian train tickets are valid for the whole trip.

Landeck

📞05442 / POP 7700

Landeck is an ordinary town with an extraordinary backdrop: framed by an amphitheatre of forested peaks, presided over by a medieval castle and bordered by the fast-flowing Inn and Sanna Rivers. The town makes a good-value base for outdoor activities and exploring the nearby Inntal and Patznauntal valleys.

⊙ Sights & Activities

Landeck attracts the odd skier to its 22km of mostly intermediate slopes (a day ski pass costs €30), but is better known for its hiking trails. The magnificent **Adlerweg** (Eagle Trail) stops off in Landeck on its 280km journey through Tyrol. Many footpaths can be accessed by taking the **Venet cable car** (adult/child one-way €10.50/6, return €12.50/7) up to Krahberg (2208m).

DON'T MISS

ROSENGARTENSCHLUCHT CIRCUIT

An easygoing family hike is the 5km (approximately three-hour) loop through the dramatic 200m-high Rosengartenschlucht (Rose Garden Ravine), where boarded walkways make for a gentle ascent and afford sterling views of a waterfall. At the top, the walk continues through forest and along a trail overlooking the Lechtaler Alps. Look out for the Blaue Grotte, a cave pool that is a startling shade of blue. In Hoch-Imst, you can board the exhilarating **Alpine Coaster** (adult/child €6.10/4.10; ⊘10am-5pm daily May-Sep, Thu-Sun Oct), touted as the world's longest alpine roller coaster, before a gradual descent back to Imst.

The trail starts and ends at the Johanneskirche (St John's Church) opposite the tourist office, which stocks maps of the walk.

ROCK STARS

Fans of geological wonders should make their way to the **Erdpyramiden** (earth columns) in the tiny village of Roppen, 7km northwest of Ötz. An hour's trudge along a narrow trail brings to you to this cluster of hoodoos – tall, thin rock spires that protrude from the forest floor. Since the last ice age, these monoliths have been gradually eroded into weird and wonderful shapes; and yes, observed from certain angles some of them most definitely look phallic.

The tourist office arranges guided walks (free with the **TirolWestCard**) and can advise on activities from llama trekking to via ferrate.

Schloss Landeck   CASTLE
(Schlossberg; adult/child €6.50/4; ☺10am-5pm Tue-Sun) Standing sentinel above Landeck, this 13th-century hilltop castle is visible from afar. The 1st-floor museum showcases everything from Celtic figurines to hand-carved *Krampus* masks, as well as a wonderful mechanised nativity scene during advent. Climb the dizzying staircase to the tower for sweeping views over Landeck and the Lechtaler Alps.

Zammer Lochputz   SCENIC AREA
(www.zammer-lochputz.at; Zams; adult/child €3.50/2.50; ☺9.30am-5.30pm May-Sep, 10am-5pm Oct) A rollercoaster of water thrashes the limestone cliffs at Zammer Lochputz gorge just outside of Landeck. Leading up through pine forest, a trail passes viewpoints and some interesting rock formations – look out for the head of a bull and a nymph.

Sport Camp Tirol   ADVENTURE SPORTS
(☎626 11; www.sportcamptirol.at; Mühlkanal 1) This is a one-stop action shop for activities like paragliding, canyoning, white-water rafting and hydrospeeding. You can also rent mountain bikes here (half-/full day €18/22) to head off on one of the tourist office's free GPS tours or tackle the downhill Inn Trail.

🛏 Sleeping & Eating

If you're staying overnight in summer, pick up the TirolWestCard for free access to the major sights, outdoor pools and the bus network.

Tramserhof   HOTEL €€
(☎622 46; www.tramserhof.at; Tramserweg 51; s/d/tr/q incl half board €58/116/174/232; P🅿☺🅰) Nestled among trees, this is a calm retreat 20 minutes' walk from the centre. The

rooms are country-style with loads of natural light and warm pine. The spa shelters a whirlpool and sauna. Tuck into organic produce at breakfast.

Hotel Mozart   HOTEL €€
(☎642 22; www.mozarthotels.at, Adamhofgasse 7; s/d €57/96; P🅿☺) It's amazing how far Amadeus travels in Austria. This particular Mozart pleases with big sunny rooms opening onto balconies. The flowery gardens and indoor pool with a little spa area invite relaxation.

Gasthof Greif   GUESTHOUSE €
(☎622 68; www.gasthof-greif.at, in German; Marktplatz 6; s/d €35/63; P🅿) Greif sits on a quiet square above the main street just down from the castle. Its 1970s-style rooms are large and tidy, and its restaurant (mains €8 to €16) serves solid Tyrolean cuisine.

Cafe Haag   CAFE €
(Maisengasse 19; snacks €3-6; ☺7.30am-7pm Mon-Fri, 8am-1pm Sat, 1-6pm Sun) Locally picked plums are the key ingredient in this cafe's divine chocolates, and the cakes are just the sugar kick needed for the uphill trudge to the castle.

Hotel Schrofenstein   AUSTRIAN €€
(☎623 95; Malserstrasse 31; mains €12-18; ☺9am-11pm; 🅰) Schrofenstein's restaurant dishes up Austrian classics from veal goulash to spinach *Spätzle* (egg noodles) in wood-panelled surrounds and on the chestnut tree–shaded terrace.

ℹ Information

The friendly staff at the **tourist office** (☎656 00; www.tirolwest.at; Malserstrasse; ☺8.30am-noon & 2-6pm Mon-Fri, 8.30am-noon Sat) can help book accommodation and have a list of local pensions.

The train station is 1.5km to the east; to get into town walk left on leaving the station and stay on the same side of the river.

Getting There & Away

Trains run roughly hourly to Innsbruck (€13.90, 50 minutes) and every two hours to Bregenz (€22, 1¾ hours). Buses head in all directions, departing from outside the train station and/or from the bus station in the centre.

The A12 into Vorarlberg passes by Landeck, burrowing into a tunnel as it approaches the town. The B171 passes through the centre of town.

The Inntal

POP 11,250

Shadowing the turquoise Inn River, the Inntal (Inn Valley) has few major sights but the scenery is beautiful, particularly around **Pfunds** with its jagged peaks and thickly forested slopes. Many homes here are similar in design to those found in the Engadine in Graubünden, Switzerland, further up the Inn Valley.

South of Pfunds, you have the choice of routes. If you continue along the Inn you'll end up in Switzerland (infrequent buses). Alternatively, if you bear south to Nauders you'll soon reach South Tyrol (Italy) by way of the Reschen Pass (open year-round). Eleven buses daily run from Landeck to Nauders (€8, one hour), where it's possible to head on with public transport to Merano in Italy, but at least three changes are required.

The Paznauntal

POP 5950

Grazing the Swiss border and running west of the Inntal, the Paznauntal (Paznaun Valley) is a dramatic landscape overshadowed by the pearly white peaks of the Silvretta range. The villages are sleepy in summer, a lull that is broken in winter when skiers descend on party-hearty resorts like Ischgl.

The valley is undoubtedly one of Austria's best ski areas, despite (or because of) its relative isolation. The **Silvretta Ski Pass** (2-day pass adult/child €87.50/49.50) covers Ischgl, Galtür, Kappl and Samnaun, a duty-free area

in Switzerland. Its summer equivalent is the **Silvretta Card** (3-day pass adult/child €36/21) comprising cable cars, lifts, public transport over the Bielerhöhe Pass into Vorarlberg, and numerous swimming pools in Ischgl and Galtür.

Around 10km from Ischgl is the uncrowded resort of **Galtür**. This unspoilt village suffered in February 1999 when an avalanche all but swept it away. A museum documenting the event has been built on the spot, the **Alpinarium Galtür** (www.alpinarium.at; adult/child €8/4; ☺10am-6pm Tue-Sun). Inside you'll find many poignant reminders of the devastation in the shape of photos, newspaper reports and some incredible video footage.

Getting There & Away

Only a secondary road (B188) runs along the valley, crossing into Vorarlberg at the Bielerhöhe Pass (toll cars/motorcycles €11.50/10.50), where the views are sensational. This pass, closed in winter, rejoins the main highway near Bludenz. Regular buses travel as far as Galtür (€7.20, 1¼ hours) from Landeck.

ISCHGL

📞 05444 / POP 1500 / ELEV 1377M

Ischgl becomes a quintessential powdersville in winter, with snow-sure slopes and a boisterous après-ski scene. The resort is a bizarre combination of rural meets raunchy; a place where lap-dancing bars, folk music and techno happily coexist. That said, summer here can be *tote Hose* (totally dead) and you may prefer to base yourself in one of the more authentic neighbouring villages.

🏃 Activities

WINTER ACTIVITIES

Silvretta Arena   SKIING

(www.silvretta.at) Ischgl is the centrepiece of the vast Silvretta Arena, offering fabulous skiing on 238km of groomed slopes, ultramodern lifts (heated seats and all) and few queues. Suited to all except absolute beginners, the resort has great intermediate runs around Idalp, tough black descents at Greitspitz and Paznauer Taya, and plenty of

WORTH A TRIP

PASS THE SCHNAPPS

If all that fresh air and activity have worked up a thirst, pop over to **Stanz** (www.brennerei dorf.at), 4km away. Set on a sunny plateau dotted with apple and plum orchards, the village has 150 houses and a mind-boggling 54 schnapps distilleries. There are a number of rustic huts where you can kick back and taste the local firewater before rolling back down to the valley.

off-piste powder to challenge experts. Skiing to Samnaun in Switzerland for lunch adds the novelty factor. Boarders can play on the half-pipe, jumps and boarder-cross at **Rennstrecke** snowpark.

Toboggan Track
TOBOGGANING

(adult/child €11.50/5) The 7km toboggan track offers a bumpy downhill dash through the snow from Idalp to Ischgl, which is particularly scenic when floodlit on Monday and Thursday nights.

SUMMER ACTIVITIES

Silvretta Mountain Bike Arena
MOUNTAIN BIKING

Few Austrian resorts can match Ischgl for mountain biking. The mammoth Silvretta Mountain Bike Arena features 1000km of bikeable territory, ranging from downhill tracks to circular trails and a technique park. Pick up a free map of the area at the tourist office.

For bike rental, try **Ischgl Bike** (www. ischgl-bike.at, in German; Ischgl 22; per day from €33) or **Silvretta Bike Academy** (www. silvretta-bikeacademy.at; Ischgl 116), which arranges freeride and day tours costing €25.

Klettersteige
WALKING

Walking is the other big draw in summer, ranging from gentle lakeside rambles to ambitious scrambling on the *Klettersteige* (fixed-rope routes) at 2872m Greitspitz and 2929m Flimspitze.

Festivals & Events

Top of the Mountain
CONCERT

This winter-season opening and closing concert has welcomed a host of stars, including pop divas Kylie Minogue and Alicia Keys in recent years.

Ironbike
SPORTS EVENT

Super-fit mountain bikers compete in this 79km obstacle course of a race in August, involving steep climbs and exhilarating descents.

Sleeping & Eating

Rates double those quoted below in the high winter season and nearly everywhere closes between seasons. Cafes, pizzerias and snack bars cluster on Dorfstrasse.

AlpVita Piz Tasna
HOTEL €€

(☑52 77; www.piztasna.at; Stöckwaldweg 5; s €53, d €94-114, half board €15; P🐕@≋) Picturesquely set on a slope, Piz Tasna gets rave reviews for its heartfelt welcome, big and comfy rooms and superb food (half board is worth the

extra). The spa has an indoor pool, saunas, herbal steam rooms and a relaxation zone with hay and water beds.

Hotel Alpenstern
HOTEL €

(☑512 01; www.alpenstern.at; Versahlweg 5; s/d €36/54; P@≋) Nice surprise: one of Ischgl's sweetest hotels is also among its cheapest. The friendly Walser family keep the modern alpine-style rooms spotless and serve generous breakfasts. In winter, the spa is great for post-ski downtime.

Paznaunerstube
GOURMET €€€

(☑600; www.trofana-royal.at; Hotel Troyana Royal, Dorfstrasse 95; menus €55-110) Celebrity chef Martin Sieberer turns every meal into a gastronomic event at this Michelin-starred hotel restaurant. In a refined wood-panelled parlour, regional specialities like milk-fed Galtür lamb are given a creative twist and paired with top wines.

Toscana
ITALIAN €€

(☑200 07; www.ristorante-toscana.at; Ischgl 9; mains €15-25; ⊙10am-2am) This sleek Italian bistro is a welcome break from fondue. Pasta, fish and meat dishes are big on herbs and flavour, and artistically presented. Check out the fine selection of Tuscan wines.

Drinking

The snow doesn't get hotter than in Ischgl, famous Europe-wide for its pumping après-ski scene. Oompah-playing barns, raunchy go-go bars and chichi clubs shake the resort. The following places, except for the Golden Eagle, close in summer.

Schatzi Bar
BAR

(Hotel Elizabeth, Fimbabahnweg 4; ⊙4-8pm) This rollicking après-ski bar is full of *Schatzis* (little treasures) in the form of go-go dancing girls in skimpy *Dirndls* that look like they've shrunk in the wash. Madness.

Niki's Stadl
BAR

(www.nikis-stadl.com, in German; Pizbuin Hotel; ⊙1pm-3am) German sing-alongs and swinging steins – it's Oktoberfest every day in this rustic barn.

Golden Eagle
PUB

(www.golden-eagle.at; Ischgl 6; ⊙8pm-2am) Great for a pint of Kilkenny or a wee dram of whisky, with a laid-back vibe and ZZ Top at full blast. Rock 'n' roll through and through.

Kuhstall
BAR

(Ischgl 80; ⊙3pm-midnight) *The* place for slope-side socialising to gear up for a big night out in Ischgl.

Trofana Alm
CLUB

(Dorfstrasse 91; ⊙3-8pm) A huge wooden barn with live Austrian bands and potent apple schnapps working the crowd into a singing, dancing, drunken frenzy.

Pacha
CLUB

(www.pacha.at; Hotel Madlein; ⊙10pm-5am) Victoria Beckham (performing), Paris Hilton (posing)...they've all been spotted at this glamorous club brimming with beautiful people.

ⓘ Information

The **tourist office** (☑050-990 100; www.ischgl. com; ⊙8am-6.30pm) stocks heaps of literature on hiking, biking and skiing in the area, plus accommodation brochures.

ⓘ Getting There & Away

Bus 4240 operates hourly between Ischgl and Landeck (€6.30, 55 minutes).

ARLBERG REGION

The wild and austerely beautiful Arlberg region, shared by Vorarlberg and Tyrol, comprises several linked resorts and offers some of Austria's finest skiing. Heralded as the cradle of alpine skiing, St Anton am Arlberg is undoubtedly the best known and most popular resort.

St Anton am Arlberg

☑05446 / POP 2270 / ELEV 1304M

Once upon a time St Anton was but a sleepy village, defined by the falling and melting of snow and the coming and going of cattle, until one day the locals beheld the virgin powder on their doorstep and discovered their happy-ever-after...In 1901 the resort founded the first ski club in the Alps and downhill skiing was born, so if ever the ski bug is going to bite you it will surely be here. Nestled at the foot of 2811m-high Valluga and strung out along the northern bank of the Rosanna River, St Anton am Arlberg is a cross between a ski bum's Shangri-La and Ibiza in fast-forward mode – the terrain fierce, the nightlife hedonistic.

◎ Sights & Activities

St Anton Museum
MUSEUM

(Rudi-Matt-Weg 10; adult/child €4/3; ⊙noon-6pm Tue-Sun) Set in attractive gardens with a trout lake, playground and minigolf course, this nostalgic museum traces St Anton's tracks back to the good old days when skis were little more than improvised wooden planks.

Arlberg Well.com
LEISURE CENTRE

(www.arlberg-well.com; adult/child €6/3, incl sauna €10; ⊙9am-9pm) You can gaze up to the Alps from the indoor and outdoor pools or warm up in the sauna complex at this striking glass-and-wood leisure centre. There's also curling (summer) and ice skating (winter), plus a tennis court and fitness centre.

Arlrock
LEISURE CENTRE

(www.arlrock.at; Bahnhofstrasse 1; ⊙11am-midnight) This all-new leisure centre by the train station has climbing and boulder walls, kids' play areas, a bowling alley and tennis courts. It's also the home base of **H2O-Adventures** (☑05446-39 37; ⊙May–mid-Oct), offering adrenalin-based activities from rafting on the Sanna River to canyoning, zip-lining and downhill mountain biking.

Winter Activities

Alpine Skiing
SKIING

St Anton is the zenith of Austria's alpine skiing, and the spacey Galzigbahn gondola, launched in 2007, has further improved conditions. The terrain is vast, covering 280km of slopes, and the skiing challenging, with fantastic backcountry opportunities and exhilarating descents including the **Kandahar** run on Galzig.

Cable cars ascend to **Valluga** (2811m), from where experts can go off-piste all the way to Lech (with a ski guide only). For fledglings, there are nursery slopes on Gampen (1850m) and Kapall (2330m). Rendl is snowboarding territory with jumps, rails and a half-pipe. A 10-minute stroll east of St Anton is **Nasserein**, where novices can test out the nursery slopes. Further east still are the quieter slopes of St Jakob, easily accessed by the Nasserein gondola.

A single **ski pass** (1-/3-/7-day pass €44.50/122/239) covers the whole Arlberg region and is valid for all 84 ski lifts.

Summer Activities

Alpine Walks
WALKING

Walking in the mountains is the most popular summertime activity, and the meadows full of wildflowers and grazing cattle are pure Heidi. A handful of cable cars and lifts (€5 to €20 one-way, €6 to €22 return) rise to the major peaks. If you're planning on going hiking, pick up a detailed booklet and map from the tourist office. Also consider purchasing a **Wanderpass** (3-/7-day pass €28/33),

St Anton am Arlberg

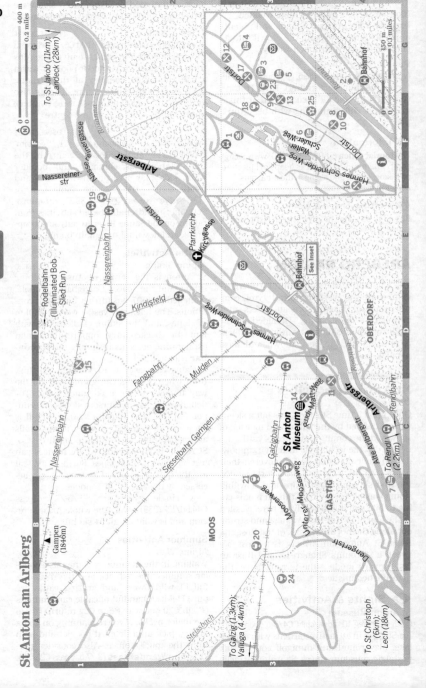

St Anton am Arlberg

providing unlimited access to all lifts, or a **St Anton Card** (3-/7-day pass €42/49), which offers the same benefits plus entrance to the town's indoor and outdoor swimming pools.

The tourist office also produces a small booklet (in German only) with a number of suggested **cycling** trails in the area.

🎉 Festivals & Events

The cows come home in their floral finery at September's **Almabtrieb**, a village-wide excuse for a party. The **Arlberg Adler** (www.arlbergadler.eu) triathlon kicks off with *der weisse Rausch* (the white thrill) ski race in April; then the Jakobilauf half-marathon in July, and the Bike Marathon in August.

🛏 Sleeping

The best places fill up in a flash in winter, so book well ahead. For cheaper pensions, try nearby Nasserein and St Jakob. Some of the smaller places only open in winter, when rates can be as much as double those quoted below.

TOP CHOICE **Altes Thönihaus** HISTORIC GUESTHOUSE €
(✆28 10; www.altes-thoenihaus.at; Im Gries 1; s/d/q €28/52/80; ☺🛜📶) Run by the affable Matt family, this listed wooden chalet dating to 1465 radiates alpine charm from every last beam and flowerbox. Fleecy rugs and pine keep the mood cosy in rooms with gleaming bathrooms and mountain-facing balconies. Downstairs there's a superb little spa and a lovingly restored *Stube*.

Himmlhof GUESTHOUSE €€
(✆232 20; www.himmlhof.com; Im Gries 9; d €94-126, tr/q €156/172; 🅿☺📶) This *himmlisch* (heavenly) chalet is oh so Tyrolean. The wood-clad rooms brim with original features (tiled ovens, four-poster beds and the like). An open fire for afternoon tea with homemade cakes and a cosy spa with a grotto-like plunge pool beckon after a day's skiing.

Lux Alpinae HOTEL €€
(✆301 08; www.luxalpinae.at; Arlbergstrasse 41; s/d €69/125; 🅿☺📶) This design hotel wings you into the 21st century with glass-walled rooms that bring the mountains indoors and industrial-chic interiors blending concrete, wood and steel. Personalised service (including a driver to take you to the slopes), a first-rate restaurant and a spa add to its appeal.

Rundeck HOTEL €€
(✆31 33; www.hotelrundeck.at; Arlbergstrasse 59; s/d €67/84; ☺@🛜📶) Clean lines, earthy tones and nutwood panelling define the streamlined rooms at design-focused Rundeck. There's a sleek spa and a backlit bar with an open fire for relaxing moments, plus a playroom for the kids.

Hotel Post HOTEL €€
(✆221 30; www.hotel-post.co.at; Walter-Schuler-Weg 2; s/d €62/114; 🅿☺@🛜📶) Right in the heart of the village, this chalet-style hotel has large, modern rooms. The meditation room, saunas and whirlpool are ideal for post-skiing, and the restaurant (mains €10 to €21) dishes up substantial Austrian fare.

Haus Moostal GUESTHOUSE €
(✆28 31; www.hausmoostal.at; Marktstrasse 14; s/d €32/60; 🅿🛜) You'll receive a warm welcome at this little guesthouse. Dressed in blond

A DASH TO DINNER

Fancy a twilight dash through the snow? Every Tuesday and Thursday evening in winter, the 4km-long **Rodelbahn** (adult/child €10/5, sled rental €8) toboggan run from Gampen to Nasserein is floodlit. Simply grab your sled and away you go! Most ruddy-faced sledders stop to defrost over schnapps and enormous portions of *Schweinshaxe* (pork knuckles) by an open fire at the halfway hut, **Rodelalm** (☎0699-1085 8855; Nassereinerstrasse 106; mains €10-16). Reservations are highly advisable.

wood furnishings, the bright rooms have squishy beds and wi-fi. There's a tiny sauna (winter only) on-site.

✖ Eating

Because of the lopsidedness of St Anton's seasons, many restaurants only open in winter, when reservations are recommended. Most places double as vibrant bars after dinner, especially along the pedestrian-only Dorfstrasse. Self-caterers have a choice of supermarkets, including the centrally located **Spar** (Dorfstrasse 66).

TOP CHOICE **Museum Restaurant** AUSTRIAN €€
(☎24 75; Rudi-Matt-Weg 10; mains €10-16; ⊘dinner; ♠) Arlberger hay soup with wildboar ham, the most succulent Tyrolean beef and trout fished fresh from the pond land on your plate at this inviting wood-panelled restaurant, housed in the picture-perfect chalet of the St Anton Museum.

Hazienda FUSION €€€
(☎29 68; www.hazienda.at; Dorfstrasse 56; mains €16-33; ⊘cafe 9am-10pm year-round, restaurant 6pm-1am winter only) A prime people-watching terrace fronts this smart restaurant-cafe hybrid. Thai-style Argentine beef filet, herby homemade pasta with sheep's cheese, proper Italian espresso – everything here strikes a perfect balance.

seitenBlick INTERNATIONAL €
(☎425 51; Kandaharweg 2; mains €8-15; ⊘10am-midnight; ♠♠♠) Warm and inviting seiten-Blick opposite the Galzigbahn is great for afternoon coffee and strudel. Or come for dinner: the creamy vanilla-garlic soup and hamburgers homemade with beef from the local butcher come recommended.

Fuhrmann Stube AUSTRIAN €€
(☎29 21; Dorfstrasse 74; mains €10-16; ⊘10am-10pm) When snow blankets the rooftops, this is a cosy hideaway for tucking into *Knödel* (dumplings) or a carnivorous *Tiroler Bauernplatte* ('Tyrolean farmers' platter').

Bobo's TEX-MEX €€
(☎27 14; www.bobos.at, in German; Dorfstrasse 60; mains €11-16; ⊘5pm-2am; ♠) Tex-Mex food and potent cocktails make Bobo's a perennial favourite. The party cranks up after fajitas and a fistful of nachos, with everything from karaoke to live bands and DJs.

Bodega TAPAS €€
(☎427 88; Dorfstrasse 40; tapas €2.50-10; ⊘3pm-1am) Tapas, vino and live music reel in the crowds to this buzzy Spanish haunt.

Floriani PIZZA €€
(☎23 30; Alte Arlbergstrasse 13; mains €7-10; ⊘dinner Tue-Sun) The pizzas – thin, crisp and filling – are the stars of the menu at this sweet and simple place.

❍ Drinking & Entertainment

St Anton is Austria's unrivalled après-ski king. Dancing on tables, *Schlager* sing-alongs, Jägermeister after Jägermeister – it's just an average night out in St Anton, where people party as hard as they ski. Pace yourself.

Mooserwirt BAR
(www.mooserwirt.at; Unterer Mooserweg 2; ⊘3.30-8pm) One word: *craaaazy*. Come teatime Mooserwirt heaves with skiers guzzling beer (the place sells around 5000L a day), dancing to DJ Gerhard's Eurotrash mix and sweating in their salopettes. The first challenge is to locate your skis, the second to use them to get back to St Anton in one piece.

Krazy Kanguruh BAR
(www.krazykanguruh.com; Mooserweg 19; ⊘10am-8pm) Owned by St Anton ski champ Mario Matt, this slopeside hot spot is loud, fun and jam-packed after 5pm. One too many tequilas will indeed send you bouncing (on skis) back to the valley.

Heustadl BAR
(www.heustadl.com; Dengerstrasse 625; ⊘9.30am-7am) Just north of Sennhütte, this shack is always fit to bursting with beery throngs. There's live music from 3pm to 6pm most

days. Yes, the bar stools have legs; yes, you are still sane if not sober.

Taps
BAR

(Mooserweg 15; ⊙10am-8pm) Taps is a pumping après-ski place with the cheapest beer on the mountain. There's a huge sun terrace for chilling and if you're lucky you will even get a free tipple of Egon's homemade schnapps (mind-blowing stuff).

Sennhütte
BAR

(www.sennhuette.at, in German; ⊙3-6pm) A sunny terrace, feisty schnapps, locals jiggling on the tables – what more après-ski could one ask for? Perhaps one-man-show Didi Diesel, who sends crowds into fits of laughter with his music, jokes and tricks.

Pub 37
PUB

(Im Gries 4; ⊙4pm-1am) The name is spot on: around 37 people can cram into St Anton's smallest and oldest pub, where Sammy keeps the drinks and smiles coming.

Piccadilly
BAR

(www.piccadilly-bar.com; Dorfstrasse 2; ⊙4pm-2am) This loud, crowded British pub with daily live music is known as Pickawilly (the mind boggles) to locals.

Fanghouse
BAR

(www.fanghouse.com; Nassereinerstrasse 6; ⊙10am-10pm) At the base of the slopes in Nasserein, this laid-back hangout has a big, sunny terrace, fun staff and lethal Jägermeister shots. The pub occasionally hosts events from live music to quiz nights.

Bar Cuba
BAR

(www.barcuba-stanton.com; Dorfstrasse 33; ⊙4pm-3am) Live music, Wednesday-night fancy-dress parties, chipper bar staff and cocktails named Cuban Cocaine and Love Juice – say no more.

Kandahar
CLUB

(Dorfstrasse 50; ⊙7pm-6am) Top British and Ibiza DJs play house and keep the dance floor packed till dawn here.

ℹ Information

The only real internet cafe is **Mailbox** (Dorfstrasse 54; per min €0.15; ⊙8.30am-8.30pm), but you can check emails for free in most ski shops. The centrally located **tourist office** (📞226 90; www.stantonamarlberg.com; Arlberg Haus; ⊙8.30am-7pm Mon-Fri, 9am-6pm Sat, 9am-noon & 3-5pm Sun) has information on outdoor activities, maps and places to stay. There's an accommodation board and a free telephone outside.

ℹ Getting There & Away

St Anton is the easiest access point to the region. The ultramodern train station is on the route between Bregenz (€17.60, 1¼ hours) and Innsbruck (€20.10, 1¼ hours), with fast trains every one or two hours. St Anton and St Christoph are close to the eastern entrance of the Arlberg Tunnel (cars and minibuses €8.50), the toll road connecting Vorarlberg and Tyrol. You can avoid the toll by taking the B197, but no vehicles with trailers are allowed on this winding road.

Buses depart from stands southwest of the tourist office.

ℹ Getting Around

BICYCLE Bicycles can be rented (half-/full day €16/23) from **Sport Alber** (Dorfstrasse 15) and **Intersport Arlberg** (Dorfstrasse 1).

BUS Free local buses go to outlying parts of the resort (such as St Jakob). Buses run to Lech and Zürs in Vorarlberg (one-way €4.70); they are hourly (till about 6pm) in winter, reducing to four a day in summer.

TAXI A minibus taxi can be shared between up to eight people; the trip from St Anton to Lech costs €37/55 in the day/night.

LOCALS' APRÈS-SKI FAVOURITES

Taps 'Après ski at its finest! Live music, an amazing sun terrace and the "boss man" Egon's lethal homemade schnapps' – *Susanne, dancer*

Fanghouse 'Jägermeister capital of St Anton. It really is fang-tastic fun here and the staff are totally crazy. Great music, no Schlager!' – *Maggie Ritson, mum of two*

Pub 37 'You have to have a beer at Pub 37. What a classic little bar – warm and cosy. Get in early as it only holds about 37 people!' – *Shane Pearce, après-ski instructor*

Heustadl 'It's the biggest and best. Top location, good all-day après-ski and a very entertaining band where the waitresses are part of the show...' – *Chris Ritson, powerline contractor*

Mooserwirt 'Seeing is believing at Mooserwirt – the lively crowd, DJs and lights make for a great après-ski experience. Bet your ski boots take you grooving...' – *Jason, chalet worker*

Vorarlberg

Best Places to Eat

» Deuring-Schlössle (p339)

» April (p345)

» Fux (p351)

» Rauch Cafe (p347)

» Wirthaus zur Fohrenburg (p348)

Best Places to Stay

» Gasthof Hirschen (p343)

» Hotel Alpenrose (p345)

» Deuring-Schlössle (p337)

» Posthotel Rössle (p349)

» Hotel Gotthard (p351)

Why Go?

If much of Vorarlberg remains unknown, it's because the locals are so modest about its charms. Oh, we only have fresh air, dairy farms, plenty of forest and a few mountains to ski on, they say with a shrug. Yes, yes and double yes, you're thinking. But then the Vorarlberger are a pretty unique lot: they speak with a Swiss-Alemannic dialect *(Vorarlbergerisch)* and swing happily between ecofriendly architecture on the cutting edge of design and deeply traditional hamlets with more cows than people.

To the west lies Bregenz on the glittering expanse of Bodensee (Lake Constance), wedged between Switzerland and Germany, while to the east the glaciated peaks of Montafon and Western Arlberg attract hikers and skiers to their rugged realms. In between is the green and almost soothingly beautiful Bregenzerwald, where the welcome is as refreshing and authentic as the scenery.

When to Go

Winter blankets the Alps in snow, with downhill and cross-country skiers heading to the twinkling slopes of Montafon, Western Arlberg and the Bregenzerwald. Bodensee is at its best from May to September, when mild temperatures make it possible to swim, cycle and laze on the beach. Come in July for Bludenz' Milka chocolate festival and medieval shindigs in Feldkirch, or August for lakeside opera at the world-renowned Bregenzer Festspiele. Crowds are few and room rates low during the shoulder seasons (May to mid-June and September to mid-December).

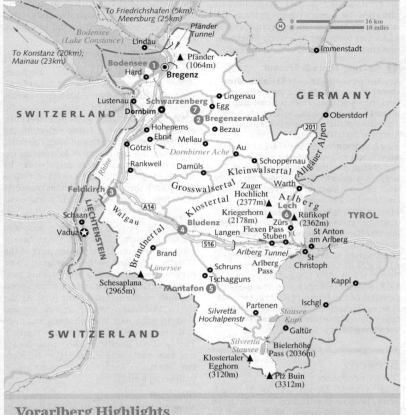

Vorarlberg Highlights

1 Splash and cycle over borders on **Bodensee** (p340), Europe's third-largest lake

2 Eat cheese, cheese and more glorious cheese in the dairy-loaded **Bregenzerwald** (p342)

3 Tiptoe back to medieval times at the castles and towers in **Feldkirch** (p344)

4 Go to purple-cow heaven gorging on Milka chocolate in **Bludenz** (p348)

5 Enjoy the rugged splendour of hiking in **Montafon** (p350)

6 Schuss with celebrities on the slopes of **Lech** (p351)

7 Contemplate Angelika Kauffmann's art in the chocolate-box village of **Schwarzenberg** (p342)

History

Vorarlberg has been inhabited since the early Stone Age but it wasn't until the Celts arrived in 400 BC, followed by the Romans in around 15 BC, that lasting settlements were maintained. Brigantium, the forerunner of Bregenz, was a Roman stronghold until around the 5th and 6th centuries, when the raiding Germanic Alemanni tribes increased their influence and effectively took over.

Peace reigned in the province until the early 15th century, when it suffered substantial damage during the Appenzell War with the Swiss Confederation. Relations with its neighbour later improved to such an extent that in 1918 Vorarlberg declared independence from Austria and sought union with Switzerland. The move was blocked by the Allied powers in the post-war reorganisation of Europe; fears that an even smaller Austria would be easily absorbed by a recovering Germany were certainly founded. Today, Vorarlberg still looks first towards its westerly neighbours, and then to Vienna, 600km to the east.

ℹ Getting There & Around

AIR Austrian Airlines flies to **St Gallen Altenrhein** (www.airport-stgallen.com) in Switzerland, the nearest airport. **Friedrichshafen airport** (www.fly-away.de), in Germany, is the closest major airport serving domestic and European destinations.

CAR & MOTORCYCLE The A14/E43 connects the province to Germany in the north and the rest of Austria via the 14km Arlberg tunnel, which runs under the Arlberg mountains. To the west, there are plenty of border crossings into Liechtenstein and Switzerland.

PUBLIC TRANSPORT Vorarlberg is broken down into Domino (individual zones), grouped into nine transport regions. A Regio travel pass covering one region costs €5.60/€13.60 for one day/week while a Maximo pass, costing €12.20/26.10, covers the entire province. Single Domino tickets cost €1.20 and a day pass is €2.20 – these cover city transport in Bregenz, Dornbirn, Götzis, Feldkirch, Bludenz, Lech and Schruns/Tschagguns. Information and timetables are available from the **Verkehrsverbund Vorarlberg** (www.vmobil.at, in German).

Bregenz

📞 05574 / POP 28,000

What a view! Ah yes, the locals proudly agree, Bregenz does indeed have the loveliest of views: before you the Bodensee, Europe's third-largest lake, spreads out like a liquid mirror; behind you the Pfänder climbs to the Alps; to the right you see Germany, to the left the faint outline of Switzerland. Just wow.

Whether contemplating avant-garde art and architecture by the new harbour, sauntering along the promenade on a summer's evening or watching opera under the stars at the much-lauded Festspiele, you can't help but think – clichéd though it sounds – that Vorarlberg's pocket-sized capital has got at least a taste of it all.

◉ Sights

TOP CHOICE **Kunsthaus Bregenz** ART GALLERY
(www.kunsthaus-bregenz.at; Karl-Tizian-Platz; adult/child €8/free; ⊙10am-6pm Tue-Sun, to 9pm Thu) Designed by Swiss architect Peter Zumthor, this giant glass and steel cube is said to resemble a lamp, reflecting the changing light of the sky and lake. The stark, open-plan interior is perfect for rotating exhibitions of contemporary art – works by British sculptor Anthony Gormley often feature. Check the website for details on everything from guided tours to kids' workshops.

Pfänder SCENIC AREA
(Steinbruchgasse 4; one-way adult/child €6.30/3.10, return €10.80/5.40; ⊙8am-7pm) A cable car whizzes to the 1064m peak of the Pfänder, a wooded mountain rearing above Bregenz and affording a breathtaking panorama of the Bodensee and the snowcapped summits of the not-so-distant Alps. At the top, a 30-minute circular trail brings you close to deer, ibex and whistling marmots at the year-round Wildpark (nature reserve). There's also a **Greifvogelflugschau** (bird of prey show; adult/child €5/2.50; ⊙11am & 2.30pm May-Sep), where feathered performers amaze with aerial feats.

Oberstadt HISTORIC AREA
Slung high above the lake is the Oberstadt, Bregenz' tiny old town of winding streets, candy-coloured houses and flowery gardens. It's still enclosed by defensive walls and the sturdy **Martinstor** (St Martin's Gate), guarded by a grotesque mummified shark.

Martinsturm MUSEUM
(St Martin's Tower; www.martinsturm.at; Martinsgasse; adult/child €1/0.50; ⊙10am-5pm Tue-Sun Apr-Oct) Not far past Martinstor is this ba-

ARCHITECTURAL TRAILBLAZER

Rural though it may seem, Vorarlberg is among the most progressive places on the planet when it comes to architecture. It all started back in the mid-1980s when a group of forward-thinking architects began calling themselves Baukünstler (building artists). Today, almost everywhere you look – private homes, hotels, office blocks, supermarkets – you'll find cutting-edge buildings of glass, wood and steel. Some, like Inatura in Dornbirn and the Kunsthaus Bregenz, make urban design statements; others, like the alpine Silvrettahaus, integrate seamlessly into the natural environment.

OPERA UNDER THE STARS

The **Bregenzer Festspiele** (Bregenz Festival; ☑407-6; www.bregenzerfestspiele.com), running from late July to late August, is the city's premier cultural festival. World-class operas, orchestral works and other highly imaginative productions are staged on the open-air Seebühne, a floating stage on the lake, in the Festspielhaus and at the Vorarlberger Landestheater. Information and tickets (€28 to €132) are up for grabs about nine months before the festival.

roque tower, topped by the largest onion dome in central Europe. It's worth seeing the 14th-century frescoes in the chapel before climbing up to the small military museum for fine views over Bregenz' rooftops. The website has details of the summer concerts which are held at the foot of the tower.

Festspielhaus LANDMARK
(Festival Hall; www.festspielhausbregenz.at; Platz der Wiener Symphoniker 1) Even if you can't bag tickets for the Bregenzer Festspiele, the Festival Hall is a must-see. All tinted glass, smooth concrete and sharp angles, this is one of Bregenz' most visible icons. Many festival performances are held on the semicircular Seebühne stage jutting out onto the lake.

Vorarlberger Landesmuseum MUSEUM
(www.vlm.at, in German; Kornmarktplatz 1) This museum romps through the region's history, art and architecture. Besides Stone Age and Roman artefacts, it contains an unrivalled collection of works by Swiss-Austrian neoclassical artist Angelika Kauffmann. The museum is closed for a complete facelift until 2013; see the website for the latest information.

🏃 **Activities**

Bregenz' shimmering centrepiece is the Bodensee, Europe's third-largest lake, straddling Austria, Switzerland and Germany. In summer, the well-marked trail that circumnavigates the lake becomes an autobahn for lycra-clad *Radfahrer* (cyclists); shoulder seasons are considerably more peaceful.

Other lakeside activities include sailing and diving at Lochau, around 6km north of town, and swimming. The most central place for a quick dip or a barbecue is the **Pipeline**, a stretch of pebbly beach north of Bregenz, so named for the large pipeline running parallel to the lake.

Vorarlberg Lines LAKE CRUISES
(www.vorarlberg-lines.at; Seestrasse) This is one of a number of companies taking you out

onto the lake from April to mid-October. There are two-hour Bodensee panorama cruises (adult/child €15.20/7.60), one-hour Bregenz trips (€9.20/4.60) and regular boat transfers to lake destinations including Lindau, Mainau, Friedrichshafen and Konstanz.

Rheindelta WALKING, CYCLING
(www.rheindelta.com, in German; Hard) Easily explored on foot or by bike, this nature reserve sits 5km south of Bregenz, where the River Rhine flows into the Bodensee. The mossy marshes, reeds and mixed woodlands attract more than 300 bird species, including curlews, grey herons and rare black-tailed godwits.

Strandbad Bregenz LIDO
(Strandweg; adult/child €3.90/1.70; ☺9am-8pm mid-May–Sep) Packed with bronzed bods, overexcited kids and flirty teens in summer, this central lido has a lakeside beach, several outdoor pools with waterslides, and activities like volleyball and table tennis.

Strandbad Hard LIDO
(www.hard-sport-freizeit.at; Hard; adult/child €3.60/1.80; ☺9am-8pm May–mid-Sep) A lakefront contender 5km south of town, this lido has outdoor pools, barbecue areas, minigolf and a secluded FKK (nudist) beach for skinny-dippers.

🛏 **Sleeping**

Stop by the tourist office for a list of private rooms (around €30 per person). Prices soar and beds are at a premium during the Bregenzer Festspiele in late July to late August, when it's highly advisable to book ahead. If Bregenz is booked solid, consider hopping over the border to Lindau in Germany, around 8km away.

Deuring-Schlössle HISTORIC HOTEL €€€
(☑478 00; www.deuring-schloessle.at; Ehre-Guta-Platz 4; s/d/ste €111/222/386; P❄@🖤) Perched above Bregenz in the Oberstadt, this is your archetypal fairy-tale hotel with turret

Bregenz

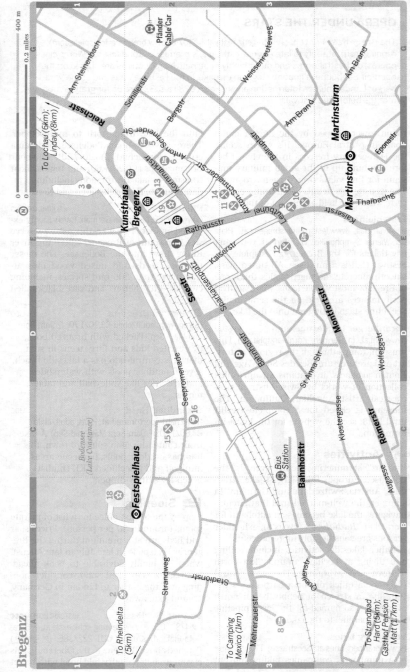

Bodensee
(Lake Constance)

Festspielhaus

Kunsthaus
Bregenz

Martinsturm

Martinstor

To Lochau (6km);
Lindau (8km)

Pfänder Cable Car

Bus
Station

To Rheindelta
(5km)

To Camping
Mexico (1km)

To Strandbad
Hard (5km);
Gasthof Pension
Matt (17km)

400 m
0.2 miles

Am Steinenbach
Schillerstr
Bergstr
Reichsstr
Anton-Schneider-Str
Kornmarktstr
Rathausstr
Kaiserstr
Seestr
Sparkassenplatz
Belruptstr
Leutbühel
Weissenreuteweg
Am Brand
Am Brand
Eponastr
Thalbachg
Kaiserstr
Montfortstr
Römerstr
Wolfeggstr
Klostergasse
Augasse
Bahnhofstr
St Anna Str
Seepromenade
Strandweg
Stadionstr
Mehrerauerstr
Quellenstr

Bregenz

◉ Top Sights

Festspielhaus	B2
Kunsthaus Bregenz	E2
Martinstor	F4
Martinsturm	F4

◉ Sights

1	Vorarlberger Landesmuseum	E2

Activities, Courses & Tours

2	Strandbad Bergenz	A1
3	Vorarlberg Lines	F1

◉ Sleeping

4	Deuring-Schlössle	F4
5	Hotel Bodensee	F2
6	Hotel Messmer	F2
7	Hotel Weisses Kreuz	E3
8	JUFA Gästehaus Bregenz	A3

◉ Eating

9	Bistro Duygu	E3
10	Cafesito	E3
	Deuring-Schlössle	(see 4)
11	Gösserbrau	E3
12	GWL Shopping Centre	E3
	Kornmesser	(see 13)
	KUB	(see 13)
13	Market	E2
14	Neubeck	E3
	Spar	(see 12)
15	Wirtshaus am See	C2

◉ Drinking

16	Beach Bar Bregenz	C2
17	Cuba	E2
	Wunderbar	(see 17)

◉ Entertainment

18	Seebühne	B1
19	Vorarlberger Landestheater	E2
20	Wohnzimmer	F3

and ivy-draped walls. Rooms have medieval charm with antiques and low beams, while marble bathrooms, designer furnishings and wi-fi bring you back to the 21st century.

Hotel Weisses Kreuz　　　HOTEL €€
(☎498 80; www.hotelweisseskreuz.at; Römerstrasse 5; s/d €119/146; P🄿🅸🆂@🛜) Service is attentive at this central pick, with a cocktail bar and a restaurant (mains €14 to €29) rolling out seasonal Austrian fare. The bright rooms are smartly kitted out with cherry wood furnishings, flat-screen TVs and organic bedding.

Gasthof Pension Matt　　　GUESTHOUSE €€
(☎717 77; www.gasthofmatt.at, in German; Wuhrbaumweg 36; s/d €50/90; P🛜) The Matt family extends a warm welcome at this guesthouse, 20 minutes' walk southwest of the station. Done in fresh lemon and lime shades, the quiet rooms have comfy beds, squeaky-clean bathrooms and wi-fi. Enjoy breakfast on the leafy terrace.

🌿 Camping Mexico　　　CAMPGROUND €
(☎732 60; www.camping-mexico.at, in German; Hechtweg 4; camp sites per adult/child/tent €7/3.50/8; ☺May-Sep; 🛜) This eco-labelled camp site by the lake uses solar energy, recycles waste and serves organic food in its restaurant. The leafy pitches offer plenty of shade. You can rent a canoe from €28 per day.

Hotel Bodensee　　　HOTEL €€
(☎423 00; www.hotel-bodensee.at; Kornmarktstrasse 22; s/d €71/126; P😊🛜) Right in the thick of things, this hotel's best rooms are spacious, tastefully decorated in muted tones and sport flat-screen TVs. Breakfast is a wholesome fresh fruit, muesli and regional produce affair.

JUFA Gästehaus Bregenz　　　HOSTEL €
(☎05708-35 40; www.jufa.at/bregenz; Mehrerauerstrasse 5; dm €27; P😊@) Housed in a former needle factory near the lake, this HI hostel now reels backpackers in with its roomy, superclean dorms. The excellent facilities include a cafe, common room and restaurant.

Hotel Messmer　　　HOTEL €€
(☎423 56; www.hotel-messmer.at, in German; Kornmarktstrasse 16; s/d €76/118; P🛜) This central hotel looks back on a 600-year history. That said, rooms are functional rather than fancy, with smallish bathrooms. Breakfasts are generous and there's free access to the sauna.

🍴 Eating

Restaurants and cafes huddle along the lakefront and the streets of the Unterstadt. In summer, little beats a picnic on the banks of the Bodensee; stock up on fresh bread, smoked fish, cheese and fruit at the weekly **market** (Kornmarktstrasse & Sparkassenplatz; ☺8am-1pm Tue & Fri).

The **GWL Shopping Centre** (Römerstrasse 2) has a Spar supermarket for self-caterers.

**TOP
CHOICE　Deuring-Schlössle**　　　GOURMET €€€
(☎478 00; www.deuring-schloessle.at; Ehre-Guta-Platz 4; mains €21-35; ☺dinner Mon-Sat)

WORTH A TRIP

TWO WHEELS, THREE COUNTRIES

When the sun's out, there's surely no better way to explore Bodensee than with your bum in a saddle. The well-marked Bodensee Cycle Path (www.bodensee-radweg.com) makes a 273km loop of the Bodensee, taking in vineyards, meadows, orchards, wetlands and historic towns. There are plenty of small beaches where you can stop for a refreshing dip in the lake. Visit the website for itineraries and maps.

A day suffices to tick off some highlights in three countries on a 30km stretch of the route. Catch a morning ferry to **Lindau**'s storybook old town in Germany, then roll along the lakeshore back to **Bregenz**. Continue southwest along a woodland path to the broad banks of the **Bregenzerach**, a beautiful meltwater river where locals bathe and fly-fish on hot days. From here it's just a short pedal to the Rheindelta wetlands and the wide bay of **Rorschach** in Switzerland, where you can stop for Swiss chocolate before catching a train back to Bregenz.

Whether by the fireside in the wood-panelled salon or in the walled garden, this restaurant is romantic stuff. The menu makes the most of organic, market-fresh produce, with specialities like *Felchen* (Bodensee whitefish) and rack of venison with sage gnocchi and lavender-orange jus. Deuring-Schlössle regularly hosts wine tasting and concert dinners.

Cafesito CAFE €
(Maurachgasse 6; bagels €3-4; ⊙7.45am-6.30pm Mon-Fri, 9am-4.30pm Sat; ☻) Tiny Cafesito does the best create-your-own bagels and smoothies in town. Lilac and yellow walls and modern art create a funky backdrop for a light lunch or cup of fair-trade coffee.

Wirtshaus am See AUSTRIAN €€
(☑422 10; www.wirtshausamsee.at; Seepromenade 2; mains €11-18) Snag a table on the lakefront terrace at this mock half-timbered villa, dishing up local specialities like buttery Bodensee whitefish and venison ragout. It's also a relaxed spot for quaffing a cold one.

Neubeck FUSION €€€
(☑436 09; www.neubeck.at; Anton-Schneider-Strasse 5; lunch €9.50, mains €21-33; ⊙Tue-Sat) Crisp white linen and soft lighting set the scene in this fin-de-siècle bistro, opening onto a leafy patio. Chef Nina Sotriffer puts a creative, herby spin on seasonal dishes like Singapore-style noodles with wild gambas and veal-stuffed agnolotti pasta tossed in sage butter.

Bistro Duygu TURKISH €
(Kirchstrasse 1; mains €6-8; ⊙10am-1am Mon-Sat, noon-9pm Sun) Locals pile into this cheery Turkish place for late-night munchies such

as lentil soup, falafel and honey-drenched baklava.

Kornmesser AUSTRIAN €€
(☑548 54; www.kornmesser.at; Kornmarktstrasse 5; lunch €7.30, mains €10-25; ⊙9.30am-midnight Tue-Sun) Baroque meets Bavaria at this attractively converted 18th-century *Gasthaus*. Wash down *Weisswürste* (herby veal sausages), suckling pig and other hearty fare with Augustiner Bräu beer in the vaulted interior or chestnut-shaded beer garden.

Gösserbrau GASTROPUB €€
(☑424 67; Anton-Schneider-Strasse 1; mains €9-23) Gösserbrau is an optical illusion: one side is a wood-panelled tavern serving Austrian fare like goulash and *Knödel* (dumplings), the other an ubercool bar. Both have Gösserbrau brews on tap.

Viva Cantina MEXICAN €€
(☑422 88; www.cantina.at; Seestrasse 7; mains €9-20 ⊙5pm-3am Tue-Sun) This colourful Mexican cantina doubles as a party place after shrimp fajitas and one too many tequilas. Retreat to the palm garden in summer.

KUB CAFE €
(Karl-Tizian-Platz; breakfast €5.50-8.50, lunch €7.60; ⊙8.30am-1.30am) Kunsthaus Bregenz' all-black cafe serves art-inspired breakfasts and morphs into a slinky cocktail bar after dark.

🍸 Drinking & Entertainment

Wunderbar BAR
(Bahnhofstrasse 4; ⊙10am-4am Mon-Sat, 2pm-1am Sun; ☎) Bordello meets neobaroque at the Wunderbar, where flickering candles illuminate blood-red walls, cherubs and velvet sofas. Browse the papers, bag a swing on the terrace or sip cocktails as smooth funk plays.

Beach Bar Bregenz
BAR

(Seepromenade; ⊘4pm-1am Mon-Fri, 2pm-2am Sat, 11am-2am Sun Jul & Aug) Cool cocktails, palm trees, chilled DJ beats – it's the Costa del Bodensee every summer at this lakefront beach bar. Work your relaxed look in a *Strandkorb* (wicker basket chair).

Cuba
BAR

(Bahnhofstrasse 9; ⊘11am-2am Sat, from 2pm Sun) Glammed up with chandeliers and a sweeping staircase, this gallery-style bar attracts a young crowd with Latin tunes and a top line-up of DJs.

Wohnzimmer
CLUB

(www.wohnzimmer.cc; Maurachgasse 3; ⊘9pm-2am Wed-Sat) Rock, electro and punk on the decks and occasional gigs are what to expect at this happening music bar and club.

Vorarlberger Landestheater
THEATRE

(428 70; www.landestheater.org, in German; Seestrasse 2) Also known as the Theater am Kornmarkt, this German-language theatre is Vorarlberg's main stage for opera, drama, comedy and musicals.

ℹ Information

Bregenz' Unterstadt has a handful of banks and *Bankomat* (ATM) machines.

Bodensee-Vorarlberg Tourism (☑434 43 15; www.bodensee-vorarlberg.com) Free regional accommodation booking service.

Main post office (Seestrasse 5)

Tourist office (☑49 59-0; www.bregenz.ws; Rathausstrasse 35a; ⊘9am-6pm Mon-Fri, to noon Sat) Information on the city and the surrounding area and can help with accommodation. Outside opening hours, brochures are stacked in front of the office.

Unfallkrankenhaus (☑4901; Josef Huter Strasse 12) Provincial hospital with emergency ward.

ℹ Getting There & Around

Bicycle

Fahrradverleih Bregenz (Bregenz Harbour; ⊘9am-7pm May-Sep) rents quality bikes for €16.50 per day and has free Bodensee cycling maps.

Bus

A daily bus service runs to Dornbirn (€2.30, 30 minutes) at least four times an hour. Buses to Feldkirch (€5.10, two hours) depart twice hourly from Monday to Friday and hourly at weekends.

Train

Four direct trains daily head for Munich (€43.50, three hours) via Lindau, while trains for Konstanz (€17.60, 1¾ hours) go via the Swiss shore of the lake and may be frequent, but require between one and four changes. There are four daily departures for Zürich (€33, 2¼ hours), all of which call in at St Gallen (€12, 50 minutes). Nine trains daily depart for Innsbruck (€31, 2½ hours), calling en route at Dornbirn (€3.60, 15 minutes), Feldkirch (€7.20, 25 minutes) and Bludenz (€11, 40 minutes).

Dornbirn & Around

Ragged, thickly wooded limestone pinnacles are the dramatic backdrop to Dornbirn, Vorarlberg's largest city. While nowhere near as appealing as Bregenz, it's worth a visit for its refreshing lack of tourists and remarkable museums.

Hohenems, 6km south of Dornbirn, sheltered a large Jewish community in the 17th century. Their numbers dwindled in the 1860s, when Jews were eligible to live anywhere under Habsburg rule.

◎ Sights & Activities

TOP CHOICE Inatura
MUSEUM

(www.inatura.at; Jahngasse 9, Dornbirn; adult/child/family €9.50/4.80/21; ⊘10am-6pm) Dornbirn's biggest draw is this hands-on museum. It's a wonderland for kids who can pet (stuffed) foxes and handle (real) spiders, whip up tornados, conduct light experiments and generally interact with science, nature and technology. There's also a climbing wall and 3D cinema.

Altstadt
HISTORIC SITE

Dornbirn's compact old town centres on the Marktplatz, where your gaze is drawn to the crooked, 17th-century **Rotes Haus**, which owes its intense red hue to an unappetising mix of ox blood and bile. Next door, the neoclassical columns and

---

MOVING ON?

For tips, recommendations and reviews, head to shop.lonelyplanet.com to purchase downloadable PDFs of the Liechtenstein chapter from Lonely Planet's *Central Europe* guide, the Graubünden chapter from Lonely Planet's *Switzerland* guide or the Bavaria chapter from Lonely Planet's *Germany* guide.

free-standing Gothic belfry of **Pfarrkirche St Martin** catch your eye.

Rolls-Royce Museum
MUSEUM

(www.rolls-royce-museum.at; adult/child €8/4; ⊙10am-6pm) Situated at the bottom of the gorge and ensconced in a 19th-century cotton mill, this museum harbours the world's largest collection of Rolls-Royces. Highlights include a reconstruction of Royce's Cooke Street factory in Manchester and a hall of fame showcasing vintage Rollers that once belonged to the likes of Queen Elizabeth, Franco and George V. Stay for tea in the ever-so-British rosewood tearoom.

Jüdisches Museum Hohenems
MUSEUM

(www.jm-hohenems.at; Schweizer Strasse 5, Hohenems; adult/child €7/4; ⊙10am-5pm Tue-Sun) Housed in the Rosenthal villa, this museum zooms in on Hohenems' long-defunct Jewish community with photos, documents and religious artefacts. The Rosenthals built up a considerable textile business in the town, and part of their wealth – especially gorgeous period furniture – is also on show.

Huddled against a tree-lined hill just outside the town on the road to Götzis is the **Jewish cemetery**; get the key from the museum.

Rappenlochschlucht
SCENIC AREA

Just 4km south of Dornbirn is the narrow Rappenlochschlucht (Rappenloch Gorge), gouged out by the thundering Dornbirner Ache. A 10-minute walk leads up to a good viewpoint and a 30-minute trail to the **Staufensee**, a turquoise lake ringed by forest.

ℹ️ Getting There & Away

Dornbirn has frequent connections to Bregenz (€3.60, 15 minutes) and Hohenems (€2, eight minutes) on the Bregenz–Innsbruck railway line. Bus 47 departs from Dornbirn train station and passes by the Rappenlochschlucht scenic area (€1.20, 30 minutes, six daily).

Bregenzerwald

The wooded limestone peaks, cow-nibbled pastures and bucolic villages of the Bregenzerwald unfold to the south of Bregenz. This rural region is great for getting back to nature for a few days, whether cheese-tasting in alpine dairies, testing out hay and herbal treatments in spa hotels, or curling up by the fireside in a cosy farmhouse. One lungful of that good clean air and you'll surely want to grab your boots, slip into your skis or get on your bike and head outdoors.

⊙ Sights

TOP CHOICE \ Angelika Kauffmann Museum
MUSEUM

(www.angelika-kauffmann.com; Hof 454, Schwarzenberg; adult/child €7/1.50; ⊙10am-5pm Tue-Sun) This ultramodern museum houses a permanent collection in winter and rotating exhibitions in summer of Swiss-Austrian neoclassical painter Angelika Kauffmann's works. The artist had strong connections to the village where her father was born.

A ticket covers entry to the neighbouring **Heimat Museum** (Heritage Museum), a pristine alpine chalet. Displays of traditional painted furniture, extraordinary headwear, hunting paraphernalia and filigree iron crosses focus on rural 19th-century life.

Bergkäserei Schoppernau
SHOW DAIRY

(www.bergkaeserei.at, in German; Unterdorf 248, Schoppernau; ⊙8.30-11am & 3-6pm Mon-Fri, to 5pm Sat) Discover cheese-making secrets (including why Emmentaler is holey) at this show dairy, famous for its award-winning tangy *Bergkäse*, matured for up to 12 months.

DON'T MISS

A DATE WITH DAISY

Elsa, Bella, Dora and sisters are there for the milking at the **Kräuterbauernhof** (☏05515-22 98; www.kuhforyou.at, in German; Argenau 116, Au; d/tr/q €44/55/66). The Erlach-Dorle family will rent you the cow of your choice (€29 per week for a minimum of two months). The price includes 8kg of cheese which they can post to your home country, regular visits and milking sessions, and a keepsake photo of your long-lashed alpine beauty. Cow or no cow, this 300-year-old farmhouse is a fantastic place to stay, with spacious apartments full of woody charm, a herb garden and plenty of dairy goodness at breakfast.

DON'T MISS

SCHUBERT IN THE SPOTLIGHT

The highly acclaimed **Schubertiade** (☏05576-720 91; www.schubertiade.at) festival brings the *Lieder* (songs) and chamber music of the great Austrian Romantic composer Franz Schubert to atmospheric venues in Schwarzenberg (mid-June to mid-September) and Hohenems (May and October). Tickets are like gold dust and should be booked well in advance.

Käse-Molke Metzler　　SHOW DAIRY
(☏0551-230 44; www.molkeprodukte.com, in German; Bruggan 1025, Egg; ⊙8.30am-noon & 2-6pm Mon-Fri, 8.30am-noon Sat) This architecturally innovative dairy churns out fresh *Wälderkäse*, arranges tastings and runs four-hour cheese-making workshops (€49, booking essential) on Saturdays.

Käsekeller Lingenau　　SHOW DAIRY
(www.kaesekeller.at; in German; Zeihenbühel 423, Lingenau; ⊙10am-6pm Mon-Fri, 9am-5pm Sat) Step into the foyer of this modern cheese-maturation cellar to glimpse robots attending to wagon wheel–sized cheeses through a glass wall. A tasting of *Bergkäse* with wine costs €5.90.

🏃 Activities

The hills buzz with hikers, climbers and cyclists in summer. Local tourist offices also arrange **themed walks**, including some geared towards families. Paragliders can launch themselves off mountains in Andelsbuch, Bezau and Au-Schoppernau; tandem flights cost around €100. You'll receive the **Bregenzerwald Guest Card** when you stay more than three nights, giving free access to lifts, buses and outdoor pools.

Downhill Skiing　　SKIING
(3-/7-day pass adult €106/201, child €53/101) Though lesser known than other Austrian ski regions, the Bregenzerwald has fine downhill skiing on 255km of slopes, well suited to beginners, intermediates and ski tourers. Lift queues are virtually nonexistent and free ski buses shuttle between resorts. Nonskiers can shuffle through snowy forests on cross-country or snowshoe trails, go winter hiking or bump downhill on toboggan runs in Au and Damüls.

🛏 Sleeping & Eating

The Bregenzerwald has some incredibly charming places to sleep and eat. Local tourist offices can help you book farmstays and holiday homes.

Gasthof Hirschen　HISTORIC HOTEL €€
TOP CHOICE (☏05512-29 44; www.hirschenschwarzen berg.at; Hof 14, Schwarzenberg; s/d €106/152; P❄🔊) This a 250-year-old dream of a *Gasthof*. The wood-shingle facade is festooned with geraniums, while inside low-ceilinged corridors lead to antique-filled nooks and individually designed rooms. *Dirndl*-clad waitresses bring spot-on Austrian fare like *Tafelspitz* (boiled beef) and Schub Schwarzenberger cheeses to the table in the award-winning restaurant (mains €14 to €27)

Bio-Pension Beer　　PENSION €€
(☏05512-20 02; Gräsalp 357, Schoppernau; s/d €38/70) The light, cheery rooms at this pension are done out in sustainable wood from the Beer family forest. You'll feel right at home at this ecofriendly country retreat, complete with pure spring water, clucking chickens and organic produce at breakfast.

Hotel Gasthof Gams　BOUTIQUE HOTEL €€€
(☏05514-22 20; www.hotel-gams.at; Platz 44, Bezau; d €198-226; P❄🔊🏊) A real glamour puss of a hotel, the Gams (chamois) whispers romance from every last gold-kissed, heart-strewn, candlelit corner. An open fire in the dreamlike Da Vinci spa, starry ceilings, a decadent restaurant (five-course menu €19) with a walk-in wine tower – this is definite honeymoon material.

ℹ Information

The **Bregenzerwald tourist office** (☏05512-23 65; www.bregenzerwald.at; Impulszentrum 1135, Egg; ⊙9am-5pm Mon-Fri, 8am-1pm Sat & Sun) should be your first port of call for details on the region's sights, activities and accommodation. The shelves are well stocked with maps and brochures.

ℹ Getting There & Away

There are eight direct bus services daily to Bezau (€4.40, one hour) from Bregenz, but for most other destinations a change at Egg is required. From Dornbirn, Schwarzenberg (€3,

25 minutes), Bezau (€3.70, 50 minutes), Mellau (€4.40, one hour), Au (€5.80, 70 minutes) and Schoppernau (€5.80, 80 minutes) can all be reached a couple of times daily (times vary from season to season). For Damüls (€7.50, 1¾ hours), a change at Au is required.

Feldkirch

📞 05522 / POP 32,000

On the banks of the turquoise Ill River, Feldkirch sits prettily at the foot of wooded mountains, vineyards and a castle-crowned hill. It's a joy to stroll the well-preserved old town, which wings you back to late medieval times with its cobbled, arcaded lanes, towers and pastel-coloured townhouses. The town springs to life in summer with pavement cafes and open-air festivals.

◎ Sights

Fortifications HISTORIC SITE

Feldkirch has several towers surviving from the old fortifications. These include the 40m-high, late-15th-century **Katzenturm** on Hirschgraben, where Vorarlberg's biggest bell (weighing 7500kg) still tolls. The **Mühletor** on Mühletorplatz, also known as the Sautor, is where the pig market was held in the Middle Ages. On Heiligkreuzbrücke, the step-gabled **Churertor**

is the gateway to the bridge that was once used to transport salt across the Ill River to Switzerland.

Schloss Schattenburg CASTLE

(www.schattenburg.at; Burggasse 1; adult/child €6/4.50; ⊙9am-noon & 1.30-5pm Mon-Fri, 10am-5pm Sat & Sun) This 13th-century hilltop castle is storybook stuff with its red turrets and creeping vines. It's a steep climb up to the ramparts, which command far-reaching views over Feldkirch's rooftops. Once the seat of the counts of Montfort, the castle now houses a small **museum** displaying religious art, costumes and weaponry.

Domkirche St Nikolaus CATHEDRAL

(Domplatz; ⊙8am-6pm) Identified by a slender spire, Feldkirch's cathedral has a large, forbidding interior complemented by late-Gothic features and dazzling stained glass. The painting on the side altar is by local lad Wolf Huber (1480–1539), a leading member of the Danube school.

FREE **Wildpark** WILDLIFE PARK

(Ardetzenweg 20; ⊙dawn-dusk) Facing the castle across the town is Ardetzenberg (631m), a heavily forested hill. At its northern end is this wildlife park, with a woodland trail and animal-friendly enclosures home to marmots, ibex and wild boar.

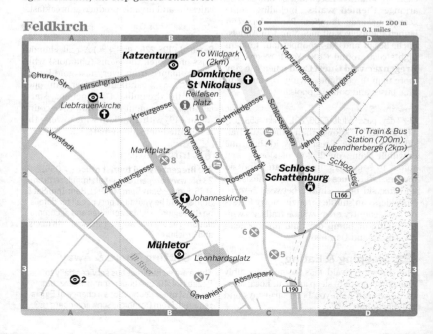

⚡ Activities

Dreiländerweg   CYCLING

The Feldkirch region is criss-crossed with cycling trails, including the 30km Dreiländerweg (Three Country Trail), taking in beautiful scenery in Austria, Switzerland and Liechtenstein. Pick up the free *Feldkircher Radwegkarte* map from the tourist office.

Bike hire is available at Gasthof Löwen (Kohlgasse 1; per day €12), 2.7km west of the centre.

🎭 Festivals & Events

Mittelaltermarkt   MEDIEVAL FESTIVAL

In late May, Feldkirch revisits the Middle Ages with troubadours, knights and non-stop feasting.

Feldkirch Festival   MUSIC FESTIVAL

(www.feldkirch.at/festival) This festival in June draws classical-music lovers to historic venues.

Gauklerfestival   FESTIVAL

Jugglers, fire-eaters and clowns entertain the crowds at this enormous street party in late July.

🛏 Sleeping

Hotel Alpenrose   BOUTIQUE HOTEL €€

(☑721 75; www.hotel-alpenrose.net; Rosengasse 4-6; s/d €80/140; ⊜@⊛) Hidden down a

quiet old-town backstreet, this 16th-century merchant's house is a touch of old-fashioned romance, with its dusky pink facade, rose garden and Biedermeier salon. The rooms blend contemporary and classic – think lots of polished wood, muted colours and flat-screen TVs.

Jugendherberge   HOSTEL €

(☑731 81; Reichsstrasse 111; dm/s/d €12.50/25.50/39; P⊜@⊛) A 700-year-old infirmary has been converted into this HI hostel, which exudes charm with its creaking beams, vaulted lounge and ivy-clad courtyard. A spiral staircase twists up to light-filled dorms with pine bunks. Buses 59, 60 and 68 stop here.

Hotel Central Löwen   HOTEL €€

(☑720 70; www.central-hotel-loewen.at; Schlossgraben 13; s/d €98/133; P⊜@⊛) Modern art cheers up the spacious rooms at this central, friendly pick. Guests can use the sauna, steam bath and pool a two-minute walk away.

Waldcamping   CAMPGROUND €

(☑76001-3190; www.waldcamping.at; Stadionstrasse 9; camp sites per adult/car/tent €6/4.20/5.15; ⊙Apr-Oct; P⊛) Pine trees shade this quiet camp site, where facilities include a barbecue area, playground and free entry to the Waldbad leisure pool. Take bus 2 from the train station to the last stop (3.5km).

🍴 Eating & Drinking

For self-caterers, there is an Interspar (Leonhardsplatz) supermarket at the southern end of the town centre.

TOP CHOICE **April**   CAFE €

(www.aprilcafe.at, in German; Neustadt 39; ⊙Thu-Tue; ⊜) Bright flower pots and upside-down watering cans guide the way to this wholesomely hip and wonderfully laid-back cafe. Bag a spot on one of the sofas or on the pocket-sized terrace for a latte adorned with flowers or butterflies (Ingo is a 'coffee artist'). Lavish breakfasts, open sandwiches and homemade cakes feature on the all-organic menu. Riojas are paired with tapas on Thursday evenings. There's a book exchange.

Möbelle   CAFE €

(Schmiedgasse 12; breakfast items €1; ⊙10am-midnight Sun-Thu, to 2am Fri & Sat; ⊛) Like the look of that groovy lamp, vase or chair? No problem. This cafe-cum–lounge bar doubles as a contemporary design store and

Driving Tour
Bregenzerwald Käsestrasse

❯ The Bregenzerwald's rolling dairy country is best explored on the Käsestrasse (Cheese Rd), which refers to the cheese-producing region rather than a specific route. This tour (40 minutes' driving without stops) takes in the highlights, threading through countryside and quaint villages, and stopping en route for silo-free buttermilk and cheese at local *Sennereien* (dairy farms). Spring through autumn is the best time to visit. See www.kaesestrasse.at (in German) for details.

Take a peek inside the huge cellars of the ultramodern **①** **Käsekeller Lingenau** to see how cheese is matured and taste flavoursome *Bergkäse* with a glass of local wine. Swing slightly south and hit the pretty village of **②** **Egg** and, 1km west, **③** **Käse-Molke Metzler**, an avant-garde dairy and farmhouse duo. Here you can sample creamy *Wälderkäse*, made from cow's and goat's milk, or call ahead to join a cheese-making workshop.

Veer southwest to the village of **④** **Schwarzenberg**, where old farmhouses tiled with wood shingles and studded with scarlet geraniums crowd the narrow streets. Contemplate art in the **⑤** **Angelika Kauffmann Museum** before lunching on cheese-rich *Kässpätzle* (egg noodles) in the wood-panelled parlour or garden at **⑥** **Gasthof Hirschen**. The narrow country lane now wends its way gently to **⑦** **Bezau**, 7km southeast, where the Bregenzerach river flows swiftly past forest-cloaked slopes rising to jagged limestone crags. The village has a handful of dairy shops where you can buy cheese and other local goodies like honey, herbs and schnapps. Continue southeast towards the Arlberg and mountainous **⑧** **Mellau**, where the tourist office organises cheese walks in summer.

Driving southeast brings you to peaceful **⑨** **Au**, affording deep views into a U-shaped valley, particularly beautiful on a golden autumn day. Round out your tour with total cheese immersion at the **⑩** **Bergkäserei Schoppernau**, where you can learn about cheese production and – if your stomach is still willing – try the famous *Bergkäse*.

DON'T MISS

POOL PARTY

Feldkirch's old public swimming pool in the Reichenfeld district has been born again as the ultra-hip Poolbar, the venue of the summertime Poolbar Festival (www.poolbar.at, in German). If you're in town in July or August, be sure to check out the top-notch line-up of mostly free events, skipping from concerts, dance and poetry slams to juggling shows and DJ nights.

everything's for sale. It's a chilled spot for an espresso, cocktail or DIY breakfast.

Wirtschaft zum Schützenhaus AUSTRIAN €€
(☑852 90; Göfiser Strasse 2; mains €10-14; ☺Thu-Mon) *Schiessen und Geniessen* (shoot and enjoy!) is the motto at this half-timbered tavern, where *Lederhosen*-clad staff bring humungous schnitzels to the table. The tree-shaded beer garden has prime views of the castle and a pet corner with fluffy rodents to keep kids amused.

Rauch Cafe CAFE €€
(Marktgasse 12-14; mains €15-26; ☺10am-1am Wed-Mon) This vaulted cafe-restaurant opens onto a buzzy terrace. If you can stomach chilli first thing, try the 'how to cure the hangover' breakfast (€10.90). The menu is a medley of Austrian staples and more imaginative dishes like homemade coffee gnocchi with a vanilla-chicory reduction. DJs spin house here after dark.

Dogana FUSION €€
(☑751 26-3; Neustadt 20; lunch €7.60, mains €18-25; ☺Tue-Sat) Mellow music plays at Dogana, with a popular terrace for alfresco snacking in summer. The menu changes seasonally but mainstays include delicious salads (try the curried *kikeriki* – chicken salad) and good-value lunches.

ℹ Information

The helpful **tourist office** (☑734 67; www.feldkirch.at; Schlossergasse 8; ☺8.30am-noon & 1.30-5.30pm Mon-Fri, 9am-noon Sat) has stacks of information and free town maps. The post office is opposite the train station.

ℹ Getting There & Away

Trains head north to Bregenz (€7.20, 30 minutes) and Dornbirn (€5.40, 25 minutes), and southeast to Bludenz (€5.40, 15 minutes). Feldkirch is the gateway to Liechtenstein's capital, Vaduz (€2.30, 40 minutes); a change at Schaan is normally necessary. Liechtenstein has a customs union with Switzerland, so you'll pass through Swiss customs before entering Liechtenstein.

Bludenz

☑05552 / POP 14,000

The Alps provide a spectacular backdrop to Bludenz, the only town in Austria – perhaps the world – that can lay claim to having purple cows; the Milka ones churned out from the Suchard factory. Gorging on chocolate aside, Bludenz' arcaded old town takes you back to its heyday as the seat of the Habsburg governors from 1418 to 1806. Bludenz also makes a good base for exploring the surrounding valleys.

◉ Sights & Activities

To explore Bludenz' attractions, join a free **city tour** organised by the tourist office, departing at 10am on Friday from mid-May till October.

St Laurentiuskirche CHURCH
(Mutterstrasse; ☺9am-5pm) Climb the covered Kirchensteig walkway up to this Gothic parish church, dominated by an octagonal onion-domed spire. There are stellar views over the town's rooftops to the Alps beyond from up here.

Stadtmuseum MUSEUM
(Kirchgasse 9; adult/child €1/free; ☺3-5pm Mon-Sat Jun-early Sep) This museum houses a small display on folk art and prehistoric finds.

Muttersberg SCENIC AREA
About 1km north of the town centre, a **cable car** (Hinterplärsch; adult/child one-way €6.60/4.20, return €11.10/6.90; ☺9am-5.30pm) rises up to this 1401m peak, the starting point for numerous hiking, Nordic-walking and cycling trails. If you don't want to walk it, catch bus 1 from in front of the train station to the cable-car station.

Alpine Skiing SKIING
There are 15 skiing areas within a 30km radius and ski bus transport to/from Bludenz

DON'T MISS

SWEET LIKE CHOCOLATE

One of Bludenz' best features can't even be seen. Almost anywhere you wander in the centre, the rich, enticing aroma of chocolate will fill your nostrils. The source of these divine smells is the Suchard chocolate factory. Unfortunately there are no guided tours but you can stock up on Milka at its **shop** (Fohrenburgstrasse 1; ⊙8-11am & 1.30-4.30pm Mon-Thu, 9-11.30am & 1.30-4pm Fri).

Bludenz' sweetest event is the **Milka Chocolate Festival** in mid-July, when 1000kg of *Schokolade* is up for grabs in prizes. There's also music, games and plenty of kids too full of sugar to control.

is sometimes included in the price of ski passes.

Walking and cycling are other popular activities; the tourist office has thick booklets on summer and winter outdoor pursuits.

Kletterhalle ROCK CLIMBING
(Untersteinstrasse 5; adult/child €6/4 plus shoe hire €0.80; ⊙hall 6am-10pm, ticket office 8am-noon & 1-5pm Mon-Fri) Practise clambering up boulders before tackling the real thing in the Alps at this excellent hall, run by the Austrian Alpine Club. The ticket office is on the 1st floor.

🛏 Sleeping

Private rooms usually offer the best value, even though a surcharge of around €3.50 per day applies for stays under three days.

Schlosshotel Dörflinger HISTORIC HOTEL €€
(☑630 16-0; www.schlosshotel.cc; Schlossplatz 5; s/d €85/130; 🅿🐕@) Clinging to the cliffs above Bludenz, this smart hotel shelters modern rooms, many with balconies. There's a mountain-facing terrace for warm evenings, free mountain-bike hire for guests and a smart restaurant (mains €16 to €23) dishing up Austrian fare.

Val Blu HOTEL €€
(☑631 06; www.valblu.at, in German; Haldenweg 2a; s/d €64/106; 🅿🐕🛜🏊) Glass walls and smooth contours define this ultramodern spa hotel, a 10-minute walk east of the centre along Untersteinstrasse. The functional, minimalist-style rooms feature wi-fi and flat-screen TVs.

Gasthof Hotel Löwen HOTEL €€
(☑322 70; www.loewen-bludenz.at; Mutterstrasse 7a; 🅿🛜) A recent makeover has brought this central hotel bang up to date. Rooms now sport parquet floors, crisp white bedding and walk-in showers.

Landhaus Muther GUESTHOUSE €
(☑657 04; www.landhaus-muther.at, in German; Alemannenstrasse 4; s/d €40/80; 🅿) Smothered in geraniums in summer, this homely chalet is fairly central. The rooms are old-style and simple, but fastidiously clean.

🍴 Eating

Wirthaus zur Fohrenburg AUSTRIAN €€
(☑685 68; www.fohrenburg.cc; Werdenbergerstrasse 53; mains €8-16; ⊙11am-2am Mon-Thu, 11am-4am Fri & Sat, 10am-3am Sun) Copper vats gleam at this cavernous brewpub-cum-beer garden. Hearty fare like *Tafelspitz* is washed down with Fohrenburger beer from the brewery opposite. Out front, Arche Nova bar is done out like a ship complete with fish lights; why a nautical theme in the Alps is anyone's guess!

Remise CAFE €
(Am Raiffeisenplatz; lunch €6.90, mains €6-10; ⊙10am-midnight) This contemporary cafe attracts arty types and serves snacks from polenta pizza to creative salads. The cultural centre next door regularly hosts exhibitions, film screenings and concerts.

Altes Rathaus CAFE €€
(Rathausgasse 1a; mains €8-15; ⊙10am-1am Mon-Sat) Opening onto a terrace under the arcades, this minimalist glass-fronted cafe rustles up cakes, steaks and cheese-rich Austrian specialities.

ℹ Information

The town centre sits on the northern bank of the Ill River. The **tourist office** (☑621 70; www.bludenz.travel; Werdenbergerstrasse 42; ⊙7.30am-noon & 2-5.30pm Mon-Thu, 7.30am-noon Fri) is five minutes' walk from the train station and has free internet access.

Across the road is the town's **post office** (Werdenbergerstrasse 37), and not far east is a small pedestrian-only shopping area.

ℹ Getting There & Away

Bludenz is on the east–west InterCity express rail route to Innsbruck (€22.50, two hours, every two hours) and Bregenz (€11, 45 minutes, hourly).

The A14 motorway passes just south of the Ill River and the town centre. Buses run down all five valleys around Bludenz.

Montafon

POP 15,500

The Montafon's pristine wilderness and potent schnapps had Ernest Hemingway in raptures when he wintered here in 1925 and 1926, skiing in blissful solitude and penning *The Sun Also Rises*. Silhouetted by the glaciated Silvretta range and crowned by the 3312m arrow of Piz Buin, the valley remains one of the most serene and unspoilt in the Austrian Alps.

Partenen marks the start of the serpentine 23km Silvretta Hochalpenstrasse (www.silvretta-bielerhoehe.at), which wends its way under peaks rising to well over 2500m before climbing over the 2036m Bielerhöhe Pass via a series of tight switchbacks. At the top of the pass is the **Silvretta Stausee** (2030m), a startlingly aquamarine reservoir, which mirrors the snowcapped peaks of Piz Buin and Klostertaler Egghorn on bright mornings.

🏃 Activities

Alpine Skiing　　　　　　　SKIING

(3-/7-day pass €107/211.50) In winter, Montafon is a magnet to families who come to carve its 243km of uncrowded pistes and go cross-country skiing, snowshoeing, ski touring and sledding. The Skipass-Montafon covers public transport and the 60 lifts in the valley.

Alpine Trails　　　　　　　　HIKING

Mile upon glorious mile of alpine trails, including the Radsattel Circuit, attract hikers in summer. Cable cars and lifts can be accessed with the regional Montafon-Silvretta-Card (3-/7-day €36/49).

🛏 Sleeping & Eating

Every village in the valley has a tourist office that can help you find a pension (expect to pay €20 to €30 per person).

TOP CHOICE Posthotel Rössle　　HISTORIC HOTEL €€

(☑05558-833 30; www.posthotel-roessle. at, in German; Dorfstrasse 4, Gaschurn; d incl half board €130-180; P❄✿) Hemingway once stayed in this 200-year-old chalet – whether with his mistress or wife remains a mystery. The friendly Kessler family will show you the guestbook he signed and the bed he slept in. Within easy reach of the Silvretta Nova ski arena, the hotel has well-kept rooms, a superb wood-panelled restaurant, indoor and outdoor pools, and a spa.

Madlenerhaus　　　　　　ALPINE HUT €

(☑05558-42 34; www.madlenerhaus.at; dm €8-10; ☉Feb-Oct) This DAV (German Alpine Club) hut at 1986m is a good-value place to bed down at Bielerhöhe. The four- to 10-bed dorms are comfy and the restaurant (mains €7 to €14) serves Austrian comfort food.

Silvrettahaus　　　　　　ALPINE HUT €€

(☑05558-42 46; www.silvretta-bielerhoehe.at; s/d €52.50/82; ☉Jul–mid-Oct & mid-Dec–Easter) For more creature comforts at 2000m, check into the architecturally innovative Silvrettahaus at Bielerhöhe, which has bright, contemporary rooms and spellbinding mountain views.

ℹ Information

Montafon Tourism (☑05556-722 530; www. montafon.at; Montafonerstrasse 21, Schruns; ☉8am-7pm Mon-Fri, 9am-5pm Sat & Sun) has the low-down on accommodation and activities in the valley.

ℹ Getting There & Away

Trains run frequently from Bludenz to Schruns (€3.20, 20 minutes), from where up to five buses daily continue onto Partenen (€3, 35 minutes) at the base of the Silvretta pass. From mid-July to mid-October, eight buses daily climb from Partenen to the Silvretta Stausee (€2.30, 35 minutes). The Silvretta Hochalpenstrasse pass is controlled by a toll road, which costs €11.50/10.50 for cars/motorcycles.

Western Arlberg

☑05583

Mountains huddle conspiratorially around the snow-sure slopes of the rugged Arlberg region, one of Austria's top ski destinations. The best-known villages are picture-postcard Lech (1450m) and its smaller twin Zürs (1716m), 6km south. Because of their relative isolation, fabulous skiing and five-star hotels, the resorts are a magnet to royalty (Princess Diana used to ski here), celebrities and anyone who pretends to be such from behind Gucci shades.

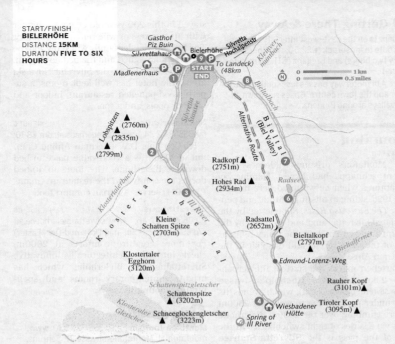

START/FINISH
BIELERHÖHE
DISTANCE **15KM**
DURATION **FIVE TO SIX HOURS**

Walking Tour
Radsattel Circuit, Bierlehöhe

This is one of Vorarlberg's most spectacular hikes, exploring two valleys linked by a pass and taking you high into the realms of 3000m mountains and glaciers. Best tackled in July or August, the route demands a moderate level of fitness. The Alpenvereinskarte 1: 25,000 map No 26 *Silvrettagruppe* covers the trail in detail.

From the ❶ **Silvretta Stausee** car park, walk over the dam to join the well-worn path skirting the western shore of the turquoise reservoir, framed by jagged, snowcapped mountains. Stick to the shoreline around the southern end of the lake, crossing one bridge over the ❷ **Klostertaler Bach**, then another over the fast-flowing ❸ **Ill River**. At the junction, turn right up the trail signed to the Wiesbadener Hütte.

The broad path to the hut shadows the east bank of the Ill towards the arrow-shaped peak of Piz Buin (3312m) at the valley head. An amphitheatre of glistening blue, heavily crevassed glaciers appears as you gradually gain height. Continue your steady ascent, stopping for refreshment on the sunny ter-

race of the ❹ **Wiesbadener Hütte** after two to 2¼ hours. At the back of the hut, veer left towards the Radsattel on a red-and-white-marked trail that becomes increasingly narrow and rough underfoot. The path zigzags steeply up the slope and over a small stream. Keep right and ascend a rise topped by a large cairn. Cross a shallow pool outlet before the final steep climb to the 2652m ❺ **Radsattel**, where a sign marks the Vorarlberg–Tyrol border, one to 1½ hours from the hut.

Drop steeply down the boulder-strewn eastern side of the pass, keeping an eye out for ibex. You will pass several small lakes including the jewel-like ❻ **Radsee** as you take the small path down to the remote meadows of the ❼ **Bieltal** (Biel Valley). Follow the path along the west bank of the babbling ❽ **Bieltalbach** stream and continue west to the Silvretta Stausee, turning right along the reservoir. Back at the main road, turn left and walk 300m to return to ❾ **Bielerhöhe** (1½ to two hours from the Radsattel).

✗ Activities

Alpine Skiing
SKIING

(1-/6-day pass €44.50/212) Remember Bridget Jones hurtling backwards down the mountain on skis in *The Edge of Reason?* That was filmed on Lech's scenic, forest-streaked runs. You can surely do a better job skiing on the Arlberg region's 280km of slopes, which are interlinked by free solar-powered buses and covered by a regional ski pass. The terrain is best suited to beginners and intermediates, with off-piste possibilities and the famous 21km *Weisse Ring* (White Ring) appealing to more advanced skiers.

Themed Walks
WALKING

From July to September, the tourist office organises free themed walks such as sunrise hikes and botanical strolls. You can also go it alone on 250km of signed hiking trails, ranging from high-Alpine treks to gentle lake walks, as well as dedicated running and Nordic walking trails.

🛏 Sleeping & Eating

Many of the hotels in Lech and Zürs are five-star, including the super-luxurious Hotel Aurelio which made Condé Nast's Hotlist in 2010. Expect prices to be 30% to 50% higher than those quoted below in the winter high season.

Hotel Gotthard
HOTEL €€

(☑35 60; www.gotthard.at; Omesberg 119, Lech; s/d/ste €75/140/180; P🐕❄🏊🐾) It's the little touches that make all the difference at this chalet hotel – from oven-warm bread at breakfast (owner Clemens is a baker) to the fluffy bathrobes in the bright, contemporary rooms. There's a spa, an indoor pool and a children's playroom.

Gästehaus Lavendel
PENSION €€

(☑26 57; www.lavendel.at; Lech 447; d €70-90, apt €75-150; 🐕🐾) The affable Mascher family make you feel at home at this cosy pension next to the ski lifts. Many of the spacious, immaculate rooms and apartments sport balconies and there's a little spa for a post-hike or après-ski unwind.

Pension Alwin
PENSION €

(☑309 30-0; www.alwin.at; Zug 309, Lech; s/d €35/64; P@) A bargain place close to the centre of Lech, this pinewood chalet features bright rooms with parquet floors. After a day on the slopes, the sauna is the perfect wind down.

Fux
FUSION €€€

(☑29 92; www.fux-mi.net; Omesberg 587, Lech; mains €28-34; 🐾) Asian art gives a decadent touch to Fux, a steakhouse-restaurant hybrid. The food is top notch, whether you go for succulent charcoal-grilled meats or Asian signatures like garlicky Chinese-style halibut with pak choi. The award-winning wine list comprises 2700 bottles.

Hûs Nr. 8
AUSTRIAN €€

(☑33 22-0; Lech 8; mains €8-16; ⊘closed Mon) Raclette and fondue are on the menu at this rustic chalet, with a small patio and playground.

Ambrosius Stüble
AUSTRIAN €€

(☑419 30; Rüfiplatz; mains €7-16) Kick back on the sunny terrace at this traditional tavern near the Rüfikopf lift. The schnitzel and *Kaiserschmarrn* (shredded pancakes) come recommended.

ℹ Information

The central **tourist office** (☑21 61-0; www.lech-zuers.at; Dorf 2, Lech; ⊘8am-6pm Mon-Sat) has bags of info on skiing and walking possibilities, and an accommodation board.

ℹ Getting There & Away

Bus

Buses run between Lech and Zürs (€1.20, seven minutes); both resorts have connections to St Anton am Arlberg. For Bludenz (€5.40, 1½ hours) and beyond, a change in Langen is required.

Car & Motorcycle

One kilometre south of Zürs is the Flexen Pass (1773m), occasionally blocked off by snow in winter, after which the road splits: the western fork leads to Stuben (1407m), the eastern one to St Anton am Arlberg in Tyrol. In summer, Lech can also be approached from the north, via the turning at Warth (1494m).

Understand Austria

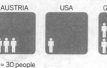

AUSTRIA   USA   GERMANY

👤 = 30 people

Austria Today

A Country of Coalitions

Austria today enjoys the kind of economic, social and political stability many other nations would dream of. Political stability has been achieved through a string of well-balanced coalition governments, especially 'grand' coalitions involving the two major parties, the Sozialdemokratische Partei Österreichs (SPÖ; Social Democrats) and the Österreichische Volkspartei (ÖVP). Since 1945, all but nine of the 26 governments have been formed by these two parties. The situation in most Austrian states is very similar. It's a remarkably robust system in which the chancellor (currently SPÖ leader Werner Faymann, b 1960) changes, but rarely the parties that form the government.

Notwithstanding, the political scene is taking unexpected directions. The SPÖ, which had governed Vienna (a city-state) alone since 1945, lost its absolute majority in late 2010 and was forced to form a coalition with Die Grünen (the Greens party), currently wracked by internal disarray. In the same election, Vienna's right-wing populist Freiheitliche Partei Österreichs (Austrian Freedom Party; FPÖ) under the party's national and Viennese head Heinz-Christian Strache (b 1969) triumphed on an anti-Islam and law-and-order platform.

In 2010 Austria's president, Heinz Fischer, was re-elected as an independent to this mostly ceremonial position, defeating the right-wing populist Barbara Rosenkranz (FPÖ).

Haider Gone – But Strache's Star Rises

As elsewhere in Europe, Austria is seeing a revival of populist, right-wing sentiments around the issues of Islam, criminality among foreigners, and immigration. These issues are nothing new, even if they take new expression under the resurgent FPÖ. One-time doyen of the populist right Jorg

---

» Population: 8.34 million

» GDP: €274.3 billion

» Inflation rate: 1.7%

» Unemployment rate: 4.5%

Etiquette

» Dress up for classical concerts, opera and upmarket restaurants.

» Give your name at the start of phone calls.

» Look people in the eye when saying *Prost* (cheers). Hosts make the first toast.

» Say *Guten Appetit* before you begin eating.

» Generally, use the formal *Sie* form of address.

» Don't say *Danke* while handing over cash to pay bills – this can be understood as 'keep the change'.

They Don't Say

» 'Hey, we're just like Germans!'

» 'Never seen a baroque church.'

» 'No grandiose plans; let's keep it small and unbureaucratic.'

» 'We don't use academic titles.'

» 'I like being at sea level.'

» Was Sisi really *Kaiserin*? Here? In Austria?'

belief systems
(% of population)

74 — Roman Catholic

12 — None

• 5 — Protestant

• 4 — Muslim

• 5 — Other

if Austria were 100 people

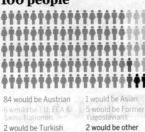

84 would be Austrian
6 would be EU, EEA & Swiss Nationals
2 would be Turkish

1 would be Asian
5 would be Former Yugoslavians
2 would be other

Haider (1950–2008) took a hard line on the foreigner issue as well as the ever-present one of bilingual signposting of towns in border regions such as Carinthia. Haider died in a car accident in 2008 while drunk and speeding. Although Haider himself had long withdrawn into Carinthia's local politics and formed his own breakaway party, the FPÖ has consistently made enormous capital out of anti-Islam, anti-foreigner sentiments, and in 2009 the party caused a furore when it coined the slogan 'Abendland in Christenhand' (The Western World in Christian Hands) for one of its election posters. With almost the same issues hogging headlines in neighbouring Germany and in France and the Netherlands, Austria is no exception but nor is it looking to be different.

Sex, Lies & Missing Money

Although in recent years a couple of high-profile cases involving sexual abuse and deprivation of freedom raised concerns at home and were reported widely abroad, Austrians have tended not to see this as an underlying social problem. Of more concern have been instances of child abuse and other immoral conduct by priests within church institutions.

On matters more worldly, Austrians look critically upon the waste of their taxes and the continuing exorbitant salaries of managers who led them into the most recent financial crisis. Youth violence and corruption were a couple of other issues on the minds of those polled in 2010 by the Linz-based Imas group. Most thought, however, that corruption was worse elsewhere.

Indeed, despite some minor political and social turbulence of late, most Austrians would probably agree that their standard of living – due to social conditions, but also because of the natural landscape – is higher than in most other places.

> 'The [Habsburg] empire is made up of health resorts; it distributes health to the whole world. Its waters are all medicinal. They are bottled and sent throughout the earth; the natives drink beer. This is self-sacrifice, apparently.' Mark Twain

---

» Top MP3s

The Magic Flute Mozart
Pierrot Lunaire Arnold Schönberg
Falco 3 Falco (original LP has full version of 'Rock Me, Amadeus'; there are various mixes too)
Superstardom Naked Lunch
The K&D Sessions Kruder & Dorfmeister

Top Travel Books

A Time of Gifts Patrick Leigh Fermor. First volume of trilogy about an epic walk from the Hook of Holland via Austria to Constantinople in 1933–34.
Vienna: The Image of a Culture in Decline Edward Crankshaw. Travel description and history.

Danube Claudio Magris. Mid-1980s Italian travel journal covering the river's length.
Last Waltz in Vienna: The Destruction of a Family 1842–1942 George Clare. Autobiographical account of a Jewish family's fate.

History

Although Austria's territorial heartland has always been modest in size, its monarchy ruled an empire that spanned continents and was once the last word in politics and high culture. How did it happen and how did it all change over time? To really understand this, it's useful to know more about the civilisations and empires that figure in its colourful past. Civilisations & Empires is therefore where this history starts. Afterwards we take a trail through themes of post-WWII neutrality (Neutral, Nice & Not Guilty), foreign invasion of its territory (The Enemy at the Gate), uprisings (To the Barricades) and Jewry (Jewish History in Austria), and along the way getting to know one of the world's most enduring family dynasties (The Empire of the Habsburgs).

Civilisations & Empires

It would be an understatement to say that alpine regions of Austria were inhospitable places during the ice age 30,000 years ago. They were virtually impenetrable for human and beast. So it's not surprising that while mammoths were lumbering across a frozen landscape, the more accessible plains and Danube Valley in Lower Austria developed into early centres of civilisation. A visit to the Naturhistorisches Museum in Vienna contains two stone Venus statuettes that are reminders of this era.

When the Celts settled in the late Iron Age (around 450 BC) they also chose the valley of the Danube River and the salt-rich regions around Salzburg, encountering Illyrians who had wandered there from the Balkan region. Gradually an Illyric-Celtic kingdom took shape, known as Noricum, that stretched from eastern Tyrol to the Danube and eastern fringes of the Alps in Carinthia.

Discover more about the history of Austria from the Babenbergs through to the country's entry into the EU in *The Austrians: A Thousand Year Odyssey* by Gordon Brook-Shepard.

Romans

The Romans, who crossed the Alps in force in 15 BC and settled south of the Danube River, carved up these regions into administrative areas and

TIMELINE	30,000–25,000 BC	5300 BC	800–400 BC
	The 30,000-year-old Venus of Galgenberg (aka Dancing Fanny) and the 25,000-year-old buxom beauty the Venus of Willendorf are crafted – both are now in Vienna's Naturhistorisches Museum.	The Neolithic 'Ötzi' dies and is mummified in a glacier in the Ötztal. He's found in 1991; several Austrian and Italian women ask to be impregnated with his frozen sperm.	The Iron Age *Hallstadtkultur* (Hallstadt culture) develops in southern Salzkammergut, where settlers work salt mines. Around 450 BC Celts arrive in the region and build on this flourishing culture.

built *Limes* (fortresses) and towns such as Carnuntum, Vindobona (the forerunner of Vienna), Brigantium (Bregenz), Juvavum (Salzburg), Flavia Solva (Leibnitz in Styria), Aguntum and Virunum (north of Klagenfurt). However, the Western Empire created by the Romans collapsed in the 5th century, leaving a vacuum that was filled by newly arriving tribes: the Germanic Alemanni in Vorarlberg, Slavs who pushed into Carinthia and Styria, and Bavarians who settled south of the Danube in Upper and Lower Austria, Tyrol and around Salzburg. The Bavarians proved to be the most successful, and by the 7th century they had most regions of Austria in their grip, creating a large German-speaking territory.

'The Viennese are neither more abstinent nor more nervous than anyone else in big cities.' Sigmund Freud

The Carolingian Empire

But at this time it was still possible to talk only about tribes, not fully fledged empires. This changed in Europe and in Austria itself with the growth of the so-called Carolingian Empire in the 6th century. This was Europe's most powerful empire in its day. It originated in western France and Belgium, grew into a heavyweight under Charlemagne (747–814) and took its inspiration from the Romans. Significantly for future Austria, Charlemagne created a buffer region in the Danube Valley, later dubbed Ostmark (Eastern March), which shored up the eastern edge of his empire, and in 800 he was crowned Kaiser (see the boxed text, p359) by the pope.

The Babenburg Dynasty

Fate took another decisive turn in 976, when the Eastern March landed in the hands of Leopold von Babenberg (940–94), a descendent of a noble Bavarian family. The Babenbergs were a skilful clan who in the 11th century expanded their small territory to include most of modern-day Lower Austria (with Vienna), and a century later Styria (1192) and much of Upper Austria. In 1156, under the Babenberg monarch Heinrich II 'Jasmirogott', the Eastern March (still a political fence at that time) was elevated to a duchy (ie with its own duke and special rights) and Vienna became its capital.

The patron saint of Austria is Saint Leopold III of Babenberg (1096–1135).

The Empire of the Habsburgs

The Babenberg dynasty ran out of heirs in 1246 when one of its rulers, Duke Friedrich II, died in battle with neighbouring Hungarians over a border dispute. This had enormous ramifications for future Austria because it led to the catapulting of another noble family, the Habsburgs, to power in Europe. In a twist of bad fortune, a Bohemian monarch of the day, Ottokar II, married Friedrich's widow and in 1273 refused to recognise the election as king another noble whose star was rising in Central Europe – the Habsburg Rudolf I (1218–91).

The distended lower jaw and lip, a family trait of the early Habsburgs, is discreetly downplayed in official portraits.

15 BC–AD 600	**795**	**976 & 996**	**1156**
Romans establish relations with Celts and Nordic tribes. Roman occupation begins in the provinces of Rhaetia, Noricum and Pannonia. Slavic, Germanic and other tribes later overrun the territories.	Charlemagne creates a buffer region in the Danube Valley, later dubbed Ostmark (Eastern March) by the Nazis; this shores up the eastern edge of his empire.	The Babenbergs are entrusted with the Eastern March in 976 and administer it as margraves; in 996 this appears for the first time in a document as Ostarrîchi.	As consolation for relinquishing Bavaria, Austria becomes a duchy (Privilegium Minus) and the Babenberg ruler Heinrich Jasomirgott (1107–77) becomes Austria's first duke, residing in Vienna.

HABSBURGS

This caused one of the most celebrated clashes in Austrian history when in 1278 the House of Habsburg and Bohemian arch rival Ottokar II (who also controlled Styria and Carinthia) fought it out on the March-feld, situated 30km northeast of Vienna. Ottokar, held up while trying to penetrate Drosendorf's fortress en route to the battle, was killed, allowing the Habsburg family to reign over the Holy Roman Empire.

That was pretty much the way things remained for over 500 years. It's only a modest simplification to say that between the era in which mammoths roamed the frozen wastes and the next important change – the arrival of 164cm, low-rise Napoleon in the early 19th century – Austria had seen early human settlers (the ones who carved those Venus statuettes), two major civilisations (Illyrians and the Celts), one Roman Empire and two families (the Babenbergs and the Habsburgs) control the land.

The French Revolution of 1789–99 was a political explosion that ushered in a new age of republicanism in Europe, and it challenged surviving feudalistic establishments like the Holy Roman Empire. Thus, although Napoleon was soundly defeated in Leipzig in 1813 and, finally, at Waterloo in 1815, his advance across Europe caused its collapse. The Habsburgs survived, however, and in the post-Napoleon Vormärz (Pre-March) years, they dominated a loose Deutscher Bund (German Alliance) comprising hundreds of small 'states' cobbled together in a period of modest cultural flourish and reactionary politics called the Biedermeier period.

Given that ordinary citizens at the time were kept on a short leash by their political masters, it's not surprising that they began to seek new freedoms. In 1848, inspired by the February 1848 revolution in France, Austrians demanded their own parliament (p363). One was created and met (without Hungary, a Habsburg possession at the time, and without parts of Italy that had been in Habsburg hands) in July that year. But revolution and a democratic parliament failed to endure in Austria.

In 1867 a dual monarchy was created in Austria and Hungary, arising out of an attempt by the Habsburgs to hold onto support for the monarchy among Hungarians by giving them a large degree of autonomy. This Austro-Hungarian Empire would grow to include core regions of Austria, Hungary, the Czech Republic, Slovakia, Slovenia, Croatia and Bosnia-Herzegovina, as well as regions like the Voivodina in Serbia, and small chunks in northern Italy, Romania, Poland and the Ukraine.

This was the so-called 'KuK' (König und Kaiser; King and Kaiser) monarchy – the Kaiser of Austria was also king of Hungary. In practice, the two countries increasingly went separate ways, united only by the dual monarch and a couple of high-level ministries like 'war' and 'foreign affairs'. This so-called 'Danube Monarchy' was the last stage of development in the Habsburg Empire before it collapsed completely in 1918.

Really mad or really handsome? The Habsburg Johanna the Mad kissed the feet of husband Philip the Handsome when his coffin was opened five weeks after his death in 1506.

1192	1246–78	1335 & 1363	1496
Styria is given to Babenberg Leopold V (1157–94) on the condition that it stays part of Austria forever. Styria then includes chunks of Slovenia and Lower and Upper Austria.	Last Babenberg dies in 1246. Habsburg Rudolf I is elected king of the Holy Roman Empire in 1273; he defeats Bohemian Ottokar II in the 1278 Battle of Marchfeld.	Bavarian Ludwig IV (1314–47) gives Carinthia to the Habsburgs in 1335; territories include Austria (Ostarrîchi), Styria and Carinthia. In 1363 Margarethe Maultasch (1318–63) dies and Tyrol is added.	Maximilian's son Philipp der Schöne (Philip the Handsome) marries Juana la Loca (Johanna the Mad) in the 'Spanish Marriage': Spain and its resource-rich Central and South American territories became Habsburg.

Marriage, not Muscle

Marriage, not muscle, was the historic key to Habsburg land grabbing. The Hungarian king Matthias Corvinus (1443–90) once adapted lines from Ovid when he wrote: 'Let others wage war but you, lucky Austria, marry! For the empires given to others by Mars are given to you by Venus.'

The age of the convenient wedding began in earnest with Maximilian I (1459–1519), whose moniker was The Last Knight because of his late predilection for medieval tournaments. His other loves were Renaissance art, his own grave (which he commissioned during his lifetime) and Albrecht Dürer (1471–1528), whom he commissioned to work on the very same grave before he stepped into it. It is now in Innsbruck's Hofkirche.

But it was Maximilian's affection for Maria of Burgundy (1457–82) that had the greatest influence on the fortunes of the Habsburgs. The two married, and when Maria fell from a horse and died as a result of a miscarriage in 1482, Burgundy, Lorraine and the Low Countries fell into Habsburg hands. In their day, these regions were the last word in culture, economic high kicking and the arts. The downside was a sticky relationship with France that stuck to the Habsburg shoe for centuries.

Carl E Schorske magically interlinks seven essays on the intellectual history of Vienna in his seminal work *Fin-de-Siècle Vienna*.

AUSTRIA & THE HOLY ROMAN EMPIRE

The Holy Roman Empire was Europe's oddest 'state'. Its foundations were laid when Charlemagne's father, Pippin, rescued a beleaguered pope and became Patricius Romanorum (Protector of Rome), making him Caesar's successor. The title 'Kaiser' is derived from 'Caesar'. Pippin, with Italian spoils on his hands (one being the present-day Vatican), gave these to the pope. Charlemagne continued this tradition as protector, and in 962, with the crowning of Otto I (912–73) as Holy Roman Emperor, the empire was officially born.

Kings in the empire were elected in political horse-trading by a handful of prince electors, but for a king to take the next step and become *Kaiser* (and protector of the pope), he had to be crowned by the pope. Depending on how feisty the pope happened to be, this brought other troubles. In 1338 enough was enough and the electors threw the pope overboard, deciding they could elect their own *Kaiser*.

In 972, just before Otto I died, borders of the empire included present-day Austria, Slovenia, Czech Republic, Germany, Holland, Belgium and much of the Italian peninsula. These borders ebbed and flowed with the times. When Rudolf I arrived in 1273, all – or what remained of it – belonged to the Habsburgs.

The empire was formally buried in 1806 when Napoleon Bonaparte tore through Europe, and by the time the Austro-Hungarian Empire (a dual monarchy of Austria and Hungary) took shape in 1867, it was little more than a dim and distant reminder of medieval times.

1517

Theology professor Martin Luther sparks the Reformation when he makes public his 95 Theses that call into question corrupt practices of the church, and most of Austria becomes Lutheran (Protestant).

1529

The first Turkish siege of Vienna takes place, undertaken by Süleyman the Magnificent, but Süleyman's forces are not strong enough to take control of the city.

RICHARD NEBESKY

» Naturhistorisches Museum, Vienna (p69)

The 'Spanish Marriage' in 1496 was another clever piece of royal bedding. When Maximilian's son Philipp der Schöne (Philip the Handsome) married Juana la Loca (Johanna the Mad; 1479–55), Spain and its resource-rich overseas territories in Central and South America became Habsburg. When their son, Ferdinand I (1503–64) married Anna of Hungary and Bohemia (1503–47), fulfilling a deal his grandfather Maximilian I had negotiated with King Vladislav II (1456–1516), Bohemia was also in the Habsburg fold. In the same deal, Maria von Habsburg (1505–58) married into this Polish-Lithuanian Jagiellonen dynasty, which traditionally purveyed kings to Poland, Bohemia and Hungary at that time. By 1526, when her husband Ludwig II (1506–26) drowned in a tributary of the Danube during the Battle of Mohács against Turks, Silesia (in Poland), Bohemia (in the Czech Republic) and Hungary were all thoroughly Habsburg.

Under Karl V (1500–58), the era of the universal monarch arrived, and the Habsburgs had added the Kingdom of Naples (southern Italy, including Sicily). That, unfortunately, was about as good as it got.

The rot set in with the Treaty of Augsburg (1555), which regulated religious bickering surrounding the Reformation. This treaty stipulated that each ruler could decide the religion of his or her own region. Not only does this explain the patchwork of Protestant and Catholic religions today in many regions that used to be part of the Holy Roman Empire, but it also made a mess of the Habsburgs because Karl V had dedicated his life to creating his so-called 'universal Catholic monarchy'. Seeing the writing clearly on the wall, he abdicated in 1556 and withdrew to a monastery in Spain to lick his wounds and die.

The spoils were divided up among Habsburgs. The brother of Karl V – Ferdinand I (the same one who had married Anna of Hungary and Bohemia) – inherited Austria and (yes, you guessed it) Hungary and Bohemia, and Karl V's only legitimate son, Philip II (1527–98) got Spain, Naples and Sicily, the Low Countries, and the overseas colonies.

Maria Theresia

If Maximilian I was the Last Knight, Maria Theresia (1717–80) was the mother of the nation. Thrust into the limelight when her father died with no male heirs, she held on to power for 40 years, while also managing to give birth to 16 children – among them Marie Antoinette, future wife of Louis XVI. Maria Theresia's fourth child, Joseph II, weighed a daunting 7kg at birth.

Although Maria Theresia undertook many enlightened reforms, she was remarkably prudish for a family that had married and copulated its way to power. One of her less popular measures was the introduction of the short-lived Commission against Immoral Conduct in 1752, which

PRINCE EUGENE

Austria's greatest military hero, Prince Eugene of Savoy, was in fact French. Refused entry to the French army by Louis XIV, Eugene went on to humiliate him on the battlefield.

1556	1618–48	1670	1683
Abandoning the idea of uniting an empire under Catholicism, Karl V abdicates – the Spanish part goes to his son Philip II, and Ferdinand I gets Austria, Bohemia and largely Turkish-occupied Hungary.	Anti-reformer Ferdinand II challenges Bohemia's confessional freedom. Habsburg counsels are thrown out of a window (the Prague Defenestration), triggering the Thirty Years' War.	Leopold I drives the Jews out of Unterer Werd in Vienna and the quarter is renamed Leopoldstadt, the name it bears today.	Turkish siege of Vienna. Christian Europe is mobilised and the threat persists until 1718, after which the Ottoman Empire gradually wanes.

raided private homes, trying to catch men entertaining loose women – the commission even tried to snare Casanova during his visit to Vienna.

Maria Theresia's low take on fornication was no doubt coloured by the conduct of her husband, Francis I, who was apparently very adept in just that field. Yet despite her husband's philandering, Maria Theresia felt she should remain loyal to her spouse, and when he died suddenly in 1765 she stayed in mourning for the rest of her life. She retreated to Schloss Schönbrunn in Vienna, left the running of the state in the hands of Joseph II (of 7kg fame), and adopted a low profile and chaste existence.

Although the last Habsburg ruler abdicated in 1918, the family is still going strong in public life.

The Modern Republics

The turmoil caused by defeat in WWI brought the monarchy to an end, laying the foundations for modern Austria. Austrians demanded a fully fledged republic, and they got one, ending 640 years of Habsburg rule.

This First Republic was the country's first experiment with truly democratic institutions, but the stigma of WWI defeat weakened it. Austria, now reduced almost to the size of the country we know today, lost access to resources beyond its own borders, which caused economic problems. Polarisation was another hurdle. This had a geographic edge in Austria: 'Rotes Wien' (Red Vienna) was controlled by a socialist city government, while rural regions were firmly in the grip of the conservative federal government of the Christian Socials. Chaos broke out in March 1933 when the Christian Socials chancellor Engelbert Dollfuss (1892–1934) dissolved parliament and, in what was virtually a putsch, prevented it from sitting.

Dollfuss' sympathies lay with the Italian dictator Benito Mussolini (1883–1945) and the Catholic Church. He banned the communist party and the pro-German Austrian Nazi Party (this favoured annexation of Austria by Germany), and when he took up the battle with the Social Democrats, he sparked the Austrian Civil War in 1934.

By 1936, however, Hitler and Mussolini had created a Rome-Berlin axis and Austria found itself between a rock and a hard place. In March 1938, Hitler's troops invaded Austria, and Hitler, an Austrian himself, ruled the country as an appendage of Germany until 1945.

Soviet, not Allied, troops liberated Vienna in March 1945, triggering a twilight period in which the Soviet Union, Britain, the USA and France occupied Austria and carved up the capital into zones – the famous 'four men in a jeep' period. It was the beginning of the Second Republic – today's Republic of Austria.

Historic Palaces

» Schloss Schönbrunn, Vienna

» Schloss Belvedere, Vienna

» Schloss Eggenberg, Graz

» Festung Hohensalzburg, Salzburg

1740–48	1752	1764	1789–99
Maria Theresia (1717–80) inherits Habsburg possessions, Prussia seizes Silesia (in Poland today) and the Austrian War of Succession starts a power struggle between Prussia and a Habsburg-controlled Austria-Hungary.	Maria Theresia introduces the short-lived Commission against Immoral Conduct, which pillages homes and attempts to snatch men entertaining loose women.	Reformer Kaiser Joseph II (1741–90) takes the throne and the Age of Enlightenment that began under Maria Theresia is in full swing. The power of the church is curbed.	French Revolution takes place, bringing a new age of republicanism to Europe and challenging feudalistic establishments such as the Holy Roman Empire.

Neutral, Nice & Not Guilty

In 1948 the British author Graham Greene flew to Vienna and roamed the bomb-damaged streets looking for inspiration for a film he had been commissioned to write about the occupation of post-WWII Vienna. As chance would have it, Greene penned the script for one of Europe's finest films about the era – *The Third Man,* starring Orson Wells as the penicillin racketeer Harry Lime. In a moment of improvisation at the end of the film, Orson Wells as Lime waxes lyrical about how under the bloody reign of the Borgias Italy produced some of its finest art. 'In Switzerland they had brotherly love, 500 years of democracy and peace, and what did they produce? The cuckoo clock.'

Postwar Austria sought the kind of Swiss stability that makes a cuckoo clock fascinating. One day in April 1945, at the instigation of the Soviet Union, the country was proclaimed a republic for the second time in its history. The constitution from 1920 was revived (in its 1929 form), and pre-Nazi laws from March 1933 came back into force; free elections were held in November 1945.

The Soviet Union insisted that Austria declare its neutrality as a condition for ending Soviet occupation in 1955. At the last minute, though, recognition of Austria's guilt for WWII was struck out of the state treaty that paved the way for neutral independence. Its neutrality differs from the Swiss 'cuckoo clock' model, however, because Austria joined the UN and has even participated in international peace-keeping forces. The Second Republic became a mostly quiet, peaceful period during which the economy enjoyed solid growth or boom conditions, Austria played a moderating role during the East–West frost, and the world forgot about the past.

Women in Austria gained the right to vote in national elections in 1919.

WHATEVER HAPPENED TO THE HABSBURGS?

They're still around. Otto von Habsburg (b 1912) is the current family head, but he renounced his claims to the Habsburg lands in 1961, a step that allowed him to re-enter Austria and launch a career in European politics.

Once asked why his name never surfaced in the tabloids, the 90-plus-year-old 'monarch' replied: 'I've not once attended a ball. I prefer to sleep at night. And if you don't go to nightclubs, you don't run into the gossip columnists.' He's something of a sporting man, too: when quizzed about who he thought would win an Austria–Hungary football match, Otto reportedly replied, 'Who are we playing?'

Most poignant is perhaps a comment by German President Paul von Hindenburg to Otto von Habsburg in 1933 (the year Hitler seized power in Germany): 'You know, your majesty, there's only one person with hostile feelings towards the Habsburgs, but he's an Austrian.'

1793

Following a marriage to French king Louis XVI (1754–93), Maria Theresia's 15th child, Marie-Antoinette – who the French call 'L'Autrichienne' (the Austrian) – is beheaded during the French Revolution.

1804–05

Napoleon (1769–1821) occupies Vienna in 1805. The Holy Roman Empire is abolished; Franz II reinvents himself as Austrian Kaiser Franz I. In 1809 the Frenchman returns to re-take Vienna.

» The Hofkirche, Innsbruck (p297)

This silence was shattered in 1986, however, and not surprisingly it was the guilt question again. When accusations surfaced that presidential candidate Kurt Waldheim had been involved in Nazi war crimes, Austria seriously confronted its Nazi past for the first time. Evidence that he had committed these crimes while a lieutenant serving with the German army in the Balkans could never be proved, but nor was Austria's elected president willing to fully explain himself or express misgivings about his wartime role.

The Enemy at the Gate

The Celts, the Romans and various tribes have all swept across borders at one time or another to lay claim to Austrian lands. In fact, Austria itself was originally founded as a border *March* to keep out tribes (see p357). The Turkish sieges, though, are the ones that really got the European imagination firing.

The Ottoman Empire viewed Vienna as 'the city of the golden apple', but it wasn't *Apfelstrüdel* they were after in their great sieges. The first, in 1529, was undertaken by Süleyman the Magnificent, but the 18-day endeavour was not sufficient to break the resolve of the city. The Turkish sultan subsequently died at the siege of Szigetvár, yet his death was kept secret for several days in an attempt to preserve the morale of his army. The subterfuge worked for a while. Messengers were led into the presence of the embalmed body, which was placed in a seated position on the throne. They then unwittingly relayed their news to the corpse.

At the head of the Turkish siege of 1683 was the general and grand vizier Kara Mustapha. Amid the 25,000 tents of the Ottoman army that surrounded Vienna he installed his 1500 concubines, guarded by 700 black eunuchs. Their luxurious quarters contained gushing fountains and regal baths, all set up in haste but with great effect.

Again, it was all to no avail, even though Vienna was only lightly defended by 10,000 men. Mustapha's overconfidence was his downfall; failing to put garrisons on Kahlenberg, he and his army were surprised by a swift attack. Mustapha was pursued from the battlefield and defeated once again, at Gran. At Belgrade he was met by the emissary of Sultan Mehmed IV. The price of failure was death, and Mustapha meekly accepted his fate. When the Austrian imperial army conquered Belgrade in 1718 the grand vizier's head was dug up and brought back to Vienna in triumph.

To the Barricades

While empires waxed and waned, Austria was wracked by revolt and resistance. Apart from frequent squabbles between sycophantic monarchs, the first large-scale uprising took place in the mid- and late-15th

> The roots of Austria's Österreich-ische Volkspartei (ÖVP; Austrian People's Party) go back to 1887; a forerunner of the Sozialdemokratische Partei Österreichs (SPÖ; Social Democratic Party of Austria) was founded a year later.

POLITICS

1809	1813 & 1815	1848	1866
In the midst of the Napoleonic occupation, Tyrol – which had fallen under Bavarian control – is the scene of another rebellion when innkeeper Andreas Hofer leads a bid for independence.	Napoleon is defeated in Leipzig in 1813 and, in his final battle, at Waterloo in 1815.	Revolution topples Chancellor Klemens von Metternich, who flees disguised as a washerwoman. Franz Joseph I abolishes many reforms. Austria's first parliament is formed.	Austria and its allied principalities in Germany fight the Austro-Prussian War (1866), which leads to victory for Prussia and creates the groundwork for a unified Germany that excludes Austria.

century, when peasants in Austria (as elsewhere in Central Europe) rose up against their nobility in the Peasants' Wars. These upheavals were spontaneous and directed at local despots, however, rather than against the empire itself. The roots of discontent could be found in a need for cash to finance defences against the Turks, or in some instances demands by an oppressive monarch during the drawn-out anti-reformation.

In April 1809, during the Napoleonic occupation, Tyrol – which had fallen into the hands of Bavaria – was the scene of another rebellion when innkeeper Andreas Hofer (1767–1810) led a rebellion for independence. For his troubles, Hofer was put on trial and executed at Napoleon's behest. His body is entombed in Innsbruck's Hofkirche.

The next show of strength from the people was the revolution of 1848. Austrians suffered badly during the system of atrophy under Klemens von Metternich, a diplomat who rose to power in the splash caused by Napoleon's fall. Metternich believed in the power of absolute monarchy and his police snapped ferociously at the heels of liberals and Austrian nationalists in the decades before revolution. This Vormärz era (also called 'Biedermeier') was culturally rich, but socially the air was heavy with political resignation and Austrians grew insular. This was about to change, not least because atrocious industrial conditions were making the country ripe for transformation. Nationalism – the best chance of liberalising societies in those days – was also threatening to chip the delicate edges of the Habsburg empire.

The sparks of the 1848 February revolution in Paris flared in Vienna in March, but, reflecting the city-country divide, failed to really ignite Austria elsewhere except in Styria. In one ironic twist, a similar revolution in Germany meant some Austrian revolutionaries supported being part of a greater, unified and liberal Germany. This was the tricky *Grossdeutsch-Kleindeutsch* (Greater Germany–Lesser Germany) question, and reflects the difficult affinity between Austrians and Germans.

The rebels demanded a parliament, and briefly they got one in May 1848. Kaiser Ferdinand I packed his bags and his family and fled to Innsbruck. This should have been the end of the Habsburgs. It wasn't. Parliament passed a bill improving the lot of the peasants, and Ferdinand cleverly sanctioned this, overnight winning the support of rural folk in the regions. Meanwhile, the Habsburgs received a popular boost when General Radetzky (1766–1858) won back Lombardy (Italy) in successful military campaigns.

In October 1848 the revolution reached fever pitch in Vienna. Although this uprising was ultimately quashed, the Habsburgs decided to dispense with Ferdinand I, replacing him with his nephew Franz Joseph I, who introduced his own monarchical constitution and dissolved the parliament in early 1849. It would only be revived properly in 1867.

Vienna's population peaked at more than two million between 1910 and 1914. After WWI, Vienna was one of the world's five largest cities.

The report of the Historical Commission's inquiry into Austria during the Nazi era can be found at www.historikerkommission.gv.at.

1867	1878	1908	1914
Weakened by loss against Prussia, Austria is now forced by Hungary to create a dual Austro-Hungarian monarchy (the Ausgleich) in 1867. Austria establishes a democratic parliament.	To prevent the Russians increasing their influence in the Balkans after they win the Russo-Turkish War of 1877–78, Austria-Hungary occupies Bosnia and Herzegovina.	Fatefully, Austria-Hungary is given a mandate to occupy and administer Bosnia and Herzegovina, with the expectation that it would later be annexed completely.	Austrian archduke Franz Ferdinand is assassinated in Sarajevo by a Serbian nationalist, triggering WWI, which sees Austria-Hungary in alliance with Germany and the Ottoman Empire.

By September 1849 it was time to weigh up the damage, count the dead and, most importantly, look at what had been won. Austria was not a democracy, because the *Kaiser* could veto the Reichstag's legislation. But revolution had swept away the last vestiges of feudalism and made state citizens out of royal subjects.

The Nazi Era

By 1927, these citizens inhabited a very different world. WWI had ended in defeat and armed paramilitary groups roamed the streets of Vienna and elsewhere engaging in bloody clashes. A July revolt broke out in 1927 when left-wing groups stormed the Justizpalast (Palace of Justice) in Vienna. This was prompted by a court's having acquitted members of a right-wing paramilitary Frontkämpfer (Front Fighters) group charged with killing two people during demonstrations. The police moved in and regained control of the building, but about 90 people died in the revolt and over 1000 were injured.

In the late 1920s and the 1930s, the stakes were raised even higher and, with the annexation of Austria by Hitler in 1938, opposition turned to resistance. As elsewhere, whenever Hitler's troops jackbooted over a border, resistance from within was extremely difficult. Communists and Social Democrats were outlawed in the early 1930s and fought from underground. Members of the Social Democratic Workers Party fought a four-day battle with police in Linz and Vienna before being banned and having their leaders arrested.

The role of Austria during WWII is one of the most controversial aspects of its modern history. Austria's home-grown brand of fascism had favoured independence, but Hitler was popular inside Austria, and Austria itself supplied a disproportionately large number of officers for the SS and the German army. In short, what Hitler and the Nazis couldn't achieve through pressure, large numbers of Austrians themselves helped achieve through their active and passive support for Nazism and Hitler's war.

Interestingly, Tyrolean resistance leaders often rallied opposition to Nazism by recalling the revolt of innkeeper Andreas Hofer in 1809 (see p363). An *Österreichisches Freiheitsbataillon* (Austrian Freedom Battalion) fought alongside the Yugoslav People's Liberation Army, and partisan groups in Styria and Carinthia maintained links with other partisans across the Yugoslavian border. Tellingly, unlike other countries, Austria had no government in exile.

Resistance increased once the war looked lost for Hitler. The Austrian Robert Bernardis (1908–44) was involved in the assassination attempt on Hitler by military brass on 20 July 1944 and was then executed by the Nazis. Another involved in that plot, Carl Szokoll (1915–2004), survived undetected. The most famous resistance group, however, was called 05,

Hella Pick's *Guilty Victim: Austria from the Holocaust to Haider* is an excellent analysis of modern-day Austria.

Take a virtual tour through Jewish history in Austria from the Middle Ages to the present in the Jewish Virtual Library at www.jewishvirtuallibrary.org/jsource/vjw/Austria.html.

1918	1920s	1934	1938
WWI ends and Karl I abdicates after the humiliating defeat; the First Republic is proclaimed in Vienna. The Habsburg empire is shaved of border nationalities; Austria keeps most German-speaking regions.	The Social Democratic Party of Austria controls 'Red Vienna', its heart set on Austro-Marxism, while the provinces are controlled by conservative forces.	Austrian politics is polarised, paralysed by paramilitary groups. In 1934 parliament is gridlocked and Austria collapses into civil war – hundreds die in three-day fighting culminating in Social Democrat defeat.	Nazi troops march into Vienna; Hitler visits his beloved Linz, and Vienna to address 200,000 ecstatic Viennese on Heldenplatz. After a rigged referendum, Austria becomes part of Hitler's *Reich*.

whose members included Austria's president from 1957 to 1965, Adolf Schärf (1890–1965).

With the Red Army approaching Vienna in 1945, 05 worked closely with Szokoll and other military figures in Operation Radetzky to liberate Vienna in the last days of the war. Although they were able to establish contact with the Red Army as it rolled towards the city, they were betrayed at the last moment and several members were strung up from street lanterns. The Red Army, not Austrians, would liberate the capital.

Jewish History in Austria

When the Nazis stomped into Vienna in March 1938, ordinary Austrians threw bouquets of flowers and cheered. A few days later, Hitler addressed tens of thousands of cheering Austrians on Vienna's Heldenplatz to declare the integration of his 'homeland' into the Third Reich. For those Jews who had not yet managed to flee the country, this must have been a depressing moment. Vienna's 'father' of modern psychoanalysis, Sigmund Freud (1856–1939), had not wanted to read the signs for a long time, but in June that year he fled to England. The 20th century's most innovative classical composer, Arnold Schönberg (1874–1951), had already been booted out of his job as a lecturer in Berlin in 1933 and fled to the US. They were just two of many prominent Austrian Jews forced into exile.

Others were not as fortunate. The Holocaust (or *Schoa*), Hitler's attempt to wipe out European Jewry, was a brutal and systematic act that saw some 65,000 Austrian Jews perish in concentration camps throughout Europe. It ruptured a Jewish history in Austria dating back to the early Middle Ages, and even today it's not really possible to talk about a 'recovery' of Jewish culture in the country.

The first mention of Jews in Vienna was in 1194, when a minter by the name of Schlom was appointed by the crown. The very same man was subsequently murdered along with 16 other Viennese Jews by zealous crusaders on their way to the Holy Land. Gradually, a ghetto grew around today's Judenplatz in Vienna, where a large synagogue stood in the 13th century.

Historically, Jews could only work in some professions. They were seldom allowed into tradesmen's guilds or to engage in agriculture, and therefore earned a living through trading goods and selling, or through money lending, which explains many of the clichés of the past and present. Two 'libels' in the Middle Ages made life difficult for Jews. One of these was the 'host desecration libel', which accused Jews of desecrating Christ by acts such as sticking pins into communion wafers and making them weep or bleed. The second was the 'blood libel', which accused Jews of drinking the blood of Christians during rituals. In 1420 these libels culminated in one of Vienna's worst pogroms, during which many Jews

1939–45	1948	1955	1955–66
War and genocide in Austria. Over 100,000 of Vienna's 180,000 Jews escape, but 65,000 die. In 1945 the Red Army liberates Vienna. Austria and Vienna are divided among the powers.	Graham Greene flies to Vienna for inspiration for a film which becomes *The Third Man*, starring Orson Wells and featuring an iconic scene on the city's Riesenrad (Ferris wheel).	Austrian *Staatsvertrag* (state treaty) is ratified. Austria declares sovereignty and neutral status, ending a decade of occupation. Post-WWII international bodies come to Vienna; the UN later sets up offices here.	'Grand coalitions' of major parties govern Austria based on a system of *Proporz* (proportion), whereby ministerial posts are divided among the major parties. This becomes a hallmark of Austrian politics.

committed collective suicide. The synagogue on Vienna's Judenplatz was destroyed and the stones of the synagogue were used for the building of the old university.

Out of the Darkness

Jews were officially banned from settling in Vienna until 1624, but this law was regularly relaxed. It did mean, however, that Vienna's Jews had a particularly rough time of it, and in 1670 when Leopold I (1640–1705) drove them out of Unterer Werd, the quarter was re-christened Leopoldstadt, the name it bears today. They returned, however, and this district remained Vienna's largest Jewish quarter until WWII.

When money was tight following the 1683 Turkish siege, Jews were encouraged to settle in town as money lenders. Interestingly, once the threat subsided from 1718, Sephardic Jews from Spain arrived and were allowed to establish their own religious community. An edict from Kaiser Joseph II (1741–90) improved conditions for Jews, and after Kaiser Franz I reinvented himself as Austria's Kaiser and allowed Jews to establish schools, some of Vienna's Jewry rose into bourgeois and literary circles.

The revolution of 1848 (see p363) brought the biggest changes, however. Vienna's Jews were at the forefront of the uprising, and it brought them freedom of religion, press and schooling. Indirectly, it also led to the founding of the *Israelitische Kultusgemeinde* (Jewish Religious Community), more than a century after the Sephardic Jews had founded their own. Today this is the main body that represents religious Jews in Austria.

Legally unfettered, Vienna's Jews nevertheless found themselves walking a high tightrope. They owed much to the Habsburg monarchy and many therefore identified with it. Many also cherished the freedoms of revolution. And all inhabited an 'Austrian-German' cultural landscape. Somewhere in there, they also lived out their strong Jewish identity.

In 1878 Jewry in Austria was shaken up again by the arrival from Budapest of Theodor Herzl (1860–1904), who founded political Zionism, a concept that brought together the ideas of the workers movement with support for a Jewish state. His book *Der Judenstaat* (The Jewish State; 1896) would later be crucial to the creation of Israel.

Beginning with Adolf Fischhof (1816–93), whose political speech on press freedom in 1848 helped trigger revolution, and continuing with Herzl and with the founding father of Austrian social democracy, Viktor Adler (1852–1918), Jews drove reforms in Austria and played a key role during the Rotes Wien (see p361) period of the 1920s and early 1930s.

This, of course, poured oil on the fires of Hitler's ideology. When Hitler's troops reached Vienna in 1938, Jews were subjected to attack and abuse. The tragedy was that the Jewish community had contributed so

1986	**1995**
Presidential candidate Kurt Waldheim (1918–2007) is accused of war crimes. Waldheim wins a tough election but is stained. Historians Commission finds Waldheim unhelpful but no proof of crimes.	Austria joins the EU in 1995, but because of guarantees in 1955 to Moscow to remain neutral it forgoes NATO membership.

JONATHAN SMITH

» The Hofburg, Vienna (p59)

When Governor Schwarzenegger allowed an execution to go ahead in California in 2005, some Austrians wanted to revoke his Austrian citizenship. Austria first abolished capital punishment in 1787.

much to Viennese cultural and political life, and now many of Vienna's non-Jewish citizens simply looked the other way.

The events that followed, culminating in the Holocaust, are etched in the collective memory of Jews everywhere: the prohibitive Nuremberg Laws, the forced sale and theft of Jewish property, *die Kristallnacht* ('The Night of Broken Glass') on 9 and 10 November 1939 when synagogues and Jewish businesses were burnt and Jews were attacked openly on the streets.

Because of this, today the Jewish community is only a fraction of its former size. About 7000 religiously affiliated Jews live in Austria, and there are about another 3000 to 5000 who are not affiliated with a community. The number was boosted by the arrival of Jews from the former Soviet Union in the 1990s. For a fascinating glimpse of Jewish life from the 13th century to today, don't miss the Jewish Museum and the Museum Judenplatz, both in Vienna.

1999	2007	2008	2010
Austria introduces the euro and abolishes the Austrian shilling as its currency, having easily satisfied the criteria for the level of debt and the inflation rate.	A grand coalition government of Social Democrats and the Austrian People's Party is formed under Alfred Gusenbauer.	Austria co-hosts football's European Cup with Switzerland.	SPÖ preferred presidential candidate Heinz Fischer is re-elected with an overwhelming majority as an independent; populist right-wing candidate Barbara Rosenkranz is resoundingly defeated.

Architecture

Thanks to the Habsburg monarchy and its obsession with creating grand works, Austria is packed with high-calibre architecture. The earliest 'architectural' signs are ancient grave mounds from the Iron Age Hallstatt culture outside Grossklein (p187), and the marginally more recent Roman ruins of Vienna and Carnuntum (p128). In later centuries and millennia, Romanesque, Gothic, Renaissance and especially baroque buildings rose up all over Austria.

Baroque – Elegantly Feral

According to one 19th-century Swiss art historian, Jacob Burckhardt, the baroque period and the Renaissance period that preceded it speak roughly the same language. The difference, however, is that the baroque speaks a dialect that has gone feral. The height of the baroque era of building was in the late 17th and early 18th century in Austria. It only moved into full swing once the Ottoman Turks had been beaten back from the gates of Vienna during the Turkish siege of 1683. It took the graceful columns and symmetry of the Renaissance and added elements of the grotesque, the burlesque and the saccharine.

A good example of this 'feral dialect' spoken by baroque architecture is the Karlskirche (Church of St Charles; p78) in Vienna. Here you find towering, decorative columns rising up on Karlsplatz and a stunning cupola painted with frescoes. The church was instigated by the Habsburg Charles VI following the plague of 1713, and it was dedicated to St Charles Borromeo, who succoured the victims of plague in Italy. It is arguably the most beautiful of the baroque masterpieces.

The architect who shaped the Karlskirche was Johann Bernhard Fischer von Erlach (1656–1723). Fischer von Erlach was Austria's first, and possibly the country's greatest, architect of the baroque era. He was born in Graz, the capital of Styria, and began working as a sculptor in his father's workshop before travelling to Rome in 1670 and spending well over a decade studying baroque styles in Italy. He returned to Austria in 1686 and in 1693 completed one of his earliest works in the capital, the magnificent Pestsäule (p82), a swirling, golden, towering pillar commemorating the end of the plague.

Fischer von Erlach's greatest talent during these early years was his interior decorative work, and in Graz he

---

c AD 40
Romans establish Carnuntum and build military outpost Vindobona, today Vienna.

11th Century
Gurk's Romanesque *Dom*, and Benedictine abbey Stift Millstatt are built (both in Carinthia); during the 12th century early versions of Vienna's Stephansdom rise up.

12th–15th Century
Gothic Stephansdom in Vienna, the Hofkirche in Innsbruck and the Domkirche in Graz are built.

16th Century
The Renaissance in Austria produces Burg Hochosterwitz and Burg Landskron in Carinthia, Schallaburg in Lower Austria, Schloss Ambras in Innsbruck and the Schweizer Tor in Vienna's Hofburg.

17th–mid-18th Century
The baroque era results in an overwhelming number of masterpieces throughout Austria, among them Schloss Belvedere and Schloss Schönbrunn in Vienna.

Mid-18th–mid-19th Century
Neoclassicism takes root and the Burgtor is built in Vienna and Schloss Grafenegg in Lower Austria.

Don't
Miss...

» Hofburg, MuseumsQuartier, Karlskirche, Schloss Schönbrunn and Kunsthistorisches Museum, Vienna

» Kunsthaus and Schloss Eggenberg, Graz

» Festung Hohensalzburg, Salzburg

» Stift Melk, Melk

» Hofburg and Hofkirche, Innsbruck

Friedensreich Hundertwasser abhorred straight lines. He claimed in his *Mould Manifesto* to have counted 546 on a razor blade. He moved towards spiritual ecology, believing that cities should be in harmony with their natural environment, a philosophy that is represented metaphorically in his 'wobbly' KunstHausWien and Hundertwasserhaus in Vienna.

was responsible for the baroque interior of the Mausoleum of Ferdinand II (p175). In 1689 he began tutoring the future Kaiser Joseph I (1678–1711) in architecture, before being appointed court architect for Vienna in 1694. Despite his high standing and connections to the royal court, he found himself without commissions, however, and worked in Germany, Britain and Holland until his favourite student, Joseph I, elevated him in 1705 to head of imperial architecture in the Habsburg-ruled lands.

Although Fischer von Erlach's original plans for Schloss Schönbrunn in Vienna would be revised, the palace is one of his true masterpieces and was built from 1700. It counts among the world's finest baroque palaces and landscaped gardens, comprising the palace itself, perfectly laid-out gardens, baroque fountains, mythological figures inspired from classical epochs and an area used for hunting game that today is Vienna's zoo.

Vienna's other baroque palace masterpiece, Schloss Belvedere (p75), was designed by Austria's second great architect of the era, Johann Lukas von Hildebrandt (1668–1745).

In his day, Hildebrandt fell into the long shadow cast by Fischer von Erlach. Like his renowned fellow architect, Hildebrandt headed the Habsburgs' *Hofbauamt* (Imperial Construction Office). His great works were not churches – although he built several of these – or grand abodes for the royal court but primarily palaces for the aristocracy. He became the architect of choice for the field marshal and statesman Prince Eugene of Savoy, and it was Prince Eugene who commissioned Hildebrandt to build for him a summer residence in Vienna. Today the magnificent ensemble of palaces and gardens comprising Schloss Belvedere is Hildebrandt's most important legacy.

The Viennese palaces and churches were a high point in the art of the baroque, but the style was of course prevalent right across Austria. In Salzburg, when fire completely destroyed the city's Romanesque cathedral the new Salzburger Dom (Salzburg Cathedral; p223) was completed in place of the former cathedral in the baroque style in 1628. Meanwhile, in Melk on the Danube River, Jakob Prandtauer (1660–1726) and his disciple Josef Munggenast (1660–1741) completed the monastery Stift Melk (p120) between 1702 and 1738. In Graz, Schloss Eggenberg (p176) was commissioned in 1625 to the Italian architect Giovanni Pietro de Pomis (1565–1633), giving Austria another fine baroque palace and gardens.

It is said that the baroque was a leveller of styles. This is ironic, because its grandeur was also an over-the-top display of power and wealth. Once the fad caught on, churches almost everywhere were pimped up and brought into line with the style.

The baroque era in Austria, as elsewhere, had begun in architecture before gradually spreading into the fine arts. The fresco paintings of Paul Troger (1698–1762) would become a feature of the late baroque. Troger is Austria's master of the baroque fresco and he worked together with Munggenast on such buildings as Stift Melk, where he created the library and marble hall frescoes, using light cleverly to deliver a sense of space.

The Austrian Kaisers Leopold I (1640–1705), Joseph I and Karl VI (1685–1740) loved the dramatic flourishes and total works of art of the early baroque. During the late 17th century the influence of Italy and Italian masters such as Solari (of Salzburger Dom fame), de Pomis (Schloss Eggenberg) and other foreigners was typical of the movement. Vorarlberg, however, was an exception, as here Austrians, Germans and Swiss played the lead roles. The height of baroque was reached during the era of Fischer von Erlach in the early 18th century, and by the reign of Maria Theresia (1717–80) from the mid-18th century Austria experienced its largest wave of conversion of older buildings into a baroque style. But this brought little in the way of new or innovative buildings. A neoclassicist movement was gaining popularity, and in Austria as elsewhere the movement left behind the saccharine hype and adopted a new style of strict lines.

Contemporary Directions

Austria is known for its historic masterpieces, but recent years have also brought interesting new designs, some of these incorporating or complementing existing historic architecture. While many of these are office buildings in the large cities, some are locations for events or are museums. Schloss Grafenegg (p115) near the Danube Valley in the lush, rolling hills of Lower Austria is a fine instance of a postmodern concert location. Here a Renaissance palace was set on the shores of a lake but rebuilt from the 1840s in its current neoclassical form. The castle and grounds have long been a venue for classical-music events, but in 2007 they were given a new component: a 15m open-air stage called the Wolkenturm (Cloud Tower), designed by Viennese architects nextENTERprise. Set in a cleft in manicured parkland, this shiny, jagged and sculpture-like stage is a natural amphitheatre and takes on the hue of the surrounding parkland.

A similar reflection of surroundings is incorporated into the postmodern Loisium Weinwelt in Langenlois (p123). This brings together a modern, upmarket hotel complex, the world of wine, and tours through historic cellars with an aluminium cube designed by New York architect Steven Holl. Meanwhile, further along the Danube River in Linz, the capital of Upper Austria, the Lentos Kunstmuseum (p153) is a cubic, postmodern construction with a glass facade that also reflects its surroundings.

This idea of the modern building reflecting or absorbing the tones of its environment contrasts with another approach in modern Austrian architecture: a building that is in a state of flux. Also in Linz, the postmodern Ars Electronica Center (p153) received an addition alongside its original modern building in 2007. The added dimension of an LED facade encloses both buildings and lights up and changes colour at night. Another example of this style is the *Kunsthaus* in Graz (p176), which quickly became a new trademark of Styria's capital. Situated alongside the Mur River, this slug-like construction – the work of British architects Peter Cook and Colin Fournier – has an exterior that changes colour through illumination. The building's modernity seeks to create an 'aesthetic dialogue' with the historic side of Graz, rising up on a bluff on the other side of the river. This dialogue is literally linked by the Murinsel (Mur Island; p176), a swirl-shaped pontoon bridge situated in the middle of the river with a cafe, a children's playground and an amphitheatre for performance.

One of the most innovative architectural works of recent years has been the MuseumsQuartier in Vienna (p69). The MuseumsQuartier has retained an attractive ensemble of 18th-century buildings that once served as the royal stables for the Habsburgs, added cafes and shops, and augmented these by new buildings, such as the dark-basalt Museum Moderner Kunst (MUMOK) and the Leopold Museum. These two museums are separated by the *Kunsthaus* and a bold public space that has grown to become a favourite gathering place in the inner city.

1815–48
A Biedermeier style casts off some of the strictness of classicism, focusing on housing with simple yet elegant exteriors and on light, curved furnishings and interior decoration.

Mid-19th Century Onward
Lingering neoclassicism spills over into other revivalist styles, giving 'neo' prefixes to Gothic, baroque, Renaissance and other architecture on Vienna's Ringstrasse and across the country.

Late 19th–Early 20th Century
Backward-looking historicism is cast aside for lighter, modern styles such as Vienna's Secession building.

20th Century
While the Secession can still be felt, the Rotes Wien (Red Vienna) period produces large-scale workers' housing, and later postmodernist and contemporary buildings like Graz' *Kunsthaus* spring up.

ADOLF LOOS

'People love everything that fulfils the desire for comfort. They hate everything that wishes to draw them out of the secure position they have earned. People therefore love houses and hate art.' Adolf Loos

Otto Wagner – Austria Shapes up for the Modern

No single architect personifies the dawning of Austria's modern age in architecture more than the Vienna-born Otto Wagner. Wagner, who for many years headed the *Hofbauamt*, ushered in a new, functional direction around the turn of the 20th century. When he was finished with Austria's capital it had a subway transport system replete with attractive art-nouveau stations, he had given the flood-prone Wien River a stone 'sarcophagus' that allowed the surrounding area to be landscaped and part of it to be given over to the Naschmarkt food market, and he had given us the Postsparkasse building and a sprinkling of other interesting designs in Vienna and its suburbs.

Wagner's style was much in keeping with the contours of his epoch. He was strongly influenced in his early years by the architects of the Ringstrasse buildings (p67) and the revivalist style (which entailed resurrecting mostly the styles of ancient Rome and Greece), and he even (unsuccessfully) submitted his own plans for the new Justizpalast (Palace of Justice) in Vienna in a Ringstrasse revivalist style. Gradually, though, Wagner grew sceptical of revivalism and spoke harshly about his early works, calling revivalism a 'stylistic, masked ball'. His buildings dispensed with 19th-century classical ornamentation and his trademark became a creative use of modern materials like glass, steel, aluminium and reinforced concrete. The 'studs' on the Postsparkasse building are the perfect example of this. Those who venture out to his 1907 Kirche am Steinhof (p80) will find another unusual masterpiece: a functional, domed art-nouveau church built in the grounds of a psychiatric institution.

One of Wagner's most functional pieces of design was the Vienna U-Bahn (subway) system. He developed the system between 1892 and 1901 during his long spell heading the construction office of Vienna and he was responsible for about 35 stations in all – stops like Josefstädter Strasse on the U6 and Karlsplatz on the U4 are superb examples. One interesting way to get a feel for Wagner's masterpieces is simply to get onto the U-Bahn and ride the U6 north from Westbahnhof. It's sometimes called Wagner's *Gesamtkunstwerk* (total work of art) – in this case, one you can literally sit on.

Back to the Future – Neoclassicism & Revivalism

Walk around the Ringstrasse of Vienna today, admire the Burgtor (Palace Gate) fronting the Hofburg (p59) on its southwest side and dating from the early 19th century, the Neue Burg (New Palace) from the late 19th century, or the parliament building designed by the Dane Theophil von Hansen (1813–91) and you may feel as though you have been cast into an idealised version of ancient Greece or Rome. Outside Vienna, the 1765 Triumphpforte (Triumphal Arch; p300) is an early work of neoclassicism in Austria and creates a similar impression.

The age of neoclassicism took root during the second half of the 18th century, and over the next 100 years buildings inspired by ancient civilisations would spring up across Austria and elsewhere in Europe. By the mid-19th century, an architectural revivalist fad had taken root that offered a pot-pourri of styles: neo-Gothic, neo-Renaissance, and even a 'neo' form of neoclassicism.

Since the early days of the Renaissance, architects had looked to the ancient Greeks for ideas. The architecture of Rome was well known, but from the 18th century, monarchs and their builders were attracted to the purer classicism of Greece, and some of these architects travelled there to experience this first-hand. One of the triggers for this newly found love of all things Greek was the discovery in 1740 of three Doric temples in southern Italy in a Greek-Roman settlement known as Paestum.

In Austria, the love of all things classical or revivalist moved into full swing from the mid-19th century. The catalyst locally was the tearing down of the old city walls that had run around the Innere Stadt (Inner City), offering the perfect opportunity to enrich the city's architecture with grand buildings.

Vienna's medieval fortress had become an anachronism by the mid-19th century and the clearings just beyond the wall had been turned into *Glacis* (exercise grounds and parkland). In stepped Emperor Franz Josef I. His idea was to replace the *Glacis* with grandiose public buildings that would reflect the power and the wealth of the Habsburg Empire. The Ringstrasse was the result. It was laid out between 1858 and 1865, and in the decade afterwards most of the impressive edifices that now line this busy thoroughfare were already being built. It is something of a shopping list of grand buildings: the Staatsoper (National Opera; built 1861–69; p100), the Museum für angewandte Kunst (MAK; Museum of Applied Arts; 1868–71; p71), the Naturhistorisches Museum (Museum of Natural History; 1872–81; p69), the Rathaus (Town Hall; 1872–83; p67), Kunsthistorisches Museum (Museum of Fine Arts; 1872–91; p68), the Parlament (1873–83; p67), Burgtheater (1874–88; p101), and the Heldenplatz section of the Hofburg's Neue Burg (1881–1908; p64).

Hansen's parliament, with its large statue of Athena out front, possibly best symbolises the spirit of the age and its love of all things classical, but also ancient Greece as a symbol of democracy. One of the finest of the Ringstrasse buildings, the Kunsthistorisches Museum, is not only a neo-Renaissance masterpiece but also a taste of movements to come. This museum, purpose-built by the Habsburgs as a repository for their finest collection of paintings, is replete with colourful lunettes, a circular ceiling recess that allows a glimpse into the cupola when you enter, and paintings by Gustav Klimt (1862–1918). WWI intervened and the empire was lost before Franz Josef's grand scheme for the Ringstrasse could be fully realised.

By then, however, Gustav Klimt and contemporaries of his generation were pushing Austria in new directions.

'Prose is architecture, not interior decoration, and the baroque is over.' Ernest Hemingway, inadvertently revealing to us what he thinks of baroque architecture (and also why he wrote about bullfights and not, say, Austrian churches).

ADOLF LOOS – 'EVERY CITY GETS THE ARCHITECTURE IT DESERVES'

In 1922 a competition was held to build 'the most beautiful and distinctive office building in the world' for the Chicago *Tribune* newspaper. The greats of the architectural world vied for the project, and one of them was Czech-born Adolf Loos (1870–1933). As fate would have it, a neo-Gothic design trumped Loos' entry, which resembled a Doric column on top of what might easily have passed for a car factory.

Loos studied in Bohemia and later Dresden, then broke out for the US, where he was employed as a mason and also did stints washing dishes. He was influenced strongly by Otto Wagner, but it is said that his time as a mason (less so as a dishwasher) heightened his sensitivity to materials. He detested ornamentation, and that's why he also locked horns with the art-nouveau crew, whose flowers and ornamental flourishes (the golden cabbage-head dome of the Secession building, for instance) were anathema to his functional, sleek designs. Space, materials and even the labour used to produce a building ('Ornament is wasted labour and therefore a waste of good health') had to be used as fully as possible. Today, anyone who squeezes into Loos' miniscule American Bar in Vienna (p95), with its mirrors, glistening onyx stone surfaces and illusion of space, will get not only a decent cocktail but a good idea of what the architect was about.

ORNAMENTS

Secession & Art Nouveau

They called it a 'temple for bullfrogs' or a temple for an anarchic art movement. Other unflattering names for the Secession building were 'the mausoleum', 'the crematorium' or, because of the golden filigreedome perched on top, 'the cabbage head'. Others still, according to today's Secession association, thought it looked like a cross between a greenhouse and an industrial blast furnace.

In 1897, 19 progressive artists broke away from the conservative artistic establishment of Vienna and formed the Vienna Secession *(Sezession)* movement. In Austria, the movement is synonymous with art nouveau. Its role models were taken from the contemporary scene in Berlin and Munich and its proponents' aim had been to shake off historicism – the revivalist trend that led to the historic throwbacks built along Vienna's Ringstrasse. At the time, the Kunstlerhaus (Artists' House) of Vienna was the last word in the arts establishment, and Secessionists, including Gustav Klimt, Josef Hoffman, Kolo Moser and Joseph M Olbrich, distanced themselves from this in order to form their association.

Olbrich, a former student of Otto Wagner, was given the honour of designing an exhibition centre for the newly formed Secessionists. The 'temple for bullfrogs' was completed in 1898 and combined sparse functionality with stylistic motifs.

Initially, Klimt, Olbrich and their various colleagues had wanted to build on the Ringstrasse, but the city authorities baulked at the idea of watering down their revivalist thoroughfare with Olbrich's daring design. They agreed, however, to the building being situated just off it – a temporary building where for 10 years the Secessionists could hold their exhibitions.

Because art nouveau was essentially an urban movement, the scenes of its greatest acts were played out in the capitals or large cities: Paris, Brussels, New York, Glasgow, Chicago and Vienna. Like the Renaissance and baroque movements before it, Secession broke down the boundaries between painting and architecture. But it was also a response to the industrial age (although it used a lot of metaphors from nature), and the new movement sought to integrate traditional craftsmanship into its philosophy. The British were its role models for the crafts, and in 1903 Josef Hoffmann und Kolo Moser founded the Wiener Werkstätte (Vienna Workshop), which worked together with Vienna's School of the Applied Arts and the Secession movement to promote their ideas.

Another feature of Secession is its international tone. Vienna was a magnet for artists from the Habsburg-ruled lands. The movement was also greatly influenced by Otto Wagner. The Secession building, for instance, may have been domed by a floral 'cabbage', but its form had the hallmarks of Otto Wagner's strictness of lines.

'Because ornamentation is no longer an organic part of our culture it no longer expresses our culture. An ornament created today has nothing to do with us, no connection to human beings and nothing to do with the world order. It's not capable of developing any further.'
Adolf Loos

Visual Arts & Music

Austria is a relatively small country, but it has a grandiose past and an exciting presence in the visual arts and in music. The reason is simple: Habsburg monarchs fostered and patronised the arts for much of the period from Rudolf I's rise to the throne in 1273 until the demise of the dynasty in the early 20th century. From the time of Maximilian I (1459–1519) the Habsburgs were avid supporters of music, which they used to underscore their own power and pomp. They were no less active in the visual arts, especially through their commissioning of fresco painters to lend colourful texture and new dimensions to their buildings. Although Vienna is the uncontested centre of the visual arts in Austria, many important works are housed in smaller museums around the country and, notably, in churches or public buildings – the latter is especially true for baroque painting.

Visual Arts

The Great Fresco Artists

The tradition of fresco painting in Austria dates back to the mid-Romanesque era of the 11th century, when frescoes appeared for the first time in churches, depicting religious scenes. Around 1200 original Romanesque frescoes were painted inside the former Dom (cathedral) in Gurk (p263) in eastern Carinthia, and in 1270 these were revamped with a 'zigzag' style, giving naturalistic figures long, flowing robes with folds; you can see some of these in Gurk today.

In the Gothic era that followed from about the 14th century (as for instance in Vienna's Stephansdom, p58), fresco painting reached spatial limits due to vaulted ceilings and large windows (this encouraged glass painting). The height of magnificent fresco painting was therefore achieved in the baroque period of the 17th and early 18th centuries, when fresco painting is associated with three major figures: Johann Michael Rottmayr (1654–1730), Daniel Gran (1694–1757) and Paul Troger (1698–1762). Today the works of these three greats predominate in Vienna and especially in Lower Austria.

**20 BC
Roman**

With the building of the fortress of Carnuntum in Lower Austria, the Romans use decorative mosaics, some of which survive today in Carnuntum's open-air museum.

**8th–12th Century
Romanesque**

Salzburg becomes the centre for frescoes, many of which have Byzantine influences.

**13th Century
Early Gothic**

A transition from Romanesque to Gothic occurs, exemplified by frescoes today found in the former cathedral of Gurk.

**14th Century
High Gothic**

Ribbed Gothic interiors and high windows leave little space for frescoes but create new opportunities for glass painting. Altar painting establishes itself in churches.

**16th Century
Danube School**

In the transition from late Gothic to the Renaissance, a Danube School of landscape painting arises from the early 16th century, later absorbed into the Renaissance

**1680–1740
High & Late
Baroque**

Fresco painting reaches dizzying heights of achievement in the age of Johann Michael Rottmayr, Paul Troger and Daniel Gran

SCHÖNBERG

The innovative composer Arnold Schönberg (1874–1951) stretched tonal conventions to snapping point with his 12-tone style of composition. The most influential of his pupils were Alban Berg (1885–1935) and Anton von Webern (1883–1945); both were born in Vienna and both continued the development of Schönberg's technique.

Rottmayr and Gran were active during the high baroque, which spans the late 17th century and early 18th century. Paul Troger, however, produced most of his work during the late baroque or rococo period from the mid-18th century. Troger spent several years in Italy learning techniques before moving to Vienna, where Rottmayr had been setting the tone for fresco painting since 1696. Over time Troger became the painter of choice for churches and monasteries in Lower Austria, and fine examples of his work survive in Stift Melk (p120), Stift Zwettl (p123) and Stift Altenburg (p123), as well as in the Dom in Klagenfurt (p250), where you can find a Troger altar painting. Schloss Schönbrunn (p78) in Vienna also has work by Troger.

Rottmayr was Austria's first and the country's foremost baroque painter. He spent his early years as a court painter to the Habsburgs in Salzburg before he moved to Vienna in 1696, dominating the scene there for the next three decades. He became the favoured fresco painter of the architect Johann Bernhard Fischer von Erlach and is often compared to the Flemish painter Peter Paul Rubens. His work brought together Italian and Flemish influences into a style that featured plenty of bouncy, joyous figures and bright colours. Fine frescoes from Rottmayr can be found in Vienna decorating the staircases in Palais Liechtenstein (p76) and in the Karlskirche (p78), where a glass lift ascends over 70m into the cupola for a close-up view. In Lower Austria his work adorns Stift Melk and Klosterneuburg.

Daniel Gran, the third in the triumvirate of baroque fresco greats, also studied in Italy, but unlike those of Troger and Rottmayr his style reined in the most extravagant features and offered a foretaste of neoclassicism – perhaps best illustrated by his ceiling fresco in the Nationalbibliothek (National Library; p63) in Vienna. As fate would have it, Gran was the son of a court chef for Leopold I. But it was his talent, not his connections, that made his fresco in the library above the apotheosis of Leopold's son, Kaiser Karl VI, one of his most important legacies to the style and age.

Schiele, Kokoschka & the Expressionists

Tulln is a sleepy town slaked by the waters of the Danube River. It has a couple of interesting churches and the Minoritenkloster (Minorite Seminary; p121), which each year presents a new exhibition on modern art. Tulln is also the home of Austria's most important expressionist painter, Egon Schiele (1890–1918), and a museum there tells the story of his life through a large collection of his paintings and sketches. Other works are held in Austria's most important museum for expressionist art, the Leopold in Vienna's MuseumsQuartier, where Schiele's art is hung alongside the expressionists Oskar Kokoschka, Klagenfurt-born Herbert Boeckl, as well as Gustav Klimt, who worked in a number of styles.

WOULD IT HAVE CHANGED HISTORY?

Vienna's Academy of Fine Arts was famous not only for being a place Oskar Kokoschka unkindly described as 'a hotbed of conservatism and somewhere you went to become an artist in a velvet skirt and beret'. In 1907 an aspiring young Adolf Hitler sat the entry exam at the academy (the exam themes were Expulsion from Paradise, Hunting, Spring, Building Workers, Death – you get the idea). There were 128 applicants in Hitler's year and 28 were successful. Not Adolf. He desolately crawled back to Linz to lick his wounds and lived from his allowance as an orphan (his mother had died) before trying and failing a second time. Disillusioned, Hitler enlisted to fight on the Western Front in WWI. The rest is history.

In his day, Schiele was one of the country's most controversial artists. He left Tulln in 1906 to attend the Vienna's Akademie der bildenden Künste (Academy of Fine Arts), one of Europe's oldest academies – and one famous, incidentally, for having turned down Adolf Hitler in 1907. Schiele co-founded a group in Vienna known as the *Neukunstgruppe* (New Art Group) and around that time his work began to resonate with the public. Although he was very strongly influenced by one of the leading forces behind the Secession movement and art nouveau in Austria, Gustav Klimt, he is much more closely associated with expressionism than Klimt. Indeed, much of Klimt's early work had revivalist flavours before he broke away from the conservative art establishment of the Künstlerhaus Wien in 1897 and moved into art nouveau.

Vienna's famous psychologist, Sigmund Freud, apparently felt no affinity with expressionists like Schiele, preferring classical art and its neoclassical incarnations, but both Freud and Schiele were bedfellows in one way: the concept of the erotic. While Freud was putting together his theories on eros and the unconscious, Schiele was capturing the erotic on canvas, often taking death and lust as his explicit themes.

He had come a long way from the conservative, idyllic Tulln countryside – a little too far, some thought. In 1912 Schiele was held in custody for three weeks and later found guilty of corrupting minors by exposing them to pornography. His arrest and imprisonment were the culmination of a series of events that saw the painter and his 17-year-old lover and model 'Wally' Neuzil flee the Vienna scene and move to Bohemia (Český Krumlov in the Czech Republic), from where the two soon fled again. Today the Tulln museum dedicated to Schiele has a reconstruction of the prison cell near St Pölton where he was imprisoned.

Like Schiele, Oskar Kokoschka, the second of the great Austrian expressionists, was born on the Danube River. Kokoschka comes from Pochlarn, near Melk. Like Klimt, he studied at the Kunstgewerbeschule (School of Applied Arts) in Vienna. Like Schiele, he was strongly influenced by Klimt, but another of his influences was Dutch post-impressionist Vincent van Gogh. From 1907 he worked in the Wiener Werkstatte (Vienna Workshop; see p374). His earliest work had features of the Secession and art-nouveau movements, but later he moved into expressionism. The Österreichische Galerie in Schloss Belvedere (Oberes Belvedere; p75) has a collection of about a dozen of his oil paintings; some of these portraits highlight Kokoschka's skill for depicting the subject's unsettled psyche without in any way resorting to bleak colours.

Kokoschka's long life was punctuated by exile and travel. He moved to Prague in 1934 to escape the extreme right-wing politics of the day; once the Nazis came to power and declared his work 'degenerate' in

VISUAL ARTS & MUSIC VISUAL ARTS

Early 19th Century Biedermeier

Amid a wave of neoclassical and revivalist painting, the Biedermeier painter Ferdinand Georg Waldmüller becomes Austria's best-known painter of the era.

1900 Art Nouveau

Vienna becomes the world's art-nouveau capital, with the likes of Gustav Klimt, Hans Makart and Kolo Moser working in the city.

1910–20 Expressionism

Seeking a new language of art, expressionists Egon Schiele and Oskar Kokoschka move to the forefront of Austrian painting.

1918–1939 New Objectivity

Post-expressionism takes root and international movements such as surrealism, futurism and cubism reach Austria, while from 1925 *Neue Sachlichkeit* (New Objectivity) moves away from the 'subjective' approach of expressionism.

1960s Viennese Actionism

After the Nazi era (when little of lasting significance was achieved), a period of post-WWII fantastic realism adopted esoteric themes; later Viennese actionism brings 'happenings': pain, death, sex and abasement move to the fore.

21st Century Contemporary

A neo-expressionist Neue Wilde (New Wild Ones) movement of the 1980s gives way to 21st-century explorations using digital graphics to complement conventional forms of painting.

1937, seizing over 400 of them in German museums, Kokoschka packed his bags for Britain and became a UK citizen.

If Kokoschka was 'degenerate' and shocked the Nazis, it was a good thing the 'brown' men and women of the Thousand Year Reich were not around to see what would come later. It was called Viennese actionism – and now even the mainstream art establishment was being sent into a state of shock.

Shocking the Republic

Art has always enjoyed a good scandal. The expressionist Egon Schiele and the architect Adolf Loos were – rightly or wrongly – embroiled in morals charges that resulted in partial convictions. Kokoschka and Klimt explored in their paintings themes of eros, homoeroticism, and adolescence and youth. One day in 1968, however, the stakes were raised significantly higher when a group of artists burst into a packed lecture hall of Vienna's university and began an action that became known as the 'Uni-Ferkelei' (University Obscenity; see p66). According to reports, at least one member of the group began masturbating, smearing themselves with excrement, flagellating and vomiting. Lovely, but was it art? One member was probably singing the Austrian national anthem, another seemed to be rambling on about computers. Court cases followed, and so too did a couple of convictions and a few months in prison for two of those involved. It was all about breaking down the taboos of society.

If some of the art of the 1960s, like the Fluxus style of happenings (picked up from a similar movement in the US), was theatrical and more like performance on an impromptu stage, actionism took a more extreme form and covered a broad spectrum. Some of it was masochistic, self-abasing or employed blood rituals. At the hard-core end of the spectrum a picture might be produced in an orgy of dramatics with colour and materials being splashed and smeared collectively from various bodily cavities while the artists ascended into ever-higher states of frenzied ecstasy. At the more harmless end, a few people might get together and squirt some paint.

Actionism doesn't lend itself to the formal gallery environment. Some of it has been caught on video – salad-smeared bodies, close-ups of urinating penises, that sort of thing – and is presented in Vienna's MUMOK (Museum Moderner Kunst; p71). The University Obscenity action survives only in a few photographs and a couple of minutes of film footage. Günter Brus (b 1978), one of the participants, was convicted of 'denigrating an Austrian symbol of state'. His colleague of the day, Oswald Wiener (b 1935), is now an author and respected academic who went on to win one of the country's most prestigious literary prizes. Meanwhile, Hermann Nisch (b 1938), who staged theatrical events in the early 1960s based on music and painting and leaned heavily on sacrificial or religious rituals, has advanced to become Austria's best-known contemporary Viennese actionist. His work can be found in Vienna's MUMOK, the Lentos Museum in Linz (p153) and in St Pölten's Landesmuseum (p124).

Music

What other country can match the musical heritage of Austria or the creative force of its great composers? Even some of the Habsburgs were gifted musicians: Leopold I (1640–1705) composed, Karl VI (1685–1740) stroked a violin, his daughter Maria Theresia (1717–80) played a respectable double bass, while her son Joseph II was a deft hand at harpsichord and cello. But it's the greats we remember: Haydn, Mozart, Beethoven, Schönberg – and yes, even that contemporary great, Falco.

For more on what's happening in contemporary music (rock, jazz, pop, electronic, world music, classical and everything between and beyond) check out the Music Austria website www.musicaustria.at/en.

Vienna Classic

Wiener Klassik (Vienna Classic), which dates back to the mid- and late 18th century, very much defines the way we perceive classical music today. In its day, the epoch marked a move away from the celestial baroque music of the royal court and the church and brought forms of classical music such as opera and symphonies to the salons and theatres of the upper-middle classes of Vienna and Austria.

The earliest of the great composers was Joseph Haydn (1732–1809; see p140), who in his long career would tutor a budding young German-born composer by the name of Ludwig van Beethoven (1770–1827). Another well-known figure of the epoch was Franz Schubert (1797–1828), and one of the least known was the female 'blind virtuoso' Maria Theresia von Paradis (1759–1824). Von Paradis received voice training from the Italian composer Antonio Salieri (1750–1825), and this is where we get to the heart of the matter during this epoch: the much-discussed but possibly fictional rivalry between Antonio Salieri and Wolfgang Amadeus Mozart (1756–91).

Mozart was born in Salzburg (see p223). He tinkled out his first tunes on the piano at the age of four years, securing a dazzling reputation as Austria's *Wunderkind*. Salieri had been appointed by the Habsburgs in 1774 to head Italian opera at the royal court in the years following Mozart's meteoric rise. The stage was set for rivalries and intrigue, and this culminated in rumors that Salieri had murdered Mozart. We will never know whether he did or not (it's extremely unlikely that he did), but this is a moot point. The interesting thing is how much art has been born of the rumors. The most recent artistic masterpiece is the film *Amadeus,* directed by Milos Formann (b 1932). It won eight Academy awards and is widely considered to be the best of its ilk.

According to an interesting article published in the mid-1990s in the *Hong Kong Medical Journal,* even Mozart himself in his final year believed he had been poisoned, saying one day on a walk through a park with his wife that someone had slipped him aqua tofana. This happens to be a slow-acting concoction of arsenic and lead that was commonly used in Italy at the time. The same year, when an anonymous wealthy nobleman asked Mozart to compose a requiem, Mozart was convinced he had been commissioned by the devil to write one for his own requiem mass. The day of reckoning came. On New Year's Eve in 1791, Mozart died (the exact cause of death is unknown), causing the plot to thicken. One German newspaper remarked casually in an article on Mozart's demise that some people thought the great composer had been poisoned.

End of story for the time being. Then, some time in the 1820s, according to the *Hong Kong Medical Journal* article, a senile and crumbling Salieri allegedly confessed that he had poisoned Mozart. A couple of years later, he swore to someone else that he hadn't. By this time, though, Salieri was ready to shuffle off this mortal coil, having become a crumbling old man with dementia. The hapless Salieri only poured more fuel onto the fires of conspiracy when he sought to hasten his shuffle in an attempted suicide. This, the conspiracy theorists cried, was due to his being wracked by guilt.

Salieri died in 1825. Now the plot shifts to Russia. The Russian poet and playwright Alexander Pushkin wrote the original play *Mozart and Salieri* in 1830. The Russian connection grew stronger when Nikolay Rimsky-Korsakov created a short opera out of this. About 150 years later the British dramatist Peter Schaffer, inspired by Pushkin, penned his *Amadeus,* and this created the basis for the screenplay of Milos Formann's film. The rumors had come a long way.

But so much for Mozart versus Salieri. The epoch of Vienna Classic was losing momentum in 19th-century Vienna and, with Mozart,

Singers, Songwriters & Indie Music

» Lonely Drifter Karen

» Marilies Jagsch

» Paperbird

» Mika Vember

» Kreisky

» Ja Panik!

» Garish

» A Life, A Song, A Cigarette

LIFE AFTER MOZART

Austria has some great musicians and contemporary acts. Although none so far has achieved the international fame of Falco (real name Hans Hölzel; 1957–98), whose 'Rock Me, Amadeus' topped the US charts in 1986, there are some great acts to check out.

Naked Lunch (www.nakedlunch.de) is probably the best-known Austrian band since Falco. Going a bit deeper into the underground, the duo Attwenger (www.attwenger.at) has a large following for its music with flavours of folk, hip hop and trance. Completing the triumvirate of relative old hands, Graz-based Rainer Binder-Krieglstein (b 1966; performs as binder & krieglstein, www.mikaella.org/bk, in German) has gone from an eclectic blend of headz, hip hop, groove and nujazz to concentrate on folk music today.

For pure hip hop, Linz-based Texta (www.texta.at, in German) is the most established in the art. The bizarre Bauchklang (www.bauchklang.com) is remarkable for using only voices – no instruments – for its reggae- and ethnic-influenced hip hop and trance. This, of course, is absolutely normal compared to the equally remarkable Fuckhead (www.fuckhead.at), who, solely for a tendency to perform in plastic robes or gear that looks suspiciously like underwear, will obviously not be everyone's cup of tea. Afterwards you might be ready to tune into the saccharine flavours of popular rocker Christina Stürmer (b 1982; www.christinastuermer.de, in German).

Salieri, Haydn, Beethoven and the other great proponents dead or dying off, Austrian society and Europe as a whole experienced a period of repressive conservatism that culminated in revolutions across the continent in 1848 aimed at liberal reform. The pre-revolutionary period was known as the Vormärz ('Pre-March' – the revolutions began in March 1848); the Vormärz sounded the final death knell for Vienna Classic and produced a creative lull in music. It was only once the noise of the revolutions had died down that a new wave of composers – the likes of Franz Liszt (1811–87), Johannes Brahms (1833–97) and Anton Bruckner (1824–96) – arrived on the scene to take the legacy of Vienna Classic and transform it into new and exciting forms.

The Austrians

Trying to put a finger on the psyche of a country that gave us the likes of psychoanalyst Sigmund Freud is surely fraught with dangers. As Freud himself said, 'I know only one thing for sure. The value judgements of human beings are...an attempt to prop up illusion with argument'. So what was he trying to tell us? Maybe that whatever we decide about Austrians on a visit, some of it will be our own narrative.

Even Freud, though, couldn't deny a few things about the Austrians' mental topography. One is the self-styled conservatism you find in the deeper rifts and valleys of its regions. On top of this come a few historical grains that irritate the Austrian psyche. Once upon a time half the world was its oyster. Now it isn't. But what Austria now lacks in land it makes up for with a grandiose bureaucracy honed with vigour since the 19th century. Inside this bureaucracy you are likely to find (apart from the odd grump) a system of dividing up posts not on merit but consensus. Austrians see themselves – probably quite rightly – as more harmony-seeking than the neighbouring Germans, but they can also be greater sticklers for convention, and public opinion is less fragmented, which has much to do with the country's size.

Austrians are self-made rather than born; strikingly 'New World' at times and also fiercely regional. Along with the national symbols, each state has its own anthem, which is sung by schoolchildren on important occasions, and each even has its own patron saint.

The Viennese are different because they see themselves first and foremost as Austrians. The capital lives and thrives from its *Wiener Schmäh* (Vienna humour), a concoction of morbid, wry, misanthropic wit, personified by rock singer Falco. Some of the local Viennese actionism art did too. Maybe it's also why one of Freud's most important works is his *Jokes and their Relation to the Unconscious* – all very serious stuff, of course, but it also happens to be a fine collection of *Schmäh*.

The Lifestyle

With their high material standard of living, a spectacular landscape on the doorstep lending itself to skiing, hiking and extreme sports, and exciting cultural metropolises, Austrians enjoy a quality of life that is the envy of other Europeans. The Viennese lifestyle brings the excitement and perks of a big city at a pace that is more relaxed than in most other European capitals. This shows in the favoured Viennese pastime of enjoying a beer, wine or coffee with friends in one of the capital's many bars, restaurants or coffee houses. Vienna is also a magnet for artists, students and professionals from all over Austria, who go there to live and work, but return to their 'homes' in the provinces regularly for a shot of country life.

The roots of tradition still reach down deep into Austrian soil outside the cities, so sometimes Austrians live up admirably to bizarre images the world has of them. Women can still be seen in the *Dirndl* (a full,

For online information on Austria's cultural life, people and movements, see the Austrian Encyclopaedia website www.aeiou.at.

National service is still compulsory for males in Austria, who can either serve their time in the military or perform civil service duties.

For a good number crunch, visit the English- and German-language pages of the government statistic internet site at www.statistik.at.

pleated skirt) with tight bodice, worn with traditional apron, bonnet, and blouse with short, puffed sleeves. Men, meanwhile, can be found drinking a beer or wine in collarless loden jackets, green hats, wide braces and shorts or knee breeches. In early summer, hardy herders plod to alpine pastures with their cattle and live in summer huts while tending their beasts. Austria also has lots of traditional festivals.

All this is packed into in a small country with the fifth-highest standard of living in the EU and the 10th in the world in terms of earnings and purchasing power. It's coupled with a generous system of social security and healthcare funded by a percentage of the pay packet, and Austrians are also among the best educated in the world; 98% of the population aged 15 and above is literate.

Sports

Peer into the pantheon of Austrian Olympic Games medallists and one thing becomes clear: Austrians are killer-bee at winter sports. Football, however, draws the largest crowds. Ice hockey, handball, tennis and motor racing also enjoy a strong following. Except for motor racing, Austrians participate in these in large numbers too.

Summer is pretty much a time for niche sports like golf (except for snow golf), paragliding, and anything to do with running, swimming and windsurfing. With the arrival of autumn and winter, things get going on the pistes.

Football

The halcyon days of Austrian football were in 1931–32 when local legend Hugo Meisl (1891–1937) coached the national team through 14 consecutive international matches undefeated. In 1932 the team lost narrowly to the England team at old Wembley and in the 1934 World Cup to Italy in the semifinal.

The national football league, the Austrian *Bundesliga* (www.bundesliga.at, in German), kicks off at the end of autumn and runs until the beginning of spring with a break during the severe winter months. Games are hardly ever sold out, so getting a ticket is rarely a problem.

A lot of Austrians also play in the German *Bundesliga*. Styrian Emmanuel 'Mad Dog' Pogatetz, who earned his moniker in the English league, was appointed captain of the national team in 2009 and today plays for Hannover 96.

DOS & DON'TS

Austria is a society of politeness; to ignore the rules is the height of rudeness. Stick to the following dos and don'ts and you'll do just fine:

» Do greet people with *Grüss Gott* or *Guten Tag*, whether it be in a social setting, shop, cafe, restaurant or information office. *Servus* is reserved for greetings only between friends or the younger generation. When departing, *Auf Wiedersehen* or *Auf Wiederschauen* is appropriate.

» Do shake hands when introduced to someone, even in younger, informal company. Likewise, shake hands when you leave.

» Do use full titles at the beginning of formal meetings; *Herr* for men and *Frau* for women is the minimum required.

» Don't cross at the traffic lights when the figure is red, even when there is no traffic in sight. Austrians rarely do it, and the cops can instantly fine you for jaywalking.

» Don't strip off or go topless at every beach in Austria. Nude bathing is limited to areas with FKK signs and if no-one else is going topless at other beaches, you shouldn't either.

Three of Austria's great sportsmen stand out for one feature: they were badly injured at the height of their careers and made sensational comebacks.

Formula One legend Niki Lauda is possibly most famous of all. He suffered horrific burns in a high-speed crash during the 1976 season, yet he was back in his car after missing only two races. That year he narrowly failed to retain the world championship, losing to James Hunt by a single point on the season's last race. He regained the title the following year, and netted his third championship win in 1984.

The somewhat bumbling side of skier Hermann Maier has led to his being likened to Superman's alter ego, Clark Kent. However, in the 1998 Nagano Olympics, Maier showed the amazing toughness that characterises his all-or-nothing skiing style. During the men's downhill competition, he misjudged a difficult curve, got too close to a gate, somersaulted 30m through the air, bounced over a fence and crashed through two safety nets before finally coming to rest. Austria held its breath as the man known as 'The Herminator' got to his feet, dusted himself down and waved at the crowd. He went on to win two gold medals in the next six days.

But worse was to come. In August 2001 Maier was involved in a horrific motorcycle crash that almost cost him his life. He nearly lost one of his legs and underwent painful operations to have it held together by a titanium rod. In January 2003, only 18 months after the accident, he went on to win the Super G (super giant slalom) at Kitzbühel – his 42nd World Cup victory.

Thomas Muster, Austria's top tennis player during the 1990s, had his kneecap crushed by a drunk driver just hours after a win at the 1989 Lipton Championship semi-final in Florida. It was doubtful he would ever play tennis again. Images of Muster hitting balls while strapped to an osteopathic bench evoked admiration and bewilderment among tennis fans. He went on to become world number one and in the process earned the nickname 'The Iron Man'.

THE AUSTRIANS SPORTS

Skiing

As much a national hobby as a sport, nothing gets an Austrian snorting more than the whiff of powder snow. It's hardly surprising, because some of the best conditions worldwide are here. Innsbruck has hosted the Winter Olympics twice (in 1964 and 1976), and World Cup ski races are annually held in Kitzbühel, St Anton am Arlberg and Schladming.

Stars of the Austrian skiing scene abound, and one person who does this literally is the ski-jumper Thomas Morgenstern (b 1986), winner of team and individual gold medals in large-hill ski-jumping events in the 2006 Winter Olympics in Torino. Another, Salzburg-born Hermann 'The Herminator' Maier, has achieved superhero status in an alpine career spanning more than a decade and bristling with medals and cups.

Austria's first true superstar, Toni Sailer, is arguably the greatest skier the country has ever produced. At 17 he claimed the Tyrolean championships at downhill, slalom and giant slalom, and four years later won gold medals in all three disciplines at the 1956 Winter Olympics in Cortina d'Ampezzo.

The Austria Sports Organisation website www. bso.or.at, in German, showcases all sports.

Other Sports

Motor racing is enormously popular as an armchair sport, and only speed limitations prevent this from spreading to the highways. No Austrian has roared around the Formula One circuit more successfully than Vienna-born star of the 1970s and '80s Niki Lauda (b 1949). Off the circuit, Lauda morphed into a local aviation mogul, and more recently founded the low-cost Niki airline and a car-rental firm.

Gone are the days when Austria could claim a tennis ace of the likes of the Styrian *Laufstier* (running bull) Thomas Muster (b 1967), although tennis is still popular, and Association of Tennis Professionals (ATP) tennis events are held in Vienna, Pörtschach am Wörthersee and Kitzbühel.

Ice hockey is also popular, and Austria's one and only superstar, Thomas Vanek (b 1984), currently plays in the National Hockey League (NHL) in the USA for the Buffalo Sabres.

Multiculturalism

With 16% of its population on foreign passports, Austria still has a lower percentage of foreigners than many other European countries such as Switzerland and the Benelux countries. But this is 6% higher than in 2006, and the trend continues to move upward: foreigners have a higher birth rate, and more people are arriving than leaving. The other important trend over recent years has been an increase in people taking the plunge to become 'neo-Austrians' (as the local statistical office quaintly puts it). A good indication of the situation on the ground is that almost 17% – or one in six people living in Austria – have a migrant background.

A tiny 1.5% of the population is made up of other national minorities, mainly from Eastern Europe. Most settled in Austria's eastern parts between the 16th and 19th centuries and include Croatians, Slovenes, Hungarians, Czechs, Slovaks and Sinti or Roma. A number of traditional languages crossed the border with them: Slovene is an official language in Carinthia, and some town signs are bilingual. Croatian and Hungarian are spoken in Burgenland.

The largest immigrant groups are Serbians, Bosnians and Croatians, who arrived in the early 1990s, and Turks or descendents of Turks who arrived as guest workers in earlier decades, mainly in the 1950s and '60s.

As a result, Vienna has some fascinating quarters, such as the 16th district, that are colourful places for a plunge into multicultural life, but immigration has also produced a backlash. Anti-foreigner campaigns have been a feature of Austrian politics since the 1990s, particularly by the right-wing nationalist Freedom Party (FPÖ), which played the anti-Turkish card with the slogan 'Home, not Islam' during the 2006 national elections. Jörg Haider's Alliance Future Austria (BZÖ), a right-wing breakaway party from the FPÖ, campaigned on the platform of a one-third reduction of the number of foreigners in Austria; this never came to fruition, and Haider died in 2008. With the increase of foreigners in the country as a whole (in Vienna specifically, the foreign-born population is roughly 31% in 2010), this campaign was clearly unsuccessful.

Religion

On the surface of things, religion would seem to play an important part in the lives of Austrians, and the country has certainly been a stronghold of Catholicism for centuries. Inquiring whether there's a church in town is bit like asking whether the pope is Catholic. In the latest census, 73.6% of the population said they were Roman Catholic, 4.7% Protestant and 4.2% Muslim. Freedom of religion is guaranteed under the constitution.

All is well for the Catholic Church, then, right? It could be worse. Religion for most Austrians means observing the major rituals such as baptism, confirmation and weddings and funerals; about one-third make it regularly to church.

'If you want to abolish Austrian capitalism, first you have to create it.' Hannes Androsch, businessman and politician

CAPITALISM

Kaffeehäuser – Austria's Living Rooms

The *Kaffeehäuser* (coffee houses) of Austria, and especially its capital Vienna, are legendary. These are as much a part of social life and the cultural fabric of the country as the diner in the United States or the local pub in Britain and Australia. The story of their evolution from the days during the Turkish siege of Vienna to today is an interesting one sprinkled with not just a few grains of fiction.

The introduction of coffee into Europe occurred around the late 16th century. The bean probably originates from the highlands of Ethiopia, where it was chewed by slaves before being cultivated for the first time systematically around the 14th and 15th centuries in southern Yemen. Its rise to fame to become the world's second-most-traded product after oil began when it spread throughout the Middle East to places like Mecca and Medina (in today's Saudi Arabia), but notably also throughout countries of Central Asia and the Middle East conquered by the Ottoman Turks. A coffee house in Constantinople (Istanbul) became known as the *kaveh* and was a place where men gathered to chew the cud on life, listen to music and play chess and the like.

'In Café Central there are creative people who can't think of anything to write; everywhere else, though, there are fewer of them.' Writer Alfred Polgar (1873–1955)

The Noble Bean Reaches Europe

The Dutch were probably the first to smuggle the coffee bean into Europe – in 1616, when they illegally carried back cultivable beans to Holland and began raising the plants in greenhouses. From Europe the coffee bean spread to the United States, where it was mentioned for the first time in 1668.

Back in Vienna in 1683, the Ottoman Turks were conducting their second great onslaught to wrest control of the Occident, the Second Turkish Siege, that saw the Turkish general and grand vizier Kara Mustafa along with his eunuchs, concubines and 25,000 tents huddled on the fringe of fortified central Vienna in the *Vorstadt* (inner suburbs; places like Josefstadt and Alsergrund today).

According to legend, a certain Georg Franz Koltschitzky dressed himself up as a Turk and brought a message behind Turkish lines from the field Marshal Karl I of Lothringen and was rewarded for his efforts with some war booty that included sacks of coffee beans. Legend also says that our clever Koltschitzky sniffed the beans and saw his chance to establish Vienna's first coffee house. Koltschitzky is also said to have been the first person to mix milk and sugar into the exotic elixir.

True connoisseurs of coffee history scorn this version and raise their hats to a spy by the name of Deodato, who because of his Armenian

COFFEE CONUNDRUMS

Ordering 'a coffee, please' won't go down well in most coffee houses. A quick glance at a menu will uncover a long list of choices, and a little time studying the options is advisable. A good coffee house will serve the cup of java on a silver platter accompanied by a glass of water and a small sweet.

The selection of coffee includes:

» **Brauner** Black but served with a tiny splash of milk; comes in *Gross* (large) or *Klein* (small)

» **Einspänner** With whipped cream, served in a glass

» **Fiaker** *Verlängerter* (see below) with rum and whipped cream

» **Kapuziner** With a little milk and perhaps a sprinkling of grated chocolate

» **Maria Theresia** With orange liqueur and whipped cream

» **Masagran, Mazagran** Cold coffee with ice and Maraschino liqueur

» **Melange** Viennese classic; served with milk, and maybe whipped cream too; similar to a cappuccino

» **Mocca, Mokka, Schwarzer** Black coffee

» **Pharisäer** Strong *Mocca* topped with whipped cream, served with a glass of rum

» **Türkische** Comes in a copper pot with coffee grounds and sugar

» **Verlängerter** *Brauner* weakened with hot water

» **Wiener Eiskaffee** Cold coffee with vanilla ice cream and whipped cream

Vienna Coffee Houses

» Postmodern: Café Drechsler (p96)

» Rustic: Café Hawelka (p96)

» Views: Café Gloriette (p98)

» Grand: Café Sacher (p96)

» Quirky: Café Jelinek (p98)

background was the perfect man to open up a coffee house with the sanction of the Habsburg monarchy. He did this in Vienna's central district at what today is Rotenturnstrasse 14. We will probably never know the truth about who did what, but we do know that coffee houses soon flourished in Vienna, and here coffee was served with a glass of water. Coffee houses in the 17th century also had a billiard table, but playing cards in them wasn't allowed until the late 18th century.

Gradually, newspapers were introduced, and from the late 18th century the *Konzertcafe* (concert cafe) took hold – places where music was played. This cast the humble coffee house into a new role of being a place where the likes of Mozart, Beethoven and later Johann Strauss (the elder) could try out their works in the equivalent of open-stage or 'unplugged' performances.

When Austria adopted Napoleon's trade embargo against Britain in 1813 it lost almost its entire source of imported coffee beans. Although alternatives like chicory, rye and barley were tried, in the end the coffee houses started serving food and wine, which is why today you can still get a light meal or a drink in a traditional coffee house.

Come the late 19th century, elegant coffee houses sprang up along Vienna's Ringstrasse and everywhere a new 'literary coffee house' developed where writers could work in a warm room. Café Grienstedl (p95) was the first, but Café Central, the favourite of writers Peter Altenberg and Alfred Polgar, and architect Adolf Loos, is the best-known literary coffee house.

The writer Stefan Zweig saw them as an inimitable 'democratic club' bearing no likeness to the real world, but your average coffee house did have a clear pecking order. At the bottom of the heap was the *piccolo* who set the tables and topped up the guest's water glass, while flirting like a gigolo with the grand ladies whenever a spare moment presented itself. The cashier (in the ideal case of coffee-house tradition, buxom, blonde and with jewellery dripping from her ears) wrote the bills and kept a watchful eye on the sugar.

At the top of the heap was the *Oberkellner* (*Herr Ober,* for short, or head waiter), who until 1800 used to be a pony-tailed fellow with a dinner jacket, white tie, laced shoes, striped stockings and often a green apron. No *Herr Ober* dresses like this today (there are hints of the old garb, but none of the kinky stuff), but they do still rule the tables and the spaces between them in their dark attire.

Today you find more of a *Konditorei* (cake shop) atmosphere, and most continue to be the living room of the Viennese. These are places where you can drink coffee or wine, eat a goulash or light meal, read the newspapers or even enjoy a lounge vibe.

'The coffee house is a place where people have to go to kill time so that time doesn't end up killing them.' Alfred Polgar

The Austrian Table

Deep in the picturesque Kamptal of Lower Austria, cheese producer Robert Paget sits in the courtyard and waxes lyrical about his buffalos and goats and about earlier visits to India, where he spent time as an agricultural aid worker. A mural of Che Guevara adorns the barn wall, a fading leftover of an event once held on his farm. Paget is Austria's only producer of buffalo mozzarella and one of the country's leading makers of goat-cheese varieties. Elsewhere, on the southern outskirts of Vienna, Andreas Gugumuck plucks a snail from the grass and explains the life cycle of this culinary star before it adorns the finest tables of Vienna, Graz, Salzburg and other food capitals. What do these two producers have in common? Both in their own way symbolise a new focus on local, seasonal produce in Austria. It can be best described as a 'slow food' movement and is an exciting part of the table experience in Austria.

Austria is famous for its Wiener schnitzel, for its tender goulash and for desserts like *Sacher Torte* (Sacher cake) and *Kaiserschmarrn* (sweet pancake with raisins). Certainly, these legendary classics are not to be missed. But, as the examples of Paget and Gugumuck suggest, the Austrian table offers a host of other delights to explore. Throw in excellent red wines from Burgenland and quality whites and reds from Lower Austria, Styria and elsewhere, and you have the makings of an exciting and unexpected culinary experience, often amid spectacular landscapes.

The Historical Angle

Classic Austrian cuisine has always been a creature that thrives on change and outside influences, especially in Vienna and in the border regions where foreign influences are strongest. Wiener schnitzel (a true Wiener schnitzel is made from veal) is rumoured – this is hotly disputed today – to have originated from the recipe for Milanese crumbed veal cutlet brought back by Field Marshal Radetzky in 1857. Goulash comes from Hungary and the dumplings served with it originate from Czech regions. *Tafelspitz* (boiled beef, served with radish) is another classic, and it also happened to be the favourite dish of Kaiser Franz Josef. When foreign guests visited Vienna's opulent Schloss Schönbrunn, he fed them French delights, and when they left he ate his schnitzels and *Tafelspitz*. This captures the essence of Austrian cuisine as a whole: pilfered by the Habsburgs wherever they reigned, localised at home, shoehorned into the imperial tradition, and given new blood by the great culinary capitals abroad, like Paris, before being restyled for the contemporary Austrian table. More recently, immigrants from Turkey and other ethnic groups arriving since 1945 have contributed new dishes, while the postmodern love for sushi and pan-Asian cuisine has brought another dimension.

For a two-course meal, excluding drinks

» €€€ More than €30

» €€ €15 to €30

» € Under €15

Regional & Seasonal

While the classic cuisine can be found in virtually all parts of Austria, regional and seasonal fare is where the really interesting table experiences begin. Because of Austria's size, you will find very many overlaps in regional specialities, but also very many differences.

Vienna

Surprisingly for a city of its size, Vienna is famous for its locally produced vegetables, the so-called *Suppengemüse* (soup vegetables such as carrots, celery and radish and various other root vegetables) that are produced on its fringes. Snail-producer Andreas Gugumuck has integrated this into the centuries-old tradition of Viennese snail production to serve quality restaurants such as Aubergine (p88). Vienna also produces its own wine.

To really get to the bottom of Viennese cuisine, however, we need to look beyond the city and its outer suburbs to the backyard of the capital: the regions surrounding it, such as the Waldviertel in Lower Austria or the Neusiedler See area in Burgenland.

Check out the www.heurigen kalender.at tool, an online *Heurigen* calendar, to plan a meal and drink.

Lower Austria

Lower Austria is the closest region to Vienna and in terms of providing local and seasonal produce it plays the most important role in the country. The Wachau region is famous for its *Marillen* (apricots), brought to the table by about 180 producers in this spectacular section of the Danube Valley. The harvest begins around mid-July, when gourmands are thrown into a state of *Marille* madness and apricots are used in sweet desserts or made into schnapps. Just north of the Danube River in Diendorf in the Kamptal, Robert Paget produces his organic cheeses (see p127), whereas north along the Kamptal and west of this in the heart of the Waldviertel, beef (some of it organically produced) is complemented by carp (www.waldviertler-karpfen.at, in German) raised in ponds. The western parts of the Waldviertel are also famous for poppy seeds, which find their way into desserts across the nation (see p122). The Ybbs region just west of the Wachau and south of the Danube is known for its trout, while in the other direction, in Lower Austria's Weinviertel, asparagus from the Marchfeld reaches the tables from about April.

South of the Danube River is the Mostviertel, an area of rolling hills in Lower Austria where fruits from the orchards are worked into juices and alcoholic, cider-like wines known as *Most*. The two mainstays are *Apfelmost* (apple wine) and *Birnenmost* (pear wine). This has an alcohol content of about 4% to 8% and, like wine, is often served *gespritz* with a shot of sparkling mineral water. Upper Austria is also a *Most* region.

Off-the-Wall Traditional

A typical Austrian dish is *Kalbs-beuschel*, made from thin slices of veal offal (lung and heart), usually with celery, carrot, onion and wine, and spiced with juniper and bay leaves. The offal is boiled, the rest is fried and then it's combined. Inventive variations on it are served with snail caviar.

Burgenland

Like Lower Austria, Burgenland is one of Austria's premier wine regions, but it is also famous for its Neusiedlersee fish – species like perch-pike, pike, carp and catfish. These have long been served on the tables here,

---

IF YOU LIKE...

» **White wine** *Grüner Veltliner* (Austria's most widespread variety) or a *Riesling* from the Wachau

» **Red wine** *Zweigelt* or *Blaufränkisch* from Burgenland

» **Rosé** *Schilcher* from Styria

» **Dessert wine** *Schilfwein* (reed wine, or 'straw' *Strohwein*) is made from grapes that spend at least three months drying on reed or straw, or *Eiswein* (ice wine) made from frost-shrivelled grapes.

where, incidentally, the food has a strong Hungarian influence in parts. The Hungarian connection partly explains why Pannonian steppe cows and a Hungarian species of woolly pig called the Mangalitza (much loved by gourmands) have respectively been supplying beef and hams for the table in recent decades. Toss in nuts and orchard produce, as well as some of Austria's most interesting wines, and the region makes for a mouth-watering trip.

Styria

Styria is also a producer of Mangalitza ham, as well as beef locally produced from *Almochsen* (meadow beef) raised on mountain meadows in the region about 30km northeast of Graz. What the visitor to Styria, however, will immediately notice is that pumpkin oil is used to dress everything from salads to meats. This healthy, dark oil has a nutty flavour and here it often stands on tables alongside the salt and pepper.

Carinthia

Further west in Carinthia, you leave the dominant wine-growing regions and enter an extremely mountainous area where cheese, hams and salamis, game, lamb and beef count among the regional produce. Wherever there are lakes you'll also find trout and other freshwater fish on the menus. Each Friday Carinthians often eat a local pasta at home known as *Kärntner Nudel*, bearing a resemblance in shape to Russian *pelmeni* and filled with anything from potato or cheese to mint, the wild parsley-like chervil, mushrooms and any number of combinations of these.

Upper Austria & Salzburg

Upper Austria is one of Austria's dumpling strongholds, variously known across the country as *Knödel* or *Klöse* and very much in keeping with the cuisine of Bavaria in Germany and Bohemia in the Czech Republic. The most famous delight from the region, though, is its *Linzer Torte,* a short-pastry pie with a grid pattern of pastry on top that goes back to the mid-17th century (see p159). Although it is inseparable from its namesake Linz, the capital of Upper Austria – all politicians have one in their baggage ready to unpack for their hosts, it seems, whenever they're in a foreign country – *Linzer Torte* is believed to have originated in Vienna. It's a moot point – indulge in this speciality, filled with redcurrant jam or other preserves.

Salzburg's most famous culinary gift to civilisation is the *Mozartkugel,* a chocolate-coated concoction of pistachio marzipan and nougat that ungraciously translates as 'Mozart's Ball'. The original *Salzburger Kugeln* (Salzburg Balls) are sold by Fürst (see p229) and are also much tastier than the translation suggests. Like their Upper Austrian counterparts, Salzburgers

---

WHEN IN...TRY...

» **Vienna** Wiener schnitzel or *Tafelspitz* (boiled beef)
» **Lower Austria** Waldviertel beef, lamb, game or fish
» **Upper Austria** *Knödel* (dumpling) – what else?
» **Carinthia** *Kärntner Nudel* (Carinthian noodle)
» **Styria** *Steirischer Backhendl* (Styrian chicken) with *Kürbisöl* (pumpkin oil)
» **Burgenland** Neusiedler See fish, local beef
» **Tyrol** *Tyroler Gröstl* (fry-up), cheese and hams
» **Vorarlberg** *Heumilch* (hay milk) dairy products
» **Salzburg** *Salzburger Nockerln, Mozartkugeln*

otherwise lean heavily towards noodle and dumpling dishes, but this gives way to fish in lakeside towns and settlements, especially in the mountainous Salzkammergut. Typical *Salzburger Nockerln,* its favourite dessert, are massive soufflé-like baked concoctions (don't even ask how many egg whites are in them!) topped with icing sugar. Don't confuse this with *Nocken* or *Nockerln,* which is a variation on the Italian gnocchi theme.

Tyrol & Vorarlberg

These two regions have one thing in common – cheese, most notably what is called locally *Heumilchkäse* (hay-milk cheese), which aficionados claim is the purest form of milk you can find. What sounds like hype around the white gold is actually a sensible, low-intensity traditional form of agriculture: the cows, goats or sheep spend the warmer months on mountain meadows eating the 50 or more types of fresh grasses and herbs found in the regions; later, they move into barns to live off the hay during the winter months. The roughly 60 producers belonging to the Austrian association (www.heumilch.at, in German) are mostly located in Tyrol and Vorarlberg, but some are also in Styria, Salzburg and Upper Austria.

Gröstl, or *Gröstel* in some other regions, is a fry-up from leftovers, usually potato, pork and onions, but there are sausage varieties and the *Innsbrucker Gröstl* or *Gröstl Kalb* has veal.

Where Austrians Eat & Drink

Austria, led by Vienna, is experiencing a renaissance in gourmet culture and a surge in the sheer number, variety and quality of places to eat. At one end of the spectrum, coffee houses – which Vienna has in abundance but are a feature of the cityscape in all large Austrian towns – also serve a handful of light or classic dishes like goulash. See p385 for more about coffee houses. The towns of Austria are brimming with farmers markets where the freshest of produce is sold from stalls.

Restaurants

The Austrian restaurant scene covers a broad spectrum of ethnic eat-in and take-away joints in the large cities, corner Italian pizza places in smaller towns, upmarket restaurant experiences where the emphasis is spread evenly among fine food, good wine and the formalities and rituals of dining (sometimes in a castle), and at the other end of the scale off-beat crossover places where you can grab a bite to eat or sit over a coffee or alcoholic drink while surfing the web on wi-fi.

Beisl or Gasthaus

The word *Beisl* (beer house) is said to be related to a Yiddish expression for 'little houses'. These are found in large numbers in Vienna and also in the regional capitals and larger cities. In rural regions this kind of place might be signposted as a *Gasthaus* or perhaps as a *Gasthof,* both being rural inns. The fare and decor in a *Beisl* or *Gasthaus* is usually traditional for the region and homely. In recent years, smarter versions of these aimed at middle-class diners – *neo-Beisln* – have sprouted up in Vienna and other cities, offering pimped-up homeliness. The food in these can be excellent, usually based on fresh, local ingredients, and in some cases organic produce. A typical *Beisl* or *Gasthaus* will serve food, beer and wine, and offer an alternative to bars or cafes as places to drink.

Heurigen

Like *Beisln* and *Kaffeehäuser, Heurigen* are an integral part of the cultural and culinary scene. These simple establishments date back to the

Eating & Drinking Hours

» **Restaurants & Beisln** 11am-3pm & 6pm-11pm or midnight

» **Heurigen** Seasonal, or lunch and/or dinner

» **Pubs & bars** 6pm-1am

» **Cafe-bars** 9am or 10am-1am

Selected Classic Mains

» *Beuschel* (offal)

» *Rindsgulasch* (beef goulash)

» *Steirisches Backhendl* (breaded chicken)

» *Tafelspitz* (boiled beef with horseradish)

» *Wild* (game)

» *Wurst* (sausage)

» *Zwiebelrostbraten* (roast beef fried in onions)

Middle Ages and have the right to sell their wine directly from their own premises in winegrowing regions.

Originally, these were only open for a short time each year and served cold meats, but today there are various types of *Heurigen*. The most traditional type is the true *Buschenshank,* which can be identified by a *Busch'n* (green wreath or branch) hanging over the door. Because they are seasonal and are open on a roster, the easiest thing to do when in a winegrowing region is to pick up the local *Heurigenkalender* (*Heurigen* calendar) from the tourist office or one of the hotels and take your pick from those currently open. September to mid-October, following the harvest, is when the new wines are sold, and this is the time to indulge in *Sturm* (literally 'storm' for its cloudy appearance and chaotic effects on drinkers), fermented grape juice with a high alcohol content and deceptively sweet, non-lethal taste. In Styria, *Sturm* is known as *Junker*.

Beyond the traditional *Buschenshank* you'll find the less traditional *Heurigen-Restaurant,* which is often open all year and serves warm as well as cold buffet food. There are many of these on the outskirts of Vienna, some in the city *(Stadtheurigen),* and even the so-called *Nobelheurigen* – upmarket versions. In the restaurant-type *Heurigen* the wine washes down food like roast pork, blood sausage, pickled vegetables, potato salad and strudel. See p94 for tips on Viennese *Heurigen*.

> **Classic Desserts**
>
> » *Apfelstrudel* (apple strudel)
> » *Kaiserschmarrn* (sweet pancake with raisins)
> » *Salzburger Nockerln* (similar to soufflé)
> » *Topfenstrudel* (curd-filled strudel)

Cooking Courses

Places offering cooking courses are rather thin on the ground, but if you're keen to learn how to bread a schnitzel the Austrian way, or roll the perfect *Knödel,* there are a few places in Vienna to check out:

Babettes (☎01-585 51 65; www.babettes.at, in German; 04, Schleifmühlgasse 17; courses €110-120; ☺10am-7pm Mon-Fri, to 5pm Sat) A food lover's dream, with a zillion cookbooks and spices, plus cooking courses to boot.

Hollerei (☎01-892 33 56; www.hollerei.at, in German; 15, Hollergasse 9, 3400 Klosterneuburg; 1½hr €25) Here you cook with the chef and eat the result.

Kocheschule 'Toni M' (☎02738-229 80; kochschule@moerwald.at; Kleine Zeile 13-17, 3483 Feuersbrunn; seminars incl 5-course meal €150) In rural Feuersbrunn (a short hop from Vienna). Offers seminars and courses almost weekly on Austrian and international cuisine.

Wrenkh Kochsalon & Restaurant (☎01-533 15 26; www.wrenkh.at, in German; 01, Bauernmarkt 10; courses from €48) Mostly vegetarian cooking in one of Vienna's first vegetarian restaurants.

EIN BIER, BITTE!

Some common beer-glass sizes and types of beer:

» *Pfiff* (0.125L)
» *Seidl, ein Glas* (0.3L)
» *Krügerl* or *Krügel, ein Grosses* (0.5L)
» *Eine Flasche*, a bottle
» *Zwickl*, unfiltered beer
» *Märzen*, a lager
» *Weizen/Weissbier*, wheat beer
» *Dunkel*, dark beer or stout
» *Pils*, pilsener
» *Radler*, lemonade shandy
» *Vom Fass*, draught beer

In Styria:

Erste Steirische Kochschule (☎03135-522 47; www.kochschule.at, in German; Hauptstrasse 168, in Kalsdorf; courses €120)

Gasthof Vitalpension Hubinger (☎03861-8114 23; www.hubinger.com; Etmissl 25, Etmissl)

Tom am Kochen (☎03454-700 99; www.trac.at, in German; Arnfelser Strasse 2, Leutschach; courses & meal €115) Day courses based on preparation of a five-course meal deep in the picturesque heart of south Styrian wine country.

Habits, Customs & Celebrations

Austrians are a polite and respectable bunch at the table, and tend to take their time over meals. More often than not, the next course will not be served until everyone at the table has finished, so don't ramble on to your neighbour while the rest of the diners are waiting.

Smoking is currently an unresolved issue and will be irksome to some visitors. If a restaurant is not completely non-smoking (most aren't), separate smoking and non-smoking rooms are required by law, but enforcement has been lax and many restaurants and coffee houses have smoking areas (*Raucherbereiche*) but not separate rooms (*Raucherzimmer*). The separate areas are sometimes useful, but sometimes they are absolutely useless. (Note that in this book a restaurant or bar is given a special non-smoking icon only if the whole restaurant is non-smoking or separate rooms exist. For more about this, see p95).

Austrians like to celebrate at the table, and St Martin's Day (11 November) is traditionally marked with the serving of *Gans* (goose), St Martin's symbol. This tasty dish is available the entire month of November. Just before *Weihnachten* (Christmas), you might like to check what's splashing in the bath-tub before you dip a toe – the Central European tradition of keeping a live *Karpfen* (carp) in store for Christmas festivities is not unknown in Austria. Seasonal celebrations are complemented by *Vanillekipferl*, crescent cookies, which have a special place in the hearts of all Austrians.

Austrians enjoy a drink, and the country has its fair share of teenage binge drinkers and alcoholics, but your average Austrian tends to take his or her time over a glass. Every drink bought deserves a *Prost* (cheers) and eye contact with your fellow drinkers; not following this custom is thought of as rude. Even worse, it's believed to result in bad sex for the next seven years.

Beer also has its own festive seasons, although the tradition has suffered in recent years. *Maibock*, a so-called *Bockbier* with an alcohol content anywhere between 5% and an astounding 10%, is brewed in spring for drinking in May, and *Festbock* is occasionally brewed in the period leading up to Christmas.

Austrian Wine

Wine in Austria comes from 16 winegrowing areas, mostly situated in the winegrowing regions of Lower Austria and Burgenland (known as the Weinland Österreich region), Styria (das Steierland) and Vienna. The fourth wine region is known as Bergland Österreich and brings together winegrowing areas in Carinthia, Tyrol, Upper Austria and Vorarlberg. Over 90% of all wine in Austria comes from Lower Austria and Burgenland, and within these two states the most interesting areas for visitors are the Danube Valley (especially the Wachau, Kremstal and Kamptal), and areas around the Neusiedler See. Krems an der Donau is the perfect Danube Valley springboard into winegrowing areas, while in Burgenland the towns Rust (on the southeastern shore of the Neusiedler See) and Mörbisch and Purbach on the north and east of the lake are the most interesting for wine and food.

In 2010 the EU Patent Office approved a beer from the Upper Austrian town of Fucking – a brew called Fucking Hell. The people of Fucking had reason to get *agitato*: there's not a brewery anywhere near the town.

While the regions' sunshine is the key to bringing the grapes to a level of ripeness for harvest, the lime soils of northern Burgenland and Styria, the volcanic soils of the Kamptal and the loess in Lower Austria also lend regional flavours to the wines.

When choosing a wine there are several things to take into account. A *Qualitätswein* (Quality Wine) is made from one or more of 35 grape varieties and is produced in one of the recognised winegrowing areas. It is distinguished by the red and white stripes on the bottle capsule. A wine that is typical of the region is labelled DAC, which is similar to the French AOC and the Italian DOC or DOCG, and if it is labelled reserve then the wine has been made for cellaring.

Some Austrian wines are chaptalised (have had sugar added), but for a wine to be labelled a *Prädikatswein* (wine with distinction) it must have natural sugar levels, be made from late-harvested grapes and be matured under particular conditions.

Eiswein is made from grapes that have frozen on the vines, *Schilfwein* (reed wine) has been dried on reeds for at least three months, the *Trockenbeerenauslese* is mostly sweetened by noble rot (the botrytis fungus), and *Ausbruch* is exclusively sweet from noble rot. *Spätlese* is late picked and fully ripe, *Auslese* is fully ripe but made from grapes that are selected, and *Beerenauslese* is wine made from overripe grapes with noble rot.

The Austrian Alps

For many people, Austria *is* the Alps and no wonder. After all, these are the alpine pastures where Julie Andrews made her twirling debut in *The Sound of Music;* the mountains that inspired Mozart's symphonies; the slopes where Hannes Schneider revolutionised downhill skiing with his Arlberg technique. Olympic legends, Hollywood blockbusters and mountaineering marvels have been made and born here for decades.

Although these Alps can't match those of Switzerland and France in height, in terms of accessibility and hut-to-hut hiking they are unrivalled. And comparatively lower elevation does not equate to lesser scenic impact, as one look at these magnificently glaciated and spectacularly rugged peaks confirms.

Kitzbühel for skiing, Salzburg for high culture, the Hohe Tauern National Park for wilderness – so many names, so many expectations. Only by heading up into the three-thousanders on foot, by bicycle or behind the wheel can you even begin to appreciate just how *big* and eminently beautiful Austria really is. One trip is never enough, which is just as well as the Austrian Alps have enough epic climbs and descents to last several lifetimes.

Alpine Landscapes

The Alps engulf almost two-thirds of the 83,858 sq km that is Austria. It's almost as though someone chalked a line straight down the middle and asked all the Alps to shuffle to the west and all the flats to slide to the east, so stark is the contrast in this land of highs and lows. Over millennia, elemental forces have dramatically shaped these mountain landscapes, etched with wondrous glaciers and forests, soaring peaks and gouged valleys.

The Austrian Alps divide neatly into three principal mountain ranges running in a west–east direction. The otherworldly karst landscapes of

Speaking of Superlatives

» Europe's highest waterfall: the 380m-high Krimmler Wasserfälle

» The world's largest accessible ice caves: Eisriesenwelt, Werfen

» The largest national park in the Alps: Hohe Tauern (1786 sq km)

» The longest glacier in the Eastern Alps: the 8km Pasterze Glacier

» Austria's highest peak: 3798m Grossglockner (literally 'Big Bell')

SEASON'S GREETINGS

Spring When the snow melts, the springtime eruption of colourful wildflowers sets senses on high alert. Look out for bell-shaped purple gentian and startlingly pink alpine roses.

Summer Stay overnight in a mountain hut, bathe in pristine alpine lakes and bring your walking boots for some highly scenic hiking on passes above 2000m.

Autumn The larch trees turn a beautiful shade of gold in late autumn and you might spot rutting stags. Come in late September for the *Almabtrieb,* where cows adorned with flowers and bells are brought down from the pastures for the winter.

Winter Snow, snow and more glorious snow. Enjoy first-class skiing, crisp mountain air and cheese-loaded alpine food. Your snug wood chalet on the mountainside awaits.

the Northern Limestone Alps, bordering Germany, reach nearly 3000m and extend almost as far east as the Wienerwald (Vienna Woods). The valley of the Inn River separates them from the granitic Central Alps, a chain which features the highest peaks in Austria dwarfed by the majestic summit of Grossglockner (3798m). The Southern Limestone Alps, which include the Karawanken Range, form a natural barrier with Italy and Slovenia.

From melt-water streams to misty falls, water is a major feature of the Austrian Alps. Mineral-rich rivers like the Enns, Salzach and Inn wend their way through broad valleys and provide a scenic backdrop for pursuits like rafting in summer. Lakes, too, come in all shapes and sizes, from glacially cold alpine tarns to the famously warm (around 28°C) waters of Wörthersee in Carinthia.

Wildlife in the Austrian Alps

Nature reigns on an impressive scale in the Austrian Alps. The further you tiptoe away from civilisation and the higher you climb, the more likely you are to find rare animals and plant life in summer. Besides a decent pair of binoculars, bring patience and a sense of adventure.

Watching Wildlife

GOLDEN EAGLES

A right pair of love birds, golden eagles stay together for life. See www.birdlife. at (in German) to find out more about these elusive raptors and other Austrian birdlife.

Dawn and dusk are the best times for a spot of wildlife-watching in the Austrian Alps, though a lot boils down to luck. High on the must-see list is the ibex, a wild goat with curved horns, which was at one stage under threat but is fortunately now breeding again. It is the master of mountain climbing and migrates to 3000m or higher in the Austrian Alps come July. The chamois, a small antelope more common than the ibex, is equally at home scampering around on mountain sides. It can leap an astounding 4m vertically and its hooves have rubber-like soles and rigid outer rims – ideal for maintaining a good grip on loose rocks.

At heights of around 2000m, listen and look out for marmots, fluffy rodents related to the squirrel and native to the Alps. This sociable animal lives in colonies of about two dozen members. Like meerkats, marmots regularly post sentries, which stand around on their hind legs looking alert. They whistle once for a predator from the air (like an eagle) and twice when a predator from the ground (such as a fox) is approaching and the whole tribe scurries to safety down a network of burrows.

Ornithologists flock to the Austrian Alps for a chance to see golden eagles, falcons and vultures – both bearded and griffin.

Endangered Species

Austria's most endangered species is the *Bayerische Kurzohrmaus* (Bavarian pine vole), which is endemic to Tyrol and found only in six lo-

---

WHAT A PICTURE

Photo ops abound in the Austrian Alps, but capturing the moment can be tricky. Here are our tips for getting that mountain shot just right:

» Make the most of the diffused early morning and evening light. Stay overnight in an alpine hut to get a head start.

» To get *really* white snow, you may need to increase the exposure.

» Get close-up wildlife photos with a telephoto zoom lens; moving too close unnerves animals. Stay calm and quiet.

» Think about composition: a hiker or a cyclist in the foreground gives your photo scale and highlights the immensity of the Alps.

» A polariser filter can help you capture that true blue sky.

» **Edelweiss** Star-shaped white flowers found on rocky crags and crevices.

» **Gentian** Bell-shaped blue flowers of the high Alps.

» **Alpine crowfoot** Early-flowering anemone-like blooms.

» **Arnica** Bright yellow daisy-like flowers found in alpine meadows.

» **Alpine roses** Hot-pink rhododendron-like flowers.

calities. Following close behind is the *Kaiseradler* (imperial eagle), at one time extinct in Austria but fortunately staging a comeback through re-immigration. The *Europäische Hornotter* (long-nosed viper) may be a venomous snake at home in Carinthia, but humans are a far greater threat to its survival than its bite will ever be to ours.

Although still teetering on the brink of extinction, the Austrian Alps' population of brown bears now reaches double figures (estimated at around 15 to 20). This is due to the efforts of organisations like Austria's Brown Bear Life Project and the WWF who have invested millions of euros into bringing the bear back to the Alps. While rarely sighted, brown bears are said to roam in central and southern mountainous regions such as Carinthia and Styria.

For the low-down on endangered species, consult the Rote Liste (www.umweltbundesamt.at, in German), collated by the Umweltbundesamt (Federal Environment Agency).

Alpine Flora

Below the tree line, much of the Austrian Alps is thickly forested. At low altitudes you can expect to find deciduous birch and beech forests, while coniferous trees such as pine, spruce and larch thrive at higher elevations. At around 2000m trees yield to *Almen* (alpine pastures) and dwarf pines; beyond 3000m only mosses and lichens cling to the stark crags.

A highlight of the Austrian Alps is its flowers, which bring a riot of scent and colour to the high pastures from May to September. The species here are hardy, with long roots to counter strong winds, bright colours to deter insects and petals to ward against frost and dehydration.

Spring brings crocuses, alpine snowbells and anemones; summer alpine roses and gentians; and autumn thistles, delphiniums and blue aconites. Tempting though it may be to pick them, these flowers really do look lovelier on the slopes and most are protected species.

Men once risked life and limb to pluck Edelweiss from the highest crags of the Alps for their sweethearts. The woolly bloom is Austria's national flower, symbolising bravery, love and strength.

National Parks in the Austrian Alps

For an area of such mind-blowing natural beauty, it may come as a surprise to learn that there are just three national parks (Hohe Tauern, Kalkalpen and Gesäuse) as well as one major nature reserve (Nockberge) in the Austrian Alps. But statistics aren't everything, particularly when one of these national parks is the magnificent Hohe Tauern, the Alps' largest and Europe's second-largest national park, which is a tour de force of 3000m peaks, immense glaciers and waterfalls.

The national-park authorities have managed to strike a good balance between preserving the wildlife and keeping local economic endeavours such as farming, hunting and tourism alive. The website www.nationalparksaustria.at has links to all national parks and a brochure in English to download.

THE AUSTRIAN ALPS NATIONAL PARKS IN THE AUSTRIAN ALPS

Best Places to (Maybe) See...

» Marmots – Kaiser-Franz-Josefs-Höhe, Grossglockner Rd

» Golden eagles – Hohe Tauern National Park

» Lynx – Nationalpark Kalkalpen

» Falcons – Nationalpark Gesäuse

» Ibex – Northern Limestone Alps

www.naturschutz.
at is a one-stop
shop for info on
Austria's land-
scape, flora and
fauna. It's in Ger-
man, but there
are a few links to
English sites.

Aside from national parks, protected areas and nature reserves are dotted all over the Austrian Alps, from the mesmerising mountainscapes of Naturpark Zillertaler Alpen in Tyrol to the lakes of the Salzkammergut. See www.naturparke.at for the low-down on Austria's nature parks.

Austria's Alpine Environment

Given the fragile ecosystem of the Austrian Alps, conservation, renewable energy and sustainable tourism are red-hot topics. In the face of retreating glaciers, melting snow, dwindling animal numbers and erosion, the people of the Alps come face-to-face with global warming and mankind's impact on the environment on a daily basis.

Measures have been in place for years to protect Austria's alpine regions, yet some forest degradation has taken place due to air and soil pollution caused by emissions from industrial plants, exhaust fumes and the use of agricultural chemicals.

The good news is that Austrians are, by and large, a green and nature-loving lot. Recently, everyone from top hoteliers in St Anton to farmers in Salzburgerland has been polishing their eco credentials by promoting recycling and solar power, clean energy and public transport.

Melting ice is a
hot topic in the
Hohe Tauern Na-
tional Park. The
Pasterze Glacier
has shrunk to half
its size over the
past 150 years
and is predicted
to disappear
entirely within
100 years.

The government has moved to minimise pollutants by banning leaded petrol, assisting businesses in waste avoidance and encouraging renewable energy, such as wind and solar power. Some buses are gas powered and environmentally friendly trams are a feature of many cities.

Global Warming

With global warming a sad reality, 'snow-sure' is becoming more wishful thinking in resorts at lower elevations in the Austrian Alps. Every year, the snow line seems to edge slightly higher and snow-making machines are constantly on standby.

A recent United Nations Environment Programme (UNEP) report on climate change warned that rising temperatures could mean that 75% of alpine glaciers will disappear within the next 45 years, and that dozens of low-lying ski resorts such as Kitzbühel (762m) will be completely cut off from their slopes by 2030. Forecasts suggest that the snowline will shift from 1200m to 1800m by 2100, a prediction that is supported by

PARK (AREA)	FEATURES	FAUNA	ACTIVITIES	BEST TIME	WEBSITE
Hohe Tauern (1786 sq km)	classic alpine scenery with 3000m mountains, glaciers, lakes, high alpine pastures	ibex, chamois, marmots, bearded vultures, golden eagles	hiking, rock climbing & mountaineering, skiing, canyoning, paragliding	year-round	www.hohe tauern.at
Gesäuse (110 sq km)	rivers, meadows, gorges, thick forest, limestone peaks	owls, eagles, falcons, deer, bats, woodpeckers	hiking, rafting, caving, mountain biking, rock climbing	spring, summer, autumn	www. national park.co.at
Kalkalpen (210 sq km)	high moors, mixed forest, rugged limestone mountains	lynx, brown bears, golden eagles, owls, woodpeckers, butterflies	hiking, cycling, rock climbing, cross-country skiing	year-round	www.kal kalpen.at
Nockberge (184 sq km)	gentle rounded peaks, alpine pastures, woodlands	marmots, snow eagles, alpine salamanders, butterflies	walking, climbing, cross-country & downhill skiing	year-round	www. national parknock berge.at

In a bid to offset the impact of skiing, many Austrian resorts are taking the green run with ecofriendly policies. For more details on reducing your carbon snowprint, see www.saveoursnow.com.

» Lech in Vorarlberg scores top points for its biomass communal heating plant, the photovoltaic panels that operate its chairlifts and its strict recycling policies.

» Zell am See launched Austria's first ISO-certified cable car at the Kitzsteinhorn glacier. It operates a free ski bus in winter and runs an ecological tree and grass planting scheme.

» Kitzbühel operates green building and climate policies, and is taking measures to reduce traffic and the use of nonrenewable energy sources.

» St Anton am Arlberg has created protected areas to reduce erosion and pumps out artificial snow without chemicals. Its excellent train connections mean fewer cars.

» Ischgl uses renewable energy; recycles in all hotels, lifts and restaurants; and has a night-time driving ban from 11pm to 6am.

» Mayrhofen operates its lifts on hydroelectricity, separates all waste and has free ski buses to reduce traffic in the village.

recent mild winters in the Alps. As well as the impact on Austria's tourist industry, the melting snow is sure to have other knock-on effects, including erosion, floods and an increased risk of avalanches.

Skiing

Austria's highly lucrative ski industry is a double-edged sword. On the one hand, resorts face mounting pressure to develop and build higher up on the peaks to survive; on the other, their very survival is threatened by global warming. For many years, ski resorts have not done the planet many favours: mechanically grading pistes disturbs wildlife and causes erosion, artificial snow affects native flora and fauna, and trucking in snow increases emissions.

However, many Austrian resorts now realise that they are walking a thin tightrope and are mitigating their environmental impact with renewable hydroelectric power, biological wastewater treatment and ecological buildings.

Want to know more about Austrian ski resorts stepping up efforts to save the environment? Check out www.saveoursnow.com.

Survival Guide

Directory A–Z

Accommodation

From simple mountain huts to five-star hotels fit for kings – you will find a wide choice of accommodation in Austria. Tourist offices invariably keep lists and details, and some arrange bookings for a small fee, while others will help free of charge.

Facilities

Most hotel rooms in Austria have their own shower, although hostels and some rock-bottom digs usually have an *Etagendousche* (corridor shower). The better rooms have bath-tubs. Very often a hotel won't have lifts; if this is important, always check ahead. Tea and coffee-making facilities are the exception rather than the rule.

Price Ranges

Accommodation prices in this book are for the high season. Listings are arranged in the order of Lonely Planet preference, taking into account key aspects like location, value for money (not simply the cheapest price), facilities, cleanliness and hospitality.

Price ranges for two people in a double room with a bathroom and including breakfast:

€€€ more than €200
€€ €80 to €200
€ below €80

Reservations & Cancellations

It's wise to book ahead at all times. Often a day or two in advance is sufficient, but reserve at least one week ahead to increase the chances of getting into your hotel of choice on Friday and Saturday nights, during the high seasons July and August, and much longer ahead at Christmas, Easter and between December and April in ski areas. Some places require email confirmation following a telephone reservation but many places are also bookable online. Confirmed reservations in writing are binding, and cancellations within several days of expected arrival often involve a fee or full payment.

Guest Cards

In some resorts (not often in cities) a *Gästekarte* (guest card) is issued if you stay overnight. This card may of-

fer discounts on things such as cable cars and admission, so check with a tourist office if you're not offered one at your resort accommodation.

Websites

There are some good international and local websites for scanning and booking accommodation. Locally, always check the city or region website in the destination chapter, as many (such as in Vienna, Salzburg and Graz) have an excellent booking function. Some useful websites:

Austrian Hotelreservation (www.austrian-hotel reservation.at)
Austrian National Tourist Office (www.austria.info)
Booking.com (www.book ing.com)
Camping in Österreich (www.campsite.at)
Expedia (www.expedia.com)
Hostelling International (www.hihostels.com)
Hostelworld (www.hostel world.com)
hotel.de (www.hotel.de)

Alpine Huts

There are over 530 of these huts in the Austrian Alps maintained by the Österreichischer Alpenverein (ÖAV; Austrian Alpine Club; www.alpenverein.at, in German) and the German Alpine Club (DAV). Huts are found at altitudes between 900m and 2700m, and may be used by the general public. Meals or cooking facilities are often available. Bed prices for nonmembers are around €26 to €44 in a dorm or €20 to €32 for a mattress on the floor. Members of the ÖAV or affiliated clubs pay half-price and have priority. Contact the ÖAV or a local tourist office for lists of huts and to make bookings.

Camping

Austria has over 490 camping grounds that offer users a range of facilities such as washing machines, electricity connections, on-site shops and, occasionally, cooking facilities. Camping gas canisters are widely available. Camp sites are often scenically situated in an out-of-the-way place by a river or lake – fine if you're exploring the countryside but inconvenient if you want to sightsee in a town. For this reason, and because of the extra gear required, camping is more viable if you have your own transport. Prices can be as low as €4 per person or small tent and as high as €10.

A majority of the camp sites close in the winter. If demand is low in spring and autumn, some camp sites shut, even though their literature says they are open, so telephone ahead to check during these periods.

Free camping in camper vans is allowed in autobahn rest areas and alongside other roads, as long as you're not causing an obstruction. It's illegal to camp in tents in these areas.

While in the country, pick up camping guides from the **Österreichischer Camping Club** (Austrian Camping Club; ☑01-713 6151; www.campingclub.at, in German; Schubertring 1-3, A-1010 Vienna) and a *Camping Map Austria* from **Österreich Werbung** (www.austria.info).

Private Rooms

Rooms in private houses are cheap (often about €40 per double) and in most towns you will see *Privat Zimmer* (private room) or *Zimmer Frei* (room free) signs. Most hosts are friendly; the level of service though is lower than in hotels. On top of this, you will find *Bauernhof* (farmhouses) in rural areas, and some *Öko-Bauernhöfe* (organic farms). Regional tourist offices are good information sources for farm stays.

Hostels

Austria is dotted with *Jugendherberge* (youth hostels) or *Jugendgästehaus* (youth guesthouses). Facilities are often excellent: four- to six-bed dorms with shower/toilet are the norm in hostels, while many guesthouses have double rooms or family rooms; internet facilities, free wi-fi and a restaurant or cafe are commonplace.

Austria has over 100 hostels affiliated with **Hostelling International** (HI; www.hihostels.com), plus a smattering of privately owned hostels. HI hostels are run by two hostel organisations (either can provide information on all HI hostels):

Österreichischer Jugendherbergsverband (ÖJHV; ☑01-533 53 53; www.oejhv.or.at; Gonzagagasse 22, Vienna; ◷9am-5pm Mon-Thu, to 3pm Fri)

Österreichischer Jugendherbergswerk (ÖJHW; ☑01-533 18 33; www.oejhw.at; Mariahilferstraße 22-24, Vienna; ◷10am-6pm Mon-Thu, to 5pm Fri).

Memberships cards are always required, except in a few private hostels, but non-members pay a surcharge of about €3.50 per night and after six nights the stamped Welcome Card counts as full membership. Most hostels accept reservations by telephone or email and are part of the worldwide computer reservations system (www.hihostels.com). Average dorm prices are about €21 per night.

Hotels & Pensions

The majority of travellers stay in either a hotel or a pension or *Gasthof* (B&B or guesthouse). All are rated by the same criteria for stars (from one to five stars). Hotels invariably offer more services, including bars, restaurants and garage parking, whereas pensions and guesthouses tend to be smaller than hotels and have fewer standardised fixtures and fittings but sometimes larger rooms.

What to expect:

Two stars Functional rooms with cheap furnishings. Most cost under €40/80 per single/double but in many cases you're better off booking a good hostel room. Often more central than a hostel and near the train station. Breakfast is unlikely to thrill. Showers are in the rooms, but they might be a booth.

Three stars Most accommodation in Austria is in this midrange category. The majority of singles cost about €60 to €70, doubles €120 to €130 (from about €70/140 in Vienna). Expect good clean rooms and a decent buffet breakfast with cold cuts of meat, cheeses, eggs and bread rolls. Usually there will be a minibar and perhaps snacks will be offered; often you have a place to sit or a desk to write on. Internet and either wi-fi or cable LAN is available, often free or inexpensively. Some specialise in catering to seminar guests. Showers and TV (often flat screen) in rooms.

Four and five star Rooms in a four-star hotel or pension are generally larger than three star and should have better sound insulation as well as contemporary or quality furnishings. Expect

BOOK YOUR STAY ONLINE

For more accommodation reviews by Lonely Planet authors, check out hotels.lonelyplanet.com/Austria. You'll find independent reviews, as well as recommendations on the best places to stay. Best of all, you can book online.

PRACTICALITIES

» **Seasonal Opening Hours** Opening hours can vary significantly between the high season (April to October) and winter – many sights and tourist offices are on reduced hours from November to March. Opening hours we provide are for the high season, so outside those months it can be useful to check ahead.

» **Seasonal Prices** In mountain resorts, high-season prices can be up to double the prices charged in the low season (May and November, which fall between the summer and winter seasons in mountains). In other towns, the difference may be 10% or less.

» **Concession Prices** Many museums and sights have concessions for families and for children (generally for children under 16 years), which are listed in this book along with practical details. Some places also have reduced student and senior citizen admission prices, which are generally slightly higher than the child's price. Children under 12 years usually receive a substantial discount on rooms they share with parents. Ask when booking. Children also travel at reduced rates on public transport.

» **Smoking** Unless a separate room has been set aside, smoking is not allowed in restaurants, wherever food is served or in all but the smallest, one-room drinking venues. In the past, controls have been lax, but since mid-2010, when authorities stepped up enforcement, venues have gradually begun to obey laws, even in provincial regions. It's legal, though, to smoke anywhere on outdoor terraces, which can be irksome on a still night among chain smokers. Whenever a hotel has designated nonsmoking rooms, we've included an icon to show this.

decent wellness facilities in a four-star option, premium facilities in five-star hotels.

Rental Accommodation

Ferienwohnungen (self-catering holiday apartments) are very common in Austrian mountain resorts, though it is often necessary to book these well in advance. The best idea is to contact a local tourist office for lists and prices.

Eco-Hotels & Eco-Farmhouses

So-called *Bio-* or *Öko-* ('eco') hotels are widespread in Austria. Most of them are located outside towns in picturesque settings. Some of the farmhouses are fully functioning farms with a few rooms; others are nominally farms that mostly make a living from overnight guests. Not a few of the hotels have wellness facilities like saunas and steam baths, and because of their rural location they often have winter skiing and activities. Generally, you will need to have your own wheels – a car or a bicycle – to reach these. Tourist offices keep lists or have a special section in their accommodation listings and on websites. The website www.biohotels. info also has a brief list.

University Accommodation

Studentenheime (student residences) are available to tourists over university summer breaks (from the beginning of July to around the end of September). Some rooms have a private bathroom but often there's no access to the communal kitchen. The widest selection is in Vienna, but tourist offices in Graz, Salzburg, Krems an der Donau and Innsbruck can point you in the right direction. Prices per person are likely to range from €20 to €75 per night and sometimes include breakfast. **Academia Hotels** (☎01-40 176 55; www.academia-hotels. co.at; Pfeilgasse 3a, Vienna) handles bookings for its residencies in Vienna, Graz and Salzburg. Book on the website or call.

Business Hours

Normal opening hours in Austria are as follows. See the practicalities for each point of interest for hours when they are different from these.

Banking From 8am or 9am until 3pm Monday to Friday, extended hours to 5.30pm on Thursdays. Many of the smaller branches close from 12.30pm to 1.30pm.

Offices & Government Departments Usually from 8am to 3.30pm, 4pm or 5pm Monday to Friday.

Post Offices From 8am to noon and 2pm to 6pm Monday to Friday; many open all day and also on Saturday from 8am to noon.

Shops Most open from 9am to 6.30pm Monday to Friday (often to 9pm Thursday and Friday in cities), from 9am to 5pm Saturday.

Restaurants Serve lunch between 11am and 3pm and dinner from 6pm to midnight, and often close in between.

Cafes Hours vary considerably and are included in our listings. A traditional cafe opens around 7.30am and shuts at about 8pm.

Pubs & Bars Close anywhere between midnight and about 4am.

Children

Facilities Facilities for travellers with kids are good. Some museums (especially in Vienna) have a children's play area; restaurants offer child portions and have high chairs; and many hotels have rooms that are connected by a door, making them especially suitable for families. In most hotels and pensions children under 12 years receive substantial discounts, depending on exact age. Midrange and better hotels have cots (but book ahead). Family- or child-friendly hotels are highlighted in reviews.

Restaurants Most midrange restaurants have a child's menu or will prepare smaller portions for children if you ask. A few have a play area.

Travelling with Babies In bigger cities, breastfeeding in public won't cause eyelids to bat. Everything you need for babies, such as formula and disposable nappies, is widely available (in *Drogerien* or drug stores).

Getting Around with Kids Rental car companies can arrange safety seats. Newer public transport, such as trams and buses in Vienna, are easily accessible for buggies and prams, but the older models can prove a nightmare. Children under six years usually travel free on public transport, or half-price until 15 years of age.

Resources Log on to www. kinderhotels.at for information on child-friendly hotels throughout the country. For helpful travelling tips, pick up a copy of Lonely Planet's *Travel with Children* by Cathy Lanigan.

Sights & Activities

Regional tourist offices often produce brochures aimed directly at families. Museums, parks and theatres often have programs for children over the summer holiday periods, and local councils occasionally put on special events and festivals for the little ones. Many museums in Vienna are free for those under 18 or 19 years. With its parks, playgrounds and great outdoors, Austria has plenty to keep the kids amused.

Some children's sights and activities:

Swimming Many lakes have a supervised beach area.

Hiking Lots of easy family walks as well as challenging ones in most places.

Cable Cars & Panoramic Walkways Freak-out or tamer varieties, great rides and lookouts aplenty.

Museums & More Good ones include Zoom (p84), Haus der Musik (p64), FriDa & FreD (p177), Schlossberg Cave Railway (p177), Ars Electronica (p153) and the Pöstlingberg (p156), Minimundus miniature park (p251) and the Marionettentheater (p238).

Going Underground Erzberg mine (p193) in Styria and the salt mines (p204) of Salzkammergut offer good underground mine experiences.

Customs Regulations

Austrian customs regulations are in line with all other EU countries. Items such as weapons, certain

Climate

Innsbruck

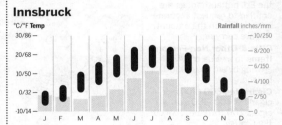

Salzburg

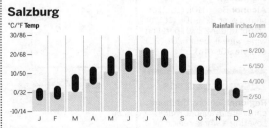

Vienna

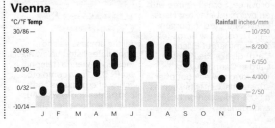

drugs (both legal and il-legal), meat, certain plant materials and animal prod-ucts are subject to strict customs control. All goods must be for personal use. The **Ministry of Finance** (http://english.bmf.gv.at) website has an overview of regulations. Below are some key guidelines for anyone 17 years or older importing items from an EU or non-EU country. The amounts in brackets are for items im-ported from outside the EU; if tobacco products don't have health warnings in the German language, these too are limited to the amounts given in brackets.

Money Amounts of over €10,000 in cash or in travel-lers cheques (or the equiva-lent in cash in a foreign currency) must be declared on entering or leaving the EU. There is no limit within the EU, but authorities are entitled to request accurate information on the amount you are carrying.

Gifts & Other Non-Personal Items To a value of €430 if arriving by air, up to €300 by land.

Cigarettes 800 (200); or cigarillos 400 (100); or cigars 200 (50); or tobacco 1kg (250g).

Alcohol Beer 110L (16L); or spirits over 22% 10L (1L); or spirits under 22%, sparkling wine, wine liqueurs 20L (2L); or wine 90L (4L).

Discount Cards

Regional Various discount cards are available, many covering a whole region or province. Some are free with an overnight stay (eg Neus-iedler See Card in Burgen-land), cost a few euros (eg Salzkammergut Erlebnis Card) or, like the Kärnten Card in Carinthia, cost €34 for one week but offer substantial benefits such as a 50% reduction on buses and trains.

Senior Cards In some cases senior travellers will be able to get discount admission to sights, but local proof is often required. It can't hurt to ask and show proof of age, though. The minimum quali-fying age for Austrians is 65 for men and 60 for women.

Student & Youth Cards International Student Identity Cards (ISIC) and European Youth Card (Euro<26; check www.euro26.org for dis-counts) will get you discounts at most museums, galleries and theatres. Admission is generally a little higher than the price for children.

Discount Rail Cards See Getting Around in the Trans-port chapter on p419 for these.

Electricity

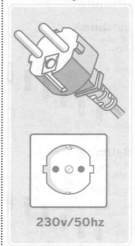

230v/50hz

Embassies & Consulates

All the embassies and consulates listed below are located in Vienna (telephone prefix 01). For a complete listing of embassies and consulates, look in the Aus-trian telephone book under *Botschaften* (embassies) or *Konsulate* (consulates).

Australia (506 74-0; www.australian-embassy.at; Mattielli-strasse 2-4)

Canada (531 38-3000; www.kanada.at; Laurenzerberg 2)

Czech Republic (899 581 11; www.mzv.cz/vienna; Penz-ingerstrasse 11-13)

France (502 75 200; www.ambafrance-at.org; Wipplinger Strasse 24-26)

Germany (711 54-0; www.wien.diplo.de/vertretung/wien; Metternichgasse 3)

Hungary (537 80-300; kom@huembvie.at; Bankgasse 4-6)

Ireland (715 42 46; www.embassyofireland.at; Roten-turmstrasse 16-18)

Italy (713 56 71; www.amb vienna.esteri.it; Ungargasse 43)

The Netherlands (589 39; www.mfa.nl/wen; 7th fl, Opernring 5)

New Zealand (consulate-general; 318 85 05; www.nzc.at; Salesianergasse 15/3)

Slovakia (318 90 55-200; www.vienna.mfa.sk; Armbrustergasse 24)

Slovenia (585 22 40; vdu@gov.si; Nibelungengasse 13)

UK (716 13-0; www.british embassy.at; Jaurèsgasse 12)

USA (313 39-0; http://austria.usembassy.gov; Boltz-manngasse 16)

Gay & Lesbian Travellers

Vienna is reasonably tolerant towards gays and lesbians, more so than the rest of the country. Austria is these days close to Western European par on attitudes towards homosexuality.

The 'Gay & Lesbian Vienna' boxed text (p99) has specific listings of publications, or-ganisations, hotels and bars for gays and lesbians. Online information (in German) can be found at www.gayboy.at, www.rainbow.or.at, www.gay.at and www.gayguide.at. The

Spartacus International Gay Guide, published by Bruno Gmünder (Berlin), is a good international directory of gay entertainment venues worldwide (mainly for men).

Health

Travelling in Austria presents very few health risks. The water everywhere can be safely drunk from the tap, and the water in the lakes and streams is for the most part excellent and poses no risk of infection.

Health Insurance If you are not an EU citizen and your country doesn't have a reciprocal arrangement with Austria for treatment costs, don't leave home without insurance. The USA, Canada, Australia and New Zealand don't have reciprocal agreements. Otherwise, expect to pay anything from €40 to €75 for a straightforward, nonurgent consultation with a doctor. Make sure you get a policy that covers you for the worst possible scenario, such as an accident requiring an emergency flight home. Find out in advance if your insurance plan will make payments directly to providers or reimburse you later for overseas health expenditures, and whether it covers all activities (like skiing or climbing). If you're an EU citizen, a European Health Insurance Card (formerly an E111 form), available from health centres, covers you for most medical care. The cards will not cover you for nonemergencies or emergency repatriation home.

Recommended Vaccinations The World Health Organization (WHO) recommends that all travellers should be covered for diphtheria, tetanus, measles, mumps, rubella and polio, as well as hepatitis B, regardless of their destination. A vaccination for tickborne encephalitis is highly advisable.

Snakes & Insects Austria has only a few poisonous snake species and bites are rare in comparison with the situation in the US and Australia. Bandage the bite, keep calm and seek medical assistance. Wasps can be a problem in midsummer but are only dangerous for those with an allergy or if you are stung in the throat. Look before you take a sip outdoors from a sweet drink. Mosquitoes can be a nuisance around lakes.

Activities-Related Dangers Hikers, skiers and climbers should take precautions to avoid sunburn, heatstroke and exhaustion, all potential dangers, especially at higher altitudes. Carry a bottle of water in summer and in winter take care to avoid hypothermia, another risk in Austria's mountains.

Sexual Health Condoms are readily available throughout Austria. Supermarkets and *Drogerien* are the cheapest places to buy these and sanitary articles. Some bars have condom dispensers. About 500 people in Austria become infected with the HIV (AIDS) virus each year. Always take precautions, such as proper use of a condom.

Tick-Borne Diseases

Ticks can carry lyme disease and encephalitis, and pose a serious outdoor hazard to health in many parts of Europe. They are usually found below 1200m in undergrowth at the forest edge or beside walking tracks.

Lyme Disease Also known as *Borreliose,* this is a bacterial infection caused by ticks and has serious long-term consequences if left untreated with antibiotics. It is often possible to recognise in the early stage (a rash or red infection around the bite). There is no vaccination against it.

Tickborne Encephalitis This is called FSME in Austria. It is a serious infection of the brain and **vaccination is highly advised** for risk groups and in risk areas (especially campers, climbers and hikers). Austrians who are in risk groups or risk areas have usually been vaccinated. Distribution of tickborne encephalitis is uneven; the website www.zecken.at (in German; go to FSME then Verbreitungsgebiete Österreich) has excellent region-by-region maps showing dangerous areas. Local pharmacists always know whether FSME is a danger in their region and can advise if you're bitten.

Precautions & Removing Ticks Wearing long trousers tucked into walking boots or socks and using a DEET-based insect repellent is the best prevention against tick bites. If a tick is found attached, press down around the tick's head with tweezers, grab the tick as close as possible to the head and rotate continuously in one direction, without pulling, until the tick releases itself. Pharmacies sell plastic or metal tweezers especially for this purpose (highly recommended for hikers). Avoid pulling the rear of the body or smearing chemicals on the tick.

Internet Access

Wi-fi This is available in most hotels of three-star quality or more. It's also available free in some cafes and bars. Often you need a password from staff. A wi-fi icon in a listing in this book means a hotel has wi-fi access either in the room or in a public area for free or for a moderate charge per day.

Network (LAN) Cable Many hotels have wi-fi in the foyer and cable access or occasionally power LAN (through the electricity socket) in rooms. A cable is usually in the room or available from reception. We mention whenever you need to bring your own. Cable-only access in hotels is noted in reviews (without the wi-fi icon).

Internet Terminals Many hotels have internet terminals that guests can use for free or for a small cost. In this book icons in reviews indicate the places.

Public Access Prices in internet cafes vary from around €4 to €8 per hour. Small towns often won't have internet cafes but the local library will probably have a terminal.

Pre-Paid Surf Sticks Not a convenient or inexpensive option yet, but this might change.

Internet on Smart Phones Available but expensive if you are roaming. GPS and navigation works fine in most areas.

Hot Spot Resources See www.freewave.at/en/hot spots for free hot spots in Vienna, and www.freewlan.at for Austria-wide hot spots.

Language Courses

Many places, including some of Austria's universities, offer German courses, and they can usually offer the option of accommodation for the duration.

Berlitz (www.berlitz.at) Offers private, intensive day and evening courses in Vienna, Wiener Neustadt, Klagenfurt, Linz and Graz.

Inlingua Sprachschule (www.inlingua.at) Courses run for a minimum of two weeks and can either be taken in the morning or some evenings. Classes are limited to seven students and individual tuition is also available. Offices in Linz, Graz, Salzburg, Innsbruck, Klagenfurt and Vorarlberg.

Legal Matters

If you are arrested, the police must inform you of your rights in a language that you understand.

In Austria, legal offences are divided into two categories: *Gerichtsdelikt* (criminal) and *Verwaltungsübertretung* (administrative). If you are suspected of having committed a criminal offence (such as assault or theft) you can be detained for a maximum of 48 hours before you are committed for trial. If you are arrested for a less serious, administrative offence, such as being drunk and disorderly or committing a breach of the peace, you will be released within 24 hours.

Drunken driving is an administrative offence, even if you have an accident. However, if someone is hurt in the accident it becomes a criminal offence. Possession of a controlled drug is usually a criminal offence. Possession of a large amount of dope (around 300g) or dealing (especially to children) could result in a five-year prison term. Prostitution is legal provided prostitutes are registered and have a permit.

Legal Advice

If you are arrested, you have the right to make one phone call to 'a person in your confidence' within Austria, and another to inform your legal counsel. If you can't afford legal representation, you can apply to the judge in writing for legal aid.

Free advice is given on legal matters in some towns; for example, during special sessions at Vienna's *Bezirksgerichte* (district courts). As a foreigner, your best bet when encountering legal problems is to contact your national consulate (see p406).

Money

Like other members of the European Monetary Union (EMU), Austria's currency is the euro, which is divided into 100 cents. There are coins for one, two, five, 10, 20 and 50 cents, and for €1 and €2. Notes come in denominations of €5, €10, €20, €50, €100, €200 and €500. The Need to Know section lists exchange rates (p19).

ATMs

Bankomaten are extremely common everywhere and accessible till midnight. Some are 24 hours. Most accept at the very least Maestro debit cards and Visa and MasterCard credit cards. There are English instructions and daily withdrawal limits of €400 with credit and debit cards. Check with your home bank before travelling for charges for using a *Bankomat;* there's usually no commission to pay at the Austrian end.

Cash & Emergency Transfers

ATMs mean that you don't need to carry large amounts of cash or use money-changing facilities. It is, however, worth keeping a small amount in a safe place for emergencies. Western Union (www.westernunion.com) money offices are available in larger towns for emergency transfers.

Credit Cards

Visa and MasterCard (Euro-Card) are accepted a little more widely than American Express (Amex) and Diners Club, although a surprising number of shops and restaurants refuse to accept any credit cards at all. Upmarket shops, hotels and restaurants will accept cards, though. Train tickets can be bought by credit card in main stations. Credit cards allow you to get cash advances at most banks.

For lost or stolen credit cards:

Amex (⏻0810 910 940)
Diners Club (⏻01-501 35 14)
MasterCard (⏻0800 21 8235)
Visa (⏻0800 200 288, wait for second dial tone & enter 800 892 8134)

Taxes & Tipping

Taxes *Mehrwertsteuer* (MWST; value-added tax) in Austria is set at 20% for most goods. Prices are always displayed inclusive of all taxes. Shops with a 'Global Refund Tax Free Shopping' sticker have the paperwork to reclaim about 13% of this tax on single purchases over €75 by non-EU citizens or residents. See www.globalrefund.com for more information. Refund desks are at the department stores Gerngross and Steffl in Vienna, and in Graz at Kastner & Öhler. Vienna and Salzburg airports also have refund desks. It's easiest to claim this before leaving the country rather than at home.

Tipping This is part of everyday life in Austria; in restaurants, bars and cafes and in taxis it's customary to give about 10%. Add the bill and the tip together and hand it over in one lump sum. It also doesn't hurt to tip hairdressers, hotel porters, cloak-room attendants, cleaning staff and tour guides one or two euros.

Public Holidays

Basically, everything shuts down on public holidays. The only establishments open are bars, cafes and restaurants, and even some of these don't open. Museums are usually – but not universally – open. The big school break is in July and August. This is a time when most families go on holiday so you'll find some places, like cities, a little quieter

and others, such as popular holiday destinations, busier. Avoid ski breaks during much of February; school pupils have a week off during that time and invariably the ski slopes are full to overflowing with kids and parents. Plan bus trips more carefully on public holidays – services are usually reduced.

New Year's Day (Neujahr) 1 January
Epiphany (Heilige Drei Könige) 6 January
Easter Monday (Ostermontag) March/April
Labour Day (Tag der Arbeit) 1 May
Whit Monday (Pfingstmontag) 6th Monday after Easter
Ascension Day (Christi Himmelfahrt) 6th Thursday after Easter
Corpus Christi (Fronleichnam) 2nd Thursday after Whitsunday
Assumption (Maria Himmelfahrt) 15 August
National Day (Nationalfeiertag) 26 October
All Saints' Day (Allerheiligen) 1 November
Immaculate Conception (Mariä Empfängnis) 8 December
Christmas Day (Christfest) 25 December
St Stephen's Day (Stephanitag) 26 December

Telephone

Country Code Austria's country code is ⏻0043.
Area Codes Each town and region has its own area code beginning with '0' (eg '01' for Vienna). Drop this when calling from outside Austria; use it for all landline calls inside Austria except for local calls or special toll and toll-free numbers.
Public Telephones These take phonecards or coins. Twenty cents is the minimum for a local call and

they are charged by length of call (and by distance rates if not local). Call centres for domestic and international calls are also widespread, and many internet cafes are geared for Skype calls.

Mobile, Free & Toll Numbers Austrian mobile (*Handy*) telephone numbers begin with 0650 or higher up to 0683 (eg 0664/plus the rest of the number). All 0800 numbers are free; 0810 and 0820 numbers cost €0.10 and €0.20 respectively per minute; and 0900 numbers are exorbitant and best avoided. Some large organisations have '050' numbers, which do not need an area code (a local call from a landline, but often expensive from a mobile phone).

International Calls

To direct-dial abroad, first telephone the overseas access code (00), then the appropriate country code, then the relevant area code (minus the initial '0' if there is one), and finally the subscriber number. International directory assistance is available on ⏻0900 11 88 77.

Tariffs for making international calls depend on the zone. To reverse the charges (call collect), you have to call a free phone number to place the call. Some of the numbers are listed below (ask directory assistance for others):

Australia (⏻0800-200 202)
Ireland (⏻0800-200 213)
New Zealand (⏻0800-200 222)
South Africa (⏻0800-200 230)
UK (⏻0800-200 209)
USA (AT&T; ⏻0800-200 288)

Roaming The *Handy* (mobile phone) network works on GSM 1800 and is compatible with GSM 900 phones; it is not compatible with systems from the US unless the mobile phone is at least a tri-band model that can receive one of these frequencies. Japanese mobile phones need to be quad-band (world phone) to work in Austria. Despite roaming agreements, there can be downtime lasting a day or more. Roaming can also get very expensive if your provider is outside the EU.

Prepaid SIM Cards Phone shops in Austrian cities sell prepaid SIM cards without further ado over the counter for about €10 (calls for about €0.10 per minute) that can be refilled at kiosks anywhere. To use one, your mobile phone must be without a SIM lock. Cheap dual-band mobile phones without a SIM lock cost about €30 to buy locally.

Phonecards & Internet Calls

There's a wide range of local and international *Telefon-Wertkarte* (phonecards), which can save you money and help you avoid messing around with change. They are available from post offices, *Tabak* and train stations. Large internet cafes have Skype software on their terminals and headphones for internet telephony, but you'll need to register and put money on your account in order to make calls to landlines or mobile phones.

Time

Austria has summer and winter time. Daylight saving time *(Sommerzeit)* begins on the last Sunday in March and all clocks are put forward by one hour. On the last Sunday in October, normal Central European Time begins and clocks are put back one hour. Note that in German *halb* is used to indicate the half-hour before the hour, hence *halb acht* means 7.30, *not* 8.30.

TIME DIFFERENCES
When it's noon in Vienna (outside daylight saving time):

Berlin, Stockholm & Paris	noon
London	11am
Los Angeles & Vancouver	3am
Moscow	2pm
New York	6am
Perth	7pm
Sydney	9pm

Tourist Information

Any town or village that tourists are likely to visit will have a centrally situated tourist office and at least one of the staff will speak English. They go by various names – *Kurort, Fremden-verkehrsverband, Verkehrs-amt, Kurverein, Tourismus-büro* or *Kurverwaltung* – but they can always be identified by a white 'i' on a green background.

Staff can answer enquiries, ranging from where and when to attend religious services for different denominations, to where to find vegetarian food or wi-fi. If you need a hotel with wi-fi in an isolated area, for instance, they can usually help you find one. Most offices have an accommodation-finding service, often free of charge. Maps, often also some great hiking and cycling maps, are available and usually free.

Some local tourist offices hold brochures on other localities, allowing you to stock up on information in advance. If you're empty-handed and arrive somewhere too late in the day to get to the tourist office, try asking at the railway ticket office, as staff there often have hotel lists or city maps. The tourist office may have a rack of brochures hung outside the door, or there may

be an accommodation board you can access even when the office is closed. Top hotels usually have a supply of useful brochures in the foyer.

Burgenland Tourismus (www.burgenland.info)
Kärnten Information (www.kaernten.at)
Niederösterreich Werbung (www.niederoesterreich.at)
Oberösterreich Tourismus (www.oberoesterreich.at)
Österreich Werbung (www.austria.info)
Salzburgerland Tourismus (www.salzburgerland.com)
Salzkammergut (www.salzkammergut.at)
Steirische Tourismus (www.steiermark.com)
Tirol Info (www.tirol.at)
Vorarlberg Tourismus (www.vorarlberg-tourism.at)

Travellers with Disabilities

The situation in Austria for travellers with disabilities is improving but is still by no means plain sailing, especially outside Vienna. Ramps leading into buildings are common but not universal; most U-Bahn stations have wheelchair lifts but on buses and trams you'll often be negotiating gaps and one or more steps.

For distance travel, ÖBB (Austrian National Railways; www.oebb.at) has a section for people with disabilities on its website. Change to the English-language option, then go to 'Planning your trip' and submenu 'Barrier-free travelling'. You can also get information and arrange your trip by calling ☑5-1717 (05-1717 inside Austria). Press 5 after the recorded message, and 5 again for 'notification of trips of wheelchair users or persons with other handicaps'. You must book at least three days in advance. No special service is available at unstaffed stations.

The detailed pamphlet *Vienna for Visitors with Disabilities* is available in German or English from **Tourist Info Wien** (Map p60; [✆]211 14-555; www.wien.info; 01, Albertinaplatz; ☉9am-7pm). A comprehensive list of places in Vienna catering to visitors with special needs can be downloaded on www.wien.info/en/travel-info/accessible-vienna. In other cities, contact the tourist office directly for more information.

Some of the more expensive (four star or above, usually) hotels have facilities tailored to travellers with disabilities; cheaper hotels invariably don't.

There is no national organisation for the disabled in Austria, but the regional tourist offices or any of the following can be contacted for more information:

Behinderten Selbsthilfe Gruppe ([✆]03332-65 405; www.bsgh.at; Sparkassenplatz 4, 8320 Hartberg, Styria)

Bizeps ([✆]01-523 89 21; www.bizeps.at, in German; Kaiserstrasse 55/3/4a, Vienna)

Faktor i ([✆]01-274 92 74; www.faktori.wuk.at, in German only; 05, Rechte Wienzeile 81, Vienna) Aimed at offering information to young people with disabilities.

Upper Austria tourist office (www.oberoesterreich.at/nohandicap, in German) Information on contacts, guides and wheelchair hire.

Visas

Visas for stays of up to three months are not required for citizens of the EU, the European Economic Area (EEA), much of Eastern Europe, Israel, USA, Canada, the majority of Central and South American nations, Japan, Korea, Malaysia, Singapore, Australia or New Zealand. All other nationalities require a visa; the **Ministry of Foreign Affairs** (www.bmaa.gv.at) website has a list of

Austrian embassies where you can apply for one.

If you wish to stay longer you should simply leave the country and re-enter. For those nationalities that require a visa, extensions cannot be organised within Austria; you'll need to leave and reapply. EU nationals can stay indefinitely but are required by law to register with the local *Magistratisches Bezirksamt* (magistrate's office) if the stay exceeds 60 days.

Austria is part of the Schengen Agreement, which includes all EU states (minus Britain and Ireland) and Switzerland. In practical terms this means a visa issued by one Schengen country is good for all the other member countries and a passport is not required to move from one to the other (a national identity card is required, though). Austrians are required to carry personal identification, and you too will need to be able to prove your identity.

Visa and passport requirements are subject to change, so always double-check before travelling. Lonely Planet's website, www.lonelyplanet.com, has links to up-to-date visa information.

Volunteering

Voluntary work is a good way to meet people and do something for the country you're visiting. In Austria, maintaining hiking trails is popular, but other volunteer projects range from joining a performance group on social issues to repairing a school fence outside Vienna. Generally, there's something for everyone, young or senior, lasting anything from a week to 18 months or more.

The key to finding a volunteer position in Austria is to hook up with the networks in your home country and/or, if you speak German, approach

an Austrian organisation directly.

Bergwald Projekt (Oesterreichischer Alpenverein; www.bergwaldprojekt.at, in German; Olympiastrasse 37, Innsbruck) Excellent volunteer work programs protecting and maintaining mountain forests in Austria, Germany and Switzerland. Generally, the Austrian programmes last one week.

Canadian Alliance for Development Initiatives and Projects (CADIP; www.cadip.org) Open to Canadian and US citizens.

Freiwilligenweb (www.freiwilligenweb.at, in German) Official Austrian government portal for volunteer work.

International Voluntary Service Great Britain (IVS; http://ivsgb.org) The UK organisation networked with the SCI.

International Voluntary Service USA (www.sci-ivs.org) The US organisation networked with the SCI.

International Volunteers for Peace (www.ivp.org.au) An Australian organisation networked with the SCI.

Service Civil International (SCI; www.sciint.org) Worldwide organisation with local networks.

Travel Tree (www.traveltree.co.uk) A UK portal for volunteers.

Work

EU, EEA and Swiss nationals can work in Austria without a work permit or residency permit, though as intending residents they need to register with the police.

Non-EU nationals need both a work permit and a residency permit, and will find it pretty hard to get either. Enquire (in German) about job possibilities via local Labour Offices; look under *'Arbeitsmarktservice'* in the *White Pages* for the closest office. The work permit needs to be applied for by your employer in Austria. Applications for residency permits must be applied for via the Austrian embassy in your home country.

Teaching is a favourite of expats; look under 'Sprach-schulen' in the Gelbe Seiten for a list of schools. Outside that profession (and bar-keeping), you'll struggle to find employment if you don't speak German. There are some useful job websites:

Arbeitsmarktservice Österreich (www.ams.or.at, in German) Austria's Labour Office.

jobpilot (www.jobpilot.at, in German) For professionals.

StepStone (www.stepstone. at, in German) Directed towards professionals.

Virtual Vienna Net (www. virtualvienna.net) Aimed at expats, with a variety of jobs, including UN listings.

Transport

GETTING THERE & AWAY

Austria is well connected to the rest of the world. Vienna and several regional capitals are served by no-frills airlines (plus regular airline services). Europe's extensive bus and train networks criss-cross the country and there are major highways from Germany and Italy. It's also possible to enter Austria by boat from Hungary, Slovakia and Germany.

Flights, tours and rail tickets can be booked online at www.lonelyplanet.com/travel_services.

Entering the Country

Paperwork A valid passport is required when entering Austria. The only exception to this rule is when entering from another Schengen country (all EU states minus Britain and Ireland); in this case, only a national identity card is required. See p411 for more on visa requirements.

Border procedures Formal border controls have been abolished for those entering from another EU country or Switzerland, but spot checks may be carried out at the border or inside Austria itself.

Air

Vienna is the main transport hub for Austria, but Graz, Linz, Klagenfurt, Salzburg and Innsbruck all receive international flights. Flights to these cities are often a cheaper option than those to the capital, as are flights to Airport Letisko (Bratislava Airport), which is only 60km east of Vienna, in Slovakia. Bregenz has no airport; your best bet is to fly into Friedrichshafen in Germany or Altenrhein in Switzerland.

For information on getting to and from airports, see the individual cities in regional chapters.

Airports & Airlines

Austrian Airlines (code OS; ☑05 1766 1000; www.aua.com; Hegelgasse 21) is the national carrier based in Vienna; member of Star Alliance (www.staralliance.com).

Among the low-cost airlines, Ryanair and Air Berlin fly to Graz, Innsbruck, Klagenfurt, Linz, Salzburg and Vienna (Ryanair to Bratislava for Vienna). See the Getting There & Away sections of individual chapters for airlines flying to/from Austria's international airports:

Airport Letisko Bratislava (BTS; ☑421 2 3303 33 53; www.airportbratislava.sk) Serves Slovakia's capital Bratislava and has good transport connections to Vienna. Used by Ryanair.

Graz (GRZ; ☑0316-29 02-0; www.flughafen-graz.at)

Innsbruck (INN; ☑0512-225 25-0; www.innsbruck-airport.com)

Klagenfurt (KLU; ☑0463-41 5 00-0; www.klagenfurt-airport.com)

Linz (LNZ; ☑07221-600-0; www.flughafen-linz.at)

Salzburg (SZG; ☑0662-85800; www.salzburg-airport.com)

Vienna (VIE; ☑01-7007 22233; www.viennaairport.com)

Land

Bus

Travelling by bus is a cheap but less comfortable way to reach Austria from other European countries. Some options are listed below.

EUROLINES

Consortium of coach companies with offices all over Europe. While the bulk of **Eurolines** (www.eurolines.at) Vienna (☑01-798 29 00; Erdbergstrasse 202); Graz (☑0316 67 11 55; Wiener Strasse 229) buses pass through Vienna, stops in Austria include Graz, Linz, Salzburg, Klagenfurt and Innsbruck.

Passes Eurolines Passes are priced according to season; 15-day pass €205 to €345 for adults, 30-day pass €310 to €455 (cheaper for those under 26). Covers 35 cities across Europe (including Vienna).

London One-way/return €86/126, 23 hours, six days per week. Buses connect

CLIMATE CHANGE & TRAVEL

Every form of transport that relies on carbon-based fuel generates CO_2, the main cause of human-induced climate change. Modern travel is dependent on aeroplanes, which might use less fuel per kilometre per person than most cars but travel much greater distances. The altitude at which aircraft emit gases (including CO_2) and particles also contributes to their climate change impact. Many websites offer 'carbon calculators' that allow people to estimate the carbon emissions generated by their journey and, for those who wish to do so, to offset the impact of the greenhouse gases emitted with contributions to portfolios of climate-friendly initiatives throughout the world. Lonely Planet offsets the carbon footprint of all staff and author travel.

London (Victoria coach station) and Vienna; anyone under 26 or over 60 gets a 10% discount on most fares and passes.

Prague One-way/return €26/47, six hours, 8am and 5pm daily.

Bratislava City and airport; one-way/return to Vienna €10/20, 75 minutes, 10 daily.

Other destinations As well as the above, Eurolines serves numerous cities in Italy, Germany and Hungary. For other destinations see www.eurolines.com.

BUSABOUT

London-based **Busabout** (☏08450 267 514; www. busabout.com; 1/2/3 loops €399/699/859) offers two passes for travel around 50 European cities from May to September. It splits stops into various 'loops' which you can combine. The **Northern Loop** includes Vienna and Salzburg, as well as Prague, Amsterdam, Paris and several German cities. A **Southern Loop** includes Innsbruck. The website gives other deals.

ÖBB INTERCITY BUS

An **ÖBB Intercity** (www. oebb.at) bus connects Klagenfurt via Villach and Udine with Venice (€25, 4½ hours, four to five times daily).

Car & Motorcycle

Numerous entry points by road from Germany, the Czech Republic, Slovakia, Hungary, Slovenia, Italy and Switzerland. Liechtenstein is so small that it has just one border-crossing point, near Feldkirch in Austria. The Alps limit the options for approaching Tyrol from the south (Switzerland and Italy). All border-crossing points are open 24 hours.

For information on Austria's road rules and regulations, see p418.

Paperwork and insurance Proof of ownership of a private vehicle and a driver's licence should always be carried while driving. EU licences are accepted in Austria; all other nationalities require a German translation or an International Driving Permit (IDP). Translations can be obtained on the spot for a small fee from automobile associations (see p417). Third-party insurance is a minimum requirement in Europe and you'll need to carry proof of this in the form of a Green Card. If you're a member of an automobile association, ask about free reciprocal benefits offered by affiliated organisations in Europe. The car must also display a sticker on the rear indicating the country of origin.

Safety requirements Carrying a warning triangle and first-aid kit in your vehicle is compulsory in Austria.

Train

Austria benefits from its central location within Europe by having excellent rail connections to all important destinations.

ONLINE TIMETABLES

Deutsche Bahn (www. bahn.de) German National Railways, with similar information. Useful for finding special deals to/from Germany.

ÖBB (www.oebb.at) Austrian National Railways, with national and international connections. Only national connections have prices unless they are special deals to and from Germany.

HARD-COPY TIMETABLES

Thomas Cook (www. thomascookpublishing.com) *Thomas Cook European Timetable* contains all train schedules, supplements and reservations information. The monthly edition can be ordered from Thomas Cook outlets or from the website – US or mainland European travellers are best off using the website. The bi-annual edition is also available from www.amazon .com and local Amazon sites.

TRAINS

Extra charges can apply on fast trains and international trains, and it is a good idea (sometimes obligatory) to make seat reservations for peak times and on certain lines.

Express and high-speed Express trains can be identified by the symbols EC (EuroCity, serving international routes) or IC (InterCity, serving national routes). The French Train à Grande

Vitesse (TGV) and the German InterCityExpress (ICE) trains are high-speed trains. Surcharges are levied for these.

Overnight trains Usually offer a choice between a *Liegewagen* (couchette) or a more expensive *Schlafwagen* (sleeping car). Long-distance trains have a dining car or snacks available.

International connections Vienna is one of the main rail hubs in Central Europe. Most services listed below for elsewhere in Austria depart at least three times daily (these prices may vary slightly depending on the type of train service).

London Fastest connection between London and Vienna is the Eurostar train to Brussels, then to Frankfurt am Main, then Vienna (total of 14 hours). Standard price is €445 (€245 to Brussels, €200 Brussels to Vienna); rates are often cheaper through www.eurostar.com. **Rail Europe Travel Centre** (www.raileurope.co.uk; British Columbia House, 1 Regent St, London; ☺10am-6pm Mon-Fri, to 5pm Sat) handles bookings for an UK£8 fee; the website books tickets from other countries.

River

Danube Tourist Commission (www.danube-river.org) has a country-by-country list of operators and agents who can book canal tours, including companies in Australia, New Zealand, the US, Canada and various European countries.

Danube Cruises

Avalon Waterways UK (☏0800 668 1802; www.avaloncruises.co.uk); Australia (www.avalonwaterways.com.au); Canada (www.avalonwaterways.ca); New Zealand (www.avalonwaterways.co.nz); USA (☏877 797 8791; www.avalonwaterways.com) International cruise operator; can also handle bookings from regions other than those shown above. Typical cruises include 13 days Vienna to Amsterdam (UK£1435), 15 days Amsterdam to Budapest with a stop in Vienna (UK£1409). Prices include flights and often free airport transfers.

Excursion Services

Twin City Liner (☏01-588 80; www.twincityliner.com; 01, Schwedenplatz, Vienna; one-way adult €17-30) Vienna to/from Bratislava, 1½ hours,

March to October. Ships dock at the DDSG quay between Marienbrücke and Schwedenbrücke in Vienna. **DDSG Blue Danube** (☏588 80; www.ddsg-blue-danube.at; Handelskai 265, Vienna; one-way/return €89/109) Hydrofoil Vienna to/from Budapest, 5½ hours, three to seven times a week April to early October.

GETTING AROUND

Transport systems in Austria are highly developed and generally very efficient, and reliable information is usually available in English. Individual bus and train *Fahrplan* (timetables) are readily available, as are helpful annual timetables.

Austria's main rail provider is the **Österreiche Bundesbahn** (ÖBB; Austrian Federal Railways; www.oebb.at), which has an extensive countrywide rail network. This is supplemented by a handful of private railways. Wherever trains don't run, a **Postbus** (www.postbus.at) usually does. Sometimes there's an overlap of services and you have a choice of bus or train. Timetables and prices for many train and bus connections

---

VIENNA'S NEW HAUPTBAHNHOF

For many years Vienna had no central train station, although most international services began and terminated in Westbahnhof or Südbahnhof. This situation has now changed and Vienna is getting a monumental *Hauptbahnhof*, built by tearing down most of the Südbahnhof and creating a new station and precinct.

The interim period Until the new *Hauptbahnhof* goes into partial service from late 2012, some trains will still begin and end at Westbahnhof (which is itself being revamped into a new station for regional trains, with offices and shops). Most of these are international trains to/from Western Europe, but some are domestic trains. The services that used to begin and end at Südbahnhof (mostly to and from Graz and other southern regions) will be diverted to Wien-Meidling until about 2012 (Meidling-Philadelphiabrücke, NOT Meidling Hauptstrasse). One section of Südbahnhof (known as Südbahnhof Ostbahn) continues to operate, mostly for trains to Bratislava and a few other places.

From late 2012 Vienna will have a *Hauptbahnhof* for international, long-distance and some regional services. Westbahnhof will become a regional station (ie for regional trains mostly from places near Vienna). Wien-Meidling will no longer get international and long-distance services.

TRAIN CONNECTION	PRICE (€)	DURATION (HR)
Belgrade-Villach	82	11
Budapest-Graz	46	5½
Dortmund-Linz	153	9 (departs from Vienna, change in Würzburg for northern Germany)
Ljubljana-Graz	34	3½ (some continue on to Zagreb and Belgrade)
Ljubljana-Villach	20	1¾
Munich-Graz	79	6 (via Salzburg)
Munich-Innsbruck	36.50	2
Munich-Salzburg	34	2
Munich-Villach	67	4½
Prague-Linz	43	5
Verona-Innsbruck	34	3½
Zagreb-Villach	38	4
Zürich-Innsbruck	51	3¾

can be found online at www.oebb.at.

Most provinces have an integrated transport system offering day passes covering regional zones for both bus and train travel.

Air

Flying within a country the size of Austria is rarely necessary. The main exception is Innsbruck in the far west of Austria. Those who, for special reasons, do need to fly will find airlines serving several routes. Airlines in Austria:

Austrian Airlines (www.austrian.com) The national carrier and its subsidiaries Tyrolean Airways and Austrian Arrows offer several flights daily between Vienna and Graz, Innsbruck, Klagenfurt, Linz and Salzburg, and also flights between Graz and Linz, and Linz and Salzburg.

Welcome Air (www.welcomeair.at) Flights from Innsbruck to Graz, along with a handful of international services. See Innsbruck (p325) for other airlines.

Bicycle

Bike touring Most regional tourist boards have bro-

chures on cycling facilities and routes within their region. Separate bike tracks are common in cities, and long-distance tracks and routes also run along many of the major valleys such as the Danube, Enns and Mur. Others follow lakes, such as the bike tracks around the Neusiedler See in Burgenland and the Wörthersee in Carinthia. The Danube cycling trail is like a Holy Grail for cyclists, following the entire length of the river in Austria between the borders with Germany and Slovakia. The Tauern Radweg is a 310km trail through the mountain landscapes of Hohe Tauern National Park. For more information on popular cycle routes, see the Austria Outdoors chapter.

Mountain biking Austria's regions are well-equipped for mountain biking of various levels of difficulty. Carinthia (around Hermagor) and northern Styria (the Gesäuse, Schladming and Mariazell) are excellent places. The Dachstein Tour can be done over three days, whereas the Nordkette Single Trail in Innsbruck is one of the toughest and most exhilarating downhill rides in the country.

Bike Transport

It's possible to take bicycles on trains with a bicycle symbol at the top of its timetable. You can't take bicycles on bus services.

Regional A ticket for a day/week on a Regionalzug (R; regional train), Regionalexpress (REX; regional express), S-Bahn (S) or RegionalS-Bahn (RB; regional S-Bahn) costs €5/10. The exception is when you buy a EURegio ticket, for which bicycle transport is free on trains with capacity and with the bicycle symbol.

Intercity and international On these trains with bicycle facilities you need to reserve ahead and place the bike in one of the special racks onboard. National tickets cost €10 (€5 discounted) and international tickets €12.

Hire

All large cities have at least one bike shop that doubles as a rental centre. In places where cycling is a popular pastime, such as the Wachau in Lower Austria and the Neusiedler See in Burgenland, almost all small towns have rental facilities. Rates vary from town to town, but expect to pay around €10 to €15 per day; see the destination chapters for specific details on bike hire.

Hire stations Some regions have summer bicycle-rental stations where you can rent and drop off a bicycle at different stations, often using a credit card. In Lower Austria and Burgenland the system is very well established. A similar network is also located around the Wörthersee in Carinthia. Vienna also has a pick-up and drop-off service using credit cards. See the destination chapters for details on local bicycle hire.

Boat

The Danube serves as a thoroughfare between Vienna

and Lower and Upper Austria. Services are generally slow, scenic excursions rather than functional means of transport. For more information on boat travel in Vienna, see p106; for Lower Austria see p111; and for Upper Austria p162. Some of the country's larger lakes, such as Bodensee and Wörthersee, have boat services.

Bus

Rail routes are often complemented by Postbus services, which really come into their own in the more inaccessible mountainous regions. Buses are fairly reliable, and usually depart from outside train stations.

Remote regions Plan a day or two ahead and travel on a weekday; services are reduced on Saturday, often nonexistent on Sunday. Pay attention to timetables on school buses in remote regions. These are excellent during the term (if a little loud and packed with kids) but don't operate outside school term.

Telephone information Inside Austria, call ☎0810 222 333 (6am to 8pm). From outside Austria, call ☎+43 1 71101.

Online information Consult www.postbus.at or www.oebb.at. Local bus stations or tourist offices usually stock free timetables for specific bus routes.

Reservations Usually unnecessary. It's possible to buy tickets in advance on some routes, but on others you can only buy tickets from the drivers.

Costs and duration Oddly, travel by Postbus can work out to be more expensive than train, especially if you have a Vorteilscard for train discounts (not valid on buses). The ÖBB intercity bus between Graz and Klagenfurt (€36) costs the same as the train but is

direct. Sometimes buses are marginally faster; mostly, though, buses are slower.

Car & Motorcycle

Roads Autobahns are marked 'A', some are pan-European 'E' roads. You can only drive on them with a *Vignette* (motorway tax; see Autobahn Tax & Tunnel Tolls). *Bundesstrassen* or 'B' roads are major roads, while *Landstrassen* (L) are places to enjoy the ride rather than get quickly from one place to another. 'L' roads are usually good for cyclists.

Seasonal closures and snow chains Some minor passes are blocked by snow from November to May. Carrying snow chains in winter is highly recommended and is compulsory in some areas.

Navigation systems These work well in Austria, but as elsewhere, use your eyes and don't rely 100% on them.

Motorcycles Motorcyclists and passengers must wear a helmet. Dipped lights must be used in daytime. You must carry a first-aid kit. The National Austrian Tourist Office has an *Austrian Classic Tour* brochure, which covers 3000km of the best roads for motorcyclists in the country.

Motorail Trains

ROUTE	PRICE (€)	TIME (HR)
Vienna-Feldkirch	99	7½
Vienna-Innsbruck	79	5¼
Vienna-Villach	65	4¼
Vienna-Lienz	73	5¾
Graz-Feldkirch	89	9
Villach-Feldkirch	79	8¾

Automobile Associations

Two automobile associations serve Austria. Both provide free 24-hour breakdown service to members and have reciprocal agreements with motoring clubs in other countries; check with your local club before leaving. Both have offices throughout Austria, and it is possible to become a member, but you must join for a year, which costs €66. For a small fee, the associations also translate non-German-language driving licences.

If you're not entitled to free assistance, you'll incur a fee for call-outs, which varies depending on the time of day.

ARBÖ (☎24hr emergency assistance 123, office 050/123 123; www.arboe.at; Mariahilfer Strasse 180, Vienna; ☻office telephone 6am-7pm daily, office premises 8am-5.30pm Mon-Fri)

ÖAMTC (☎24hr emergency assistance 120, office 01-711 99-0; www.oeamtc.at; Schubertring 1-3, Vienna; ☻8am-6pm Mon-Fri, 9am-1pm Sat)

Bring Your Own Vehicle

You need to have proof of ownership papers and third-party insurance. The car must also display a sticker on the rear indicating the country of origin.

Driving Licence

A licence should always be carried; see p414 for more information. If it's not in German, you need to carry a translation or International Driving Permit (IDP) as well.

Hire

Minimum requirements

Minimum age for hiring small cars is 19 years, for prestige models 25 years. A valid licence issued at least a year ago is necessary. If you plan to take the car across the border, especially into Eastern Europe, let

	Bad Ischl	Bregenz	Bruck an der Mur	Eisenstadt	Graz	Innsbruck	Kitzbühel	Klagenfurt	Krems	Kufstein	Landeck	Lienz	Linz	Salzburg	St Pölten	Vienna	Villach
Bregenz	432																
Bruck an der Mur	170	577															
Eisenstadt	297	704	127														
Graz	193	600	54	175													
Innsbruck	239	193	384	511	407												
Kitzbühel	191	300	275	469	400	113											
Klagenfurt	245	510	145	298	133	322	264										
Krems	222	626	175	132	229	433	372	320									
Kufstein	161	271	331	460	356	78	37	286	355								
Landeck	316	117	461	588	484	77	186	394	510	155							
Lienz	232	424	266	393	277	178	94	144	432	142	248						
Linz	103	507	190	246	237	314	247	253	145	236	391	359					
Salzburg	58	374	228	362	264	181	129	223	257	103	258	180	138				
St Pölten	206	610	140	123	194	417	356	285	32	339	494	416	129	241			
Vienna	266	670	145	50	191	477	420	316	79	399	554	411	189	301	66		
Villach	250	486	178	335	170	287	226	37	353	251	370	109	330	188	318	353	
Wiener Neustadt	268	675	98	31	146	482	441	267	137	431	559	364	237	339	114	53	316

the rental company know beforehand and double-check for any add-on fees and age requirements. Although companies accept any licence that is written in Latin letters, a translation or International Driving Permit (IDP) is required by the traffic police for any non-EU license not in German.

Where to hire It is much easier to hire in large cities. Small towns either have no hire companies or a very limited number of vehicles and can be expensive and booked out. If you've got time, shop around for small companies as they can be cheaper (but more restrictive conditions often apply).

Insurance Third-party insurance is a minimum requirement in Austria. All companies offer Personal Accident Insurance (PAI) for occupants and Collision Damage Waiver (CDW) for an additional charge. PAI may not be necessary if you or your passengers hold personal travel insurance.

COMPANIES

Avis (☑01-601 87-0; www.avis.at)

EasyMotion (☑0900 240 120; www.laudamotion.com, in German) Expensive 0900 telephone. Use the web.

Europcar (☑0810 911 911; www.europcar.at)

Hertz (☑01-795 32; www.hertz.at)

Holiday Autos (www.holidayautos.com) Often offers very low rates and has offices or representatives in over 20 countries. By booking early, prices can be about 60% of those charged by the international companies.

Megadrive (☑05/0105-4124; www.megadrive.at, in German) Formerly Denzeldrive. Good network in major cities, often cheaper.

Sixt (☑0810 977 424; www.sixt.at, in German)

Autobahn Tax & Tunnel Tolls

A *Vignette* is imposed on all autobahns; charges for cars below 3.5 tonnes are €7.90 for 10 days, €22.90 for two months and €76.20 for one year. For motorbikes expect to pay €4.50 for 10 days, €11.50 for two months and €30.40 for one year. *Vignitte* can be purchased from motoring organisations, border crossings, petrol stations, post offices and *Tabak* shops.

Anything above 3.5 tonnes is charged per kilometre. The system uses a GO-Box, available from petrol stations along the autobahn for €5, which records the kilometres you travel via an electronic tolling system. A minimum of €75 must be loaded onto the box (plus a €5 fee the first time you load), with a maximum amount of €500). Information on the system and prices can be found online at www.go-maut.at.

A toll (*not* covered by the motorway tax) is levied on some mountain roads and tunnels. For a full list of toll roads, consult one of the automobile organisations.

Road & Parking Rules

Drive on the right-hand side of the road. The minimum driving age is 18.

Alcohol The penalty for drink-driving – driving with over 0.05% BAC (blood-alcohol concentration) – is a hefty on-the-spot fine and confiscation of your driving licence.

Children Those under the age of 14 who are shorter than 1.5m must have a special seat or restraint.

Fines Can be paid on the spot, but ask for a receipt.

Giving way Give way to the right at all times except when a priority road sign indicates otherwise or one street has a raised border running across it (the vehicle entering from such a street must give way). Note: the give way to the right rule also applies at T-junctions.

Helmets Compulsory for motorcyclists and their passengers, not for cyclists.

Parking Most town centres have designated *Kurzparkzone* (short-term parking zone), where on-street parking is limited to a maximum of 1½ or three hours (depending upon the place) between certain specified times. *Parkschein* (parking vouchers) for such zones can be purchased from *Tabak* shops or pavement dispensers and then displayed on the windscreen. Outside the specified time, parking in the *Kurzparkzone* is free.

Seat belts Compulsory.

Speed limits Fifty kilometres per hour in built-up areas, 130km/h on auto-bahns and 100km/h on other roads. In some places, the speed on country roads is restricted to 70km/h.

Speed limits at night Except for the A1 between Vienna and Salzburg and the A2 between Vienna and Villach, the speed limit on autobahns from 10pm to 5am is 110km/h.

Trams These always have priority. Vehicles should wait behind while trams slow down and stop for passengers.

Local Transport

Austria's local transport infrastructure is excellent, inexpensive and safe.

Fines They're stiff if you don't have a ticket – about €60 is common, and controls are frequent, especially in the provincial capitals.

Hours In Vienna, the metro runs all night on Friday and Saturday nights. From Sunday night to Thursday night it stops around midnight or 12.30am. No other towns have metro systems. These rely on buses and often a tram network. Bus services are complemented by a few night bus lines. Tram and bus services in most places run from about 5am to 11pm or midnight.

Stop request You usually need to press the stop-request button, often even in trams.

Taxis Austrians mostly call ahead or use taxi ranks. Flagging down a taxi usually works, though. Drivers always expect a 10% tip.

Tickets Ticketing systems and prices vary from region to region. Often they're sold from machines at stops. In Graz you buy them on machines in trams, in Salzburg you can buy them from the driver. Universally, tickets are cheaper from any *Tabak* shop, also known as a *Trafik*. Passes for single trips, 24 hours and several days or a week are usually available.

Train

While the country bemoans the state of its 'rundown' rail system, travellers praise it to the heavens. It's good by any standard, and if you use a discount card (see Rail Passes) it's inexpensive.

ÖBB (☑05/17 17; www.oebb.at) is the main operator, supplemented by a handful of private lines. Call to book a ticket or get information on long-distance trains 24 hours, or on regional train and bus services from 7am to 10pm.

Reservations Cost €3.50 for most 2nd-class express services within Austria. If you haven't reserved ahead, check (before you sit) whether your intended seat has been reserved by someone else. Reservations are recommended for weekend travel.

USEFUL TRAIN TERMS

Abfahrt Departure

Ankunft Arrival

Bahnhof (Bf) Station

Bahnsteig Track (the track number)

Einfache Fahrt ('hin') One-way

Erste Klasse First class

Fahrkarte (Fahrausweis) Ticket

Gleis Platform

Hauptbahnhof (Hbf) Main station

Retour Return

Speisewagen Dining carriage

Täglich Daily

Umsteigen Change of trains

Wagen Carriage

Zweite Klasse Second class

Disabled passengers Use the ☑05/1717 number from 7am to 10pm for special travel assistance (you can do this while booking your ticket by telephone). If you've already got a ticket, call the number and press '5' (*Spezialauskünfte*) in the menu selection, and '5' again to register for assistance at a station. Staff at stations will help with boarding and alighting. Do this at least 24 hours ahead of travel (72 hours ahead for international services).

Smoking Not allowed on trains.

Etiquette The ÖBB takes a strong stand on putting your feet on the seats. You can be fined for it.

Costs

In this book, the fares quoted are always those for 2nd class. Depending on the exact route, a fare can vary slightly.

Tickets Purchase before boarding the train. Amex, Visa, MasterCard, JCB and Diners Club, as well as cash and EC/Maestro cards, are accepted at all stations and in ticket machines.

Boarding without a ticket If you board and go immediately to the conductor, only a €3 surcharge will be applied to the normal price of the ticket. If you don't do this, a fee and fine totalling €95 will have to be paid (unless you board at an unstaffed station or the ticket machine is out of order).

Children Children aged six to 15 travel half-price; younger kids travel free if they don't take up a seat.

Pets Kept in suitable containers, these travel free; larger pets travel half-price.

Breaking your journey One-way tickets for journeys of 100km or less are valid for only one day and the journey can't be broken. For trips of 101km or more, the ticket is valid for one month and you can alight en route. This is worth doing, as longer trips cost less per kilometre. Return tickets of up to 100km each way are valid for one day; tickets for longer journeys are valid for one month, though the initial outward journey must still be completed within six days. A return fare is usually the equivalent price of two one-way tickets.

Rail Passes

Depending on the amount of travelling you intend to do in Austria and your residency status, rail passes can be a good deal.

VORTEILSCARD

These Austrian National Railways discount tickets can be purchased by anyone. They offer a 45% discount on inland trains for tickets purchased at the counter and 50% if you buy at a ticket machine. After purchasing one (bring a photo and your passport or other ID), you receive a temporary card and can begin using it right away. The plastic permanent card is posted to your home address. It's valid for one year, but not on buses.

Classic (€100) For those over 26.

Family (€20) Valid for up to two adults and any number of children. The children must be travelling with you.

Jugend <26 (€20) For those under 26.

Senior (€27) For women over 60 years and men over 65 years.

EURAIL PASS

Only available to non-European residents, Eurail passes are valid for unlimited 1st-class travel on national railways and some private lines in 21 countries taking in Western Europe (the UK is not included) as well as Hungary and Romania. Those under 26 receive substantial discounts. See www.eurail.com for all options.

Global Pass From 15 consecutive days within a three-month period (US$669) and upwards in 15-day batches to a maximum of three months' travel (90 consecutive days; US$1889).

Flexi Pass Offers 10 non-consecutive days ($795) or 15 non-consecutive days ($1045) within a two-month period.

Eurail Select Pass Allows you to tailor a rail trip in three, four or five of 24 bordering countries.

Regional Pass Combine Austria with Croatia/Slovenia, Germany, Hungary, the Czech Republic or Switzerland for four to 10 days within a two-month period; 10 days' 2nd-class travel in Austria and Germany is US$495 for those over 26 years.

Country Pass For Austria this is valid for three to eight days within one month; from $145 to $229 in 2nd class for those over 26 years.

INTERRAIL

Passes are for European citizens or anyone who has lived in Europe for at least six months. Those under 26 receive substantial discounts. See www.interrail-net.com for all options.

One Country Pass Austria Adult 2nd class three/four/six/eight days within a month €172/191/252/290.

InterRail Global Flexi Valid for a certain number of days in up to 30 countries within a 10- or 22-day period; five days' travel in 10 days costs €249, 10 days' travel in 22 days costs €359.

Language

WANT MORE?

For in-depth language information and handy phrases, check out Lonely Planet's *German Phrasebook*. You'll find it at **shop.lonelyplanet.com**, or you can buy Lonely Planet's iPhone phrasebooks at the Apple App Store.

The national language of Austria is German, though there are a few regional dialects. For example, the dialect spoken in Vorarlberg is much closer to Swiss German (Schwyzertütsch) – a language all but incomprehensible to most non-Swiss – than it is to the standard High German (Hochdeutsch) dialect. Nevertheless, Austrians can easily switch from their dialect to High German.

There are many words and expressions in German that are used only by Austrians, some throughout the country and others only in particular regions, although they'll probably be understood elsewhere. Most of these would not automatically be understood by non-Austrian German speakers. On the other hand, the 'standard' German equivalents would be understood by all Austrians. The greetings and farewells included in this chapter are specific to Austria.

Pronunciation

It's easy to pronounce German because almost all sounds are also found in English. If you read our coloured pronunciation guides as if they were English, you'll be understood.

Note that the vowel ü sounds like the 'ee' in 'see' but with rounded lips. As for the consonants, the kh sound is pronounced like a hiss from the back of the throat (as in the Scottish *loch*). The r sound is pronounced at the back of the throat, almost like saying a g sound, but with some friction – a bit like gargling.

As a general rule, word stress in German falls mostly on the first syllable. In our pronunciation guides the stressed syllable is indicated with italics.

BASICS

German has polite and informal forms for 'you' (*Sie* and *du* respectively). When addressing people you don't know well, use the polite form (though younger people will be less inclined to expect it). In this language guide the polite form is used unless indicated with 'inf' (for 'informal') in brackets.

Hello.	*Servus.*	zer·vus
Goodbye.	*Auf Wiedersehen.*	owf vee·der·zay·en
Yes.	*Ja.*	yah
No.	*Nein.*	nain
Please.	*Bitte.*	bi·te
Thank you.	*Danke.*	dang·ke
You're welcome.	*Bitte (sehr).*	bi·te (zair)
Excuse me.	*Entschuldigung.*	ent·shul·di·gung
Sorry.	*Entschuldigung.*	ent·shul·di·gung

How are you?
Wie geht es Ihnen/dir? — vee gayt es ee·nen/deer (pol/inf)

Fine, thanks. And you?
Danke, gut. Und Ihnen/dir? — dang·ke goot unt ee·nen/deer (pol/inf)

What's your name?
Wie ist Ihr Name? — vee ist eer nah·me (pol)
Wie heißt du? — vee haist doo (inf)

My name is ...
Mein Name ist ... — main nah·me ist ... (pol)
Ich heiße ... — ikh hai·se ... (inf)

Do you speak English?
Sprechen Sie Englisch? shpre·khen zee eng·lish

I (don't) understand.
Ich verstehe (nicht). ikh fer·shtay·e (nikht)

ACCOMMODATION

Do you have a ... room?
Haben Sie ein ...? hah·ben zee ain ...

How much is it per night/person?
Wie viel kostet es vee feel kos·tet es
pro Nacht/Person? praw nakht/per·zawn

camp site	Campingplatz	kem·ping·plats
guesthouse	Pension	pahng·zyawn
hotel	Hotel	ho·tel
inn	Gasthof	gast·hawf
youth hostel	Jugend-herberge	yoo·gent·her·ber·ge

air-con	Klimaanlage	klee·ma·an·lah·ge
bathroom	Badezimmer	bah·de·tsi·mer
double room	Doppelzimmer	do·pel·tsi·mer
single room	Einzelzimmer	ain·tsel·tsi·mer
window	Fenster	fens·ter

DIRECTIONS

Where's (a bank)?
Wo ist (eine Bank)? vaw ist (ai·ne bangk)

What's the address?
Wie ist die Adresse? vee ist dee a·dre·se

Can you please write it down?
Könnten Sie das bitte kern·ten zee das bi·te
aufschreiben? owf·shrai·ben

Can you show me (on the map)?
Können Sie mir ker·nen zee es meer
(auf der Karte) zeigen? (owf dair kar·te) tsai·gen

at the corner	an der Ecke	an dair e·ke
at the traffic lights	bei der Ampel	bai dair am·pel
behind ...	hinter ...	hin·ter ...
far away	weit weg	vait vek
in front of ...	vor ...	fawr ...
left/right	links/rechts	lingks/rekhts
near	nahe	nah·e
next to ...	neben ...	nay·ben ...
opposite ...	gegenüber ...	gay·gen·ü·ber ...
straight ahead	geradeaus	ge·rah·de·ows

EATING & DRINKING

A table for (two) people, please.
Einen Tisch für (zwei) ai·nen tish für (tsvai)
Personen, bitte. per·zaw·nen bi·te

KEY PATTERNS

To get by in German, mix and match these simple patterns with words of your choice:

When's (the next flight)?
Wann ist (der van ist (dair
nächste Flug)? naykhs·te flook)

Where's (the station)?
Wo ist (der vaw ist (dair
Bahnhof)? bahn·hawf)

Where can I (buy a ticket)?
Wo kann ich (eine vaw kan ikh (ai·ne
Fahrkarte kaufen)? fahr·kar·te kow·fen)

Do you have (a map)?
Haben Sie (eine hah·ben zee (ai·ne
Karte)? kar·te)

Is there (a toilet)?
Gibt es (eine gipt es (ai·ne
Toilette)? to·a·le·te)

I'd like (a coffee).
Ich möchte ikh merkh·te
(einen Kaffee). (ai·nen ka·fay)

I'd like (to hire a car).
Ich möchte ikh merkh·te
(ein Auto mieten). (ain ow·to mee·ten)

Can I (enter)?
Darf ich darf ikh
(hereinkommen)? (her·ein·ko·men)

Could you please (help me)?
Könnten Sie (mir kern·ten zee (meer
helfen)? hel·fen)

Do I have to (book a seat)?
Muss ich (einen Platz mus ikh (ai·nen plats
reservieren lassen)? re·zer·vee·ren la·sen)

What would you recommend?
Was empfehlen Sie? vas emp·fay·len zee

What's in that dish?
Was ist in diesem vas ist in dee·zem
Gericht? ge·rikht

I don't eat ...
Ich esse kein ... ikh e·se kain ...

Bon appétit.
Guten Appetit. goo·ten a·pe·teet

Cheers!
Prost! prawst

That was delicious!
Das war sehr lecker! das vahr zair le·ker

The bill, please.
Die Rechnung, bitte. dee rekh·nung bi·te

Key Words

appetisers	Vorspeisen	fawr·shpai·zen
ashtray	Aschenbecher	a·shen·be·kher
bar	Kneipe	knai·pe

ham	Schinken	shing·ken
hare	Hase	hah·ze
lamb	Lamm	lam
liver	Leber	lay·ber
minced meat	Hackfleisch	hak·flaish
plaice	Scholle	sho·le
pork	Schweinfleisch	shvai·n·flaish
salmon	Lachs	laks
tongue	Zunge	tsung·e
trout	Forelle	fo·re·le
tuna	Thunfisch	toon·fish
turkey	Puter	poo·ter
veal	Kalbfleisch	kalp·flaish
venison	Hirsch	hirsh

Signs

Ausgang	Exit
Damen	Women
Eingang	Entrance
Geschlossen	Closed
Herren	Men
Offen	Open
Toiletten	Toilets
Verboten	Prohibited

bottle	Flasche	fla·she
bowl	Schüssel	shü·sel
breakfast	Frühstück	frü·shtük
cold	kalt	kalt
cup	Tasse	ta·se
dinner	Abendessen	ah·bent·e·sen
drink list	Getränke-karte	ge·treng·ke·kar·te
food	Essen	e·sen
fork	Gabel	gah·bel
glass	Glas	glahs
grocery store	Lebensmittel-laden	lay·bens·mi·tel·lah·den
hot (warm)	heiß	hais
knife	Messer	me·ser
local speciality	örtliche Spezialität	ert·li·khe shpe·tsya·li·tayt
lunch	Mittagessen	mi·tahk·e·sen
main courses	Hauptgerichte	howpt·ge·rikh·te
menu	Speisekarte	shpai·ze·kar·te
market	Markt	markt
plate	Teller	te·ler
restaurant	Restaurant	res·to·rang
spicy	würzig	vür·tsikh
spoon	Löffel	ler·fel
vegetarian food	vegetarisches Essen	ve·ge·tah·ri·shes e·sen
with/without	mit/ohne	mit/aw·ne

Meat & Fish

bacon	Speck	shpek
beef	Rindfleisch	rint·flaish
brains	Hirn	heern
carp	Karpfen	karp·fen
chicken	Huhn	hoon
duck	Ente	en·te
eel	Aal	ahl
fish	Fisch	fish
goose	Gans	gans

Fruit & Vegetables

apple	Apfel	ap·fel
apricot	Aprikose	a·pri·ko·ze
asparagus	Spargel	shpar·gel
banana	Banane	ba·nah·ne
beans	Bohnen	baw·nen
beetroot	Rote Rübe	raw·te rü·be
cabbage	Kohl	hawl
carrots	Karotten	ka·ro·ten
cherries	Kirschen	kir·shen
corn	Mais	mais
cucumber	Gurke	gur·ke
garlic	Knoblauch	knawp·lowkh
grapes	Trauben	trow·ben
green beans	Fisolen	fee·zo·len
mushrooms	Pilze	pil·tse
onions	Zwiebeln	tsvee·beln
pear	Birne	bir·ne
peas	Erbsen	erp·sen
peppers	Paprika	pap·ri·kah
pineapple	Ananas	a·na·nas
plums	Zwetschgen	tsvech·gen
potatoes	Kartoffeln	kar·to·feln
raspberries	Himbeeren	him·bee·ren
spinach	Spinat	shpi·naht
strawberries	Erdbeeren	ert·bee·ren
tomatoes	Tomaten	to·mah·ten

Other

bread	Brot	brawt
butter	Butter	bu·ter
cheese	Käse	kay·ze
chocolate	Schokolade	sho·ko·lah·de

cream	*Sahne*	*zah*·ne
dumplings	*Knödel*	*kner*·del
eggs	*Eier*	*ai*·er
honey	*Honig*	*haw*·nikh
jam	*Marmelade*	*mar·me·lah·*de
mustard	*Senf*	zenf
nut	*Nuss*	nus
oil	*Öl*	erl
pasta	*Nudeln*	*noo*·deln
pepper	*Pfeffer*	*pfe*·fer
rice	*Reis*	rais
salad	*Salat*	za·*laht*
salt	*Salz*	zalts
sugar	*Zucker*	*tsu*·ker

Drinks

beer	*Bier*	beer
coffee	*Kaffee*	ka·*fay*
(orange) juice	*(Orangen-) saft*	(o·*rahng·*zhen·) zaft
milk	*Milch*	milkh
tea	*Tee*	tay
(mineral) water	*(Mineral-) wasser*	(mi·ne·*rahl·*) va·ser
red wine	*Rotwein*	*rawt*·vain
white wine	*Weißwein*	*vais*·vain

EMERGENCIES

Help!
Hilfe! — hil·fe

Leave me alone!
Lassen Sie mich in Ruhe! — la·sen zee mikh in *roo*·e

I'm lost.
Ich habe mich verirrt. — ikh *hah*·be mikh fer·*irt*

Call the police!
Rufen Sie die Polizei! — roo·fen zee dee po·li·*tsai*

Call a doctor!
Rufen Sie einen Arzt! — roo·fen zee *ai*·nen artst

I'm sick.
Ich bin krank. — ikh bin krangk

It hurts here.
Es tut hier weh. — es toot heer *vay*

Question Words

How?	*Wie?*	vee
What?	*Was?*	vas
When?	*Wann?*	van
Where?	*Wo?*	vaw
Who?	*Wer?*	vair
Why?	*Warum?*	va·*rum*

I'm allergic to (antibiotics).
Ich bin allergisch gegen (Antibiotika). — ikh bin a·*lair*·gish *gay*·gen (an·ti·bi·*aw*·ti·ka)

SHOPPING & SERVICES

I'd like to buy ...
Ich möchte ... kaufen. — ikh *merkh*·te ... *kow*·fen

I'm just looking.
Ich schaue mich nur um. — ikh *show*·e mikh noor um

Can I look at it?
Können Sie es mir zeigen? — *ker*·nen zee es meer *tsai*·gen

How much is this?
Wie viel kostet das? — vee feel *kos*·tet das

That's too expensive.
Das ist zu teuer. — das ist tsoo *toy*·er

Can you lower the price?
Können Sie mit dem Preis heruntergehen? — *ker*·nen zee mit dem prais he·*run*·ter·gay·en

There's a mistake in the bill.
Da ist ein Fehler in der Rechnung. — dah ist ain *fay*·ler in dair *rekh*·nung

ATM	*Geldautomat*	*gelt*·ow·to·maht
credit card	*Kreditkarte*	kre·*deet*·kar·te
internet cafe	*Internet-Café*	in·ter·net·ka·fay
PIN	*Geheimnummer*	ge·*haim*·nu·mer
post office	*Postamt*	*post*·amt
tourist office	*Fremden-verkehrsbüro*	*frem*·den·fer·*kairs*·bü·raw

TIME & DATES

What time is it?
Wie spät ist es? — vee shpayt ist es

It's (one) o'clock.
Es ist (ein) Uhr. — es ist (ain) oor

Half past one.
Halb zwei. — halp tsvai (lit: 'half two')

morning	*Morgen*	*mor*·gen
afternoon	*Nachmittag*	*nahkh*·mi·tahk
evening	*Abend*	*ah*·bent
yesterday	*gestern*	*ges*·tern
today	*heute*	*hoy*·te
tomorrow	*morgen*	*mor*·gen
Monday	*Montag*	*mawn*·tahk
Tuesday	*Dienstag*	*deens*·tahk
Wednesday	*Mittwoch*	*mit*·vokh
Thursday	*Donnerstag*	*do*·ners·tahk
Friday	*Freitag*	*frai*·tahk
Saturday	*Samstag*	*zams*·tahk
Sunday	*Sonntag*	*zon*·tahk

Numbers		
1	*eins*	ains
2	*zwei*	tsvai
3	*drei*	drai
4	*vier*	feer
5	*fünf*	fünf
6	*sechs*	zeks
7	*sieben*	zee·ben
8	*acht*	akht
9	*neun*	noyn
10	*zehn*	tsayn
20	*zwanzig*	tsvan·tsikh
30	*dreißig*	drai·sikh
40	*vierzig*	feer·tsikh
50	*fünfzig*	fünf·tsikh
60	*sechzig*	zekh·tsikh
70	*siebzig*	zeep·tsikh
80	*achtzig*	akht·tsikh
90	*neunzig*	noyn·tsikh
100	*hundert*	hun·dert
1000	*tausend*	tow·sent

January	*Januar*	yan·u·ahr
February	*Februar*	fay·bru·ahr
March	*März*	merts
April	*April*	a·pril
May	*Mai*	mai
June	*Juni*	yoo·ni
July	*Juli*	yoo·li
August	*August*	ow·gust
September	*September*	zep·tem·ber
October	*Oktober*	ok·taw·ber
November	*November*	no·vem·ber
December	*Dezember*	de·tsem·ber

TRANSPORT

Public Transport

boat	*Boot*	bawt
bus	*Bus*	bus
plane	*Flugzeug*	flook·tsoyk
train	*Zug*	tsook

At what time does it leave/arrive?
Wann fährt es ab?/ van fairt es ap/
Wann kommt es an? van komt es an

I want to go to ...
Ich mochte nach ... ikh merkh·te nahkh ...
fahren. fah·ren

Does it stop at ...?
Hält es in ...? helt es in ...

I want to get off here.
Ich mochte hier ikh merkh·te heer
aussteigen. ows·shtai·gen

one-way ticket	*einfache Fahrkarte*	ain·fa·khe fahr·kar·te
return ticket	*Rückfahrkarte*	rük·fahr·kar·te

first	*erste*	ers·te
last	*letzte*	lets·te
next	*nächste*	naykhs·te

aisle seat	*Platz am Gang*	plats am gang
platform	*Bahnsteig*	bahn·shtaik
ticket office	*Fahrkarten- verkauf*	fahr·kar·ten- fer·kowf
timetable	*Fahrplan*	fahr·plahn
train station	*Bahnhof*	bahn·hawf
window seat	*Fensterplatz*	fens·ter·plats

Driving & Cycling

I'd like to hire a ...	*Ich möchte ein ... mieten.*	ikh merkh·te ain ... mee·ten
4WD	*Allrad- fahrzeug*	al·raht- fahr·tsoyk
bicycle	*Fahrrad*	fahr·raht
car	*Auto*	ain ow·to
motorcycle	*Motorrad*	maw·tor·raht

child seat	*Kindersitz*	kin·der·zits
helmet	*Helm*	helm
mechanic	*Mechaniker*	me·khah·ni·ker
petrol/gas	*Benzin*	ben·tseen
pump	*Luftpumpe*	luft·pum·pe
service station	*Tankstelle*	tangk·shte·le

Does this road go to ...?
Führt diese Strasse fürt dee·ze shtrah·se
nach ...? nahkh ...

(How long) Can I park here?
(Wie lange) Kann ich (vee lang·e) kan ikh
hier parken? heer par·ken

The car has broken down (at ...).
Ich habe (in ...) eine ikh hah·be (in ...) ai·ne
Panne mit meinem Auto. pa·ne mit mai·nem ow·to

I have a flat tyre.
Ich habe eine ikh hah·be ai·ne
Reifenpanne. rai·fen·pa·ne

I've run out of petrol.
Ich habe kein Benzin ikh hah·be kain ben·tseen
mehr. mair

behind the scenes

SEND US YOUR FEEDBACK

We love to hear from travellers – your comments keep us on our toes and help make our books better. Our well-travelled team reads every word on what you loved or loathed about this book. Although we cannot reply individually to postal submissions, we always guarantee that your feedback goes straight to the appropriate authors, in time for the next edition. Each person who sends us information is thanked in the next edition – and the most useful submissions are rewarded with a free book.

Visit **lonelyplanet.com/contact** to submit your updates and suggestions or to ask for help. Our award-winning website also features inspirational travel stories, news and discussions.

Note: We may edit, reproduce and incorporate your comments in Lonely Planet products such as guidebooks, websites and digital products, so let us know if you don't want your comments reproduced or your name acknowledged. For a copy of our privacy policy visit lonelyplanet.com/privacy.

OUR READERS

Many thanks to the travellers who used the last edition and wrote to us with helpful hints, useful advice and interesting anecdotes:
David and Susan Bratt, Bernhard Bouzek, Douglas Campbell, Patricia Cook, Alex Davies, Joana Estilita, Rahel Seraina Imbach Ferner, Elizabeth Fox, Carlo Gandolfi, Gareth Hamilton, Hanna Hoffmann, Julia Jander, Henninger Jeannot, Richard Kelly, Martin Kohl, Tim Nowotny, Alex Sacco, Andrea Schopper, Valerie Schnee, Paul Souter, Mario Toups, Rebecca Turi, Bart Von Wien, Jack Whitehead, Robert Wijdeveld

AUTHOR THANKS

Anthony Haywood

Many thanks to the help of the very many informed staff at information offices and other places around my regions, to Robert Paget and Gert Prix for contributing their local knowledge, to Susie and Ruprecht in Graz (and Maribor) for their friendship, tips and music. Last but not least thanks to Lonely Planet's in-house editors and cartos, especially Paula Hardy, Joe Bindloss and Herman So, and to my coauthors Caroline Sieg and Kerry Christiani for their excellent work.

Caroline Sieg

Thanks to my parents for instilling in me a lifelong zest for travel. Thanks mucho to Paula Hardy for giving me this gig and *Vielen Dank* to Rafed & Company for a few truly excellent nights on the town and showing me how proper Viennese party it up. And this guide is dedicated to Jules – the biggest Austria fan I know and one of the best friends I could ever wish for.

Kerry Christiani

Special thanks to my husband, Andy, for being with me every step of the way on this book. Big thanks to my interviewees: puppeteer Gretl Aicher (Salzburg), mountaineering legend Peter Habeler (Tyrol), baker Fritz Rath (Linz), and the après-ski instructors in St Anton including Maggie Ritson and Shane Pearce. Thanks to all the tourism professionals who made the road to research smooth, especially Sabine Günterseder (Upper Austria Tourism), Monika Reichel (Salzburg Information) and Nicholas Boekdrukker (Innsbruck Tourism). At Lonely Planet, thanks go to Paula Hardy, Joe Bindloss, Herman So and coauthors Anthony and Caroline for being so great to work with.

ACKNOWLEDGMENTS

Climate map data adapted from Peel MC, Finlayson BL & McMahon TA (2007) 'Updated World Map of the Köppen-Geiger Climate Classification', *Hydrology and Earth System Sciences*, 11, 163344.

Vienna U & S bahn map © 2010

Cover photograph: Chapel at the base of the Austrian Alps, Tyrol, Schmid Reinhard/4Corners

Many of the images in this guide are available for licensing from Lonely Planet Images: www.lonelyplanetimages.com.

BEHIND THE SCENES

THIS BOOK

This 6th edition of Lonely Planet's *Austria* guidebook was coordinated by Anthony Haywood, with contributions from coauthors Caroline Sieg and Kerry Christiani. Anthony and Kerry also worked on the 5th edition, while the 4th edition was written by Neal Bedford and Gemma Pitcher. The first three editions were written by Mark Honan. This guidebook was commissioned in Lonely Planet's London office, and produced by the following:

Commissioning Editors Paula Hardy, Joe Bindloss

Coordinating Editors Sarah Bailey, Helen Koehne

Coordinating Cartographers Jacqueline Nguyen, Jennifer Johnston

Coordinating Layout Designer Nicholas Colicchia

Managing Editors Imogen Bannister, Sasha Baskett

Managing Cartographers Shahara Ahmed, Herman So, Mandy Sierp

Managing Layout Designers Jane Hart, Celia Wood

Senior Editors Helen Christinis, Katie Lynch, Susan Paterson

Assisting Editors Janet Austin, Alice Barker

Assisting Cartographers Julie Dodkins, Valentina Kremenchutskaya

Cover Research Naomi Parker

Internal Image Research Rebeccea Skinner

Language Content Branislava Vladisavljevic

Thanks to Mark Adams, Yvonne Bischofberger, David Connolly, Melanie Dankel, Stefanie Di Trocchio, Janine Eberle, Brigitte Ellemor, Joshua Geoghegan, Mark Germanchis, Michelle Glynn, Lauren Hunt, Laura Jane, David Kemp, Yvonne Kirk, Nic Lehman, John Mazzocchi, Wayne Murphy, Trent Paton, Adrian Persoglia, Piers Pickard, Averil Robertson, Lachlan Ross, Michael Ruff, Julie Sheridan, Laura Stansfeld, John Taufa, Sam Trafford, Juan Winata, Emily Wolman, Nick Wood

index